ASIA SMALL AND MEDIUM-SIZED ENTERPRISE MONITOR 2020

VOLUME I—COUNTRY AND REGIONAL REVIEWS

OCTOBER 2020

ASIAN DEVELOPMENT BANK

ADB

6 ADB Avenue, Mandaluyong City, 1550 Metro Manila, Philippines
Tel +63 2 8632 4444; Fax +63 2 8636 2444
www.adb.org

ISBN 978-92-9262-421-7 (print); 978-92-9262-422-4 (electronic); 978-92-9262-423-1 (ebook)
Publication Stock No. TCS200290-2
http://dx.doi.org/10.22617/TCS200290-2

Notes:
In this publication, "$" refers to United States dollars.

ADB recognizes "Hong Kong" as Hong Kong, China; "China" as the People's Republic of China; "Korea" as the Republic of Korea; "Vietnam" as Viet Nam; and "Hanoi" as Ha Noi.

Cover design by Claudette Rodrigo.

Printed on recycled paper

Contents

Tables, Figures, and Boxes	iv
Foreword	ix
Acknowledgments	x
Data Contributors	xi
Abbreviations	xiv
Rationale and Methodology	1
Highlights	6
Regional Review: Southeast Asia	10
Country Reviews	
1. Brunei Darussalam	54
2. Cambodia	71
3. Indonesia	92
4. Lao People's Democratic Republic	117
5. Malaysia	135
6. Myanmar	157
7. Philippines	176
8. Singapore	199
9. Thailand	214
10. Viet Nam	237

Tables, Figures, and Boxes

Tables

Regional Review

2.1 MSME Definitions in Southeast Asia 12
2.2 Assistance and Infrastructure for MSME Access to Finance 27
2.3 Financial Infrastructure 36
2.4 Policies and Regulations 40

Brunei Darussalam

3.1 MSME Definition 67
3.2 MSME Landscape 67
3.3 Bank Credit 68
3.4 Nonbank Finance 69
3.5 Policies and Regulations 70

Cambodia

4.1 MSME Definition 88
4.2 MSME Landscape 88
4.3 Bank Credit 89
4.4 Nonbank Finance 89
4.5 Capital Markets 90
4.6 Policies and Regulations 91

Indonesia

5.1 MSME Definition 111
5.2 MSME Landscape 111
5.3 Bank Credit 112
5.4 Public Finance and Guarantees 112
5.5 Nonbank Finance 113
5.6 Capital Markets 114
5.7 Listing Requirements—Indonesia Stock Exchange 114
5.8 Policies and Regulations 115

Lao People's Democratic Republic

6.1 MSME Definition 131
6.2 MSME Landscape 131
6.3 Bank Credit 132
6.4 Nonbank Finance 133
6.5 Capital Markets 133
6.6 Policies and Regulations 134

Malaysia
7.1 MSME Definition 152
7.2 MSME Landscape 152
7.3 Bank Credit 153
7.4 Public Finance and Guarantees 154
7.5 Nonbank Finance 154
7.6 Capital Markets 155
7.7 Listing Requirements—Bursa Malaysia 155
7.8 Policies and Regulations 156

Myanmar
8.1 SME Definition 172
8.2 SME Landscape 172
8.3 Bank Credit 173
8.4 Nonbank Finance 174
8.5 Capital Markets 174
8.6 Policies and Regulations 175

Philippines
9.1 MSME Definition 192
9.2 MSME Landscape 192
9.3 Bank Credit 193
9.3a Compliance with MSME Loans Required 193
9.3b Microfinance Exposures of Microfinance-Oriented and Engaged Banks 194
9.3c Retail Loans to Barangay Micro Business Enterprises 194
9.4 Public Finance and Guarantees 194
9.5 Nonbank Finance 195
9.6 Capital Markets 195
9.7 Listing Requirements—Philippine Stock Exchange 196
9.8 Policies and Regulations 197

Singapore
10.1 SME Definition 210
10.2 SME Landscape 210
10.3 Bank Credit 211
10.4 Nonbank Finance 212
10.5 Capital Markets 212
10.6 Policies and Regulations 213

Thailand
11.1 MSME Definition 231
11.2 MSME Landscape 231
11.3 Bank Credit 232
11.4 Public Finance and Guarantees 232
11.5 Credit Guarantee Schemes—Thai Credit Guarantee Corporation 233
11.6 Nonbank Finance 233
11.7 Capital Markets 234
11.8 Listing Requirements—Stock Exchange of Thailand 234
11.9 Policies and Regulations 235

Viet Nam
12.1 MSME Definition 253
12.2 MSME Landscape 253
12.3 Bank Credit 254
12.4 Nonbank Finance 255
12.5 Capital Markets 256
12.6 Listing Requirements—Hanoi Stock Exchange 256
12.7 Policies and Regulations 257

Figures

Rationale and Methodology
1.1 Key Components of the Asia SME Monitor 3
1.2 Data Processing Flow 5

Regional Review
2.1 Number of MSMEs 13
2.2 Employment by MSMEs 14
2.3 MSME Contribution to Gross Domestic Product 16
2.4 MSME Exports 18
2.5 Mobile and Internet Penetration, 2018 19
2.6 Bank Credit 22
2.7 MSME Nonperforming Loans 23
2.8 Credit Guarantees, 2018 and 2019 25
2.9 Nonbank Finance 29
2.10 Nonbank Finance Institutions—Nonperforming Financing 30
2.11 Equity Markets for MSMEs 34

Brunei Darussalam
3.1 Number of MSMEs 55
3.2 Employment by MSMEs 56
3.3 MSME Contribution to Gross Domestic Product 56
3.4 Bank Loans 60
3.5 MSME Loans 62
3.6 Nonbank Finance 63

Cambodia
4.1 Number of MSMEs 73
4.2 Employment by MSMEs 74
4.3 Bank Loans 79
4.4 Nonbank Finance 80
4.5 Equity Market 83

Indonesia
5.1 Number of MSMEs 93
5.2 Employment by MSMEs 94
5.3 MSME Contribution to Gross Domestic Product 95
5.4 MSME Exports 96
5.5 MSME Loans 100

5.6 Credit Guarantees—Kredit Usaha Rakyat 102
5.7 Nonbank Finance 103
5.8 Peer-to-Peer Lending in Indonesia 106
5.9 Equity Market 107

Lao People's Democratic Republic
6.1 Number of MSMEs 119
6.2 Employment by MSMEs 119
6.3 MSME Loans 123
6.4 Nonbank Finance 125
6.5 Equity Market 127

Malaysia
7.1 Number of MSMEs 136
7.2 Employment by MSMEs 137
7.3 MSME Contribution to Gross Domestic Product 138
7.4 MSME Exports 139
7.5 MSME Loans 142
7.6 Public Finance and Guarantees 144
7.7 Nonbank Finance 145
7.8 Equity Markets 148

Myanmar
8.1 Number of SMEs 158
8.2 Employment by Enterprises 160
8.3 SME Loans 163
8.4 SME Loans—Small and Medium Industrial Development Bank 164
8.5 Nonbank Finance—Microfinance Institutions 166
8.6 Equity Market 168

Philippines
9.1 Number of MSMEs 177
9.2 Employment by MSMEs 178
9.3 MSME Loans 181
9.4 Public Finance and Guarantees 183
9.5 Nonbank Finance 185
9.6 Equity Market 187

Singapore
10.1 Number of SMEs 201
10.2 Employment by SMEs 201
10.3 SME Value Added 201
10.4 SME Loans 204
10.5 Nonbank Finance—Finance Companies 205
10.6 Equity Market 207

Thailand
11.1 Number of MSMEs 215
11.2 Employment by MSMEs 216
11.3 MSME Contribution to Gross Domestic Product 217
11.4 MSME Exports and Imports 218
11.5 MSME Loans 221
11.6 Credit Guarantees—Thai Credit Guarantee Corporation 223
11.7 Number of Nonbank Finance Institutions 223
11.8 Equity Markets 225

Viet Nam
12.1 Number of MSMEs 238
12.2 Employment by MSMEs 239
12.3 Bank Loans 244
12.4 Nonbank Finance 247
12.5 Equity Market 249

Boxes

Indonesia
5.1 Gojek Supports MSME Growth in Indonesia 97
5.2 Bahana Alta Ventura Channels Government Programs to Support MSMEs 104

Malaysia
7.1 Technology Park Malaysia Supports Technology-Based MSMEs 140

Thailand
11.1 The National Innovation Agency Supports Technology-Based Innovation by MSMEs 228

Foreword

Asia's robust and sustainable economic growth has helped alleviate poverty and transformed many low-income countries into middle-income economies. The growth momentum in developing Asia, however, has gradually decelerated since 2018 due to increasing global trade tensions, economic uncertainty, and the coronavirus disease (COVID-19) shock. Our region faces greater downside risks to its economic outlook, which currently forecasts a healthy rebound in 2021 from this year's contraction. But the economic disruption has also energized several opportunities. At the national level, micro, small, and medium-sized enterprises (MSMEs) can play a more central role in recovering from economic contraction and promoting sustainable economic growth in Asia and the Pacific.

MSMEs are the backbone of Asia's economy. They stimulate domestic demand, create jobs, innovate and compete nationally, and potentially, regionally. Access to finance and expanded markets remain at the core of MSME growth. Asia's economic transformation and pandemic recovery offer the chance to accelerate business opportunities for MSMEs to learn how to digitize and embrace digital financial services and e-commerce, without abandoning the traditional MSME strengths in wholesale and retail trade, agribusiness, food processing, accommodation, and other service-related business. A recovery in demand, trade, and investment is needed, and MSMEs should be at its heart.

MSME development remains key to promoting inclusive growth in developing Asia. The design of MSME policies has become more challenging due to the complexity of the MSME business climate and the rapidly changing external environment. Governments are well aware of these changes, monitoring shifts in business sentiment and adjusting policies accordingly. Asian Development Bank (ADB) developing member countries (DMCs) need timely access to high-quality multicountry analytical data and examples of their peers' best practices on MSME development to design the most appropriate MSME policy support. ADB is in the good position to provide this data and policy advice, given its long experience and expertise in programs and projects that support MSME development across Asia and the Pacific.

With this in mind, ADB launched the Asia Small and Medium-Sized Enterprise Monitor (ASM) in 2014 and the second edition in 2015 covering 20 DMCs from five ADB subregions. This 2020 edition upgrades the ASM by extending analytical coverage to both financial and nonfinancial topics critical to MSME development. Focusing on Southeast Asia, ASM 2020 comprises four volumes: (i) country and regional reviews, (ii) a special chapter surveying the widespread effects of COVID-19 on MSME businesses in selected developing Asian economies, (iii) a thematic chapter analyzing the impact of finance technology-based loans to tricycle drivers in the Philippines, and (iv) a new technical chapter presenting ADB's Small and Medium-Sized Enterprise Development Index (SME-DI). We sincerely hope this Volume I of ASM 2020 will provide analytical support to governments in their efforts to promote evidence-based policy design on MSME development.

Yasuyuki Sawada
Chief Economist and Director General
Economic Research and Regional Cooperation Department
Asian Development Bank

Acknowledgments

The Asia Small and Medium-Sized Enterprise Monitor (ASM) 2020 was prepared by Shigehiro Shinozaki, senior economist, Economic Research and Regional Cooperation Department (ERCD) of the Asian Development Bank (ADB). The work was supervised by Joseph Ernest Zveglich Jr., deputy chief economist, and supported by Satoru Yamadera from ERCD's financial cooperation and integration team. The ASM team comprised Shigehiro Shinozaki, team leader; Michael Troilo, ADB consultant and associate professor of international business and finance, University of Tulsa, United States; Josephine Penaflor Ferre, ADB consultant; Chona Plete Guatlo, ADB consultant; and Junray Bautista, ADB consultant. Administrative support was provided by Richard Supangan and Maria Frederika Bautista.

Shigehiro Shinozaki wrote the rationale and methodology, highlights, regional review, and country reports for Brunei Darussalam, Indonesia, Malaysia, the Philippines, and Thailand, and co-authored country reports for Lao People's Democratic Republic (Lao PDR) and Viet Nam. Michael Troilo authored country reports for Cambodia, Myanmar, and Singapore, and co-authored country reports for Lao PDR and Viet Nam. Josephine Penaflor Ferre and Chona Plete Guatlo led the preparation of the ASM database.

We thank all data contributors for their solid reviews of respective country chapters incorporated in this report despite the difficult time caused by COVID-19 pandemic.

Data Contributors in Participating Developing Member Countries of the Asian Development Bank

Country	Data Contributors
Brunei Darussalam	Autoriti Monetari Brunei Darussalam; Bank Usahawan; Darussalam Enterprise; Department of Economic Planning and Statistics; Ministry of Energy, Manpower, and Industry; Ministry of Finance and Economy; National Chamber of Commerce and Industry; Youth Entrepreneur Association Brunei
Cambodia	In Channy, ACLEDA Bank Plc.; Nguon Mengtech, Cambodia Chamber of Commerce; Kea Borann, Cambodia Microfinance Association; Hong Sok Hour, Cambodia Securities Exchange; Oeur Sothearoath, Credit Bureau Cambodia; Oknha Te Taingpor, Federation of Associations for Small and Medium Enterprises of Cambodia; Hort Pheng, General Department of SMEs and Handicraft - Ministry of Industry, Science, Technology and Innovation; Veng Sakhon, Ministry of Agriculture Forestry and Fisheries; Tekreth Kamrang, Ministry of Commerce; Vongsey Vissoth, Ministry of Economy and Finance; Chea Chanto, National Bank of Cambodia; Hang Lina, National Institute of Statistics; Sou Socheat, Securities and Exchange Commission of Cambodia; Kong Marry, Techo Startup Center
Indonesia	Budi Hanoto, Bank Indonesia; Muhamad Sidik Heruwibowo, Bahana Artha Ventura; Kecuk Suhariyanto, Bandan Pusat Statistik; Gede Edy Prasetya, Coordinating Ministry for Economic Affairs; Inarno Djajadi, Indonesia Stock Exchange; Muhammad Lutfi, Indonesia National Chamber of Commerce and Industry; Siti Astrid Kusumawardhani, Gojek; Rendra Z. Idris, Otoritas Jasa Keuangan; Rully Indrawan, Ministry of Cooperatives and SMEs; Hadi Prabowo, Ministry of Home Affairs; Achmad Sigit Dwiwahjono, Ministry of Industry; Oke Nurwan, Dipl.Ing, Ministry of Trade; Yohanes Arts Abimanyu, PEFINDO Credit Bureau
Lao People's Democratic Republic	Phanthaboun Sayaphet, Bank of the Lao PDR; Akhom Praseuth, Lao Development Bank; Pamouane Phetthany, Lao Microfinance Association; Oudet Souvannavong, Lao National Chamber of Commerce and Industry; Saysamone Chanthachack, Lao Securities Commission Office; Vanhkham Voravong, Lao Securities Exchange; Phonesaly Souksavath, Lao Statistics Bureau; Bountheung Douangsavanh, Ministry of Industry and Commerce - Department of SME Promotions; Buavanh Vilavong, Ministry of Industry and Commerce - Department of Industry and Handicraft; Ministry of Industry and Commerce – Enterprise Registration and Management Department; Sisomboun Ounavong, Ministry of Planning and Investment

Country	Data Contributors
Malaysia	Datuk Nor Shamsiah binti Mohd Yunus, Bank Negara Malaysia; Datuk Muhamad Umar Swift, Bursa Malaysia; KC Wong, Credit Bureau Malaysia; Mohd Uzir Mahidin, Department of Statistics; Surina Shukri, Malaysia Digital Economy Corporation; Azrai Bin Shuib, Malaysian Business Angel Network; Shaun Cheah, Malaysian International Chamber of Commerce and Industry; Datuk Seri Mohd Redzuan bin Md Yusof, Ministry of Entrepreneur Development and Cooperatives; Datuk Syed Zaid Albar, Securities Commission Malaysia; Aria Putera Ismail, SME Bank; Noor Azmi Mat Said, SME Corporation Malaysia; Sharbani Harun, Technology Park Malaysia
Myanmar	Kyaw Kyaw Maung, Central Bank of Myanmar; San Myint, Central Statistical Organization; Aye Aye Win, Directorate of Industrial Supervision and Inspection - Ministry of Industry; Thant Zin Lwin, Directorate of Investment and Company Administration; Zaw Naing, Financial Regulatory Department - Ministry of Planning and Finance; Sandar Oo, Myanma Insurance; Cherry Lwin, Myanmar Investment and Commercial Bank; Takashi Yamaguchi, Myanmar Securities Exchange Centre; Aye Aye Win, Myanmar SME Development Agency; Tin Tin Ohn, Securities and Exchange Commission of Myanmar; Ye Myat Min, Seed Myanmar; Zeya Nyunt, SME Development Bank; Yin Zaw Myo, Yangon Stock Exchange
Philippines	Pia Bernadette Roman Tayag, Bangko Sentral ng Pilipinas; Jerry Clavesillas, Bureau of Small and Medium Enterprise Development, Department of Trade and Industry; Ray Elevazo, Cooperative Development Authority; Jaime Casto Jose Garchitorena, Credit Information Corporation; Carlos Dominguez III, Department of Finance; Emmy Lou Delfin, Industry Development Bureau - Department of Information and Communications Technology; Benedicto Yujuico, Philippine Chamber of Commerce and Industry; Enrico Paringit, Philippine Council for Industry, Energy and Emerging Technology Research and Development - Department of Science and Technology; Alberto Pascual, Philippine Guarantee Corporation; Claire Dennis Mapa, Philippine Statistics Authority; Ramon Monzon, Philippine Stock Exchange Inc.; Emilio Benito Aquino, Securities and Exchange Commission; Ma. Luna Cacanando, Small Business Corporation - Department of Trade and Industry; Edgar Garcia, Technology Application and Promotion Institute - Department of Science and Technology
Singapore	Ted Tan, Enterprise Singapore; Wong Wee Kim, Singapore Department of Statistics – Ministry of Trade and Industry; Lee Jinglun, Monetary Authority of Singapore; Neo Wee Ling, Singapore Exchange
Thailand	Wimonkan Kosumas, Office of Small and Medium Enterprises Promotion; Wanpen Poonwong, National Statistical Office; Veerathai Santiprabhob, Bank of Thailand; Ruenvadee Suwanmongkol, Securities and Exchange Commission; Kailin Sarasin, Thai Chamber of Commerce; Pakorn Peetathawatchai, The Stock Exchange of Thailand; Wimol Chatameena, Thai Credit Guarantee Corporation; Lavaron Sangsnit, The Fiscal Policy Office - Ministry of Finance; Nartnaree Rattapat, Small and Medium Enterprise Development Bank of Thailand; Surapol Opasatien, National Credit Bureau; Pun-Arj Chairatana, National Innovation Agency

Country	Data Contributors
Viet Nam	Bui Anh Tuan, Agency for Business Registration – Ministry of Planning and Investment; Bui Thu Thuy, Agency for Enterprise Development – Ministry of Planning and Investment; Pham Dinh Thuy, General Statistics Office of Vietnam; Nguyen Thanh Long, Hanoi Stock Exchange; Trinh Phong Lan, Ministry of Finance; Pham Thi Hong Hanh, Ministry of Science and Technology; Lan Nguyen, Private Credit Bureau; To Huy Vu, State Bank of Vietnam; Vu Chi Dzung, State Securities Commission of Viet Nam; Pham Hoang Tien, Vietnam Chamber of Commerce and Industry; Nguyen Duc Nam, Vietnam Development Bank; Hung Manh Nguyen, Vietnam Trade Promotion Agency; Hien Tu Thu, Women Innovative Startup and Entrepreneurship

Abbreviations

ADB	—	Asian Development Bank
AIM	—	alternative investment market
AITI	—	Authority for Info-Communications Technology Industry (Brunei Darussalam)
AMBD	—	Autoriti Monetari Brunei Darussalam
ASEAN	—	Association of Southeast Asian Nations
ASENSO	—	Access of Small Enterprises to Sound Lending Opportunity (Philippines)
BMBE	—	barangay micro business enterprise
BNM	—	Bank Negara Malaysia
BOL	—	Bank of the Lao PDR
BSMED	—	Bureau of Small and Medium Enterprise Development (Philippines)
BSP	—	Bangko Sentral ng Pilipinas
C2C	—	company-to-company
CAGR	—	compounded annual growth rate
CBC	—	Credit Bureau Cambodia
CBM	—	Credit Bureau Malaysia
CBM	—	Central Bank of Myanmar
CCC	—	Cambodia Chamber of Commerce
CDA	—	Cooperative Development Authority (Philippines)
CFB	—	cash flow base
CGC	—	Credit Guarantee Corporation Malaysia Berhad
CIC	—	Credit Information Center
CIES	—	Cambodia Inter-censal Economic Survey
CSX	—	Cambodia Securities Exchange
DARe	—	Darussalam Enterprise
DBU	—	Domestic Banking Unit
DERM	—	Department of Enterprise Registration and Management (Lao PDR)
DFI	—	development financial institutions
DFS	—	digital financial service
DICA	—	Directorate of Investment and Company Administration (Myanmar)
DKN	—	Dasar Keusahawanan Nasional (National Entrepreneurship Policy, Malaysia)
DLT	—	distributed ledger technology
DOSMEP	—	Department of Small and Medium Enterprise Promotion (Lao PDR)
DOST	—	Department of Science and Technology (Philippines)
DTI	—	Department of Trade and Industry (Philippines)
EBITDA	—	earnings before interest, taxes, depreciation, and amortization
ECF	—	equity crowdfunding
EDF	—	Entrepreneurial Development Fund (Cambodia)
FDI	—	foreign direct investment

FIS	—	Financial Information Services Sdn Bhd (Malaysia)
FISC	—	Financial Inclusion Steering Committee (Philippines)
FPO	—	Fiscal Policy Office (Thailand)
FRD	—	Financial Regulatory Department (Myanmar)
GDP	—	gross domestic product
GPN	—	Gerbang Pembayaran Nasional (National Payment Gateway, Indonesia)
GVA	—	gross value added
HNX	—	Hanoi Stock Exchange
ICT	—	information and communications technology
IDX	—	Indonesia Stock Exchange
IFC	—	International Finance Corporation
IFS	—	International Financial Statistics
IMDA	—	Infocomm Media Development Authority (Singapore)
IMF	—	International Monetary Fund
IPO	—	initial public offering
IT-BPO	—	information technology-business process outsourcing
JICA	—	Japan International Cooperation Agency
KUR	—	Kredit Usaha Rakyat (People's Business Credit, Indonesia)
Lao PDR	—	Lao People's Democratic Republic
LDB	—	Lao Development Bank
LEAP	—	Leading Entrepreneur Accelerator Platform (Malaysia)
LNCCI	—	Lao National Chamber of Commerce and Industry
LSCO	—	Lao Securities Commission Office
LSX	—	Lao Securities Exchange
MAFF	—	Ministry of Agriculture, Forestry, and Fisheries (Cambodia)
MAS	—	Monetary Authority of Singapore
MDEC	—	Malaysia Digital Economy Corporation
MDI	—	microfinance deposit-taking institution
MEB	—	Myanma Economic Bank (Myanmar)
MEDAC	—	Ministry of Entrepreneur Development and Cooperatives (Malaysia)
MEF	—	Ministry of Economy and Finance (Cambodia)
MFA	—	(Lao) Microfinance Association
MFI	—	microfinance institution
MICB	—	Myanma Investment and Commercial Bank
MISTI	—	Ministry of Industry, Science, Technology, and Innovation (Cambodia)
MNRC	—	Microfinance NGOs Regulatory Council (Philippines)
MOFE	—	Ministry of Finance and Economy (Brunei Darussalam)
MOIC	—	Ministry of Industry and Commerce (Lao PDR)
MOPFI	—	Ministry of Planning, Finance, and Industry (Myanmar)
MOST	—	Ministry of Science and Technology (Thailand)
MOST	—	Ministry of Science and Technology (Viet Nam)
MSB	—	money service business
MSDP	—	Myanmar Sustainable Development Plan
MSE	—	micro and small enterprise
MSEC	—	Myanmar Securities Exchange Center
MSME	—	micro, small, and medium-sized enterprise
MSMED Council	—	Micro, Small, and Medium Enterprise Development Council (Philippines)
MTI	—	Ministry of Trade and Industry (Singapore)

NBC	—	National Bank of Cambodia
NBFI	—	nonbank finance institution
NCCI	—	National Chamber of Commerce and Industry (Brunei Darussalam)
NGO	—	nongovernment organization
NPF	—	nonperforming financing
NPL	—	nonperforming loan
NSDP	—	National Strategic Development Plan (Cambodia)
NSFI	—	National Strategy for Financial Inclusion (Philippines)
NSSLA	—	non-stock savings and loan associations
OECD	—	Organisation for Economic Co-operation and Development
OJK	—	Otoritas Jasa Keuangan (Financial Services Authority, Indonesia)
OSMEP	—	Office of Small and Medium Enterprises Promotion (Thailand)
OSS	—	one stop service
P2P	—	peer-to-peer
PCB	—	private credit bureau
PCCI	—	Philippine Chamber of Commerce and Industry
PGS	—	portfolio guarantee scheme
PNM	—	PT Permodalan Nasional Madani (Indonesia)
PRC	—	People's Republic of China
PSE	—	Philippine Stock Exchange
R&D	—	research and development
SBC	—	Small Business Corporation (Philippines)
SBV	—	State Bank of Vietnam
SCM	—	Securities Commission Malaysia
SDF	—	Skill Development Fund (Cambodia)
SEC	—	Securities and Exchange Commission (Philippines)
SEC	—	Securities and Exchange Commission (Thailand)
SECC	—	Securities and Exchange Commission of Cambodia
SECM	—	Securities and Exchange Commission of Myanmar
SET	—	Stock Exchange of Thailand
SFI	—	specialized financial institution
SME	—	small and medium-sized enterprise
SMEDA	—	SME Development Agency (Myanmar)
SMEDB	—	SME Development Bank (Thailand)
SMI	—	small and medium industries
SMIDB	—	Small and Medium Industrial Development Bank (Myanmar)
SNKI	—	National Financial Inclusion Strategy (Indonesia)
SSC	—	State Securities Commission (Viet Nam)
TCC	—	Thai Chamber of Commerce
TCG	—	Thai Credit Guarantee Corporation
TSC	—	Techo Startup Center (Cambodia)
UPCoM	—	Unlisted Public CoMpanies (Viet Nam)
US	—	United States
VCCI	—	Vietnam Chamber of Commerce and Industry
VDB	—	Vietnam Development Bank
VIETRADE	—	Vietnam Trade Promotion Agency
YSX	—	Yangon Stock Exchange

Rationale and Methodology

Awareness of Issues

Economic growth in developing Asia has helped alleviate poverty and graduated many countries to middle-income status. However, growth has been slowing—from 5.9% in 2018 to 5.1% in 2019—due to increased global trade tensions and economic uncertainty. A 0.1% contraction is expected in 2020[1] largely caused by the coronavirus disease (COVID-19) pandemic and associated lockdowns in many economies. This has sharply increased the downside risks to the region's growth outlook. Although growth in developing Asia is forecast to rebound to 6.2% in 2021, the shocks of 2020 require implementing a new model that minimizes damage and maximizes the opportunities and benefits from changing external circumstances—to create a resilient national base. This is where micro, small, and medium-sized enterprises (MSMEs) can play a more central role in recovering from economic contraction and promoting sustainable economic growth across the region.

MSMEs are a driving force behind developing Asia's economies, accounting for an average 97% of all enterprises and 69% of the national labor force. Their contribution to growth momentum, however, is limited, averaging 41% of each country's gross domestic product.[2] Asia's past economic expansion brought with it business opportunities for MSMEs to grow. Increased foreign direct investment inflows since the 2007–2008 global financial crisis encouraged the entry of large multinational firms into developing Asia, which created new demands for MSME domestic products and services—typically in supporting industries or for parts and components suppliers. Accordingly, it was expected to improve labor productivity if MSMEs actively joined global value chains. However, the COVID-19 pandemic that emerged in early 2020 has brought a shockwave to MSME growth in the region, causing a decline in domestic and foreign demand on, and investments in, MSME products and services. MSMEs are fragile entities easily disrupted by external shocks—such as economic and financial crises, disasters, and sudden changes of business environment (like reaction to a pandemic).

MSME development policy is key to achieving inclusive growth. MSME policy design has grown more challenging given the complexity of the MSME business environment and the rapidly evolving external environment. Liberalized trade and investment brought about by economic integration and expansion, and the advent of advanced technologies has promoted the structural change needed for the MSME business model to shift from a domestic focus to being globally competitive. The shift requires new policy solutions for emerging growth-oriented MSMEs. A changing external environment accelerated by the Fourth Industrial Revolution[3] and foreign direct investment inflows will create more opportunities for MSMEs to do business in developing Asia. Meanwhile, the changing external environment forced by sudden shocks such as COVID-19 will require appropriate and timely assistance for MSMEs to survive. Properly designed policy support can help these opportunities materialize and for shocks to

---

1 ADB. 2020. *Asian Development Outlook 2020 Supplement: Lockdown, Loosening, and Asia's Growth Prospects.* Manila. https://www.adb.org/publications/ado-supplement-june-2020.

2 Data for Southeast Asian countries from ADB Asia Small and Medium-Sized Enterprise Monitor 2020.

3 According to the World Economic Forum's definition (2018), a Fourth Industrial Revolution is an age in which scientific and technological breakthroughs are disrupting industries, blurring geographical boundaries, and challenging existing regulatory frameworks.

be absorbed. Thus, governments need to constantly monitor the evolving business climate to design workable and enforceable policy support for MSME development.

Governments in Asian Development Bank (ADB) developing member countries (DMCs) are seeking timely access to high-quality multicountry analytical data and other countries' best practices on MSME development so they can effectively assess and implement enforceable MSME policies. ADB is in the best position to provide data and policy advice, given its long-term expertise and projects supporting MSME development across the region.

Concept of the Asia Small and Medium-Sized Enterprise Monitor

The Asia Small and Medium-Sized Enterprise Monitor (ASM) is a knowledge-sharing product developed as a key resource for MSME development policies in Asia and the Pacific. The ASM, as an annual periodical, reviews financial and nonfinancial conditions of MSMEs at country and regional levels. The ASM has several main objectives: (i) provide in-depth analyses on MSME sector, finance, and policy interventions; (ii) exchange county best practices and experiences on MSME development; and (iii) present timely comparative financial and nonfinancial data on MSMEs. Its target clientele are DMC policymakers responsible for MSME development and access to finance. The ASM supports DMC governments in promoting evidence-based policy design on MSME development.

The ASM project continues to follow its phased approach. The Phase 1 project (September 2012–May 2014) designed a feasible framework for a MSME data platform for Asia and the Pacific. As a pilot product, the inaugural ASM 2013 was published in April 2014 with 14 countries from five ADB regions: (i) Kazakhstan in Central Asia; (ii) the People's Republic of China (PRC) and the Republic of Korea (ROK) in East Asia; (iii) Bangladesh, India, and Sri Lanka in South Asia; (iv) Cambodia, Indonesia, Malaysia, the Philippines, Thailand, and Viet Nam in Southeast Asia; and (v) Papua New Guinea and Solomon Islands in the Pacific.

The Phase 2 project (July 2014–September 2015) improved the ASM platform based on feedback from DMC partner institutions, expanded country coverage, and designed a pilot online ASM database (for internal use only). With the success of the inaugural volume of ASM 2013, ASM 2014 (second edition) was published in September 2015 covering 20 DMCs from five ADB regions: (i) Kazakhstan, the Kyrgyz Republic, and Tajikistan in Central Asia; (ii) the PRC, ROK, and Mongolia in East Asia; (iii) Bangladesh, India, and Sri Lanka in South Asia; (iv) Cambodia, Indonesia, the Lao People's Democratic Republic (Lao PDR), Malaysia, Myanmar, the Philippines, Thailand, and Viet Nam in Southeast Asia; and (v) Fiji, Papua New Guinea, and Solomon Islands in the Pacific.

After Phase 2, ADB conducted evaluation surveys for both DMCs and ADB operations, and received positive feedback from both external and internal clients asking for regularizing the ASM publication. In July 2019, after a 4-year interval, the ASM project moved into Phase 3 as a multiyear project, strengthening its global reach and data comparability, and developing a user-friendly online data portal. As the ASM 2013 and 2014 focused specifically on MSME access to finance, ASM 2020 upgrades prior ASM products by extending its analytical coverage to nonfinancial issues on MSME development.

The new ASM would normally comprise three key components: (i) country and regional reviews, (ii) thematic analysis, and (iii) technical assessments (Figure 1.1). Because of the pandemic impact, however, ADB added a special chapter component to ASM 2020.

Country and regional reviews offer in-depth analyses on financial and nonfinancial issues of a country's MSME development. Each has three review dimensions with 14 subdimensions for analysis: (i) MSME development (scale of MSMEs, employment, business productivity, market access, technology and innovation, and networking and support); (ii) access to finance (bank credit, public financing and guarantees, nonbank financing, digital financial services, capital markets, and financial infrastructure); and (iii) policies and regulations (MSME development and financial inclusion). This component analyzes these dimensions based on data collected from DMC partner institutions by using a standardized ASM data request form. This report is Volume I of the ASM 2020.

As mentioned, for ASM 2020, given the emergency needs of DMC governments, ADB prepared a **special chapter** titled "COVID-19 Impact on Micro, Small, and Medium-Sized Enterprises in Developing Asia." This special study is based on the findings from rapid MSME surveys conducted in March–May 2020 in Indonesia, the Lao PDR, the Philippines, and Thailand. It is Volume II of ASM 2020.

The **thematic analysis** explores each country's best practices related to MSME development by using an impact evaluation approach—an approach that assesses how an intervention affects particular conditions compared with non-intervention. This is a useful analytical tool to evaluate the impact of policy interventions on MSME development at the national level. The analysis will also be used as a pilot project exercise for MSME development in DMCs. This component is Volume III of the ASM 2020.

Technical assessment is a new feature. It aims to design and test a new composite index called the Small and Medium-Sized Enterprise Development Index (SME-DI) to measure two dimensions affecting MSME development, finance and non-finance areas, by using multivariate analysis based on country data received in the ASM project. This component is Volume IV of ASM 2020.

Figure 1.1: Key Components of the Asia SME Monitor

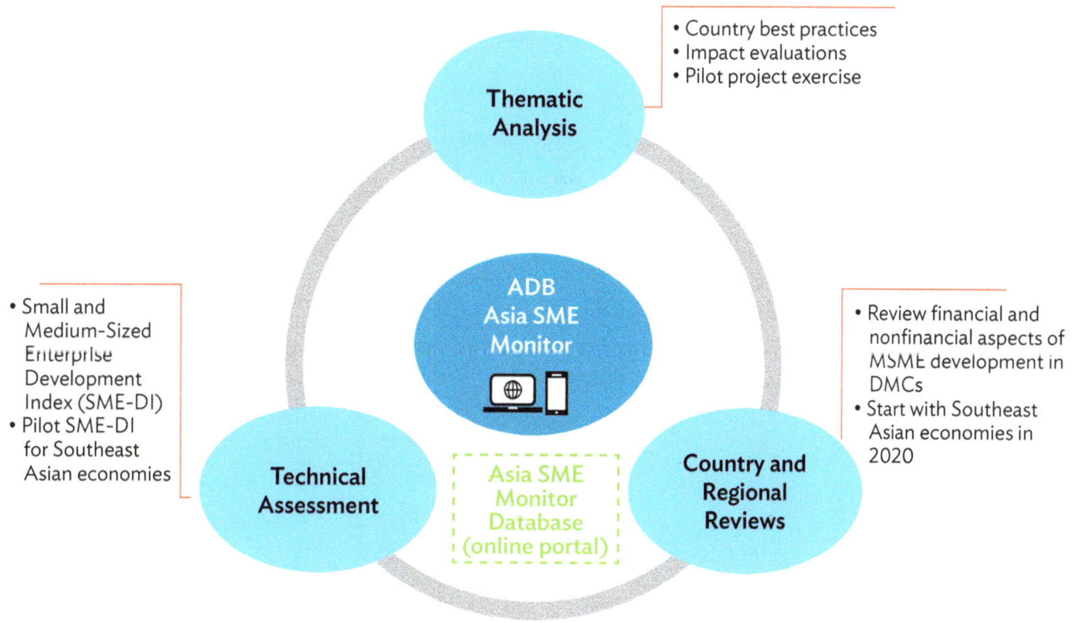

ADB = Asian Development Bank, DMC = developing member country, MSME = micro, small, and medium-sized enterprise.
Source: ADB.

Data Processing

To collect reliable and accurate data with periodic updates, ADB first built up strategic partnerships with key institutions that hold MSME data, including SME agencies, relevant line ministries, statistics offices, central banks, financial authorities, SME banks, and chambers of commerce (Figure 1.2). To systematically compile the data, ADB prepared a Standardized Data Request Form for collecting MSME data from partner institutions, comprising two separate forms on finance and nonfinance. Missing data and information from the data forms were supplemented by surveys and field research. For the ASM 2020, field missions were conducted in July–October 2019 in Brunei Darussalam, Cambodia, Indonesia, the Lao PDR, Malaysia, Myanmar, the Philippines, Thailand, and Viet Nam. ADB held online communications with Singapore for data collection and verification. All data collected were interactively reviewed and finalized by an ADB team and DMC partner institutions. Volume I country and regional data are downloadable from the ADB Asia SME Monitor database (online data portal). The ASM also has a feedback mechanism for participating DMCs through training programs. The training module will be developed based on the ASM findings.

Moving Forward

The ASM 2020 strategically targets Southeast Asian countries to assess the feasibility of the new ASM framework. The ASM 2021 and 2022 will expand country coverage to South Asian countries and Central Asian countries, respectively.

The ASM aims to support DMC policymakers on MSME development as its main beneficiaries, but also expects additional audiences. For instance, ASM expects that analyzed data on MSME development and access to finance will contribute to increasing analytical outputs on MSMEs from academia; thus, it will promote global and regional dialogues on MSME policies and financial inclusion. Using ASM data, ADB operations supporting MSME development in DMCs would be effectively implemented, timely capturing MSME demand. As indirect effects, the ASM may help financial institutions improve financing and investment strategies for MSME clients by better understanding critical issues on financing MSMEs, which will improve funding and the MSME business environment.

Besides the ASM, there are several global MSME data initiatives. For instance, the Organisation for Economic Co-operation and Development (OECD) has issued an annual SME scoreboard since 2011, focusing on bank credit and nonbank finance in 43 countries which include five ADB DMCs (Georgia, Kazakhstan, Malaysia, the PRC, and Thailand). The International Finance Corporation has issued an ad hoc report on the MSME finance gap covering 128 countries, including 29 ADB DMCs. The Economic Research Institute for ASEAN and East Asia has issued the ASEAN SME Policy Index in collaboration with OECD, providing six scale ratings to eight policy dimensions based on descriptive analysis. The DMC governments often utilize the World Bank Doing Business Report to measure the effectiveness of the enabling business environment for MSMEs in developing Asia. The ASM will avoid duplication with existing MSME data initiatives, but adds value through its close collaboration and partnerships with DMCs.

Figure 1.2: Data Processing Flow

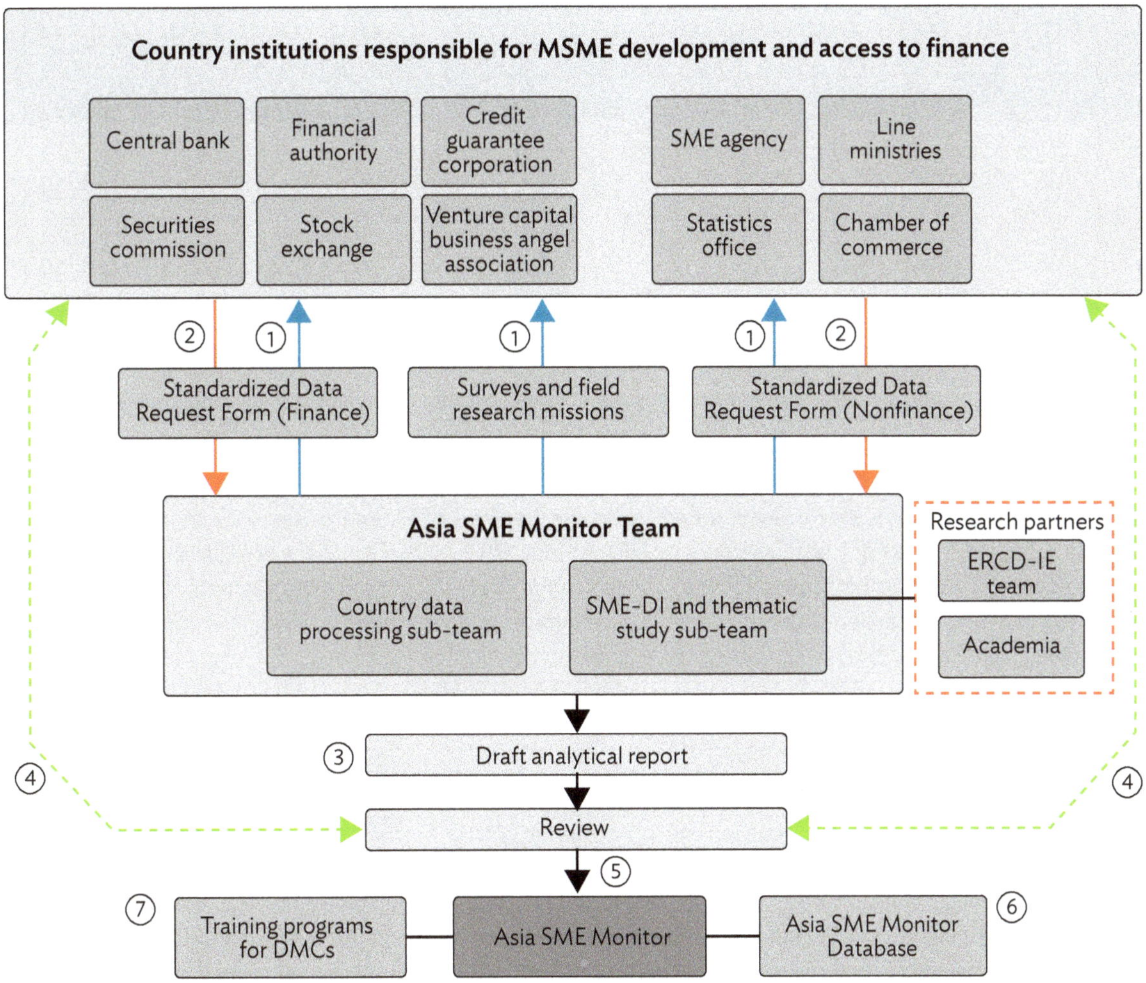

DMC = developing member country, ERCD = Economic Research and Regional Cooperation Department of Asian Development Bank, MSME = micro, small, and medium-sized enterprise, SME = small and medium-sized enterprise, SME-DI = Small and Medium-Sized Enterprise Development Index.

1 The standardized data request forms are delivered to respective counterpart institutions in participating DMCs (one for SME agency, line ministries, statistics office, and chamber of commerce; another for central bank, financial authorities, financial institutions, and finance/investment related associations).

2 Country counterpart institutions complete the data forms and return them to the Asia SME Monitor (ASM) team.

3 Based on collected data from counterpart institutions, the ASM team prepares draft country papers.

4 Draft country papers are sent out for review to the counterpart institutions or a focal entity in the participating country. After the necessary revisions reflecting feedback from counterpart institutions, country papers are finalized.

5 All country papers, together with the analytical paper and a thematic study, are consolidated into the single product.

6 Country and regional data under the ASM are downloadable from ADB ASM database (online data portal).

7 ASM is disseminated through the launch seminar at a selected DMC, ADB headquarters, and/or virtual conference. Training programs based on key findings from the ASM are elaborated for requested DMCs as back-to-back events with the dissemination seminar or as stand-alone events.

Source: Asian Development Bank.

Highlights

Southeast Asia's robust growth over the past 10 years has been underpinned by micro, small, and medium-sized enterprises (MSMEs); strengthening their role through structural reform will be critical in maintaining the region's dynamism.

Using national classifications, MSMEs accounted for an average 97% of all enterprises, 69% of the total workforce, and 41% of a country's gross domestic product (GDP) during 2010–2019. The share of MSME employees to total employees and MSME contributions to GDP expanded moderately. The impact of the novel coronavirus disease (COVID-19) in 2020 exacerbated already growing global trade tensions and economic uncertainty in the region. In many ways, MSMEs hold the key to economic recovery in developing Asia.

Entrepreneurship development is key for accelerating inclusive growth in developing Asia.

In Southeast Asia, 61%–89% of MSMEs are in services, many engaged in traditional wholesale and retail trade. Their operations are typically low-technology and domestically focused with little drive among owners to expand their business. Young entrepreneurs, start-ups, and technology-based MSMEs are far more growth-oriented, have innovative mindsets, and look to tap regional and global markets. However, they remain a small fraction of MSMEs in Southeast Asia. It is crucial to foster this MSME segment to ignite resilient and inclusive growth at both national and regional levels.

Local MSMEs have the potential to create more jobs.

In Southeast Asia, 72%–85% of MSMEs operate in rural areas. They absorb 70%–84% of MSME employees in their countries. Thus, their growth is crucial for providing jobs for the unemployed or informal workforces. Improved basic infrastructure in rural areas—such as electricity, internet penetration, and transportation—can attract more workers with new and innovative business ideas to outside national capital regions.

Promoting MSME internationalization through participation in global value chains will boost national productivity; however, it requires well-organized government support.

In Southeast Asia, just a small number of MSMEs have been exposed or have access to global markets. MSMEs contributed an average 20% of a country's export value during 2010–2018. Participation in global value chains is limited. Access to markets remains a major challenge. Developing agricultural value chains should be a core policy, especially for food processing. Enhanced MSME internationalization brings with it new risks—such as changing or volatile foreign demand—made abundantly clear by the ongoing COVID-19 crisis. MSMEs are fragile, prone to disruption from external shocks. This requires a well-organized government support mechanism covering international trade (such as trade insurance).

Asia's rapid shift into using digital transactions for MSMEs should be further encouraged, bolstered by the post-COVID-19 business model that lessens physical contact.

The expansion of digital services nationwide has promoted the rapid development of e-commerce in Southeast Asia, bringing new business opportunities to start-ups and MSMEs overall. However, it remains at an early stage of development. MSME online presence is rare in most countries, while the majority still prefer traditional ways of doing business through personal contact. Digital technology offers a way to grow MSMEs by creating new and innovative businesses. Several countries in the region have launched assistance programs such as Indonesia's *E-Smart IKM* program, Malaysia's *Accelerating SME eCommerce Adoption* program, Philippine's *digitaljobsPH* program, and Singapore's *SMEs Go Digital* program.

Access to finance is the central factor underlying MSME growth; limited access to formal financial services remains a critical structural problem.

The MSME credit market is small and is growing slowly across Southeast Asia, affected by slower domestic economic growth generally. Bank loans to MSMEs averaged 14.8% of a country's GDP and 16.9% of total bank lending during 2010–2019, contracting at a compound annual rate of 1.3% and 0.3%, respectively. MSME nonperforming loans accounted for an average 4.1% of total MSME bank loans, above the average 2.0% nonperforming loan ratio for banks, yet it has been declining faster (decreasing at a compound annual rate of 2.5% against 0.7% for total bank loans).

Public finance plays a critical role in narrowing the MSME financing gap; it also acts as an emergency assistance tool for MSMEs during and after financial crises, disasters, and other shocks.

Public financing for MSMEs runs through various direct or indirect lending modalities, such as specialized banks, special funds, soft loan programs, and/or refinancing facilities, together with interest rate subsidies, mandatory lending, and/or credit guarantees. This government financial assistance for MSMEs often focuses on thematic or priority groups such as women-led MSMEs, agribusiness, technology-based start-ups, young entrepreneurs, and rural MSMEs. More importantly, this public financing acts as an emergency assistance tool for MSMEs to retain their business and survive, particularly when unexpected events strike—such as economic and financial crises, disasters, and/or forced changes in the business environment (the COVID-19 pandemic response).

Nonbank finance is a viable substitute for bank credit in financing MSME working capital; it remains small but growing.

The nonbank finance industry is small in scale but growing. Nonbank finance institutions (NBFIs)—including microfinance institutions, credit cooperatives, finance companies, pawnshops, and leasing companies—do not clearly target MSMEs as major clients but are viable substitutes for banks in financing MSME working capital. In Southeast Asia, NBFI financing accounted for an average 3.9% of a country's GDP and 8.6% of total bank lending during 2010–2019 (a compound annual growth of 13.1% and 3.2%, respectively). The average share of nonperforming financing to total NBFI financing was a negligible 0.8% (but slightly increasing at a compound annual growth of 0.7%).

As digital finance increases across developing Asia, governments have begun regulating peer-to-peer (P2P) lending and equity crowdfunding as well as establishing basic digital finance infrastructure.

Digital financial services (DFS) have spread widely across Southeast Asia, offering new financing opportunities for MSMEs while accelerating national financial inclusion. The number of finance technology or fintech firms has been increasing, while most still operate informally. In response, central banks and financial authorities have started formulating DFS regulatory and policy frameworks, addressing branchless/agent banking, P2P lending platforms, equity crowdfunding, and cybersecurity. Countries in the region have focused first on developing national payment systems as basic DFS infrastructure.

MSME capital markets have reached the stage for further development.

Dedicated MSME stock markets exist in several Southeast Asian countries—such as Indonesia (Acceleration Board), Malaysia (ACE and LEAP markets), the Philippines (SME Board), and Thailand (mai)—as an alternative funding source for viable, innovative small firms. Equity markets that MSMEs can tap remain small but are gradually expanding. Their market capitalization averaged 8.1% of a country's GDP during 2010–2019 (a compound annual growth of 1.0%). Key development challenges for MSME capital markets include market liquidity, listing costs, issuer quality, capital market literacy, and the growth mindset of MSME owners.

Intragovernmental policy coordination is an essential part of implementing comprehensive policy frameworks on MSME development and financial inclusion; greater synergy among policy actions can emerge from more extensive coordination among public-private stakeholders.

MSME development is a government policy priority to boost economic diversification and inclusive growth. In Southeast Asia, most countries have developed long-term strategies for MSME development in line with national economic development strategies and goals. Central banks promote financial inclusion to achieve national inclusive growth strategies and address DFS solutions for MSMEs. There are relatively good policy coordination mechanisms for MSME development and access to finance at the national and regional level. However, policy coordination among central government authorities and between central and local governments should be further strengthened to increase policy synergy. In addition, given the emerging risks associated with DFS—such as cybersecurity—extensive coordination between financial regulators, government authorities, and the private sector would maximize the benefits of inclusive finance.

Southeast Asia

Regional Review

Overview

Southeast Asian economy[4] has been underpinned by micro, small, and medium-sized enterprises (MSMEs). They stimulate domestic demand, job creation, innovation, and competition. The region's slowing economic growth can be recovered by strengthening dynamics of MSMEs. Based on national firm classifications, MSMEs in Southeast Asia accounted for an average 97.2% of all enterprises, 69.4% of the total workforce, and 41.1% of a country's gross domestic product (GDP) during 2010–2019. The share of MSMEs to total enterprises slightly declined across the region, dropping at a compound annual rate of 0.3%. Meanwhile, the share of MSME employees to total employees rose by 0.8%, and MSMEs' contribution to GDP expanded by 2.3% at a compound annual rate. During 2010–2018, MSMEs contributed 20.4% of a country's export value on average (a compound annual decline of 0.05%).

Access to finance is essential for MSMEs to grow further. But their access to formal financial services is limited—a structural problem in most countries. Across Southeast Asia, bank lending to MSMEs was equivalent to an average 14.8% of a country's GDP and 16.9% of total bank lending during 2010–2019 (a compound annual decline of 1.3% and 0.3%, respectively). The MSME credit market is small with sluggish growth, the result of slowing national economic growth. The MSME nonperforming loans (NPLs) accounted for an average 4.1% of total MSME bank loans, above the overall bank average NPL ratio of 2.0%. Yet both declined over the period—MSME NPL ratio fell at a compound annual rate of 2.5% against 0.7% for total bank loans.

The nonbank finance industry is small but growing. While nonbank finance institutions (NBFIs)—which include microfinance institutions, credit cooperatives, finance companies, pawnshops, and leasing companies—do not clearly target MSMEs as major clients, they are a viable substitute for banks in financing MSME working capital. During 2010–2019, NBFI financing accounted for an average 3.9% of a country's GDP (a compound annual growth of 13.1%) and 8.6% of total bank lending (3.2%). The share of nonperforming financing to total NBFI financing averaged a negligible 0.8% (yet it rose slightly at a compound annual growth of 0.7%).

Equity markets that MSMEs can tap are small but expanding gradually in Southeast Asia. A dedicated MSME stock market has been created in several countries such as Indonesia, Malaysia, the Philippines, and Thailand as an alternative funding source for viable and innovative small firms. Their market capitalization averaged 8.1% of the country's GDP during 2010–2019 (a compound annual growth of 1.0%). Digital financial services (DFS) have spread widely across the region and should help fill some of the unmet demand from MSMEs. Financial authorities have begun regulating peer-to-peer (P2P) lending platforms and equity crowdfunding.

MSME development is a policy priority for governments as they seek economic diversification and inclusive growth. In Southeast Asia, most countries have long-term strategies for MSME development in line with their national economic development strategies and goals. Central banks promote financial inclusion as part of national inclusive growth strategies, helping organize DFS solutions for MSMEs.

[4] Southeast Asian countries observed in the Asia Small and Medium-Sized Enterprise Monitor 2020 are Brunei Darussalam, Cambodia, Indonesia, the Lao People's Democratic Republic (Lao PDR), Malaysia, Myanmar, the Philippines, Singapore, Thailand, and Viet Nam.

The 10 Association of Southeast Asian Nations (ASEAN) members created an ASEAN Economic Community (AEC) in 2015 to accelerate a regional economic integration.[5] The AEC holds the ASEAN Coordinating Committee on Micro, Small and Medium Enterprises and the Working Committee on Financial Inclusion to promote MSME development and financial inclusion in the region, respectively. ASEAN's long-term MSME development strategy (2016–2025) has five goals: (i) promote productivity, technology, and innovation; (ii) increase access to finance; (iii) enhance market access and internationalization; (iv) enhance the policy and regulatory environment; and (v) promote entrepreneurship and human capital development. Along with this regional strategy, Southeast Asian countries offer a relatively good policy coordination mechanism for MSME development and access to finance at national and regional levels.

1. MSME Development

Micro, Small, and Medium-Sized Enterprises in Southeast Asia, 2010–2019

	Percentage share	*Compound annual growth*
• **Number of MSMEs to total enterprises**	***97.2%***	***-0.3%***
• **MSME employees to total employees**	***69.4%***	***+0.8%***
• **MSME contribution to national GDP**	***41.1%***	***+2.3%***
• **MSME export to total export value***	***20.4%***	***-0.05%***

GDP = gross domestic product; MSME = micro, small, and medium-sized enterprise. Reporting countries only.
* 2010–2018.

Scale of MSMEs

In Southeast Asia, MSMEs are classified using a combination of four criteria: number of employees, net or total assets, annual sales turnover, and capital invested. All 10 countries covered use an employment threshold to classify MSMEs, either as stipulated by law or for statistical purposes—seven countries use sales turnover, five use assets, and two use invested capital (Table 2.1). In defining MSMEs, the level of employment, assets, turnover, and capital differs by country and by industrial sector (Cambodia, the Lao PDR, Malaysia, Myanmar, Thailand, and Viet Nam). This makes it difficult to discuss MSMEs across countries due to the lack of a standardized definition. This report relies upon national definitions of MSMEs. Myanmar and Singapore do not classify microenterprises, but this chapter collectively uses "MSME" throughout.

MSMEs dominate the business environment. In Southeast Asia, MSMEs accounted for an average 97.2% of a country's total enterprises during 2010–2019. The share of MSMEs to total enterprises declined slightly (a negligible compound annual decline of 0.3%). By country, the number of MSMEs increased sharply in Viet Nam (a compound annual growth of 13.8%), followed by Cambodia (6.4%), Myanmar (5.0%), and Malaysia (4.3%) (Figure 2.1A).[6] Within the region, only Myanmar (89.9%) had less than 97% of its enterprises MSMEs.

5 The Association of Southeast Asian Nations (ASEAN) was founded by Indonesia, Malaysia, the Philippines, Singapore, and Thailand in 1967. Brunei Darussalam joined the ASEAN in 1984, followed by Viet Nam in 1995, the Lao PDR and Myanmar in 1997, and Cambodia in 1999.

6 Compound annual growth is calculated based on latest available data. See Notes for Figure 2.1.

Table 2.1: MSME Definitions in Southeast Asia

Country	Category	Definition: Employee	Definition: Asset	Definition: Turnover	Definition: Capital	Definition: By Sector	Definition: Others	Legal Basis	Remarks
Brunei Darussalam	Micro, small, and medium-sized firm	√							Utilized by statistics office.
		√	√	√			√ (loan size)		Utilized by financial regulatory authority.
Cambodia	Micro, small, and medium-sized firm	√	√			√			Small and Medium Enterprise Development Policy and Five-year Implementation Plan 2020–2024 [Forthcoming]
Indonesia	Micro, small, and medium-sized firm		√	√				√	Law No.20/2008 on Micro, Small and Medium-sized Enterprises
		√							Utilized by statistics office.
Lao People's Democratic Republic	Micro, small, and medium-sized firm	√	√	√		√		√	Decree No.25/GOL/2017/on SME Classification
Malaysia	Micro, small, and medium-sized firm	√		√		√		√	National SME Development Council Directive 2005
Myanmar	Small, and medium-sized firm	√			√	√		√	SME Development Law No.23/2015
Philippines	Micro, small, and medium-sized firm		√					√	Small and Medium Enterprise Development Council Resolution No.01 Series of 2003
		√							Utilized by statistics office.
Singapore	Small, and medium-sized firm	√		√					Utilized by statistics office.
Thailand	Micro, small, and medium-sized firm	√		√		√		√	Ministerial Regulation on SME Definition/B.E.2562 (2019)
Viet Nam	Micro, small, and medium-sized firm	√		√	√	√		√	Law No.04/2017/QH14 on Support for Small and Medium-sized Enterprises; Decree No.39/2018/ND-CP

MSME = micro, small, and medium-sized enterprise; SME = small and medium-sized enterprise.
Source: Compilation from Country Reviews of Asia SME Monitor 2020.

By sector, the majority of MSMEs are engaged in services, especially wholesale and retail trade. In Southeast Asia, 61%–89% of MSMEs by country belong to the services sector—which combines wholesale and retail trade with "other services" such as accommodation and food services—while manufacturing (which includes food processing) accounted for just 5%–17% of MSMEs by country (Figure 2.1B).[7] Most MSMEs in Southeast Asia are typically low-technology businesses operating in domestic markets, and their business owners tend to be less growth oriented.[8] A small fraction of MSMEs in the region involve young entrepreneurs, start-ups, and technology-based firms. They are more growth oriented, innovative, and often aim to join global markets. It is essential to promote these MSMEs to build more resilient and inclusive growth at the national level.

MSMEs are spread widely outside of the country's capital. In Southeast Asia, 72%–85% of MSMEs operate in rural areas with the remaining 15%–28% based in capital cities (Figure 2.1C).[9] The spread of local MSMEs is critical to diversify national economies. In many countries, a lack of basic infrastructure (such as electricity and transportation) is the primary barrier to rural business development. Digital infrastructure (such as broadband internet) is also lacking in most rural areas, access to which is critical for developing innovative rural-based businesses.

Gender data of MSMEs is not available in Southeast Asia, except for Malaysia, where 2015 census data found that a relatively small 20% of MSMEs were owned by women. Throughout the region, many MSMEs remain unregistered and operate informally, creating barriers to business development, particularly globally (footnote 8). Business formalization is a critical agenda for MSME development at the national level. Countries such as the Lao PDR and Viet Nam have reformed their business registration systems to encourage more MSMEs to join.

7 Wholesale and retail trade in Malaysia includes transportation and storage, telecommunication, and real estate. No sector data is available for Myanmar and Singapore.
8 Based on interviews with partner institutions in nine Southeast Asian countries (except Singapore) during July and October 2019.
9 Capitals include Phnom Penh (Cambodia), Vientiane (Lao PDR), Kuala Lumpur (Malaysia), Yangon (Myanmar), National Capital Region (the Philippines), Bangkok (Thailand); reporting countries only.

Figure 2.1: Number of MSMEs

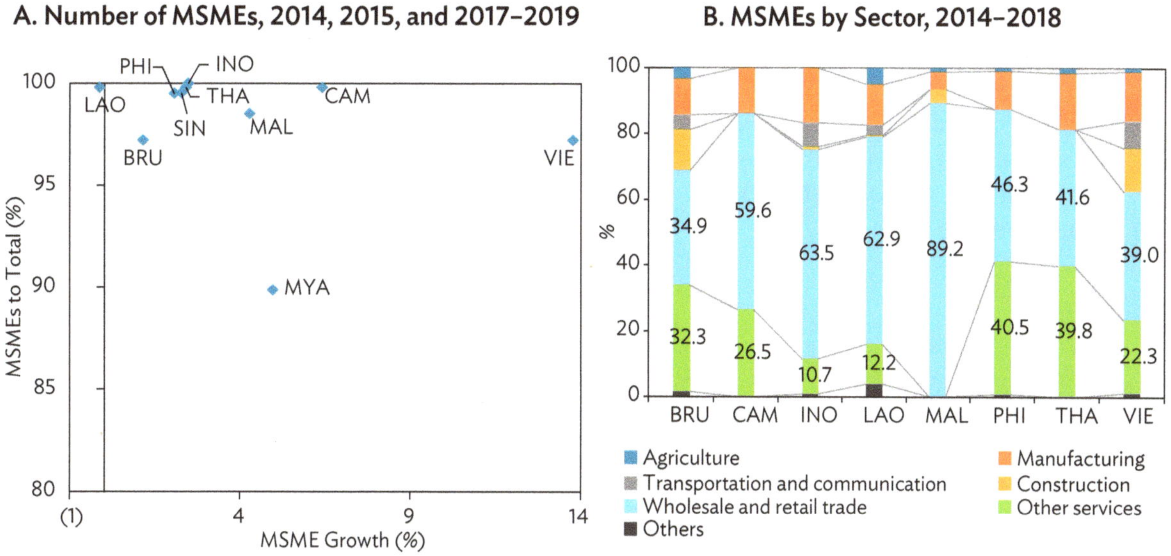

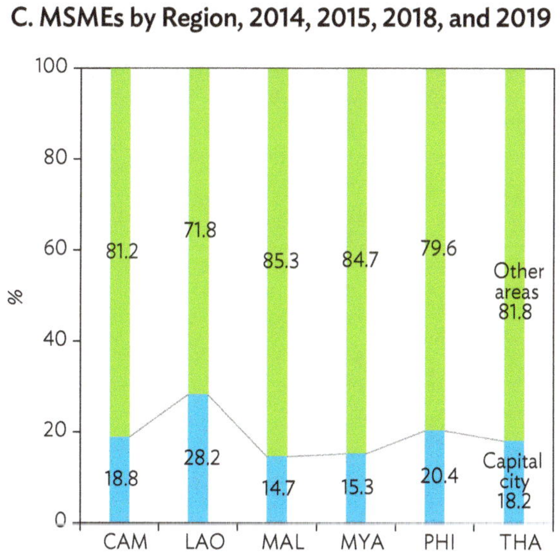

BRU = Brunei Darussalam; CAM = Cambodia; INO = Indonesia; LAO = Lao PDR; MAL = Malaysia; MSME = micro, small, and medium-sized enterprise; MYA = Myanmar; PHI = Philippines; SIN = Singapore; THA = Thailand; VIE = Viet Nam.

Notes: For Figure 2.1A, data refer to the latest available year (end-of-year): 2014 for CAM; 2015 for MAL; 2017 for BRU; 2018 for INO, LAO, PHI, THA, and VIE; 2019 for MYA (March) and SIN. MSME growth (%) refers to compound annual growth during past and latest available data. Data covers: 2009–2014 for CAM; 2003–2015 for MAL; 2010–2017 for BRU; 2006–2018 for LAO and PHI; 2007–2018 for THA and VIE; 2010–2018 for INO; 2006–2019 for MYA (fiscal year); 2014–2019 for SIN. For Figure 2.1B, data refer to the latest available year (end-of-year): 2014 for CAM; 2015 for MAL; 2016 for INO; 2017 for BRU; 2018 for LAO, PHI, THA, and VIE. Wholesale and retail trade in MAL includes transportation and storage, telecommunication, and real estate. For Figure 2.1C, data refer to the latest available year (end-of-year): 2014 for CAM; 2015 for MAL; 2018 for LAO, PHI, and THA; 2019 for MYA (March).

Source: ADB Asia SME Monitor 2020 database.

Employment

The employment by MSMEs accounted for an average 69.4% of a country's workforce during 2010–2019 in Southeast Asia. The share of MSME employees to the total has grown slightly (a compound annual growth of 0.8%). By country, MSME employees sharply increased in Viet Nam (a compound annual growth of 6.4%), followed by the Lao PDR (5.9%), the Philippines (4.6%), Thailand (4.2%), and Cambodia (4.1%) (Figure 2.2A).[10] In 2018, Indonesian MSMEs accounted for 97.0% of the workforce, the highest among Southeast Asian countries, followed by Thailand (85.5%) and the Lao PDR (82.4%). MSMEs in Viet Nam absorbed just 38.0%.

By sector, the majority of MSME workers are in services, especially wholesale and retail trade, which makes sense given the large number of MSMEs in the services sector. In Southeast Asia, 44%–85% of MSME employees

[10] Compound annual growth is calculated based on latest available data. See Notes for Figure 2.2.

by country work in services, while manufacturing accounted for 10%–26% of MSMEs by country in the region (Figure 2.2B) (footnote 7). In Viet Nam, manufacturing is the largest employer with more than 25% of the workforce.

By domestic region, MSME employees are spread widely outside the capital, similar to the spread of MSMEs in rural areas. Across the region, 70%–84% of MSME employees by country work in rural areas with the remaining 16%–30% in the capital (Figure 2.2C) (footnote 9). Given that local MSMEs hold much promise in creating new jobs, they are critical in absorbing the unemployed or informal workers. Improving basic rural infrastructure such as electricity, internet access, and transportation will attract better skilled workers to new and innovative local businesses outside the capital.

Figure 2.2: Employment by MSMEs

A. MSME Employees, 2014 and 2017–2019

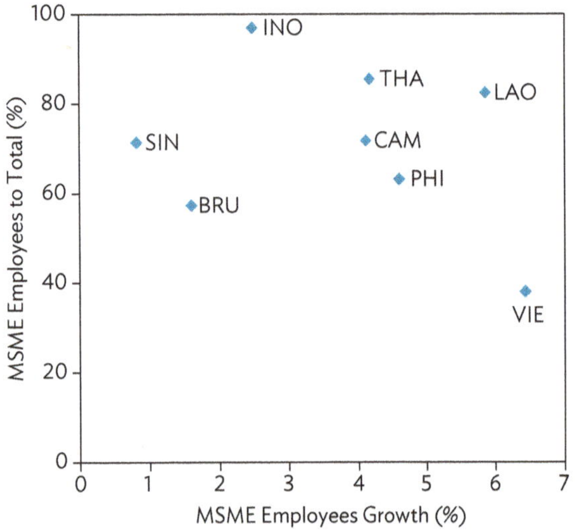

B. MSME Employees by Sector, 2013, 2014, and 2016–2018

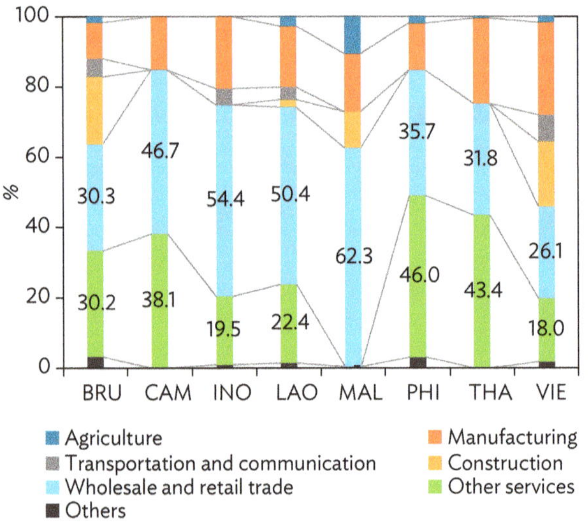

C. MSME Employees by Region, 2014, 2015, and 2018

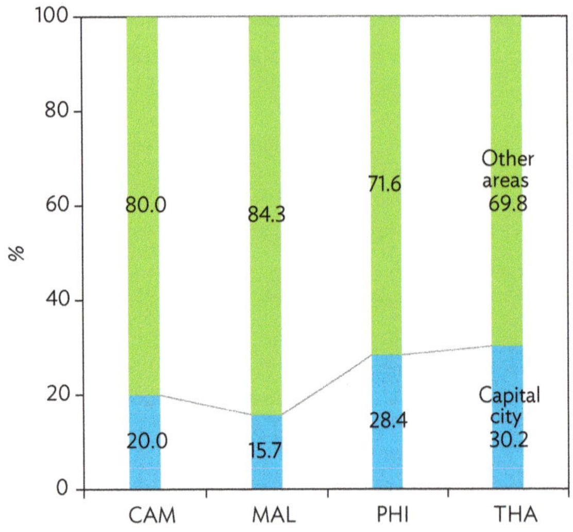

BRU = Brunei Darussalam; CAM = Cambodia; INO = Indonesia; LAO = Lao PDR; MAL = Malaysia; MSME = micro, small, and medium-sized enterprise; PHI = Philippines; SIN = Singapore; THA = Thailand; VIE = Viet Nam.

Notes: For Figure 2.2A, data refer to the latest available year (end-of year): 2014 for CAM; 2017 for BRU; 2018 for INO, LAO, PHI, THA, and VIE; 2019 for SIN. MSME employees growth (%) refers to compound annual growth during past and latest available data. Data covers: 2009–2014 for CAM; 2010–2017 for BRU; 2006–2018 for LAO and PHI; 2007–2018 for THA and VIE; 2010–2018 for INO; 2014–2019 for SIN. For Figure 2.2B, data refer to the latest available year (end-of-year): 2013 for LAO; 2014 for CAM; 2016 for INO; 2017 for BRU; 2018 for MAL, PHI, THA, and VIE. Wholesale and retail trade in MAL includes transportation and storage, telecommunication, and real estate. For Figure 2.2C, data refer to the latest available year (end-of-year): 2014 for CAM, 2015 for MAL, 2018 for PHI and THA.

Source: ADB Asia SME Monitor 2020 database.

The share of female employees to total MSME workers remained small in Malaysia (33.6%) in 2015 (Census 2016), while they held a relatively large share in Cambodia (54.0%) in 2014 (Census 2014). Gender data is not available for other countries, but given the share of female employees to total employees (ranging from 31% to 47%), it is unlikely to be large.

Business Productivity

As a region, Southeast Asia's economic growth slowed from 5.3% in 2017 to 5.1% in 2018 and 4.4% in 2019, as global trade tensions and global economic uncertainty increased. In 2020, the novel coronavirus disease (COVID-19) caused major disruptions to global, regional, and national economies—Southeast Asia's economy is expected to contract 2.7% in 2020.[11] MSMEs are the backbone of national economies, but they are highly susceptible to external shocks. This report (Volume I) analyzes MSMEs as of the end of 2019. A more definitive description of the COVID-19 impact on MSMEs will appear in the 2021 edition.

In Southeast Asia, MSMEs contributed an average 41.1% of a country's gross domestic product (GDP) during 2010–2019.[12] MSME contributions to GDP have expanded moderately (a compound annual growth of 2.3%). Indonesian MSMEs contributed a relatively high 61.1% to GDP in 2018, increasing at a 14.2% compound annual growth rate during 2010–2018 (Figure 2.3A).[13] MSMEs in Brunei Darussalam, Malaysia, Thailand, and Singapore contributed 35%–45% of the country's GDP (a compound annual growth ranging from 2.8%–9.1%). The share of MSME GDP to a country's GDP has gradually increased over time in Indonesia, Thailand, and Malaysia (Figure 2.3B). It fell in Singapore, while it generally increased in Brunei Darussalam. In US dollar terms, Indonesian MSMEs recorded $592 billion in 2018, followed by Thailand ($216 billion), Singapore ($149 billion), and Malaysia ($126 billion) (Figure 2.3C).[14]

By sector, services (including wholesale and retail trade and other services) was the major contributor of MSME GDP, ranging 60%–71% of a country's MSME GDP in 2018, followed by manufacturing (19%–27%) (Figure 2.3D). In Malaysia, MSMEs in agriculture accounted for 10% of MSME GDP in 2018.

[11] ADB. 2020. *Asian Development Outlook 2020 Supplement (June 2020)*. Manila.

[12] Time series data of MSMEs' GDP are available in five countries only (Brunei Darussalam, Indonesia, Malaysia, Singapore, and Thailand). For Malaysia, MSMEs' GDP figures are based on real GDP at constant 2005 price.

[13] Compound annual growth is calculated based on latest available data. See Notes for Figure 2.3.

[14] Exchange rates of local currency to US dollar refer to end-of-year currency rates from the International Monetary Fund/International Financial Statistics (IMF/IFS) in designated years.

Figure 2.3: MSME Contribution to Gross Domestic Product

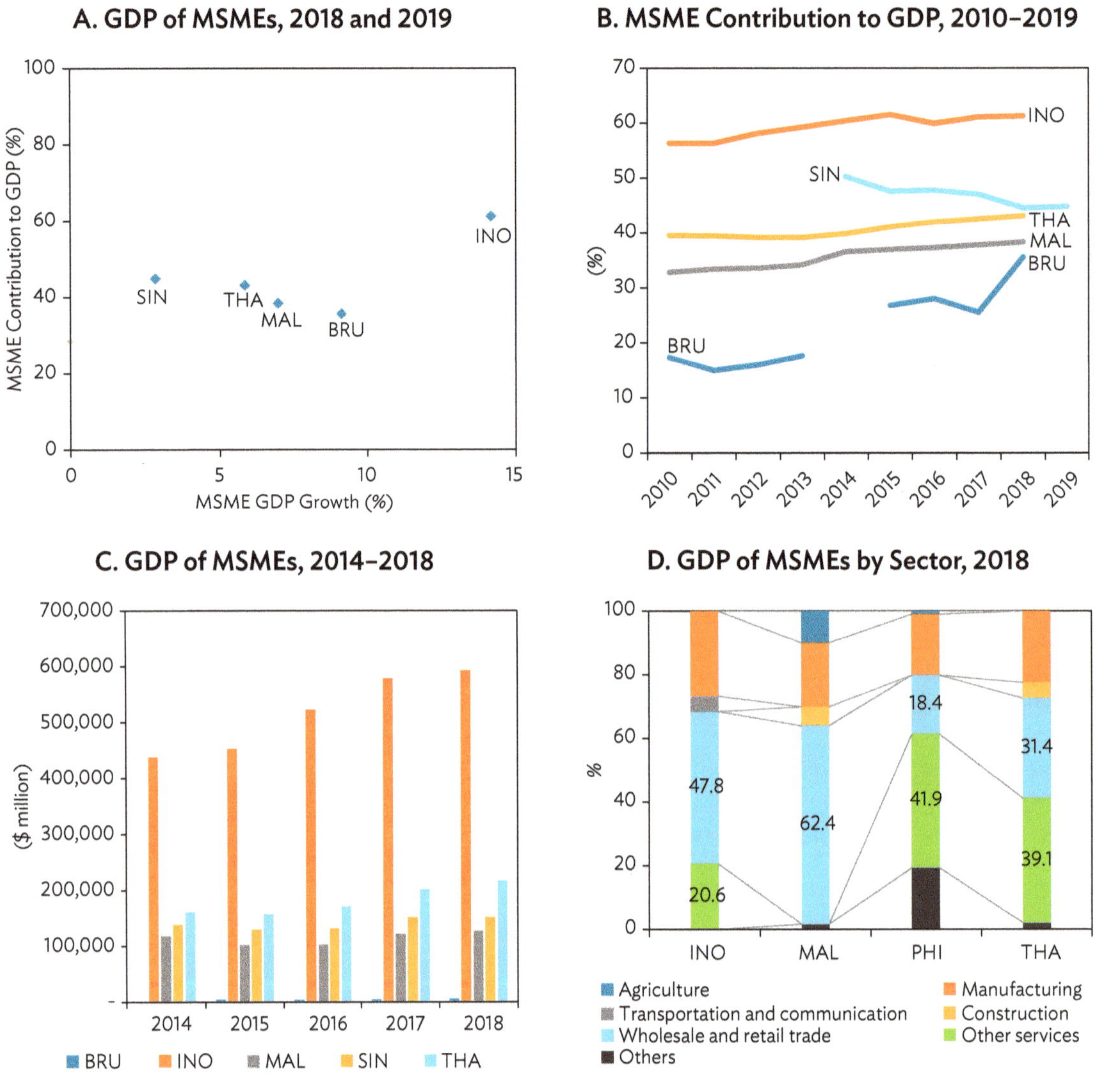

BRU = Brunei Darussalam; GDP = gross domestic product; INO = Indonesia; MAL = Malaysia; MSME = micro, small, and medium-sized enterprise; SIN = Singapore; THA = Thailand.

Notes: For Figure 2.3A, data refer to the latest available year (end-of-year): 2018 for BRU, INO, MAL, and THA; 2019 for SIN. MSME GDP growth (%) refers to compound annual growth during past and latest available data. Data covers: 2003–2018 for MAL; 2007–2018 for THA; 2010–2018 for BRU and INO; 2014–2019 for SIN. For Figure 2.3B, data for SIN are until 2019 and, data for other countries are until 2018. For BRU, data in 2014 is not available. For Figure 2.3C, exchange rates of local currency to US dollar refer to end-of-year currency rates from the International Monetary Fund International Financial Statistics in designated years. For Figure 2.3D, data refer to the latest available year (end-of-year): 2006 for PHI; 2016 for INO; 2018 for MAL and THA. Wholesale and retail trade in MAL includes transportation and storage, telecommunication, and real estate.

Source: ADB Asia SME Monitor 2020 database.

Market Access

Most Southeast Asian MSMEs operate within small domestic markets in relatively stable businesses such as wholesale and retail trade, accommodation, and restaurants. They normally use their own market channels with few links to other businesses or business partners. Only a small portion of MSMEs are exposed to global markets. MSME participation in global value chains is limited for each country observed. Access to markets remains a major challenge for MSMEs in the region.

On average, MSMEs contributed 20.4% of a country's export value during 2010–2018—the share has been largely stable (a compound annual contraction of 0.05%).[15] By country, MSMEs in Thailand accounted for 28.7% of export value in 2018, followed by Malaysia (17.3%) and Indonesia (14.4%). While MSME exports remain small in scale, they grew at a compound annual rate of 7.7% in Indonesia, followed by Malaysia (4.9%) and Thailand (3.6%) (Figure 2.4A).[16] The share of MSME export to total export value has been relatively stable, though with a slight decline since 2017 (Figure 2.4B). Exports in the region remain volatile, affected by shifting foreign demand. Escalating trade tensions between the United States (US) and the PRC have skewed or weakened foreign demand. In US dollars, MSMEs in Thailand exported a high of $72 billion in 2018, followed by Malaysia ($42 billion) and Indonesia ($20 billion) (Figure 2.4C) (footnote 14).

Promoting internationalization of MSMEs through assisting their participation in global value chains is one key to unlock new productivity and inclusive growth. Thailand promotes specific industrial clusters as high-potential production bases, for example, in automotive and parts, electronics, digital industries, agro-processing, and garments, providing more global business opportunities for MSMEs. Malaysia has several support programs to promote MSME internationalization, such as SME Go Global, Market Development Grant, and export training programs. In Indonesia, some handicrafts and wooden furniture industries have created export business clusters. A good example is a teak wood furniture cluster in Jepara, Central Java. Viet Nam has set MSME internationalization as a policy target, whereby the government offers export training and connects domestic MSMEs with global supply chains through trade promotion activities.

In Brunei Darussalam and the Philippines, developing agricultural value chains is an important policy priority, especially in food processing. The Brunei Darussalam government supports a *halal* certification program for export quality food products, promoting the internationalization of agribusinesses, including MSMEs. In the Philippines, the central bank supports agriculture value chain financing as part of its financial inclusion initiative.

To enhance MSME market access, several countries (such as Brunei Darussalam and Viet Nam) promote MSME participation in government projects. In Brunei Darussalam, MSMEs, especially material suppliers, have started participating in government procurement for construction projects; however, understanding project cost structures is a major challenge for them to actively participate.

15 Time series data of MSME export values are available for three countries (Indonesia, Malaysia, and Thailand).
16 Compound annual growth is calculated based on latest available data. See Notes for Figure 2.4.

Figure 2.4: MSME Exports

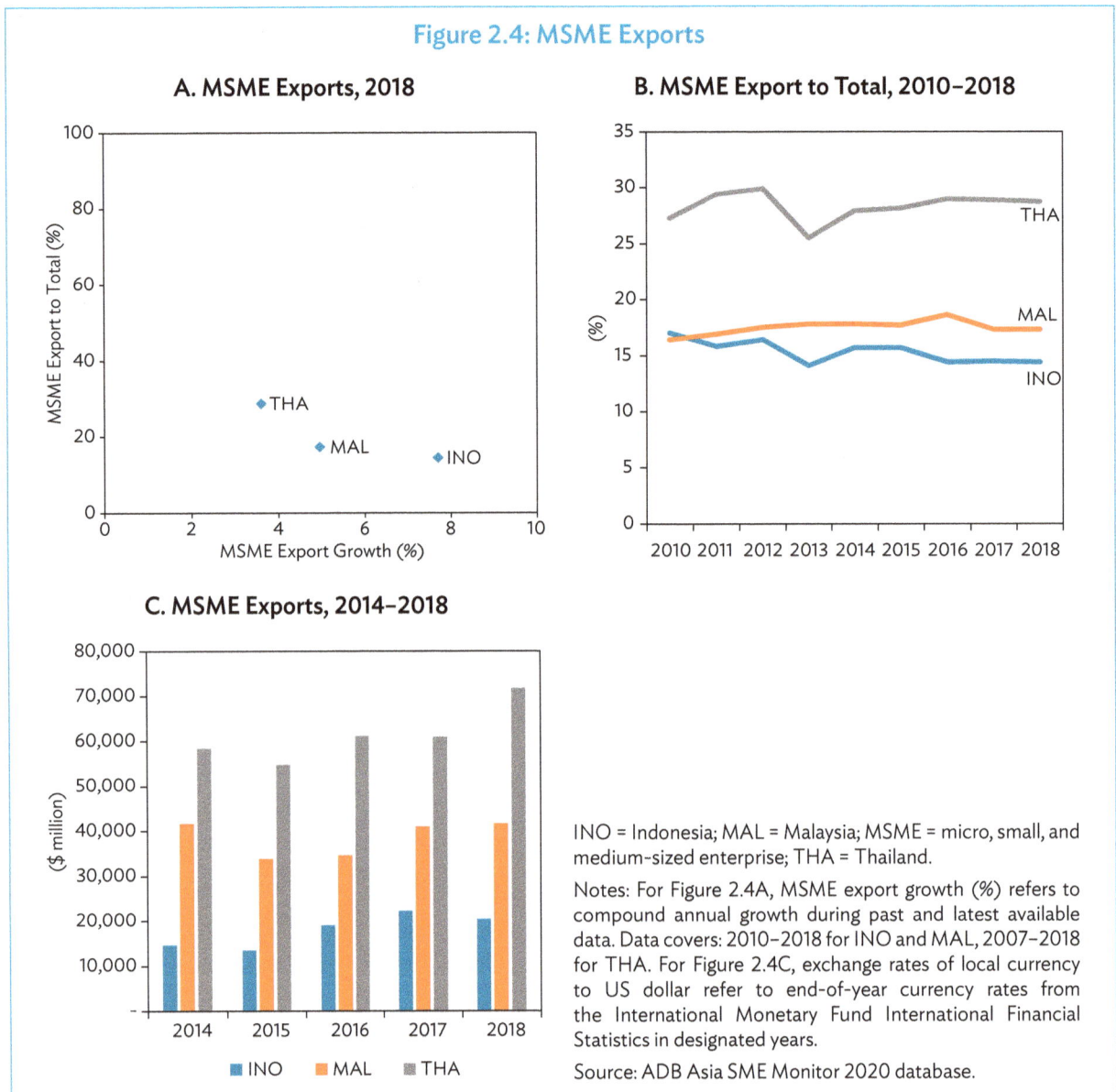

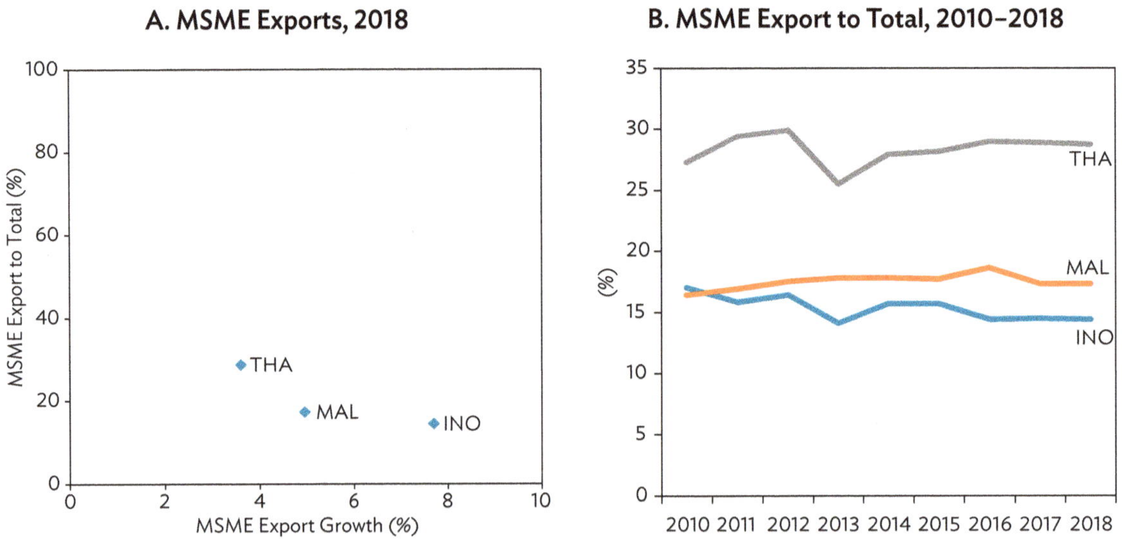

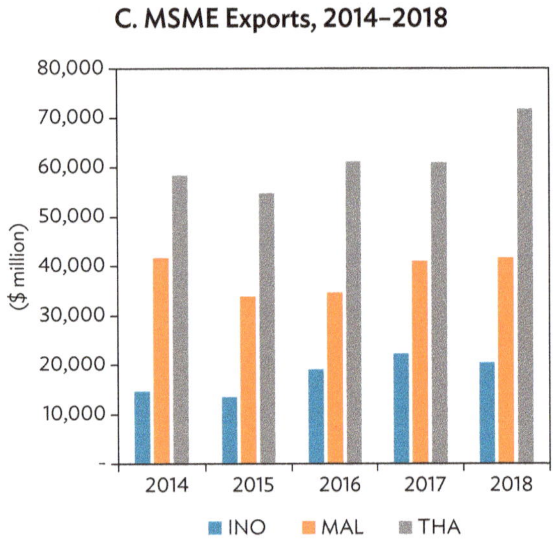

INO = Indonesia; MAL = Malaysia; MSME = micro, small, and medium-sized enterprise; THA = Thailand.

Notes: For Figure 2.4A, MSME export growth (%) refers to compound annual growth during past and latest available data. Data covers: 2010–2018 for INO and MAL, 2007–2018 for THA. For Figure 2.4C, exchange rates of local currency to US dollar refer to end-of-year currency rates from the International Monetary Fund International Financial Statistics in designated years.

Source: ADB Asia SME Monitor 2020 database.

Technology and Innovation

Digital technology has clearly contributed to the growth of MSMEs in Southeast Asia, providing the tools that help create new and innovative businesses. Internet and mobile phone penetration has sharply increased across the region. In 2018, there were more than 119 mobile cellular subscriptions per 100 people, except in the Lao PDR (52), while individual internet use varied greatly by country (26% in the Lao PDR to 95% in Brunei Darussalam) (Figure 2.5). Increased digital access has promoted the development of e-commerce businesses in the region, bringing new business opportunities to start-ups and MSMEs.[17]

Although still in its early stages, domestic e-commerce providers and mobile-based businesses have multiplied across Southeast Asia. Examples include online shopping platforms such as Lazada in Singapore and Tokopedia in Indonesia,

[17] E-commerce refers to buying and selling goods and services through the internet via digital platforms.

and mobile-based ride-hailing services such as Grab in Singapore, Gojek in Indonesia, and Angkas in the Philippines. Ride-hailing businesses also provide online food delivery services through partnering restaurants and MSME merchants. The larger and established Singapore-based e-commerce players actively participate in global markets.

However, MSME online presence remains to be developed in most countries in the region, with the majority of MSMEs preferring traditional ways of doing business. For instance, in the Lao PDR, limited internet connectivity, high costs of internet use, and lack of a regulatory framework for e-commerce business contributed to the slow development of domestic e-commerce and digital industry.[18] Business innovation has also yet to appear in most MSMEs in the region. In Malaysia, for instance, a 2015 census survey found only 1.3% of MSMEs held patents, trademarks, or copyrights and only 0.9% spent on research and development (R&D) for business innovation.

Many countries have launched assistance programs and strategies for MSMEs to adopt technology, innovation and expand e-commerce. Cambodia's Techno Startup Center supports start-ups in developing new and innovative businesses (incubation) for e-commerce and technology-based agribusinesses. Indonesia's *E-Smart IKM* program helps small industries expand market access through e-commerce. Malaysia has an *Accelerating SME eCommerce Adoption* program. The Philippines' *digitaljobsPH* program offers training for online freelancers and MSMEs to encourage their e-commerce business. Singapore has an *SMEs Go Digital* program to help create digital solutions. Thailand's SME promotion master plan encourages a shift from traditional to "smart" MSMEs, promoting the use of e-commerce for their marketing. Viet Nam's Master Plan 844 directs state-owned enterprises to work with technology-based start-ups, opening up public procurement opportunities for MSMEs.

Figure 2.5: Mobile and Internet Penetration, 2018

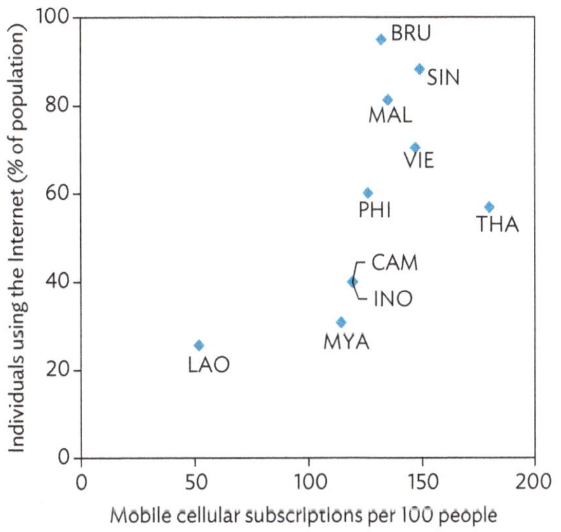

BRU = Brunei Darussalam, CAM = Cambodia, INO = Indonesia, LAO = Lao PDR, MAL = Malaysia, MYA = Myanmar, PHI = Philippines, SIN = Singapore, THA = Thailand, VIE = Viet Nam.

Source: World Development Indicators. https://data.worldbank.org/indicator/.

[18] As of August 2018, there was no e-commerce business registered in the Lao PDR.

Networking and Support

There are several autonomous business communities in Southeast Asia that support development of MSMEs and entrepreneurship through business linkages, networking, and incubation programs that offer office space and skill training for enterprises. National chambers of commerce are the primary providers of private sector business development services and networking opportunities. They often advocate on behalf of business with governments through national councils (in Malaysia, the Philippines, Singapore, and Viet Nam). There are also special-purpose associations that support young entrepreneurs (Brunei Darussalam and Thailand), women-led businesses (Indonesia and Viet Nam), and e-commerce start-ups (Indonesia). These private sector communities do not normally offer direct financial assistance to MSMEs, but on some occasions connect them to financial institutions as part of their business development services.

Several government authorities in the region also provide various capacity development programs to MSMEs on their own or in collaboration with international donors, generally focusing on technical and skill development. However, no country has a comprehensive national system for business development services.

To support MSME development, some countries use local business support centers; such as MSME Service Centers sponsored by the Chamber of Commerce in the Lao PDR, Negosyo Centers (local business centers) organized by the Government of the Philippines, and Member Development Centers organized by the Chamber of Commerce in Thailand. These centers provide hands-on support for MSMEs in accessing domestic markets and offer local training, incubation, and advisory services.

2. Access to Finance

Micro, Small, and Medium-Sized Enterprises in Southeast Asia, 2010–2019

Bank credit	*Percentage share*	*Compound annual growth*
• **MSME loans to national GDP**	***14.8%***	***-1.3%***
• **MSME loans to total bank loans**	***16.9%***	***-0.3%***
• **MSME NPLs to total MSME loans**	***4.1%***	***-2.5%***
Nonbank and market-based finance		
• **NBFI financing to national GDP**	***3.9%***	***+13.1%***
• **NBFI financing to total bank loans**	***8.6%***	***+3.2%***
• **NBFI NPF to total financing**	***0.8%***	***+0.7%***
• **MSME market capitalization to GDP**	***8.1%***	***+1.0%***

GDP = gross domestic product; MSME = micro, small, and medium-sized enterprise; NBFI = nonbank finance institution; NPF = nonperforming financing; NPL = nonperforming loan. Reporting countries only.

Bank Credit

Access to finance is critical for MSME growth. But limited access to formal financial services remains a serious, structural problem for MSMEs. During 2010–2019, bank loans to MSMEs in Southeast Asia averaged 14.8% of a country's GDP (a compound annual contraction of 1.3%), and they averaged 16.9% of total bank lending (a compound annual contraction of 0.3%). The MSME credit market is small, its sluggish growth a reflection of the overall slowing growth of national economies. MSME nonperforming loans (NPLs) averaged 4.1% of outstanding MSME bank loans (a compound annual decline of 2.5%), higher than the 2.0% NPL ratio for all bank lending (a compound annual decline of 0.7%).

By country, bank loans to MSMEs in 2019 was equivalent to 30.3% of Thailand's GDP, followed by Malaysia (18.5%), Singapore (15.1% [2018]), the Lao PDR (8.5%), Indonesia (7.0%), the Philippines (3.2%), and Myanmar (1.0% [2018]) (Figure 2.6A). MSME bank loans to total bank lending in 2019 reached 30.9% in Thailand, followed by the Lao PDR (19.8%), Indonesia (19.6%), Malaysia (14.6%), the Philippines (6.1%), Singapore (5.8% [2018]), and Myanmar (4.8%). In US dollar terms, Thailand's MSME lending was $218 billion in 2019, followed by Indonesia ($80 billion), Malaysia ($68 billion), Singapore ($57 billion), the Philippines ($12 billion), the Lao PDR ($1.6 billion), and Myanmar ($772 million) (Figure 2.6B) (footnote 14). High-income (Singapore) and upper middle-income (Indonesia, Malaysia, and Thailand) countries provided relatively large amounts of bank credit to MSMEs, while (lower middle-income) Lao PDR had a relatively large share of MSME credit to total bank lending.[19]

With the exception of the Lao PDR, bank loans to MSMEs continued to increase. The compound annual growth rate was high in Myanmar (24.2%; 2017–2019), followed by Indonesia (11.7%; 2011–2019), Thailand (7.7%; 2007–2019), the Philippines (7.3%; 2008–2019), Malaysia (6.7%; 2007–2019), and Singapore (6.1%; 2010–2019). The Lao PDR contracted by 1.4% (2015–2019). However, the shares of MSME loans to GDP and total bank loans have been shrinking over time, except in Indonesia and Myanmar (Figures 2.6C and 2.6D). In Indonesia, Kredit Usaha Rakyat (KUR), a public guaranteed loan scheme for MSMEs, supports the growth of MSME loans; nonetheless, MSME loan growth has been decelerating, reflecting the slowing growth of the national economy. In Myanmar, the Small and Medium Industrial Development Bank, a private sector bank, supports MSME loan growth; but MSME loans remain quite small compared with other countries.

In 2019, the MSME services sector—including wholesale and retail trade and "other services"—was the main borrower of bank loans across Southeast Asia, ranging 53%–67% of a country's MSME bank lending. This was followed by manufacturing (8%–30%) (Figure 2.6E). In Singapore, MSMEs in agriculture held the largest share of MSME credit (37%) in June 2019.

Commercial banks mostly rely on real estate security as collateral for loans. Movable assets such as machinery and inventory are also used as collateral for bank loans in many countries, but usually at the bank's discretion. In Myanmar, the central bank limits the amount of collateral required for loans and also allows for non-collateralized lending.

[19] World Bank country income classification (https://datahelpdesk.worldbank.org/knowledgebase/articles/906519).

Figure 2.6: Bank Credit

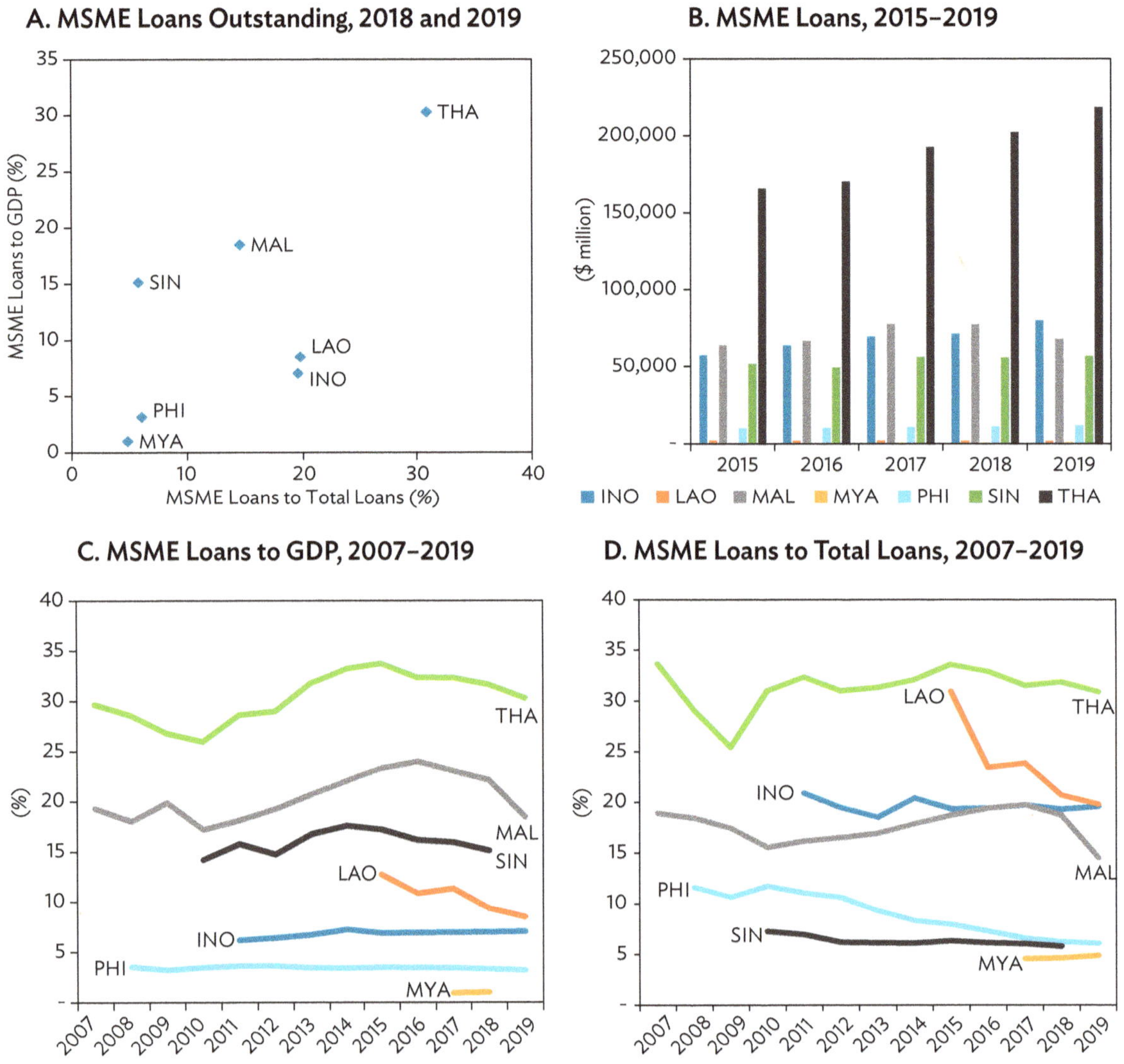

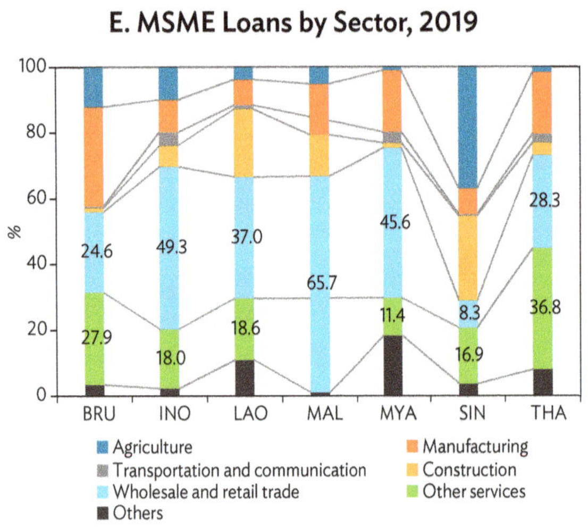

BRU = Brunei Darussalam; GDP = gross domestic product; INO = Indonesia; LAO = Lao PDR; MAL = Malaysia; MSME = micro, small, and medium-sized enterprise; MYA = Myanmar; PHI = Philippines; SIN = Singapore; THA = Thailand.

Notes: For Figure 2.6A, data for SIN as of end-2018; for the rest as of end-2019 (except MYA using fiscal year). Data (% of GDP) for MYA as of 2018 (fiscal year). For Figures 2.6B and 2.6E, data for SIN in 2019 are as of end-June. For Figure 2.6B, exchange rates of local currency to US dollar refer to end-of-year currency rates from the International Monetary Fund International Financial Statistics in designated years. For Figure 2.6C, data for MYA (fiscal year) and SIN (end-of-year) are until 2018. For Figure 2.6D, data for SIN are until 2018. For Figure 2.6E, wholesale and retail trade in MAL includes transportation and storage, telecommunication, and real estate.

Source: ADB Asia SME Monitor 2020 database.

The share of MSME NPLs to total MSME loans was higher than for non-MSMEs in 2019. By country, the MSME NPL ratio was 5.8% in the Philippines, 4.7% in Thailand, 4.2% in Singapore, 3.7% in Malaysia, and 3.6% in Indonesia; all higher than the overall NPL ratio for banks (Figure 2.7A). The spread between the MSME NPL ratio and gross bank NPL ratio was 3.7% in the Philippines, 2.2% in Singapore, 2.1% in Malaysia, 1.7% in Thailand, and 1.1% in Indonesia.

MSME NPLs have increased except Malaysia. The compound annual growth rate of MSME NPLs was high in Singapore (19.7%, 2010–2019), followed by Indonesia (12.5%, 2011–2019), the Philippines (3.4%, 2010–2019), Thailand (2.3%, 2009–2019), with Malaysia contracting 1.2% (2007–2019) (Figure 2.7A). The growth of MSME NPLs was higher than gross bank NPLs in Singapore (gross bank NPL compound annual growth of 12.1%), Thailand (2.1%), and Malaysia (−3.2%), while it was lower in Indonesia (14.6%) and the Philippines (5.9%). However, the share of MSME NPLs to total MSME loans has been decreasing moderately over time in Malaysia, the Philippines, and Thailand (Figure 2.7B).

Figure 2.7: MSME Nonperforming Loans

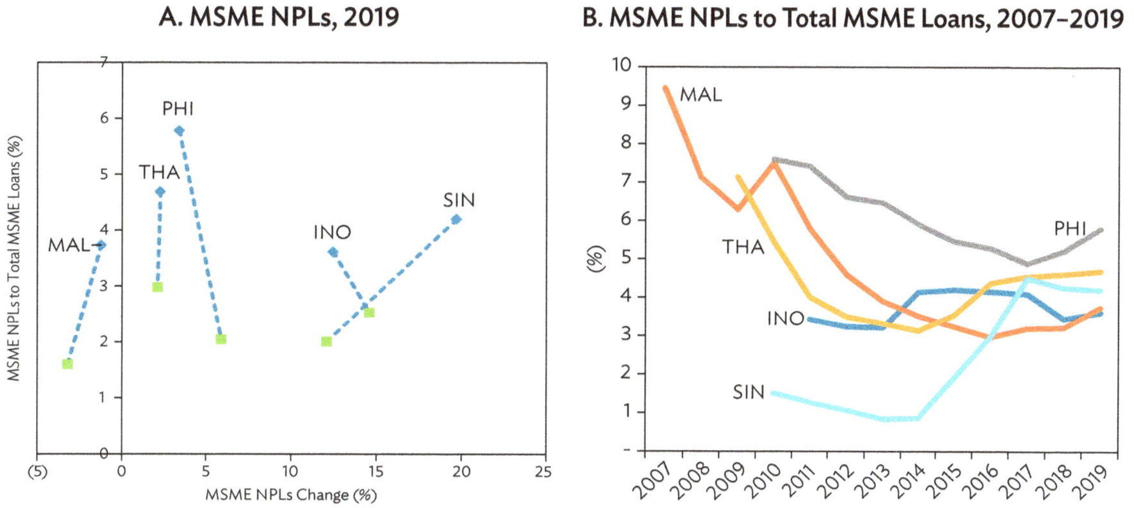

INO = Indonesia; MAL = Malaysia; MSME = micro, small, and medium-sized enterprise; NPL = nonperforming loan; PHI = Philippines; SIN = Singapore; THA = Thailand.

Notes: For Figures 2.7A and 2.7B, data for SIN in 2019 are as of end-June. For Figure 2.7A, ◆ = MSME NPLs, ■ = banks' gross NPLs. NPL change (%) refers to compound annual change (latest available data). For MSME NPLs, data covers 2011–2019 for INO, 2007–2019 for MAL, 2010–2019 for PHI, 2010–June 2019 for SIN, and 2009–2019 for THA. For banks' gross NPLs, the same data ranges except PHI (2008–2019) and SIN (2018--end of 2019).

Source: ADB Asia SME Monitor 2020 database.

Public Financing and Guarantees

Public financing plays a critical role in narrowing the financing gap faced by MSMEs. It comes via various modalities—such as direct or indirect lending to MSMEs through specialized banks, special funds, soft loan programs, and/or refinancing facilities, along with interest rate subsidies, mandatory lending, and/or credit guarantees. Government financial assistance for MSMEs often focuses on thematic or priority groups—such as women-led MSMEs, agribusiness, technology-based start-ups, young entrepreneurs, and rural firms. More importantly, public financing acts as an emergency assistance tool for MSMEs when confronted by external shocks—such as economic and financial crises, disasters, and/or other disruptions to the business environment (e.g., the COVID-19 pandemic). Financial assistance measures and related financial infrastructure and policies to support MSME access to finance in Southeast Asia are summarized in Table 2.2.

a. Specialized banks for MSMEs

The majority of Southeast Asian countries have a specialized bank dedicated to MSMEs; most are state-owned banks. In Brunei Darussalam, the government established an Islamic compliant SME Bank (Bank Usahawan) in 2017. Cambodia launched a state-owned SME Bank in April 2020, which offers guaranteed loans at below-market rates for MSMEs. In the Lao PDR, the government appointed a state-owned Lao Development Bank as an MSME-focused bank in 2008. Malaysia's state-owned SME Bank, launched in 2005, offers Islamic financing to MSMEs. In Myanmar, in addition to state-owned banks offering subsidized loans to MSMEs, there is the private sector Small and Medium Industrial Bank, established in 1996 as a dedicated bank for financing MSMEs. Thailand has the Small and Medium Enterprise Development Bank, a specialized financial institution established by the government in 2002, which offers subsidized loans to MSMEs. In Viet Nam, the state-owned Vietnam Development Bank (undergoing restructuring in 2020), while not specializing in MSMEs, helps service some of their financing needs.

b. Soft loan programs

Most countries offer soft loan programs, special funds, and/or refinancing schemes for MSMEs. The Lao PDR's SME Promotion Fund, restructured in 2018, offers financial intermediation loans via six participating commercial banks, offering concessional loans with subsidized interest rates up to 10 years. Since 1993, Malaysia's central bank has managed special funds to facilitate concessional MSME loans—there were 26 government funds with interest rate subsidies (as of end-2018) including an Islamic compliant SME Financing Scheme—with a non-collateral microcredit program since 2005. In Myanmar, the Japan International Cooperation Agency (JICA) offers two-step (financial intermediation) loans at below-market rates for MSMEs. In the Philippines, the government-funded Access of Small Enterprises to Sound Lending Opportunity (ASENSO) program for MSMEs has been operating since 2003, with a P3 Program (Pondo sa Pagbababago at Pag-Asenso) launched in 2017 to finance unserved or underserved microenterprises and entrepreneurs in the poorest provinces. The Singapore government streamlined existing firm-level financing schemes in 2019 under its Enterprise Financing Scheme, which includes SME working capital loans and credit risk sharing with participating financial institutions. Viet Nam has 10 state-owned MSME funds, which include the SME Development Fund and Credit Guarantee Fund. There are also several thematic financing programs for MSMEs in Southeast Asia such as Malaysia's SME Bank financing program for women entrepreneurs and Viet Nam's Fund for Science and Technology Innovation addressing high-tech MSMEs.

c. Mandatory lending scheme

Some countries set mandatory MSME lending targets. Since 2012, Indonesia's mandatory lending requires banks to allocate 20% of their loan portfolios to MSMEs—with target milestones of 5% by 2015, 10% by 2016, 15% by 2017, and 20% by 2018. Banks can meet their targets by either direct lending or indirectly channeling loans to MSMEs via linkage or intermediation loan programs or syndicated bank loans. In the Philippines, the 1991 Magna Carta mandated banks to allocate 10% of their loan portfolio to MSMEs but expired in 2018, while the Philippine Innovation Act of 2019 sets 4% in new mandatory lending for innovation activities targeting start-ups and MSMEs.

d. Credit guarantees

Credit guarantees are a popular tool for governments to help narrow MSME financing gaps. Most countries in Southeast Asia have credit guarantee schemes supporting MSME access to finance. In 2017, Indonesia launched KUR, a public guaranteed loan scheme for MSMEs, backing both non-collateral and collateral loans (with government interest rate subsidies). In Malaysia, MSME credit guarantees are mainly provided by the private Credit Guarantee Corporation Malaysia Berhad (CGC) and Prokhas (based on government guarantee funds). The centralized Philippine Guarantee Corporation (PhilGuarantee) was established in September 2019, combining five existing guarantee corporations (including the Small Business Corporation [SBC], which was a major credit guarantor for MSMEs). The state-funded Thai Credit Guarantee Corporation (TCG) provides three major MSME products: portfolio guarantees, guarantees for start-ups and innovative businesses, and guarantees for micro community businesses. Viet Nam runs a state-owned Credit Guarantee Fund for MSMEs.

In 2018, the share of guaranteed loans to total MSME loans was 22.1% in Malaysia (CGC), followed by Indonesia (13.8% for KUR, 2019), Thailand (5.9% for TCG, 2019), and the Philippines (0.01% for SBC, 2019) (Figure 2.8).[20] The growth of guaranteed loans was highest in Indonesia (a compound annual growth rate of 34.1% for KUR, 2009–2019), followed by Thailand (26.9% for TCG, 2007–2019) and Malaysia (5.6% for CGC, 2007–2018). The Philippines compound annual rate for MSME guarantees contracted 4.2% during 2007–2019, largely due to the centralization process.

Figure 2.8: Credit Guarantees, 2018 and 2019

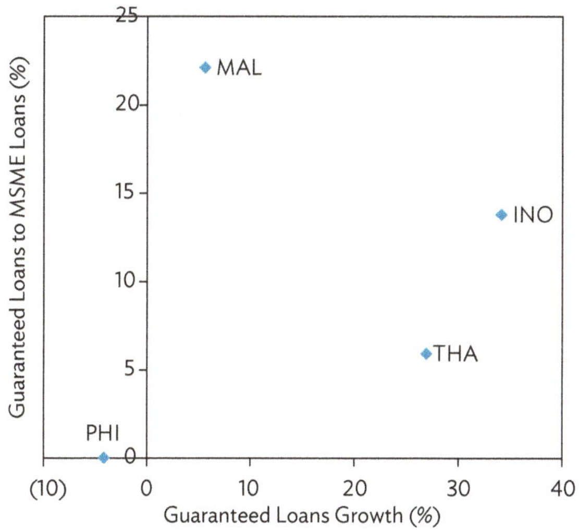

INO = Indonesia; MAL = Malaysia; MSME = micro, small, and medium-sized enterprise; THA = Thailand.

Notes: Data refer to the latest available year: end-2018 for MAL (Credit Guarantee Corporation), August 2019 for PHI (Small Business Corporation), and end-2019 for Indonesia (Kredit Usaha Rakyat) and Thailand (Thai Credit Guarantee Corporation). Guaranteed loans growth (%) refers to compound annual growth during past and latest available data. Data covers: 2007–2018 for MAL; 2007–2019 for PHI and THA; 2009–2019 for INO.

Source: ADB Asia SME Monitor 2020 database.

e. Emergency financial assistance: COVID-19 response

MSMEs are the backbone of national economies, but they are fragile entities easily disrupted by external shocks. In particular, the extent of access to finance seriously influences MSME survival rates in emergencies, such as economic and financial crises, flooding, and other disasters, where public financing plays a critical role of rescuing MSMEs devastated by such unexpected events.

In 2020, the COVID-19 pandemic derailed global, regional, and national economies. Quarantines strictly limited people's movements to control the virus spread. Travel bans, temporary school and business closures, and physical distancing slowed economic activities. Private business cut back production and service delivery. Workers were temporarily laid off. Working capital dried up, while prolonged containment measures increased the risk of business

20 The data for the Philippines referred to existing credit guarantees for MSMEs by Small Business Corporation (SBC) as of August 2019; after September 2019, no more new guarantees were provided by SBC.

failure and bankruptcy. MSMEs are at greater risk due to abrupt supply chain disruptions and tightened financial conditions.

Every government in Southeast Asia acted quickly to contain the spread of COVID-19 and curb the economic disruption through large-scale stimulus packages. Containment measures began in late February 2020 in Indonesia with government implementing emergency fiscal packages covering health expenditures (procurement of medical equipment), social assistance (providing food), and economic assistance (including financial assistance to MSMEs). The Lao PDR started containment measures on 23 March, including travel bans, school closures, and prohibiting mass gatherings. It implemented a total lockdown on 1–20 April with several extensions during May. The government offered tax relief, debt restructuring, and new loans for individuals and MSMEs. The Philippines imposed strict lockdowns and quarantines, beginning 16 March, including an Enhanced Community Quarantine in the capital region and other high-risk provinces, with various extensions in various forms through August. The government provided a comprehensive set of support measures for households and businesses—such as an emergency subsidy program for families and wage supplements to employees of small businesses. Thailand began containment measures on 26 March, including travel bans and a curfew extended to the end of June. Government measures included tax relief, cash handouts to workers, and debt restructuring and new MSME lending.

These initial national responses were clearly in the right direction, given the emergency need to contain the virus. ADB's rapid MSME surveys,[21] however, revealed that the majority of MSMEs in the Philippines (70.6% of those surveyed) and the Lao PDR (61.1%), and nearly half in Indonesia (48.6%) and Thailand (41.1%), suspended operations a month after the virus outbreak and national quarantine measures enforced. The remaining half (or less) continued to operate but faced supply disruptions given low demand. Domestic demand for MSME products fell 40% in Thailand and the Lao PDR, and 30% in the Philippines and Indonesia. Supply disruptions were cited by more than 30% of MSMEs in Thailand and the Philippines, and less than 20% in Indonesia and the Lao PDR. Accordingly, MSMEs in all countries surveyed reported a serious lack of funds to retain business operations, with many stating they had no cash or savings remaining, or would run out funds within a month.

All countries surveyed reported MSMEs had tremendous difficulty in raising enough working capital to survive. In response, central banks and financial authorities quickly offered liquidity support for financial institutions through reduced policy rates and/or capital injections to banks. At the same time, banks offered debt restructuring for existing loans by extending loan tenures and/or reducing interest rates, as well as deferring debt repayments (principal). They provided new loans to MSMEs through refinancing facilities or via special credit guarantee schemes. Table 2.2 provides a summary of the region's government emergency financial assistance to MSMEs in response to COVID-19.

21 ADB conducted rapid online MSME surveys in Indonesia, the Lao PDR, the Philippines, and Thailand during March and May 2020 to assess the initial impact of COVID-19 and associated quarantine measures on MSMEs. The detailed findings from these surveys are in Volume II of the Asia Small and Medium-Sized Enterprise Monitor 2020.

Table 2.2: Assistance and Infrastructure for MSME Access to Finance

Item		Bank Credit						Public Finance			Nonbank Finance			Digital Finance			
		Refinancing facilities to banks	Credit guarantees/ credir risk sharing	Mandatory lending to MSMEs	Interest rate subsidy	Credit bureaus/ credit information system	Secured transaction legal system	Specialized bank for MSMEs	Direct lending/ special funds/ soft loans	Focused groups financing	MFI development support	NBFI industry development (except MFIs)	Consumer/ client protection policies	Branchless/ agent banking strategy	Peer-to-peer (P2P) lending regulations	Equity crowdfunding (ECF) regulations	National payment system and digital infrastructure
Lower-middle-income economies	CAM		(CGS planned)			√		√ (SME Bank)			√		√	√ (mobile banking)			√ (Retail Pay)
	LAO	√	(drafting law)		√	√	√ (to be amended)	√ (LDB)	√		√		√	√			
	MYA	√ (JICA 2-step loans)	√ (MI; CGF planned)		√	(in process)	(drafting law)	√ (SMIDB)**	√		√			√ (mobile banking)			(brainstorming)
	PHI	√ (P3)	√	√*	√	√	√		√		√	√	√	√			√ (NRPS; PhilSys)
	VIE		√		√	√		√ (VDB)	√	√ (tech-MSMEs)	√	√			(brainstorming)	(brainstorming)	
Upper-middle-income economies	INO		√	√	√	√			√		√	√	√	√	√	√	√ (GPN)
	MAL	√	√		√	√	(preparing)	√ (SME Bank)	√	√ (women entrepreneurs)				√	√	√	√ (PayNet)
	THA	√	√		√	√	√	√ (SMEDB)					√	√	√	√	√ (PromtPay)
High-income economies	BRU					√	√	√ (SME Bank)	√ (co-matching grant)						√	√	(pilot testing)
	SIN	√	√			√	√		√ (EFS)					√ (digital banking)			√

Item		Capital Markets			Financial education programs and training	Dedicated financial inclusion strategy	Emergency Assistance (Response to COVID-19)					
		Equity markets that MSMEs can tap	Venture capital and private equity investments	Tax incentive for MSME issuers/ investors			Liquidity support for financial institutions/capital injection	Debt restructuring/ deferral of debt payments	Relaxed lending conditions/ interest rate reduction	New lending to MSMEs/ emergency refinaning facility	Special credit guarantees	Regulatory forbearance
Lower-middle-income economies	CAM			√	√	√	√	√	√	√		√
	LAO				√	√	√	√	√	√		√
	MYA				√	√	√		√	√		√
	PHI	√ (SME Board)			√	√	√	√	√	√	√	√
	VIE	√ (UPCoM)	√		√	√	√	√	√	√		√
Upper-middle-income economies	INO	√ (Acceleration Board)	√		√	√	√	√	√	√	√	√
	MAL	√ (ACE and LEAP)	√		√	√	√	√	√	√	√	√
	THA	√ (mai)	√	√ (VC/BA)	√		√	√	√	√	√	√
High-income economies	BRU						√	√				
	SIN	√ (Catalist)	√				√	√		√		√

BRU = Brunei Darussalam; CAM = Cambodia; CGF = credit guarantee fund; CGS = credit guarantee scheme; COVID-19 = coronavirus disease; GSB = Gerbang Pembayaran Nasional; INO = Indonesia; JICA = Japan International Cooperation Agency; LAO = Lao PDR; LDB = Lao Development Bank; MAL = Malaysia; MSME = micro, small, and medium-sized enterprise; MYA = Myanmar; PHI = Philippines; RPS = National Retail Payment System; SIN = Singapore; SMEPDF = Small and Medium Enterprise Development Bank; SMIDB = Small and Medium Industrial Development Bank; THA = Thailand; VDB = Vietnam Development Bank; VIE = Viet Nam. * PHI: Magna Carta (including a mandatory lending allocation to MSMEs) expired in June 2018. A new mandatory lending scheme for innovation activities (including start-ups and MSMEs) was enacted in April 2019. ** Private sector bank.

Note: World Bank country classification by income (https://datahelpdesk.worldbank.org/knowledgebase/articles/906519).

Source: ADB Asia SME Monitor 2020 database.

Nonbank Financing

The nonbank finance sector is small but growing. Nonbank finance institutions (NBFIs)—including microfinance institutions, credit cooperatives, finance companies, pawnshops, and leasing companies—do not specifically target MSMEs as major clients but act as viable substitutes for banks in providing MSME working capital. In Southeast Asia, NBFI financing accounted for an average 3.9% of a country's GDP during 2010–2019 (a compound annual growth rate of 13.1%) and 8.6% of total bank lending (3.2%). The average share of nonperforming financing (NPF) to total NBFI financing was a negligible 0.8%, but increased slightly at a compound annual growth rate of 0.7%.

By country, NBFI financing[22] in 2019 was 27.9% of GDP in Cambodia, followed by Brunei Darussalam (8.4%), Indonesia (3.2%), the Lao PDR (3.2% [2018]), the Philippines (3.0% [2018]), Singapore (2.9%), Myanmar (2.4% [2018]), Viet Nam (1.8%), and Malaysia (0.1% [2018]) (Figure 2.9A). Compared with total bank lending, NBFI financing in 2019 was 29.8% of total bank lending in Cambodia, followed by Brunei Darussalam (27.9%), Indonesia (11.3%), the Lao PDR (8.5%), Myanmar (7.7% [September 2019]), the Philippines (2.2%), Viet Nam (1.3% [June 2019]), Singapore (1.1% [August 2019]), and Malaysia (0.1% [2018]). Microfinance institutions (MFIs) dominate nonbank financing in Cambodia, followed by leasing companies, with both leading NBFI growth. In Brunei Darussalam, while small in number (two finance companies and one pawnbroker), the nonbank finance industry held a relatively high share of GDP and total bank lending.

In US dollar terms, nonbank finance in Indonesia reached $36 billion in 2019, followed by Singapore ($11 billion), Cambodia ($7.5 billion), Viet Nam ($4.4 billion), the Philippines ($4.2 billion), Myanmar ($1.2 billion), Brunei Darussalam ($1.1 billion), and the Lao PDR ($0.7 billion) (Figure 2.9B).[23] Although still small in size, NBFIs in Indonesia—such as finance companies, MFIs, and government pawnshops—offer various financing options for the traditionally underserved, including low-income households and MSMEs, especially in rural areas. In Singapore, finance companies are the primary form of nonbank financing. In Viet Nam, People's Credit Funds and MFIs are the leading form of nonbank financing. People's Credit Funds, introduced in 1993, are credit institutions established on a voluntary basis in the form of cooperatives. In the Philippines, NBFIs include finance companies, MFIs, credit unions and cooperatives, pawnshops, and non-stock savings and loan associations (NSSLAs) (there is no financing data on finance companies and MFIs, thus NBFI financing figures are incomplete). In Myanmar, MFIs are growing rapidly. Among NBFIs in the Lao PDR, MFIs and leasing companies are the most prominent for financing MSMEs.

Nonbank financing has grown rapidly across Southeast Asia (except Malaysia). Compound annual growth is high in the Lao PDR (70.8%, 2010–2019), followed by Myanmar (70.5%, 2012–September 2019), the Philippines (41.7%, 2009–2019), Cambodia (38.4%, 2007–2019), Viet Nam (18.7%, 2010–June 2019), Singapore (7.2%, 2010–August 2019), Indonesia (5.9%, 2016–2019), and Brunei Darussalam (0.9%, 2010–2019). Malaysia had a compound annual contraction of 5.1% during 2007–2018.

The nonbank finance industry, especially MFIs, has been increasing in Cambodia, the Lao PDR, Myanmar, and Viet Nam (CLMV). The share of NBFI financing to GDP sharply increased in Cambodia (a compound annual growth of 25.9%, 2007–2019), the Lao PDR (51.5%, 2010–2019), Myanmar (71.5%, 2012–2018), and Viet Nam (7.9%, 2012–June 2019) (Figure 2.9C). The nonbank finance industry in Cambodia, the Lao PDR, Myanmar, and Viet Nam also grew faster than the banking sector. The share of NBFI financing to total bank loans grew at a compound annual growth of 9.8% in Cambodia (2007–2019), the Lao PDR (41.5%, 2010–2019), Myanmar

[22] NBFI data differs by country: Brunei Darussalam includes finance companies and pawnbrokers; Cambodia microfinance institutions and leasing companies; Indonesia finance companies, microfinance institutions, and government pawnshops; Lao PDR microfinance institutions, pawnshops, and leasing companies; Malaysia venture capital, private equity, factoring, and leasing companies; Myanmar microfinance institutions; the Philippines credit unions and cooperatives (2015–2018), pawnshops (2009–2018), and nonstock savings and loans associations (NSSLAs; 2014–2019); Singapore finance companies; and Viet Nam People's Credit Funds and MFIs.

[23] Ibid, footnote 14.

(25.0%, 2012–September 2019), and Viet Nam (1.7%, 2012–June 2019) (Figure 2.9D). The share also increased in Indonesia (7.0%, 2016–2019).

Figure 2.9: Nonbank Finance

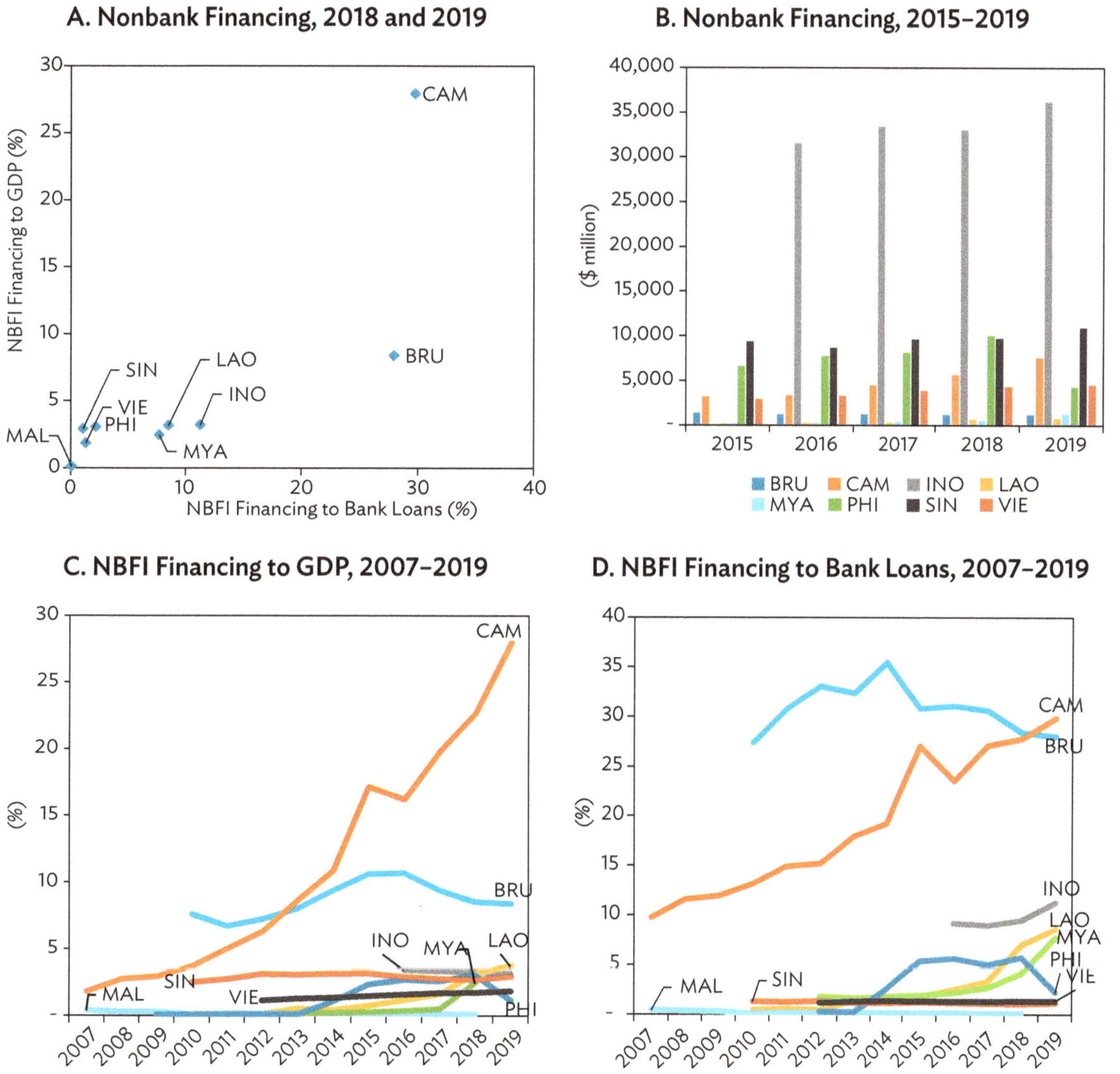

BRU = Brunei Darussalam, CAM = Cambodia, GDP = gross domestic product, INO = Indonesia, LAO = Lao PDR, MAL = Malaysia, MYA = Myanmar, PHI = Philippines, NBFI = nonbank finance institution, SIN = Singapore, VIE = Viet Nam.

Notes: NBFI data varies by country: Brunei Darussalam (finance companies and pawnbrokers); Cambodia (microfinance institutions and leasing companies); Indonesia (finance companies, microfinance institutions, and government pawnshops); the Lao PDR (microfinance institutions, pawnshops, and leasing companies); Malaysia (venture capital, private equity, factoring, and leasing companies); Myanmar (microfinance institutions); Philippines (credit unions and cooperatives [2015–2018], pawnshops [2009–2018], and nonstock savings and loans associations [NSSLAs, 2014–2019]); Singapore (finance companies); Viet Nam (People's Credit Funds and microfinance institutions). For Figure 2.9A, data (% of GDP) for LAO, MAL, MYA, and PHI are as of 2018 and for the rest as of 2019; data (% of bank loans) for MAL is as of 2018; others as of 2019. For Figures 2.9A and 2.9B, data in 2019 are as of September for MYA, August for SIN, June for VIE, and end-of-year for the rest. For Figure 2.9B, exchange rates of local currency to US dollar refer to end-of-year currency rates from the International Monetary Fund International Financial Statistics in designated years. For Figure 2.9C, data for MYA and MAL are until 2018. For Figure 2.9D, data for MAL are until 2018.

Source: ADB Asia SME Monitor 2020 database.

The share of NBFI nonperforming financing to total financing is relatively low in Southeast Asia. By country, the NBFI nonperforming financing ratio was 0.4% in Viet Nam in 2019, 0.8% in Myanmar, 0.9% in Cambodia, 1.1% in Brunei Darussalam, and 2.4% in Indonesia (Figure 2.10A). However, nonperforming financing amounts have increased, except in Indonesia. The compound annual growth rate in Myanmar was 137% (2012–September 2019), followed by Viet Nam (111%, 2011–June 2019), Cambodia (57%, 2007–2019), and Brunei Darussalam (3.2%, 2010–2019). Indonesia's nonperforming financing fell at a compound annual rate of 4.9% (2016–2019) (Figure 2.10A). The share of NBFI nonperforming financing to total financing has increased slightly over time, except in Indonesia (Figure 2.10B).

Figure 2.10: Nonbank Finance Institutions—Nonperforming Financing

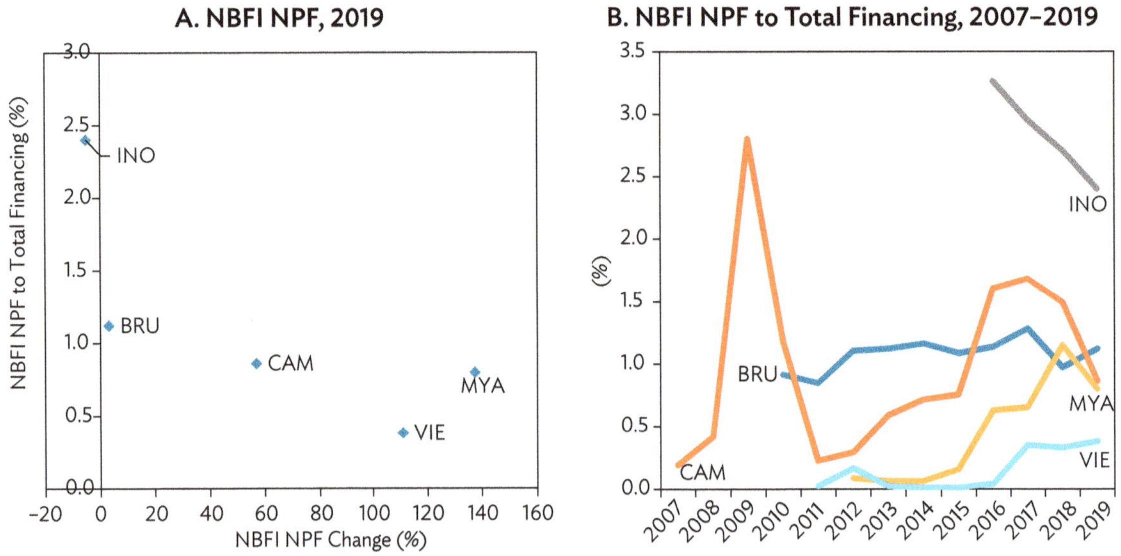

BRU = Brunei Darussalam, CAM = Cambodia, INO = Indonesia, MYA = Myanmar, NBFI = nonbank finance institution, NPF = nonperforming financing, VIE = Viet Nam.

Notes: For Figures 2.10A and 2.10B, data in 2019 are as of September for MYA and June for VIE. NBFI NPF change (%) refers to compound annual growth during past and latest available data. Data cover 2010–2019 for BRU, 2007–2019 for CAM, 2016–2019 for INO, 2012–September 2019 for MYA, 2011–June 2019 for VIE.

Source: ADB Asia SME Monitor 2020 database.

Digital Financial Services

Digital financial services (DFS) have spread widely across Southeast Asia. They have the potential to fill the large unmet financing demand from MSMEs and to accelerate financial inclusion. The number of fintech firms has been increasing, although most still operate informally. The region's central banks and financial authorities are building DFS regulatory and policy frameworks that address branchless/agent banking, P2P lending platforms, equity crowdfunding (ECF), and cybersecurity. Table 2.2 offers a summary of DFS development in Southeast Asia.

Each country focused first on developing a national payment system as the basis for DFS infrastructure. Brunei Darussalam has pilot tested digital payments using regulatory sandboxes. In 2020, Cambodia is expected to launch Retail Pay, a real-time fund transfer system. Interoperable national payment gateways have been launched in Indonesia (Gerbang Pembayaran Nasional [GPN] in 2017), Malaysia (PayNet in 2019), the Philippines (National

Retail Payment System [NRPS] in 2018), and Thailand (PromptPay in 2017). The Philippines is establishing a single national identification (ID) system (PhilSys) for citizens and full-time residents, which should simplify government and private transactions. Thailand has also developed a national digital ID (NDID) system, being pilot tested as of end-2019. Below is a DFS summary by country:

- **Brunei Darussalam** established a DFS regulatory and policy framework in 2017–2019, including regulations on P2P lending and ECF, guidelines on fintech regulatory sandboxes, cybersecurity strategies, and a digital payment roadmap. As of end-2019, there was no registration on P2P lending and ECF.

- **Cambodia**'s Financial Sector Development Strategy for 2016–2025 and the National Financial Inclusion Strategy for 2019–2025 incorporate DFS strategies, addressing mobile banking.

- **Indonesia** promotes DFS and non-cash transactions as part of policy actions under its national financial inclusion strategy. Regulations on P2P lending and ECF were established in 2016 and 2018, respectively. The financial services authority, or Otoritas Jasa Keuangan (OJK), licensed 164 P2P lenders and 2 ECFs as of 2019. Indonesia has two schemes of agent banking: the central bank's e-money-based *Layanan Keuangan Digital,* and OJK's branchless/agent *Laku Pandai* system. Indonesia is aligning regulations covering two systems.

- **The Lao PDR** has prepared fintech regulations, but had not implemented them as of end-2019. The central bank promotes branchless and e-banking under its 2018–2025 financial inclusion roadmap.

- In **Malaysia**, DFS is a strategic target under the 2011 Financial Inclusion Framework. Regulations covering ECF were launched in 2015, while those covering P2P lending in 2016. As of end-2019, there were 11 P2P lenders and 10 ECFs registered with the Securities Commission Malaysia. An agent banking system was launched in 2012 to let customers access banking services through third-party agents such as retail outlets and post offices.

- **Myanmar** is preparing a national financial inclusion strategy, addressing DFS solutions such as mobile and branchless banking. The national payment gateway is being prepared using standardized quick response (QR) codes.

- In **the Philippines**, the central bank promotes a digital financial ecosystem as part of its financial inclusion strategy. It uses two types of branchless banking providers: cash agents and branch-lite units, both launched in 2017. Cash agents accept and disburse cash to clients for and on behalf of banks. Branch-lite units can be a branch annex, office, or place of business where a bank can offer limited products and services to local clients.

- **Singapore**'s e-payment system is well developed using several national platforms. As of 2019, there were more than 1,100 fintech firms operating in the country. By January 2020, the Monetary Authority of Singapore received 21 applications for five available digital banking licenses.

- **Thailand**'s securities commission supervises crowdfunding platforms, while the central bank supervises P2P lenders. Regulations on fintech and digital finance platforms, including P2P lending and ECF, were enacted in 2019. As of October 2019, there were two licensed ECFs (*Live* and *Sinwattana*). The central bank promotes agent banking under its Financial Sector Master Plan.

- In **Viet Nam**, DFS solutions remain nascent. The central bank's Fintech Working Group is determining how best to promote and supervise P2P lending, while the securities commission is conducting a feasibility study on crowdfunding.

Most countries in the region continue to formulate and implement DFS regulatory and supervisory frameworks. A key challenge is to develop digital literacy and education outreach systems to create a sufficiently knowledgeable customer base, including MSMEs, so financial institutions and DFS providers can establish the "trust" required to build a vibrant fintech industry. MSME demand for DFS is strong, as it requires no collateral and offers fast, low-cost access to simple financial transactions and loans. Increasing fintech and bank collaboration creates synergies for delivering more demand-driven financial services.

Capital Markets

Equity markets that MSMEs can tap remain small yet are expanding gradually in Southeast Asia. A dedicated MSME stock market has been created in several countries such as Indonesia, Malaysia, the Philippines, and Thailand as an alternative funding source for viable and innovative small firms. Their market capitalization averaged 8.1% of a country's GDP during 2010–2019 (a compound annual growth rate of 1.0%).

By country, the market capitalization in 2019 of equity markets available to MSMEs (MSME markets) was 14.8% of GDP in Viet Nam, followed by the Lao PDR (5.9%), Cambodia (2.6%), Singapore (1.9%), Myanmar (1.7% [2018]), Malaysia (1.4%), Thailand (1.3%), and the Philippines (0.1%) (Figure 2.11A). MSME market capitalization grew at a compound annual growth rate of 71.0% in Viet Nam (2009–2019), followed by the Philippines (28.7%, 2004–2019), Cambodia (26.6%, 2012–2019), Thailand (15.5%, 2007–2019), Malaysia (14.9%, 2009–2019), Singapore (9.6%, 2008–2019), the Lao PDR (9.5%, 2011–2019), and Myanmar (2.4%, 2016–2019). In US dollar terms, MSME market capitalization in Viet Nam reached $39 billion in 2019, followed by Singapore ($7.3 billion), Thailand ($7.1 billion), Malaysia ($5.2 billion), the Lao PDR ($1.1 billion), Cambodia ($0.7 billion), Myanmar ($0.4 billion), and the Philippines ($0.2 billion) (Figure 2.11B) (footnote 14).

The growth in MSME market capitalization to GDP increased sharply in Viet Nam, while remained relatively stable or declined over time in other countries (Figure 2.11C). The number of listed companies in MSME markets also increased sharply in Viet Nam, while other markets have seen relatively stagnant growth of new issuers (Figure 2.11D).

In Southeast Asia, MSME equity markets can be roughly classified into three categories: (i) the market board of the stock exchange that offers concessional listing requirements for MSMEs, (ii) a sponsor-driven alternative investment market (AIM), and (iii) a dedicated MSME market. The first two types are not a specialized market board for MSMEs but relaxes listing requirements—such as minimum paid-up capital, operating profits, business track records, and audited financial reports—to attract MSME issuers. The AIM-typed market uses more sophisticated risk-hedge mechanisms by involving qualified sponsors and advisors. The dedicated MSME market has more concessional listing requirements than other stock exchange boards.

Stock markets in Cambodia, the Lao PDR, and Myanmar are classified as type (i); they are the main boards open to all enterprises including MSMEs. Viet Nam's UPCoM market can be classified into the type (i), as it is a venue for MSME equity financing. Indonesia's main board also qualifies, as it offers concessional listing requirements for MSMEs. There were 25 initial public offerings by MSMEs on the Indonesia Stock Exchange as of end-2019—main board data for Indonesia is not included in Figure 2.11 as a dedicated stock market was launched in 2019. The type (i) markets are overviewed as follows:

- **Cambodia**'s stock exchange began operations in 2012, with five companies listed as of end-2019. MSMEs can tap the growth board at the Cambodia Securities Exchange under eased listing requirements. There are capital market dissemination and incubator programs marketing MSMEs to capital markets. A tax incentive scheme (adopted in 2019) offers a corporate tax deduction for issuers, helping attract MSMEs to capital markets.

- **The Lao PDR** has no dedicated equity market for MSMEs, but the securities commission started brainstorming on it. The stock exchange opened in 2010, with 11 companies listed as of end-2019. Tax incentives (a corporate tax deduction and capital gains exemption) adopted in 2019 aim to attract more issuers and investors to capital markets.

- **Myanmar**'s stock exchange began operations in 2015, with five companies listed as of end-2019. There is no specialized board for MSMEs and no plan to discuss it as of end-2019.

- **Viet Nam** has a stock market for unlisted public companies and privatized state-owned enterprises, called UPCoM ("Unlisted Public CoMpany") under the Hanoi Stock Exchange. The UPCoM commenced its operation in 2009, with 872 companies registered as of end-2019. It is not a dedicated MSME market but an equity financing venue accessible for MSMEs, offering concessional requirements for registration.

Singapore, Malaysia, and Thailand have developed the AIM-typed market for growing enterprises. The type (ii) markets are overviewed as follows:

- **Singapore** features highly developed capital markets, with the Catalist market an equity finance venue that MSMEs can tap. Launched in 2007, Catalist is a sponsor-supervised listing platform for fast-growing local and international companies, modeled on the London Stock Exchange's Alternative Investment Market. Catalist had 216 listed companies as of end-2019.

- **Malaysia** has multitiered equity markets, including ACE ("Access, Certainty, Efficiency") and LEAP ("Leading Entrepreneur Accelerator Platform") markets that MSMEs can tap. The ACE market, launched in 2009, is a sponsor-driven market designated for companies with growth prospects (129 companies listed as of end-2019). The LEAP market, launched in 2017, is an advisor-driven market for emerging companies and MSMEs (28 companies listed as of end-2019)—it could also be classified as type (iii). Only sophisticated investors (e.g., registered high-net-worth investors) can invest in the LEAP market.

- **Thailand** has the market for alternative investment (mai), Launched in 1998, it has supported financing MSMEs, with 169 companies listed as of end-2019. The mai has demonstrated the flow of its listed companies to the main board of stock exchange, playing the critical role of supporting the growth cycle of enterprises. Total 26 previously listed companies graduated from the mai to the main board. The securities commission began a capital market literacy program in 2017 to attract more issuers, while the stock exchange launched a Social Impact Platform in 2016 for matching potential issuers from social enterprises.

Indonesia and the Philippines (along with Malaysia's LEAP market) have a dedicated equity market for MSMEs. The type (iii) markets are overviewed as follows:

- **Indonesia** launched a dedicated MSME market named the Acceleration Board at the Indonesia Stock Exchange in 2019 with eased listing requirements. The stock exchange has an incubator program that helps MSMEs tap capital markets. As of January 2020, the Acceleration Board had one listed company.

- **The Philippines** created an SME Board at the Philippine Stock Exchange in 2001, with five companies listed as of end-2019. The stock exchange is working to ease listing rules and offer capital market literacy and training programs to attract more MSMEs to the SME Board.

There is no national stock exchange in Brunei Darussalam, while a capital market law was enacted in 2013. Following the Financial Sector Blueprint 2016–2025, work continues on establishing a national stock exchange (as of end-2019).

There are several challenges to develop MSME capital markets in the region. Regulators and stock exchanges describe seven main challenges: (i) low market liquidity, (ii) high costs for listing (corporate governance requirements), (iii) quality of issuers (poor accounting), (iv) tax compliance, (v) MSME owners' mindset not looking for growth, (vi) limited number of qualified sponsors and advisors (Malaysia), and (vii) weak capital market literacy among MSMEs.[24]

Figure 2.11: Equity Markets for MSMEs

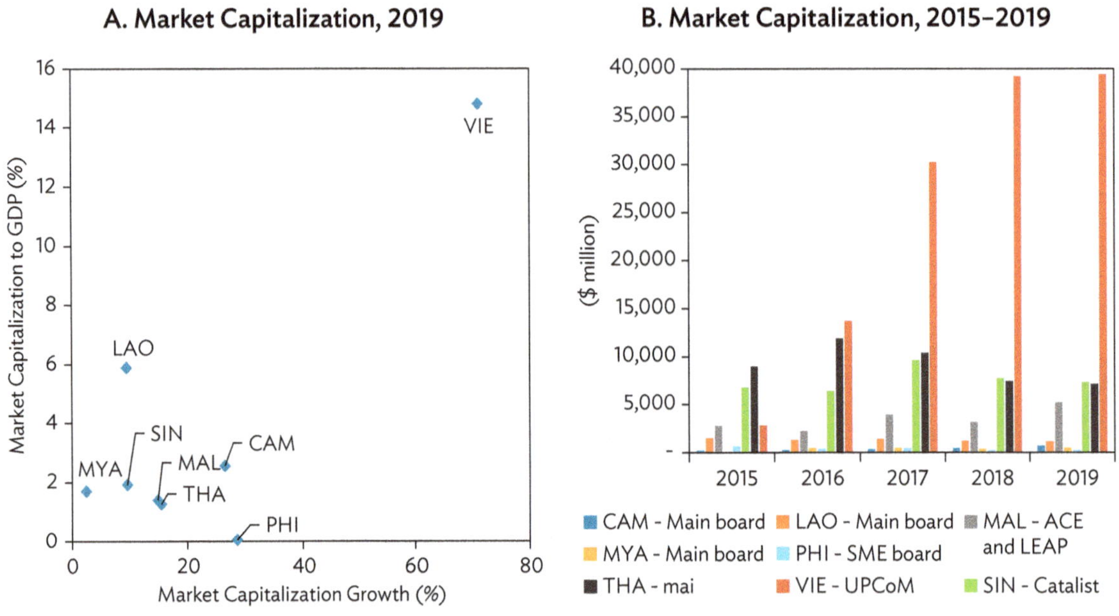

24 Ibid, footnote 8.

C. Market Capitalization to GDP, 2007–2019

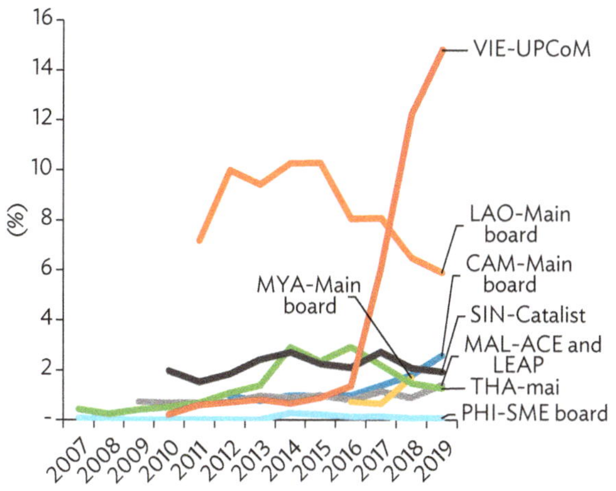

D. Number of Listed Companies, 2007–2019

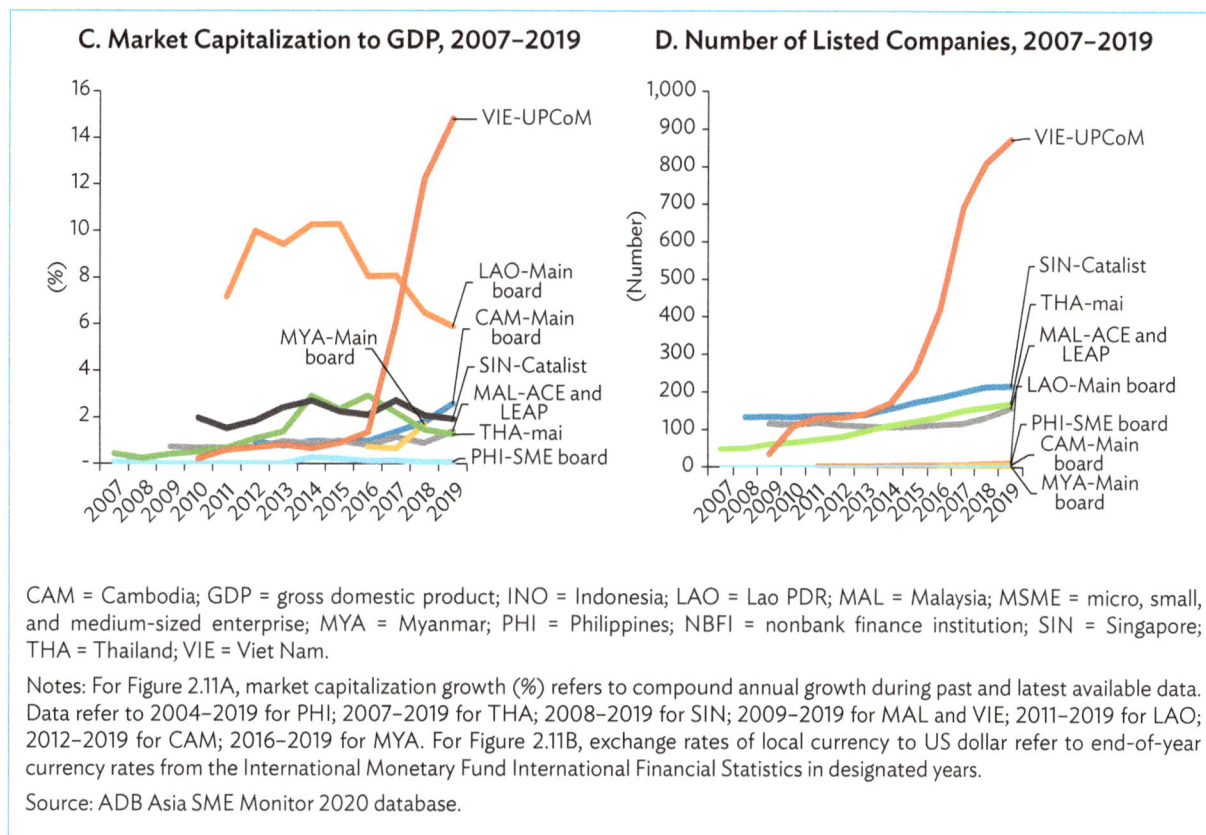

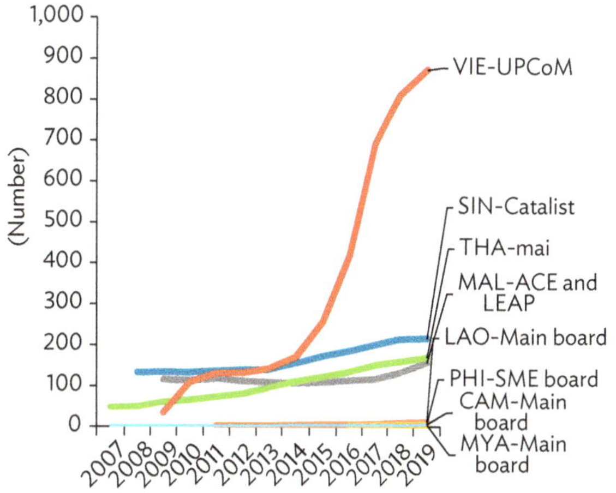

CAM = Cambodia; GDP = gross domestic product; INO = Indonesia; LAO = Lao PDR; MAL = Malaysia; MSME = micro, small, and medium-sized enterprise; MYA = Myanmar; PHI = Philippines; NBFI = nonbank finance institution; SIN = Singapore; THA = Thailand; VIE = Viet Nam.

Notes: For Figure 2.11A, market capitalization growth (%) refers to compound annual growth during past and latest available data. Data refer to 2004–2019 for PHI; 2007–2019 for THA; 2008–2019 for SIN; 2009–2019 for MAL and VIE; 2011–2019 for LAO; 2012–2019 for CAM; 2016–2019 for MYA. For Figure 2.11B, exchange rates of local currency to US dollar refer to end-of-year currency rates from the International Monetary Fund International Financial Statistics in designated years.

Source: ADB Asia SME Monitor 2020 database.

Financial Infrastructure

Credit bureaus and collateral registries operate in many Southeast Asian countries, supporting risk-based credit delivery and asset-based finance. A well-functioning secured transaction legal system helps MSMEs access credit by using their personal properties as loan collateral.

The region's credit bureau systems can be classified into four types: (i) a public entity operated by the central bank or financial authority, (ii) a private business, (iii) a single bureau in the country, and (iv) multiple bureaus in the country (Table 2.3A). The credit bureau in Brunei Darussalam and the Lao PDR is a single public entity. The bureau in Cambodia, the Philippines, and Thailand is a single private business. Indonesia, Malaysia, and Viet Nam have multiple credit bureaus, mixing both public and private entities. Singapore has several private credit bureaus. There are pros and cons for having a single or multiple credit bureaus operating. Countries with several credit bureaus worry about competition and low profitability, while there is the belief that competition enhances service quality of bureaus. Countries with single credit bureau stress that a centralized system is best able to manage quality credit data for financial institution clients.

Half of the countries in Southeast Asia either have yet to introduce a secured lending legal system or reform an existing one (Table 2.3B). The Lao PDR is amending its current secured transaction law to establish a collateral registry.

Table 2.3: Financial Infrastructure

A. Credit Bureau System

Item	Credit Bureau	
	Single	Plural
Public	Brunei Darussalam Lao PDR	Indonesia (1) Malaysia (1) Viet Nam (1)
Private	Cambodia Philippines Thailand	Indonesia (1) Malaysia (7) Singapore (3) Viet Nam (1)

B. Secured Transaction System

Item	Secured Transaction	
	Regulation	No regulation
Collateral registry	Brunei Darussalam Philippines Thailand	
No collateral registry	Lao PDR Singapore	Cambodia Indonesia Myanmar Viet Nam

Lao PDR = Lao People's Democratic Republic.

Notes: For Table 2.3A, ( ) = number of institutions. For Table 2.3B, Malaysia is reforming a secured lending legal system with a centralized collateral registry (as of end-2019).

Source: Compiled from country reviews of Asia Small and Medium-Sized Enterprise Monitor 2020.

Country's practices on financial data infrastructure are overviewed as follows:

- **Brunei Darussalam:** A credit bureau has been operating since 2012 under the financial authority. It provides consolidated credit information and credit scoring services to members only (licensed banks and NBFIs). An online collateral registry started in 2016, listing movable assets such as personal property and intellectual property rights.

- **Cambodia:** Financial information infrastructure is being developed through various policies. A private credit bureau, Credit Bureau Cambodia, opened in 2012. The credit bureau handles individual and corporate accounts. Roughly 68% of its commercial loan portfolio covers MSMEs, while individual accounts include a large number of MSME owner accounts. As of end-2019, no secured lending legal system has been established.

- **Indonesia:** The credit reporting system has two streams: (i) a public credit registry managed by OJK and (ii) a private credit bureau (PEFINDO). OJK receives data from financial institutions through its financial information services system (SLIK), from which OJK produces standardized credit information for financial institutions. PEFINDO mostly serves individual debtors and large firms as MSMEs typically lack financial statements. MSME data are mostly captured within individual consumer data. As of end-2019, no legal system on secured lending or a collateral registry system had been established.

- **Lao PDR:** A credit information bureau opened in 2010 under the central bank. The 1994 Secured Transactions Law was implemented only after 2011, once movable assets such as inventory, accounts receivable, and intellectual property rights became available as loan collateral. This law is being amended, in part to establish a collateral registry.

- **Malaysia:** A public credit registry began operations in 1982 under central bank supervision. The Central Credit Reference Information System (CCRIS), launched in 2001, aggregates credit data from financial institutions. In addition, there are seven private credit bureaus, with Credit Bureau Malaysia covering MSMEs. A secured lending legal system has yet to be fully developed; by end-2019, the government was preparing a modern and unified movable property security interest legislation and a centralized collateral registry for movable assets.

- **Myanmar:** A privately owned credit bureau is scheduled to begin operations in 2020, backed by the 2018 establishment law on credit bureau. There is as yet no collateral registry. The government is drafting the Secured Transaction Law, expected to go into effect in 2020.

- **Philippines:** The credit bureau and secured lending legal system supports MSME access to finance. Credit Information Corporation, a central repository of credit information founded in 2008, offers standardized credit information for member financial institutions. The Personal Property Security Act, enacted in 2018, allows financial institutions to use movable assets—such as receivables, equipment, inventory, and intellectual property rights—as collateral for MSME loans.

- **Singapore:** The three credit bureaus include the Credit Bureau Singapore (the largest), the Consumer Credit Bureau (sponsored by the Post Office Savings Bank), and the Singapore Commercial Credit Bureau (which covers both individual and corporate accounts). All types of immovable and movable assets—including real estate, receivables, and equity stocks—are eligible as collateral for loans under Singapore law.

- **Thailand:** The credit bureau system developed after the 1997–1998 Asian financial crisis. The National Credit Bureau, a private sector credit bureau established in 2005, supplies information on consumers and corporates exclusively to members, and runs an SME credit scoring service. The 2015 Business Collateral Act covers the centralized collateral registry, which was created in 2015. Movable assets, such as machinery and equipment, are used as loan collateral.

- **Viet Nam:** Two credit bureaus operate in Viet Nam: (i) the central bank's Credit Information Center, the country's major provider of credit information; and (ii) the central bank-licensed Private Credit Bureau (PCB) established in 2007, which mainly covers individual accounts. There is no secured transaction legal system and thus, no collateral registry. The acceptance of movable assets as collateral for loans is at a bank's discretion.

3. Policies and Regulations

MSME development is a government policy priority to help build greater economic diversification and inclusive growth. Most Southeast Asian countries have long-term strategies for MSME development in line with their national economic development strategies and goals. Central banks promote financial inclusion as part of their national inclusive growth strategies, promoting DFS solutions for MSMEs. Table 2.4 summarizes policies and regulations on MSME development and access to finance in Southeast Asian countries.

MSME Development

a. Medium- and long-term national MSME policies

In Southeast Asia, MSME development policies are either aligned with or are a part of long-term national development policies. Of the 10 Southeast Asian countries observed, six have a comprehensive MSME development framework: Cambodia (SME Development Policy and Five-year Implementation Plan 2020–2024); the Lao PDR (SME Development Plan for 2021–2025, forthcoming); Malaysia (National Entrepreneurship Policy [DNK] 2030); the Philippines (MSME Development Plan 2017–2022); Thailand (Fourth SMEs Promotion Plan 2017–2021); and Viet Nam (Five-year SME Development Plan). As of end-2019, Brunei Darussalam was preparing an Industry Roadmap that addresses MSME development. In Indonesia, several line ministries implement MSME development policies under the National Long-term Development Plan 2005–2025. The Myanmar Sustainable Development Plan 2018–2030 stipulates MSME development. And in Singapore, MSME development policy is part of the development of the enterprise ecosystem under the Ministry of Trade and Industry's Economic Strategy.

Each country's MSME policy covers thematic areas: (i) entrepreneurship development, especially for youth and women; (ii) technology and innovation, facilitating a shift from traditional MSMEs to "smart" firms; (iii) internationalizing MSMEs to improve market access; (iv) MSME human capital and skill development; and (v) access to finance. Malaysia and Viet Nam have MSME policies that address the formalization of informal businesses (promoting business registration) to accelerate their national inclusive growth strategies. Thailand's budget system covering all MSME policies was centralized in 2017 (the SME Promotion Integrated Budget). For financial assistance, several governments have created special funds for MSME development, such as the Entrepreneurship Development Fund (EDF) and Skill Development Fund (SDF) in Cambodia, the SME Promotion Fund in the Lao PDR, and the SME Development Fund in Viet Nam.

b. Policy coordination, implementation, and monitoring

Every country has a focal government authority for MSME development policies: (i) the Ministry of Economy and Finance in Brunei Darussalam; (ii) the Ministry of Industry, Science, Technology and Innovation in Cambodia; (iii) the Ministry of Cooperatives and SMEs in Indonesia; (iv) Department of SME Promotion (DOSMEP) under the Ministry of Industry and Commerce in the Lao PDR; (v) the Ministry of Entrepreneur Development and Cooperatives in Malaysia; (vi) SME Development Department under the Ministry of Industry in Myanmar; (vii) the Philippines Bureau of SME Development (BSMED) under the Department of Trade and Industry; (viii) Singapore's Ministry of Trade and Industry; (ix) the Office of SME Promotion (OSMEP) in Thailand; and (x) the Ministry of Planning and Investment in Viet Nam.

Of the 10 countries, eight have intragovernmental policy coordination bodies: (i) National MSME Taskforce in Brunei Darussalam; (ii) Subcommittee on SMEs in Cambodia; (iii) SME Promotion and Development and National Productivity Committee in the Lao PDR; (iv) National Entrepreneur and SME Development Council (NESDC) in Malaysia; (v) SME Development Central Committee in Myanmar; (vi) MSME Development Council (MSMED Council) in the Philippines; (vii) National Board of SMEs Promotion in Thailand; and (viii) SMEs Development Promotion Council in Viet Nam.

Five countries use a separate policy-implementing agency for MSMEs: (i) Darussalam Enterprise (DARe) in Brunei Darussalam; (ii) SME Corporation Malaysia; (iii) SME Development Agency in Myanmar; (iv) Enterprise Singapore (13 SME Centers); and (v) Agency for Enterprise Development in Viet Nam. In the Philippines, BSMED monitors MSMEs using regional networks of business support centers (Negosyo Centers) in all provinces and municipalities.

Financial Inclusion

a. National financial inclusion strategies

Seven countries in Southeast Asia have comprehensive national financial inclusion strategies: (i) National Financial Inclusion Strategy 2019–2025 in Cambodia; (ii) National Strategy for Financial Inclusion (SNKI) launched in 2016 in Indonesia; (iii) Financial Inclusion Roadmap 2018–2025 in the Lao PDR; (iv) Malaysia's Financial Inclusion Framework (through 2020); (v) Myanmar Financial Inclusion Roadmap 2014–2020; (vi) National Strategy for Financial Inclusion (NSFI) launched in 2015 in the Philippines; and (vii) National Financial Inclusion Strategy until 2025 in Viet Nam. Brunei Darussalam and Thailand have yet to develop a comprehensive national financial inclusion strategy, though their mid-term financial sector development plans cover key financial inclusion policies: (i) the Financial Sector Blueprint 2016–2025 in Brunei Darussalam and (ii) the Financial Sector Master Plan Phase III for 2017–2021 in Thailand. Singapore has no financial inclusion strategy.

National financial inclusion strategies in the region generally have several common components: (i) developing alternative and innovative financial products and services for MSMEs, focusing on DFS solutions or fintech innovation such as branchless/agent banking; (ii) enhancing financial literacy among MSMEs; and (iii) consumer protection. As thematic areas for financial inclusion, the Philippines focuses on agriculture value chain finance; and Thailand addresses credit database enhancement and financial infrastructure development. Financing young entrepreneurs, women-led start-ups, and rural MSMEs are common themes for financial inclusion across the region.

b. Policy coordination, implementation, and monitoring

Financial authorities and central banks coordinate and implement financial inclusion policies in Southeast Asia: (i) Autoriti Monetari Brunei Darussalam (AMBD); (ii) National Bank of Cambodia; (iii) OJK in Indonesia, together with the Coordinating Ministry of Economic Affairs; (iv) Bank of the Lao PDR; (v) Bank Negara Malaysia; (vi) Financial Regulatory Department of the Ministry of Planning and Finance in Myanmar; (vii) Bangko Sentral Pilipinas in the Philippines; (viii) Bank of Thailand; and (ix) State Bank of Vietnam. Although there is no financial inclusion strategy in Singapore, the Monetary Authority of Singapore is responsible for financial sector development and stability, and supporting the enterprise ecosystem in the country.

There are intragovernmental policy coordination bodies focusing on financial inclusion in Indonesia and the Philippines: (i) the National Council of Inclusive Finance in Indonesia and (ii) the Financial Inclusion Steering Committee in the Philippines. For Malaysia, Bank Negara Malaysia developed a Financial Inclusion Index as a benchmark to measure the implementation level of financial inclusion strategies.

Across the region, countries generally have good policy coordination mechanisms for MSME development and access to finance at both national and regional levels. However, in some countries, policy coordination among central government authorities and between central and local governments should be strengthened further to build greater policy synergies. In addition, given the emerging risks associated with DFS, such as cybersecurity, extensive coordination between financial regulators, government authorities, and the private sector would bring more benefits from inclusive finance.

Table 2.4: Policies and Regulations

Country		Regulators and Policymakers	Regulations	Policies
Brunei Darussalam	SME Promotion	Ministry of Finance and Economy		(1) Wawasan Brunei 2035 (long-term national development plan)
		Darussalam Enterprise (DARe) [policy implementing agency]	Darussalam Enterprise Order of 2016	(2) National Digital Strategy 2016–2020
		National MSME Task Force [policy coordination body]	...	
	Banking Sector	Autoriti Monetari Brunei Darussalam [banks, NBFIs, and capital markets]	Autoriti Monetari Brunei Darussalam Order of 2010	(3) Financial Sector Blueprint 2016–2025
			Secured Transaction Order of 2016	
	Nonbank Sector		Pawnbrokers Order of 2002 [amended, 2005]	
			Moneylenders Act, Chapter 62	
	Digital Finance		Guidelines on Fintech Regulatory Sandbox (2017)	(4) Digital Payment Roadmap 2019–2025
			Notice on Equity Based Crowdfunding (ECF) Platform Operators (2017)	
			Notice on Early Detection of Cyber Intrusion and Incident Reporting (2017)	(5) Cybersecurity Strategy 2017–2020
			Notice on Peer to Peer Financing (P2P) Platform Operators (2019)	
	Capital Markets		Securities Markets Order of 2013	
Cambodia	SME Promotion	Ministry of Industry, Science, Technology and Innovation	...	(1) National Strategic Development Plan (NSDP) - Rectangular Strategy - Phase IV 2018-2023
		Sub-committee on Small and Medium Enterprises [policy coordination body]	Resolutions No.45 S.S.R (2007) and No.27 S.S.R (2008)	(2) Small and Medium Enterprise Development Policy and Five-year Implementation Plan 2020-2024 [Forthcoming]
				(3) Industrial Development Policy 2015-2025
	Banking Sector	National Bank of Cambodia (central bank) [banks and MFIs]	Law on Banking and Financial Institutions (1999)	(4) Financial Sector Development Strategy 2016-2025
	Nonbank Sector		Prakas on Licensing of Microfinance Institutions	(5) National Financial Inclusion Strategy 2019-2025
			Prakas on Licensing of Microfinance Deposit-taking Institutions	
		Ministry of Economy and Finance [pawnshop, insurance, and real estate]	Prakas on Financial Leasing Companies	
		Securities and Exchange Commission of Cambodia	Prakas on Licensing to Pawn Busines, Buying-Selling of Pawn Pledges and Liens by Cession	
	Capital Markets		Law on the Issuance and Trading of Non-Government Securities (2007) [Securities Law]	
Indonesia	SME Promotion	Ministry of Cooperatives and SMEs	Law No.20/2008 on Micro, Small and Medium-sized Enterprises	(1) Masterplan for Acceleration and Expansion of Indonesia Economic Development 2011-2025 (MP3EI) (2011)
			Law No.25/1992 on Cooperatives	
		Ministry of Industry	Government Regulation No.14/2015 on Master Plan of National Industry Development 2015-2035	(2) Master Plan of National Industry Development 2015-2035
		Ministry of Trade	...	
		Ministry of Home Affairs	...	
	Banking Sector	National Council of Inclusive Finance [financial inclusion policy coordination]	Presidential Regulation No. 82/2016 on National Strategy for Inclusive Finance	(3) National Strategy for Financial Inclusion (SNKI) (2016)
		Coordinating Ministry of Economic Affairs [public guaranteed loans (KUR)]	Coordinating Ministry for Economic Affairs Regulation No.11/2017 on KUR Implemention Guidelines (amended, 2019)	
		Bank Indonesia (central bank)	Bank Indonesia Regulation No.14/22/PBI/2012 on Financing and Technical Assistance by Commercial Banks in Developing MSMEs [amended, 2015]	
		Financial Services Authority (OJK) [banks, NBFIs, and capital markets]	Law No.7/1992 and Law No.10/1998 (amendment) on Banking	(4) Indonesian Financial Services Sector Masterplan (2015-2019)
			OJK Regulation No.40/POJK.03 /2019 on Quality Assessment of Commercial Bank Assets	
	Nonbank Sector		Law No. 1/2016 on Guarantee Institutions	
			Law No.1/2013 on Microfinance Institutions	
			OJK Regulation No.35/POJK.05/2015 on Business Operations of Venture Capital Company	
	Digital Finance		OJK Regulation No.19/ POJK.03/2014 on Branchless Banking (LAKU PANDAI)	
			OJK Regulation No.77/POJK.01/2016 on Information Technology-Based Lending Services (LPMUBTI) [P2P]	
			OJK Regulation No.13/POJK.02/2018 on Digital Financial Innovation in the Financial Services Sector	
			OJK Regulation No.37/POJK.04/2018 on Equity Crowdfunding [ECF]	
	Capital Markets		Law No.8/1995 on Capital Market	
			Decision of the Directors of PT Bursa Efek Indonesia No II-V on Trading Regulation for Listing Share on the Acceleration Board	
Lao People's Democratic Republic	SME Promotion	Department of SME Promotion, Ministry of Industry and Commerce (MOIC)	Decree No.42/PM/2004 on the Promotion and Development of Small and Medium sized Enterprises	(1) SME Development Plan 2016-2020; SME Development Plan 2021-2025 (forthcoming)
		Department of Industry and Commerce, MOIC [policy implementing agency at local level]	Law No.011/NA/2011 on Small and Medium sized Enterprises Promotion	
		SME Promotion and Development and National Productivity Committee [policy coordination body]	Decree No.25/GOL/2017/on SME Classification	
	Banking Sector	Bank of the Lao PDR (central bank) [banks and NBFIs]	Law No.05/NA/1995 on the Bank of the Lao PDR	(2) Lao PDR Financial Inclusion Roadmap 2018-2025
			Law No.03/NA/2006 on Commercial Banks	
			Law No.06/NA/2005 on Secured Transactions	
	Nonbank Sector		Decree No.460/G/2012 on Microfinance Institutions	
			Regulation No.02/BOL/2008 for Non-Deposit Taking Microfinance Institutions	
			Regulation No.03/BOL/2008 for Savings and Credit Unions	
			Regulation No.04/BOL/2008 for Deposit Taking Microfinance Institutions	
	Capital Markets	Lao Securities Commission Office	Law No.21/NA/2012 on Securities	(3) Strategic Plan for Capital Market Development 2016-2025
			Law No.33/NA on the Approval of the Law on Securities	
Malaysia	SME Promotion	Ministry of Entrepreneur Development and Cooperatives	...	(1) Shared Prosperity Vision 2030
				(2) National Entrepreneurship Policy 2030 (DKN 2030)
		SME Corporation Malaysia (SME Corp.) [policy implementing agency]	Small and Medium Enterprises Corporation Malaysia Act 1995	(3) Malaysia Productivity Blueprint (2017)
				(4) National eCommerce Strategic Roadmap (2016)
		National Entrepreneur and SME Development Council (NESDC) [policy coordination body]	National SME Development Council Directive 2005	(5) SME Masterplan 2012–2020
	Banking Sector	Bank Negara Malaysia (central bank) [banks and NBFIs]	Development Financial Institutions Act 2002	(6) Financial Sector Blueprint 2011–2020
			Financial Services Act 2014	
	Digital Finance		Agent Banking Act 2012	(7) Financial Inclusion Framework (2011)
	Nonbank Sector			
	Capital Markets	Securities Commission Malaysia [VC, PE, and capital markets]	Capital Markets and Services Act 2007 [P2P and ECF covered]	(8) Capital Market Masterplan 2 (2011)

continued on next page

Table 2.4 continued

Country		Regulators and Policymakers	Regulations	Policies
Myanmar	SME Promotion	SME Development Department, Ministry of Industry	Private Industrial Enterprise Law No.22/1990	(1) Myanmar Sustainable Development Plan (MSDP) 2018–2030
			Law Amending the Promotion of Cottage Industries Law No.14/2010	
		SMEs Development Central Committee [policy coordinating body]	SME Development Law No.23/2015	
		SMEs Development Working Committee		
		Directorate of Investment and Company Administration (DICA)	Myanmar Companies Law No.29/2017	
	Banking Sector	Central Bank of Myanmar [banks and NBFIs]	Financial Institutions of Myanmar Law No.16/1990	(2) Myanmar Financial Inclusion Roadmap 2014–2020
			Myanmar Agricultural and Rural Development Bank Law No.17/1991	
			Savings Banks Law No.5/1992	
			Secured Transaction Law [Forthcoming]	
	Nonbank Sector		Financial Institutions Law No. 20/2016	
		Financial Regulatory Department, Ministry of Planning and Finance [NBFIs]	Cooperative Society Law No.9/1992	
			Microfinance Law No.13/2011	
	Capital Markets	Securities and Exchange Commission, Ministry of Planning and Finance	Securities Exchange Law No.20/2013	
Philippines	SME Promotion	Department of Trade and Industry (DTI)	Magna Carta for Micro, Small and Medium Enterprises (R.A. No.6977 of 1991, and several amendments until 2014)	(1) Philippine Development Plan (2017–2022)
		Bureau of Small and Medium Enterprise Development (BSMED), DTI	Barangay Micro Business Enterprises Act of 2002 (R.A. No.9178 as amended by R.A. No.10644 of 2014)	(2) Micro, Small and Medium Enterprise Development Plan (2017-2022)
		Micro, Small and Medium Enterprise Development Council (MSMED Council) [policy coordinating body]	Small and Medium Enterprise Development Council Resolution No.01 Series of 2003 [MSME definition]	
			Go Negosyo Act of 2014 (R.A. No.10644)	
			Philippine Innovation Act of 2019 (R.A. No.11293)	
			Innovative Startup Act of 2019 (R.A. No.11337)	
	Banking Sector	Financial Inclusion Steering Committee [financial inclusion policy coordination]	...	(3) The National Strategy for Financial Inclusion (2015)
		Bangko Sentral ng Pilipinas (central bank) [banks and NBFIs]	General Banking Law of 2000 (R.A. No.8791)	
			Credit Information Systems Act of 2008 (R.A. No.9510)	
			Personal Property Security Act of 2018 (R.A. No.11057)	
	Nonbank Sector		Pawnshop Regulation Act of 1973 (Presidential Decree No.114)	
			Non-Stock Savings and Loan Association Act of 1997 (R.A. No.8367)	
		Cooperative Development Authority [credit unions and cooperatives]	Philippine Cooperative Code of 2008 (R.A. No.9520)	
			Cooperative Development Authority Charter Act of 2019 (R.A. No.11364)	
		Microfinance NGO Regulatory Council [NGO-MFI policy coordination]	Microfinance NGOs Act of 2015 (R.A. No.10693)	
	Capital Markets	Securities and Exchange Commission	Securities Regulation Code of 2000 (R.A. No.8799, Implementing Rules and Regulation in 2015)	
Singapore	SME Promotion	Enterprise Singapore	Enterprise Singapore Board Act (2018)	(1) Enterprise Singapore Strategic Plan (2) Ministry of Trade and Industry Economic Strategy (3) Industry Transformation Maps
		Ministry of Trade and Industry		
	Banking Sector	Monetary Authority of Singapore [banks, NBFIs, and capital markets]	Banking Act 41 of 1970 (Chapter 19, as amended in 2008)	
			Credit Bureau Act No,27 of 2016	
	Nonbank Sector		Finance Companbies Act 43 of 1967 (Chapter 108, as amended in 2011)	
			Hire-Purchase Act 1 of 1969 (Chapter 125, as amended in 2014)	
	Digital Finance		Electronic Transactions Act (2010)	
			Personal Data Protection Act (2012)	
	Capital Markets		Securities and Futures Act 42 of 2001 (Chapter 289, as amended in 2006)	
Thailand	SME Promotion	Office of National Economic and Social Development Board (NESDB)	SMEs Promotion Act B.E.2543 (2000) [amended by No.2/B.E.2561 (2018)]	(1) Thailand 4.0 (2016)
			Ministerial Regulation on SME Definition/B.E.2562 (2019)	(2) National Strategy 2018-2037 and Master Plan (2019)
		National Board of SMEs Promotion [policy coordination body]	Electronic Transactions Act B.E.2544 (2001) and amendments	(3) The Twelfth National Economic and Social Development Plan (2017–2021)
			Bankruptcy Act B.E.2559 (2016)	
		Office of Small and Medium Enterprises Promotion (OSMEP) [policy implementing agency]		(4) The Fourth SMEs Promotion Plan (2017–2021)
	Banking Sector	Fiscal Policy Office, Ministry of Finance [state-owned banks]	SME Development Bank of Thailand Act B.E.2545 (2002)	(5) Policy Guidelines for the Specialized Financial Institutions with regards to SMEs (2016–2020)
		Bank of Thailand (central bank) [banks and NBFIs]	Financial Institution Business Act B.E.2551 (2008)	(6) The Bank of Thailand's 3-Year Strategic Plan (2017–2019)
	Nonbank Sector		Small Industry Credit Guarantee Corporation Act B.E.2534 (1991) and No.2/B.E.2560 (2017)	(7) Financial Sector Master Plan Phase III (2016–2020)
			Credit Information Business Act B.E.2545 (2002) [amended in 2008]	
			Business Collateral Act B.E. 2558 (2015)	
			Payment Systems Act B.E.2560 (2017)	(8) Payment Systems Roadmap No. 4 (2019–2021)
	Digital Finance		Bank of Thailand Notification No.4/B.E.2562 on the Determination of Rules, Procedures, and Conditions for Peer-to-Peer Lending Businesses and Platforms (2019) [P2P]	
		Securities and Exchange Commission	Securities and Exchange Commission Notification No.21/B.E.2562 on the Offering of Securities for Sale through Crowdfunding Portals (2019) [ECF]	
			Securities and Exchange Commission Rules on Digital Asset Exchange B.E.2562 (2019)	
	Capital Markets		Securities and Exchange Act B.E.2535 (1992)	(9) The Third Thai Capital Market Development Plan (2016–2021)

continued on next page

Table 2.4 continued

Country		Regulators and Policymakers	Regulations	Policies
Viet Nam	SME Promotion	SME Development Promotion Council [policy coordination body]	Law No.04/2017/QH14 on Support for Small and Medium-sized Enterprises (SME Support Law)	(1) Five-year Socio-Economic Development Plan of 2016–2020
		Ministry of Planning and Investment (MPI)	Decree No.39/2018/ND-CP on Guidelines for the SME Support Law	(2) Five-year SME Development Plan 2011–2015
		Agency for Enterprise Development, MPI [policy implementing agency]	Decree No.55/2019/ND-CP providing legal assistance for SME	
		Ministry of Science and Technology [tech-based MSMEs]	Law No.21/2008 on High Technology [SMEs targeted]	(3) Master Plan 844 [innovative start-ups targeted]
			Decree No.13/2019/ND-CP on Science and Technology Enterprises [tax breaks]	
		Ministry of Industry and Trade	...	
	Banking Sector	Ministry of Finance [state-owned financial institutions and state-run funds]	Decree No.39/2019/ND-CP on organization and operation of Small and Medium Enterprise Development Fund and relevant documents	(4) National Financial Inclusion Strategy until 2025 (2020)
			Decree No.34/2018/ND-CP on Establishment and Operation of Credit Guarantee Funds and relevant documents	
			Decree No.38/2018/ND-CP on Investment for Small and Medium Startups and Innovative Firms	
			Decree No.03/2011/ND-CP on Promulgating the Regulation on Guaranteeing Commercial Bank Loans to SMEs	
		State Bank of Vietnam (central bank) [banks and NBFIs]	Law No.47/2010/QH12 on Credit Institutions	
			Prime Minister Decision No.254/2012/QD-TTg on Approving the Project on Restructuring the System on Credit Institutions During 2011–2015	
	Nonbank Sector		Decree No.165/2007/ND-CP on Microfinance Institutions	
			Prime Minister Decision No.2195/2011/QD-TTg on Approving the Proposal for Building and Developing the Microfinance System in Vietnam up to 2020	
			Decree No.48/2001/ND-CP on People's Credit Fund	
			Law No.18/2003/QD on Cooperatives	
	Capital Markets	State Securities Commission of Vietnam	Law No.54/2019/QH14 on Securities	(5) Restructuring securities and insurance markets by 2020 and vision to 2025 (2019)

KUR = Kredit Usaha Rakyat, MFI = microfinance institution, MSME = micro, small, and medium-sized enterprise, NBFI = nonbank finance institution, NGO = nongovernment organization.

Source: Compiled from country reviews of Asia Small and Medium-Sized Enterprise Monitor 2020.

Data Tables

A. MSME Landscape

A1. Number of MSMEs

Country	2003	2004	2005	2006	2007	2008	2009	2010	2011	2012	2013	2014	2015	2016	2017	2018	2019
Brunei Darussalam	--	--	--	--	--	--	--	5,427	--	--	--	--	5,248	5,721	5,876	--	--
Cambodia	--	--	--	--	--	--	376,069	--	462,582	--	--	512,870	--	--	--	--	--
Indonesia	--	--	--	--	--	--	--	52,764,750	54,114,821	55,206,444	56,534,592	57,895,721	59,262,772	61,651,177	62,922,617	64,194,057	--
Lao People's Democratic Republic	--	--	--	126,717	--	--	--	--	--	--	124,510	--	--	--	--	124,567	--
Malaysia	548,267	--	--	--	--	--	--	638,790	--	--	--	--	907,065	--	--	--	--
Myanmar	--	--	--	39,949	40,811	40,529	40,396	39,272	38,978	38,590	38,654	39,062	39,162	59,694	61,949	71,290	75,116
Philippines	--	--	--	780,469	781,201	758,436	777,357	774,664	816,759	940,886	937,327	942,925	896,839	911,768	920,677	998,342	--
Singapore	--	--	--	--	--	--	--	--	--	--	--	242,800	246,200	247,400	253,300	263,800	271,800
Thailand	--	--	--	--	2,366,227	2,827,633	2,896,106	2,913,167	2,646,549	2,730,591	2,763,997	2,736,744	2,765,986	3,004,679	3,046,790	3,077,822	--
Viet Nam	--	--	--	--	143,622	186,379	230,365	272,283	316,941	338,916	365,181	393,915	433,453	495,010	544,212	593,629	--

MSME = micro, small, and medium-sized enterprise. Note: End-of-year data. For Myanmar, fiscal year starts in April and ends in March of the following year.

Source: ADB Asia SME Monitor 2020 database.

A2. MSMEs to Total (%)

Country	2003	2004	2005	2006	2007	2008	2009	2010	2011	2012	2013	2014	2015	2016	2017	2018	2019
Brunei Darussalam	--	--	--	--	--	--	--	97.5	--	--	--	--	96.6	97.0	97.2	--	--
Cambodia	--	--	--	--	--	--	99.8	--	99.8	--	--	99.8	--	--	--	--	--
Indonesia	--	--	--	--	--	--	--	99.99	99.99	99.99	99.99	99.99	99.99	99.99	99.99	99.99	--
Lao People's Democratic Republic	--	--	--	99.8	--	--	--	--	--	--	99.8	--	--	--	--	99.8	--
Malaysia	99.2	--	--	--	--	--	--	98.5	--	--	--	--	98.5	--	--	--	--
Myanmar	--	--	--	92.0	92.0	91.8	91.6	90.3	89.1	88.4	87.9	87.4	87.1	90.2	89.6	90.1	89.9
Philippines	--	--	--	99.7	99.7	99.6	99.6	99.6	99.6	99.6	99.6	99.6	99.5	99.6	99.6	99.5	--
Singapore	--	--	--	--	--	--	--	--	--	--	--	99.5	99.4	99.5	99.5	99.5	99.5
Thailand	--	--	--	--	99.6	99.7	99.8	99.6	99.8	97.2	97.2	99.7	99.7	99.7	99.8	99.8	--
Viet Nam	--	--	--	--	96.3	97.0	97.4	97.5	97.6	97.7	97.8	97.9	98.0	98.0	97.1	97.2	--

MSME = micro, small, and medium-sized enterprise. Note: End-of-year data. For Myanmar, fiscal year starts in April and ends in March of the following year.

Source: ADB Asia SME Monitor 2020 database.

A3. MSMEs by Sector (% share, latest available year)

Item	Brunei Darussalam	Cambodia	Indonesia	Lao People's Democratic Republic	Malaysia	Myanmar	Philippines	Singapore	Thailand	Viet Nam
Agriculture	3.3	--	--	4.9	1.1	--	0.9	--	1.5	1.1
Manufacturing	11.1	13.9	16.7	12.4	5.3	--	11.7	--	17.1	15.1
Transportation and communication	4.4	--	7.3	3.1	--	--	--	--	--	8.0
Construction	12.4	--	0.9	0.5	4.3	--	--	--	--	13.3
Wholesale and retail trade	34.9	55.6	63.5	62.9	89.2*	--	46.3	--	41.6	39.0
Other services	32.3	26.5	10.7	12.2	--	--	40.5	--	39.8	22.3
Others	1.6	--	0.9	3.9	0.1	--	0.8	--	--	1.2

MSME = micro, small, and medium-sized enterprise. * Includes transportation and storage, telecommunication, and real estate.

Note: Data for Cambodia: 2014; data for Malaysia: 2015; data for Indonesia: 2016; data for Brunei Darussalam: 2017; data for the Lao PDR, the Philippines, Thailand, and Viet Nam: 2018. End-of-year data.

Source: ADB Asia SME Monitor 2020 database.

A4. MSMEs by Region (% share, latest available year)

Item	Brunei Darussalam	Cambodia	Indonesia	Lao People's Democratic Republic	Malaysia	Myanmar	Philippines	Singapore	Thailand	Viet Nam
Capital city	--	18.8	--	28.2	14.7	15.3	20.4	--	18.2	--
Other areas	--	81.2	--	71.8	85.3	84.7	79.6	--	81.8	--

MSME = micro, small, and medium-sized enterprise. Note: Data for Cambodia: 2014; data for Malaysia: 2015; data for the Lao PDR, the Philippines, and Thailand: 2018; data for Myanmar: 2019. End-of-year data. For Myanmar, fiscal year starts in April and ends in March of the following year. Capital city: Phnom Penh in Cambodia, Vientiane in the Lao PDR, Kuala Lumpur in Malaysia, Yangon in Myanmar, National Capital Region in the Philippines, Bangkok in Thailand.

Source: ADB Asia SME Monitor 2020 database.

A5. Number of Employees by MSMEs

Country	2003	2004	2005	2006	2007	2008	2009	2010	2011	2012	2013	2014	2015	2016	2017	2018	2019
Brunei Darussalam	--	--	--	--	--	--	--	59,179	--	--	--	--	64,722	65,486	66,123	--	--
Cambodia	--	--	--	--	--	--	1,099,647	--	1,158,871	--	--	1,345,100	--	--	--	--	--
Indonesia	--	--	--	--	--	--	--	96,193,623	98,238,913	101,722,458	107,657,509	114,144,082	123,229,386	112,828,610	116,431,224	116,978,631	--
Lao People's Democratic Republic	--	--	--	238,703	--	--	--	--	--	--	472,231	--	--	--	--	472,529	--
Malaysia	--	--	--	--	--	--	--	--	--	--	--	--	--	--	--	--	--
Myanmar	--	--	--	--	--	--	--	--	--	--	--	--	--	--	--	--	--
Philippines	--	--	--	3,327,855	3,355,742	3,395,505	3,595,641	3,532,935	3,872,406	4,930,851	4,770,445	4,891,836	4,784,870	4,879,179	4,922,251	5,714,262	--
Singapore	--	--	--	--	--	--	--	--	--	--	--	2,400,000	2,500,000	2,500,000	2,500,000	2,500,000	2,500,000
Thailand	--	--	--	--	8,900,567	--	9,701,354	10,507,507	10,995,977	11,783,143	11,414,702	10,501,166	10,749,735	11,747,093	13,088,802	13,950,241	--
Viet Nam	--	--	--	--	2,834,950	3,347,883	3,872,711	4,394,037	5,060,430	5,107,958	5,179,702	5,321,882	5,682,980	6,205,320	5,538,134	5,627,952	--

MSME = micro, small, and medium-sized enterprise. Note: End-of-year data.

Source: ADB Asia SME Monitor 2020 database.

A6. MSME Employees to Total (%)

Country	2003	2004	2005	2006	2007	2008	2009	2010	2011	2012	2013	2014	2015	2016	2017	2018	2019
Brunei Darussalam	--	--	--	--	--	--	--	59.4	--	--	--	--	55.1	56.5	57.3	--	--
Cambodia	--	--	--	--	--	--	74.8	--	72.0	--	--	71.8	--	--	--	--	--
Indonesia	--	--	--	--	--	--	--	97.3	97.3	97.2	97.2	97.0	96.7	97.0	96.8	97.0	--
Lao People's Democratic Republic	--	--	--	87.4	--	--	--	--	--	--	82.9	--	--	--	--	82.4	--
Malaysia	56.4	56.6	56.8	56.9	58.2	58.9	58.0	55.5	57.3	57.2	57.5	63.8	64.5	65.3	66.0	66.2	--
Myanmar	--	--	--	--	--	--	--	--	--	--	--	--	--	--	--	--	--
Philippines	--	--	--	66.8	64.7	61.2	63.2	62.3	61.0	64.9	63.7	62.8	61.6	63.3	62.8	63.2	--
Singapore	--	--	--	--	--	--	--	--	--	--	--	70.6	73.5	73.5	73.5	71.4	71.4
Thailand	--	--	--	--	76.0	--	78.2	77.9	83.9	81.0	81.0	80.3	80.4	78.5	82.2	85.5	--
Viet Nam	--	--	--	--	39.2	42.1	44.4	45.1	46.8	46.4	45.2	44.2	44.2	44.3	38.1	38.0	--

MSME = micro, small, and medium-sized enterprise. Note: End-of-year data.

Source: ADB Asia SME Monitor 2020 database.

A7. MSME Employees by Sector (% share, latest available year)

Item	Brunei Darussalam	Cambodia	Indonesia	Lao People's Democratic Republic	Malaysia	Myanmar	Philippines	Singapore	Thailand	Viet Nam
Agriculture	1.7	--	--	2.7	10.7	--	1.9	--	0.5	1.7
Manufacturing	10.3	15.2	20.5	17.4	16.4	--	13.4	--	24.3	26.4
Transportation and communication	5.1	--	4.7	3.6	--	--	--	--	--	7.4
Construction	19.2	--	--	2.0	10.3	--	--	--	--	18.6
Wholesale and retail trade	30.3	46.7	54.4	50.4	62.3*	--	35.7	--	31.8	26.1
Other services	30.2	38.1	19.5	22.4	--	--	46.0	--	43.4	18.0
Others	3.1	--	0.9	1.4	0.3	--	3.0	--	--	1.7

MSME = micro, small, and medium-sized enterprise. * Includes transportation and storage, telecommunication, and real estate.
Note: Data for the Lao PDR: 2013; data for Cambodia: 2014; data for Indonesia: 2016; data for Brunei Darussalam: 2017; data for Malaysia, the Philippines, Thailand, and Viet Nam: 2018. End-of-year data.
Source: ADB Asia SME Monitor 2020 database.

A8. MSME Employees by Region (% share, latest available year)

Item	Brunei Darussalam	Cambodia	Indonesia	Lao People's Democratic Republic	Malaysia	Myanmar	Philippines	Singapore	Thailand	Viet Nam
Capital city	--	20.0	--	--	15.7	--	28.4	--	30.2	--
Other areas	--	80.0	--	--	84.3	--	71.6	--	69.8	--

MSME = micro, small, and medium-sized enterprise.
Note: Data for Cambodia: 2014; data for Malaysia: 2015; data for the Philippines and Thailand: 2018. End-of-year data. Capital city: Phnom Penh in Cambodia, Kuala Lumpur in Malaysia, National Capital Region in the Philippines, Bangkok in Thailand.
Source: ADB Asia SME Monitor 2020 database.

A9-1. GDP of MSMEs (local currency)

Country	2003	2004	2005	2006	2007	2008	2009	2010	2011	2012	2013	2014	2015	2016	2017	2018	2019
Brunei Darussalam	--	--	--	--	--	--	--	3,233	3,472	3,808	3,984	--	4,765	4,409	4,271	6,497	--
Cambodia	--	--	--	--	--	--	--	--	--	--	--	--	--	--	--	--	--
Indonesia	--	--	--	--	--	--	--	2,969,346	3,411,575	4,321,830	4,869,568	5,440,008	6,228,285	7,009,283	7,820,283	8,573,895	--
Lao People's Democratic Republic	--	--	--	--	--	--	--	--	--	--	--	--	--	--	--	--	--
Malaysia	190,199	205,999	220,213	234,359	257,883	274,766	275,324	298,180	319,832	339,121	360,916	409,776	435,072	458,686	491,159	521,721	--
Myanmar	--	--	--	--	--	--	--	--	--	--	--	--	--	--	--	--	--
Philippines	--	--	--	751,543	--	--	--	--	--	--	--	--	--	--	--	--	--
Singapore	--	--	--	--	--	--	--	--	--	--	--	180	181	189	200	204	207
Thailand	--	--	--	--	3,758,130	3,863,743	3,858,146	4,258,542	4,445,932	4,831,990	5,044,252	5,261,090	5,631,426	6,099,185	6,557,750	7,013,971	--
Viet Nam	--	--	--	--	--	--	--	--	--	--	--	--	--	--	--	--	--

GDP = gross domestic product, MSME = micro, small, and medium-sized enterprise.
Note: End-of-year data. Brunei Darussalam: B$ million; Indonesia: Rp billion; Malaysia: RM million (real GDP); Philippines: P million; Singapore: S$ billion; Thailand: B million.
Source: ADB Asia SME Monitor 2020 database.

A9-2. GDP of MSMEs ($ million)

Country	2003	2004	2005	2006	2007	2008	2009	2010	2011	2012	2013	2014	2015	2016	2017	2018	2019
Brunei Darussalam	--	--	--	--	--	--	--	2,503	2,669	3,113	3,139	--	3,370	3,049	3,195	4,747	--
Cambodia	--	--	--	--	--	--	--	--	--	--	--	--	--	--	--	--	--
Indonesia	--	--	--	--	--	--	--	330,258	376,221	446,932	399,505	437,300	451,489	521,679	577,228	592,079	--
Lao People's Democratic Republic	--	--	--	--	--	--	--	--	--	--	--	--	--	--	--	--	--
Malaysia	50,052	54,2[illegible]0	58,257	66,362	77,993	79,320	80,398	96,702	100,671	110,887	109,985	117,246	101,368	102,248	120,916	126,065	--
Myanmar	--	--	--	--	--	--	--	--	--	--	--	--	--	--	--	--	--
Philippines	--	--	--	15,305	--	--	--	--	--	--	--	--	--	--	--	--	--
Singapore	--	--	--	--	--	--	--	--	--	--	--	136,229	128,015	130,678	149,633	149,472	153,652
Thailand	--	--	--	--	111,456	110,716	115,792	141,239	140,289	157,745	153,724	159,606	156,044	170,222	200,660	216,148	--
Viet Nam	--	--	--	--	--	--	--	--	--	--	--	--	--	--	--	--	--

GDP = gross domestic product, MSME = micro, small, and medium-sized enterprise.
Note: End-of-year data. Exchange rates of local currency to US dollar refer to end-of-year currency rates from the International Monetary Fund (IMF) International Financial Statistics in designated years.
Source: ADB Asia SME Monitor 2020 database.

A10. MSME Contribution to GDP (%)

Country	2003	2004	2005	2006	2007	2008	2009	2010	2011	2012	2013	2014	2015	2016	2017	2018	2019
Brunei Darussalam	--	--	--	--	--	--	--	17.3	14.9	16.0	17.6	--	26.8	28.0	25.5	35.5	--
Cambodia	--	--	--	--	--	--	--	--	--	--	--	--	--	--	--	--	--
Indonesia	--	--	--	--	--	--	--	56.2	56.2	58.0	59.1	60.3	61.4	59.8	60.9	61.1	--
Lao People's Democratic Republic	--	--	--	--	--	--	--	--	--	--	--	--	--	--	--	--	--
Malaysia	29.3	25.7	30.2	30.4	31.5	32.0	32.6	32.8	33.4	33.6	34.2	36.6	37.0	37.3	37.8	38.3	--
Myanmar	--	--	--	--	--	--	--	--	--	--	--	--	--	--	--	--	--
Philippines	--	--	--	35.7	--	--	--	--	--	--	--	--	--	--	--	--	--
Singapore	--	--	--	--	--	--	--	--	--	--	--	50.1	47.5	47.7	46.9	44.4	44.7
Thailand	--	--	--	--	41.4	39.8	39.9	39.4	39.3	39.1	39.1	39.8	41.0	41.9	42.4	43.0	--
Viet Nam	--	--	--	--	--	--	--	--	--	--	--	--	--	--	--	--	--

GDP = gross domestic product, MSME = micro, small, and medium-sized enterprise. Note: End-of-year data.
Source: ADB Asia SME Monitor 2020 database.

A11. MSME GDP by Sector (% share, latest available year)

Item	Brunei Darussalam	Cambodia	Indonesia	Lao People's Democratic Republic	Malaysia	Myanmar	Philippines	Singapore	Thailand	Viet Nam
Agriculture	--	--	--	--	10.1	--	1.0	--	--	--
Manufacturing	--	--	26.8	--	20.1	--	19.3	--	22.6	--
Transportation and communication	--	--	4.8	--	--	--	--	--	--	--
Construction	--	--	--	--	5.9	--	--	--	4.9	--
Wholesale and retail trade	--	--	47.8	--	62.4*	--	18.4	--	31.4	--
Other services	--	--	20.6	--	--	--	41.9	--	39.1	--
Others	--	--	--	--	1.6	--	19.3	--	2.0	--

GDP = gross domestic product, MSME = micro, small, and medium-sized enterprise. * Includes transportation and storage, telecommunication, and real estate.
Note: End-of-year data. Data for the Philippines: 2006; data for Indonesia: 2016; data for Malaysia and Thailand: 2018.
Source: ADB Asia SME Monitor 2020 database.

A12. MSME GDP by Region (% share, latest available year)

Item	Brunei Darussalam	Cambodia	Indonesia	Lao People's Democratic Republic	Malaysia	Myanmar	Philippines	Singapore	Thailand	Viet Nam
Capital city	--	--	--	--	23.0	--	--	--	--	--
Other areas	--	--	--	--	77.0	--	--	--	--	--

GDP = gross domestic product, MSME = micro, small, and medium-sized enterprise.
Note: End-of-year data. Data for Malaysia: 2015. Capital city: Kuala Lumpur in Malaysia.
Source: ADB Asia SME Monitor 2020 database.

A13-1. MSME Export Value (local currency)

Country	2003	2004	2005	2006	2007	2008	2009	2010	2011	2012	2013	2014	2015	2016	2017	2018	2019
Brunei Darussalam	--	--	--	--	--	--	--	--	--	--	--	--	--	--	--	--	--
Cambodia	--	--	--	--	--	--	--	--	--	--	--	--	--	--	--	--	--
Indonesia	--	--	--	--	--	--	--	162,255	175,895	187,442	166,627	182,113	185,975	255,126	301,630	293,841	--
Lao People's Democratic Republic	--	--	--	--	--	--	--	--	--	--	--	1,238	--	--	--	--	--
Malaysia	--	--	--	--	--	--	--	116,800	131,000	134,700	136,900	145,200	145,000	155,100	166,200	171,900	--
Myanmar	--	--	--	--	--	--	--	--	--	--	--	--	--	--	--	--	--
Philippines	--	--	--	--	--	--	--	--	--	--	--	--	--	--	--	--	--
Singapore	--	--	--	--	--	--	--	--	--	--	--	--	--	--	--	--	--
Thailand	--	--	--	--	1,576,000	1,691,000	1,564,000	1,669,000	1,971,000	2,065,460	1,761,800	1,922,500	1,978,300	2,190,500	1,990,420	2,325,852	--
Viet Nam	--	--	--	--	--	--	--	--	--	--	--	--	--	--	--	--	--

MSME = micro, small, and medium-sized enterprise.
Note: End-of-year data. Indonesia: Rp billion; Lao PDR: KN million; Malaysia: RM million; Thailand: B million.
Source: ADB Asia SME Monitor 2020 database.

A13-2. MSME Export Value ($ million)

Country	2003	2004	2005	2006	2007	2008	2009	2010	2011	2012	2013	2014	2015	2016	2017	2018	2019
Brunei Darussalam	--	--	--	--	--	--	--	--	--	--	--	--	--	--	--	--	--
Cambodia	--	--	--	--	--	--	--	--	--	--	--	--	--	--	--	--	--
Indonesia	--	--	--	--	--	--	--	18,046	19,397	19,384	13,670	14,639	13,481	18,988	22,264	20,291	--
Lao People's Democratic Republic	--	--	--	--	--	--	--	--	--	--	--	0.2	--	--	--	--	--
Malaysia	--	--	--	--	--	--	--	37,879	41,234	44,045	41,719	41,545	33,784	34,574	40,916	41,537	--
Myanmar	--	--	--	--	--	--	--	--	--	--	--	--	--	--	--	--	--
Philippines	--	--	--	--	--	--	--	--	--	--	--	--	--	--	--	--	--
Singapore	--	--	--	--	--	--	--	--	--	--	--	--	--	--	--	--	--
Thailand	--	--	--	--	46,740	48,456	46,939	55,354	62,194	67,429	53,691	58,323	54,818	61,135	60,905	71,675	--
Viet Nam	--	--	--	--	--	--	--	--	--	--	--	--	--	--	--	--	--

MSME = micro, small, and medium-sized enterprise.
Note: End-of-year data. Exchange rates of local currency to US dollar refer to end-of-year currency rates from the International Monetary Fund International Financial Statistics in designated years.
Source: ADB Asia SME Monitor 2020 database.

A14. MSME Exports to Total (%)

Country	2003	2004	2005	2006	2007	2008	2009	2010	2011	2012	2013	2014	2015	2016	2017	2018	2019
Brunei Darussalam	--	--	--	--	--	--	--	--	--	--	--	--	--	--	--	--	--
Cambodia	--	--	--	--	--	--	--	--	--	--	--	--	--	--	--	--	--
Indonesia	--	--	--	--	--	--	--	17.0	15.8	16.4	14.1	15.7	15.7	14.4	14.5	14.4	--
Lao People's Democratic Republic	--	--	--	--	--	--	--	--	--	--	--	--	--	--	--	--	--
Malaysia	--	--	--	--	--	--	--	16.4	16.9	17.5	17.8	17.8	17.7	18.6	17.3	17.3	--
Myanmar	--	--	--	--	--	--	--	--	--	--	--	--	--	--	--	--	--
Philippines	--	--	--	--	--	--	--	--	--	--	--	--	--	--	--	--	--
Singapore	--	--	--	--	--	--	--	--	--	--	--	--	--	--	--	--	--
Thailand	--	--	--	--	30.1	28.9	30.1	27.3	29.4	29.9	25.5	27.9	28.2	29.0	28.9	28.7	--
Viet Nam	--	--	--	--	--	--	--	--	--	--	--	--	--	--	--	--	--

MSME = micro, small, and medium-sized enterprise.
Note: End-of-year data.
Source: ADB Asia SME Monitor 2020 database.

B. MSME Access to Finance (Banking)

B1-1. MSME Bank Loans Outstanding (local currency)

Country	2003	2004	2005	2006	2007	2008	2009	2010	2011	2012	2013	2014	2015	2016	2017	2018	2019
Brunei Darussalam	--	--	--	--	--	--	--	--	--	--	--	--	--	--	--	3,304,913	8,996,023
Cambodia	--	--	--	--	--	--	--	--	--	--	--	--	--	--	--	--	--
Indonesia	--	--	--	--	--	--	--	--	458,164	526,397	608,823	763,307	790,467	856,997	942,388	1,032,643	1,111,340
Lao People's Democratic Republic	--	--	--	--	--	--	--	--	--	--	--	--	14,919	13,997	15,939	14,241	14,104
Malaysia	--	--	--	--	127,984	138,859	141,608	141,159	165,316	187,039	211,038	243,708	274,412	299,733	315,660	320,140	278,701
Myanmar	--	--	--	--	--	--	--	--	--	--	--	--	--	--	733,235	896,840	1,131,665
Philippines	--	--	--	--	--	270,526	257,894	311,452	351,693	384,082	395,031	425,155	461,650	496,863	532,198	577,719	588,837
Singapore	--	--	--	--	--	--	--	46,424	55,381	54,371	64,468	70,130	72,835	71,135	75,207	76,159	76,590
Thailand	--	--	--	--	2,688	2,768	2,585	3,594	4,272	4,627	5,123	5,460	5,974	6,096	6,288	6,560	6,581
Viet Nam	--	--	--	--	--	--	--	--	--	--	--	--	--	--	--	--	--

MSME = micro, small, and medium-sized enterprise. Note: End-of-year data. For Myanmar, fiscal year which starts in April and ends in March of the following year. Data for Singapore as of end-June. Brunei Darussalam: B$; Indonesia: Rp billion; Lao PDR: KN billion; Malaysia: RM million; Myanmar: MK million; Philippines: P million; Singapore: S$ million; Thailand: B billion.
Source: ADB Asia SME Monitor 2020 database.

B1-2. MSME Bank Loans Outstanding ($ million)

Country	2003	2004	2005	2006	2007	2008	2009	2010	2011	2012	2013	2014	2015	2016	2017	2018	2019
Brunei Darussalam	--	--	--	--	--	--	--	--	--	--	--	--	--	--	--	2.4	6.7
Cambodia	--	--	--	--	--	--	--	--	--	--	--	--	--	--	--	--	--
Indonesia	--	--	--	--	--	--	--	--	50,525	54,436	49,949	61,359	57,301	63,784	69,559	71,310	79,947
Lao People's Democratic Republic	--	--	--	--	--	--	--	--	--	--	--	--	1,831	1,710	1,922	1,669	1,592
Malaysia	--	--	--	--	38,707	40,086	41,351	45,779	52,035	61,159	64,311	69,730	63,936	66,815	77,710	77,356	68,100
Myanmar	--	--	--	--	--	--	--	--	--	--	--	--	--	--	538	579	772
Philippines	--	--	--	--	--	5,697	5,563	7,097	8,006	9,324	8,894	9,529	9,788	9,975	10,660	10,957	11,604
Singapore	--	--	--	--	--	--	--	36,057	42,578	44,439	50,951	53,077	51,514	49,184	56,268	55,802	56,851
Thailand	--	--	--	--	79,714	79,319	77,586	119,201	134,802	151,040	156,137	165,626	165,550	170,122	192,415	202,155	218,260
Viet Nam	--	--	--	--	--	--	--	--	--	--	--	--	--	--	--	--	--

MSME = micro, small, and medium-sized enterprise. Note: End-of-year data. For Myanmar, fiscal year starts in April and ends in March of the following year. Data for Singapore as of end-June. Exchange rates of local currency to US dollar refer to end-of-year currency rates from the International Monetary Fund International Financial Statistics in designated years.
Source: ADB Asia SME Monitor 2020 database.

B2. MSME Bank Loans to Total (%)

Country	2003	2004	2005	2006	2007	2008	2009	2010	2011	2012	2013	2014	2015	2016	2017	2018	2019
Brunei Darussalam	--	--	--	--	--	--	--	--	--	--	--	--	--	--	--	0.1	0.2
Cambodia	--	--	--	--	--	--	--	--	--	--	--	--	--	--	--	--	--
Indonesia	--	--	--	--	--	--	--	--	20.8	19.4	18.5	20.4	19.3	19.4	19.7	19.3	19.6
Lao People's Democratic Republic	--	--	--	--	--	--	--	--	--	--	--	--	30.9	23.4	23.8	20.6	19.8
Malaysia	--	--	--	--	18.9	18.4	17.4	15.5	16.2	16.5	16.9	17.9	18.7	19.4	19.8	18.7	14.6
Myanmar	--	--	--	--	--	--	--	--	--	--	--	--	--	--	4.5	4.6	4.8
Philippines	--	--	--	--	--	11.6	10.6	11.7	11.0	10.6	9.3	8.3	7.9	7.2	6.6	6.2	6.1
Singapore	--	--	--	--	--	--	--	7.2	7.0	6.2	6.1	6.1	6.3	6.2	6.0	5.8	--
Thailand	--	--	--	--	33.6	29.1	25.4	30.9	32.3	30.9	31.3	32.1	33.5	32.9	31.5	31.8	30.9
Viet Nam	--	--	--	--	--	--	--	--	--	--	--	--	--	--	--	--	--

MSME = micro, small, and medium-sized enterprise. Note: End-of-year data. For Myanmar, fiscal year starts in April and ends in March of the following year.
Source: ADB Asia SME Monitor 2020 database.

B3. MSME Bank Loans to GDP (%)

Country	2003	2004	2005	2006	2007	2008	2009	2010	2011	2012	2013	2014	2015	2016	2017	2018	2019
Brunei Darussalam	--	--	--	--	--	--	--	--	--	--	--	--	--	--	--	0.0	0.1
Cambodia	--	--	--	--	--	--	--	--	--	--	--	--	--	--	--	--	--
Indonesia	--	--	--	--	--	--	--	--	6.2	6.4	6.7	7.2	6.9	6.9	6.9	7.0	7.0
Lao People's Democratic Republic	--	--	--	--	--	--	--	--	--	--	--	--	12.7	10.8	11.3	9.3	8.5
Malaysia	--	--	--	--	19.3	18.0	19.9	17.2	18.1	19.3	20.7	22.0	23.3	24.0	23.0	22.1	18.5
Myanmar	--	--	--	--	--	--	--	--	--	--	--	--	--	--	0.9	1.0	--
Philippines	--	--	--	--	--	3.5	3.2	3.5	3.6	3.6	3.4	3.4	3.5	3.4	3.4	3.3	3.2
Singapore	--	--	--	--	--	--	--	14.2	15.8	14.7	16.8	17.6	17.2	16.2	15.9	15.1	--
Thailand	--	--	--	--	29.6	28.5	26.8	25.9	28.6	29.0	31.8	33.2	33.7	32.3	32.3	31.6	30.3
Viet Nam	--	--	--	--	--	--	--	--	--	--	--	--	--	--	--	--	--

GDP = gross domestic product, MSME = micro, small, and medium-sized enterprise.
Note: End-of-year data. For Myanmar, fiscal year starts in April and ends in March of the following year. Data for Singapore as of end-June.
Source: ADB Asia SME Monitor 2020 database.

B4. MSME Bank Loans by Sector (% share, latest available year)

Item	Brunei Darussalam	Cambodia	Indonesia	Lao People's Democratic Republic	Malaysia	Myanmar	Philippines	Singapore	Thailand	Viet Nam
Agriculture	12.2	--	9.9	3.8	5.1	1.0	--	37.0	1.5	--
Manufacturing	30.2	--	10.0	7.9	15.6	18.9	--	7.9	18.9	--
Transportation and communication	0.4	--	4.0	1.1	--	3.4	--	0.4	2.6	--
Construction	1.2	--	6.5	20.7	12.5	1.5	--	25.9	3.8	--
Wholesale and retail trade	24.6	--	49.3	37.0	65.7*	45.6	--	8.3	28.3	--
Other services	27.9	--	18.0	18.6		11.4	--	16.9	36.8	--
Others	3.5	--	2.3	11.0	1.1	18.3	--	3.7	8.0	--

MSME = micro, small, and medium-sized enterprise.

Note: Data in end-2019. For Singapore, June 2019. For Myanmar, fiscal year starts in April and ends in March of the following year. Data for Brunei Darussalam refers to SME Bank data only.

Source: ADB Asia SME Monitor 2020 database.

B5. MSME Bank Loans by Region (% share, latest available year)

Item	Brunei Darussalam	Cambodia	Indonesia	Lao People's Democratic Republic	Malaysia	Myanmar	Philippines	Singapore	Thailand	Viet Nam
Capital city	96.0	--	--	--	--	--	--	--	--	--
Other areas	4.0	--	--	--	--	--	--	--	--	--

MSME = micro, small, and medium-sized enterprise.

Note: Data in end-2019. Data for Brunei Darussalam refers to SME Bank data only. Capital city: Bandar Seri Begawan in Brunei Darussalam.

Source: ADB Asia SME Monitor 2020 database.

B6-1. Nonperforming MSME Bank Loans (local currency)

Country	2003	2004	2005	2006	2007	2008	2009	2010	2011	2012	2013	2014	2015	2016	2017	2018	2019
Brunei Darussalam	--	--	--	--	--	--	--	--	--	--	--	--	--	--	--	--	--
Cambodia	--	--	--	--	--	--	--	--	--	--	--	--	--	--	--	--	--
Indonesia	--	--	--	--	--	--	--	--	15,674	17,011	19,515	31,560	33,208	35,597	38,520	35,504	40,089
Lao People's Democratic Republic	--	--	--	--	--	--	--	--	--	--	--	--	--	--	--	--	--
Malaysia	--	--	--	--	12,083	9,882	8,895	10,590	9,552	8,574	8,216	8,553	8,880	8,874	10,065	10,261	10,399
Myanmar	--	--	--	--	--	--	--	--	--	--	--	--	--	--	--	--	--
Philippines	--	--	--	--	--	--	--	23,656	26,078	25,347	25,512	25,097	25,209	26,217	25,989	30,030	32,020
Singapore	--	--	--	--	--	--	--	696	698	574	536	602	1,379	2,115	3,380	3,233	3,211
Thailand	--	--	--	--	--	--	184	153	130	125	136	137	164	205	220	230	231
Viet Nam	--	--	--	--	--	--	--	--	--	--	--	--	--	--	--	--	--

MSME = micro, small, and medium-sized enterprise.

Note: End-of-year data. Data for Singapore as of end-June. Indonesia: Rp billion; Malaysia: RM million; Philippines: P million; Singapore: S$ million; Thailand: B billion.

Source: ADB Asia SME Monitor 2020 database.

B6-2. Nonperforming MSME Bank Loans ($ million)

Country	2003	2004	2005	2006	2007	2008	2009	2010	2011	2012	2013	2014	2015	2016	2017	2018	2019
Brunei Darussalam	--	--	--	--	--	--	--	--	--	--	--	--	--	--	--	--	--
Cambodia	--	--	--	--	--	--	--	--	--	--	--	--	--	--	--	--	--
Indonesia	--	--	--	--	--	--	--	--	1,728	1,759	1,601	2,537	2,407	2,649	2,843	2,452	2,884
Lao People's Democratic Republic	--	--	--	--	--	--	--	--	--	--	--	--	--	--	--	--	--
Malaysia	--	--	--	--	3,654	2,853	2,597	3,434	3,006	2,804	2,504	2,447	2,069	1,978	2,478	2,479	2,541
Myanmar	--	--	--	--	--	--	--	--	--	--	--	--	--	--	--	--	--
Philippines	--	--	--	--	--	--	--	539	594	615	574	562	534	526	521	570	631
Singapore	--	--	--	--	--	--	--	541	536	469	424	455	976	1,463	2,529	2,369	2,383
Thailand	--	--	--	--	--	--	5,530	5,060	4,091	4,078	4,149	4,164	4,535	5,727	6,722	7,076	7,667
Viet Nam	--	--	--	--	--	--	--	--	--	--	--	--	--	--	--	--	--

MSME = micro, small, and medium-sized enterprise.

Note: End-of-year data. Data for Singapore as of end-June. Exchange rates of local currency to US dollar refer to end-of-year currency rates from the International Monetary Fund International Financial Statistics in designated years.

Source: ADB Asia SME Monitor 2020 database.

B7. MSME Nonperforming Loans to Total MSME Bank Loans (%)

Country	2003	2004	2005	2006	2007	2008	2009	2010	2011	2012	2013	2014	2015	2016	2017	2018	2019
Brunei Darussalam	--	--	--	--	--	--	--	--	--	--	--	--	--	--	--	--	--
Cambodia	--	--	--	--	--	--	--	--	--	--	--	--	--	--	--	--	--
Indonesia	--	--	--	--	--	--	--	--	3.4	3.2	3.2	4.1	4.2	4.2	4.1	3.4	3.6
Lao People's Democratic Republic	--	--	--	--	--	--	--	--	--	--	--	--	--	--	--	--	--
Malaysia	--	--	--	--	9.4	7.1	6.3	7.5	5.8	4.6	3.9	3.5	3.2	3.0	3.2	3.2	3.7
Myanmar	--	--	--	--	--	--	--	--	--	--	--	--	--	--	--	--	--
Philippines	--	--	--	--	--	--	--	7.6	7.4	6.6	6.5	5.9	5.5	5.3	4.9	5.2	5.8
Singapore	--	--	--	--	--	--	--	1.5	1.3	1.1	0.8	0.9	1.9	3.0	4.5	4.2	4.2
Thailand	--	--	--	--	--	--	7.1	5.4	4.0	3.5	3.3	3.1	3.5	4.4	4.5	4.6	4.7
Viet Nam	--	--	--	--	--	--	--	--	--	--	--	--	--	--	--	--	--

MSME = micro, small, and medium-sized enterprise. Note: End-of-year data. Data for Singapore as of end-June.
Source: ADB Asia SME Monitor 2020 database.

B8-1. Outstanding Guaranteed Loans (local currency)

Country	2003	2004	2005	2006	2007	2008	2009	2010	2011	2012	2013	2014	2015	2016	2017	2018	2019
Brunei Darussalam	--	--	--	--	--	--	--	--	--	--	--	--	--	--	--	--	--
Cambodia	--	--	--	--	--	--	--	--	--	--	--	--	--	--	--	--	--
Indonesia	--	--	--	--	--	--	8,154	5,010	30,486	40,760	47,422	49,546	22,757	70,669	75,004	125,912	153,180
Lao People's Democratic Republic	--	--	--	--	--	--	--	--	--	--	--	--	--	--	--	--	--
Malaysia	--	--	--	--	38.8	41.8	44.9	47.4	50.3	51.4	52.9	56.1	59.5	63.7	67.1	70.8	--
Myanmar	--	--	--	--	--	--	--	--	--	--	--	--	--	--	--	--	--
Philippines	--	--	--	215.0	131.3	107.8	58.3	66.9	26.4	125.6	80.3	175.0	229.7	123.3	594.9	185.2	78.4
Singapore	--	--	--	--	--	--	--	--	--	--	--	--	--	--	--	--	--
Thailand	--	--	--	--	22.3	21.9	39.9	72.9	113.0	180.5	243.6	269.5	308.9	331.0	353.9	373.8	388.7
Viet Nam	--	--	--	--	--	--	--	--	--	--	--	--	--	--	--	--	--

Note: End-of-year data. For the Philippines, data in 2019 as of August. Indonesia: Rp billion; Malaysia: RM million (data from Credit Guarantee Corporation); Philippines: P million (data from Small Business Corporation; guaranteed loans approved); Thailand: B billion.
Source: ADB Asia SME Monitor 2020 database.

B8-2. Outstanding Guaranteed Loans ($ million)

Country	2003	2004	2005	2006	2007	2008	2009	2010	2011	2012	2013	2014	2015	2016	2017	2018	2019
Brunei Darussalam	--	--	--	--	--	--	--	--	--	--	--	--	--	--	--	--	--
Cambodia	--	--	--	--	--	--	--	--	--	--	--	--	--	--	--	--	--
Indonesia	--	--	--	--	--	--	867	557	3,362	4,215	3,891	3,983	1,650	5,260	5,536	8,695	11,019
Lao People's Democratic Republic	--	--	--	--	--	--	--	--	--	--	--	--	--	--	--	--	--
Malaysia	--	--	--	--	11,734	12,067	13,111	15,371	15,819	16,807	16,121	16,052	13,863	14,200	16,514	17,099	--
Myanmar	--	--	--	--	--	--	--	--	--	--	--	--	--	--	--	--	--
Philippines	--	--	--	4.2	2.8	2.4	1.2	1.5	0.6	3.0	1.9	3.9	5.0	2.6	11.8	3.5	1.5
Singapore	--	--	--	--	--	--	--	--	--	--	--	--	--	--	--	--	--
Thailand	--	--	--	--	660	626	1,197	2,418	3,567	5,891	7,425	8,177	8,561	9,238	10,828	11,520	12,890
Viet Nam	--	--	--	--	--	--	--	--	--	--	--	--	--	--	--	--	--

Note: End-of-year data. For the Philippines, data in 2019 as of August. Exchange rates of local currency to US dollar refer to end-of-year currency rates from the International Monetary Fund International Financial Statistics in designated years.
Source: ADB Asia SME Monitor 2020 database.

B8-3. Number of MSMEs Guaranteed

Country	2003	2004	2005	2006	2007	2008	2009	2010	2011	2012	2013	2014	2015	2016	2017	2018	2019
Brunei Darussalam	--	--	--	--	--	--	--	--	--	--	--	--	--	--	--	--	--
Cambodia	--	--	--	--	--	--	--	--	--	--	--	--	--	--	--	--	--
Indonesia	--	--	--	--	3,623	1,652,965	718,320	1,437,650	1,909,912	1,962,121	2,347,429	2,443,907	722,621	4,362,599	4,086,971	4,440,028	4,729,531
Lao People's Democratic Republic	--	--	--	--	--	--	--	--	--	--	--	--	--	--	--	--	--
Malaysia	--	--	--	--	13,004	10,368	14,073	7,670	7,504	2,152	2,368	6,839	8,225	7,568	8,637	8,999	--
Myanmar	--	--	--														
Philippines	--	--	--	54	43	36	17	10	9	44	22	91	142	181	14,799	327	80
Singapore	--	--	--	--	--	--	--	--	--	--	--	--	--	--	--	--	--
Thailand	--	--	--	--	--	--	--	--	--	--	--	--	--	--	--	--	--
Viet Nam	--	--	--	--	--	--	--	--	--	--	--	--	--	--	--	--	--

MSME = micro, small, and medium-sized enterprise. Note: End-of-year data. For the Philippines, data in 2019 as of August.
Source: ADB Asia SME Monitor 2020 database.

C. MSME Access to Finance (Nonbanking)

C1-1. NBFI Financing, Total (local currency)

Country	2003	2004	2005	2006	2007	2008	2009	2010	2011	2012	2013	2014	2015	2016	2017	2018	2019
Brunei Darussalam	--	--	--	--	--	--	--	1,415	1,562	1,716	1,815	2,023	1,881	1,677	1,570	1,552	1,537
Cambodia	--	--	--	--	617,271	1,130,585	1,244,970	1,724,841	2,591,263	3,538,889	5,261,752	7,299,407	12,589,330	13,146,529	17,761,787	22,527,051	30,527,095
Indonesia	--	--	--	--	--	--	--	--	--	--	--	--	--	423,125	452,049	477,589	503,199
Lao People's Democratic Republic	--	--	--	--	--	--	--	49,209	93,042	103,110	459,065	430,988	835,488	1,461,276	2,196,508	4,808,287	6,075,379
Malaysia	--	--	--	--	2,479,000	2,276,611	2,097,352	553,233	952,883	1,129,848	1,363,741	1,486,810	1,392,280	1,641,471	1,244,832	1,386,277	--
Myanmar	--	--	--	--	--	--	--	--	--	49,194	67,245	110,069	169,293	260,948	426,016	793,197	1,800,232
Philippines	--	--	--	--	--	--	6,544	5,947	7,711	8,876	8,538	130,201	310,467	382,749	403,599	527,932	213,452
Singapore	--	--	--	--	--	--	--	8,058	9,460	11,312	11,654	12,385	13,252	12,547	12,849	13,254	14,712
Thailand	--	--	--	--	--	--	--	--	--	--	--	--	--	--	--	--	--
Viet Nam	--	--	--	--	--	--	--	23,708,082	29,076,880	36,450,034	45,557,772	53,221,190	61,880,958	71,700,966	84,896,048	96,140,373	102,086,556

NBFI = nonbank finance institution.

Note: End-of-year data. For Myanmar, fiscal year starts in April and ends in March of the following year. Data in 2019 as of September for Myanmar, August for Singapore, and June for Viet Nam. Brunei Darussalam: B$ million (finance companies and pawnbrokers); Cambodia: KR million (microfinance institutions and leasing companies); Indonesia: Rp billion (finance companies, microfinance institutions, and government pawnshops); Lao PDR: KN million (microfinance institutions, pawnshops, and leasing companies); Malaysia: RM '000 (private equity, venture capital, factoring, and leasing companies); Myanmar: MK million (microfinance institutions); Philippines: P million (credit unions and cooperatives [2015–2018], pawnshops [2009–2018], and nonstock savings and loans associations [NSSLAs; 2014–2019]); Singapore: S$ million (finance companies); Viet Nam: D million (People's Credit Funds and microfinance institutions).

Source: ADB Asia SME Monitor 2020 database.

C1-2. NBFI Financing, Total ($ million)

Country	2003	2004	2005	2006	2007	2008	2009	2010	2011	2012	2013	2014	2015	2016	2017	2018	2019
Brunei Darussalam	--	--	--	--	--	--	--	1,095	1,201	1,402	1,430	1,531	1,331	1,159	1,174	1,134	1,139
Cambodia	--	--	--	--	154	277	299	--	642	886	1,317	1,791	3,107	3,250	4,395	5,586	7,475
Indonesia	--	--	--	--	--	--	--	--	--	--	--	--	--	31,492	33,366	32,980	36,199
Lao People's Democratic Republic	--	--	--	--	--	--	--	6	12	13	57	53	103	179	265	564	686
Malaysia	--	--	--	--	750	657,220	612,455	179,417	299,932	369,443	415,585	425,411	324,390	365,910	306,458	334,971	--
Myanmar	--	--	--	--	--	--	--	--	--	58	68	107	130	192	313	512	1,228
Philippines	--	--	--	--	--	--	141	136	176	215	192	2,918	6,582	7,684	8,084	10,013	4,206
Singapore	--	--	--	--	--	--	--	6,259	7,273	9,245	9,210	9,374	9,372	8,675	9,613	9,712	10,921
Thailand	--	--	--	--	--	--	--	--	--	--	--	--	--	--	--	--	--
Viet Nam	--	--	--	--	--	--	--	1,252	1,396	1,750	2,166	2,505	2,827	3,236	3,786	4,212	4,409

NBFI = nonbank finance institution.

Note: End-of-year data. For Myanmar, fiscal year starts in April and ends in March of the following year. Data in 2019 as of September for Myanmar, August for Singapore, and June for Viet Nam. Exchange rates of local currency to US dollar refer to end-of-year currency rates from the International Monetary Fund International Financial Statistics in designated years.

Source: ADB Asia SME Monitor 2020 database.

C2. NBFI Financing to Bank Loans (%)

Country	2003	2004	2005	2006	2007	2008	2009	2010	2011	2012	2013	2014	2015	2016	2017	2018	2019
Brunei Darussalam	--	--	--	--	--	--	--	27.3	30.7	33.0	32.3	35.4	30.8	31.0	30.6	28.3	27.9
Cambodia	--	--	--	--	9.7	11.5	11.9	13.1	14.8	15.2	17.9	19.2	27.0	23.5	27.1	27.7	29.8
Indonesia	--	--	--	--	--	--	--	--	--	--	--	--	--	9.2	9.0	9.5	11.3
Lao People's Democratic Republic	--	--	--	--	--	--	--	0.4	0.5	0.4	1.3	1.1	1.7	2.4	3.3	7.0	8.5
Malaysia	--	--	--	--	0.4	0.3	0.3	0.1	0.1	0.1	0.1	0.1	0.1	0.1	0.1	0.1	--
Myanmar	--	--	--	--	--	--	--	--	--	1.7	1.6	1.7	1.9	2.1	2.6	4.1	7.7
Philippines	--	--	--	--	--	--	--	--	--	0.2	0.2	2.5	5.3	5.6	5.0	5.7	2.2
Singapore	--	--	--	--	--	--	--	1.3	1.2	1.3	1.1	1.1	1.2	1.1	1.0	1.0	1.1
Thailand	--	--	--	--	--	--	--	--	--	--	--	--	--	--	--	--	--
Viet Nam	--	--	--	--	--	--	--	--	--	1.2	1.3	1.3	1.3	1.3	1.3	1.3	1.3

NBFI = nonbank finance institution.

Note: End-of-year data. For Myanmar, fiscal year starts in April and ends in March of the following year. Data in 2019 as of September for Myanmar, August for Singapore, and June for Viet Nam.

Source: ADB Asia SME Monitor 2020 database.

C3. NBFI Financing to GDP (%)

Country	2003	2004	2005	2006	2007	2008	2009	2010	2011	2012	2013	2014	2015	2016	2017	2018	2019
Brunei Darussalam	--	--	--	--	--	--	--	7.6	6.7	7.2	8.0	9.3	10.6	10.6	9.4	8.5	8.4
Cambodia	--	--	--	--	1.8	2.7	2.9	3.7	5.0	6.2	8.6	10.8	17.1	16.2	19.8	22.6	27.9
Indonesia	--	--	--	--	--	--	--	--	--	--	--	--	--	3.4	3.3	3.2	3.2
Lao People's Democratic Republic	--	--	--	--	--	--	--	0.1	0.1	0.1	0.5	0.4	0.7	1.1	1.6	3.2	3.7
Malaysia	--	--	--	--	0.4	0.3	0.3	0.1	0.1	0.1	0.1	0.1	0.1	0.1	0.1	0.1	--
Myanmar	--	--	--	--	--	--	--	--	--	0.1	0.1	0.2	0.2	0.3	0.5	2.4	--
Philippines	--	--	--	--	--	--	0.1	0.1	0.1	0.1	0.1	1.0	2.3	2.6	2.6	3.0	1.1
Singapore	--	--	--	--	--	--	--	2.5	2.7	3.1	3.0	3.1	3.1	2.9	2.7	2.6	2.9
Thailand	--	--	--	--	--	--	--	--	--	--	--	--	--	--	--	--	--
Viet Nam	--	--	--	--	--	--	--	--	--	1.1	1.3	1.4	1.5	1.6	1.7	1.7	1.8

GDP = gross domestic product, NBFI = nonbank finance institution.

Note: End-of-year data. For Myanmar, fiscal year starts in April and ends in March of the following year. Data in 2019 as of August for Singapore and June for Viet Nam.

Source: ADB Asia SME Monitor 2020 database.

C4-1. Nonperforming NBFI Financing (local currency)

Country	2003	2004	2005	2006	2007	2008	2009	2010	2011	2012	2013	2014	2015	2016	2017	2018	2019
Brunei Darussalam	--	--	--	--	--	--	--	13	13	19	20	24	20	19	20	15	17
Cambodia	--	--	--	--	1,171	4,719	34,847	20,361	5,753	10,284	30,880	52,119	94,788	210,885	298,210	335,399	262,692
Indonesia	--	--	--	--	--	--	--	--	--	--	--	--	--	12,644	12,260	11,810	10,864
Lao People's Democratic Republic	--	--	--	--	--	--	--	--	--	--	--	--	--	--	--	--	--
Malaysia	--	--	--	--	--	--	--	--	--	--	--	--	--	--	--	--	--
Myanmar	--	--	--	--	--	--	--	--	--	42	41	68	258	1,645	2,769	9,085	14,376
Philippines	--	--	--	--	--	--	--	--	--	--	--	--	--	--	--	--	--
Singapore	--	--	--	--	--	--	--	--	--	--	--	--	--	--	--	--	--
Thailand	--	--	--	--	--	--	--	--	--	--	--	--	--	--	--	--	--
Viet Nam	--	--	--	--	--	--	--	--	84	912	140	87	115	554	16,319	18,669	22,761

NBFI = nonbank finance institution.

Note: End-of-year data. For Myanmar, fiscal year starts in April and ends in March of the following year. Data in 2019 as of September for Myanmar and June for Viet Nam. Brunei Darussalam: B$ million (finance companies and pawnbrokers); Cambodia: KR million (microfinance institutions and leasing companies); Indonesia: Rp billion (finance companies only); Myanmar: MK million (microfinance institutions); Viet Nam: D million (microfinance institutions only).

Source: ADB Asia SME Monitor 2020 database.

C4-2. Nonperforming NBFI Financing ($ million)

Country	2003	2004	2005	2006	2007	2008	2009	2010	2011	2012	2013	2014	2015	2016	2017	2018	2019
Brunei Darussalam	--	--	--	--	--	--	--	10.0	10.1	15.5	16.0	17.8	14.4	13.2	15.1	11.0	12.8
Cambodia	--	--	--	--	0.3	1.2	8.4	5.0	1.4	2.6	7.7	12.8	23.4	52.1	73.8	83.2	64.3
Indonesia	--	--	--	--	--	--	--	--	--	--	--	--	--	941.0	904.9	815.6	781.5
Lao People's Democratic Republic	--	--	--	--	--	--	--	--	--	--	--	--	--	--	--	--	--
Malaysia	--	--	--	--	--	--	--	--	--	--	--	--	--	--	--	--	--
Myanmar	--	--	--	--	--	--	--	--	--	0.05	0.04	0.07	0.20	1.21	2.03	5.86	9.81
Philippines	--	--	--	--	--	--	--	--	--	--	--	--	--	--	--	--	--
Singapore	--	--	--	--	--	--	--	--	--	--	--	--	--	--	--	--	--
Thailand	--	--	--	--	--	--	--	--	--	--	--	--	--	--	--	--	--
Viet Nam	--	--	--	--	--	--	--	--	0.004	0.044	0.007	0.004	0.005	0.025	0.728	0.818	0.983

NBFI = nonbank finance institution.

Note: End-of-year data. For Myanmar, fiscal year starts in April and ends in March of the following year. Data in 2019 as of September for Myanmar and June for Viet Nam. Exchange rates of local currency to US dollar refer to end-of-year currency rates from the International Monetary Fund International Financial Statistics in designated years.

Source: ADB Asia SME Monitor 2020 database.

C5. NBFI NPF to Total Financing (%)

Country	2003	2004	2005	2006	2007	2008	2009	2010	2011	2012	2013	2014	2015	2016	2017	2018	2019
Brunei Darussalam	--	--	--	--	--	--	--	0.91	0.84	1.10	1.12	1.16	1.08	1.14	1.28	0.97	1.12
Cambodia	--	--	--	--	0.19	0.42	2.80	1.18	0.22	0.29	0.59	0.71	0.75	1.60	1.68	1.49	0.86
Indonesia	--	--	--	--	--	--	--	--	--	--	--	--	--	3.26	2.96	2.71	2.40
Lao People's Democratic Republic	--	--	--	--	--	--	--	--	--	--	--	--	--	--	--	--	--
Malaysia	--	--	--	--	--	--	--	--	--	--	--	--	--	--	--	--	--
Myanmar	--	--	--	--	--	--	--	--	--	0.09	0.06	0.06	0.15	0.63	0.65	1.15	0.80
Philippines	--	--	--	--	--	--	--	--	--	--	--	--	--	--	--	--	--
Singapore	--	--	--	--	--	--	--	--	--	--	--	--	--	--	--	--	--
Thailand	--	--	--	--	--	--	--	--	--	--	--	--	--	--	--	--	--
Viet Nam	--	--	--	--	--	--	--	--	0.02	0.16	0.02	0.01	0.01	0.04	0.35	0.33	0.38

NBFI = nonbank finance institution, NPF = nonperforming financing.

Note: End-of-year data. For Myanmar, fiscal year starts in April and ends in March of the following year. Data in 2019 as of September for Myanmar and June for Viet Nam.

Source: ADB Asia SME Monitor 2020 database.

C6. NBFI Financing by Sector (% share, latest available year)

Item	Brunei Darussalam	Cambodia	Indonesia	Lao People's Democratic Republic	Malaysia	Myanmar	Philippines	Singapore	Thailand	Viet Nam
Agriculture	--	19.4	4.4	13.0	--	30.8	--	--	--	--
Manufacturing	--	0.8	8.8	0.2	5.9	10.5	--	--	--	--
Transportation and communication	96.9	5.7	7.8	0.1	22.7	--	--	--	--	--
Construction	--	3.5	3.4	2.6	--	--	--	--	--	--
Wholesale and retail trade	--	18.3	19.9	25.5	--	33.2	--	--	--	--
Other services	--	14.5	5.2	4.9	49.6*	25.6	--	--	--	--
Others	3.1	37.7	50.5	53.7	21.8	--	--	--	--	--

NBFI = nonbank finance institution. * Other services in Malaysia refer to life sciences.

Note: Data as of end-2019. For Myanmar, data as of September 2019. For Brunei Darussalam and Indonesia, finance companies only. For Cambodia, the Lao PDR, and Myanmar, microfinance institutions only.

Source: ADB Asia SME Monitor 2020 database.

C7. NBFI Financing by Region (% share, latest available year)

Item	Brunei Darussalam	Cambodia	Indonesia	Lao People's Democratic Republic	Malaysia	Myanmar	Philippines	Singapore	Thailand	Viet Nam
Capital city	--	11.8	--	--	--	99.3	--	--	--	--
Other areas	--	88.2	--	--	--	0.7	--	--	--	--

NBFI = nonbank finance institution. Note: end-2019 for Cambodia 2019. September 2019 for Myanmar. For both countries, microfinance institutions only.

Source: ADB Asia SME Monitor 2020 database.

C8-1. Market Capitalization (local currency)

Country	2003	2004	2005	2006	2007	2008	2009	2010	2011	2012	2013	2014	2015	2016	2017	2018	2019
BRU (no exchange market)	--	--	--	--	--	--	--	--	--	--	--	--	--	--	--	--	--
CAM - Main board	--	--	--	--	--	--	--	--	--	539,234	466,176	658,682	716,387	804,539	1,230,678	1,771,677	2,805,807
INO - Main board	--	--	--	--	1,988,326	1,076,491	2,019,375	3,247,097	3,537,294	4,126,995	4,219,020	5,228,043	4,872,702	5,753,613	7,052,389	7,023,497	7,265,016
LAO - Main board	--	--	--	--	--	--	--	--	4,638,300	8,136,540	8,826,800	10,968,690	12,047,100	10,414,100	11,352,400	9,868,000	9,618,492
MAL - ACE	--	--	--	--	--	--	5,293	5,761	6,415	6,935	9,865	9,665	11,853	9,956	15,646	12,141	18,829
MAL - LEAP	--	--	--	--	--	--	--	--	--	--	--	--	--	--	213	920	2,435
MYA - Main board	--	--	--	--	--	--	--	--	--	--	--	--	--	583,957	578,721	554,599	627,449
PHI - SME board	--	263	290	322	4,509	2,226	335	549	713	586	871	34,470	28,513	17,029	20,657	11,308	11,587
SIN - Catalist	--	--	--	--	--	3,562	5,325	6,462	5,347	6,782	9,326	10,791	9,521	9,233	12,819	10,534	9,809
THA - mai	--	--	--	--	38	22	39	55	77	133	177	383	323	425	339	241	215
VIE - UPCoM	--	--	--	--	--	--	4,259,814	16,237,680	22,663,598	28,868,424	25,745,000	37,169,559	61,033,252	303,359,258	677,705,000	893,777,000	911,940,645

BRU = Brunei Darussalam; CAM = Cambodia; INO = Indonesia; LAO = Lao PDR; MAL = Malaysia; MYA = Myanmar; PHI = Philippines; SIN = Singapore; SME = small and medium-sized enterprise; THA = Thailand; VIE = Viet Nam.

Note: End-of-year data. Cambodia: KR million; Indonesia: Rp billion; Lao PDR: KN million; Malaysia: RM million; Myanmar: MK million; Philippines: P million; Singapore: S$ million; Thailand: B billion; Viet Nam: D million.

Source: ADB Asia SME Monitor 2020 database.

C8-2. Market Capitalization ($ million)

Country	2003	2004	2005	2006	2007	2008	2009	2010	2011	2012	2013	2014	2015	2016	2017	2018	2019
BRU (no exchange market)	--	--	--	--	--	--	--	--	--	--	--	--	--	--	--	--	--
CAM - Main board	--	--	--	--	--	--	--	--	--	135	117	162	177	199	305	439	687
INO - Main board	--	--	--	--	211,097	98,310	214,827	361,150	390,085	426,783	346,133	420,261	353,222	428,224	520,548	485,015	522,625
LAO - Main board	--	--	--	--	--	--	--	--	578	1,019	1,100	1,357	1,479	1,272	1,369	1,157	1,085
MAL - ACE	--	--	--	--	--	--	1,546	1,868	2,019	2,268	3,006	2,765	2,762	2,219	3,852	2,934	4,601
MAL - LEAP	--	--	--	--	--	--	--	--	--	--	--	--	--	--	52	222	595
MYA - Main board	--	--	--	--	--	--	--	--	--	--	--	--	--	430	425	358	428
PHI - SME board	--	5	5	7	109	47	7	13	16	14	20	773	605	342	414	214	228
SIN - Catalist	--	--	--	--	--	2,475	3,795	5,019	4,111	5,543	7,371	8,167	6,734	6,384	9,591	7,718	7,281
THA - mai	--	--	--	--	1,135	635	1,174	1,828	2,439	4,342	5,405	11,621	8,963	11,872	10,368	7,421	7,135
VIE - UPCoM	--	--	--	--	--	--	237	858	1,088	1,386	1,224	1,749	2,788	13,690	30,221	39,158	39,384

BRU = Brunei Darussalam; CAM = Cambodia; INO = Indonesia; LAO = Lao PDR; MAL = Malaysia; MYA = Myanmar; PHI = Philippines; SIN = Singapore; SME = small and medium-sized enterprise; THA = Thailand; VIE = Viet Nam.

Note: End-of-year data. Exchange rates of local currency to US dollar refer to end-of-year currency rates from the International Monetary Fund International Financial Statistics in designated years.

Source: ADB Asia SME Monitor 2020 database.

C9. Market Capitalization to GDP (%)

Country	2003	2004	2005	2006	2007	2008	2009	2010	2011	2012	2013	2014	2015	2016	2017	2018	2019
BRU (no exchange market)	--	--	--	--	--	--	--	--	--	--	--	--	--	--	--	--	--
CAM - Main board	--	--	--	--	--	--	--	--	--	1.0	0.8	1.0	1.0	1.0	1.4	1.8	2.6
INO - Main board	--	--	--	--	50.3	21.8	36.0	47.3	45.2	47.9	44.2	49.5	42.3	46.4	51.9	47.3	45.9
LAO - Main board	--	--	--	--	--	--	--	--	7.2	10.0	9.4	10.3	10.3	8.1	8.1	6.5	5.9
MAL - ACE	--	--	--	--	--	--	0.7	0.7	0.7	0.7	1.0	0.9	1.0	0.8	1.1	0.8	1.2
MAL - LEAP	--	--	--	--	--	--	--	--	--	--	--	--	--	--	0.0	0.1	0.2
MYA - Main board	--	--	--	--	--	--	--	--	--	--	--	--	--	0.7	0.6	1.7	--
PHI - SME board	--	0.005	0.005	0.005	0.065	0.029	0.004	0.006	0.007	0.006	0.008	0.273	0.214	0.118	0.131	0.065	0.062
SIN - Catalist	--	--	--	--	--	--	--	2.0	1.5	1.8	2.4	2.7	2.2	2.1	2.7	2.1	1.9
THA - mai	--	--	--	--	0.4	0.2	0.4	0.5	0.7	1.1	1.4	2.9	2.4	2.9	2.2	1.5	1.3
VIE - UPCoM	--	--	--	--	--	--	--	0.2	0.6	0.7	0.8	0.7	0.9	1.4	6.1	12.2	14.8

BRU = Brunei Darussalam; CAM = Cambodia; GDP = gross domestic product; INO = Indonesia; LAO = Lao PDR; MAL = Malaysia; MYA = Myanmar; PHI = Philippines; SIN = Singapore; SME = small and medium-sized enterprise; THA = Thailand; VIE = Viet Nam.

Note: End-of-year data.

Source: ADB Asia SME Monitor 2020 database.

C10. Number of Listed Companies

Country	2003	2004	2005	2006	2007	2008	2009	2010	2011	2012	2013	2014	2015	2016	2017	2018	2019
BRU (no exchange market)	--	--	--	--	--	--	--	--	--	--	--	--	--	--	--	--	--
CAM - Main board	--	--	--	--	--	--	--	--	--	1	1	2	3	4	5	5	5
INO - Main board	--	--	--	--	383	396	398	420	440	459	483	506	521	537	566	619	668
LAO - Main board	--	--	--	--	--	--	--	--	2	2	3	4	5	5	6	9	11
MAL - ACE	--	--	--	--	--	--	116	113	119	112	109	107	109	113	115	119	129
MAL - LEAP	--	--	--	--	--	--	--	--	--	--	--	--	--	--	2	13	28
MYA - Main board	--	--	--	--	--	--	--	--	--	--	--	--	--	3	4	5	5
PHI - SME board	--	3	3	3	2	2	2	2	2	2	2	4	4	4	4	4	5
SIN - Catalist	--	--	--	--	--	133	134	133	136	139	139	155	172	185	200	214	216
THA - mai	--	--	--	--	48	49	60	66	73	81	95	111	122	134	150	159	169
VIE - UPCoM	--	--	--	--	--	--	34	109	131	132	142	169	256	417	690	810	872

BRU = Brunei Darussalam; CAM = Cambodia; INO = Indonesia; LAO = Lao PDR; MAL = Malaysia; MYA = Myanmar; PHI = Philippines; SIN = Singapore; SME = small and medium-sized enterprise; THA = Thailand; VIE = Viet Nam.

Note: End-of-year data.

Source: ADB Asia SME Monitor 2020 database.

Country Review

Brunei Darussalam

Overview

Brunei Darussalam is a small country comprising four districts. Its working age population was 369,837 in 2019.[25] Its gross domestic product (GDP) highly relies on the oil and gas industry and related exports; annual growth was 3.9% in 2019.[26] The government is trying to diversify the economy toward a more sustainable economic growth. It recognizes the role micro, small, and medium-sized enterprises (MSMEs) play as a driver of growth. In 2017, MSMEs accounted for 97.2% of enterprises and employed 57.3% of the workforce. In 2018, they contributed 35.5% of GDP. Most MSMEs belong to the services sector and are dominated by traditional wholesale and retail trade. The market for bank credit has grown, but MSME lending and alternative finance markets have yet to be developed. A national MSME policy framework is being prepared.

1. MSME Development

- The number of active registered MSMEs is small but growing. The majority of MSMEs are in traditional trade and services.
- Job absorption by formal MSMEs is limited. Most workers are in the informal sector or engaged in informal household businesses.
- The MSME contribution to GDP is limited and fragile; the dynamics of MSMEs should be strengthened to boost national productivity.
- The government has worked to enhance market access for MSMEs by promoting agricultural value chains and MSME participation in government projects, among others.
- Digital technology continues to create business opportunities for domestic enterprises and start-ups; e-commerce is expanding rapidly, though largely led by foreign service providers.
- Autonomous business communities support MSME and entrepreneurship development by promoting business linkages, networking, and incubation programs.

Scale of MSMEs

The Department of Economic Planning and Statistics under the Ministry of Finance and Economy (MOFE) compiles MSME statistics, based on the national MSME definition set by the Ministry of Industry and Primary Resources. MSME categories are defined by employment thresholds: (i) a microenterprise employs up to four persons, (ii) a small enterprise has 5–19 persons employed, and (iii) a medium-sized enterprise is a firm with 20–99 employees (Table 3.1).

[25] Government of Brunei Darussalam, Department of Economic Planning and Statistics. 2020. *Report of the Labour Force Survey 2019*. Working age population refers to those aged 15 years old and above.

[26] Government of Brunei Darussalam, Department of Economic Planning and Statistics. 2020. *Gross Domestic Product Fourth Quarter 2019*.

Only active enterprises that registered with the Registry of Companies and Business Names are included in MSME statistics. The latest census indicating MSME data is the Annual Census of Enterprises 2017.

There were 5,876 MSMEs in Brunei Darussalam in 2017, with 2,442 microenterprises and 3,434 small enterprises (Figure 3.1A and Table 3.2). MSMEs accounted for 97.2% of total active enterprises registered in the Registry of Companies and Business Names, a 2.7% increase from 2016.

By sector in 2017, 71.6% of MSMEs were in services (34.9% for wholesale and retail trade, 4.4% for transportation and communication, and 32.3% for "other" services represented by accommodation and food services), followed by construction such as material suppliers (12.4%) and manufacturing (11.1%) (Figure 3.1B). MSME data by district is unavailable.

Figure 3.1: Number of MSMEs

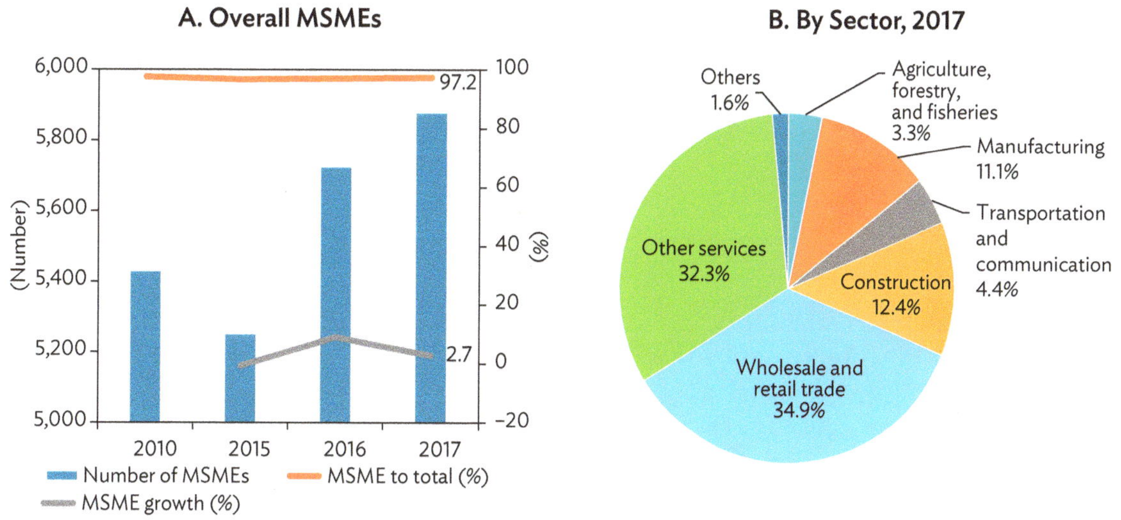

MSME =micro, small, and medium-sized enterprise.

Source: ADB Asia SME Monitor 2020 database. Data from Department of Economic Planning and Statistics.

Employment

MSMEs accounted for 57.3% of the total workforce in 2017, a 1.0% growth in employees from 2016. At the end of 2017, there were 115,329 people employed by the private sector, of which 5,911 worked in microenterprises, with another 60,212 people employed by small and medium-sized enterprises (SMEs), for an MSME total of 66,123 employees (Figure 3.2A). However, while the number of MSME employees is increasing, a small number of large firms in the oil and gas sector (171 firms in 2017) still absorb a large portion (42.7%) of the country's total workforce in 2017. With a working age population (aged 15 years old and over) of 369,837 in 2019, the majority of country's workforce is likely employed by the informal sector or engaged in informal household businesses.

By sector in 2017, 65.6% of MSME employees worked in the services sector (30.3% for wholesale and retail trade, 5.1% for transportation and communication, and 30.2% for other services), followed by construction (19.2%) and manufacturing (10.3%) (Figure 3.2B). MSME data by district is unavailable.

Figure 3.2: Employment by MSMEs

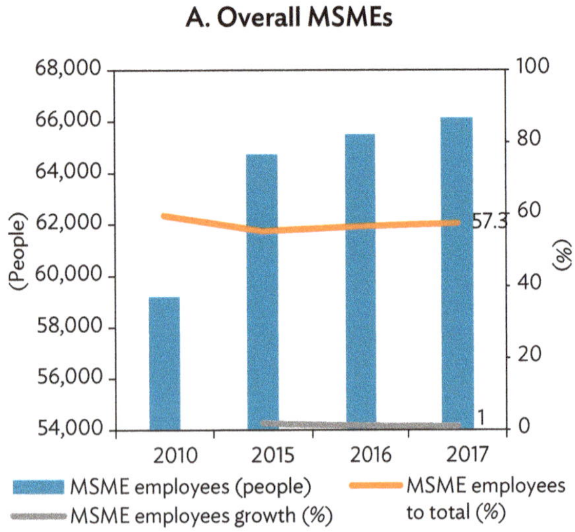

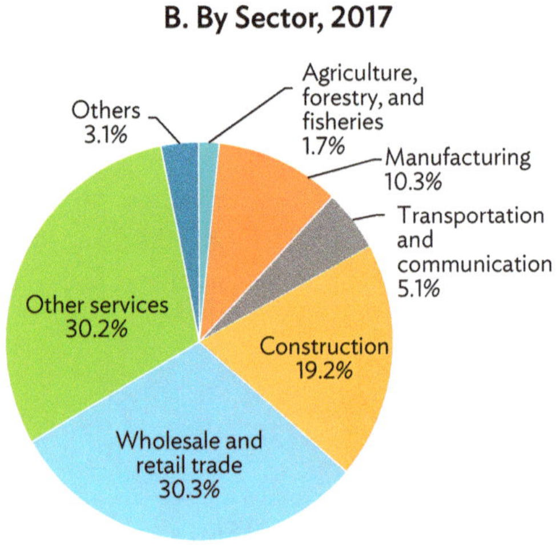

MSME =micro, small, and medium-sized enterprise.

Source: ADB Asia SME Monitor 2020 database. Data from Department of Economic Planning and Statistics.

Business Productivity

In 2017, the Brunei Darussalam economy recovered from the negative growth affected by the decline in oil and gas production and related exports from 2013 to 2016. The return to growth has been supported by increasing household consumption and a rebound in exports. The MSME contribution to GDP fell by 7.5% in 2016, but recovered with a sharp 52.1% increase in 2018 (from 2017), amounting to B$6.5 billion ($4.7 billion)[27] (Figure 3.3). The growth was supported by increased domestic demand. Although the MSME share of GDP remains limited (35.5% in 2018), it rose substantially (from 25.5% in 2017). Large-scale exports related to the oil and gas industry continue to drive the national economy, suggesting the need to strengthen the dynamics of MSMEs to further boost national productivity.

Figure 3.3: MSME Contribution to Gross Domestic Product

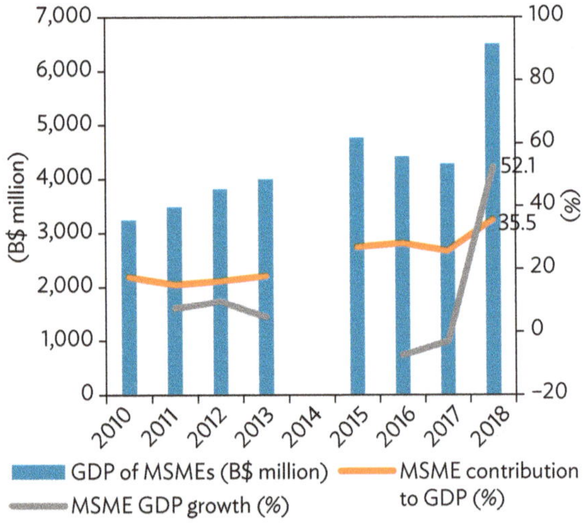

GDP = gross domestic product; MSME = micro, small, and medium-sized enterprise.

Source: ADB Asia SME Monitor 2020 database. Data from Department of Economic Planning and Development.

27 IMF International Finance Statistics. Exchange rates, national currency per US dollar, end of period.

Market Access

MSMEs in Brunei Darussalam typically operate within the small domestic market in stable businesses such as trade, accommodation, and restaurants, with only a small portion exposed to global markets. Domestic MSMEs have yet to participate in global value chains.

Developing agricultural value chains is an important policy agenda in Brunei Darussalam, especially for food processing such as shrimp, catfish, and corned beef. Supported by the *halal* certification program, food products, especially *halal* products, are of high export quality and hold the potential to internationalize agribusiness. The *halal* industry has also expanded into several products including cosmetics and pharmaceuticals. *Halal* branding will serve as a conduit for MSMEs to access international markets.

To enhance MSME market access, the government is promoting MSME participation in government projects. For example, MSMEs in material supply have started participating in government procurement for construction projects. Understanding costs of government projects is a major challenge for MSMEs. Generally, they need more funds to participate in government projects. There is still room to improve the procedure for government-to-commerce payments—addressing late payments is frequently raised at the business help desk operated by Darussalam Enterprise (DARe), a government agency for MSME support. This led MOFE to establish a Vendor Clinic in 2016 for inquiries, clarifications, and complaints about delayed payments for the supply and service delivery to the government.

Technology and Innovation

Digital connectivity has expanded across Brunei Darussalam. In 2018, mobile subscriptions reached 565,949 (or 131.9 per 100 people), a 3.9% increase in number from 2017.[28] Individual internet use also surged, from 71.2% of total population in 2015 to 94.9% in 2017 (the latest available year).

Accordingly, e-commerce has been rapidly expanding. The Authority for Info-Communications Technology Industry (AITI) reports that 76% of the population uses e-commerce.[29] Clothing and accessories are the most popular online purchases, followed by travel services, cosmetics, and health care. Major e-commerce service providers include foreign companies such as eBay (US), Zalora (Singapore), Amazon (US), AliExpress (PRC), and Lazada (Singapore, owned by the PRC's Alibaba Group). Domestic e-commerce providers and digital industries are being developed in the country.

The Ministry of Transport and Infocommunications and the AITI promote the transformation to the digital economy under the National Digital Strategy 2016–2020.

Networking and Support

There are autonomous business networking communities that support MSME development in Brunei Darussalam. The National Chamber of Commerce and Industry (NCCI)—which includes the Brunei Malay Chamber of Commerce and Industry and the Chinese Chamber of Commerce and Industry—was established in 1985 to guide and assist enterprises in the country. The NCCI has 1,300 members, all MSMEs based on the employment thresholds that define MSMEs (firms with fewer than 100 employees). NCCI member firms are mainly from the agriculture, tourism, food and beverage, and services sectors, especially wholesale and retail trade. There is one

[28] World Bank database (https://data.worldbank.org/indicator/). Accessed on 30 March 2020.

[29] The E-Commerce Survey for Consumers in Brunei Darussalam 2018 Report.

fintech company (*Chynge*, a payment platform provider) which is under the central bank's financial regulatory sandbox (as of October 2019). The NCCI offers (i) business matching services among members (available even outside the NCCI), (ii) training programs (upon request with a small fee), and (iii) integrity checks of businesses.

The Brunei Malay Chamber of Commerce and Industry plans to launch an incubation program for youth in 2020. The program offers business planning support, organizes workshops (3- and 6-month training programs), provides office space for two to three groups of enterprises, and connects young people to financial institutions. The NCCI also monitors enterprises for 6 months to find viable business models and targets fresh university graduates.

The Young Entrepreneurs Association of Brunei, established in 2000, supports entrepreneurs by facilitating business linkages locally and internationally. The association has a network of more than 170 young entrepreneurs at various stages of growth and across diverse industries—including information and communications technology (ICT), fashion, food processing, and the oil and gas industry, among others. Agribusiness offers promising opportunities for young entrepreneurs. Given the Sultanate's strong Islamic brand, Islamic-based entrepreneurship could become lucrative. Start-ups such as Al-Huffaz Management (Islamic education matching), Tarbiyyah Global (Islamic program for children), and Mindplus (digital learning platform) are examples of the trend.

The number of entrepreneurs is increasing, pushed by the government's commitment to develop a business ecosystem and reduce the relatively high level of unemployment (6.8% in 2019), by making entrepreneurship a more attractive career path. The government's I-Ready Apprenticeship Program connects unemployed graduates to various public and private sector industries, opening opportunities for MSMEs to scale up manpower with less financial burden—as the government provides a monthly allowance to participating graduates for a maximum of 3 years.

However, developing entrepreneurship has faced various challenges, such as a lack of large businesses for MSMEs to service, regular consumer outflow to neighboring Malaysian provinces of Sabah and Sarawak, entrepreneurs' lack of international exposure, limited financing capabilities, and low tolerance to hardship.

While the majority of microenterprises are owned by women, only a small fraction are prepared to grow. Further government support on capacity building and networking for women-led businesses would help them prepare to scale up.

2. Access to Finance

- MSME access to bank credit is limited; however, while the central bank does not offer comprehensive financial support to MSMEs, the government-owned SME Bank and the government's agency DARe serve unmet MSME demand for financing.
- There is no active credit guarantee scheme in the country.
- The nonbank finance industry is small and has yet to fulfill MSME financing needs; all licensed finance companies and pawnbrokers are bank subsidiaries.
- A comprehensive regulatory and policy framework for digital financial services was established between 2017 and 2019; but there are as yet no domestic-oriented fintech firms.
- There is no national stock exchange in Brunei Darussalam; although work to establish a stock exchange is progressing.
- A credit bureau and collateral registry currently support risk-based credit delivery and asset-based finance by financial institutions.

Bank Credit

The banking sector is small in scale, but it dominates the financial system. In 2019, it held B$18.6 billion ($13.8 billion) (footnote 27) in assets, or 83.5% of total financial institution assets.[30] Licensed commercial banks include Islamic and conventional banks. At end-2019, seven licensed commercial banks were operating in the country—two locally incorporated banks (Baiduri Bank Berhad and Bank Islam Brunei Darussalam Berhad) and five foreign bank branches. In addition, two financial institutions supervised but not licensed by the central bank are operating: the Islamic Trust Fund (Perbadanan Tabung Amanah Islam Brunei Berhad) and the SME Bank (Table 3.3). Islamic banking is a major component of the banking system. In 2019, for example, the Bank Islam Brunei Darussalam Berhad and the Islamic Trust Fund accounted for 65.1% of commercial bank assets, with the remaining 34.9% held by conventional banks.

The Autoriti Monetari Brunei Darussalam (AMBD)—the central bank created in 2011—regulates and supervises licensed commercial banks, nonbank finance institutions, and capital market institutions. AMBD uses a risk-based bank supervisory framework based on Basel II (an international banking supervisory framework). Although AMBD has no comprehensive financial support measures directed at MSMEs, the Financial Sector Blueprint 2016–2025 addresses support for MSMEs and innovative services under a pillar of "competitive and innovative financial institutions and services."

The specialized bank for financing MSMEs, Bank Usahawan (SME Bank), was established by the government in 2017. AMBD supervises SME Bank, albeit minimally, as part of its financial stability mandate whereby the bank is subject to certain prudential requirements.

Since 2018, the bank credit market has recovered from the growth contraction affected by the oil and gas industry's decline. Bank loans outstanding amounted to B$5,473 million ($4,000 million) in 2018 and B$5,889 million ($4,363 million) in 2019, a 6.7% and 7.6% increase from the previous year, respectively (Figure 3.4). The share of total commercial bank loans to GDP was 32.0% at the end of 2019, while the loan to deposit ratio was 37.6%. The demand on bank credit remains stable. By type, lending to individual households accounted for 52.3% of the total loan portfolio, while business lending accounted for 47.7% at the end of 2019. Within the corporate sector, services

[30] Autoriti Monetari Brunei Darussalam. 2019 Financial Stability Report.

(including gas- and oil-related services) was the most active borrower. The nonperforming loan (NPL) ratio is decreasing but remains high (4.6% at end-2019).

There is no aggregate MSME credit data in bank credit statistics. According to AMBD, however, 6% of total loans and 14% of total business lending are MSME credit, based on internal research.[31] Major MSME borrowers include restaurants and the wholesale and retail trade sector. AMBD classifies MSMEs for credit based on assets, sales, loan size, and number of employees: (i) asset size (micro less than B$60,000, small less than B$600,000, medium less than B$3 million); (ii) annual gross sales (micro less than B$100,000, small less than B$1 million, medium less than B$5 million); (iii) loan size (micro less than B$30,000, small less than B$300,000, medium less than B$1 million); and (iv) number of employees (differs from MOFE levels—micro fewer than 10, small fewer than 30, medium fewer than 100). The average annual lending rate of MSME credit is 6.5%. The average loan size is B$89,000. Loan term data is not available. While there are no rules or collateral requirements set by AMBD, there are certain rules on eligible collateral and valuation requirements for the computation of Accounting for Credit Losses by the banking industry.

Figure 3.4: Bank Loans

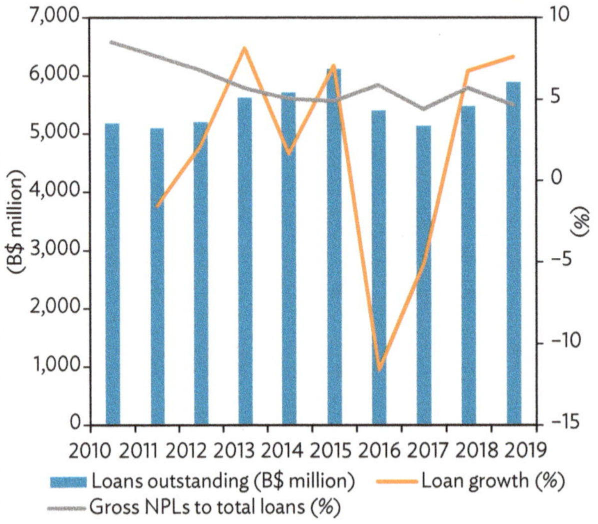

NPL = nonperforming loan.

Source: ADB Asia SME Monitor 2020 database. Data from Autoriti Monetari Brunei Darussalam.

Public Financing and Guarantees

a. Grant program

DARe's "co-matching scheme" was launched in June 2019, and offers financial assistance to MSMEs and start-ups. Under the scheme, DARe finances 70% of the total project cost (at a maximum B$20,000) initiated by the participating firm. The co-matching grant falls under two categories: (i) up to B$10,000 financial assistance for start-ups that registered within 12 months and are categorized as micro or small enterprises (firms with fewer than 20 employees); and (ii) up to B$20,000 assistance for expanding MSMEs (firms with fewer than 100 employees).

[31] Interview with the Autoriti Monetari Brunei Darussalam on 14 October 2019.

b. Specialized bank for MSMEs

The SME Bank is a *Syariah*-compliant bank created by the MOFE in 2017 and is not subject to the Islamic Banking Order of 2008. The SME Bank uses its own definition for MSME credit, based on loan size: (i) credit less than B$20,000 for microenterprise loans; (ii) credit less than B$100,000 for small enterprise loans; and (iii) credit more than B$100,000 for medium-sized enterprise loans.

Total MSME loans outstanding amounted to B$9.0 million ($6.7 million) at the end of 2019, a 172.2% increase from end-2018 (Figure 3.5A). SME Bank's MSME loans are relatively new to the credit market, accounting for only 0.15% of commercial bank loans outstanding. The SME Bank had 166 active MSME borrowers as of end-2019. By sector, 30.2% went toward food processing (manufacturing) in 2019, followed by other services including pharmaceuticals and cosmetics (27.9%), wholesale and retail trade including restaurants and catering (24.6%), and agriculture (12.2%) (Figure 3.5B). According to SME Bank,[32] beverage and agribusiness (food processing) are the most promising sectors for lending (for example, fish exporters supplying Japanese sushi). Technology-based MSMEs remain a small share of borrowers, as they are at early stages of development.

The average loan size for microenterprises is B$1,000. The lending rate ranges 6%–10% per annum, which is the same as commercial banks. In 2019, the average annual lending rate was 9% for microenterprises and 7% for SME loans. The loan tenure was a minimum of 6 months, with a maximum of 7 years, and averaged 4 years. Ninety percent of MSME loans were short-term and mid-term (up to 5 years) with the remaining 10% long-term (more than 5 years). By purpose, 87% were for working capital with the remaining 13% for capital investment. MSMEs operating in the capital, Bandar Seri Begawan, received 96% of loans granted.

The advantage of SME Bank credit is fast loan processing—1 week for short-term loans and 3 weeks for long-term loans, but none exceeding 1 month. This is faster than other commercial banks. As opposed to collateral-based commercial bank loans, the SME Bank offers cash flow-based loans. Only when needed, SME Bank requires collateral for loans (including movable assets) and third-party guarantees from family. Collateral-based and third-party guaranteed loans account for 8%–9% of total lending. The SME Bank uses a direct marketing strategy that brings clients together and follows upon client recommendations (it also promotes its loan products and services in supermarkets).

c. Credit guarantees

There is no active credit guarantee scheme in Brunei Darussalam. There were credit guarantee schemes in the past, but they were transferred to the SME Bank when it was created. Today they are inactive due to (i) a misalignment of the system to the high MSME credit NPLs and (ii) the slow and long process of guaranteeing loans (3–4 months on average, 6 months in some cases). The past scheme offered 100% government guarantees, in some cases taken up by commercial banks.

32 Interview with chief executive officer of the SME Bank (Bank Usahawan) on 15 October 2019.

Figure 3.5: MSME Loans

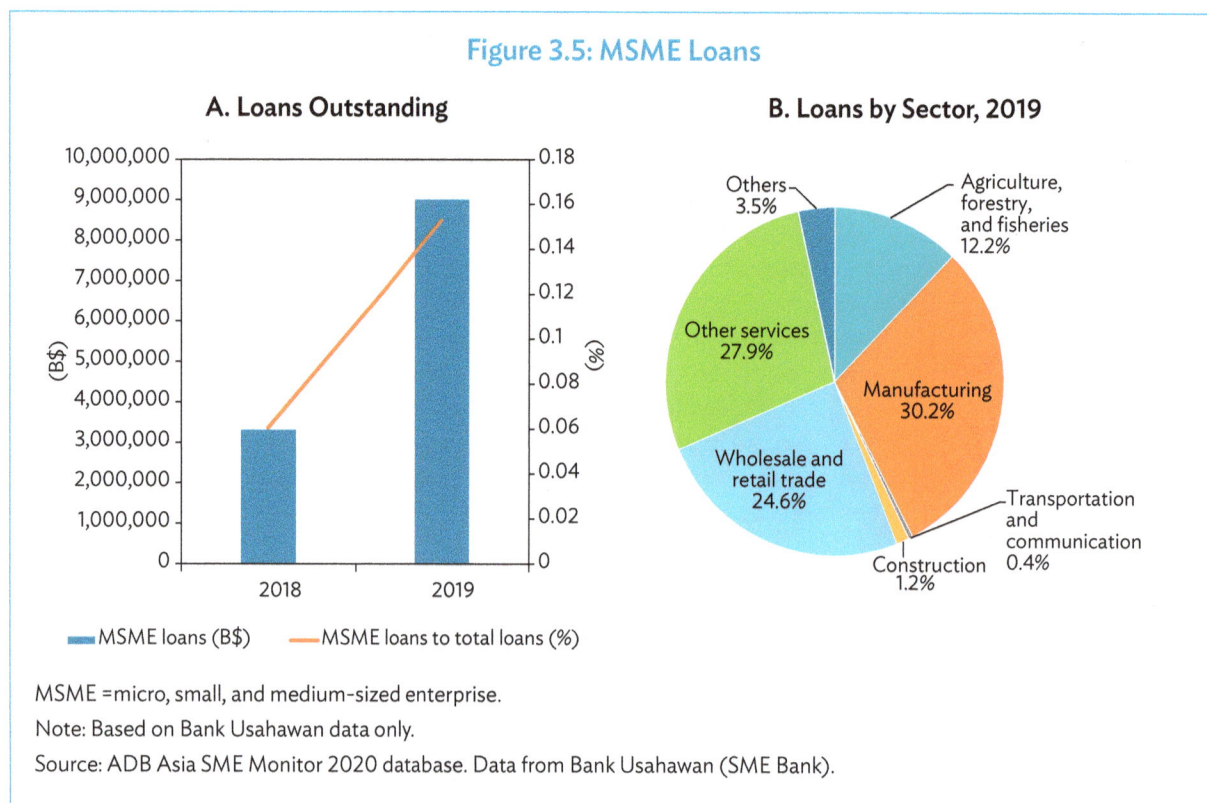

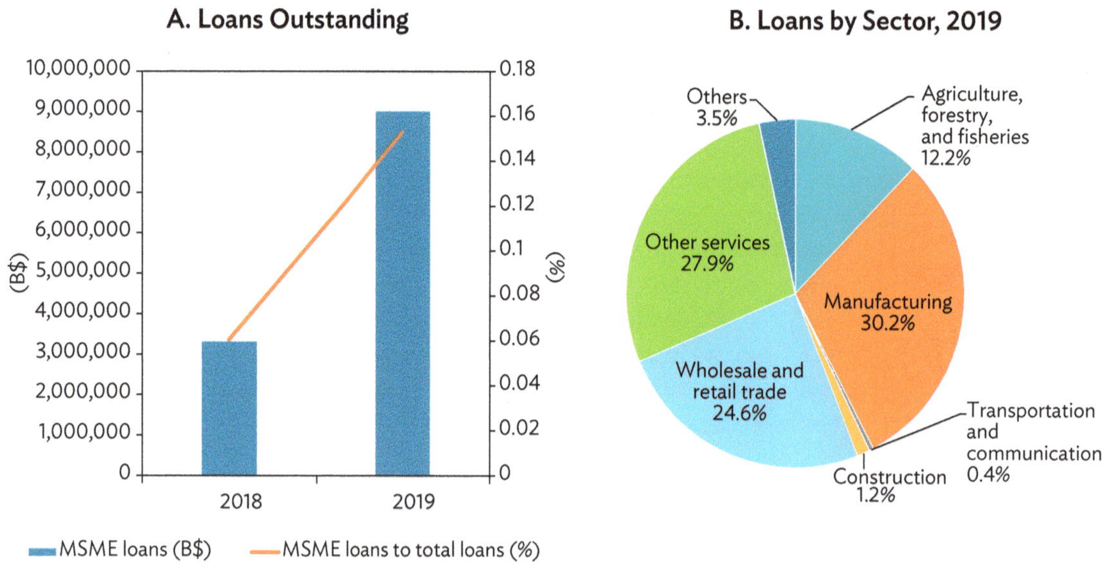

MSME =micro, small, and medium-sized enterprise.

Note: Based on Bank Usahawan data only.

Source: ADB Asia SME Monitor 2020 database. Data from Bank Usahawan (SME Bank).

Nonbank Financing

The nonbank finance industry in Brunei Darussalam is quite small in scale. Only two finance companies (one Islamic and one non-Islamic) and one Islamic-based pawnbroker were licensed by AMBD as of the end of 2019. They are all subsidiaries of local commercial banks. There is no factoring firm operating in the country. The licensed finance companies also service leasing operations (hire-purchase).

At end-2019, finance companies accounted for 8.6% of financial sector assets (footnote 30). The total financing outstanding of finance companies amounted to B$1.5 billion ($1.1 billion) (Figure 3.6A and Table 3.4). Finance company loans accounted for 8.3% of GDP in 2019 with its share decreasing. Automobile loans took up 96.9% of finance company loans in 2019, with the remaining 3.1% for consumer durables. Loan maturities are between 6 months and 1 year. Pawnbroking finance totaled B$15.1 million ($11.2 million), meeting demand from individual borrowers (Figure 3.6B). Although there is no data on MSME financing, AMBD estimates around 20% of nonbank finance institution (NBFI) loans are for MSMEs, mostly for working capital (footnote 31).

Figure 3.6: Nonbank Finance

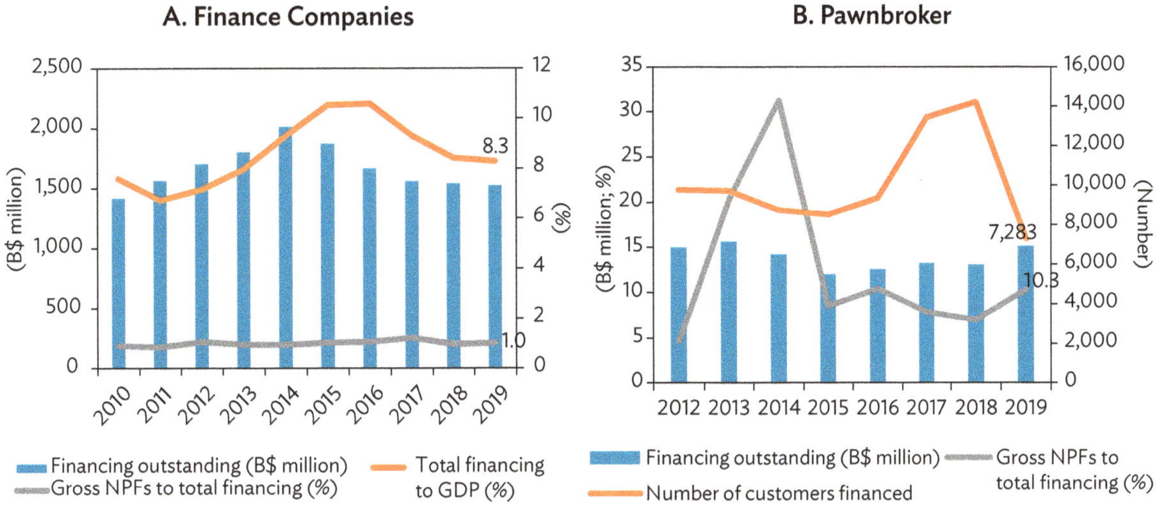

GDP = gross domestic product, NPF = nonperforming financing.

Source: ADB Asia SME Monitor 2020 database. Data from Autoriti Monetari Brunei Darussalam.

Digital Financial Services

A comprehensive regulatory and policy framework on digital financial services (DFS) or fintech was established between 2017 and 2019 to meet Financial Sector Blueprint 2016–2025 recommendations. It included regulations on equity crowdfunding (ECF) and peer-to-peer (P2P) lending platforms, guidelines on fintech regulatory sandboxes, cybersecurity strategies for 2017–2020, and the digital payment roadmap for 2019–2025. As of the end of 2019, there were no ECF and P2P lending platforms registrations with the AMBD. There is no interoperable national payment system. Only Bank Islam Brunei Darussalam Berhad has developed an e-payment system using quick response (QR) codes. DFS remain under development, with digital finance literacy a key to further development.

Capital Markets

Brunei Darussalam has no national stock exchange. Following the Financial Sector Blueprint 2016–2025, work on establishing a national stock exchange is progressing, spearheaded by the MOFE. Creating a national stock exchange will allow the economy to grow, diversify, and expand business, as it offers alternative financing for businesses, especially growth capital for viable MSMEs.

The Securities Markets Order of 2013 is the capital market law, providing licenses for capital market intermediaries and procedures on the public offering of securities and market operations. These apply to securities exchanges, clearing houses, a central securities depository, trading facilities, and credit rating agencies. As of the end of 2019, AMBD licensed eight capital market intermediaries, including three brokers/dealers and five investment management and advisory firms. With no domestic securities market, licensed brokers/dealers trade stocks and bonds on international markets in Hong Kong, China; Malaysia; Singapore; and the US.

The Securities Markets Order of 2013 also allows the issuance of Islamic bonds, or *sukuk* (*Syariah*-compliant bonds). The Islamic Financial Services Board defines *sukuk* as certificates representing a proportional undivided ownership in *Syariah*-compliant tangible assets, usufructs, or services (assets could be specific projects invested by Muslim and/or non-Muslim investors). *Sukuk* issuance remains small in Brunei Darussalam, but there is high potential demand. Most *sukuk* issuance thus far has been sovereign. For instance, AMBD issued *sukuk* in 2018 to construct its office building, with the issue giving investors beneficial ownership of the underlying assets. Corporate *sukuk* is a potential capital market instrument that can be tapped by viable MSMEs.

AMBD is a member of the International Organization of Securities Commissions (IOSCO) and a signatory of the latter's Multilateral Memorandum of Understanding Concerning Consultation and Cooperation and the Exchange of Information in 2016.

Financial Infrastructure

A credit bureau was established in September 2012, based on Section 42A of the AMBD Order of 2010. It operates under AMBD's Regulatory and Supervision Department. The credit bureau collects credit information and identification details on a regular basis from participating financial institutions, including data on basic personal profiles, credit account details, loans outstanding, and payment history. It provides consolidated credit information exclusively to its members (all licensed commercial banks, finance companies, and the Islamic Trust Fund) by way of a credit report. The SME Bank is not a member of the credit bureau. As of October 2019, data covering 12,000 companies were held by the credit bureau. The credit bureau has extended its services to credit scoring since 2018, it has provided consumer and commercial credit scores for member financial institutions.

The Secured Transaction Order of 2016 provides the legal basis for the secured transaction system in the country, which allows the establishment of a notice-based collateral registry for movable assets. Based on the law, AMBD established an online collateral registry in December 2016, which lists any type of movable assets, including personal properties and intellectual property rights. The secured transaction system helps individuals and businesses, especially MSMEs, access credit by using personal property as collateral for loans.

3. Policies and Regulations

- Wawasan Brunei 2035 offers a long-term national development vision to achieve a dynamic and sustainable economy by 2035.
- MSME development is a government policy priority to help meet its goal of economic diversification; a national MSME task force will be part of the government's upcoming Industry Roadmap.
- Promoting youth and women entrepreneurs is key to support the MSME sector.
- Fostering fintech is a core component of the Financial Sector Blueprint 2016–2025; strategies on digital payments and cybersecurity have been separately launched.
- Key elements of a financial inclusion strategy are incorporated in the Financial Sector Blueprint 2016–2025, aligned with the long-term national development plan; it would be worth considering the creation of a holistic and comprehensive strategy for effective policy support on inclusive finance.

MSME Development

Wawasan Brunei 2035 provides a long-term national development vision which, among others, aims to achieve a dynamic and sustainable economy by 2035. It stipulates development strategies to be accomplished by 2035, focusing on 13 areas: education, economy, security, institutional development, local business development, infrastructure development, social security, the environment, health, religion, land use, infrastructure and ICT, and manpower planning (Table 3.5).

MSME development is a government policy priority. The economy is highly dependent on the oil and gas industry and related exports. Economic growth dropped sharply in 2016, affected by falling oil and gas prices. Wawasan Brunei 2035 addresses the need for economic diversification. Fostering non-oil sectors is critical if economic transformation is to move forward, where MSMEs play a key role.

The MOFE is the focal ministry for MSME development in the country, with DARe an implementing agency for national MSME support policies. By the end of 2019, there was no national policy framework for MSMEs. But the government is preparing an Industry Roadmap, with the MOFE preparing to establish a National MSME Task Force to develop national MSME policies. The task force will be headed by the Permanent Secretary for Industry at the MOFE.

To support the country's entrepreneurs, an interministerial steering committee was established in 2018 to oversee the Brunei Darussalam youth entrepreneurship ecosystem, which houses all national business development initiatives. An action plan was outlined to develop ecosystem initiatives in four ways: (i) promoting ecosystem assistance to expand the pipeline of young entrepreneurs; (ii) identifying young entrepreneurs; (iii) engaging with them to assess their growth potential and the further assistance required, to increase engagement and participation within the ecosystem; and (iv) supporting further business growth as relevant programs progress.

To increase opportunities for youths to start, own, manage, and run a business, a wide range of programs are available through various agencies. Capacity building and shared support services such as a mentorship network have been offered. Financing schemes are available to address the needs of entrepreneurs to secure capital to start and grow their business. Infrastructure such as ready-built factories, office premises, and co-working spaces are available for entrepreneurs to use and leverage. Furthermore, contracts from both the public and private sectors have been ring-fenced for competitive bidding by young entrepreneurs.

The government also continues to focus on promoting women entrepreneurship. There are no restrictions on land ownership and no discrepancies in salaries between genders. Women occupy 70% of firms' senior management positions in the country.[33] Social media entrepreneurs are mostly women, for instance. Entrepreneurial sectors are mainly in food and beverage, and fashion. One challenge to promote women entrepreneurship is expanding the number of women with higher education degrees (currently one-third of men).

DARe is the government statutory body that spearheads the growth of local MSMEs to increase their contribution to GDP, employment, and exports. While DARe is a self-funding body, it works closely with the government through a board chaired by the MOFE minister.

DARe helps enterprises grow using a pro-business ecosystem that helps in five ways: (i) building business knowledge, skills, and capacity through enterprise development programs; (ii) working with both government agencies and business communities to improve the business environment; (iii) facilitating access to domestic and international markets to create new opportunities for businesses; (iv) providing land and ready-built factories for businesses at competitive rates; and (v) promoting an entrepreneurial culture by sharing and recognizing success to inspire resilient future entrepreneurs.

33 Interview with the Ministry of Energy, Manpower and Industry on 15 October 2019. Hereinafter of this paragraph refers to this interview.

Financial Inclusion

As yet, there is no specific national financial inclusion strategy in Brunei Darussalam. But the Financial Sector Blueprint 2016–2025 covers key elements of financial inclusion. The blueprint guides the country's financial sector development to 2025 and offers a strategic five pillar framework in line with the Wawasan Brunei 2035: (i) monetary and financial stability, (ii) competitive and innovative financial institutions and services, (iii) robust and modern infrastructure, (iv) enhanced international integration, and (v) human capital development. Pillar II includes support for MSMEs and innovative services to address development of fintech or DFS solutions that enhance MSME access to finance. AMBD is responsible for coordinating with relevant ministries and stakeholders the blueprint's implementation as part of Wawasan Brunei 2035.

Following the blueprint, AMBD established a FinTech Unit in October 2016, which formulates regulations and strategies in support of fintech and MSME access to finance. It facilitates the use of financial technology within the national financial system. The FinTech Unit opened a one-stop virtual facilitation office (the FinTech Office) in March 2017. It serves as a single window on matters related to fintech for any interested parties.

AMBD issued its FinTech Regulatory Sandbox Guidelines in February 2017 to help fintech firms test and develop innovative DFS through regulatory sandboxes that offer the eased regulatory environment over a limited period. The regulatory sandboxes include pilot testing for digital payment and Islamic fintech solutions.

For fintech regulations, Notices[34] on ECF and P2P lending platforms were enacted in August 2017 and April 2019, respectively.

As part of the blueprint, AMBD launched the Digital Payment Roadmap 2019–2025 in December 2018, which aims to create a digital payment ecosystem within the national payment system. It addresses three strategic actions: (i) balancing regulation and innovation, (ii) adopting open digital payments, and (iii) building public awareness and education. To implement the first strategy, regulations encourage the digitization of payments and competition, while strengthening consumer protection. The Digital Payment Committee was created to boost collaboration between government authorities and market stakeholders, and to provide an information platform on digital payments. Regulatory sandboxes are also promoted within the digital payment system. The second strategy encourages the development of an interoperable payment hub using a secure and low-cost model. It will increase accessibility, including for MSMEs. The third strategy enhances digital finance literacy and training to build trust in digital finance. It encompasses strengthening cybersecurity as well.

AMBD launched its Cybersecurity Strategy 2017–2020 in July 2017, focusing on five strategic actions: (i) setting the strategy, (ii) strengthening governance, (iii) enhancing the process, (iv) developing the people, and (v) using the right technology. AMBD issued a Notice on Early Detection of Cyber Intrusion and Incident Reporting in October 2017. It requires financial institutions to have robust capabilities to proactively detect cyber intrusions to enable quick response and recovery.

Overall, the key elements of the financial inclusion strategy are incorporated in the blueprint, aligning with the long-term Wawasan Brunei 2035 national development plan. Stand-alone regulations that directly or indirectly support MSME access to finance have been identified, such as the Secured Transaction Order of 2016 and the series of fintech regulations. However, a comprehensive regulatory and policy framework on MSME access to finance or financial inclusion has yet to be formulated. The creation of a holistic financial inclusion strategy would be worth considering for effective policy support for inclusive finance in Brunei Darussalam.

[34] "Notice" is legally binding in Brunei Darussalam.

Data Tables

Table 3.1: MSME Definition

Item	Micro	Small	Medium
Number of employees	0-4 employees	5-19 employees	20-99 employees

Source: ADB Asia SME Monitor 2020 database. Data from Department of Economic Planning and Statistics (internal definition).

Item	Micro	Small	Medium
1. Assets	less than B$60,000	less than B$600,000	less than B$3 million
2. Annual sales	less than B$100,000	less than B$1 million	less than B$5 million
3. Loan size	less than B$30,000	than B$300,000	less than B$1 million
4. Employment	less than 10	small - less than 30	less than 100

MSMEs = micro, small, and medium-sized enterprises.

Note: Priority benchmark for MSME classification follows the order from 1 to 4.

Source: ADB Asia SME Monitor 2020 database. Data from Autoriti Monetari Brunei Darussalam (internal definition).

Table 3.2: MSME Landscape

End of period data

Item	2010	2011	2012	2013	2014	2015	2016	2017	2018	2019
NUMBER OF ENTERPRISES										
Number of enterprises, total	5,566	--	--	--	--	5,434	5,896	6,047	--	--
Number of microenterprises	2,216	--	--	--	--	1,917	2,337	2,442	--	--
Number of SMEs	3,211	--	--	--	--	3,331	3,384	3,434	--	--
Number of large enterprises	139	--	--	--	--	186	175	171	--	--
MSME to total (%)	97.5	--	--	--	--	96.6	97.0	97.2	--	--
MSME growth (%)	--	--	--	--	--	(3.3)	9.0	2.7	--	--
MSMEs by sector (% share)										
Agriculture, forestry, and fisheries	5.3	--	--	--	--	3.9	3.5	3.3	--	--
Manufacturing	12.6	--	--	--	--	10.7	11.1	11.1	--	--
Transportation and communication	4.6	--	--	--	--	4.8	4.5	4.4	--	--
Construction	12.0	--	--	--	--	14.5	12.7	12.4	--	--
Wholesale and retail trade	34.7	--	--	--	--	33.9	34.9	34.9	--	--
Other services	29.7	--	--	--	--	30.8	31.9	32.3	--	--
Others	1.0	--	--	--	--	1.4	1.5	1.6	--	--
Number of MSMEs by region (% share)										
Capital city	--	--	--	--	--	--	--	--	--	--
Others	--	--	--	--	--	--	--	--	--	--
EMPLOYMENT										
Number of employment, total	99,607	--	--	--	--	117,453	115,985	115,329	--	--
Number of employment by microenterprises	5,395	--	--	--	--	4,827	5,700	5,911	--	--
Number of employment by SMEs	53,784	--	--	--	--	59,895	59,786	60,212	--	--
Number of employment by large enterprises	40,428	--	--	--	--	52,731	50,499	49,206	--	--
MSME employees to total (%)	59.4	--	--	--	--	55.1	56.5	57.3	--	--
MSME employees growth (%)	--	--	--	--	--	1.8	1.2	1.0	--	--
Share of female employees to total employees (%)	31.0	--	--	--	--	30.2	30.8	31.1	--	--
Employment by MSME by sector (% share)										
Agriculture, forestry, and fisheries	2.7	--	--	--	--	1.9	1.9	1.7	--	--
Manufacturing	10.6	--	--	--	--	10.0	10.1	10.3	--	--
Transportation and communication	5.0	--	--	--	--	5.5	5.4	5.1	--	--
Construction	18.9	--	--	--	--	20.0	19.1	19.2	--	--
Wholesale and retail trade	31.3	--	--	--	--	30.0	30.6	30.3	--	--
Other services	29.4	--	--	--	--	29.4	29.9	30.2	--	--
Others	2.0	--	--	--	--	3.1	3.0	3.1	--	--
Employment by MSMEs by region (% share)										
Capital city	--	--	--	--	--	--	--	--	--	--
Others	--	--	--	--	--	--	--	--	--	--
CONTRIBUTION TO GDP										
MSMEs contribution to GDP (B$ million)	3,233	3,472	3,808	3,984	--	4,765	4,409	4,271	6,497	--
MSMEs contribution to GDP (% share)	17.3	14.9	16.0	17.6	--	26.8	28.0	25.5	35.5	--
MSME GDP growth (%)	--	7.4	9.7	4.6	--	--	(7.5)	(3.1)	52.1	--
MSME GDP by sector (% share)										
Agriculture, forestry, and fisheries	--	--	--	--	--	--	--	--	--	--
Manufacturing	--	--	--	--	--	--	--	--	--	--
Transportation and communication	--	--	--	--	--	--	--	--	--	--
Construction	--	--	--	--	--	--	--	--	--	--
Wholesale and retail trade	--	--	--	--	--	--	--	--	--	--
Other services	--	--	--	--	--	--	--	--	--	--
Others	--	--	--	--	--	--	--	--	--	--
MSME GDP by region (% share)										
Capital city	--	--	--	--	--	--	--	--	--	--
Others	--	--	--	--	--	--	--	--	--	--
EXPORTS										
Total export value (B$ million)	12,118	15,678	16,221	14,309	13,438	8,715	6,790	7,712	8,872	9,886
Total export growth (%)	--	29.4	3.5	(11.8)	(6.1)	(35.1)	(22.1)	13.6	15.0	11.4
MSME export value (B$ million)	--	--	--	--	--	--	--	--	--	--
MSME export to total export value (%)	--	--	--	--	--	--	--	--	--	--
MSME export growth (%)	--	--	--	--	--	--	--	--	--	--
IMPORTS										
Total import value (B$ million)	3,457	4,528	4,455	4,521	4,556	4,448	3,689	4,257	5,622	6,957
Total import growth (%)	--	31.0	(1.6)	1.5	0.8	(2.4)	(17.1)	15.4	32.1	23.7
MSME import value (B$ million)	--	--	--	--	--	--	--	--	--	--
MSME import to total import value (%)	--	--	--	--	--	--	--	--	--	--
MSME import growth (%)	--	--	--	--	--	--	--	--	--	--

GDP = gross domestic product; MSME =micro, small, and medium-sized enterprise.

Source: ADB Asia SME Monitor 2020 database. Data from Department of Economic Planning and Statistics

Table 3.3: Bank Credit

End of period data

Item	2010	2011	2012	2013	2014	2015	2016	2017	2018	2019
COMMERCIAL BANKS										
Number of commercial banks	9	9	9	9	8	8	9	10	9	9
Locally incorporated banks	2	2	2	2	2	2	2	2	2	2
Foreign bank branches	6	6	6	6	5	5	6	6	5	5
Financial institutions supervised by AMBD but not licenced*	1	1	1	1	1	1	1	2	2	2
Credit										
Loans outstanding, total (B$ million)	5,173	5,092	5,200	5,621	5,712	6,115	5,404	5,130	5,473	5,889
Loans outstanding in domestic currency (B$ million)	5,079	4,642	4,688	5,081	5,063	5,505	4,939	4,738	4,938	5,024
Loans outstanding in foreign currency (B$ million)	94	450	512	540	649	610	465	392	536	865
Loan growth (%)	--	(1.6)	2.1	8.1	1.6	7.0	(11.6)	(5.1)	6.7	7.6
Total commercial bank loans to GDP (%)	27.7	21.9	21.8	24.8	26.4	34.4	34.3	30.6	29.9	32.0
Lending rate (%)**	5.5	5.5	5.5	5.5	5.5	5.5	5.5	5.5	5.5	5.5
Gross nonperforming loans (NPLs) (B$ million)	440	388	353	319	287	300	318	226	312	273
Gross NPLs to total loans (%)	8.5	7.6	6.8	5.7	5.0	4.9	5.9	4.4	5.7	4.6
Deposits										
Deposits, total (B$ million)	14,926	18,928	17,338	16,737	16,011	14,244	15,094	14,859	15,331	15,678
Deposits in domestic currency (B$ million)	12,074	16,098	14,538	14,163	13,432	11,696	12,319	12,123	12,873	13,599
Deposits in foreign currency (B$ million)	2,852	2,830	2,800	2,574	2,579	2,548	2,775	2,735	2,458	2,079
Deposit rate (%)	0.4	0.4	0.2	0.3	0.3	0.3	0.3	0.3	0.3	0.3
MSME LOANS - SME Bank										
MSME loans outstanding, total (B$)	--	--	--	--	--	--	--	--	3,304,913	8,996,023
Micro loans	--	--	--	--	--	--	--	--	178,613	1,115,666
SME loans	--	--	--	--	--	--	--	--	3,126,300	7,880,357
MSME loans to total loans outstanding (%)	--	--	--	--	--	--	--	--	0.06	0.15
MSME loans to GDP (%)	--	--	--	--	--	--	--	--	0.02	0.05
MSME loan growth (%)	--	--	--	--	--	--	--	--	--	172.2
MSME lending rate (%)	--	--	--	--	--	--	--	--	--	--
Micro loans	--	--	--	--	--	--	--	--	9.0	9.0
SME loans	--	--	--	--	--	--	--	--	7.0	7.0
Nonperforming MSME loans (NPLs) (B$)	--	--	--	--	--	--	--	--	--	--
MSME NPLs to total SME loans (%)	--	--	--	--	--	--	--	--	--	--
Number of MSME loan borrowers	--	--	--	--	--	--	--	--	45	166
Micro loans	--	--	--	--	--	--	--	--	17	96
SME loans	--	--	--	--	--	--	--	--	28	70
MSME loan borrowers to total bank borrowers (%)	--	--	--	--	--	--	--	--	--	--
MSME loan rejection rate (% of total applications)	--	--	--	--	--	--	--	--	--	--
Number of MSME savings account in banks	--	--	--	--	--	--	--	--	--	--
Guaranteed MSME loans (B$)	--	--	--	--	--	--	--	--	--	--
Non-collateral MSME loans (B$)	--	--	--	--	--	--	--	--	--	--
SME loans disbursed by sector (% share) - SME Bank										
Agriculture, forestry, and fisheries	--	--	--	--	--	--	--	--	6.5	12.2
Manufacturing	--	--	--	--	--	--	--	--	33.9	30.2
Transportation and communication	--	--	--	--	--	--	--	--	--	0.4
Construction	--	--	--	--	--	--	--	--	--	1.2
Wholesale and retail trade	--	--	--	--	--	--	--	--	26.1	24.6
Other services	--	--	--	--	--	--	--	--	22.2	27.9
Others	--	--	--	--	--	--	--	--	11.2	3.5
SME loans disbursed by region (% share) - SME Bank										
Capital city	--	--	--	--	--	--	--	--	100.0	96.0
Others	--	--	--	--	--	--	--	--	--	4.0
SME loans disbursed by type of use (% share) - SME Bank										
For working capital	--	--	--	--	--	--	--	--	72.0	87.0
For capital investment	--	--	--	--	--	--	--	--	28.0	13.0
SME loans disbursed by tenor (% share) - SME Bank										
Less than 1 year	--	--	--	--	--	--	--	--	--	3.0
1-5 years	--	--	--	--	--	--	--	--	100.0	87.0
More than 5 years	--	--	--	--	--	--	--	--	--	10.0

AMBD = Autoriti Monetari Brunei Darussalam; GDP = gross domestic product; MSME =micro, small, and medium-sized enterprise, NPL = nonperforming loan.

* Islamic Trust Fund and SME Bank. ** Prime lending rate.

Source: ADB Asia SME Monitor 2020 database. Data from AMBD and Bank Usahawan (SME Bank).

Table 3.4: Nonbank Finance

End of period data

Item	2010	2011	2012	2013	2014	2015	2016	2017	2018	2019
NUMBER OF NONBANK FINANCE INSTITUTIONS										
Microfinance institutions	--	--	--	--	--	--	--	--	--	--
Credit unions/cooperatives	--	--	--	--	--	--	--	--	--	--
Finance companies	3	3	3	3	3	3	3	3	2	2
Pawnshops	--	--	1	1	1	1	1	1	1	1
Leasing companies	--	--	--	--	--	--	--	--	--	--
Factoring companies	--	--	--	--	--	--	--	--	--	--
Insurance companies	--	--	--	--	--	--	--	--	--	--
Others	--	--	--	--	--	--	--	--	--	--
FINANCE COMPANIES										
Financing outstanding, total (B$ million)	1,415	1,562	1,701	1,799	2,009	1,869	1,664	1,556	1,539	1,522
Total financing to GDP (%)	7.6	6.7	7.1	7.9	9.3	10.5	10.6	9.3	8.4	8.3
Annual financing rate (%, on average)	--	--	--	--	--	--	--	--	--	--
Gross nonperforming financing (NPFs) (B$ million)	12.9	13.2	18.2	17.2	19.1	19.4	17.8	19.1	15.1	15.6
Gross NPFs to total financing (%)	0.9	0.8	1.1	1.0	1.0	1.0	1.1	1.2	1.0	1.0
Number of customers financed, total	--	--	--	--	--	--	--	--	--	--
Financing outstanding by sector (% share)										
Agriculture, forestry, and fisheries	--	--	--	--	--	--	--	--	--	--
Manufacturing	--	--	--	--	--	--	--	--	--	--
Transportation and communication	--	95.0	95.6	95.2	96.1	95.4	95.3	95.6	96.4	96.9
Construction	--	--	--	--	--	--	--	--	--	--
Wholesale and retail trade	--	--	--	--	--	--	--	--	--	--
Other services	--	--	--	--	--	--	--	--	--	--
Others	--	5.0	4.4	4.8	3.9	4.6	4.7	4.4	3.6	3.1
Financing outstanding by region (% share)										
Capital city	--	--	--	--	--	--	--	--	--	--
Others	--	--	--	--	--	--	--	--	--	--
PAWNBROKER										
Financing outstanding, total (B$ million)	--	--	15.0	15.6	14.2	12.0	12.6	13.2	13.0	15.1
Total financing to GDP (%)	--	--	0.06	0.07	0.07	0.07	0.08	0.08	0.07	0.08
Annual financing rate (%, on average)	--	--	--	--	--	--	--	--	--	--
Gross nonperforming financing (NPFs) (B$ million)	--	--	0.7	3.2	4.4	1.0	1.3	1.0	0.0	1.6
Gross NPFs to total financing (%)	--	--	4.6	20.3	31.2	8.5	10.4	7.8	7.0	10.3
Number of customers financed, total	--	--	9,764	9,716	8,734	8,507	9,344	13,413	14,193	7,283
Financing outstanding by sector (% share)										
Agriculture, forestry, and fisheries	--	--	--	--	--	--	--	--	--	--
Manufacturing	--	--	--	--	--	--	--	--	--	--
Transportation and communication	--	--	--	--	--	--	--	--	--	--
Construction	--	--	--	--	--	--	--	--	--	--
Wholesale and retail trade	--	--	--	--	--	--	--	--	--	--
Other services	--	--	--	--	--	--	--	--	--	--
Others	--	--	100.0	100.0	100.0	100.0	100.0	100.0	100.0	100.0
Financing outstanding by region (% share)										
Capital city	--	--	--	--	--	--	--	--	--	--
Others	--	--	--	--	--	--	--	--	--	--

GDP = gross domestic product, NPF = nonperforming finance.
Source: ADB Asia SME Monitor 2020 database. Data from Autoriti Monetari Brunei Darussalam.

Table 3.5: Policies and Regulations

Regulations	
Name	**Outline**
Nonfinance Regulations	
Darussalam Enterprise Order of 2016	Establishment of Darussalam Enterprise, as the national body for MSME development.
Finance Regulations	
Autoriti Monetari Brunei Darussalam Order of 2010	Stipulate the roles and functions of Autoriti Monetari Brunei Darussalam, including the establishment of a credit bureau.
Securities Markets Order of 2013	Provide licenses for capital market intermediaries and procedures on public offering of securities and market operations for securities exchanges, clearing houses, a central securities depository, trading facilities, and credit rating agencies.
Secured Transaction Order of 2016	Provide the legal basis on the secured transaction system, including the legal requirements for the establishment of a collateral registry for movable assets.
Pawnbrokers Order of 2002; Pawnbrokers (Amendment) Order of 2005	Provide licenses for pawnbrokers.
Moneylenders Act, Chapter 62	Provide licenses for moneylenders.
Gudelines No.FTU/G-1/2017/1 on Fintech Regulatory Sandbox (February 2017)	Guide pilot testing of innovative financial technologies in the market and ease the regulatory environment for applied fintech firms during the limited testing period.
Notice* on Equity Based Crowdfunding (ECF) Platform Operators (August 2017)	Stipulate the requirements for applicants who intend to operate an ECF Platform in Brunei Darussalam. An applicant must apply for a Capital Market Services Licence, allowing it to carry out the regulated activities of dealing and arranging deals in investments and investment advice.
Notice* on Early Detection of Cyber Intrusion and Incident Reporting (October 2017)	Require financial institutions to have robust capabilities to proactively detect cyber intrusions to enable quick response and recovery.
Notice* on Peer-to-Peer (P2P) Financing Platform Operators (April 2019)	Stipulate the requirements for applicants who intend to operate a P2P platform in Brunei Darussalam. An applicant must apply for a Capital Market Services Licence, allowing it to carry out the regulated activities of dealing and arranging deals in investments and investment advice.

Regulators and Policymakers	
Name	**Responsibility**
Autoriti Monetari Brunei Darussalam (AMBD)	Improve the financial sector infrastructure and financial intermediation necessary to support economic diversification in Brunei Darussalam.
Ministry of Energy, Manpower, and Industry (MEMI)	Develop the private sector, and promote their business capability and the growth of local enterprises. The Industry portfolio under the MEMI transferred to the MOFE in November 2019.
Ministry of Finance and Economy (MOFE)	The MOFE is a focal ministry for MSME development in the country. A National MSME Task Force is under preparation in the MOEF. The MOFE established the SME Bank.
Darussalam Enterprise (DARe)	A government statutory body and an implementing agency for national MSME support policies.
Department of Economic Planning and Statistics (DEPS), MOFE	Compile MSME data through the Economic Census of Enterprises.
National MSME Task Force	National coordinating body for MSME policy formulation.

Policies		
Name	**Responsible Entity**	**Outline**
Wawasan Brunei 2035 (long-term national development plan)	Government	Stipulate development strategies to be accomplished by 2035, focusing on 13 areas: education, the economy, security, institutional development, local business development, infrastructure development, social security, the environment, health, religion, land use, infrastructure and information and communications technology, and manpower planning.
National Digital Strategy 2016–2020	MOC and AITI	Promote the transformation to the digital economy.
Financial Sector Blueprint 2016–2025	AMBD	Guide financial sector development by 2025 and offer a strategic framework that comprises the five pillars in line with the Wawasan Brunei 2035: (i) monetary and financial stability, (ii) competitive and innovative financial institutions and services, (iii) robust and modern infrastructure, (iv) enhanced international integration, and (v) human capital development.
Digital Payment Roadmap 2019–2025	AMBD	Aim to create a digital payment ecosystem in the national payment system. The roadmap addresses three strategic actions: (i) balancing regulation and innovation, (ii) adoption of open digital payment, and (iii) public awareness and education.
Cybersecurity Strategy 2017–2020	AMBD	Stipulate five strategic actions: (i) setting the strategy, (ii) strengthening governance, (iii) enhancing the process, (iv) developing the people, and (v) using the right technology.

* Notice is legally binding. MOC = Ministry of Communications, AITI = Authority for Info-Communications Technology Industry.

Source: ADB Asia SME Monitor 2020 database. Data from AMBD, MEMI, and DARe.

Country Review
Cambodia

Overview

Cambodia had a population of 15.3 million in 2019.[35] The economy has sustained average growth of 7% between 2015 and 2019, expanding by 7.1% in 2019.[36] Micro, small, and medium-sized enterprises (MSMEs) remain the staple of the business community, accounting for 99.8% of Cambodian firms. The main challenges for continued MSME development are access to finance, development of human capital and skills, market access, and adoption of the latest technology. The government launched an SME Bank in April 2020 to expand MSME access to finance and develop credit guarantee schemes for MSMEs. Although nonbank finance remains small, microfinance institutions play a critical role in supplying MSME working capital, especially in agriculture. The government's SME Development Plan supports its medium-term National Strategic Development Plan 2018–2023 (NSDP). It also adopted a National Financial Inclusion Strategy 2019–2025 to promote digital financial services.

1. MSME Development

- A new MSME definition will be formalized in 2020, setting employment and asset thresholds by sector; 99.8% of Cambodia's firms are MSMEs, mostly microenterprises, with wholesale and retail trade having the largest share.
- Microenterprise workers account for much of the MSME labor pool, with half of the workforce engaged in wholesale and retail trade; while MSMEs are increasing in the capital, Phnom Penh, the rate of new jobs created is expected to decline. MSMEs employ many female workers.
- MSMEs accounted for a half the annual sales of Cambodian firms and nearly 80% of profits.
- Major policy challenges include enhancing MSME productivity and enabling market access; the government is actively training MSMEs in agriculture and food processing to reach international quality standards.
- The government is building an entrepreneurial ecosystem with networks of centers for incubating, accelerating, and launching new businesses.
- The Cambodia Chamber of Commerce is the primary private sector provider of business development services and networking opportunities; it also plays a critical role as principal private sector representative when advising the government on policy.

Scale of MSMEs

The General Directorate of Small and Medium Enterprises and Handicraft—under the Ministry of Industry, Science, Technology, and Innovation (MISTI)—will include its recently drafted Small and Medium Enterprise Development Policy and Five-year Implementation Plan 2020–2024 as a crucial element of the government's overall Industrial Development Policy 2015–2025. It categorizes MSMEs based on industrial activity, productive assets, and full-time employees (Table 4.1).[37] Productive assets exclude assets such as land and buildings that are owned by the entity but not directly involved in production.

[35] Government of Cambodia, National Institute of Statistics. 2019. *General Population Census of the Kingdom of Cambodia 2019*. Data as of 3 March 2019.

[36] ADB. 2020. *Asian Development Outlook 2020 Supplement (June 2020)*. Manila.

[37] The new MSME definition refers to a full-time equivalent (FTE) workforce count to determine full-time employees. FTE refers to the ratio of the total number of paid hours during a period (part-time, full-time, contracted) to the total number of working hours.

The new definition differentiates MSMEs by sector. The International Standard Industrial Classification Rev.4 Code: C taxonomy is the basis for categorizing industrial activity. In manufacturing, a firm with fewer than 500 full-time employees and productive assets of less than $1 million[38] is classified as an MSME. In agriculture, forestry, and fishing; wholesale and retail trade; and other industrial activities, a firm with fewer than 200 full-time employees and productive assets of less than $1 million is an MSME. In "other services," a firm with fewer than 100 full-time employees and productive assets of less than $1 million is an MSME. A firm with more employees or greater assets is classified as a large firm.

The new MSME definition will be used beginning 2020. Previously, there was no formal MSME definition, but convention held that a microenterprise had fewer than 10 full-time employees and less than $50,000 in productive assets, a small enterprise had 10–50 full-time employees and assets less than $250,000, and a medium-sized enterprise 51–100 full-time employees and assets less than $500,000.[39]

The most recent firm data comes from the Cambodia Inter-censal Economic Survey 2014 (CIES 2014) administered by the National Institute of Statistics under the Ministry of Planning. The CIES 2014 reported that there were 513,759 establishments in Cambodia, of which 44,171 employed 5–9 people, 14,511 employed 10–99, 895 employed 100–999, and 145 employed 1,000 or more.[40] Three-quarters of the firms were either sole proprietorships (33.0%) or owned by two individuals (40.8%), with average employment across all firms of 3.6 workers. Women were involved in 61.0% of the firms. Ninety-nine percent were Cambodian-owned, with 74.8% home businesses. It was estimated that 92.9% were unregistered. However, the Ministry of Commerce reported 9,606 registered companies with 3,941 newly registered in 2019.

Using the pre-2020 definition (up to 100 full-time employees and less than $500,000 in assets excluding land), 99.8% of the total were MSMEs in 2014, with 97.6% microenterprises and 2.2% small and medium-sized enterprises (SMEs); the remaining 0.2% were large enterprises. In 2009, there were 376,069 MSMEs, increasing 23.0% to 462,582 in 2011 and 10.9% to 512,870 in 2014 (Figure 4.1A and Table 4.2).

By industry, 59.6% of MSMEs were in wholesale and retail trade in 2014, 26.5% in other services, and 13.9% in manufacturing (Figure 4.1B). Wholesale and retail trade (including motor vehicle and motorcycle repair) held the largest share of microenterprises (60.7%), followed by manufacturing (14.0%) and accommodation and food services (10.9%) (CIES 2014). For SMEs, education held the largest share (33.7%). Half of Cambodia's large enterprises were in manufacturing.

By region, 18.8% of MSMEs in 2014 were located in Phnom Penh, with the remaining 81.2% in rural areas such as Kampong Cham, Kandal, Siem Reap, and Takeo. Cambodia's MSMEs were increasingly concentrated in the capital as compared to 2011 (18.2% in Phnom Penh).

38 The MSME definition uses US dollar amounts for asset thresholds.

39 This definition refers to an MSME definition proposed in the Small and Medium Enterprise Development Framework of 2005.

40 Cambodia Inter-censal Economic Survey 2014: Analysis of the Survey Results Report No.2 Analysis by Scale. p.xxxi. September 2015.

Figure 4.1: Number of MSMEs

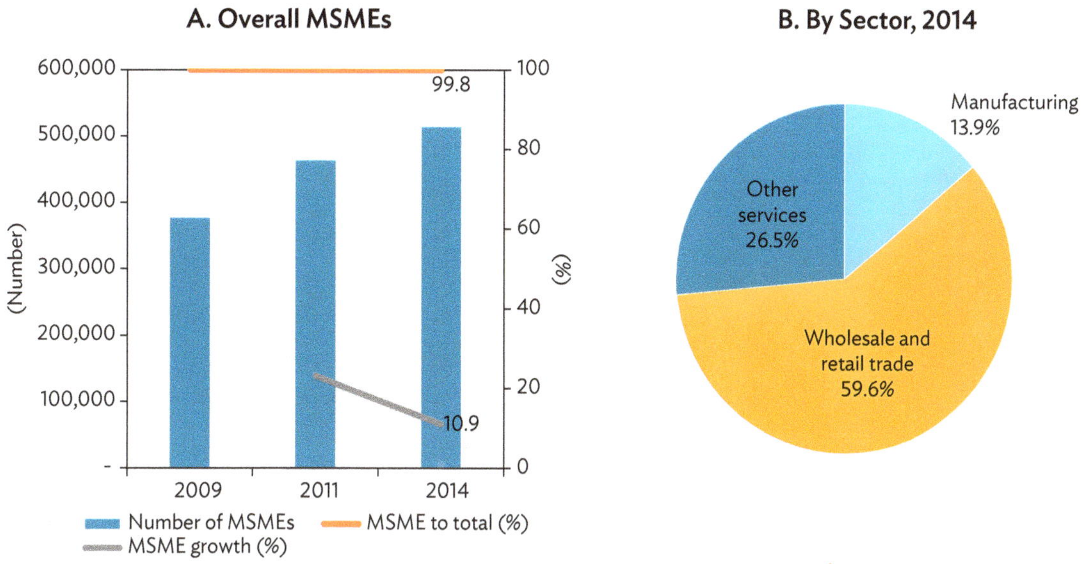

MSME = micro, small, and medium-sized enterprise.

Source: ADB Asia SME Monitor 2020 database. Data from MSME Department, Ministry of Industry, Science, Technology, and Innovation and National Institute of Statistics.

Employment

According to the CIES 2014, the workforce in 2014 was more than 1.87 million. Microenterprises employed 58.3% of the total with an average of 2.2 employees per establishment, SMEs employed 13.4% with an average of 22.3 employees per establishment, and large enterprises employed 28.2% with an average of 595.9 employees per establishment. From 1.1 million workers in 2009, the number of MSME employees increased 5.4% (to 1.16 million) in 2011, and 16.1% (1.35 million) in 2014 (Figure 4.2A). MSME employees accounted for 74.8% of total employees in 2009, 72.0% in 2011, and 71.8% in 2014.

Microenterprises had the largest share (81.3%) of MSME labor. By sector, wholesale and retail trade employed 46.7% of the MSME workforce, followed by other services (38.1%) and manufacturing (the remaining 15.2%) (Figure 4.2B). Although 37.2% of SME employees were in education, they accounted for only 10.1% of the total, with manufacturing and accommodation and food services also with more than 10%.

By region, 20% of MSME employees worked in the capital city Phnom Penh in 2014, with the remaining 80% outside in areas such as Kampong Cham and Siem Reap. The share of MSME workers in rural areas was higher than in 2011 (76.6%). The trend seems to be that while the share of MSMEs in Phnom Penh is rising, its share of MSME workers is declining.

By gender, female MSME employees accounted for 54.0% of all MSME employees in 2014, down slightly from 2011 (54.8%). However, with the female share of total employment at 42.7% in 2014, MSMEs are a major provider of jobs for women.

Figure 4.2: Employment by MSMEs

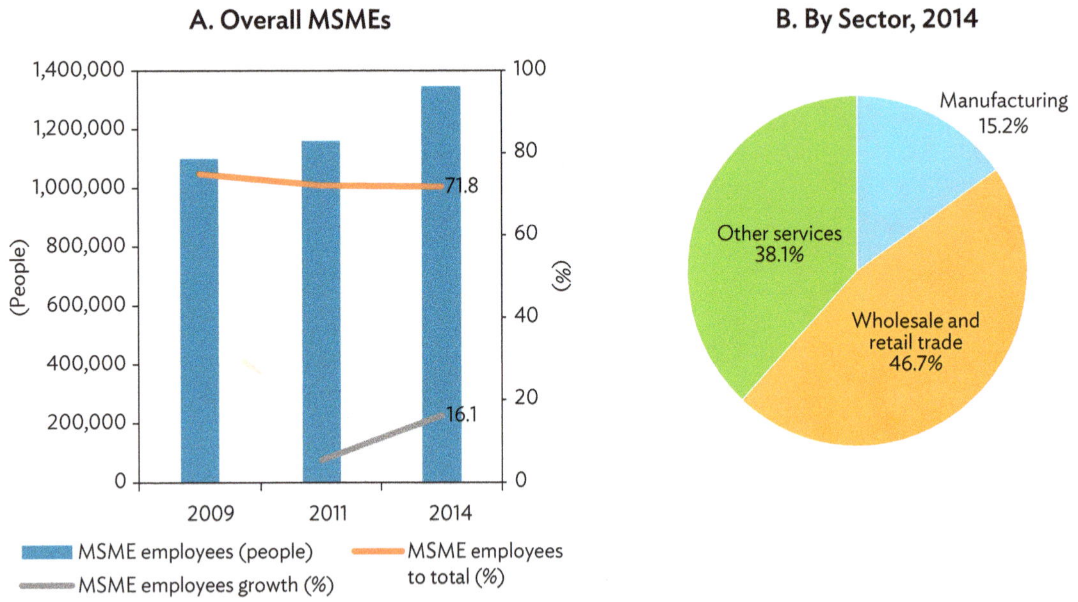

MSME = micro, small, and medium-sized enterprise.

Source: ADB Asia SME Monitor 2020 database. Data from MSME Department, Ministry of Industry, Science, Technology, and Innovation and National Institute of Statistics.

Business Productivity

The CIES 2014 reported annual sales of Cambodian entities in 2014 of $22.6 billion. Of this amount, microenterprises contributed 36.1%, SMEs 13.7%, and large firms 50.2%. Annual expenses were $18.8 billion, with microenterprises accounting for 31.9%, SMEs 12.3%, and large firms 55.8%. Of a total $2.4 billion in wages, microenterprises paid 8.7%, SMEs 15.1%, while large firms accounted for 76.2%. Microenterprises earned 57% of the $3.8 billion in profits, SMEs 20.4%, and large firms 22.6%. Large firms paid 98.4% of the $175.7 million in profit taxes.

According to the Ministry of Economy and Finance (MEF), as of end-2019, the largest share of GDP by sector was other services (22.2%), followed by agriculture, forestry, and fisheries (20.8%); manufacturing (16.7%); and construction (14.6%). These four sectors accounted for 74.0%–75.2% of GDP each year since 2014. However, the share of agriculture, forestry, and fisheries fell by 27.8% (from 28.9% in 2014 to 20.8% in 2019), while construction increased 71.1% (from 8.5% in 2014 to 14.6% in 2019). A data breakdown on MSMEs is unavailable.

Market Access

While agricultural products and food processing are major sources of Cambodian productivity and exports, for most MSMEs meeting international quality standards remains a challenge. According to stakeholders such as the Ministry of Agriculture, Forestry, and Fisheries (MAFF), while there are myriad opportunities for Cambodian firms, building the capacity and capability to take advantage remains a challenge.

For example, agriculture cooperatives (coops) are a mainstay of the sector's structure. While they are large in number (857), they lack the means to effectively support their members in terms of product quality.[41] These self-supporting groups attract farmers seeking both technical and financial assistance. Yet the coops lack both the technical and financial resources to satisfy either domestic or foreign demand. Access to markets is a major hurdle. As incomes grow, consumers demand safer and better-quality food. With farmers still learning to meet higher quality requirements, Cambodia imports food—with the exception of rice, which is exported.

MAFF provides training sessions on pertinent topics such as product marketing, increasing crop yields, and improving record keeping, among others. They are conducted by MAFF at all coops via provincial governments. Some coops have proven more business-savvy than others and are better able to access markets. Thus, MAFF is constantly trying to find ways to motivate better coop performance.

The Federation of Associations for MSMEs of Cambodia (FAMSMEC) also assists with market access. One initiative promotes business matching through an exhibition for the food processing industry. The first exhibition concluded in August 2019 with over 1,500 MSMEs participating. AusAid provided the funding via the Cambodia Agricultural Value Chain Program. The Young Entrepreneur Association also participated.

Overseas trade fairs are another FAMSMEC initiative. The Food and Ingredient Association sponsors two trips a year for 50 members, all expenses paid, to an Association of Southeast Asian Nations (ASEAN) trade exhibition. Processing and Packaging (ProPak) Asia sponsored two trips to Germany, each taking 40 members.

While there are no data on MSME exports and imports, there are data covering total exports and imports for 2009–2018 (Table 4.2). Exports climbed from KR13.1 trillion ($3.1 billion)[42] in 2009 to KR52.3 trillion ($13.0 billion) in 2018, an overall increase of 300% at an annual compound growth rate of 16.7%. Imports expanded from KR20.3 trillion ($4.9 billion) in 2009 to KR75.8 trillion ($18.8 billion) in 2018, an overall gain of 273% at an annual compound growth rate of 15.8%.

Technology and Innovation

Cambodia is in the process of building a budding entrepreneurship ecosystem under the MEF.[43] The first step is to coach potential entrepreneurs on how to turn ideas into business models—the "incubation" stage. As of end-2019, there were 20 incubators across Cambodia. The second step in the process is "acceleration," which moves ideas into actual products. MEF oversees the Techo Startup Center (TSC), launched in April 2019, which transforms business ideas into Minimum Viable Products, something that can be bought and sold. Once an entrepreneur can demonstrate a Minimum Viable Product is viable at scale, then they move to the finance stage of seeking venture capital and the launch of a new business.

TSC has 17 staff, of which 70% have an engineering background in areas such as software development, artificial intelligence, big data, and blockchain technology. TSC wants to hire more personnel to increase throughput, as the current staff can only serve 5–10 start-ups.

TSC seeks out business models that are either scalable platforms or "fast fails" (it becomes immediately apparent if a concept won't work). TSC has found scalable platforms for potential start-ups in services, media, and e-commerce. As of April 2020, it also said it will focus on AgriTech acceleration.

---

41 According to the Ministry of Commerce, this view is from Think.COOP, 22 November 2018, published by the International Labour Organization.

42 End-of-year currency rates from the International Monetary Fund/International Financial Statistics (IMF/IFS) in the designated years are used to convert Cambodian riel to US dollars.

43 From 2011 to 2018, there were 300 start-ups in Cambodia, of which 50 remain active.

One TSC project is subcomponent 2.2 of the Sustainable Assets for Agriculture Markets Business and Trade. Called the Digital Technology and Enterprise for Rural Value Chain, it aims to (i) empower the rural economy through technology, (ii) improve accessibility of agricultural products to markets using digital technology, and (iii) partner with key participants and start-ups to solve production and distribution problems across the value chain. A data-driven digital platform—the Khmer Agri Suit (KAS)—will connect key value chain participants via a suite of components (KAS-CORE, KAS-AI, KAS-IAM, KAS-PORTAL, KAS-KUMRONG, KAS-FRESH, KAS-TRACK, and KAS-WEATHER).

Another project is Start-up Cambodia, building a network of start-ups similar to other countries, such as Start-up Estonia, to connect with other start-ups across ASEAN to exchange experiences. A third project is the Cambodia Data eXchange or CamDX, which allows secure multilateral data exchange between various information systems over the internet. By adopting Estonia's X-Road model, CamDX is a unified yet decentralized data exchange platform between information systems that offers a standardized and secure way to provide and consume services. Online Business Registration (OBR)—the first to use CamDX—combines at least four main relevant information systems into a single portal allowing business owners to register and receive licenses to operate their business more efficiently and effectively. The CamDX portal distributes data registered by business owners to respective information systems within the Ministry of Commerce, the General Department of Taxation, and the Ministry of Labour and Vocational Training. The single portal uses CamDigiKey as its authentication service.

The MEF launched the Entrepreneurial Development Fund (EDF) in February 2019 (under Prakas No.136/SHV/BrK) with an initial $5 million capitalization, of which at least $4 million is available for grants. As the name suggests, it provides financial assistance to entrepreneurs, with a grant size ranging $10,000–$25,000. MEF is still determining whether grants will be "free money" or if the EDF will take a small equity stake in return. Selection criteria are still being developed.

The MEF is also developing a long-term Digital Economy Framework, expected in 2020, which spans 20 years, with the first 10 years focusing on developing digital infrastructure and connectivity. The framework covers several key areas including:

- continuing development of digital financial services (DFS) and mobile payments;
- upgrading the physical infrastructure needed to support the digital economy and the timely delivery of goods and services;
- promoting entrepreneurial start-ups and digital skill development to ensure digital literacy (e.g., public awareness as well as particular courses, on coding);[44]
- developing software platforms and cybersecurity;
- creating a digital government to improve transparency and support the digital economy. with government services increasingly digitized to boost efficiency; and
- developing the appropriate laws and regulations, including an E-Commerce Law and other statutes covering cybercrime and data protection.

[44] The World Bank is supporting a visit of TSC staff to Silicon Valley in the US to learn more about digital skill development.

Networking and Support

The Cambodia Chamber of Commerce (CCC) was established by law in 1995 to be the primary provider of business networking in the country. The CCC is the principal representative of the private sector. There are three categories of members:

- **Elected members.** The CCC invites only 40 members to this category, representing four key sectors: commercial, agriculture, service, and industry and handicrafts. Elected members pay monthly dues of $100 ($1,200 annually). Only elected members have voting rights. There are four to five MSMEs elected members (10%–12.5%).

- **Advisory members.** Also limited to 40 members, they are distributed equally across the four key sectors. MSMEs are 90% of this category. They do not pay dues, but are welcome to donate, and serve on a voluntary basis for the mutual benefit of the members and the CCC.

- **Auxiliary members.** Numbering 5,000, they pay dues of $50 and are distributed across all industry sectors. MSMEs are 100% of this category.

The principal benefit of joining the CCC is to meet foreign investors. The CCC holds monthly events with 60–70 participants where visiting investors interact with members. It also receives 15–20 member (on average) overseas delegations, following the Prime Minister's trips abroad (10 trips annually).

The World Bank funded the first Government/Private Sector Forum in 1999 to foster closer cooperation between business and government. Working groups include stakeholders from government ministries and the private sector to solve problems facing a particular industry, e.g., construction. In 2006, the CCC became the representative of the private sector and selected members of working groups. The initial eight working groups expanded to 13 by 2019.

Working group subcommittees meet twice a month to dissect and discuss issues, with the full working group meeting two to three times a year. Each working group presents its findings to the Prime Minister, who acts as arbitrator between the private sector and government, and ultimately resolves each issue more in favor of the private sector or the government based on working group findings.

2. Access to Finance

- Overall, bank credit has shown robust expansion, with services—particularly wholesale and retail trade—as the largest borrowers; the central bank estimates MSME borrowings are 70% of the total and rising.
- The government launched an SME Bank in April 2020 to expand MSME access to finance; the bank is expected to offer MSMEs credit guarantee schemes.
- Although nonbank finance is small, microfinance institutions (MFIs) dominate formal nonbank financing, with their lending portfolios growing significantly; agriculture consumes much MFI credit, but it is decreasing.
- The Financial Sector Development Strategy 2016–2025 offers a blueprint for financial inclusion, including the use of digital financial services; the strategy is expected to be renewed in 2020.
- Securities markets are in an infant stage of development; ongoing regulatory reforms are expected to attract more issuers and investors, while the stock exchange promotes training and incubator programs.
- Financial infrastructure remains underdeveloped and is a key area for policy interventions; there is an active private credit bureau in the country.

The National Bank of Cambodia (NBC) regulates and supervises bank and nonbank financing—including microfinance, financial leasing companies, rural credit institutions, payment service institutions, and money changers. The MEF oversees insurance and pawnshops. The Securities and Exchange Commission of Cambodia (SECC) regulates and supervises the securities market. Both the NBC and SECC are at the forefront of MSME finance using new financing mechanisms, regulation reforms, and education and training.

Bank Credit

The number of banks climbed from 24 in 2007 to 62 in 2019, an increase of 158.3% (a compound annual growth rate of 8.2%). Demand for credit remains high, particularly among MSMEs. According to the NBC, as of the first quarter of 2019, MSMEs held 70% of total loan accounts, a decrease from 75% in 2018; however, the NBC surmised that, by loan value, the MSME share may have actually grown (there are no publicly available data on MSME bank credit).

The amount of available credit has grown steadily. From 2007 to 2019, outstanding loans increased from KR6.3 trillion ($1.6 billion) (footnote 42) to KR102.5 trillion ($25.1 billion) (Figure 4.3A and Table 4.3), an overall increase of 1,517.9% (at a compound annual growth rate of 26.1%). Year-on-year loan growth ranges from a high of 82.7% in 2006–2007 to a low of 5.2% in 2008–2009. Loan growth was 24.3% in 2017–2018 and 23.9% in 2018–2019. As a percentage of GDP, the commercial loan share has grown steadily, from 17.9% in 2007 to 92.0% in 2019, an overall increase of 415.0% (a compound annual growth rate of 14.6%).

The nonperforming loan (NPL) ratio dropped from 3.4% in 2007 to 2.0% as of end-2019, a 43.0% decline (a compound annual rate of –4.6%). The highest was 4.4% in 2009; the lowest 2.0% in 2019.

By sector, "other services" (including accommodation and food services), and wholesale and retail trade were the two largest borrowers throughout the 2008–2019 period (Figure 4.3B). In 2019, they accounted for 48.5% and 26.4%, respectively, followed by construction (9.5%), and agriculture, forestry, and fisheries (7.3%). Over the 2008–2019 period, other services and trade combined accounted for 67.6%–74.9% of bank credit. Bank credit to other services increased by 12.7% over the period, while loans to trade fell by 9.5%. Loans to construction grew 20.4% while agriculture, forestry, and fisheries grew 39.9%.

ACLEDA, the largest commercial bank, is the primary source of MSME bank credit. ACLEDA started in 1993 as an MFI, becoming a specialty bank in 2000 and a commercial bank in 2003. By 2010, it had become the country's largest bank. By 2019, it had shifted its focus to financing SMEs, given the intense competition for larger clients. ACLEDA defines SMEs by loan size: (i) up to $50,000 as a small business loan and (ii) from $50,000 to $1 million as a medium-sized enterprise business loan. The bank's charter limits loan size to 5% of the bank's net worth, or $44.8 million as of March 2020.

Figure 4.3: Bank Loans

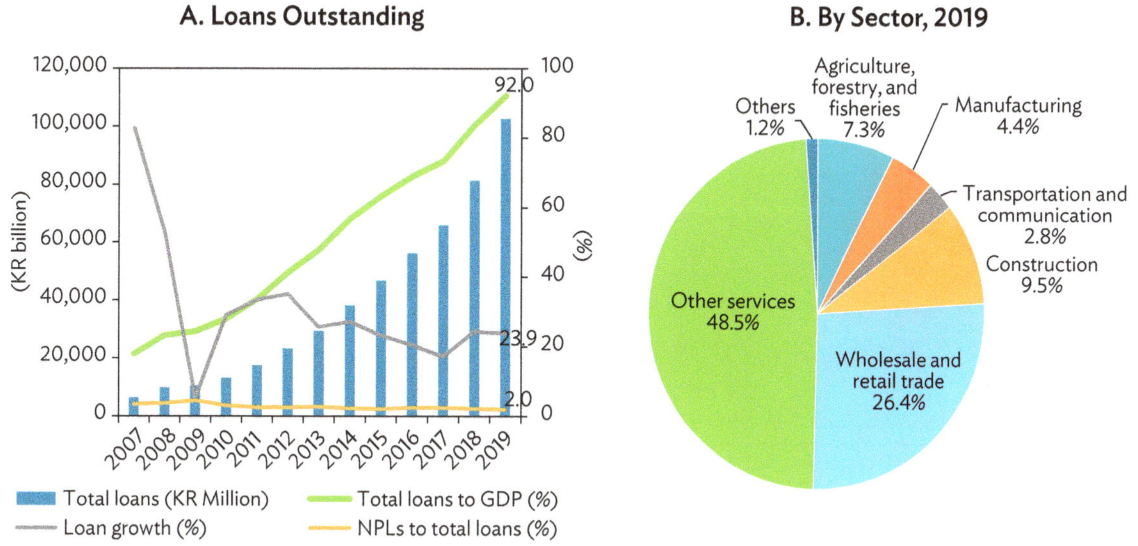

GDP = gross domestic product, NPL = nonperforming loan.

Source: ADB Asia SME Monitor 2020 database. Data from National Bank of Cambodia.

The average small business loan was $8,400 at the end of 2019, and $8,465 as of March 2020. The average loan size for SMEs combined was $13,068 at the end of 2019 and $13,367 in March 2020. The average interest rate was 11.8%, with a range of 6%–18%, with the latter capped by law. The average maturity was 4 years. Both small and medium-sized business loans have a maximum 6-year maturity.

ACLEDA's loan portfolio was $3.7 billion at the end of 2019 and $3.8 billion as of March 2020. Small business loans accounted for $1.9 billion (50.1%) of the loan balance at the end of 2019 and $2 billion (51.1%) in March 2020. Medium-sized loans accounted for $1.2 billion (32.1%) at the end of 2019 and $1.2 billion (32.0%) in March 2020. Consumer loans and mortgages accounted for the remaining $0.7 billion (17.8%) at the end of 2019 and $0.6 billion (16.9%) in March 2020. The NPL ratio was moderately low at 1.1% on average in 2019 and 1.09% in March 2020. NPL ratio was 0.8% and 0.7% for small business loans, and 2.0% and 1.9% for medium-sized business loans in the same period, respectively.

As of end-2019, ACLEDA's loan portfolio accounted for 14.8% of the national loan portfolio. Its 403,055 account holders were 50% of the national total, with savings deposits accounting for 16.6%. ACLEDA's 2.3 million savings accounts were 50.3% of the national total. By sector, retail trade was the largest at 34.4%, followed by agriculture (19.7%), services (21.6%), and the remaining sectors (24.3%).

There is high loan demand from MSMEs. ACLEDA says SME credit grew 18.4% from 2017 to 2018, versus 15.4% for their entire loan portfolio (for 2018–2019, total loans grew 6.5%).

Real property was the only collateral accepted until the Secured Transaction Law was passed in 2007, which allowed movable property such as cars and motorcycles as collateral; banks have final discretion over what they will ultimately accept. ACLEDA says almost 100% of its MSME loans involve collateral, with less than 5% using movable property as collateral. The loan-to-value ratio is 50%–75%. The NBC says that, to increase financial inclusion, there is an effort to promote the factoring of inventory as collateral. The Ministry of Commerce holds the national collateral registry.

Public Financing and Guarantees

The government launched the state-owned SME Bank on 3 April 2020 as a policy bank with an initial capitalization of $100 million to support MSME access to finance. There is a plan for the SME Bank to offer credit guarantee schemes. While its purpose is to implement government policy, it is supposed to function as a commercial bank. It will offer guaranteed loans at below-market interest rates, including concessional loans focusing on priority sectors. SME Bank will collaborate with branches of other banks to implement government policies.

Nonbank Financing

MFIs dominate nonbank financing, although leasing companies also have a presence. The number of MFIs increased from 17 in 2007 to 83 in 2019 (Figure 4.4A and Table 4.4), an overall gain of 388.2% (a compound annual growth rate of 14.1%). Leasing companies grew from just one in 2012 to 15 in 2019 (Figure 4.4B).

From 2007 to 2019, MFI loans increased significantly from KR617.3 billion ($154 million) to KR29.4 trillion ($7.2 billion), or an overall increase of 4,656% (a compound annual growth rate of 38.0%). MFI loans increased by KR5.0 trillion from 2014 to 2015 before leveling off for a year. They jumped by KR4.5 trillion from 2016 to 2017, and another KR4.6 trillion from 2017 to 2018 before rising KR7.5 trillion from 2018 to 2019.

Figure 4.4: Nonbank Finance

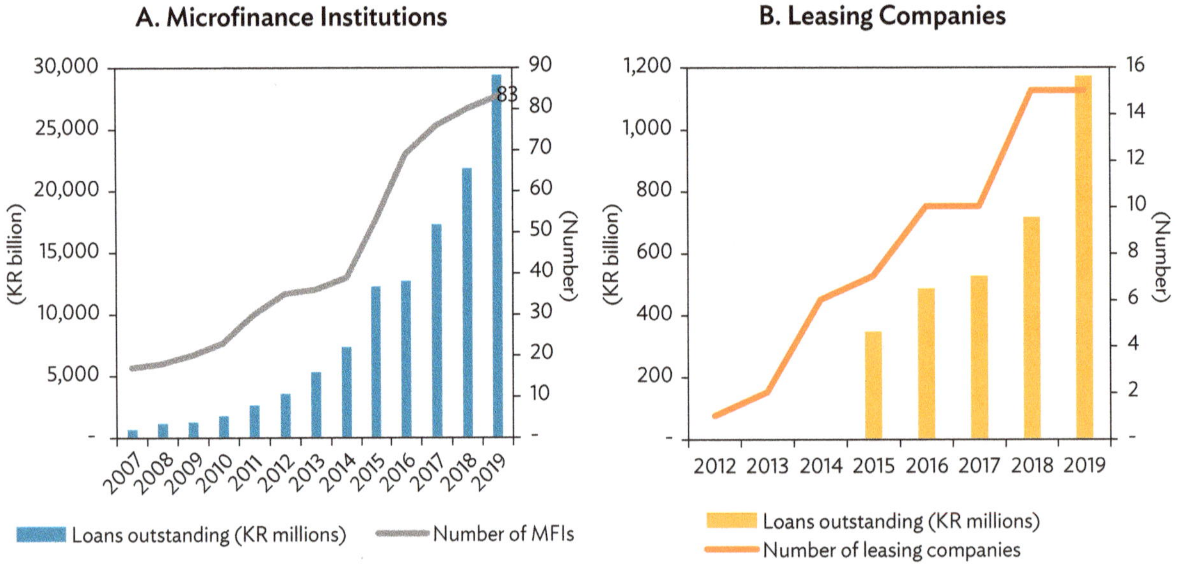

Source: ADB Asia SME Monitor 2020 database. Data from National Bank of Cambodia.

Lending data for leasing companies is available for 2015–2019. Loans increased from KR345 billion ($85 million) to KR1.2 trillion ($286 million), an overall gain of 239% (a compound annual growth rate of 35.7%).

According to NBC data, MFI loans totaled 1.8% of GDP in 2007, rising to 26.5% in 2019, an increase of 1,402% (a compound annual growth rate of 25.3%). The MFI loan share of bank loans was 9.7% in 2007, increasing to 28.6% by 2019, an increase of 194% (a compound annual growth rate of 9.4%). The number of borrowers grew from 0.6 million to 2.1 million over the period, an increase of 251.2% (a compound annual growth rate of 11.0%). The MFI NPL ratio was just 0.8% in 2019.

By sector, loans to others (all other sectors not otherwise specified) accounted for 37.7% of MFI loans in 2019, followed by agriculture, forestry, and fisheries (19.4%) and wholesale and retail trade (18.3%). For 2007–2019, loans to agriculture fell by 57.1% (a compound annual decreasing rate of 6.8%), while loans to others climbed 278.1% (a compound annual growth rate of 11.7%).

According to the Cambodia Microfinance Association, MFIs offer three main products:

- **Agricultural loans (small group lending).** The average loan size runs from $1,000 to a maximum $1,500. The interest rate is 18% (capped) plus a 5% fee, with a 12-month maturity.

- **Individual consumption loans.** Sometimes used by microenterprises when owners mix personal and business credit—the average loan size is $5,000 with a maximum of $100,000. The interest rate is 15%–18% with a 2%–3% fee. The loan term is up to 3 years.

- **MSME loans.** The average loan size is $10,000 with a maximum of $500,000. The interest rate is 10%–15% with a 1% fee. The loan term is an average 5 years with a maximum of 10 years.

The NPL ratio is 1.5% for nearly every product. Repayment is monthly. While agriculture loans do not typically require collateral, the other two types do. Real estate is the most common form of collateral; MFIs accept movable assets, though rarely.

Digital Financial Services

The national Financial Sector Development Strategy for 2016–2025, will be renewed in 2020. It addresses financial inclusion and incorporates digital financial services (DFS). The initial DFS development stage focusses on payment systems, both domestic and foreign. NBC introduced a Fast Payment system to allow near- and real-time fund transfers between and among commercial banks and microfinance deposit-taking institutions. Cambodian Shared Switch (a system facilitating interbank debit card transactions) and the Retail Pay system (a real time fund transfer system) have had a soft launch, with official launch scheduled for 2020. Mobile banking phone applications exist, but the degree of penetration remains unknown; NBC says that usage is increasing each year. According to the MEF, ACLEDA has been the most aggressive in expanding mobile banking, but this has occurred almost entirely in urban areas.

In terms of physical infrastructure, ACLEDA has 262 branches nationwide, at least one in every district of every province. It has the largest ATM network (which helps facilitate electronic infrastructure), accounting for 20% of the national total. ACLEDA's mobile phone application (app) has over one million registered users, or 9% of the adult population. The app can handle regular transactions such as bill payments and fund transfers. In 2020, the app may be able to let users apply for loans and preapprovals. While competitors also have mobile phone apps, ACLEDA's is easiest to use, with a $6 monthly fee.

MFIs have mobile phone banking apps that can handle a variety of transactions, and penetration is increasing. There are payment services institutions with agents to assist MFIs with mobile payments. These include WING (7,000 agents), TrueMoney (7,000 to 8,000), and E-Money (5,000).

The TSC is assisting with the development of national DFS policies. For example, it has begun researching other countries to find DFS best practices and solutions.

Capital Markets

The Cambodia Securities Exchange (CSX) began operations in 2012. There were five listed companies as of end-2019. The Debt Securities Listing Rule was promulgated on 26 December 2017. The first listed bond of HKL MFI was on 5 December 2018. In 2019, two more bonds listed, LOLC MFI and ABA Bank.

The CSX initially targeted large companies, but many could not list due to tax compliance issues. For example, Cambodia's tax system uses sales revenue as its tax base for income, so under-reporting is prevalent. In early 2019, a subdecree on Tax Incentives in Securities Sector was adopted to deal with the issue. The incentives provided include a 50% reduction on income tax for 3 years and a 10 year tax amnesty. Previously, listing on the main board required 3 years of audited financial statements, but the SECC amended the Prakas on equity issuance to lower the requirement to 2 years if they list on the main board and 1 year to list on the "growth" board. Previously, tax authorities could request up to 10 years of financial records, a major disincentive to list. The new regulations should allow more MSMEs to list on the CSX growth board.

In addition to regulatory reform, the SECC and CSX introduced other initiatives for companies, particularly MSMEs, to list. One CSX-sponsored program invites business owners to meet investors in an informal setting on an ad hoc basis. Since it began in 2017, there have been 10 meetings, involving 30 speakers and 1,000 participants. The SECC organizes an Excellence Program, which promotes MSME competitiveness and sustainability through support and knowledge sharing. Issues include how and why to legalize companies, and how to meet corporate governance and international financial reporting standards. The program helps speed the process for companies going public. Participants receive training and consultation for free from the SECC and other stakeholders, including the CSX, underwriters, law firms, and accounting firms.

Markets have been erratic since 2012. For example, the CSX Composite Index fell by 48.3% between 2012 and 2017, only to rebound by 121.1% between 2017 and 2019 (Figure 4.5A and Table 4.5). For 2012–2019 the index grew 14.3% (a compound annual growth rate of 1.9%). Market capitalization increased 420.3% (a compound annual growth rate of 26.6%), from KR539.2 billion ($135 million) to KR2.8 trillion ($687 million). The increase in trading value over the period has also been impressive, with overall growth of 177.8% (a compound annual growth rate of 15.7%). There was high volatility, with a decline of 86.8% from 2012 to 2015 (KR53.5 billion to KR7.0 billion), followed by a sharp recovery to KR148.9 billion ($36 million) in 2019. Trading volumes expanded 123.7% (a compound annual growth rate of 12.2%), from 6.9 million shares in 2012 to 15.5 million shares in 2019.

Listing has been slow (Figure 4.5B). It takes between 1.5 years and 4 years to prepare an initial public offering (IPO). Just one new company listed each year from 2014 to 2017 to reach the 2019 total of five listed firms.

There are successful start-ups in the capital market. While there are few tech-startups, they are young, innovative, and ambitious. Venture capital is nascent and unregulated. CSX cites five to six venture capital funds, with two to three foreign-owned. There are no professional business angel networks, just an informal group which pools their money to invest in start-ups.

CSX runs a listing incubator program to prepare companies to list. It involves free consultations on financial reporting, accounting, and corporate governance, among others. Since its start in 2016, it has served 10 companies in education, trading, and services. They contact CSX to start the process; both large companies and MSMEs participate.

The CSX cites several obstacles to capital market development: (i) low liquidity, (ii) issuer quality, (iii) tax compliance, and (iv) trading currency. For example, until August 2019, banks could not list, although they are usually the strongest candidates to tap capital markets. In August 2019, however, ABA Bank held a bond listing, and ACLEDA Bank is planning an IPO (April 2020), expecting the increase of issuer quality. The tax incentive subdecree of January 2019 is a step in the right direction to encourage tax compliance. Cambodian riel is a trading currency in the stock market instead of US dollars, which is an issue of trading to attract more foreign investors.

CSX is helping firms learn how attract more external growth financing—a modest investment goes through several financing rounds to accumulate a far greater amount of capital. But this sequence requires clean company books for tax compliance and financial reporting. Income taxes reduced by 20% in 2018 and further by 50% in 2019, reducing the corporate income tax rate from 20% to 10%. CSX is cooperating with the Stock Exchange of Thailand to offer depository receipts; while expected to start in 2020, time will be needed for implementation and to comply with regulations.

Figure 4.5: Equity Market

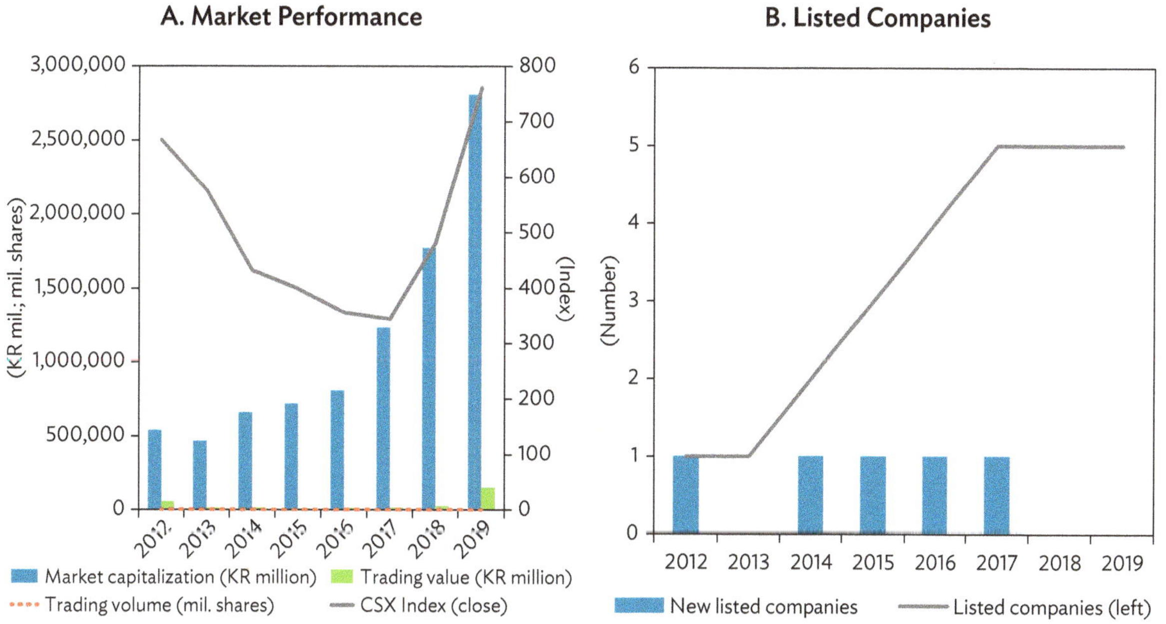

Source: ADB Asia SME Monitor 2020 database. Data from Cambodia Securities Exchange (CSX).

SECC data show foreign investors hold 17% of total accounts and comprise 50% of trading volume. Among institutional investors, insurance companies are starting to invest in bonds. The national pension fund does not participate in capital markets, using savings accounts contributions.

Financial Infrastructure

Credit Bureau Cambodia (CBC) has been in operation since 2012. As of end-2019, CBC had 161 members, including commercial and specialized banks, MFIs, and rural credit institutions (100% of formal lending institutions). Members must upload their full credit information at least monthly; for account openings and closures, updates occur weekly. In addition, members must check their credit boards to understand borrower conditions. In July 2019, the CBC launched a commercial credit platform.

CBC covers 5 million consumers out of an adult population of 9 million. According to the NBC, as of end-2019 there were 4 million active borrowers in Cambodia with a total of 3.3 million active accounts. In addition, there were 4,000 commercial accounts. CBC estimates that 68% of the loans in their portfolio belong to MSMEs. As for commercial reporting, CBC had more than 21,000 legal entities in its database at end-2019. There were 1,283 companies holding 5,371 active commercial loan accounts in the market.

The consumer credit report includes a consumer profile, demographic data, account information, number of accounts, credit limits, tenure of outstanding loans, loan amounts, repayment history, and employment details. As of July 2019, 200 consumers per month checked their credit reports. While this is small, it is a dramatic increase from 2017–2018, when only 10–20 people would have their credit checked. Starting January 2019, the general public could also request their credit report from CBC through its authorized agents, ACLEDA and AMK. According to the NBC, 3,172 personal credit reports were issued to the general public in 2019.

The financial infrastructure needed to promote MSME access to finance remains underdeveloped. Key institutions such as credit guarantee schemes and credit bureaus are either in the planning or nascent stage. Capital markets have made strides since 2014 yet remain relatively illiquid. The venture capital sector and business angel networks have yet to be developed. Use of fintech on any measurable scale is likely several years in the future. Given this infrastructure, NBC has adopted those elements of Basel I, II, and III that it can without causing too much of a burden.

3. Policies and Regulations

- The government has articulated its medium-term development vision in its National Strategic Development Plan 2018–2023 (NSDP).
- MSME development is engrained within the NSDP's private sector development and employment component: the government has an SME Development Plan and Five-year Implementation Plan to support the NSDP.
- The government's Industrial Development Policy 2015–2025 incorporates financial development and overall development in its framework.
- The Agriculture Strategic Development Plan, under the Ministry of Agriculture, Forestry, and Fisheries, supports the NSDP and the many agriculture MSMEs.
- The government adopted a National Financial Inclusion Strategy 2019–2025 in 2019; the central bank's Financial Sector Development Strategy 2016–2025, with financial inclusion as one of its pillars.

MSME Development

The government articulated its medium-term socioeconomic development vision in its NSDP—Rectangular Strategy-Phase IV 2018–2023, released September 2018. The strategy is "rectangular" as each of its four major components consists of four "sides," or subcomponents. The four major components are (i) human resource development, (ii) economic diversification, (iii) private sector development and employment, and (iv) inclusive and sustainable development. According to the National Institute of Statistics, the promotion of private sector development and employment is primarily driven by MSMEs.

There are several line ministries involved with achieving NSDP objectives. For example, MISTI has drafted (as of November 2019) a Small and Medium Enterprise Development Policy and Five-year Implementation Plan 2020–2024, which has five strategic imperatives: (i) enhance policy and regulatory environment; (ii) promote entrepreneurship and human capital development; (iii) promote productivity, technology, and innovation; (iv) enhance foreign access and internationalization; and (v) increase access to finance. The plan specifies key performance indicators for monitoring and evaluating policy implementation, such as setting formal MSME registration targets and assessing MSME owner satisfaction with government services.

The Industrial Development Policy 2015–2025 has four primary objectives covering financial and overall development: (i) attracting foreign direct investment and mobilizing domestic private investment for expanding industrial development, export market development, and promoting development of technology and technology transfer; (ii) developing and modernizing MSMEs by expanding and strengthening manufacturing, modernizing and officially registering enterprises, promoting technology, and strengthening industrial linkages between domestic and foreign enterprises (specifically in agro-industries); (iii) improving the legal environment to enhance competitiveness, such as improving the investment climate and promoting trade facilitation, providing market information, and reducing business transaction fees; and (iv) coordinating support policies, such as human resource development, skills training and industrial relations, urbanization, land management and use (in line with the Land Policy and the National Policy on Land Management), infrastructure development (which includes transport/logistics systems and digital connectivity, electricity and clean water supply), and other supporting services (such as public, social, and financial services).

There are a variety of incentive schemes to motivate MSMEs and other stakeholders to achieve these strategic directions. For example, one proposal is to arrange apprenticeships between potential entrepreneurs and relevant MSMEs for women and youth, especially in high-priority sectors such as manufacturing and agriculture.

The MAFF promulgates its Agriculture Strategic Development Plan in support of national development objectives, including the many MSMEs in agriculture. It has five elements: (i) enhancing agricultural productivity and diversification, along with expanding agribusiness; (ii) promoting animal health and commercial production; (iii) strengthening sustainable fishery resource management and development; (iv) strengthening sustainable forestry and wildlife resource management and development; and (v) effectively strengthening institutional management and supporting service and human resource development.

Funds are available for MSME training under the MEF and other agencies. For example, under the Skill Development Fund (SDF), the government contributed $5 million for 3 years (with ADB adding $9.6 million) to provide critical skills training identified by the private sector (such as technical skills to operate machinery). ADB also provides technical support

The SDF has two main objectives: (i) address skills mismatches and (ii) alleviate the shortage of skilled labor. Of the $9.6 million ADB contributes over 3 years, $7 million is for training and $2.6 million for operations. Training is demand-driven; the private sector identifies a deficiency and the fund covers 75% of the cost. The SDF has served 600 students from 12 vocational-technical schools. Initially, few MSMEs were involved; but there were more in the second round. MSMEs receive 60%–70% of the funding. The SDF tries different approaches to skill-building. It tests which methods work and which do not, and adjusts the curriculum accordingly. Prominent training sectors include information and communications technology (ICT) and manufacturing assembly. Primary skills include computer programming and soft skills.

The MEF noted that many MSMEs lack the commitment to improve skills—a major constraint to further expansion—and a lack of absorptive capacity. The government is willing to contribute $5 million annually to the fund, but there are few workers and/or MSMEs willing to participate.

The Entrepreneurship Development Fund (EDF) is another MEF initiative to develop MSMEs. The government provides $5 million annually to construct an ecosystem for MSMEs, involving business matching and incubators, among others. The EDF has two major objectives: (i) improve the entrepreneurial culture and (ii) build capacity, particularly access to finance and improved productivity. The EDF supports the TSC incubator.

Other agencies involved in MSME development include the Ministry of Post and Telecommunications, which has a $4 million fund to support start-ups and MSMEs in ICT. The Ministry of Labor and Vocational Training also provides training from the supply side (versus the SDF's focus on demand).

The CCC had an extensive arbitration training curriculum from 2008 to 2012. Twenty-five participants would travel to Germany and Italy twice a year to attend seminars and arbitration hearings. In July 2019, the PRC invited the CCC to meet in Kunming to revive the training, and it has offered to establish an arbitration center in Phnom Penh in the near future. The CCC also started e-commerce training in 2019 in partnership with the Singapore government; 40 members attended in July 2019.

In the long term, the MEF envisions a Skill Development Committee that spans multiple agencies, departments, and stakeholders. The committee would plan strategy and coordinate efforts to build workforce skills. In addition, an entrepreneurship promotion center, the Khmer Enterprise, will assist start-ups with capacity building in areas such as tax compliance, accounting and bookkeeping, and financial reporting.

The CCC cites four of the greatest challenges facing MSME development:

- Access to finance: 90% of MSMEs have a lack of adequate financial reporting, collateral, and credit history; they rely on loans from family and friends when they need capital.
- Electricity costs remain high, despite government efforts that lowered tariffs since 2017. The MEF estimates that electricity costs in Cambodia are 14% higher than in Thailand and 20% above those in the Lao PDR as of end-April 2020.
- Shipping and logistics costs are high.
- Access to technology: Cambodia wants to connect to the world, and there are tech-savvy young people who are willing to start a new venture; but overall they are few in number.

Financial Inclusion

On 12 July 2019, the government adopted a National Financial Inclusion Strategy for 2019–2025, in part to boost MSME access to finance. The strategy complements the existing Financial Sector Development Strategy 2016–2025 and the Rectangular Strategy-Phase IV. According to the strategy, only 59% of Cambodian adults have access to formal financial services, another 12% use informal finance with the remaining 29% unbanked. The key barrier to financial inclusion is the low level of financial literacy. A variety of interventions are being proposed. The strategy will focus on increasing use of four financial products: savings, payments, credit, and insurance.

The policies aim to increase access to quality formal financial services and reduce the financial exclusion of women by half (from 27% to 13%). They also aim to increase usage of formal financial services from 59% to 70% by 2025 and improve household welfare. They support economic growth in several ways: (i) encourage savings in formal financial institutions, (ii) promote innovative credit products for MSMEs, (iii) enable the expansion of payment system capabilities, (iv) improve broader access to insurance, (v) strengthen the capacity of financial sector regulators, and (vi) increase consumer empowerment and protection along with financial sector transparency.

The NBC is in its third round of financial development (the first began in 2006). The current Financial Sector Development Strategy 2016–2025 has six objectives: (i) financial stability, (ii) crisis preparedness, (iii) banking supervision, (iv) identifying and preventing money laundering and other illegal or terrorist activity, (v) consumer protection, and (vi) financial inclusion (this explicitly ties NBC development work to widening access to finance within the context of the NSDP).

While Cambodia continues to develop, the government is using its development vision to coordinate various line ministries in support of MSME development. MISTI and MAFF have their own strategic plans to further MSME development, both overall and within their specific jurisdictions, while NBC focuses upon financial inclusion and financial development.

Data Tables

Table 4.1: MSME Definition

A. Definition until 2019

Item	Micro	Small	Medium
Assets	$50,000 and below	$50,000 - $250,000	$250,000 - $500,000
Number of employees	Fewer than 10	10-50	51-100

Source: ADB Asia SME Monitor 2020 database. Data from Small and Medium Enterprise Development Framework of 2005.

B. Definition after 2020

Sector	Item	Micro	Small	Medium
Manufacturing	FTE Workforce Count	1-2	3-49	50-499
	Assets (excluding land)	$50,000 and below	$50,000 - $500,000	$500,000 - $1,000,000
Agriculture, Forestry and Fishing	FTE Workforce Count	1-2	3-49	50-199
	Assets	$50,000 and below	$50,000 - $500,000	$500,000 - $1,000,000
Wholesale and Retail Trade	FTE Workforce Count	1-2	3-49	50-199
	Assets (excluding land and buildings)	$50,000 and below	$50,000 - $500,000	$500,000 - $1,000,000
Other Services	FTE Workforce Count	1-4	5-49	50-99
	Assets (excluding land)	$50,000 and below	$50,000 - $500,000	$500,000 - $1,000,000
Other Activities	FTE Workforce Count	1-9	10-49	50-199
	Assets	$50,000 and below	$50,000 - $500,000	$500,000 - $1,000,000

FTE = full-time equivalent, MSME = micro, small, and medium-sized enterprise.

Notes: FTE refers to the ratio of the total number of paid hours during a period (part-time, full-time, contracted) by the number of working hours in that same period. The MSME definition uses US dollar amounts for asset thresholds.

Source: ADB Asia SME Monitor 2020 database. Data from Small and Medium Enterprise Development Policy and Five-Year Implementation Plan 2020-2024, Forthcoming.

Table 4.2: MSME Landscape

End of period data

Item	2009	2010	2011	2012	2013	2014	2015	2016	2017	2018	2019
NUMBER OF ENTERPRISES											
Number of enterprises, total	376,761	--	463,363	--	--	513,759	--	--	--	--	--
Number of MSMEs	376,069	--	462,582	--	--	512,870	--	--	--	--	--
Number of large enterprises	692	--	781	--	--	889	--	--	--	--	--
MSME to total (%)	99.8	--	99.8	--	--	99.8	--	--	--	--	--
MSME growth (%)	--	--	23.0	--	--	10.9	--	--	--	--	--
MSMEs by sector (% share)											
Agriculture, forestry, and fisheries	--	--	--	--	--	--	--	--	--	--	--
Manufacturing	22.4	--	15.3	--	--	13.9	--	--	--	--	--
Transportation and communication	--	--	--	--	--	--	--	--	--	--	--
Construction	--	--	--	--	--	--	--	--	--	--	--
Wholesale and retail trade	52.7	--	58.0	--	--	59.6	--	--	--	--	--
Other services	24.9	--	26.7	--	--	26.5	--	--	--	--	--
Others	--	--	--	--	--	--	--	--	--	--	--
Number of MSMEs by region (% share)											
Capital city	--	--	18.2	--	--	18.8	--	--	--	--	--
Others	--	--	81.8	--	--	81.2	--	--	--	--	--
EMPLOYMENT											
Number of employment, total	1,469,712	--	1,610,610	--	--	1,874,670	--	--	--	--	--
Number of employment by MSMEs	1,099,647	--	1,158,871	--	--	1,345,100	--	--	--	--	--
Number of employment by large enterprises	370,065	--	451,739	--	--	529,570	--	--	--	--	--
MSME employees to total (%)	74.8	--	72.0	--	--	71.8	--	--	--	--	--
MSME employees growth (%)	--	--	5.4	--	--	16.1	--	--	--	--	--
Share of female employees to total employees (%)*	43.3	42.3	51.1	42.6	42.2	42.7	43.7	33.3	33.3	--	--
Employment by MSME by sector (% share)											
Agriculture, forestry, and fisheries	--	--	--	--	--	--	--	--	--	--	--
Manufacturing	21.3	--	16.0	--	--	15.2	--	--	--	--	--
Transportation and communication	--	--	--	--	--	--	--	--	--	--	--
Construction	--	--	--	--	--	--	--	--	--	--	--
Wholesale and retail trade	39.1	--	44.2	--	--	46.7	--	--	--	--	--
Other services	39.6	--	39.8	--	--	38.1	--	--	--	--	--
Others	--	--	--	--	--	--	--	--	--	--	--
Employment by MSMEs by region (% share)											
Capital city	--	--	23.4	--	--	20.0	--	--	--	--	--
Others	--	--	76.6	--	--	80.0	--	--	--	--	--
CONTRIBUTION TO GDP											
MSMEs contribution to GDP (KR million)	--	--	--	--	--	--	--	--	--	--	--
MSMEs contribution to GDP (% share)	--	--	--	--	--	--	--	--	--	--	--
MSME GDP growth (%)	--	--	--	--	--	--	--	--	--	--	--
MSME GDP by sector (% share)											
Agriculture, forestry, and fisheries	--	--	--	--	--	--	--	--	--	--	--
Manufacturing	--	--	--	--	--	--	--	--	--	--	--
Transportation and communication	--	--	--	--	--	--	--	--	--	--	--
Construction	--	--	--	--	--	--	--	--	--	--	--
Wholesale and retail trade	--	--	--	--	--	--	--	--	--	--	--
Other services	--	--	--	--	--	--	--	--	--	--	--
Others	--	--	--	--	--	--	--	--	--	--	--
MSME GDP by region (% share)											
Capital city	--	--	--	--	--	--	--	--	--	--	--
Others	--	--	--	--	--	--	--	--	--	--	--
EXPORTS											
Total export value (KR million)	13,071,036	15,810,632	20,359,192	22,706,700	28,140,259	33,291,042	37,826,036	41,548,852	45,360,352	52,278,563	--
Total export growth (%)	(8.5)	21.0	28.8	11.5	23.9	18.3	13.6	9.8	9.2	15.3	--
MSME export value (KR million)	--	--	--	--	--	--	--	--	--	--	--
MSME export to total export value (%)	--	--	--	--	--	--	--	--	--	--	--
MSME export growth (%)	--	--	--	--	--	--	--	--	--	--	--
IMPORTS											
Total import value (KR million)	20,318,192	26,686,033	32,908,906	36,800,327	42,665,094	48,989,593	53,824,767	57,105,987	62,649,795	75,846,469	--
Total import growth (%)	(3.9)	31.3	23.3	11.8	15.9	14.8	9.9	6.1	9.7	21.1	--
MSME import value (KR million)	--	--	--	--	--	--	--	--	--	--	--
MSME import to total import value (%)	--	--	--	--	--	--	--	--	--	--	--
MSME import growth (%)	--	--	--	--	--	--	--	--	--	--	--

GDP = gross domestic product, MSME = micro, small, and medium-sized enterprise.

* Data refer to average wage employment across sectors.

Source: ADB Asia SME Monitor 2020 database. Data from Nationwide Establishment Listing of Cambodia 2009; Economic Census of Cambodia 2011 and 2014; Small and Medium Enterprise Department, Ministry of Industry, Science, Technology and Innovation; National Insitute of Statistics.

Table 4.3: Bank Credit

End of period data

Item	2007	2008	2009	2010	2011	2012	2013	2014	2015	2016	2017	2018	2019
COMMERCIAL BANKS													
Number of commercial banks - total	24	30	33	35	35	39	43	44	47	51	54	56	62
State-owned banks	--	--	--	--	--	--	--	--	--	--	--	--	--
Private sector banks	24	30	33	35	35	39	43	44	47	51	54	56	62
Credit													
Loans outstanding, total (KR million)	6,334,702	9,803,683	10,466,705	13,135,307	17,474,377	23,354,231	29,370,349	38,080,618	46,632,379	56,019,054	65,659,251	81,242,164	102,489,233
Loans outstanding in domestic currency (KR million)	142,444	189,759	285,345	336,493	394,650	392,539	435,873	449,306	597,045	839,765	1,296,746	3,526,195	10,962,193
Loans outstanding in foreign currency (KR million)	6,117,253	9,554,169	9,977,441	12,663,776	17,050,077	23,059,975	29,013,608	37,976,772	47,802,745	55,545,144	66,287,046	80,289,835	95,653,543
Loan growth (%)	82.7	52.7	5.2	29.1	33.5	35.1	25.8	27.1	23.2	20.5	17.2	24.3	23.9
Total commercial bank loans to GDP (%)	17.9	23.2	24.3	27.9	33.6	41.2	47.7	56.7	63.2	68.8	73.3	83.5	92.0
Lending rate in domestic currency loan (%)	--	--	23.0	22.5	19.4	26.7	25.7	20.5	20.1	21.5	15.5	9.5	8.7
Lending rate in foreign currency loan (%)	--	--	16.4	17.2	15.4	13.4	11.1	11.6	8.3	12.0	10.7	7.1	8.0
Gross nonperforming loans (NPLs) (KR million)	218,012	360,291	457,434	400,570	424,682	571,504	791,761	844,332	946,406	1,345,064	1,593,065	1,800,911	2,012,117
Gross NPLs to total loans (%)	3.4	3.7	4.4	3.0	2.4	2.4	2.7	2.2	2.0	2.4	2.3	2.1	2.0
Loans outstanding by sector (% share)													
Agriculture, forestry, and fisheries	--	5.3	6.7	6.7	8.9	9.6	9.7	10.7	10.7	10.7	10.3	8.9	7.3
Manufacturing	--	10.0	8.7	8.7	9.2	9.3	11.0	9.6	7.6	6.8	6.3	5.4	4.4
Transportation and communication	--	3.9	4.6	4.6	4.5	4.6	2.9	2.1	2.4	2.8	2.7	2.8	2.8
Construction	--	7.9	8.6	7.0	7.4	7.5	7.7	7.3	7.2	8.6	9.3	9.2	9.5
Wholesale and retail trade	--	29.1	31.1	35.4	32.4	33.2	32.9	32.4	32.0	31.6	30.0	27.5	26.4
Other services*	--	43.0	39.7	36.6	36.3	34.5	34.7	36.9	38.9	38.2	40.2	45.3	48.5
Others**	--	0.9	0.6	1.0	1.3	1.3	1.2	1.0	1.3	1.2	1.1	0.9	1.2
Deposits													
Deposits, total (KR million)	9,997,426	10,708,815	14,792,869	19,156,265	23,968,635	30,866,488	35,893,242	47,895,095	55,979,084	65,373,537	78,656,057	98,663,143	117,221,817
Deposits in domestic currency (KR million)	239,517	380,275	475,599	541,322	725,149	1,050,725	1,327,907	1,662,641	597,045	3,295,703	4,131,657	5,445,853	7,507,403
Deposits in foreign currency (KR million)	9,682,955	9,906,742	13,365,967	16,937,903	20,248,702	25,859,875	28,876,053	38,064,388	47,802,745	52,404,076	65,552,786	83,231,042	96,050,854
Deposit rate in foreign currency (%)	--	--	5.3	4.4	4.3	4.4	4.3	4.1	4.6	4.5	4.4	4.8	5.0
Deposit rate in domestic currency (%)	--	--	6.5	6.6	6.1	5.9	5.8	5.8	6.1	6.3	5.7	6.3	6.0

GDP = gross domestic product, MSME = micro, small, and medium-sized enterprise.

* Includes the following: hotels and restaurants, other non-financial services, real estate activities, rental and operational leasing activities, owner-occupied housing only, financial institutions, personal lending, other lending, and credit cards. ** Includes utilities, and mining and quarrying.

Source: ADB Asia SME Monitor 2020 database. Data from National Bank of Cambodia.

Table 4.4: Nonbank Finance

End of period data

Item	2007	2008	2009	2010	2011	2012	2013	2014	2015	2016	2017	2018	2019
NUMBER OF NONBANK FINANCE INSTITUTIONS													
Microfinance institutions	17	18	20	23	30	35	36	39	53	69	76	80	83
Credit unions/cooperatives	--	--	--	--	--	--	--	--	--	--	--	--	--
Finance companies	--	--	--	--	--	--	--	--	--	--	--	--	--
Pawnshops	--	--	--	--	--	--	--	--	--	--	--	--	--
Leasing companies	--	--	--	--	--	1	2	6	7	10	10	15	15
Factoring companies	--	--	--	--	--	--	--	--	--	--	--	--	--
Insurance companies	--	--	--	--	--	--	--	--	--	--	--	--	--
Others	--	--	--	--	--	--	--	--	--	--	--	--	--
MICROFINANCE INSTITUTIONS													
Financing outstanding, total (KR million)	617,271	1,130,585	1,244,970	1,724,841	2,591,263	3,538,889	5,261,752	7,299,407	12,244,357	12,661,490	17,236,445	21,813,240	29,357,486
Total financing to GDP (%)	1.8	2.7	2.9	3.7	5.0	6.0	8.5	10.7	16.7	15.6	19.2	21.9	26.5
Annual financing rate (%, on average)	--	--	--	--	--	31.8	32.4	31.4	31.2	31.2	20.7	18.9	16.9
Gross nonperforming financing (NPFs) (KR million)	1,171	4,719	34,847	20,361	5,753	10,284	30,880	52,119	94,788	182,117	270,395	275,483	224,340
Gross NPFs to total financing (%)	0.2	0.4	2.8	1.2	0.2	0.3	0.6	0.7	0.8	1.4	1.6	1.3	0.8
Number of customers financed, total	600,485	825,652	871,412	978,077	1,141,913	1,301,680	1,550,616	1,774,815	2,037,424	1,889,914	1,776,467	1,872,916	2,109,170
Financing outstanding by sector (% share)													
Agriculture, forestry, and fisheries	45.2	43.8	42.2	42.4	41.2	39.4	38.0	37.6	35.2	33.3	31.4	21.2	19.4
Manufacturing	--	--	--	--	--	--	--	--	--	--	--	--	0.8
Transportation and communication	3.8	4.0	3.6	3.7	3.0	4.5	3.7	3.9	3.4	4.3	5.7	5.1	5.7
Construction	1.8	1.8	2.3	2.6	2.8	3.7	4.9	4.4	3.7	3.2	4.9	4.2	3.5
Wholesale and retail trade	32.5	33.3	35.4	28.8	25.7	24.2	22.8	20.6	19.4	18.5	0.9	17.7	18.3
Other services	6.8	7.4	7.8	9.4	10.4	10.3	10.6	10.1	10.7	9.9	12.9	11.0	14.5
Others	10.0	9.7	8.7	13.1	16.9	17.8	20.0	23.4	27.6	30.8	44.2	40.8	37.7
Financing outstanding by region (% share)													
Capital city	--	--	--	--	--	--	--	--	--	--	14.9	12.5	11.8
Others	--	--	--	--	--	--	--	--	--	--	85.1	87.5	88.2
LEASING COMPANIES													
Financing outstanding, total (KR million)					--	--	--	--	344,974	405,039	525,343	713,810	1,169,609
Total financing to GDP (%)	--	--	--	--	--	--	--	--	0.5	0.6	0.6	0.7	1.1
Annual financing rate (%, on average)	--	--	--	--	--	--	--	--	--	--	--	--	--
Gross nonperforming financing (NPFs) (KR million)	--	--	--	--	--	--	--	--	--	28,769	27,815	59,916	38,352
Gross NPFs to total financing (%)	--	--	--	--	--	--	--	--	5.3	5.9	5.3	8.4	3.3
Number of customers financed, total	--	--	--	--	--	--	--	--	43,413	61,372	64,252	72,921	95,769
Financing outstanding by sector (% share)													
Agriculture, forestry, and fisheries	--	--	--	--	--	--	--	--	28.1	23.4	19.9	7.5	9.3
Manufacturing	--	--	--	--	--	--	--	--	--	--	--	--	--
Transportation and communication	--	--	--	--	--	--	--	--	2.6	6.4	4.6	9.3	14.2
Construction	--	--	--	--	--	--	--	--	14.7	12.8	7.7	7.2	6.9
Wholesale and retail trade	--	--	--	--	--	--	--	--	16.5	13.6	5.0	6.7	6.1
Other services	--	--	--	--	--	--	--	--	6.7	5.0	2.1	6.0	17.9
Others	--	--	--	--	--	--	--	--	31.3	38.8	60.7	63.4	45.5
Financing outstanding by region (% share)													
Capital city	--	--	--	--	--	--	--	--	--	--	--	--	--
Others	--	--	--	--	--	--	--	--	--	--	--	--	--

GDP = gross domestic product.

Source: ADB Asia SME Monitor 2020 database. Data from National Bank of Cambodia.

Table 4.5: Capital Markets

End of period data

Item	2012*	2013	2014	2015	2016	2017	2018	2019
EQUITY MARKET								
Main Board								
Index	667	576	432	399	356	345	481	762
Market capitalization (KR million)	539,234	466,176	658,682	716,388	804,540	1,230,679	1,771,678	2,805,807
Growth (%)	--	(13.5)	41.3	8.8	12.3	53.0	44.0	58.4
Trading value (KR million)	53,590	13,720	12,113	7,040	10,024	12,570	24,902	148,879
Trading volume (million shares)	6.9	2.2	1.8	1.4	2.6	3.6	3.8	15.5
Number of listed companies	1	1	2	3	4	5	5	5
Number of IPOs	1	0	1	1	1	1	0	0
Number of delisted companies	0	0	0	0	0	0	0	0

IPO = initial public offering.
* The first trading date was 18 April 2012. Thus, data from 18 April to 31 December for 2012.
Source: ADB Asia SME Monitor 2020 database. Data from Cambodia Securities Exchange.

Table 4.6: Policies and Regulations

Name	Responsible Entity	Outline
Regulations		
Name		Outline
Nonfinance regulations		
Resolution Number 45 S.S.R (August 2007)		Establishing the SME Sub-Committee (or Sub-Steering Committee on small and medium enterprises [SMEs]).
Resolution Number 27 S.S.R (November 2008)		Recomposition of the SME Sub-Committee (or Sub-Steering Committee on SMEs).
Prakas Number 078 MOC/M2002		The Prakas requires small enterprises not registered under the Law on Commercial Rules and Registration to obtain a license to operate commercial activities and services through Ministry of Commerce's provincial-municipal departments.
Finance regulations		
The Law on Banking and Financial Institutions		Regulations of banks and financial institutions; SME definition.
The Law on the Issuance and Trading of Non-Government Securities		Regulate securities exchange.
Prakas on Licensing of Microfinance Institutions		Microfinance institutions (MFIs) registration and licensing.
Prakas on Licensing of Microfinance Deposit-taking Institutions		MFI deposit-taking institution registration and licensing.
Prakas on Financial Leasing Companies		Guidance for financial leasing companies.
Prakas on Credit Reporting		Framework for establishment of a credit reporting system.
Prakas on Introduction of Financial Reporting Template for SMEs		Issues templates for SME application for financing with banking institutions.
Prakas on Licensing to Pawn Business, Buying-Selling of Pawn Pledges and Liens by Cession		Licensing of pawn businesses.
Anukret of Tax Incentives for Securities Sector		Granting of tax incentives to equity and debt issuing companies.
Regulators and Policymakers		
Name		Responsibility
Sub-committee on Small and Medium Enterprises, Royal Government of Cambodia (RGC)		Inter-ministerial coordination body that led the formulation and implementation of the 2005 SME Development Framework.
Ministry of Agriculture, Forestry and Fisheries (MAFF)		Develop and implement agricultural development policy.
Ministry of Industry, Science, Technology and Innovation (MISTI)		Regulate the SME sector.
Royal Government of Cambodia (RGC)		Introduced banking regulation and bank restructuring programs.
National Bank of Cambodia (NBC)		Regulate and supervise banks and microfinance institutions.
Ministry of Economy and Finance (MOEF)		Regulate and supervise pawnshops, insurance, and real estate.
Securities and Exchange Commission of Cambodia (SECC)		Regulate and supervise the capital market.
Policies		
Name	Responsible Entity	Outline
Nonfinance policies		
SME Development Framework 2005 (February 2006)	MIME	1) Establish an incentive policy and support for SMEs. 2) Prepare a strategy to increase competitiveness capacity for SMEs. 3) Prepare an action plan, promote and support SMEs, as well as follow up and review the implementation. 4) Promote the preparation of regulations on the management of SMEs. 5) Implement other roles related to the promotion and support of SMEs.
SME Development Strategic Framework 2010–2015	MIME	1) Establish the right condition for business and policy environment (e.g., encourage entry and diversification of businesses through easing the cost of starting and doing business). 2) Promote and create opportunities for skill development and technology adoption in SME sector through establishing and implementing a policy and strategic framework on technology adoption. 3) Develop effective mechanism and legal instruments to support and provide incentives to potential SME sectors. 4) Promote business development services focusing on SMEs. 5) Promote industrial and SME clusters.
Small and Medium Enterprise Development Policy and Five-year Implementation Plan 2020-2024, Forthcoming	MISTI	1) Enhance policy and regulatory environment. 2) Promote productivity, technology, and innovation. 3) Promote entrepreneurship and human capital development. 4) Enhance foreign market access and internalization. 5) Increase access to finance.
National Strategic Development Plan 2014–2018 (July 2014)	MISTI	1) Improving investment environment for large industries and SMEs. 2) Strengthening good governance for SMEs through transparent law enforcement. 3) Promoting competitiveness in the SMEs. 4) Setting up a financial service system for SMEs. 5) Enhancing productivity aligned with national, regional, and international standards. 6) Creating enterprise clusters for SMEs. 7) Formulating industrial development policy. 8) Updating the SMEs Development Framework. 9) Aligning private sector development and investment policies with SME and industrial development policy. 10) Adoption of Law on Special Economic Zones. 11) Promoting industrial corridor development along the main national roads. 12) Strengthening the development process in extractive industry, fiscal revenue management, regulatory framework, capacity building, and institutional coordination. 13) Human resource development especially skill training for the industrial sector.
National Strategic Development Plan (NSDP) - Rectangular Strategy - Phase IV 2018-2023 (September 2018)	RGC	1) Human resource development. 2) Economic diversifications. 3) Promotion of private sector development and employment. 4) Inclusive and sustainable development.
Agriculture Strategic Development Plan (ASDP), 2019–2023	MAFF	1) Enhancement of agricultural productivity and diversification, and agribusiness expansion. 2) Promotion of animal health and commercial production. 3) Strengthening of sustainable fisheries resource management and development. 4) Strengthening of sustainable forestry and wildlife resource management and development. 5) Increased effectiveness of strengthening institutional management, supporting service and human resource development.
Industrial Development Policy 2014–2024 (March 2014)	RGC	1) Review framework mechanism for SME development. 2) Regular information on available support to SMEs. 3) Establishing research and development (R&D) fund to meet demands for R&D development. 4) Provides skill training. 5) Enhancing SME corporate governance. 6) Provide other support to SMEs to facilitate their access to finance and new technologies. 7) Improve capacity of national productivity center to promote productivity and quality SMEs.
Industrial Development Policy 2015–2025 (March 2015)	RGC	1) Attracting foreign direct investment and mobilizing domestic private investment for industrial development, export market development and expansion, and promotion of technology development and transfer. 2) Developing and modernizing SMEs by way of expanding and strengthening the manufacturing base, modernizing and officially registering enterprises, promoting technology development and transfer, and strengthening industrial linkages between domestic and foreign enterprises specifically in the agro-industrial sector. 3) Improving the legal environment to enhance competitiveness by way of improving the investment climate and promoting trade facilitation, providing market information and reducing business transactional fees. 4) Coordinating supporting policies such as human resource development, skills training and industrial relations improvement, implementation of land management, urbanization and land use plan in line with the Land Policy and the National Policy on Land Management together with infrastructure development, including transport/logistics system and digital connectivity, electricity and clean water supply; and other supporting services such as public services, social services and financial services.
Finance policies		
Financial Sector Development Strategy 2006–2015, First Update (2006)	NBC	1) Facilitate the development of finance. 2) Integrate informal and formal sectors. 3) Increase benefits to the poor. 4) Increase resource mobilization. 5) Facilitate savings and investment. 6) Improve resource allocation.
Financial Sector Development Strategy 2016–2025, Third Update (October 2016)	NBC	1) Financial stability. 2) Crisis preparedness. 3) Banking supervision. 4) Anti-money laundering and combating the financing terrorsim. 5) Consumer protection. 6) Financial inclusion.
National Financial Inclusion Strategy 2019–2025 (July 2019)	NBC	1) Encourage savings in formal financial institutions. 2) Promote innovative credit products for SMEs. 3) Enable the expansion of payment system capabilities. 4) Improve broader access to insurance. 5) Strengthen the capacity of the financial sector regulators. 6) Increase consumer empowerment and protection, and financial sector transparency.

MIME = Ministry of Industry, Mines, and Energy; MSME = micro, small, and medium-sized enterprise.
Source: ADB Asia SME Monitor 2020 database. Data from SME Development Framework 2005, SME Development Strategic Framework 2010-2015, Financial Sector Development Strategy (2006-2015), Financial Sector Development Strategy (2011-2012), Rectangular Strategy Phase III (2013).

Country Review
Indonesia

Overview

Indonesia has a working age population of 133 million, with a robust economy growing 5.0% in 2019.[45] That growth is underpinned by micro, small, and medium-sized enterprises (MSMEs) which account for 99.9% of total enterprises across the archipelago. In 2018, 97% of the workforce worked for MSMEs, which contributed 61% to the country's gross domestic product (GDP). Traditional wholesale and retail trade dominates the MSME sector. But emerging technology-based start-ups have given MSMEs greater prominence in the Indonesian economy. MSME access to formal financial services has improved moderately, backed by comprehensive government policy support under a national financial inclusion strategy. Venture capital has expanded, much of it invested in high-growth start-ups and digital industries. A dedicated stock market for small and medium-sized enterprises (SMEs) was created in 2019 to accommodate investor demand. Digital financial services spread widely across the archipelago. Financial authorities are now regulating peer-to-peer lenders and equity crowdfunding. MSME policies are being aligned with the national mid-term development plan.

1. MSME Development

- The services sector has the highest growth potential among MSMEs, especially digital technology-based start-ups.
- Growth of the number of workers employed by MSMEs has slowed; wholesale and retail trade is the largest employer among MSMEs.
- The Indonesian economy remains robust, driven by MSMEs and their steadily increasing labor productivity.
- MSME exports remain small, yet hold much potential; internationalizing MSMEs and cluster development can enhance their global market access.
- E-commerce and other digital services have surged, led by domestic start-ups and increasingly adding value to the economy.
- Autonomous business networking communities are expanding, supporting MSME development, especially among young entrepreneurs and start-ups.

Scale of MSMEs

In Indonesia, an MSME is defined as a productive entity owned by an individual or individual business unit with maximum net assets, excluding land and buildings, of Rp10 billion, or with maximum annual sales of Rp50 billion (Law No.20/2008 on Micro, Small, and Medium-sized Enterprises) (Table 5.1). Subsidiaries or branches directly or indirectly owned or controlled by larger firms are excluded, as are foreign-owned and/or foreign-invested firms.

The number of MSMEs has consistently increased for more than a decade—expanding over 2% year-on-year. As of end-2018, there were 64 million MSMEs, accounting for 99.9% of all Indonesian enterprises (Figure 5.1A and

45 Badan Pusat Statistik. Statistical Yearbook of Indonesia 2020. Working age population refers to people aged 15 years and over.

Table 5.2). While the government has not updated annual sector data since 2013, data on MSMEs are available based on the Economic Census 2016, but only for non-agriculture sectors.[46] As of 2012, around half of MSMEs were engaged in agriculture, forestry, and fisheries. Within non-agriculture sectors in 2016, 63.5% of micro and small firms were in wholesale and retail trade (including hotels and restaurants), followed by manufacturing (16.7%); other services—which include finance, real estate, professional, rental, education, health, and art—(10.7%); and transportation and telecommunications (7.3%) (Figure 5.1B). MSME data by region are unavailable.

The services sector holds the highest growth potential among MSMEs, especially digital technology-based start-ups. The Indonesian Agency for Creative Economy[47] (BEKRAF) says the creative economy contributed Rp1,106 trillion (7.5% of GDP) in 2018, with a projected 9.5% increase to Rp1,211 trillion in 2019. The agency projected a 20%–30% growth in the number of start-ups in 2019,[48] given the high demand for digital solutions in business. Although still small, technology-based start-ups are the most promising MSME segment for boosting national productivity and accelerating job creation.

The Indonesian Chamber of Commerce and Industry (KADIN), with two million MSME members, cites two major challenges for MSME development: (i) business registration and (ii) access to finance.[49] It says many MSMEs remain unregistered and operate informally, creating barriers to business development, especially in international trade, with finance the top barrier for MSMEs to survive and grow.

Figure 5.1: Number of MSMEs

A. Overall MSMEs

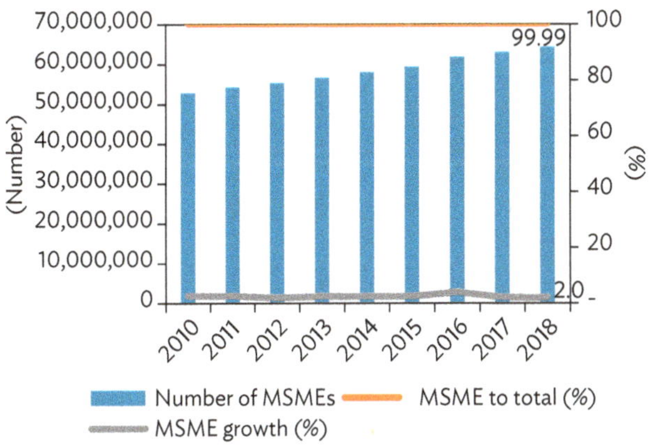

MSME = micro, small, and medium-sized enterprise.

Source: ADB Asia SME Monitor 2020 database. Data from the Ministry of Cooperatives and SMEs.

B. Micro and Small Firms by Sector, 2016

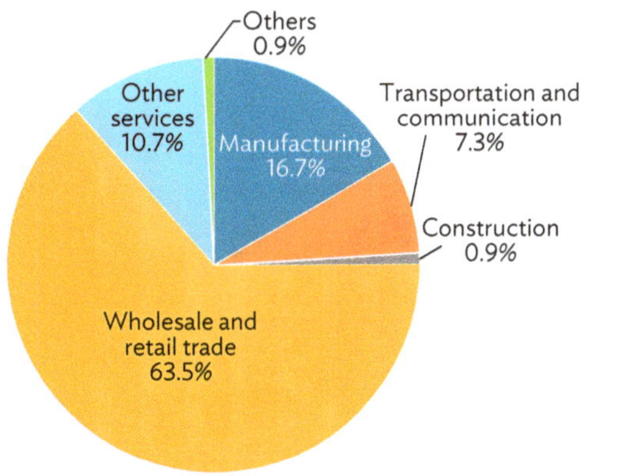

Notes. Data on agriculture, forestry, and fisheries are excluded. "Others" include medium-sized firms.

Source: ADB Asia SME Monitor 2020 database. Data from Badan Pusat Statistik, Economic Census 2016.

---

46 Non-agriculture sectors include manufacturing; transportation and communication; construction; wholesale and retail trade (including accommodation and food services); other services (financial, real estate, professional, rental, education, health, art, and other services); and others (mining and quarrying; electricity, gas, steam, and air conditioning systems; and water supply, sewerage, waste management, and remediation; only this segment includes data on medium-sized firms).

47 The creative economy consists of 16 subsectors: architecture, interior design, visual design, product design, film/animation/video, photography, craft, culinary, music, fashion, application/game developers, publishing, advertising, television/radio, performing arts, and fine arts. These subsectors include start-ups using digital technology.

48 *The Jakarta Post*, 16 April 2019. https://www.thejakartapost.com/news/2019/04/16/number-of-start-ups-projected-to-grow-20-30-percent-this-year-bekraf-says.html

49 Interview with chairman of Indonesian Chamber of Commerce and Industry (KADIN) on 17 July 2019.

Employment

At the end of 2018, MSMEs employed 117 million workers (97% of Indonesia's workforce) (Figure 5.2A). The share of MSME employees to the total has not changed much for more than a decade. However, growth in the number of MSME employees has been slowing (0.5% in 2018), tracing the slower overall growth of the labor market. Annual sector data have been unavailable since 2013. The Economic Census 2016 gives the latest available data for business sectors, excluding agriculture, forestry, and fisheries. Based on the 2012 sector composition, around 40% of MSME employees are likely in agriculture, forestry, and fisheries. In 2016, 54.4% of those employed by micro and small firms in non-agriculture sectors were in wholesale and retail trade, followed by manufacturing (20.5%), other services (19.5%), and transportation and communications (4.7%) (Figure 5.2B). Regional distribution data are unavailable.

In general, female labor force participation has been growing, increasing from 51% in 2009 to 55.4% in 2018. However, this remains below the 83% male participation in 2018 (ASEAN Statistical Yearbook 2019). Female workers accounted for 38.5% of the total workers in Indonesia in 2019 (Badan Pusat Statistik Statistical Yearbook of Indonesia 2020). With 97% of the workforce employed by MSMEs, female workers unlikely represent MSME workers. There remains an opportunity for females to create more jobs, especially by developing women entrepreneurs and promoting female-led start-ups.

Figure 5.2: Employment by MSMEs

A. Overall MSMEs

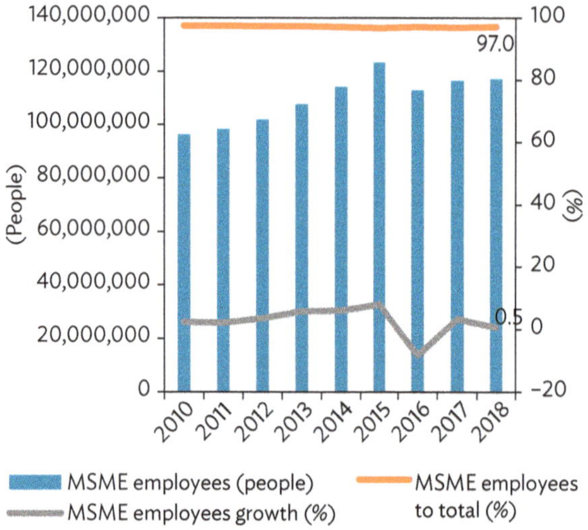

MSME = micro, small, and medium-sized enterprise.

Source: ADB Asia SME Monitor 2020 database. Data from the Ministry of Cooperatives and SMEs.

B. Micro and Small Firms by Sector, 2016

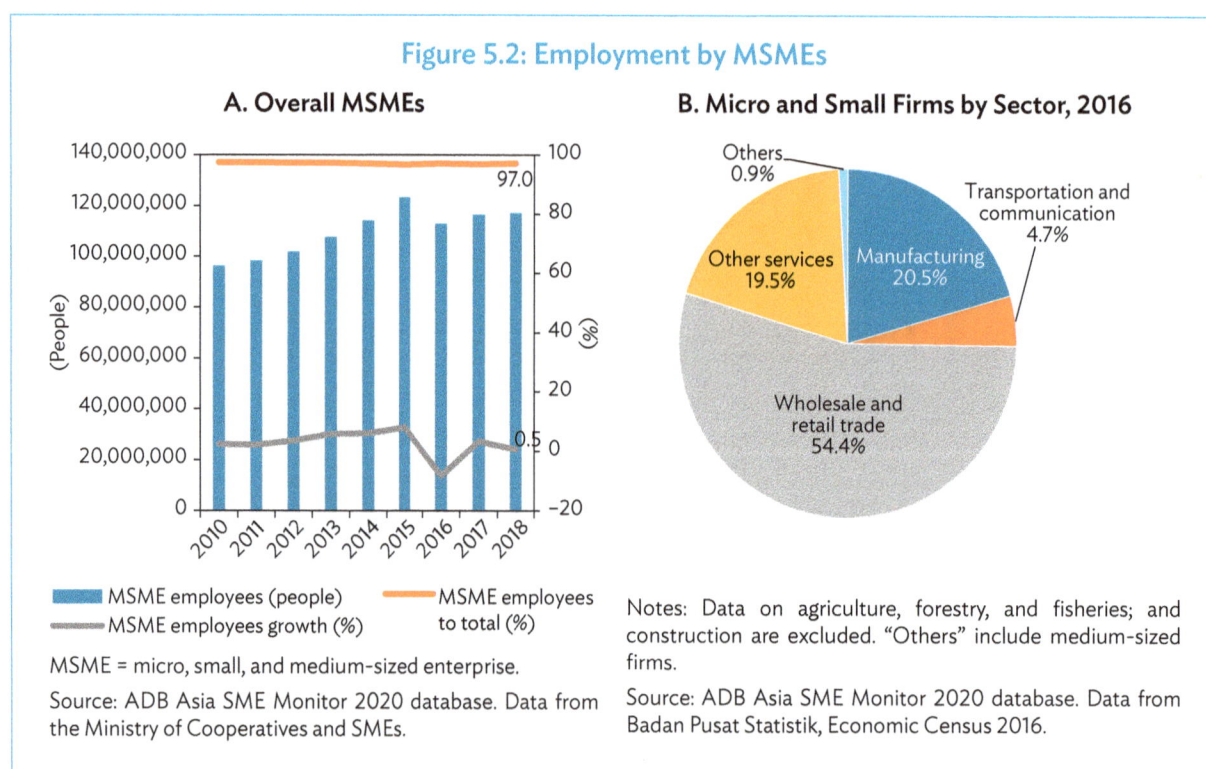

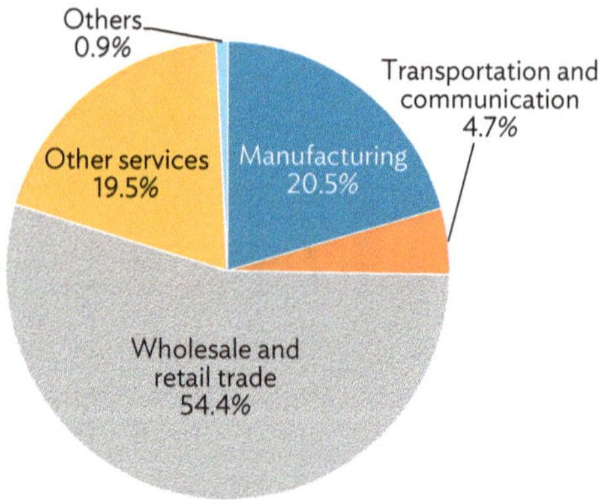

Notes: Data on agriculture, forestry, and fisheries; and construction are excluded. "Others" include medium-sized firms.

Source: ADB Asia SME Monitor 2020 database. Data from Badan Pusat Statistik, Economic Census 2016.

Business Productivity

Declining exports with major trading partners—such as the PRC and the US—has contributed to Indonesia's slower economic growth. Rather, it has been MSME output that has underpinned Indonesia's robust 5% growth. In 2018, MSMEs contributed Rp8,574 trillion (61.1%) of GDP, a 4.8 percentage point increase over 2010 (Figure 5.3A). Although decelerating since 2016, MSME output growth remained a high 9.6% in 2018. The slowdown in international trade has not critically affected MSME productivity. Labor productivity in MSMEs, calculated as MSME gross value added per capita, has been steadily increasing on the whole, rising to Rp73.3 million in 2018, a 137% increase over the

Figure 5.3: MSME Contribution to Gross Domestic Product

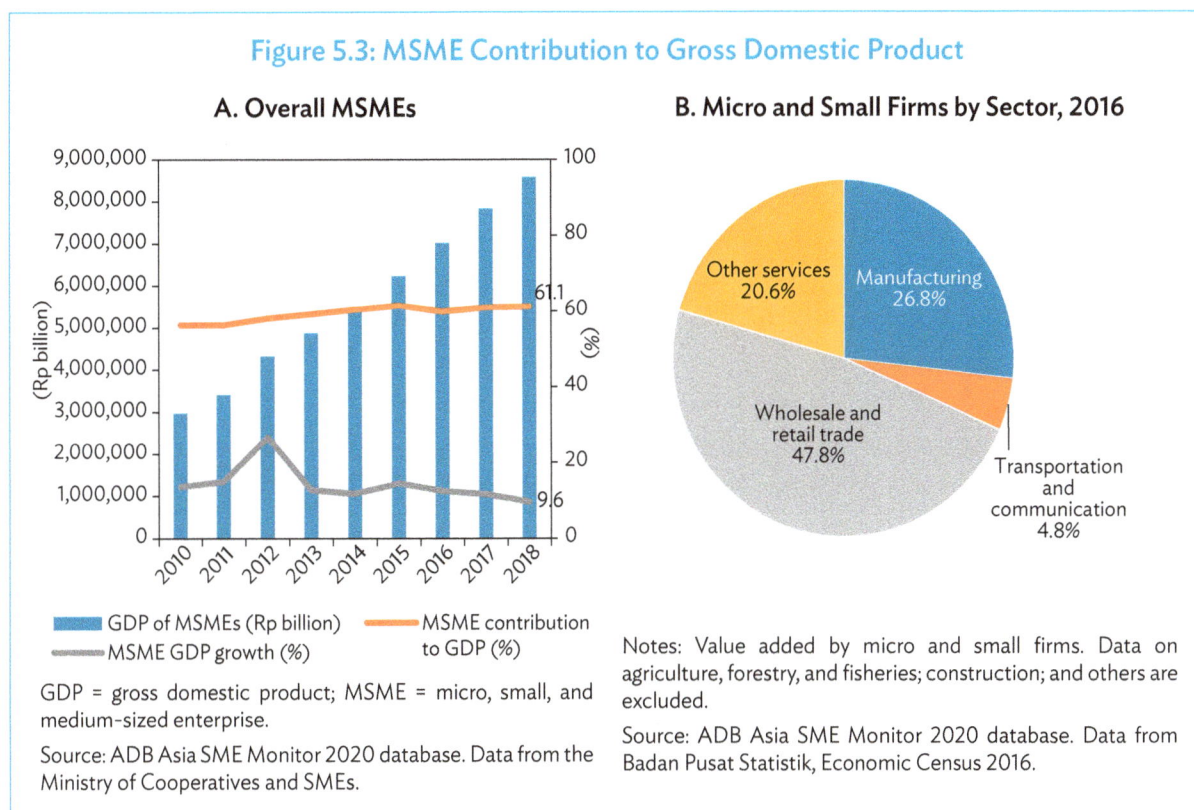

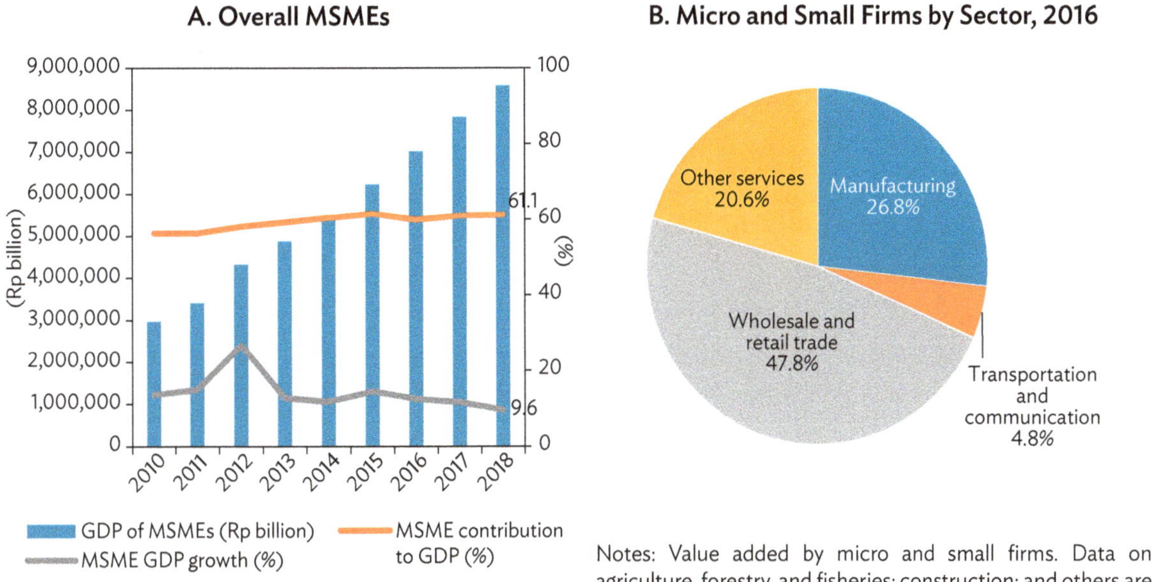

GDP = gross domestic product; MSME = micro, small, and medium-sized enterprise.

Source: ADB Asia SME Monitor 2020 database. Data from the Ministry of Cooperatives and SMEs.

Notes: Value added by micro and small firms. Data on agriculture, forestry, and fisheries; construction; and others are excluded.

Source: ADB Asia SME Monitor 2020 database. Data from Badan Pusat Statistik, Economic Census 2016.

Rp30.9 million in 2010. Based on the 2012 sector composition, around a quarter of MSME's GDP likely comes from agriculture, forestry, and fisheries. In 2016, 47.8% of micro and small firms' GDP in non-agriculture sectors derived from wholesale and retail trade, followed by manufacturing (26.8%), other services (20.6%), and transportation and communications (4.8%) (Figure 5.3B). Again, regional distribution data are unavailable.

Market Access

Most MSMEs serve domestic markets. Those serving global markets are a small fraction of the total. In 2018, MSMEs accounted for 14.4% of total export value (Rp294 trillion), a 2.6% decrease from 2017 (Rp302 trillion) (Figure 5.4A). MSME exports have been shrinking, caused by lower demand, especially from the PRC, the US, and Europe.

The export industry remains volatile, directly influenced by foreign demand. But the growth trend between MSMEs and non-MSMEs differs. MSME exports tend to grow as total exports decline, and vice versa. For instance, total exports decreased during 2014 and 2016, while MSME exports increased during the same period (Figure 5.4B). By contrast, although growth is slowing, total exports increased by 6.6% in 2018, while MSME exports decreased by 2.6%. This suggests that MSME exports supplement large firm-led exports.

MSME export sectors include food, beverages, textiles, shoes, handicrafts, and furniture. Some handicrafts and wooden furniture industries have built business clusters for exporting. A good example is the teak wood furniture cluster in Jepara, Central Java. MSME participation in global value chains remains limited due to a lack of business and management capacity; however, there is large potential for MSMEs to tap global value chains if policy support measures are well designed and implemented for internationalizing MSMEs and industrial cluster development. Fostering the MSME export industry will contribute to developing a more stable export environment.

Figure 5.4: MSME Exports

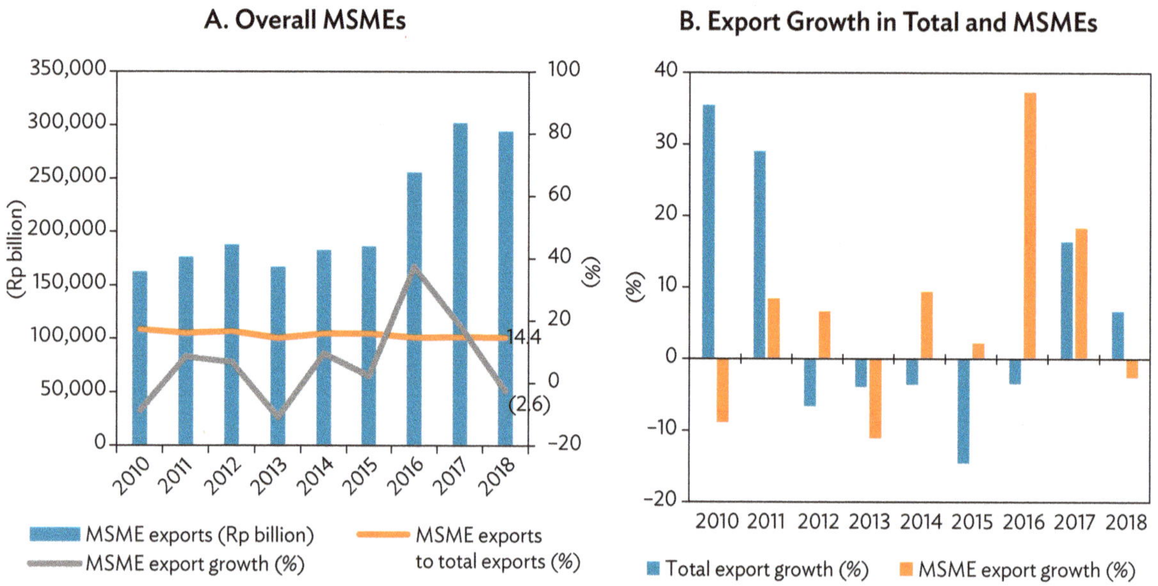

MSME = micro, small, and medium-sized enterprise.

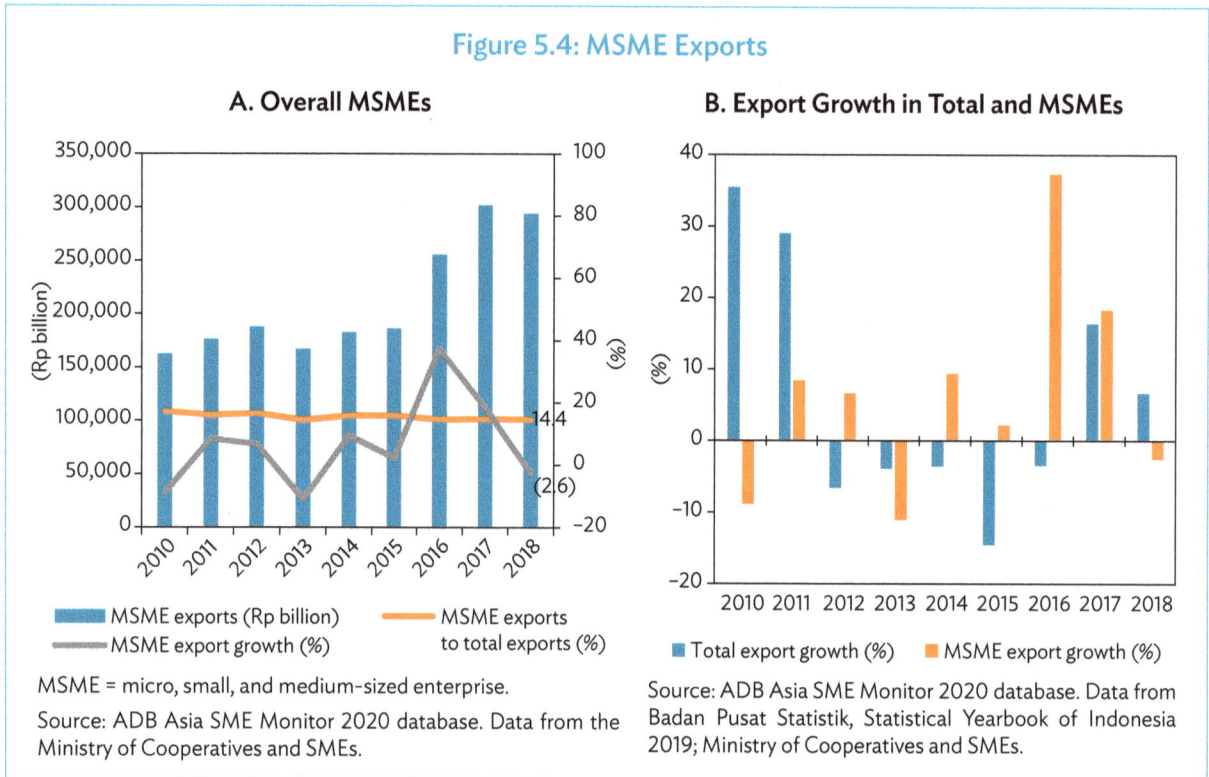

Source: ADB Asia SME Monitor 2020 database. Data from the Ministry of Cooperatives and SMEs.

Source: ADB Asia SME Monitor 2020 database. Data from Badan Pusat Statistik, Statistical Yearbook of Indonesia 2019; Ministry of Cooperatives and SMEs.

Technology and Innovation

The embrace of digital technology has clearly contributed to the growth of MSMEs, creating a swathe of new start-ups. Internet and mobile phone penetration have increased sharply. Individual internet use tripled since 2010, from 10.9% of the total population to 39.8% in 2018 (World Development Indicators). Mobile cellular subscriptions reached 119.8 per 100 people in 2018, well above 87.4 in 2010. The rising digital penetration has driven the development of domestic e-commerce businesses such as Tokopedia and Bukalapak, and mobile-based ride-hailing services such as Gojek (Box 5.1), along with other digital services such as bill payments and e-ticketing.

JP Morgan (2019 Payments Trend) estimated that Indonesia's e-commerce market is worth $13.6 billion, and is expected to grow 34.6% annually to 2021. Indonesia's Gojek and Singapore's Grab offer a variety of services, including transportation, food delivery, and other on-demand online services. Customer demand continues to rise. According to research conducted by the University of Indonesia in 2019, Gojek partners create $3 billion annually in value added to the economy. Technology-based MSMEs and start-ups play an important role in boosting the national economy and create a base for more quality jobs.

The government supports e-commerce development. Since 2017, the Ministry of Industry has developed *E-Smart IKM* to expand market access for small and medium industries (SMI) and increase the share of Indonesian products in e-commerce. Its integrated database system connects national industrial information (including SMI profiles and their products) with e-commerce platforms such as Tokopedia and Bukalapak. This helps open the digital world to SMIs, allowing them to increasingly use digital information tools, digital payments, and digital customer relations management. By the end of 2019, the system helped more than 10,000 SMIs across Indonesia raise their sales value over Rp3.2 trillion in various markets.

Box 5.1: Gojek Supports MSME Growth in Indonesia

Gojek started as a call center for on-demand *ojek* (motorcycle taxi) service in 2010, founded by three technical staff, managing 20 drivers. It launched its Gojek mobile application (app) in 2015, offering on-demand ride-hailing, logistics, and food delivery services. Gojek has now become one of the fastest-growing apps in Indonesia and Southeast Asia, offering more than 20 different services, working with more than 500,000 merchants and 2 million driver partners across the region. Its mobile app has been downloaded by more than 170 million people.

Gojek has also developed a global business. It operates in five countries: Gojek in Indonesia, GoViet in Viet Nam (launched in September 2018), Gojek in Singapore (November 2018), GET in Thailand (February 2019), and it is present in the Philippines through its acquisition of digital payments company Coins.ph.

Gojek is creating an ecosystem of app users, merchants, and service providers to address a large and unique opportunity in Southeast Asia. This self-reinforcing ecosystem creates a strong network effect, which drives more transaction volume, which in turn retains merchants, service providers, and users on the platform, and drives growth. Its Allocation System technology addresses daily problems faced in countries across the region, which enabled it to reach one million bookings in 240 days in Indonesia, 52 days in Singapore, and 47 days in Viet Nam.

Its 20 service options include not just transportation and logistics services but also food and medicine delivery, online shopping, mobile payments, massages and cleaning services, ticket booking, and digital donations (https://www.gojek.com/).

Gojek supports the growth of micro, small, and medium-sized enterprises (MSMEs) in Indonesia, which in turn drives the growth of Gojek's business. For instance, 98% of merchants of food delivery services (GoFood) are MSMEs. Gojek connects MSMEs to millions of potential customers and enables them to build trust and access new markets, information, logistics, and even financial services.

MSMEs can enter the digital economy through GoFood. The Demographic Institute of the Faculty of Economics and Business of the University of Indonesia found that 9 out of 10 MSMEs registered went digital with GoFood. The majority of MSMEs lacked digital assets before partnering with GoFood; many of them run their businesses only from physical stores (73%) or street stalls/shops (20%). After joining GoFood, 93% of the MSMEs went digital. Gojek helps MSMEs effectively improve and develop their business. According to the survey of MSME partners, 93% of the respondents (GoFood partners) cited an increase in transaction volume after becoming a Gojek partner, 7% had no change, with no partner seeing transaction volume drop. Some 85% of those surveyed re-invest their profits back into business, and 21% purchase goods for the company. The customer survey also revealed that users felt (i) ease of mobility (83% of respondents), (ii) convenience of not paying for parking and gas (77%), and (iii) time efficiency (76%) as benefits from Gojek's ride-hailing services.

Gojek has helped the national economy as well. According to the University of Indonesia, Gojek partners contribute around $3.9 billion annually to the Indonesian economy. Gojek driver income contributes an estimated $1.7 billion a year to the economy. Driver income increased by 42%–45% after joining Gojek. For partners in GoLife (customized services from massage, therapy, and home maintenance, among others), their income is estimated to contribute $84.5 million annually to the national economy. Their income increased by 72% after they joined Gojek. GoFood merchant income contributes $1.2 billion per annum to the national economy. In terms of revenue classification, 53% of GoFood partners said their businesses scaled up from micro to small business, and small to medium-sized business after partnering GoFood, according to the survey.

Gojek offers partners several benefits. Gojek drivers in Indonesia can access several private financial services with affordable prices, for example, private health insurance provided by Allianz at $0.16 per day for drivers and their families, which covers inpatient, outpatient, and immunization services. Gojek also partners with Indonesia's social protection scheme (BPJS Ketenagakerjaan) to provide driver partners with workplace protection against accidents.

In August 2019, Gojek was ranked 11th out of 52 companies in Fortune's annual "Change the World" list, becoming the only company from Southeast Asia to make the list twice.

continued on next page

Box 5.1 continued

In Indonesia and global markets, Gojek has faced a competitive environment for the mobile-based ride-hailing services. For instance, Singapore-based Grab is a major competitor. Similar business models have appeared across developing Asia, such as Angkas in the Philippines. The human factor remains a major challenge in this business model. Adding value through diversified service options must evolve with user demand. That is key for the business to survive and continue to grow.

Source: Interview with vice-president of Gojek on 19 July 2019. Data updated in March 2020.

Networking and Support

Indonesia has several business associations. The Indonesian Chamber of Commerce and Industry (KADIN), established in 1968, is the largest with two million MSME members. Beginning in 2009, it launched a Business Support Desk to promote private sector development, offering (i) business matching between entrepreneurs and investors within its network; (ii) training and business information; and (iii) market research and advisory services, through a network of 34 regional chambers, 514 district branches, and 200 business associations.

Although not specifically designed for MSMEs, the Employers' Association of Indonesia (APINDO) supports Indonesian business owners and entrepreneurs to protect and empower business and competitiveness through training and an array of business certification programs. It is led by 26 provincial boards and 173 district boards across the country.

With the rapid growth of e-commerce, leading domestic start-ups established the Indonesian E-Commerce Association in 2012 to strengthen relationships among e-commerce players and further develop the e-commerce industry by expanding public awareness and developing human resources in the industry and advanced technologies. There are also several small associations active in Indonesia, led by young entrepreneurs and start-ups.

The Indonesia Business Women Association (IWAPI) supports women-led MSMEs and entrepreneurs. Founded in 1975, it has 30,000 members, mostly MSMEs. The association offers business networking, training, business information, and advisory services.

Aside from private sector initiatives on business networking and support, several government authorities such as the Ministry of Cooperatives and SMEs, the Ministry of Industry, and the Ministry of Trade also have a variety of capacity development programs for MSMEs, either individually or in collaboration with international donor communities. They generally focus on technical and skill development. The Ministry of Research and Technology offers a technology business incubation program that applies innovative university research to start-ups for pilot testing. There is no comprehensive national system for business development services.

2. Access to Finance

- MSMEs are receiving more bank credit, but its growth has been sluggish, reflecting the slower growth of the Indonesian economy.
- Public guaranteed loans (KUR) and mandatory lending schemes strongly support the growth of MSME credit.
- Microfinance institutions and the state-owned PT Permodalan Nasional Madani (PNM) are active nonbank finance lenders to MSMEs; venture capital has expanded, led by foreign-owned firms, focusing on high-growth start-ups and digital industries.
- Digital payments have spread rapidly across the country, supported by the national payment switch established in 2017; financial authorities have begun regulating peer-to-peer (P2P) lenders and equity crowdfunding.
- A dedicated stock exchange for SMEs (the Acceleration Board) was launched in 2019 under the Indonesia Stock Exchange; the new board offers concessional listing requirements for SMEs with support from the special incubation program for IPOs.
- While public and private credit bureaus exist, there is no legal structure covering secured lending.

Bank Credit

As of end-2019, 110 commercial banks were operating in Indonesia: 4 state-owned banks, 60 private sector commercial banks, 27 regional development banks, 11 joint venture banks, and 8 foreign-owned banks (Table 5.3). The number of commercial banks is decreasing, while new entrants in financial markets, such as fintech lending firms, have been surging.

Bank credit growth has been slowing, reflecting slower economic growth of the country. Accordingly, while the MSME credit market has expanded, its growth has been sluggish. MSME loans outstanding reached Rp1,111 trillion as of end-2019, a 7.6% increase, but down from the 9.6% growth in 2018 (Figure 5.5A). Shrinking MSME exports as international demand fell was behind the slower MSME credit growth. Nonetheless, the growth of MSME loans exceeded overall bank credit growth (6.1% in 2019), supported by Kredit Usaha Rakyat (KUR), the public guaranteed loan scheme for MSMEs.

The ratio of MSME loans to total bank loans has hardly changed since 2011 (19.6% as of end-2019). The share of MSME loans to GDP was 7.0% in 2019, still relatively small. The ratio of nonperforming MSME loans to total MSME loans rose to 3.6% in 2019 from 3.4% in 2018. It was higher than overall nonperforming loans to total bank loans (2.5%). By sector, wholesale and retail trade is the most active MSME borrower, holding 49.3% of MSME loans in 2019. It is followed by other services (18.0%), manufacturing (10.0%), and agriculture (9.9%) (Figure 5.5B). By loan purpose, working capital financing accounted for 72.0% with the remaining 28.0% for investment capital.

Commercial banks rely heavily on real estate as loan collateral. Movable assets such as machinery and inventory are also used as collateral, but it is at a bank's discretion. As there is no systematic collateral registry system in Indonesia, commercial banks use movable assets registered by private notaries as collateral for lending.

Figure 5.5: MSME Loans

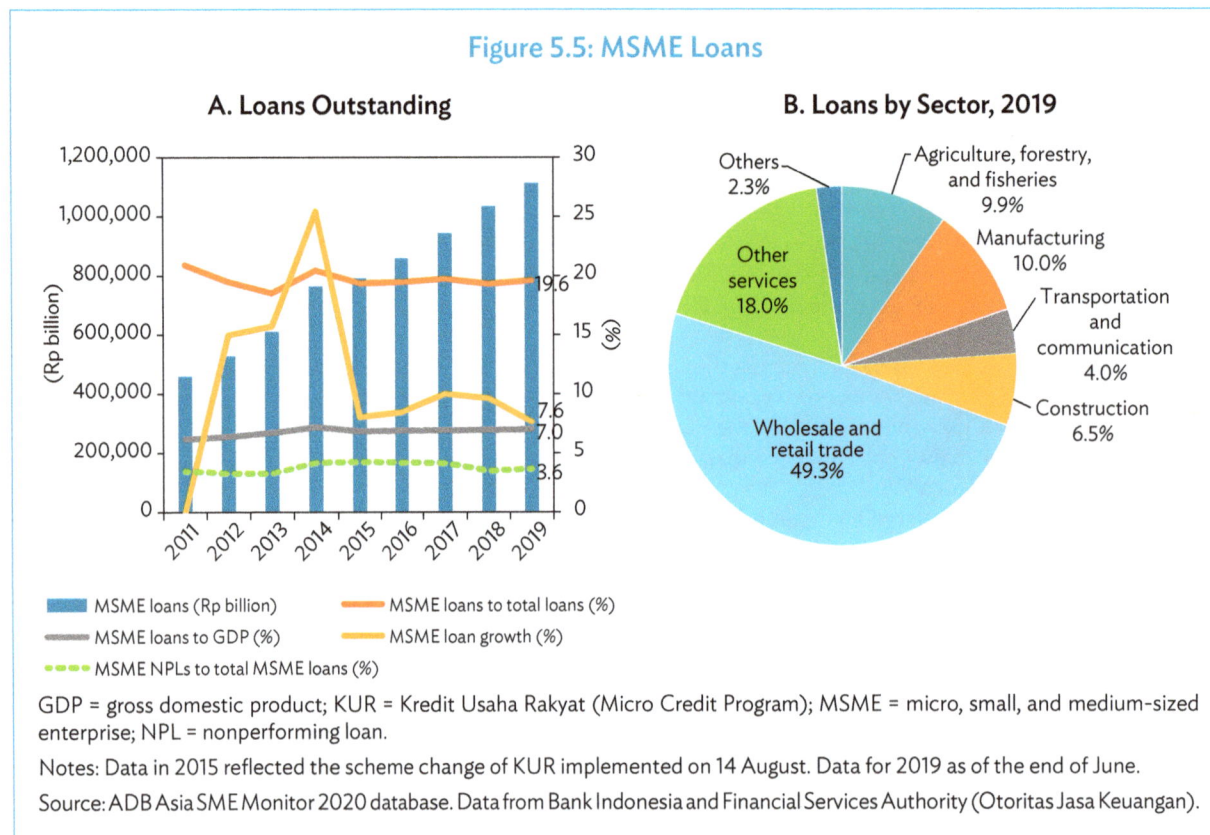

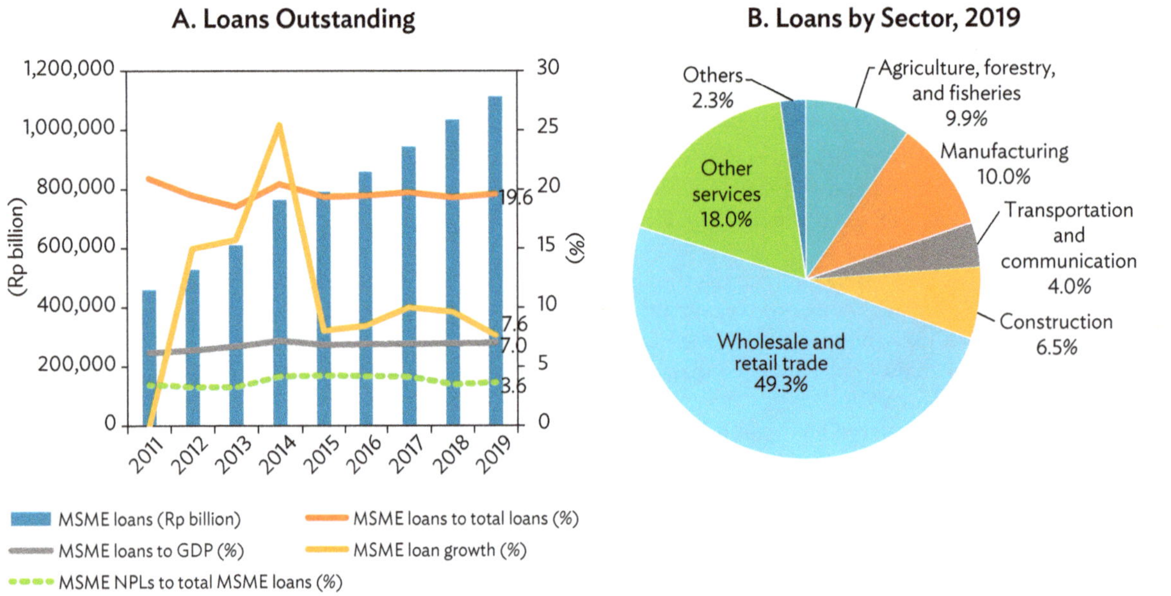

GDP = gross domestic product; KUR = Kredit Usaha Rakyat (Micro Credit Program); MSME = micro, small, and medium-sized enterprise; NPL = nonperforming loan.

Notes: Data in 2015 reflected the scheme change of KUR implemented on 14 August. Data for 2019 as of the end of June.

Source: ADB Asia SME Monitor 2020 database. Data from Bank Indonesia and Financial Services Authority (Otoritas Jasa Keuangan).

Public Financing and Guarantees

a. Public credit guarantees and interest rate subsidy

KUR was launched in 2007 as a public guaranteed loan scheme designed for MSMEs, offering partial guarantees of 70%–80% of the credit applied with concessional lending rates. There are two generations of KUR programs. The first generation (from 2007 to 2014) required a 3.25% guarantee fee per annum (p.a.) of the loan amount, with 4 guarantors (Askrindo, Jamkrindo, and 2 local guarantee corporations) and 33 participating banks (7 commercial banks and 26 regional development banks). The second generation (since 2015) uses government interest rate subsidies.

The first generation of KUR programs covered 12.4 million MSME credit agreements, with accumulated disbursement of guaranteed loans amounting to Rp178.8 trillion from 2007 to 2014. The KUR lending rate started from 24% p.a. for KUR Mikro (micro) in 2007, falling to 22% p.a. for KUR Mikro and 13% p.a. for KUR Retel (retail) in 2014. KUR Mikro offered loans of a maximum Rp20 million with no collateral required, while KUR Retel offered loans ranging between Rp20 million and Rp500 million with required collateral. The loan tenor for the first generation KUR was 3–6 years for working capital and 5–10 years for investment capital financing.

The second generation of KUR loans was offered at lending rate of 12% p.a. with interest rate subsidies in 2015, which started with two national guarantors (Askrindo and Jamkrindo) and seven commercial banks. In 2016 and 2017, the KUR lending rate was reduced to 9% p.a. with an interest rate subsidy. It was further reduced to 7% p.a. with a subsidy of Rp11 trillion for both 2018 and 2019, and reduced to 6% p.a. in 2020. This is an especially low rate as compared with the normal commercial bank rate of more than 10%.

KUR has four product lines: KUR Mikro and KUR IMW (migrant worker) offer non-collateral loans while KUR Kecil (small) and KUR Khusus (special) offer collateral loans at the distributor's discretion. KUR targeted a minimum 60% of KUR loans allocated to production (manufacturing) in 2019, with the same target continuing for 2020 .

KUR's nonperforming loan (NPL) ratio is capped at 5% of total KUR loans, but it has done exceptionally well. In 2019, KUR's NPL ratio was 1.1%, with loan disbursements of Rp140 trillion (its accumulated lending since 2007 is Rp646 trillion) (Figure 5.6A and Table 5.4). KUR loans disbursed dropped sharply in 2015, largely due to the generational switch implemented on 14 August 2015. In 2019, KUR loans accounted for 13.8% of total MSME lending by commercial banks.

KUR loan borrowers have steadily increased. The accumulated number of MSMEs guaranteed reached 30.8 million in 2019 (Figure 5.6B). Ten percent of KUR loans are delivered for new MSME borrowers and 90% are for MSME repeaters. When KUR was launched, the program was availed only for new MSME customers. In 2019, 43 financial institutions (banks and nonbank financial institutions) distributed KUR loans with 10 guarantors (two national guarantors, two Islamic guarantors, and six local guarantee corporations). The top three KUR distributors in 2019 were Bank Rakyat Indonesia, Bank Mandiri, and Bank Negara Indonesia, all state-owned banks.

b. Mandatory lending scheme

Mandatory lending to MSMEs started in 2012 to increase MSME access to bank credit. It requires banks to allocate 20% of their loan portfolios to MSMEs with target milestones of 5% by 2015, 10% by 2016, 15% by 2017, and 20% by 2018. Banks could achieve targets by directly lending to MSMEs or indirectly channeling loans to them via linkages or intermediation loan programs, as well as via syndicated bank loans. Bank Indonesia, the central bank, is responsible for monitoring bank compliance with mandatory lending. As of end-2019, the overall compliance ratio of banks was 20.5%, slightly exceeding the target. Among the three bank categories (domestic, joint venture banks, and foreign banks), domestic banks complied with the 20% obligation; however, joint venture banks and foreign banks were below target due to the fall in exports (by regulation, joint venture banks and foreign banks include MSME non-oil and gas export loans as part of their target compliance).

Bank Indonesia provides incentives and disincentives as well as written warnings for non-compliance to commercial banks. The incentives included training for banks and MSMEs, facilitating the use of credit ratings for MSMEs, and awarding banks with the best MSME financing performance. *Syariah* banks that failed to comply were obliged to provide capacity development training to MSMEs. Bank Indonesia provided incentives related to the minimum statutory reserves for conventional commercial banks, easing the upper limit of the loans-to-funding ratio. Disincentives came in the form of reduced interest paid on conventional commercial bank reserves held at Bank Indonesia. The incentives and disincentives for conventional commercial banks were terminated in 2018. Bank Indonesia will continue to issue accommodative macroprudential policy, including the one that focuses on MSMEs.

Figure 5.6: Credit Guarantees—Kredit Usaha Rakyat

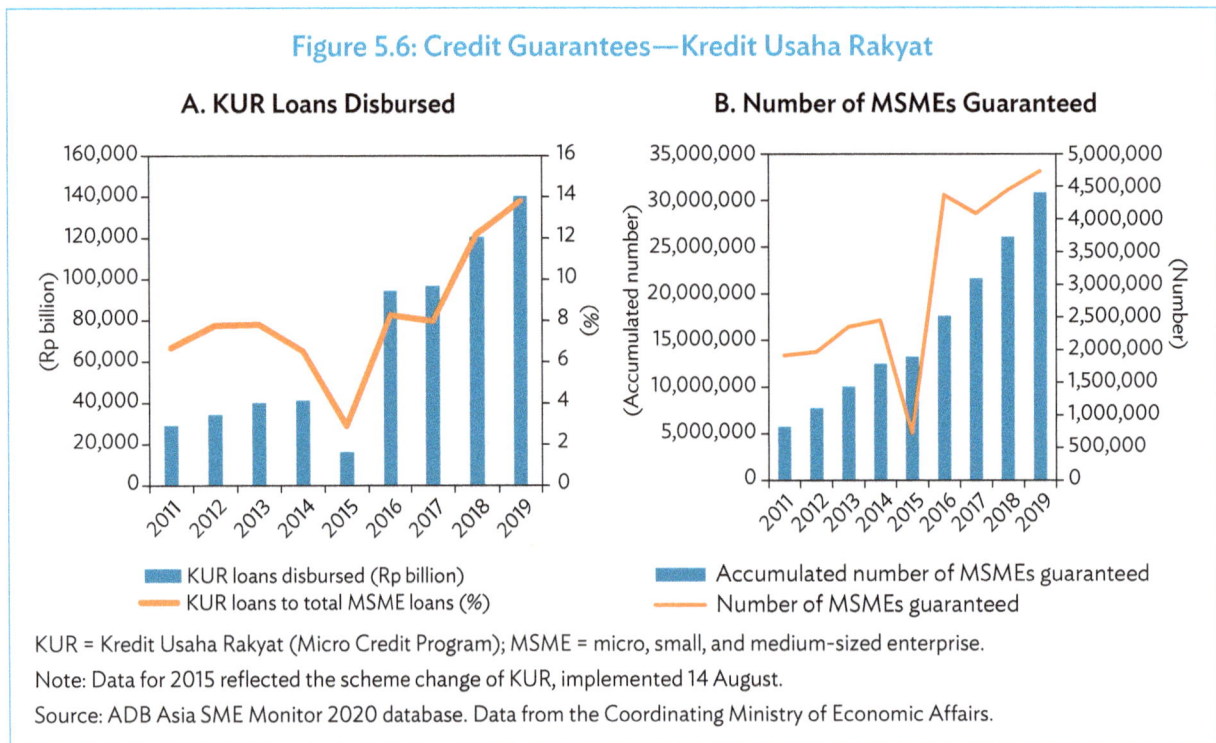

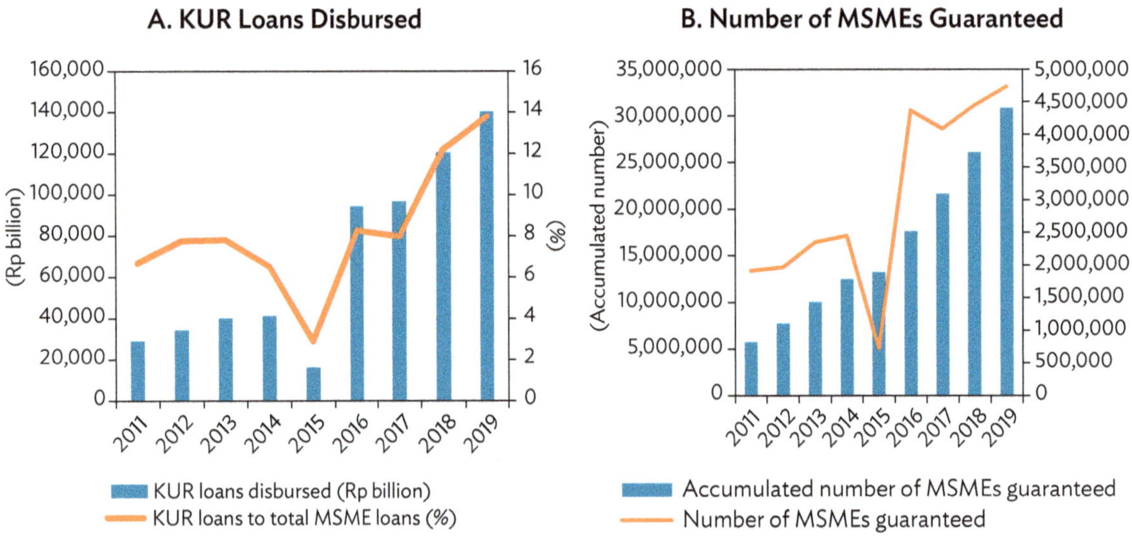

KUR = Kredit Usaha Rakyat (Micro Credit Program); MSME = micro, small, and medium-sized enterprise.

Note: Data for 2015 reflected the scheme change of KUR, implemented 14 August.

Source: ADB Asia SME Monitor 2020 database. Data from the Coordinating Ministry of Economic Affairs.

Nonbank Financing

The nonbank finance industry in Indonesia is relatively small. As of end-2019, 204 microfinance institutions (MFIs), 184 multi-finance companies, 83 pawnshops (state-owned Pegadaian and private pawnshops), 60 venture capital companies, and 22 credit guarantee corporations operate in Indonesia. They are directly or indirectly financing MSMEs and start-ups. In addition, PT Permodalan Nasional Madani (PNM), a state-owned finance company, services MSMEs.

Total financing of finance companies amounted to Rp452.2 trillion, 8.1% of the total bank loans outstanding in 2019 (Figure 5.7A and Table 5.5).[50] By business activity, multipurpose financing accounted for 60.8% of the total amount financed by finance companies in 2019, followed by investment financing (29.8%), working capital financing (5.9%), and *syariah* financing (3.5%). Nonperforming financing was 2.4% of the total financing in 2019, slightly down from 2.7% in 2018.

Among nonbank finance institutions (NBFIs), MFIs and PNM are the most active lenders to MSMEs. MFIs offer microcredit and related financial services to the traditionally underserved, including MSMEs and low-income segments of the population, especially in rural areas. Total MFI loans outstanding amounted to Rp615.9 billion in 2019, a 32% increase from Rp466.5 billion in 2018 (Figure 5.7B). The Microfinance Law (Law No.1/2013) allowed two types of legal forms: (i) savings and loan cooperatives and (ii) limited liability companies. But foreign-owned MFIs are not allowed to operate by law. Operating areas and business coverage of MFIs are restricted by type of license. Many MFIs still operate informally as they failed to register with the Financial Services Authority (Otoritas Jasa Keuangan, or OJK) due to a lack of legal documents. PNM was founded in 1999 as a state-owned finance

[50] The Financial Services Authority (OJK) introduced a new data classification system on nonbank finance institutions (NBFIs) in 2016. Due to this change of statistical methodology, NBFI data based on new classification, except microfinance institutions (MFIs), can be tracked back to 2016. For MFIs, due to the change of statistical methodology in 2014, data can be tracked from 2015.

company that aims to support MSMEs. PNM has offered a group lending program for women-led microbusinesses since 2015.

Pawnshops also support MSMEs, especially in rural areas, although their business does not specifically target MSMEs. Pawnshops are mostly located in Java. State-owned Pegadaian has dominated Indonesia's pawnshop market, with 4,123 business units across the country as of end-2019. Pegadaian offers microcredit programs to MSMEs as well. Pegadaian loans outstanding amounted to Rp50.4 trillion in 2019, a 23.3% increase from 2018 (Figure 5.7B). For other NBFIs, multi-finance companies offer leasing, factoring, credit card financing, and consumer financing, and supplement MSME credit gaps.

The venture capital industry has been growing rapidly, led mainly by foreign venture capitalists and domestic conglomerates with foreign partnerships. Their investments focus on high-growth start-ups, especially e-commerce and digital industries. According to a Google–A.T.Kearney Study in 2017,[51] 72% of venture capital investment by value came from foreign investors (the US, Japan, and the PRC) with the remaining 28% coming from domestic investors (domestic conglomerates and state-owned enterprises). From 2012 to August 2017, 58% of investment by value went to e-commerce businesses, followed by transportation (38%).

Although no statistical data is available, informal money lenders are deeply rooted in the Indonesian economy. Bank Indonesia says money lenders cause many problems, especially with their extremely high interest rates. But no national regulations exist covering the high interest rates of informal operations. Greater consumer education could ease these money lender issues.

Figure 5.7: Nonbank Finance

A. Finance Companies | **B. Pawnshops and Microfinance Institutions**

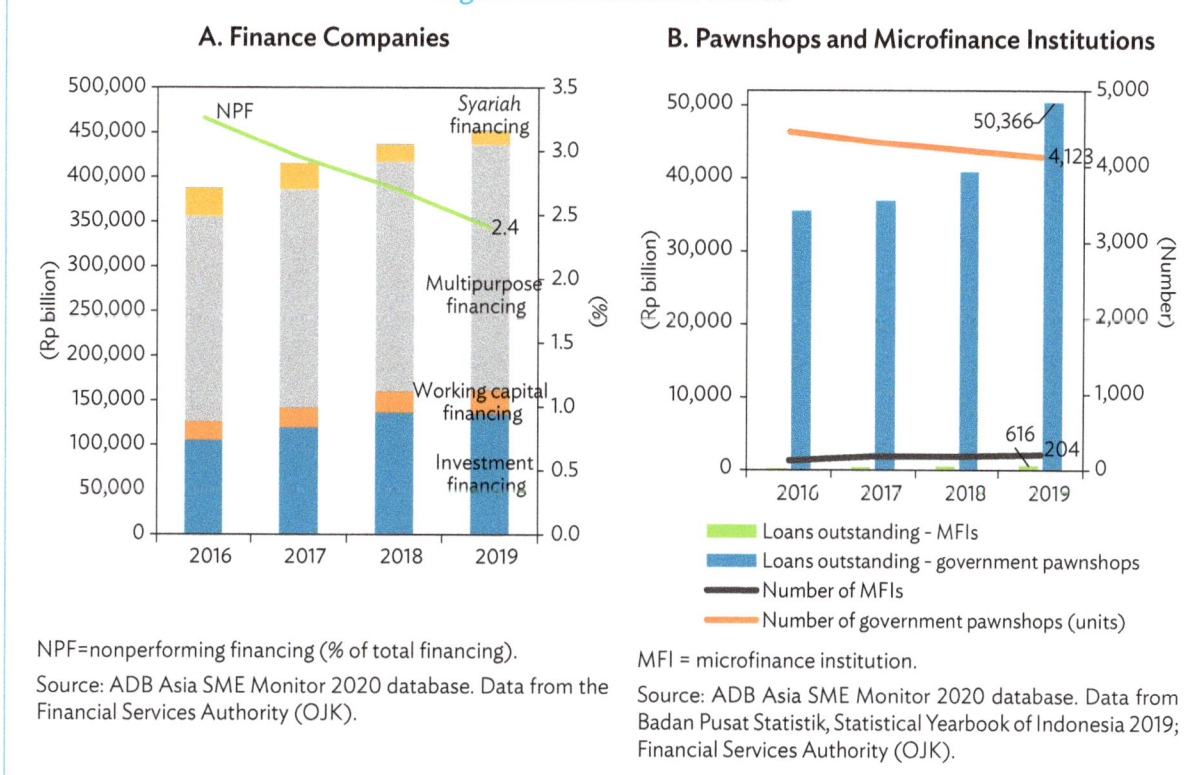

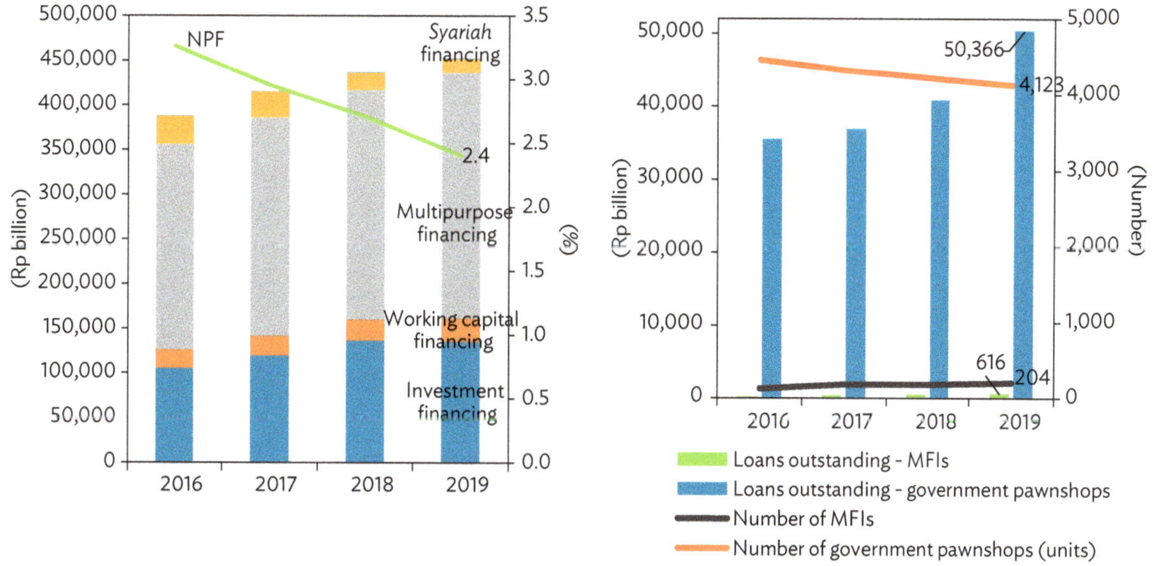

NPF=nonperforming financing (% of total financing).

Source: ADB Asia SME Monitor 2020 database. Data from the Financial Services Authority (OJK).

MFI = microfinance institution.

Source: ADB Asia SME Monitor 2020 database. Data from Badan Pusat Statistik, Statistical Yearbook of Indonesia 2019; Financial Services Authority (OJK).

51 Google and A.T.Kearney. 2017. Indonesia Venture Capital Outlook 2017.

Box 5.2: Bahana Alta Ventura Channels Government Programs to Support MSMEs

Bahana Artha Ventura (BAV) is a leading venture capital company in Indonesia, with 25 regional venture capital networks across the country. BAV business comprises government programs and commercial programs (including profit sharing lending). There are two government programs: (i) the Linkage Program (ultra-micro, or UMi) and (ii) the Community Development Partnership Program (PKBL).

- The UMi program came out of the Coordinating Ministry of Economic Affairs (CMEA) Decree on Linkage Program (Pembiayaan Ultra Mikro [UMi] KPPN Metro No.22/PMK 05/2017), enacted on 23 February 2017. BAV, PT Permodalan Nasional Madani (PNM), and Pegadaian are implementing agencies of the program. The Indonesia Investment Agency (PIP) finances BAV at a 2% per annum (p.a.) interest rate, and BAV finances 30 partner cooperatives with 4% p.a. interest rate (a 2% net profit). Partner cooperatives then lend to borrowers, mainly micro, small, and medium-sized enterprises (MSMEs), at a 4%+ p.a. interest rate, but must be lower than their existing lending rates. Loans are a maximum Rp10 million with maturities of 6–12-months. Repayments are made monthly. There are no nonperforming loans. One BAV officer monitors borrower repayments. In case of default, credit guarantee corporations cover the loss. UMi is growing with strong demand (10 million potential customers). BAV targets total disbursement of Rp1.3 trillion.

- PKBL is a state-owned enterprise (SOE) lending program to MSMEs using 25 BAV regional venture capital companies (PMVDs). They use company-to-company lending with BAV supporting SOE lending. The regulation is PKBL-BUMN Perbihan Peratum Menteri, Peraturan Menteri BUMN PER-02/MBU/7/2017 dated 5 July 2017. SOEs transfer funds to PMVDs with a 3% p.a. interest rate, and PMVDs on-lend to MSME borrowers at a 3% p.a. interest rate. Loans are at a maximum Rp200 million with a maximum 3-year maturity. BAV is obliged to return 2%–5% of its profits to the community as part of its corporate social responsibility. BAV receives 80%–90% of the SOE funding rate as fees (2.4%–2.7%) and repays the remaining 10%–20% (0.3%–0.6% interest rate plus principal) back to SOEs.

Besides these government programs, BAV has its own financing programs for MSMEs: (i) private equity finance and (ii) lending for MSME products. There is only one ongoing private equity finance project for a medical and health care start-up. The lending program to MSME products offers a maximum 17% p.a. interest rate with a maximum maturity of 3 years.

The law defines three types of venture capital business: (i) equity participation, (ii) profit-sharing loans, and (iii) fee benefits. However, domestic venture capital firms are mostly working with entities that channel government programs, while allowing active equity participation and profit-sharing loans. Foreign-led venture capital firms have dominated private equity investments in high-growth start-ups, especially e-commerce and digital industries. Domestic venture capital companies face critical challenges to survive, particularly funding for business. A venture capital association (AMVESINDO) aims to create a conducive ecosystem for Indonesian start-ups.

Source: Interview with senior manager of Bahana Alta Ventura on 18 July 2019.

Digital Financial Services

Digital financial services (DFS) have rapidly spread across the archipelago. Although still a relatively small share, adults (aged 15 and above) with mobile money accounts rose from 0.4% of the population in 2014 to 3.1% in 2017 (Global Findex 2018). An interoperable national payments gateway (Gerbang Pembayaran Nasional, GPN) was launched in 2017 to promote low-cost digital transactions. The data obtained through the system has also helped improve consumer protection. GPN supports the development of a digital payment ecosystem in the country. In 2017, 34.6% of Indonesian adults made or received digital payments, up from 22.4% in 2014. By end-2019, 54 million GPN cards had been distributed to the general public, an average increase of 31% per month from April 2018 to December 2019. However, other than payments, mobile and internet banking and other DFS have yet to be well developed.

Promoting DFS and non-cash transactions is part of Indonesia's national financial inclusion strategy. Branchless banking or agent banking plays a critical role by offering financial services to the unbanked, including MSME owners, especially in rural areas. There are two systems of agent banking: (i) digital transactions using server-based e-money called *Layanan Keuangan Digital* led by Bank Indonesia and (ii) an agent banking system using basic savings accounts called *Laku Pandai* led by OJK. By January 2020, Bank Indonesia scheme offered payments, fund transfers, and savings services through 12.7 million e-money accounts in five banks and five NBFIs with 527,030 agents. Transactions are limited to Rp20 million for *Layanan Keuangan Digital*. Meanwhile, *Laku Pandai* offers wider services including payments, fund transfers, savings, microcredit, and insurance. As of end-2019, there were 25.4 million savings accounts in 31 banks with 1.2 million agents. Transactions are limited to Rp60 million per year and Rp5 million per month. More than Rp5 million in credit can be approved in a month, but the total transaction per year remains limited to Rp60 million. Bank Indonesia and OJK plan to harmonize regulations on the two systems to increase synergy and effectiveness.

OJK has three main DFS regulations on peer-to-peer (P2P) lending, equity crowdfunding (ECF), and financial innovation operators.

The P2P regulation (OJK Regulation No.77/POJK.01/2016) allows Indonesian limited liability and cooperative companies to operate P2P lending services. Foreign ownership is limited to 85% of the company's paid-up capital. P2P lenders are considered financial institutions by regulation. They need to obtain a registration certificate and then a business license within a year of registration. The maximum P2P lending amount is Rp2 billion per borrower. In 2019, 164 P2P lenders were registered and licensed by OJK. As of end-2019, accumulated loans disbursed by P2P lenders was Rp81.5 trillion, and loans outstanding reached Rp13.2 trillion, more than double the Rp5 trillion in 2018 (Figure 5.8A). The total borrowers of P2P lending also rose sharply from 4.3 million (number of accounts) in 2018 to 18 million by end-2019 (Figure 5.8B). P2P lending has yet to become popular outside of Java.

The ECF regulation (OJK Regulation No.37/POJK.04/2018) defines ECF as a share-offering service used by firms and issuers to sell their shares to investors through an open electronic system network (platform). The ECF provider is required to obtain a registration certificate from the Ministry of Communication and Information Technology and a business license from the OJK. The ECF provider should be a limited liability company or cooperative with minimum capital of Rp2.5 billion. Issuers have to be registered as a limited company and can raise a maximum Rp10 billion per year. Although ECF is a capital market activity, offered shares through the platform are not considered a public offering under the Capital Market Law (Law No.8/1995). Investors, except for institutional investors, can buy shares through the platform up to 5% or 10% of their total income per year, depending on investor size. As of end-November 2019, two companies received ECF licenses from OJK.

The OJK Regulation on Digital Financial Innovation in the Financial Services Sector (No.13/POJK.02/2018) regulates financial innovation operators by registering to facilitate innovation in the DFS ecosystem. Registered financial innovation operators can apply to OJK's regulatory sandbox.

Fintech companies have been increasing in Indonesia. OJK and Bank Indonesia support the development of fintech firms and promote collaboration among fintech firms, commercial banks, and NBFIs in developing the payment system. Bank Indonesia has issued regulations related to payment transaction processes including fintech payments. OJK started licensing P2P lenders and ECF providers, while most fintech companies remain informal entities.

Bank Indonesia offers a free mobile accounting application called SI APIK (the Financial Statements Application Information System). It helps MSMEs prepare financial statements required by banks. The system had 14,989 users by end-2019, helping MSMEs improve business transparency and access formal financial services. Bank Indonesia has provided training on preparing simple financial statements to 1,069 participants, including MSMEs and college students.

Figure 5.8: Peer-to-Peer Lending in Indonesia

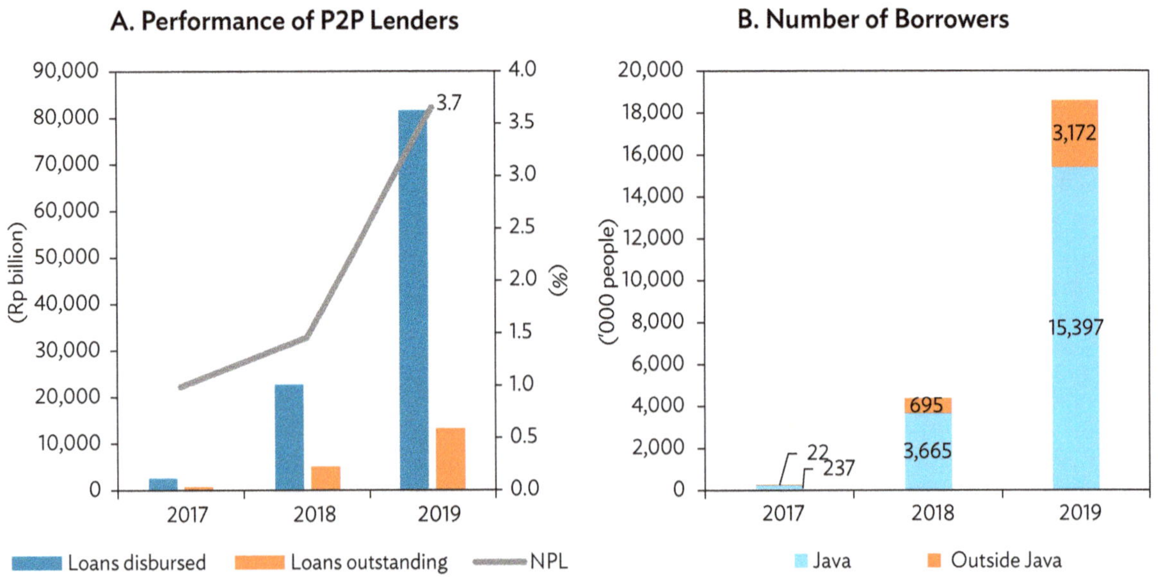

NPL=nonperforming loan (overdue more than 90 days), P2P = peer-to-peer.

Source: ADB Asia SME Monitor 2020 database. Data from the Financial Services Authority.

Capital Markets

Indonesia's equity market has seen growth stunted, affected by shrinking international trade with key foreign markets such as the PRC and the US, and by slower domestic economic growth. As of end-2019, market capitalization of the main board was Rp7,265 trillion, a 3.4% increase from 2018 (Figure 5.9A). The number of listed companies has been steadily increasing (668 companies in 2019), backed by a growing number of SME initial public offerings (IPOs) (Figure 5.9B). There were 25 SME IPOs (accumulated number) as of end-2019.

The capital market definition of SMEs differs from the national definition of MSMEs (Law No.20/2008). The OJK regulation of 2017 (No.53/POJK.04/2017) defines SMEs in the capital market by total asset thresholds and the SMEs controller. Before 2017, OJK used a single classification of SMEs (a company with total assets of not more than Rp100 billion, as defined in the Bapepam LK Rule No. IX.C.7). The new regulation created two separate segments of small-asset enterprises and medium-asset enterprises, which statistically contributed to the increased number of SME IPOs in 2018. In the capital market, a company with total assets of a maximum Rp50 billion is classified as a small enterprise, while the company with total assets up to Rp250 billion is categorized as a medium-sized enterprise. SMEs in the capital market must not be controlled by other companies not defined as SMEs by the OJK regulation.

In 2019, the Indonesia Stock Exchange (IDX) launched a dedicated stock exchange for SMEs called the Acceleration Board, following OJK regulations on public offering and capital increase by SMEs (No.53/POJK.04/2017 and No.54/POJK.04/2017). Issuers who can list on the new board must be SMEs as defined above. As of end-January 2020, the Acceleration Board had one listed company (PT Tourindo Guide Indonesia tbk, a digital tourism service provider; listed 8 January 2020). SMEs can raise a maximum Rp250 billion from the new market.

The Acceleration Board aims to expand financing opportunities for SMEs through the capital market. To this end, the new board focuses on developing the primary (issuing) market for SMEs. SME issuers enjoy several benefits: (i) free registration in the first year and (ii) support for connecting to private equity finance opportunities. Listing requirements are concessional compared with the main board and the development board (Table 5.7). For SME issuers, some specific corporate governance requirements for listing are exempted for 6–12 months, e.g., requirements for holding an independent board of commissioners, corporate secretary, audit committee, and unit of internal audit. SME issuers can bypass some operating requirements, but must disclose operating revenues. Non-profitable SMEs can tap the Acceleration Board, but need to demonstrate projected operating profits within 6 years. A minimum 1 year audited financial report is required, but if the company has operated for less than a year, an independent auditor can audit the company's financial report since the company posted revenue. There is no minimum capital requirement for SMEs to list on the new board. The ratio of shares owned by non-controlling and non-majority shareholders must be less than 20% of the total shares. And there should be at least 300 shareholders.

To develop an investor base for the new board, IDX has held periodic discussions with international venture capital companies. The key challenge for the new board is market size. Cost may not be a big factor (5% fees for issues). IDX launched an incubator program in 2019 to support SMEs tap the stock exchange market. IDX has three incubator offices in Jakarta, Bandung, and Surabaya, with 102 participants. Their support focuses on a Road-to-IPO program with a curriculum of: deepening IPO and listing regulations, public offerings structure, preparation for meetings with anchor investors, legal aspects of the company, and accounting matters.

Figure 5.9: Equity Market

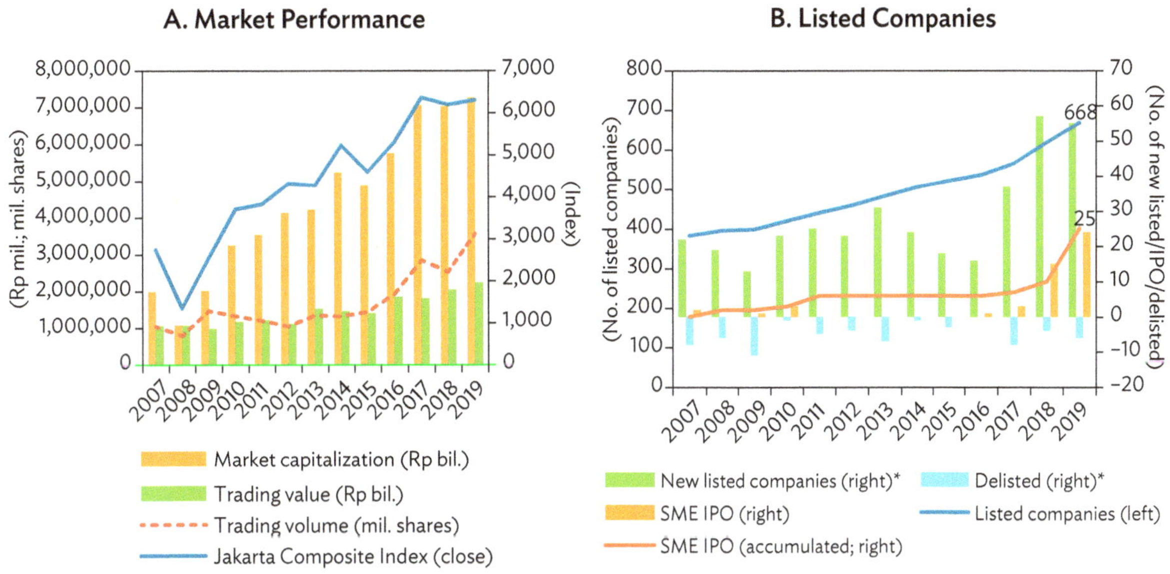

IPO = initial public offering, SME = small and medium-sized enterprise.

Source: ADB Asia SME Monitor 2020 database. Data from Indonesia Stock Exchange.

Financial Infrastructure

The national credit reporting system comprises two streams: (i) a public credit registry initiated by OJK and (ii) a private credit bureau (PEFINDO Credit Bureau). For the public credit registry, OJK receives data from financial institutions through its financial information services system called SLIK. Based on the data received, OJK produces and distributes standard credit information for financial institutions and societies. For the private credit bureau, PEFINDO Credit Bureau receives data from both SLIK and other sources, such as financial institutions (non-SLIK members), NBFIs, savings and loan cooperatives, P2P lending platforms, and public agencies. Based on the data received, PEFINDO Credit Bureau delivers comprehensive credit information and credit scoring (IdReport and IdScore) for financial institutions, NBFIs, and societies.

Credit bureaus offer several benefits: (i) minimize asymmetric information for supporting risk management of financial institutions, (ii) reduce adverse selection and moral hazard in the provision of funds, (iii) prevent NPLs, (iv) decrease credit acquisition costs, (v) encourage risk-based pricing and reputational collateral, and (vi) improve inclusive financing.

As of February 2020, PEFINDO Credit Bureau members included 97 banks (including regional and rural banks), 68 finance services, 65 P2P lending platforms, 15 savings and loan cooperatives, 8 securities houses, 12 other financial institutions, and 6 nonfinancial institutions. Company data are mostly individual debtors and large enterprises, as SMEs typically have no financial statements. SME data are largely included in individual consumer data.

For the credit scoring system, the IdScore indicates the borrower's capability in fulfilling its credit obligations, with scores ranging from 250 to 900 (the higher the score, the lower the risk). It also reports the default probability (0%–100%) of the borrower within the next 1 year, with a risk category of A1–E3. The credit rating system is designed for non-SMEs, but the bureau plans to introduce SME scoring.

There is no legal structure for secured lending and a collateral registry system in Indonesia. Commercial banks can accept both movable and immovable assets registered by private notaries as collateral for loans.

3. Policies and Regulations

- MSME development policies, initiated by line ministries, align with the National Mid-term Development Plan 2015–2019; however, policy coordination among central government authorities and between central and local governments should be strengthened to create better synergy across policies.
- The national financial inclusion system is well organized, with a central coordinating body with thematic working groups; this enables authorities to make strategic course corrections easily.
- Promoting digital finance is part of the financial inclusion strategy; given its associated risks, extensive coordination among financial regulators, government authorities, and private sector stakeholders is needed to reap greater benefits from inclusive finance.

MSME Development

The National Mid-term Development Plan 2015–2019 was launched in 2015 (Presidential Regulation No.2/2015) as part of the National Long-term Development Plan 2005–2025 (Law No.17/2007). The mid-term plan set economic development targets to 2019—such as 8.0% GDP growth, 4.0%–5.0% unemployment rate, and $250.5 billion in non-oil and gas exports. However, several factors, such as recent trade tensions and the drop in global trade generally, made these targets unattainable. In 2019, GDP growth was 5.0%, continuing its moderating trend. Unemployment among people aged 15 and older has been decreasing slightly, but remained at 5.3% in 2019. The export value of goods was $167 billion in 2019. The government has paid great attention to develop MSMEs to boost national productivity, create more jobs with poverty alleviation, and encourage more international trade.

MSME development policies initiated by line ministries all align with the National Mid-term Development Plan 2015–2019. The Ministry of Cooperatives and SMEs is dedicated to craft Indonesia's MSME policies. Other line ministries such as the Ministry of Industry and the Ministry of Trade have their own policy frameworks for MSME support. MSME policy coordination among central government authorities and between central and local governments should be strengthened further to create greater synergy between policy actions initiated by line ministries.

The Ministry of Cooperatives and SMEs laid out its 2015–2019 vison and mission of "Creating Healthy, Strong, Resilient and Independent Cooperatives and SMEs to Contribute to the National Economy," following the National Mid-term Development Plan 2015–2019. It addresses three major missions: (i) building healthy and quality cooperative institutions, (ii) fostering SMEs that can create jobs and greater income distribution, and (iii) creating cooperatives and SMEs that encourage economic growth and poverty alleviation. It also set five strategic directions: (i) improving the quality of human resources, (ii) increasing access to finance, (iii) increasing productivity, (iv) strengthening business capacity, and (v) protecting business for cooperatives and SMEs. The ministry grants a cooperative certificate (NIK) to cooperatives to monitor their activities, offers education and training programs for cooperatives and SMEs, and facilitates access to KUR and revolving funds.

The Ministry of Industry has a special policy framework for SME manufacturers (small and medium industries, or SMI), with the goal of increasing SMI business units by 1% annually, or 30,000 business units per year. The SMI development strategy has three components: (i) using domestic raw materials and resources for production; (ii) attracting a quality workforce; and (iii) utilizing technology and innovation to produce low-cost, high-quality products. Based on the Master Plan of National Industry Development 2015–2035, the Ministry of Industry has established SMI centers, targeting one center for each district and city, and allocated industrial estates for SMIs to more evenly distribute industrial development across the archipelago. The master plan sets numeric targets for SMIs, for example, increasing SME centers to 1,305 units in 2020–2024 and 2,285 units in 2025–2035, and providing 10 units of industrial estate for SMIs in 2020–2024 and 15 units in 2025–2035.

The Ministry of Trade's Master Plan 2011–2025 supports SMEs in various ways by promoting business partnerships with universities, governments, and industries. It provides technical assistance for selected SME business sectors such as fisheries and tourism, and connects them to financial institutions (credit cooperatives) to improve access to finance. The Ministry of Home Affairs has issued guidelines on issuing business licenses for micro and small enterprises (Ministerial Regulation No.83/2014).

Financial Inclusion

Financial inclusion is a policy priority to accelerate country's inclusive growth. The National Strategy for Financial Inclusion was launched in 2012 during the Yudhoyono administration. The strategy was revised in 2016 under the Jokowi administration in line with the National Mid-term Development Plan 2015–2019, where financial inclusion is defined as "a condition where all members of society have access to quality formal financial services that are timely, smooth, and safe at affordable fees in accordance with the needs and abilities in order to improve public prosperity." The National Financial Inclusion Strategy 2016 (SNKI) aimed to have 75% of adults financially included by the end of 2019.

SNKI had nine principles for inclusive finance: (i) *leadership* of the government and financial authorities, (ii) *diversity* of available financial services, (iii) *innovation* using technology to expand access to finance, (iv) *protection* of all stakeholders with consumer protection, (v) *empowerment* through developing financial literacy, (vi) *cooperation* and coordination among all stakeholders including public and private sectors, (vii) *knowledge* to promote evidence-based policy formulation, (viii) *proportionality* for policy framework and risk-based regulations, and (ix) a *framework* based on international regulatory standards.

Three groups are targeted in the SNKI: (i) low-income communities (the lowest 40% of the community); (ii) micro and small businesses as in the MSME Law (No.20/2008); and (iii) cross-community groups including migrant workers, women, socially excluded and disabled groups, economically remote areas, and students and youth.

SNKI has five policy pillars: (i) financial education; (ii) public property rights (improving loan collateral, such as land titling and copyright/patent certification); (iii) financial distribution channels and intermediary facilities (for example, digital financial services and value chain financing); (iv) government financial services (including KUR and non-cash subsidies and payments); and (v) consumer protection. These pillars must be supported by three foundations: (i) policy and regulatory support from government authorities and regulators; (ii) financial information infrastructure and technology; and (iii) organizations and mechanisms able to encourage the implementation of coordinated, integrated activities.

For country-wide coordination, the National Council of Inclusive Finance was established in 2016, chaired by the Coordinating Ministry of Economic Affairs as secretariat. SNKI implementation is supported by seven working groups for (i) financial education, (ii) public property rights, (iii) financial distribution channels and intermediary facilities, (iv) government financial services, (v) consumer protection, (vi) policies and regulations, and (vii) financial information technology and infrastructure. The Coordinating Ministry of Economic Affairs also chairs the National Committee on MSMEs, responsible for policy coordination with KUR.

The Financial Services Authority (OJK) is the country's single financial regulator and supervisor, comprising three supervisory units—banking, NBFIs, and capital markets. OJK is responsible for all financial regulations to implement SNKI in close coordination with Bank Indonesia (Table 5.8).

Bank Indonesia, as central bank, is mandated to maintain prices, financial system stability, and payment systems. To do this, it also issues regulations to protect consumers, especially those affected by its policies and regulations. Bank Indonesia plans to thoroughly review its current consumer protection framework and revise it based on emerging trends. Bank Indonesia is formulating a new regulation covering consumer protection to address market conduct, consumer education, and handling complaints.

Overall, the national financial inclusion system is well coordinated, with a central coordination body with thematic working groups. SNKI has well-designed components to spin cycles of access, usage, and monitoring and evaluation. This enables government authorities to easily make course corrections within its financial inclusion strategy. Promoting digital financial services is a key component of the strategy, creating greater opportunities for MSMEs to access low-cost finance and help fill unmet financing demand. But new issues and risks have emerged such as the need for better cybersecurity. To cope with these issues is a timely fashion, greater and more extensive coordination among financial regulators, government authorities, and private sector stakeholders will be needed to reap more benefits from inclusive finance.

Data Tables

Table 5.1: MSME Definition

Item	Micro	Small	Medium
Net assets (land and building excluded)	Less than Rp50 million	Rp50 million–Rp500 million	Rp500 million–Rp10 billion
Total annual sales value	Less than Rp300 million	Rp300.0 million–Rp2.5 billion	Rp2.5 billion to Rp50.0 billion

Note: A micro, small, and medium-sized enterprise (MSME) should be a productive entity owned by an individual or individual business unit that excludes any subsidiary firm or branch office that is directly or indirectly owned and/or controlled by or being a part of larger firm. Foreign-owned and/or foreign-invested firms are not regarded as MSMEs regardless of meeting the abovementioned criteria.

Source: ADB Asia SME Monitor 2020 database. Data from Law No.20/2008 on Micro, Small, and Medium-sized Enterprises.

Item	Micro	Small	Medium
Employment	1–4 people	5–19 people	20–99 people

MSME = micro, small, and medium-sized enterprise.

Source: ADB Asia SME Monitor 2020 database. Data from Badan Pusat Statistik.

Table 5.2: MSME Landscape

End of period data

Item	2010*	2011	2012	2013	2014	2015	2016**	2017	2018	2019
NUMBER OF ENTERPRISES										
Number of enterprises, total	52,769,426	54,119,971	55,211,396	56,539,560	57,900,787	59,267,759	61,656,547	62,928,077	64,199,606	--
Number of MSMEs	52,764,750	54,114,821	55,206,444	56,534,592	57,895,721	59,262,772	61,651,177	62,922,617	64,194,057	--
Number of large enterprises	4,676	5,150	4,952	4,968	5,066	4,987	5,370	5,460	5,550	--
MSME to total (%)	99.99	99.99	99.99	99.99	99.99	99.99	99.99	99.99	99.99	--
MSME growth (%)	2.5	2.6	2.0	2.4	2.4	2.4	4.0	2.1	2.0	--
MSMEs by sector (% share)										
Agriculture, forestry, and fisheries	50.0	49.6	48.8	--	--	--	--	--	--	--
Manufacturing	6.2	6.4	6.4	--	--	--	16.7	--	--	--
Transportation and communication	6.5	6.5	6.9	--	--	--	7.3	--	--	--
Construction	--	--	--	--	--	--	0.9	--	--	--
Wholesale and retail trade***	29.4	29.6	28.8	--	--	--	63.5	--	--	--
Other services	6.3	6.4	6.9	--	--	--	10.7	--	--	--
Others	1.6	1.6	2.1	--	--	--	0.9	--	--	--
Number of MSMEs by region (% share)										
Capital city	--	--	--	--	--	--	--	--	--	--
Others	--	--	--	--	--	--	--	--	--	--
EMPLOYMENT										
Number of employment, total	98,885,997	100,991,962	104,613,681	110,808,154	117,681,244	127,423,437	116,273,356	120,260,177	120,598,138	--
Number of employment by MSMEs	96,193,623	98,238,913	101,722,458	107,657,509	114,144,082	123,229,386	112,828,610	116,431,224	116,978,631	--
Number of employment by large enterprises	2,692,374	2,753,049	2,891,224	3,150,645	3,537,162	4,194,051	3,444,746	3,828,953	3,619,507	--
MSME employees to total (%)	97.3	97.3	97.2	97.2	97.0	96.7	97.0	96.8	97.0	--
MSME employees growth (%)	2.3	2.1	3.5	5.8	6.0	8.0	(8.4)	3.2	0.5	--
Share of female employees to total employees (%)	--	--	--	--	--	--	--	--	38.7	38.5
Employment by MSME by sector (% share)										
Agriculture, forestry, and fisheries	44.2	43.1	42.4	--	--	--	--	--	--	--
Manufacturing	11.5	11.7	11.7	--	--	--	20.5	--	--	--
Transportation and communication	6.1	5.8	6.9	--	--	--	4.7	--	--	--
Construction	--	--	--	--	--	--	--	--	--	--
Wholesale and retail trade***	22.6	22.5	21.7	--	--	--	54.4	--	--	--
Other services	9.7	10.9	10.5	--	--	--	19.5	--	--	--
Others	5.9	6.0	6.8	--	--	--	0.9	--	--	--
Employment by MSMEs by region (% share)										
Capital city	--	--	--	--	--	--	--	--	--	--
Others	--	--	--	--	--	--	--	--	--	--
CONTRIBUTION TO GDP										
GDP of MSMEs (Rp billion)	2,969,346	3,411,575	4,321,830	4,869,568	5,440,008	6,228,285	7,009,283	7,820,283	8,573,895	--
MSME contribution to GDP (%)	56.2	56.2	58.0	59.1	60.3	61.4	59.8	60.9	61.1	--
MSME GDP growth (%)	13.6	14.9	26.7	12.7	11.7	14.5	12.5	11.6	9.6	--
Labor productivity (Rp million)	30.9	34.7	42.5	45.2	47.7	50.5	62.1	67.2	73.3	--
MSME GDP by sector (% share)										
Agriculture, forestry, and fisheries	27.6	27.7	23.4	--	--	--	--	--	--	--
Manufacturing	16.3	15.4	18.2	--	--	--	26.8	--	--	--
Transportation and communication	5.6	5.6	5.1	--	--	--	4.8	--	--	--
Construction	--	--	--	--	--	--	--	--	--	--
Wholesale and retail trade***	24.1	24.9	26.6	--	--	--	47.8	--	--	--
Other services	16.7	16.9	16.8	--	--	--	20.6	--	--	--
Others	9.6	9.6	9.6	--	--	--	--	--	--	--
MSME GDP by region (% share)										
Capital city	--	--	--	--	--	--	--	--	--	--
Others	--	--	--	--	--	--	--	--	--	--
EXPORTS										
Total export value ($ million)	157,779	203,497	190,020	182,552	175,980	150,366	145,134	168,828	180,013	--
Total export growth (%)	--	29.0	(6.6)	(3.9)	(3.6)	(14.6)	(3.5)	16.3	6.6	--
MSME export value (Rp billion)	162,255	175,895	187,442	166,627	182,113	185,975	255,126	301,630	293,841	--
MSME exports to total export value (%)	17.0	15.8	16.4	14.1	15.7	15.7	14.4	14.5	14.4	--
MSME export growth (%)	(8.9)	8.4	6.6	(11.1)	9.3	2.1	37.2	18.2	(2.6)	--
IMPORTS										
Total import value ($ million)	135,663	177,436	191,690	186,629	178,179	142,695	135,653	156,986	188,711	--
Total Import growth (%)	--	30.8	8.0	(2.6)	(4.5)	(19.9)	(4.9)	15.7	20.2	--
MSME import value (Rp billion)	--	--	--	--	--	--	--	--	--	--
Share of MSME import to total import value (%)	--	--	--	--	--	--	--	--	--	--
MSME import annual growth (%)	--	--	--	--	--	--	--	--	--	--

GDP = gross domestic product; MSME = micro, small, and medium-sized enterprise.

* The Ministry of Cooperatives and SMEs revamped data, tracked back to 2010. Annual sector data were also revamped but not available after 2013 as a survey of the business sector was stopped. ** Sector data in 2016 are based on the Economic Census 2016 (only for non-agriculture sectors). *** Wholesale and retail trade includes hotel and restaurant.

Source: ADB Asia SME Monitor 2020 database. Data from the Ministry of Cooperatives and SMEs, and Badan Pusat Statistik.

Table 5.3: Bank Credit

End of period data

Item	2011	2012	2013	2014	2015	2016	2017	2018	2019
COMMERCIAL BANKS									
Number of commercial banks, total	120	120	120	119	118	116	115	115	110
State-owned banks	4	4	4	4	4	4	4	4	4
Foreign exchange commercial banks	36	36	36	38	39	42	42	42	41
Non-foreign exchange commercial banks	30	30	30	29	27	21	21	21	19
Regional development banks	26	26	26	26	26	27	27	27	27
Joint venture banks	14	14	14	12	12	12	12	12	11
Foreign-owned banks	10	10	10	10	10	10	9	9	8
Credit									
Loans outstanding, total (Rp billion)	2,200,094	2,707,862	3,319,842	3,674,427	4,057,106	4,376,603	4,735,387	5,294,669	5,616,992
Loans outstanding in domestic currency (Rp billion)	--	--	--	--	--	--	--	--	--
Loans outstanding in foreign currency (Rp billion)	--	--	--	--	--	--	--	--	--
Loan growth (%)	24.6	23.1	22.6	10.7	10.4	7.9	8.2	11.8	6.1
Total commercial bank loans to GDP (%)	28.1	31.4	34.8	34.8	35.2	35.3	34.9	35.7	35.5
Lending rate (%)*	12.4	11.8	11.7	12.6	12.7	11.9	11.1	10.5	10.4
Gross nonperforming loans (NPLs) (Rp billion)	47,695	50,595.0	55,998.0	79,866.0	101,896.6	130,369.0	125,319.6	126,723.0	141,834.4
Gross NPLs to total loans (%)	2.2	1.9	1.7	2.2	2.5	3.0	2.6	2.4	2.5
Deposits									
Deposits, total (Rp billion)	568,400	662,000	729,400	766,600	858,200	988,600	1,051,100	1,110,300	--
Deposits in domestic currency (Rp billion)	--	--	--	--	--	--	--	--	--
Deposits in foreign currency (Rp billion)	--	--	--	--	--	--	--	--	--
Deposit rate (%)*	6.9	5.9	6.3	8.8	8.3	7.2	6.5	6.1	6.7
MSME LOANS									
MSME loans outstanding, total (Rp billion)	458,164	526,397	608,823	763,307	790,467	856,997	942,388	1,032,643	1,111,340
MSME loans to total loans outstanding (%)	20.8	19.4	18.5	20.4	19.3	19.4	19.7	19.3	19.6
MSME loans to GDP (%)	6.2	6.4	6.7	7.2	6.9	6.9	6.9	7.0	7.0
MSME loan growth (%)	--	14.9	15.7	25.4	8.0	8.4	10.0	9.6	7.6
MSME lending rate (%)	--	--	--	--	--	--	--	--	--
Nonperforming MSME loans (NPLs) (Rp billion)	15,674	17,011	19,515	31,560	33,208	35,597	38,520	35,504	40,089
MSME NPLs to total MSME loans (%)	3.4	3.2	3.2	4.1	4.2	4.2	4.1	3.4	3.6
Number of MSME loan borrowers	--	--	--	--	--	--	--	--	--
MSME loan borrowers to total bank borrowers (%)	--	--	--	--	--	--	--	--	--
MSME loan rejection rate (% of total applications)	--	--	--	--	--	--	--	--	--
Number of MSME savings account in banks	--	--	--	--	--	--	--	--	--
Guaranteed MSME loans (Rp billion)	--	--	--	--	--	--	--	--	--
Non-collateral MSME loans (Rp billion)	--	--	--	--	--	--	--	--	--
MSME loans outstanding by sector (% share)									
Agriculture, forestry, and fisheries	6.5	8.3	8.5	8.7	8.1	8.2	8.8	9.1	9.9
Manufacturing	11.4	11.3	9.9	9.6	10.0	10.3	10.3	9.9	10.0
Transportation and communication	4.0	3.9	4.0	4.1	3.6	3.4	3.5	3.9	4.0
Construction	5.3	5.8	6.4	6.2	6.1	6.3	6.7	7.0	6.5
Wholesale and retail trade	46.4	49.9	56.0	53.7	52.2	52.7	51.2	50.2	49.3
Other services	13.9	13.9	14.0	15.2	17.9	17.3	17.5	17.9	18.0
Others	12.5	6.9	1.2	2.4	1.9	1.8	1.9	2.0	2.3
MSME loans outstanding by region (% share)									
Capital city	--	--	--	--	--	--	--	--	--
Others	--	--	--	--	--	--	--	--	--
MSME loans outstanding by type of use (% share)									
For working capital	77.7	76.6	72.9	73.1	72.2	72.8	74.0	74.2	72.0
For capital investment	22.3	23.4	27.1	26.9	27.8	27.2	26.0	25.8	28.0
MSME loans outstanding by tenor (% share)									
Less than 1 year	--	--	--	--	--	--	--	--	--
1-5 years	--	--	--	--	--	--	--	--	--
More than 5 years	--	--	--	--	--	--	--	--	--

MSME = micro, small, and medium-sized enterprise.

Notes: Since January 2011, MSME credits are calculated based on fair value. MSME loans outstanding in 2014 has included MSME loans from *syariah* banks since September 2014. * Based on International Monetary Fund/International Financial Statistics (IMF/IFS) data on other depository corporations rates (percent per annum).

Source: ADB Asia SME Monitor 2020 database. Data from Bank Indonesia, Otoritas Jasa Keuangan (Financial Services Authority), and IMF/IFS.

Table 5.4: Public Finance and Guarantees

End of period data

Item	2007	2008	2009	2010	2011	2012	2013	2014	2015	2016	2017	2018	2019
Kredit Usaha Rakyat (KUR; Micro Credit Program)													
Outstanding guaranteed loans (Rp billion)	--	--	8,154	5,010	30,486	40,760	47,422	49,546	22,757	70,669	75,004	125,912	153,180
Growth (%)	--	--	--	(38.6)	508.6	33.7	16.3	4.5	(54.1)	210.5	6.1	67.9	21.7
Guaranteed loans approved (Rp billion)	--	--	--	--	--	--	--	--	--	--	--	--	--
Guaranteed loans disbursed (Rp billion)	982	11,475	4,733	17,229	29,003	34,230	40,047	41,149	16,050	94,409	96,714	120,349	140,073
Accumulated guaranteed loans disbursed (Rp billion)	982	12,457	17,189	34,418	63,421	97,651	137,698	178,847	194,897	289,306	386,020	506,368	646,441
Number of MSMEs guaranteed	3,623	1,652,965	718,320	1,437,650	1,909,912	1,962,121	2,347,429	2,443,907	722,621	4,362,599	4,086,971	4,440,028	4,729,531
Accumulated number of MSMEs guaranteed	--	--	--	--	5,722,470	7,684,591	10,032,020	12,475,927	13,198,548	17,561,147	21,648,118	26,088,146	30,817,677
Nonperforming KUR (% of total KUR loans)	--	--	3.4	2.5	2.1	3.6	3.2	3.3	--	0.4	1.1	1.0	1.1
MSME access to guarantees (% of total MSMEs)	--	--	--	--	--	--	--	--	--	--	--	--	--
Guaranteed loans to MSME loans (%)	--	--	--	--	6.7	7.7	7.8	6.5	2.9	8.2	8.0	12.2	13.8

MSME = micro, small, and medium-sized enterprise.

Source: ADB Asia SME Monitor 2020 database. Data from Coordinating Ministry of Economic Affairs, Bank Indonesia, and Otoritas Jasa Keuangan (Financial Services Authority).

Table 5.5: Nonbank Finance

End of period data

Item	2016	2017	2018	2019
Number of Nonbank Finance Institutions				
Insurance	--	152	151	150
Life insurance companies	--	61	60	60
General insurance companies	--	79	79	78
Reinsurance companies	--	7	7	7
Mandatory insurance	--	3	3	3
Social insurance	--	2	2	2
Financing	68	262	252	246
Multifinance companies	--	193	185	184
Venture capital companies	66	67	65	60
Multifinance infrastructure companies	2	2	2	2
Pension Fund	--	237	233	227
Employer pension fund that operates fixed-benefit pension funds	--	169	164	159
Employer pension fund that operates fixed-contribution pension funds	--	44	44	42
Financial institution pension fund that operates fixed contribution pension funds	--	24	25	26
Special Financial Institutions	--	44	117	109
Indonesia exim bank	--	1	1	1
Pawnshop institutions	--	17	91	83
Guarantee institutions	--	23	22	22
Secondary mortgage financing	--	1	1	1
PT. PNM (SME's and ultra micro financing)	--	1	1	1
PT. Danareksa (advisory and investment banking, equity/debt offering)	--	1	1	1
NBFI Support Services	--	238	237	230
Insurance brokerage companies	--	168	167	161
Reinsurance brokerage companies	--	43	43	42
Loss adjuster companies	--	27	27	27
Microfinance institutions	129	180	183	204
Government pawnshops	4,455	4,322	4,221	4,123
Fintech companies (P2P lenders)	--	--	--	164
Finance Companies				
Total financing (Rp billion)	387,505	414,836	436,267	452,216
Investment financing	104,986	119,041	136,208	134,825
Working capital financing	20,977	22,827	24,037	26,474
Multipurpose financing	230,154	244,084	256,417	274,836
Other financing based on OJK approval	21	128	133	159
Syariah financing	31,367	28,757	19,472	15,922
By type (% share)				
Investment financing	27.1	28.7	31.2	29.8
Working capital financing	5.4	5.5	5.5	5.9
Multipurpose financing	59.4	58.8	58.8	60.8
Other financing based on OJK approval	0.0	0.0	0.0	0.0
Syariah financing	8.1	6.9	4.5	3.5
By sector (% share)				
Agriculture, forestry, and fisheries	4.8	4.8	4.1	4.4
Manufacturing	7.6	8.9	8.5	8.8
Transportation and communication	6.3	6.9	7.7	7.8
Construction	2.6	3.4	3.6	3.4
Wholesale and retail trade	10.0	16.7	17.1	19.9
Other services	4.3	5.1	4.6	5.2
Others	64.3	54.2	54.4	50.5
Nonperforming financing ratio (%)				
Total financing	3.3	3.0	2.7	2.4
Investment financing	5.3	4.2	3.6	3.1
Working capital financing	2.7	3.1	1.7	2.0
Multipurpose financing	2.4	2.1	2.0	1.8
Other financing based on OJK approval	0.0	0.8	1.1	0.8
Syariah financing	3.4	5.2	7.5	6.9
Microfinance Institutions				
Loans outstanding (Rp billion)	156	330	467	616
Government Pawnshops				
Loans outstanding (Rp billion)	35,465	36,882	40,856	50,366

MSME = micro, small, and medium-sized enterprise.

Note: Nonbank finance data has been reclassified based on new business activities (POJK 35/POJK.05/2018) and new economy sector (SEOJK 3/SEOJK.05/2016) since 2016.

Source: ADB Asia SME Monitor 2020 database. Data from Otoritas Jasa Keuangan (Financial Services Authority).

Table 5.6: Capital Markets

End of period data

Item	2007	2008	2009	2010	2011	2012	2013	2014	2015	2016	2017	2018	2019
EQUITY MARKET													
Main Board													
Index: Jakarta Composite Index	2,746	1,355	2,534	3,704	3,822	4,317	4,274	5,227	4,593	5,297	6,356	6,194	6,300
Market capitalization (Rp billion)	1,988,326	1,076,491	2,019,375	3,247,097	3,537,294	4,126,995	4,219,020	5,228,043	4,872,702	5,753,613	7,052,389	7,023,497	7,265,016
Growth (%)	--	(45.9)	87.6	60.8	8.9	16.7	2.2	23.9	(6.8)	18.1	22.6	(0.4)	3.4
Trading value (Rp billion)	1,050,154	1,064,528	975,135	1,176,237	1,223,441	1,116,113	1,522,122	1,453,392	1,406,362	1,844,588	1,809,592	2,040,086	2,230,919
Trading volume (million shares)	1,039,542	787,846	1,467,659	1,330,865	1,203,550	1,053,762	1,342,657	1,327,016	1,446,314	1,925,420	2,844,846	2,536,279	3,562,369
Number of listed companies (accumulated)	383	396	398	420	440	459	483	506	521	537	566	619	668
SMEs listed (accumulated)	0	2	2	3	6	6	6	6	6	6	7	10	25
Number of IPOs	22	19	13	23	25	23	31	24	18	16	37	57	55
SME IPOs*	2	0	1	3	0	0	0	0	0	1	3	15	24
Number of delisted companies	8	6	11	1	5	4	7	1	3	0	8	4	6

IPO=initial public offering, SME=small and medium-sized enterprise.

* Before July 2017, data used total asset below Rp100 billion to define the SME in accordance with Bapepam Rule IX.C.7. After July 2017, data used total asset below Rp250 billion for SME classification in accordance with OJK Rule POJK53.

Source: ADB Asia SME Monitor 2020 database. Data from Indonesia Stock Exchange.

Table 5.7: Listing Requirements—Indonesia Stock Exchange

Criteria	Stock		
	Main Board	Development Board	Acceleration Board
Issuer	Limited liability company	Limited liability company	Limited liability company
Independent board of commissioners	Required	Required	• 6-month grace period for medium-sized enterprise. • 1-year grace period for small enterprise.
Corporate secretary	Required	Required	• 6-month grace period for medium-sized enterprise. • 1-year grace period for small enterprise.
Audit committee and unit of internal audit	Required	Required	• 6-month grace period for medium-sized enterprise. • 1-year grace period for small enterprise.
Operating period	36 months	12 months	Since posting operating revenues.
Operating profit	Minimum 1 year.	May experience loss, but should have operating and net profit in 2 years based on projection.	May suffer loss, but should have operating profit in maximum 6 years based on projection.
Audited financial report	Minimum 3 years, unqualified opinion.	Minimum 12 months, unqualified opinion.	Minimum 1 year or since establishment if less than 1 year, unqualified opinion.
Capital requirement	Net tangible asset*: minimum Rp100 billion.	a) net tangible asset minimum Rp5 billion; or b) net profit minimum Rp1 billion and market capitalization minimum Rp100 billion; or c) revenue minimum Rp40 billion and market capitalization minimum Rp200 billion.	n/a
Number of shares owned by non-controlling and non-majority shareholders	Minimum 300 million shares and: • 20% of total shares, for equity <Rp500 billion. • 15% of total shares, for equity Rp500 billion–Rp2 trillion. • 10% of total shares, for equity >Rp2 trillion.	Minimum 150 million shares and: • 20% of total shares, for equity <Rp500 billion. • 15% of total shares, for equity Rp500 billion–Rp2 trillion. • 10% of total shares, for equity >Rp2 trillion.	Minimum 20% of total shares.
Minimum offering price	Rp100	Rp100	Rp50
Number of shareholders	≥1,000 parties	≥500 parties	≥300 parties
Underwriting scheme	Full commitment	Full commitment	Best effort

Source: ADB Asia SME Monitor 2020 database. Data from Indonesia Stock Exchange.

Table 5.8: Policies and Regulations

Regulations	
Name	**Outline**
MSME development	
Law No.20/2008 on Micro, Small and Medium-sized Enterprises	MSME definition and the government obligation to promote the MSME sector.
Presidential Decree No.98/2014 on Licensing for Micro and Small Business	Licensing for micro and small businesses.
Ministry of Home Affairs Regulation No. 83/2014 on Guildelines for the Issuance of Micro and Small Business License	Guildelines for issuing business licenses for micro and small businesses.
Presidential Regulation No.2/2015 on National Mid-term Development Plan 2015-2018	Formulation of the National Mid-term Development Plan 2015-2019. MSME policies are aligned with this.
Government Regulation No.14/2015 on Master Plan of National Industry Development 2015-2035	Formulation of the Master Plan of National Industry Development 2015-2035, including industrial estate and centers for small and medium industry.
Minister of Industry Regulation Number 64/M-IND/PER/7/2016	Define industrial classification based on the number of manpower and investment value.
Banking sector	
Law No.7/1992 and Law No.10/1998 (amendment) on Banking	Regulation on commercial banks.
Bank Indonesia Regulation No.14/22/PBI/2012 on Financing and Technical Assistance by Commercial Banks in Developing MSMEs (amendment of Regulation No.17/12/PBI/2015)	Mandatory bank lending to MSMEs: 20% of banks' loan portfolios by 2018.
Presidential Decree No.14/2015 on Financing Committee for MSME juncto Presidential Decree No.19/2015 on Amendment of Presidential Decree No.14/2015	Regulation on the Financing Committee for MSME.
OJK Regulation No.40/POJK.03 /2019 on Quality Assessment of Commercial Bank Assets	Assessment criterion on the quality of MSME loans included (based on the timeliness of principal/interest payments).
OJK Regulation No.19/ POJK.03/2014 on Branchless Banking (LAKU PANDAI)	Regulation on branchless banking (Laku Pandai) comprising three programs: (i) saving (BSA; Basic Saving Account), (ii) credit/financing to micro customers, and (iii) other financial products (e.g., micro insurance).
OJK Circular No.42/SEOJK.03/2016 on Guidelines for Risk-Based Assets Calculating for Credit Risk Using a Standard Approach	Lowering risk weighted in Risk Weight Asset (RWA) for MSME loans.
OJK Circular No.14/SEOJK.03/2016 on Opening of Commercial Bank Networks Based on Capital Core	Providing incentives for banks with MSME loans to open a bank office network.
OJK Regulation No.14/POJK.03/2018 on Assets Quality Assessment of Commercial Banks to Encourage Development of Housing Sector and Foreign Exchange	Assessment criterion on the quality of loans to export-oriented micro/small businesses included (based on the timeliness of principal/interest payments).
OJK Regulation No.17/POJK.03/2018 on Business Activities and Office Network of Commercial Bank Based on Core Capital	Obligation for commercial banks to fulfill the ratio of productive setor loans (including MSME loans).
Presidential Regulation No. 82/2016 on National Strategy for Inclusive Finance	Regulation outlining the National Financial Inclusive Strategies (2016).
Nonbank finance sector	
Presidential Regulation No.9/2009 on Financing Institutions	Regulation on nonbank financial institutions (NBFIs).
Law No.1/2013 on Microfinance Institutions	Regulation on microfinance institutions (MFIs).
Government Regulation No.89/2014 on Loan Interest Rate or Yield of Financing and MFI's Business Coverage	Regulation on loan conditions and activities of MFIs.
OJK Regulations No.12/POJK.05/2014 and No. 61/POJK.05/2015 on Business Licensing and Institutional Matters of MFIs	Licensing for MFIs.
OJK Regulation No.13/POJK.05/2014 and No. 62/POJK.05/2015 on Business Management of MFIs	Regulation on business management of MFIs.
OJK Regulation No.14/POJK.05/2014 on Fostering and Supervision of MFIs	Regulation on MFI promotion.
Law No.25/1992 on Cooperatives.	Regulation on cooperatives.
OJK Regulation No.35/POJK.05/2015 on Business Operations of Venture Capital Company	Regulation on business operations of venture capital companies. Venture capital companies should have a business portfolio that is placed in a Business Partner Company (PPU; Perusahaan Pasangan Usaha) that is included in the category of MSMEs at least 5% of the total business portfolio.
OJK Regulation No.77/POJK.01/2016 on Information Technology-Based Lending Services (LPMUBTI)	Regulation on fintech peer-to-peer (P2P) lending platforms.
OJK Regulation No.13/POJK.02/2018 on Digital Financial Innovation in the Financial Services Sector	Regulation on facilitating innovation in the digital financial services ecosystem.
OJK Regulation No.37/POJK.04/2018 on Equity Crowdfunding	Regulation on equity crowdfunding (definition and activities).
Capital markets	
Law No.8/1995 on Capital Market	Regulation on capital markets.
Decision of the Directors of PT Bursa Efek Indonesia (Indonesia Stock Exchange) No II-V on Trading Regulation for Listing Share on the Acceleration Board	Regulation on specific provisions for listing share on the Acceleration Board (specialized SME board).
OJK Regulation No.53/POJK.04/2017 on Registration Statements in the Context of a Public Offering and Capital Increase with Providing Pre-emptive Rights by Issuers with Small Scale Assets or Issuers with Middle Scale Assets	Regulation on registration statements in public offering and capital increase with providing preemptive rights by issuers with small-scale and middle-scale assets.
"OJK Regulation No.54/POJK.04/2017 on Prospectus Forms and Contents in the Context of Public Offerings and Capital Increase by Providing Preemptive Rights toSubscribe Securities, by Issuers with Small or Medium-Sized Assets"	Regulation to adjust the format and content of prospectus in public offerings to enable small-scale/medium-scale issuers to access the capital market.
Public finance and guarantees	
Law No. 1/2016 on Guarantee Institutions	Regulation on credit guarantee and reguarantee institutions.
OJK Regulation No.1/2017 on the Business Licensing and Institutional Matters of Guarantee Institutions	Licensing for guarantee institutions.
OJK Regulation No.2/2017 on the Business Management of Guarantee Institutions	Regulation on activities of guarantee institutions.
OJK Regulation No.3/2017 on the Good Corporate Governance of Guarantee Institutions	Regulation on inspection for guarantee institutions.
Coordinating Ministry for Economic Affairs Regulation No.11/2017 on KUR Implemention Guidelines (amended by Regulation No.08/2019)	Guidelines for implementing the KUR (Micro Credit Program).
Regulators and Policymakers	
Name	**Responsibility**
Bank Indonesia (BI)	Implement MSME access to finance and financial inclusion policies.
Financial Services Authority (OJK; Otoritas Jasa Keuangan)	Regulate and supervise banks, NBFIs, and capital markets.
Coordinating Ministry of Economic Affairs (CMEA)	Responsible for monitoring the KUR program and coordinating the national financial inclusion strategy.
Ministry of Cooperatives and SMEs (MCSME)	Regulate and supervise cooperatives and MSMEs.

continued on next page

Table 5.8 continued

Ministry of Industry (MOI)		Regulate and supervise manufacturing industry including small and medium industry.
Ministry of Trade (MOT)		Regulate and supervise trade businesses, including SME exporters.
Ministry of Home Affairs (MOHA)		Coordinate domestic/internal affairs, including SME development issues.
Policies		
Name	**Responsible Entity**	**Outline**
MSME development		
Instruction of the President of the Republic of Indonesia No.6/2007 and No.5/2008 (Economic Policy Package I & II)	Government	A comprehensive economic policy package prepared by all economic ministries/agencies [Strengthening the MSME sector] (extract) 1) Access to finance (strengthening revolving fund, credit guarantee institutions, MFIs, effective implementation of KUR, development of financing schemes for MSMEs, *Syariah* product development, etc.). 2) Access to market. 3) Capacity development of human resources. 4) Deregulation.
Masterplan for Acceleration and Expansion of Indonesia Economic Development 2011-2025 (MP3EI) (2011)	Government	1) Developing the regional economic potential in six Indonesia economic corridors: Sumatra Economic Corridor, Java Economic Corridor, Kalimantan Economic Corridor, Sulawesi Economic Corridor, Bali Nusa Tenggara Economic Corridor, and Papua Kepulauan Maluku Economic Corridor. 2) Strengthening national connectivity locally and internationally. 3) Strengthening human resource capacity and national science and technology to support the development of main programs in every economic corridor.
Creating Healthy, Strong, Resilient and Independent Cooperatives and SMEs to Contribute to the National Economy (2015–2019 vison and mission)	MCSME	Strategic directions: 1) Improving the quality of human resources. 2) Increasing access to finance. 3) Increasing productivity. 4) Strengthening business capacity. 5) Protecting business for cooperatives and SMEs.
Master Plan of National Industry Development 2015-2035 (2015)	MOI	SME related strategies: 1) Developing central region of industrial growth, industrial-designated regions, industrial estates and centers of small and medium industry. 2) Providing the affirmative action such as policy formulation, strengthening institutional capacity, and providing facilities to small and medium industry.
Access to finance		
Joint Decree on MFI Promotion Strategy (2009)	BI MCSME MOF MOHA	1) Database on informal MFIs. 2) Formalization of informal MFIs. 3) Human resource development. 4) Strengthening supervision. 5) Support for formalized MFIs.
The Capital Market and Non Bank Financial Industry Master Plan 2010–2014 (2010)	MOF	1) Easily accessible, efficient, and competitive source of funds: (a) Reduce constraints on business communities to access capital market for source of funds. (b) Increase public accessibility to finance and guarantee institutions. (c) Improve the role of professionals, supporting institutions, and underwriters in public offering. 2) Conducive and attractive investment climate as well as reliable risk management. 3) A stable, resilient, and liquid industry. 4) Fair and transparent regulatory framework which guarantees legal certainty.
National Strategy for Financial Inclusion (2012)	Government	Increase public access to financial services among all layers of the population Target groups: 1) Low-income poor. 2) Working poor/MSMEs. 3) Near-poor.
National Strategy for Financial Inclusion (SNKI) (2016)	Government	Key components: 1) Financial education. 2) Public property rights (improvement of collateral for loans, e.g., land titling and copyright/patent certificate). 3) Financial distribution channels and intermediary facilities (e.g., digital financial services and value chain financing). 4) Government financial services (including KUR and non-cash subsidy and payment). 5) Customer protection.
Indonesian Financial Services Sector Masterplan (2015-2019)	OJK	Primary focuses: 1) Optimizing the supporting role of the financial services sector in accelerating domestic economic growth (contributive). 2) Safeguarding financial system stability as a foundation of sustainable development (stable). 3) Attaining public financial well-being and nurturing equitable development (inclusive).

BI=Bank Indonesia, CMEA=Coordinating Ministry of Economic Affairs, MCSME=Ministry of Cooperatives and SMEs, MFI=microfinance institution, MSME=micro, small, and medium-sized enterprise, MOF=Ministry of Finance, MOHA=Ministry of Home Affairs, OJK=Otoritas Jasa Keuangan (Financial Services Authority).

Source: ADB Asia SME Monitor 2020 database. Data from Bank Indonesia, Otritas Jasa Keuangan, and Coordinating Ministry of Economic Affairs.

Country Review

Lao People's Democratic Republic

Overview

The Lao People's Democratic Republic (Lao PDR) has a working age population (ages 15–64) of 4.4 million. The economy recorded robust growth of 6.2% in 2018, but it slowed to 5.0% in 2019.[52] Micro, small, and medium-sized enterprises (MSMEs) remain a staple of the business community, with 99.8% of the total number of firms. Bank credit to MSMEs has been slowing since 2018, affected by moderating economic growth. The nonbank finance industry has yet to fill the unmet financing demand from MSMEs. Meanwhile, the central bank has formulated a national financial inclusion strategy, addressing the development of alternative finance models or digital finance service solutions to unserved/underserved groups, including MSMEs. While the government has worked to develop MSMEs through its mid-term development plan, significant challenges remain. Chief among these are access to finance, development of human capital and skills, access to markets, and adoption of the latest technology.

1. MSME Development

- MSMEs are typically engaged in traditional trade; more than half of microenterprises are considered part of the informal economy, and reforms are underway to, for example, ease the registration process so they can join the formal economy and take advantage of its benefits.
- The number of MSME employees has been declining compared with non-MSMEs; while trading firms are the largest MSME employer, "other services" shows the greatest potential for growth based upon recent trends.
- Access to markets remains a major challenge for MSMEs, and thus a growing policy issue; with the energy sector dominating exports, greater MSME export can help diversify the economy and their participation in global value chains can stimulate more robust growth.
- There remains much untapped potential in technology and innovation, as limited internet connectivity slows development of e-commerce and the digital industry; MSMEs need the capacity to use digital technology and contribute more to innovative business.
- The chamber of commerce is a major provider of business development services and networking opportunities to MSMEs.

Scale of MSMEs

On 21 December 2011, the National Assembly passed Law No.011 on the Promotion of Small and Medium Sized Enterprises. The law classified MSMEs producing commercial goods, conducting trade, and providing services by annual average number of employees, total assets, and annual turnover (revenue). It said, "the government shall issue decisions on MSME classification in each stage of development as appropriate."

Prior to Decree No.25 in 2017, the government defined small and medium-sized enterprises (SMEs) based on Prime Minister Decree No.42 of 2004, with no microenterprise category. That changed in January 2017, when

[52] ADB. 2020. *Asian Development Outlook 2020 Supplement (June 2020)*. Manila.

the Department of Small and Medium Enterprise Promotion (DOSMEP), under the Ministry of Industry and Commerce (MOIC), defined MSMEs pursuant to Law No.011 and Decree No.25.

The decree defined MSMEs by industry (Table 6.1). For manufacturing (the production of commercial goods), for instance, a microenterprise is a firm with up to five employees, no more than KN100 million in total assets, and with maximum annual revenue of KN400 million. A small enterprise has 6–50 employees, up to KN1 billion in assets, and a maximum KN2 billion in turnover. A medium-sized enterprise has 51–99 employees, up to KN4 billion in assets, and KN4 billion or less in revenue. However, these definitions are not yet reflected in MSME statistics, which continue to use the old 2004 SME definition.[53] Throughout this report, the term "MSME" is collectively used.

The number of MSMEs, and their share of total enterprises, has been relatively constant since 2006. The Lao Statistics Bureau collects data every 5–7 years (there is data for 2006, 2013, and 2018). There were 126,717 MSMEs in 2006, 124,510 in 2013, and 124,567 in 2018 (Figure 6.1A and Table 6.2). As a share of total enterprises, MSMEs represent 99.8% of the Lao PDR firms for each year. MSME growth fell by 1.7% between 2006 and 2013, edging up by 0.05% from 2013 to 2018.

Wholesale and retail trade (including the repair business) is the largest sector, accounting for 62.9% of MSMEs in 2018, followed by manufacturing (12.4%) and other services (12.2%) (Figure 6.1B). The services sector (trade plus other services) accounted for 75.2%. The share of other services—which includes accommodation, food services, tourism, and financial services—surged between 2006 and 2013, before declining from 2013 to 2018 (by 35%, from 18.9% to 12.2%). In 2019, slowing tourism growth and short electricity supply (caused by the 2018 hydroelectric dam collapse and flooding) accelerated the slowdown. Most manufacturing MSMEs are in food processing, garments, cement and construction materials, and wood furniture (more than 60% of total MSME production).[54]

The most recent MSME data by region is for 2013. Back then, 28.2% of MSMEs were located in the capital city, Vientiane, 24.0% in the north region, 32.3% in the central region, with the remaining 15.5% in the south region.

The Lao PDR enterprises must register with the MOIC and obtain a business license from the government authority responsible for their industry. According to the Department of Enterprise Registration and Management (DERM) under the MOIC, 136,201 firms registered from August 2008 through July 2019.[55] The number of registered enterprises, mainly MSMEs, has been increasing. DERM began monitoring registered enterprises frequently (monthly) since 2017. It has made efforts to improve the business registration by introducing an online system.

There is no data available on the informal economy, but the Lao National Chamber of Commerce and Industry (LNCCI) estimates that more than half of microenterprises operating in the Lao PDR are considered informal, making it difficult to count microenterprises accurately.[56] Nonetheless, these firms must still report to a local official and pay a small tax, even if not in official statistics.

[53] Decree No.42 of 2004 defined a small enterprise as having fewer than 20 employees, up to KN250 million in total assets, and up to KN400 million in annual turnover; a medium-sized enterprise had 20-99 employees, up to KN1.2 billion in total assets, and up to KN1.0 billion in turnover.

[54] Interview with deputy director general of the Department of Industry and Handicrafts on 30 July 2019.

[55] Interview with director of the Department of Enterprise Registration and Management on 30 July 2019.

[56] Interview with the secretary general of the Lao National Chamber of Commerce and Industry on 1 August 2019.

Figure 6.1: Number of MSMEs

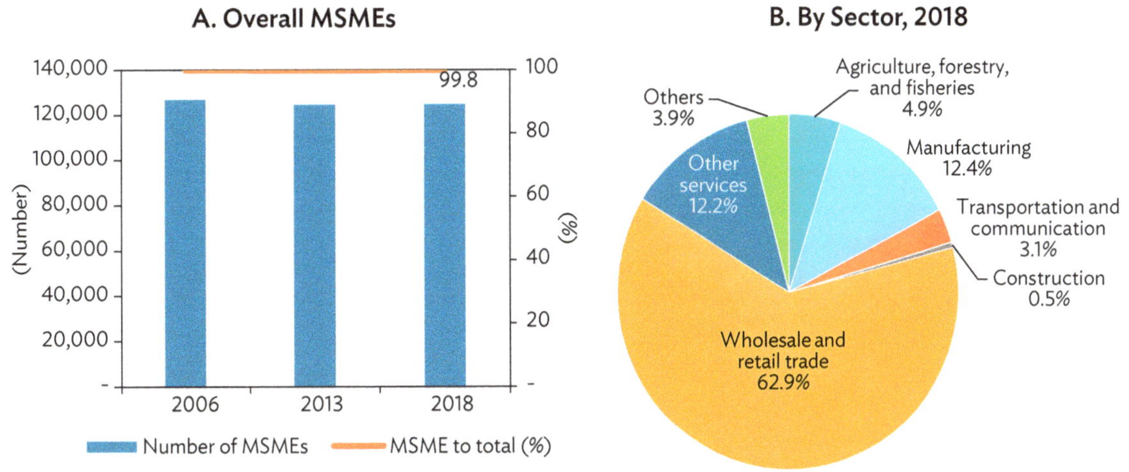

MSME = micro, small, and medium-sized enterprise.

Source: ADB Asia SME Monitor 2020 database. Data from the Ministry of Industry and Commerce.

Employment

MSMEs employed 238,703 people in 2006, 472,231 in 2013, and 472,529 in 2018. These figures represent 87.4%, 82.9%, and 82.4% of total employment, respectively (Figure 6.2A), with a decreasing trend in share of MSME employment to total workforce. The latest available data on MSME employment by sector is 2013. Wholesale and retail trade accounted for half of MSME employment, while other services employed 22.4% and manufacturing 17.4% (Figure 6.2B). The services sector (trade plus other services) absorbed 72.8% of the workforce. From 2006 to 2013, the employment share for wholesale and retail trade remained stable, while other services (accommodation, food services, tourism, and financial services) grew by 69.8%, suggesting other services has the most potential for job creation. Given the declining share of other services to the total number of MSMEs in 2018, it appears absolute employment in other services declined as well. Based on the 2013 data, manufacturing had yet to create enough MSME jobs.

Figure 6.2: Employment by MSMEs

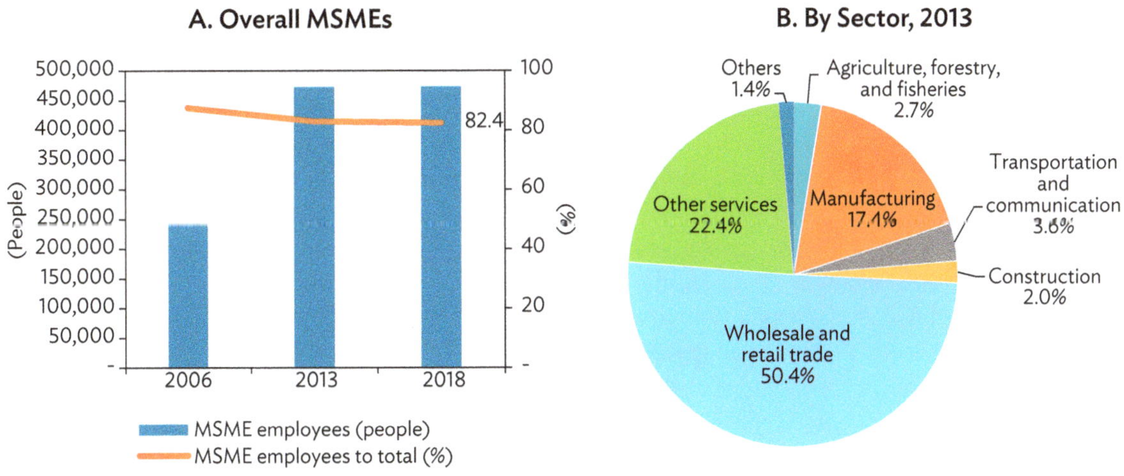

MSME = micro, small, and medium-sized enterprise.

Source: ADB Asia SME Monitor 2020 database. Data from the Ministry of Industry and Commerce.

Business Productivity

Nominal gross domestic product (GDP) was KN152 trillion in 2018, with real GDP growth remaining a robust 6.2% in 2018 but slowing to 5.0% in 2019. There are no data on MSME contributions to GDP by value or percentage share. This also applies to MSME labor productivity, manufacturing value added, and applicable subcategories such as regional and sector MSME contributions. However, overall sector data are available. In 2018, other services contributed the largest portion of GDP (29.8%), followed by energy and mines (19.3%) and agriculture, forestry, and fisheries (17.7%). Wholesale and retail trade, dominated by MSMEs, contributed 13.8% to GDP, up 0.8 percentage points from 13.0% in 2017.

Market Access

MSMEs mostly operate domestically with a limited customer base and little exposed to global markets. According to the LNCCI and the MOIC, among others, access to markets remains a major challenge for MSMEs. Very few MSMEs are able to participate in global supply chains. Estimates from the myriad stakeholders interviewed in 2019 suggest that less than 1% of MSMEs have joined global supply chains. They also generally agree no more than 10% of MSMEs export at all. Overall export and import data for 2006–2018 (in US dollars) shows exports increased by 500.3% (a compound annual growth rate of 16.1%) from $882 million in 2006 to $5.3 billion in 2018 (Table 6.2). Imports climbed by 481.5% (a compound annual growth rate of 15.8%), from $1.1 billion in 2006 to $6.2 billion in 2018. Slowing growth of electricity generation (a key export), however, pushed down exports in 2019, suggesting the need for developing more MSME exports to ensure more robust and diversified export growth.

The Investment Promotion Department (IPD) of the Ministry of Planning and Investment is trying to attract more investment in the Lao PDR, focusing on mega projects in transportation and energy infrastructure. Given their small size and a lack of financial capability, however, MSMEs are not eligible to participate in these infrastructure projects. There are no preferential measures such as tax incentives or simplified procurement procedures for MSMEs to participate in infrastructure projects. And there are no policy measures on investing in domestic MSME-led projects. DOSMEP addressed MSMEs' market access and expansion beyond traditional trade in its mid-term SME development plan, but concrete action plans have yet to be implemented.

Technology and Innovation

Information and communications technology (ICT) has rapidly spread across the country, although it remains in an infant stage of development. In 2018, there were 3.7 million mobile cellular subscriptions, or 83% of the 4.4 million working age population.[57] In 2017, 25.5% of the population used the internet. While increasing rapidly, there is still limited internet connectivity in the country.[58] E-commerce business -buying and selling goods and services through the Internet and the digital platform- has yet to come to the Lao PDR. As of August 2018, there were no e-commerce businesses registered at DERM. The limited internet connectivity, high cost of internet use, and lack of an e-commerce regulatory framework are behind the slow development of e-commerce and the digital service industry. MSMEs engaged in traditional trade will require some digital literacy to use this technology to upgrade their business. DOSMEP says that enhancing productivity, technology, and innovation is the greatest challenge to MSME development (it is the top pillar of the SME Development Plan for 2016–2020).[59]

[57] Laos Statistical Information Service (https://laosis.lsb.gov.la/) and World Bank database (https://data.worldbank.org/indicator/). Accessed on 30 March 2020.

[58] World Bank database (https://data.worldbank.org/indicator/). Accessed on 30 March 2020.

[59] Interview with deputy director general of the Department of SME Promotion under the Ministry of Industry and Commerce on 30 July 2019.

Networking and Support

LNCCI offers business development services, networking opportunities, and business incubation opportunities to members. It has 4,000 corporate members, 99% of which are MSMEs. They are mainly in trading, manufacturing, hospitality, and pharmaceuticals.

LNCCI sponsors three MSME Service Centers. The first was launched in Vientiane in 2017, with two additional offices opened in Champasa and Luang Prabang at the end of August 2019. These service centers have two functions, both related to market access: to help MSMEs access the domestic market and to help MSMEs export to Association of Southeast Asian Nations (ASEAN) countries. Less than 10% of LNCCI members export, attributed to higher operating costs (a cultural preference to buy assets rather than lease them). The service centers plan to provide MSME incubator space. The Vientiane service center will provide workspace for start-ups free of charge for the first 6 months (they will pay a nominal rent of $100/month afterward). It will accommodate up to 10 start-ups simultaneously.

LNCCI has two financing plans awaiting approval from the Bank of the Lao PDR. The first is an investment scheme whereby LNCCI requests large firms to invest in start-ups, making a pool of quasi-venture capitalists/ business angels. A selection committee of local banks, investors representing large companies, and the LNCCI Secretariat will evaluate proposals and decide the investment amount. The second supports entrepreneurs prior to start-up phase. A maximum amount of $1,000 seed capital will back promising new ideas. A business plan competition will be held with a $7,000 cash prize for the winner.

2. Access to Finance

- Bank credit growth decelerated due to the flood-induced economic slowdown in 2018, which included a decline in MSME bank credit.
- A specialized state-owned bank helps MSMEs access concessional loans; efforts to establish credit guarantees are underway, and the government has expanded financial intermediation loans to MSMEs through an SME Promotion Fund.
- The nonbank finance industry is small in scale and has yet to fill the unmet financing demand from MSMEs; microfinance institutions and leasing companies are the primary sources of formal nonbank financing for MSMEs.
- Digital financial services are in their infancy, as fintech-related regulations have yet to be implemented; nonetheless, the central bank is promoting branchless banking under its financial inclusion roadmap; but MSMEs remain unfamiliar with fintech as digital finance literacy needs to be strengthened.
- Capital markets are not a funding source for growing MSMEs and start-ups; there is no dedicated MSME equity market, although the securities commission has started brainstorming about a new board for MSMEs.
- Financial infrastructure needed to promote access to finance remains underdeveloped, with a credit bureau and collateral registry either at the nascent or planning stage; financial authorities and the private sector have initiated training and education in financial literacy to increase access to finance for MSMEs.

Every stakeholder interviewed mentioned access to finance as the main barrier to MSME development. Government agencies and the private sector are addressing the problem with plans to create a credit guarantee scheme, establish a credit bureau, and provide financial education and digital literacy targeting MSMEs.

Bank Credit

There were 42 commercial banks in the Lao PDR as of end-2019, comprising 7 private sector banks; 3 state-owned banks; and 32 others including joint venture banks, foreign subsidiary banks, and foreign bank branches. The Bank of the Lao PDR (BOL), the central bank, regulates and supervises both banks and nonbank finance institutions.

The bank credit market has been growing steadily, but growth has decelerated since 2018, when a hydroelectric dam collapse caused catastrophic flooding in Champasak and Attapeu provinces. The flooding limited the country's ability to generate electricity in 2019 and reduced export earnings along with economic growth generally. This hurt the corporate credit market. The limited electricity generation and supply also affected MSME business operations, performance, and banks credit delivery in 2018 and 2019.

MSME loans outstanding amounted to KN14.1 trillion ($1.6 billion)[60] as of end-2019, 1.0% less than end-2018 (Figure 6.3A and Table 6.3). The share of MSME loans to total outstanding bank loans has been falling, down from 30.9% in 2015 to 19.8% by end-2019 (a 36.0% drop). It declined from 30.9% in 2015 to 23.4% in 2016 (down 24.2%). In 2017, the MSME loan percentage climbed slightly to 23.8% before falling to 20.6% in 2018. MSME loans as a percentage of GDP was 12.7% in 2015, falling to 8.5% in 2019, a drop of 33.2%.

By sector as of end-2019, wholesale and retail trade accounted for the largest share of MSME loans (37.0%), followed by construction (20.7%) and other services (18.6%) (Figure 6.3B). According to BOL data for 2015–2019, the percentage of loans in wholesale and retail trade ranged from 33.2% to 38.0%. For construction, it ranged from 14.1% to 20.7%, and for other services, from 16.1% to 18.6%. Construction climbed from 14.1% in 2016 to 17.7% in 2017 and 2018, then increased again in 2019 to 20.7%. Services increased more evenly over the period. Others declined 44.5% from 19.8% in 2015 to 11.0% at end-2019.

Nonperforming loans (NPLs) as a percentage of total loans were stable during 2015–2019 (3.1%).[61] The average lending rate for MSMEs is 14% per annum against 9% for large firms. Commercial banks normally take mandatory deposit and real estate security as collateral for MSME loans. It is up to the bank's discretion to accept movable collateral such as inventory or machinery.

The BOL has partly introduced Basel II for banking supervision, and has established a new committee to study the Basel capital accord in part to assess the impact Basel II has on the MSME credit market.

60 The figures throughout this report with US dollar equivalents are converted from Laotian kip into $ using International Monetary Fund/ International Financial Statistics (IMF/IFS) end-of-year currency exchange rates.

61 All banks in the Lao PDR use the same criteria for nonperforming loans (NPLs): (i) Level 1: 90 days delayed repayment; (ii) Level 2: delinquent 180 days (6 months); and (iii) Level 3: delinquent 360 days (1 year).

Figure 6.3: MSME Loans

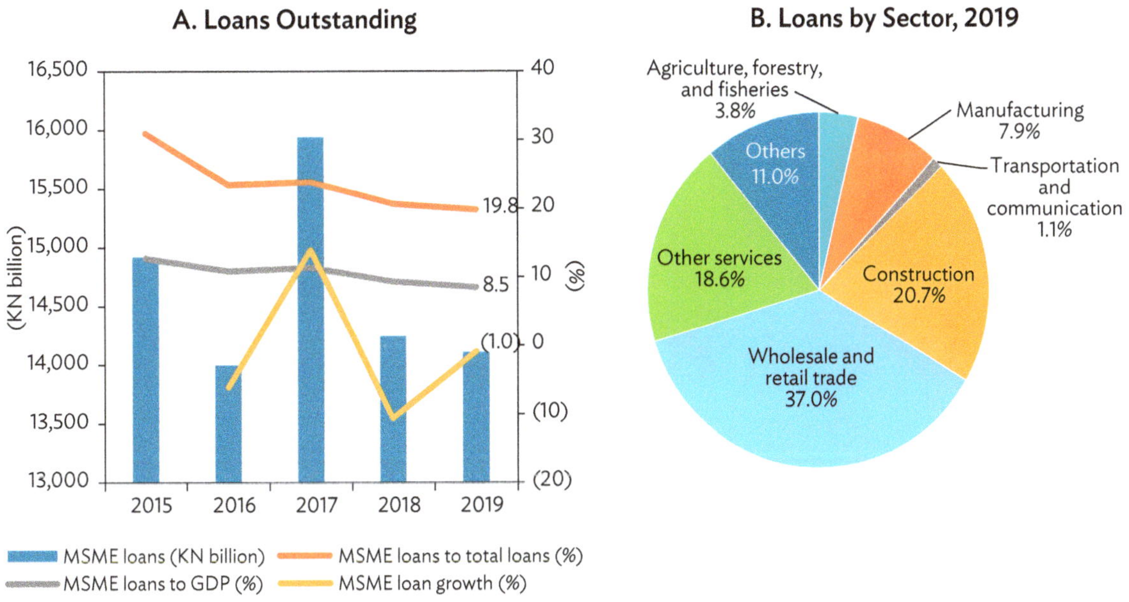

MSME = micro, small, and medium-sized enterprise.

Source: ADB Asia SME Monitor 2020 database. Data from Bank of the Lao PDR.

Public Financing and Guarantees

a. Specialized bank for MSMEs

An alternative source of bank credit is the Lao Development Bank (LDB), one of three state-owned banks (owned by the Ministry of Finance). It was established in 2003 with the merger of two commercial banks. In 2008, the Ministry of Finance appointed LDB as an MSME-focused bank. LDB has 18 branch offices and 76 service units.

MSMEs comprise about 99.5% of LDB lending with large firms taking up the rest (which helps LDB earn profits). By share, MSMEs account for 65%, while large firms account for 35%. By sector, the most active MSME borrowers are construction material suppliers, followed by wholesale and retail trade, agriculture, and services. The biggest large firm borrowers are in construction.

LDB uses the asset criteria of the national definition for MSME lending. Target priority sectors for MSME lending follow government priorities. The annual lending rate for MSMEs is 10% on average but 6.5% if via the SME Promotion Fund. Average loan tenor is 3 years or less, with a maximum 5 years. LDB accepts only real estate (land and buildings) as collateral for loans. Movable assets are not accepted. The loan-to-value ratio is 60% of collateral value. LDB also offers US dollar- and Thai Baht-denominated loans to MSMEs, besides local currency (kip) loans.

The NPL ratio for MSME loans was 4.6% as of August 2019, and it is rising. LDB's NPL ratio is based on 90 days delayed repayment (Level 1 criterion). If the borrower cannot repay the loan, LDB will discuss with the borrower and restructure the loan as necessary. In certain circumstances, the borrower may need to sell properties or other assets to repay the loan if there has been no progress on repayment. LDB does not provide credit guarantees.

b. Credit guarantees

Efforts to establish credit guarantees are underway, but remain nascent. The BOL has a working group to develop a credit guarantee scheme. The group, with the support of the People's Bank of China (PRC), drafted legislation to create a credit guarantee scheme, which the National Assembly finalized in 2019 and plans to pass in 2020.

c. Soft loan programs

BOL is working closely with the MOIC to promote MSME access to finance through the SME Promotion Fund (SME Fund). The SME Promotion Law of 2011 proposed establishing an SME Promotion and Development Fund, which began providing financial support in 2012. The government reformed the statutes governing fund in late 2018 and through 2019 to ease access and make compliance easier (and to conform to the 2017 criteria defining MSMEs). As a result, Prime Minister Decree No.299/GOV of 2019 was issued to make the SME Fund operate more effectively.

The SME Fund is part of DOSMEP and has its own administration and management regulations (adopted by the SME Fund Board of Directors). The contributing capital of the fund is $47 million (including $20 million from the World Bank, $4 million from ADB, and $23 million equivalent [KN200 billion] from the government). The SME Fund does not lend directly to MSMEs; it channels loans to small businesses via six participating commercial banks. DOSMEP estimates that over 200 MSMEs have benefited from SME Fund-assisted loans since its 2012 inception to June 2019. Demand for SME Fund financing remains strong.

The lending rate is 5.5%–10% per annum, supported by a 3%–5% subsidy (regular commercial lending rates are 9%–15% per year). The government is considering further interest rate reductions to increase access. The loan tenor can be up to 10 years. Priority sectors include agriculture, industry and handicrafts, tourism, and specific sectors as decided by participating banks. Participating banks conclude a memorandum of understanding with the SME Fund recognizing these sectors as priorities for MSME lending.

Nonbank Financing

The nonbank finance industry is small and has yet to fill the unmet financing demand from MSMEs. There are a variety of nonbank financing options for MSMEs, including microfinance institutions (MFIs), leasing companies, pawnshops, money transfer shops, and others, although they do not necessarily target MSMEs for their business. As of end-2019, there were 96 MFIs, 29 leasing companies, 26 credit unions/cooperatives, 26 pawnshops, and 5 money transfer shops registered with the BOL (Table 6.4). Total financing outstanding of nonbank finance institutions (NBFIs)—combining MFIs, leasing companies, and pawnshops—was KN6.1 billion in 2019, or 8.5% of total bank loans outstanding.

MFIs and leasing companies are the most prominent in financing MSMEs, while both have seen dramatic growth in their loan portfolios. The compound annual growth rate of financing by leasing companies was 59.9% during 2013–2019, while it was 43.8% for MFIs, although for 2010–2019.

MFI loans grew from KN49.2 billion ($6 million) in 2010 to KN1.3 trillion ($146 million) in 2019, an increase of 2,530% (Figure 6.4A). However, the growth pace of MFI loans outstanding has slowed since 2016. The number of MFI loan accounts (borrowers) increased from 18,958 to 97,573; a percentage change of 415% (a compound annual growth rate of 20.0%). By sector as of 2019, those categorized as others (sectors not specified elsewhere, including households, materials and technical supplies) held the largest share at 53.7%, followed by wholesale and retail trade (25.5%) and agriculture, forestry, and fishing (13.0%) (Figure 6.4B). From 2013 to 2019, sectors categorized as others grew 150.1% (a compound annual growth rate of 16.5%), while wholesale and retail trade declined 57.9% (a compound annual decrease of 13.4%), from 60.5% in 2013 to 25.5% in 2019. Agriculture, forestry, and fisheries declined 6.7%, from 13.9% in 2013 to 13.0% in 2019.

Financing outstanding for leasing companies was KN4.8 billion in 2019, a 27.3% increase from the end of 2018, accounting for 78.6% of total NBFI financing. Registered leasing companies are all foreign-owned. For pawnshops, financing outstanding amounted to KN 6.3 billion in 2019, less than 1% of NBFI financing. Since 2018, pawnshop financing leapt 135.6%.

Both the data and conditions for lending are more accessible for MFIs than for other nonbank sources, in part because the Lao Microfinance Association (MFA) represents their interests. With 95 members, including both deposit-taking and non-deposit-taking MFIs, and savings and credit unions; MFA membership accounts for 90% of licensed MFIs. According to the MFA, the average MFI loan size of MFIs is KN5 million, with loan maturities up to 3 years. The average interest rate is higher than the commercial bank loan rate of 14%, though the exact figure is unknown. The NPL ratio was 4% as of 2018 (by law it cannot exceed 5%). Its main customers are younger people and small business owners. Regional growth areas include Luang Prabang in the north; portions of the center region; and the five southern provinces of Attepeu, Champasak, Salavan, Savannakhet, and Xekong. The MFA noted that with a few large MFIs dominated the market, competition could be improved. This is causing an increasing number of informal MFIs to enter. By nature, these informal MFIs are unregulated and could pose a threat to the financial soundness of the microfinance industry in the Lao PDR.

Figure 6.4: Nonbank Finance

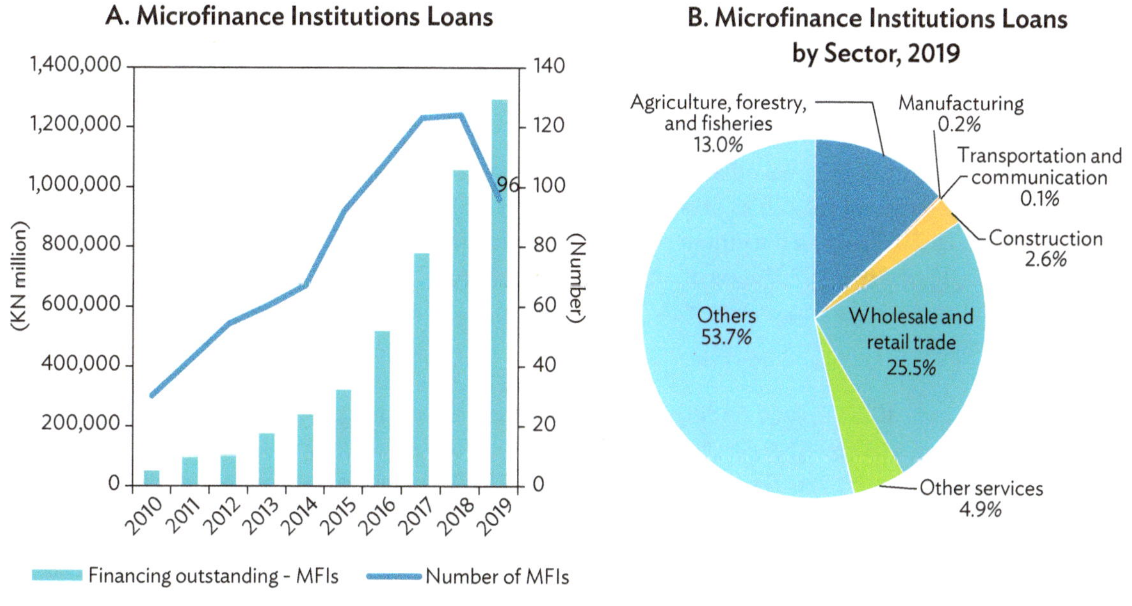

MFI = microfinance institution.

Source: ADB Asia SME Monitor 2020 database. Data from Bank of the Lao PDR.

Digital Financial Services

Digital financial services (DFS) such as e-wallet, mobile banking, and crowdfunding are in their infancy. People in the Lao PDR are unfamiliar with fintech and will need time to adapt. There is an interoperable national payments system using quick response (QR) codes, but as of July 2019 it was not fully implemented.

The BOL is promoting branchless banking or agent banking under its Financial Inclusion Roadmap (2018–2025). Branchless banking enables customers to access banking services through third-party agents such as retail outlets. BOL launched a branchless banking pilot program in 2017, with 418 agents participating as of July 2019. E-banking is also being prepared. The BOL pointed out, however, that most MSMEs are not ready to use digital platforms or new arrangements for banking services.[62] Digital finance literacy needs to be strengthened. Fintech-related regulations need to be implemented.

MFIs have a strong interest in DFS, according to the MFA, which is preparing a concept note on DFS for the microfinance industry as part of its 2020 strategic plan.[63]

Capital Markets

Capital markets are small in scale in the Lao PDR and have yet to become a funding venue for growing MSMEs and start-ups. While there is no dedicated equity market for MSMEs, the Lao Securities Commission Office (LSCO) began studying the idea.

The Lao Securities Exchange (LSX) was launched in 2010 as a joint venture between the BOL and Korea Exchange. There are four securities companies (three brokers/underwriters and one financial advisory company), three custodian banks (the Industrial and Commercial Bank of China, Bank of China, and Bangkok Bank), nine asset valuators, and one credit rating agency active in the main market. The APM (LAO) Securities Company, a Thailand–Lao PDR joint venture, provides financial consulting services. Only common stocks and government bonds are traded on the LSX.

The LSX Composite Index (close) peaked at 1,414 in 2014 after trading began in January 2011. It has declined sharply since 2015 (the index was at 728 as of end-2019) (Figure 6.5A and Table 6.5). Investor confidence in the market fell during 2012–2017, with a maximum one initial public offering (IPO) each year (Figure 6.5B). There were three IPOs in 2018 and two in 2019. As of end-2019, there were 11 companies listed on the LSX. Of these, three are in financial services, two in energy, two in construction, and one each in agriculture, manufacturing, real estate, and services.

Market capitalization grew 107.4% since trading began (a compound annual growth rate of 9.5%), from KN4.6 trillion ($578.5 million) in 2011 to KN9.6 trillion ($1.1 billion) in 2019. Market capitalization peaked in 2015 at KN12.0 trillion before sliding 20.2%. Trading value decreased 75.4% (a compound annual decrease of 16.1%), from KN301.5 billion to KN74.0 billion. Trading volume dropped 52.8% (a compound annual decrease of 9.0%) from 40.0 million shares to 18.9 million shares. The investor base includes 15,353 securities accounts. Individual investors represent 99% of the total, while the remaining 1% are institutional investors. Domestic accounts are 78% of the total, with 22% held by foreign investors—Thailand (8%), the PRC (5%), Japan (4%), the Republic of Korea (2%), and others (3%).

[62] Interview with acting director of Bank of the Lao PDR on 31 July 2019.

[63] Interview with executive director of the Lao Microfinance Association on 2 August 2019.

LSCO is brainstorming a new market board for growth enterprises and start-ups—to deepen the country's capital markets and to recover investor confidence in the stock exchange. In 2018, LSCO completed a phase 1 feasibility study on a possible equity finance venue for MSMEs. A key facet of the study was the potential for an alternative investment market (AIM) for MSMEs with the financial capacity and sophistication to list shares. MSME demand for equity finance is unclear, as no study or survey has been undertaken. The phase 2 study is ongoing (as of August 2019).

Critical challenges for capital market development in the Lao PDR are low liquidity and high costs for corporate governance requirements for issuers, particularly for boards of directors. LSCO is partnering with the Thai Institute of Directors Association to study the issue of high costs. To improve liquidity more demand from issuers must be created that attracts more investors. LSX, in conjunction with LSCO and the MOIC, is working to identify potential issuers and train them in capital market literacy.

To attract more issuers and investors, LSCO worked with the Ministry of Finance to offer tax incentives, which were approved in 2019 and implemented in 2020. For issuers, for example, income tax was reduced from 20% to 13% for 4 years. For investors, taxes on capital gains or dividends were exempted. These exemptions have no expiry date. Value-added taxes are also exempted.

Bond trading has been primarily in government bonds. There have been a few corporate bonds issued to date, but no recent trading activity. Neither LSX nor LSCO has data on venture capital and business angel investors, though there is interest in developing venture capital funds as part of the Lao Capital Market Strategic Plan 2016–2025. As of 2019, neither LSX nor LSCO had plans for equity crowdfunding or peer-to-peer lending.

Figure 6.5: Equity Market

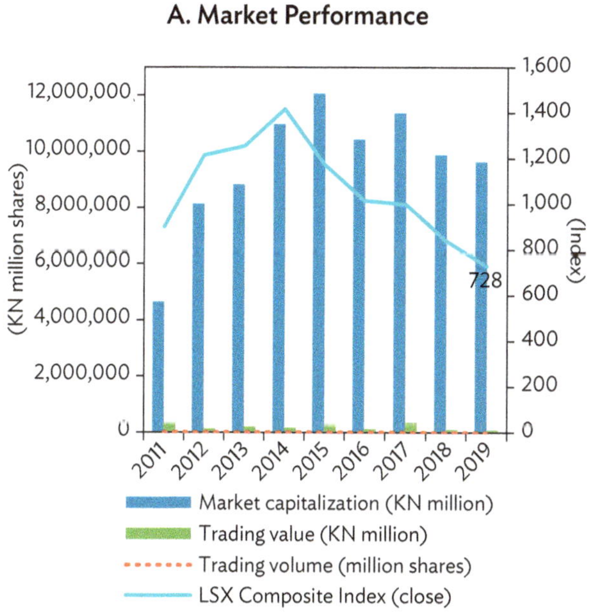

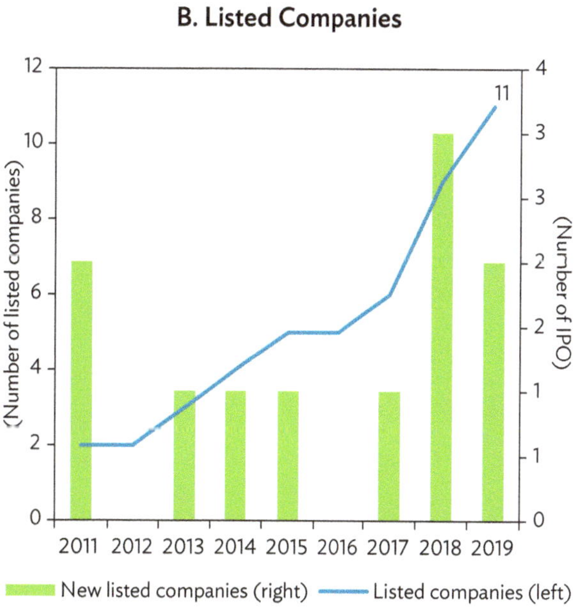

Source: ADB Asia SME Monitor 2020 database. Data from Lao Securities Exchange (LSX).

Financial Infrastructure

The financial infrastructure needed to promote MSME access to finance remains underdeveloped. Key institutions such as a credit bureau and collateral registry are either nascent or at the planning stage. Capital markets have progressed yet remain illiquid. The venture capital industry and business angel networks have yet to be developed. Use of fintech on any measurable scale is likely several years in the future.

A credit information bureau (CIB) already exists under the BOL.[64] Its data are updated monthly online and are open for firms to review their own information. Banks can access the data freely, but interested third parties must request authorization. The Secured Transactions Law was originally enacted in 1994 and amended in 2005, but was implemented after 2011. Under the law, movable assets such as inventory, accounts receivable, and intellectual property rights are available as loan collateral. The Ministry of Finance is preparing an amendment to the law, which includes the establishment of a collateral registry.

Training MSMEs in financial and capital market literacy is critical for increasing access to finance. Several organizations have stated, as part of their mission, to educate and train MSMEs, both in financial and management matters. LSCO offers capital market literacy programs to educate local firms on how to tap the LSX. They use television commercials and advertisements for this purpose, and organize on average 21 training seminars a year. The LNCCI is heavily involved in training MSME owners and employees. From January-June 2019, it provided training to 600 MSMEs, comprising 1,300 individuals, to improve their access to finance. Some of the topics include how to apply for a loan, enhance bookkeeping, generate proper financial records, and write a business plan. MFA also offers extensive training. It conducts capacity building for MFIs twice a year using a curriculum of eight standardized modules that cover topics such as accounting, performance management, and client protection. Since 2015, the MFA has had 485 attendees (as of August 2019).

3. Policies and Regulations

- MSME development efforts are well coordinated among various departments within the Ministry of Industry and Commerce and are aligned to promote national development goals and objectives; however, coordination between central and local MSME policy units formally started in 2018 and is as yet unproven.
- The central bank finalized its Financial Inclusion Roadmap (2018–2025), which addresses credit availability, consumer empowerment, village funds, payment ecosystem, and branchless banking, among others. Policies need to be developed on digital financial services, including promulgation of fintech regulations and continued efforts to boost financial literary.
- The securities commission developed the Lao Strategic Plan for Capital Market Development 2016–2025, which is under ongoing review; the development of the equity market as well as the private equity and venture capital industry should be a focal point for future policy.

MSME Development

The National Assembly approved the 8th Five-Year National Socio-Economic Development Plan 2016–2020 in April 2016. This plan articulates a vision for 2030, whereby the Lao PDR becomes a "developing country with upper-middle income and with innovative, green, and sustainable economic growth." It embraces a 10-year strategy ending 2025 that consists of seven separate strategies focused on quality, graduating least-developed country status, human development, sustainability and efficiency, an enhanced government

[64] A credit information bureau started operation in November 2010.

role in social affairs under the rule of law, regional and international integration, and industrialization and modernization. The plan sets specific targets, such as a poverty rate of 10% by 2020 (compared to 23.2% in 2013), real annual GDP growth of at least 7.5%, and exports of goods and services contributing 15% of GDP per year, among others. For MSMEs, the plan calls for enhancing management skills and competitiveness, science and technology, labor productivity and the level of education, World Bank Ease of Doing Business rating, and regional integration. These do not have specific numerical targets and fall under the Legal Framework and Human Resources Development section of the plan.

To achieve these national long-term objectives, various government agencies designed their own plans or updated previous plans on MSME development. The MOIC has promulgated MSME development plans since 2006. The latest plan is the SME Development Plan 2016–2020. It consists of seven initiatives, ranked in order of priority: (i) promote productivity, technology, and innovation; (ii) promote access to finance; (iii) promote access to business development services; (iv) promote market access and expansion; (v) promote entrepreneurship and development; (vi) create a favorable environment for establishing business and operations; and (vii) refine customs, tax, and financing policies.

DOSMEP, under the MOIC, is responsible for executing the plan (and assisting in the creation of the next plan—the SME Development Plan for 2021–2025). To help build a favorable environment for MSMEs, DOSMEP established three SME Service Centers (one in Vientiane and two outside the capital) that dispense free advisory services, including marketing and business development. The LNCCI manages these centers.

Another DOSMEP-supported initiative is business registration reform. DERM has reduced the registration process from 15 working days to 5 working days. There is now just one serial number for both registration and tax authorities so it will be easier to monitor businesses. Online registration is available, but full implementation will be completed by 2022. There are 123 registration offices operating across the country.

In 2018, MOIC established an SME Trade Promotion Office in each of the 17 provinces. These offices promote the SME Development Plan; in particular linking and synergizing work between the central SME development plan and provincial development plans.

The Department of Industry and Handicrafts (DOIH), also under the MOIC, developed a short-term Manufacturing Development Plan for 2019–2020 and a medium-term Industry and Commerce Development Plan for 2021–2025. The short-term strategy prioritizes agriculture (such as rice mills) and garments/textiles. The medium-term plan focuses on the high potential for job creation.

Financial Inclusion

There are two separate initiatives on financial inclusion, one focused on the national banking system and the other targeting capital markets. The BOL set ambitious goals in its Lao PDR Financial Inclusion Roadmap (2018–2025), which was finalized in August 2019. The roadmap has five priorities: (i) improving the availability and sustainability of credit, which focuses on strengthening credit information, diverse credit products, and supporting MSME access to finance; (ii) consumer protection and empowerment, which includes financial literacy; (iii) strengthening village funds, which are semiformal financial institutions established and supervised by provincial governments (also called village banks[65]); (iv) developing a payment ecosystem, which promotes an interoperable national payments system; and (v) extending the outreach of banks and other financial service providers, which includes promoting agent/branchless banking (a pilot project has been operating since 2017).

[65] Village funds/village banks are not supervised by the BOL.

As mentioned, DFS is in its infancy, and the requisite financial education to make its use profitable is still needed. Policymakers need to consider these areas, as there are ample benefits from both lower costs and increased access. In particular, the government should work to establish fintech regulations.

LSCO developed the Lao Strategic Plan for Capital Market Development 2016–2025 in 2014. The plan has eight overall targets: (i) ensuring the necessary conditions and environment required for enterprises to raise capital through capital markets; (ii) creating capital market instruments and procedures that support enterprise reform, especially to improve, strengthen, and enhance competitiveness of state-owned enterprises; (iii) developing a comprehensive regulatory framework suitable for the domestic capital market conditions in line with international practices; (iv) ensuring that the LSX Securities Depository Center and securities intermediaries operate smoothly with limited risk, with the ability to integrate regionally and internationally; (v) developing modern ICT systems that are well-suited to the desired level of capital market growth; (vi) increasing participation from the public, expanding the investor base, and ensuring a greater balance between institutional and individual investors; (vii) having sufficient quantity and quality of capital market regulators, experts at the LSX, the securities depository center, and securities professionals; and (viii) being able to integrate the Lao PDR capital market regionally and internationally.

These will also help the MOIC objective of making MSMEs more competitive—and is another instance of agencies cooperating to coordinate policies that advance MSME development. As mentioned, LSCO, LSX, and MOIC are identifying potential stock issuers and training them in capital market literacy.

The capital market strategic plan will also touch on private equity; however, there is no clear strategy yet regarding venture capital. This is another policy area to consider, as private equity remains important for the high-tech sector and start-ups.

Overall, policies supporting MSME development—and the related coordination among government ministries and departments—are at a more advanced stage than those for financial inclusion. Developing policies for financial inclusion will likely require more familiarity with frontier technology such as fintech. For now, gains in MSME development are more likely in relatively low-tech sectors such as agriculture and garments.

Data Tables

Table 6.1: MSME Definition

Sector	Item	Micro	Small	Medium
Production of commercial goods	Annual average number of employees	1-5	6-50	51-99
	Total assets (KN)	Not exceed 100 million	Not exceed 1 billion	Not exceed 4 billion
	Annual turnover (KN)	Not exceed 400 million	Not exceed 2 billion	Not exceed 4 billion
Trade	Annual average number of employees	1-5	6-50	51-99
	Total assets (KN)	Not exceed 150 million	Not exceed 1 billion	Not exceed 4 billion
	Annual turnover (KN)	Not exceed 400 million	Not exceed 3 billion	Not exceed 6 billion
Service	Annual average number of employees	1-5	6-50	51-99
	Total assets (KN)	Not exceed 200 million	Not exceed 1.5 billion	Not exceed 6 billion
	Annual turnover (KN)	Not exceed 400 million	Not exceed 1.5 billion	Not exceed 4 billion

MSME = micro, small, and medium-sized enterprise.
Source: ADB Asia SME Monitor 2020 database. Data from Decree No.25/GOL/2017 on SME classification (enacted on 16 January 2017).

Table 6.2: MSME Landscape

End of period data

Item	2006	2007	2008	2009	2010	2011	2012	2013	2014	2015	2016	2017	2018	2019
NUMBER OF ENTERPRISES														
Number of enterprises, total	126,913	--	--	--	--	--	--	124,808	--	--	--	--	124,837	--
Number of MSMEs	126,717	--	--	--	--	--	--	124,510	--	--	--	--	124,567	--
Number of large enterprises	196	--	--	--	--	--	--	298	--	--	--	--	270	--
MSME to total (%)	99.8	--	--	--	--	--	--	99.8	--	--	--	--	99.8	--
MSME growth (%)	--	--	--	--	--	--	--	(1.7)	--	--	--	--	0.05	--
MSMEs by sector (% share)														
Agriculture, forestry, and fisheries	3.4	--	--	--	--	--	--	1.7	--	--	--	--	4.9	--
Manufacturing	19.1	--	--	--	--	--	--	12.4	--	--	--	--	12.4	--
Transportation and communication	3.7	--	--	--	--	--	--	3.1	--	--	--	--	3.1	--
Construction	0.5	--	--	--	--	--	--	0.5	--	--	--	--	0.5	--
Wholesale and retail trade	64.5	--	--	--	--	--	--	62.9	--	--	--	--	62.9	--
Other services	8.3	--	--	--	--	--	--	18.9	--	--	--	--	12.2	--
Others	0.5	--	--	--	--	--	--	0.4	--	--	--	--	3.9	--
Number of MSMEs by region (% share)														
Capital city	--	--	--	--	--	--	--	28.2	--	--	--	--	--	--
Others	--	--	--	--	--	--	--	71.8	--	--	--	--	--	--
EMPLOYMENT*														
Number of employment, total	273,126	--	--	--	--	--	--	569,912	--	--	--	--	573,475	--
Number of employment by MSMEs	238,703	--	--	--	--	--	--	472,231	--	--	--	--	472,529	--
Number of employment by large enterprises	34,423	--	--	--	--	--	--	97,681	--	--	--	--	100,946	--
MSME employees to total (%)	87.4	--	--	--	--	--	--	82.9	--	--	--	--	82.4	--
MSME employees growth (%)	--	--	--	--	--	--	--	97.8	--	--	--	--	0.1	--
Share of female employees to total employees (%)	--	--	--	--	--	--	--	--	--	--	--	--	--	--
Employment by MSME by sector (% share)														
Agriculture, forestry, and fisheries	4.8	--	--	--	--	--	--	2.7	--	--	--	--	--	--
Manufacturing	22.8	--	--	--	--	--	--	17.4	--	--	--	--	--	--
Transportation and communication	4.5	--	--	--	--	--	--	3.6	--	--	--	--	--	--
Construction	1.9	--	--	--	--	--	--	2.0	--	--	--	--	--	--
Wholesale and retail trade	51.1	--	--	--	--	--	--	50.4	--	--	--	--	--	--
Other services	13.2	--	--	--	--	--	--	22.4	--	--	--	--	--	--
Others	1.7	--	--	--	--	--	--	1.4	--	--	--	--	--	--
Employment by MSMEs by region (% share)														
Capital city	--	--	--	--	--	--	--	--	--	--	--	--	--	--
Others	--	--	--	--	--	--	--	--	--	--	--	--	--	--
CONTRIBUTION TO GDP														
MSMEs contribution to GDP (KN million)	--	--	--	--	--	--	--	--	--	--	--	--	--	--
MSMEs contribution to GDP (%)	--	--	--	--	--	--	--	--	--	--	--	--	--	--
MSME GDP growth (%)	--	--	--	--	--	--	--	--	--	--	--	--	--	--
MSME GDP by sector (% share)														
Agriculture, forestry, and fisheries	--	--	--	--	--	--	--	--	--	--	--	--	--	--
Manufacturing	--	--	--	--	--	--	--	--	--	--	--	--	--	--
Transportation and communication	--	--	--	--	--	--	--	--	--	--	--	--	--	--
Construction	--	--	--	--	--	--	--	--	--	--	--	--	--	--
Wholesale and retail trade	--	--	--	--	--	--	--	--	--	--	--	--	--	--
Other services	--	--	--	--	--	--	--	--	--	--	--	--	--	--
Others	--	--	--	--	--	--	--	--	--	--	--	--	--	--
MSME GDP by region (% share)														
Capital city	--	--	--	--	--	--	--	--	--	--	--	--	--	--
Others	--	--	--	--	--	--	--	--	--	--	--	--	--	--
EXPORTS														
Total export value ($ million)**	882	923	1,092	1,053	1,746	2,190	2,191	2,264	3,276	3,653	4,245	4,873	5,295	--
Total export growth (%)	--	4.6	18.3	(3.6)	65.9	25.4	0.1	3.3	44.7	11.5	16.2	14.8	8.7	--
MSME export value (KN million)	--	--	--	--	--	--	--	--	1,237.8	--	--	--	--	--
MSME export to total export value (%)	--	--	--	--	--	--	--	--	--	--	--	--	--	--
MSME export growth (%)	--	--	--	--	--	--	--	--	--	--	--	--	--	--
IMPORTS														
Total import value ($ million)***	1,060	1,065	1,403	1,461	2,060	2,404	3,046	3,051	4,976	5,675	5,372	5,667	6,164	--
Total import growth (%)	--	0.5	31.7	4.1	41.0	16.7	26.7	0.1	63.1	14.1	(5.3)	5.5	8.8	--
MSME import value (KN million)	--	--	--	--	--	--	--	--	--	--	--	--	--	--
MSME import to total import value (%)	--	--	--	--	--	--	--	--	--	--	--	--	--	--
MSME import growth (%)	--	--	--	--	--	--	--	--	--	--	--	--	--	--

GDP = gross domestic product, MSME = micro, small, and medium-sized enterprise.
* Based on permanent Lao labors, except for temporary employees and foreign labors. ** Refers to exports fob. *** Refers to imports cif; For 2017 onward, the compilation methodology shifted from cif to fob.
Note: SME definition revised including the new segment of microenterprise since 2017. However, data in 2018 and after have yet to reflect the new definition but follow the old definition.
Source: ADB Asia SME Monitor 2020 database. Data from the Ministry of Industry and Commerce.

Table 6.3: Bank Credit

End of period data

Item	2007	2008	2009	2010	2011	2012	2013	2014	2015	2016	2017	2018	2019
COMMERCIAL BANKS													
Number of commercial banks	16	21	23	23	23	30	31	33	39	41	41	41	42
Private sector banks	3	5	5	5	5	6	7	7	7	7	7	7	7
State-owned banks	3	3	3	3	3	3	3	3	3	3	3	3	3
Others*	10	13	15	15	15	21	21	23	29	31	31	31	32
Credit													
Loans outstanding, total (KN billion)	3,797	6,214	8,831	13,170	19,106	25,566	35,424	40,290	48,291	59,745	66,939	69,053	71,369
Loans outstanding in domestic currency (KN billion)	--	--	--	--	--	--	--	--	--	--	--	--	--
Loans outstanding in foreign currency (KN billion)	--	--	--	--	--	--	--	--	--	--	--	--	--
Loan growth (%)	23.7	63.7	42.1	49.1	45.1	33.8	38.6	13.7	19.9	23.7	12.0	3.2	3.4
Total commercial bank loans to GDP (%)	9.4	13.4	17.7	23.6	29.5	31.3	37.7	37.7	41.2	46.2	47.6	45.3	45.5
Lending rate (%)**	--	--	14.4	14.5	12.2	13.9	13.5	12.8	11.8	9.4	9.3	9.2	18.6
Gross nonperforming loans (NPLs) (KN billion)	--	--	--	--	--	--	--	1,007	1,468	1,792	2,055	2,154	2,220
Gross NPLs to total loans (%)	--	--	--	--	--	--	--	2.5	3.0	3.0	3.1	3.1	3.1
Deposits													
Deposits, total (KN billion)***	1,227	1,492	1,705	2,461	2,325	2,524	2,301	3,031	3,863	3,472	4,104	4,064	5,204
Deposits in domestic currency (KN billion)	--	--	--	--	--	--	--	--	--	--	--	--	--
Deposits in foreign currency (KN billion)	--	--	--	--	--	--	--	--	--	--	--	--	--
Deposit rate (%)**	--	6.1	5.7	5.5	5.4	5.2	5.4	3.1	4.5	3.1	3.0	3.0	3.0
MSME LOANS													
MSME loans outstanding, total (KN billion)	--	--	--	--	--	--	--	--	14,919	13,997	15,939	14,241	14,104
MSME loans to total loans outstanding (%)	--	--	--	--	--	--	--	--	30.9	23.4	23.8	20.6	19.8
MSME loans to GDP (%)	--	--	--	--	--	--	--	--	12.7	10.8	11.3	9.3	8.5
MSME loan growth (%)	--	--	--	--	--	--	--	--	--	(6.2)	13.9	(10.7)	(1.0)
MSME lending rate (%)	--	--	--	--	--	--	--	--	--	--	--	--	--
Nonperforming MSME loans (NPLs) (KN billion)	--	--	--	--	--	--	--	--	--	--	--	--	--
MSME NPLs to total MSME loans (%)	--	--	--	--	--	--	--	--	--	--	--	--	--
Number of MSME loan borrowers	--	--	--	--	--	--	--	--	--	--	--	--	--
MSME loan borrowers to total bank borrowers (%)	--	--	--	--	--	--	--	--	--	--	--	--	--
MSME loan rejection rate (% of total applications)	--	--	--	--	--	--	--	--	--	--	--	--	--
Number of MSME savings account in banks	--	--	--	--	--	--	--	--	--	--	--	--	--
Guaranteed MSME loans (KN billion)	--	--	--	--	--	--	--	--	--	--	--	--	--
Non-collateral MSME loans (KN billion)	--	--	--	--	--	--	--	--	--	--	--	--	--
MSME loans outstanding by sector (% share)													
Agriculture, forestry, and fisheries	--	--	--	--	--	--	--	--	4.1	7.0	4.3	3.7	3.8
Manufacturing	--	--	--	--	--	--	--	--	8.9	8.3	7.6	9.4	7.9
Transportation and communication	--	--	--	--	--	--	--	--	3.8	2.6	3.4	1.7	1.1
Construction	--	--	--	--	--	--	--	--	14.2	14.1	17.7	18.0	20.7
Wholesale and retail trade	--	--	--	--	--	--	--	--	33.2	36.8	37.0	38.0	37.0
Other services	--	--	--	--	--	--	--	--	16.1	17.0	17.5	17.2	18.6
Others	--	--	--	--	--	--	--	--	19.8	14.2	12.4	12.1	11.0
MSME loans outstanding by region (% share)													
Capital city	--	--	--	--	--	--	--	--	--	--	--	--	--
Others	--	--	--	--	--	--	--	--	--	--	--	--	--
MSME loans outstanding by type of use (% share)													
For working capital	--	--	--	--	--	--	--	--	--	--	--	--	--
For capital investment	--	--	--	--	--	--	--	--	--	--	--	--	--
MSME loans outstanding by tenor (% share)													
Less than 1 year	--	--	--	--	--	--	--	--	--	--	--	--	--
1-5 years	--	--	--	--	--	--	--	--	--	--	--	--	--
More than 5 years	--	--	--	--	--	--	--	--	--	--	--	--	--

GDP = gross domestic product, MSME = micro, small, and medium-sized enterprise.

* Others include joint state commercial banks, subsidiary banks, and foreign commercial bank branches.

** Lending rate is based on minimum lending rate and deposit rate is based on 3-month deposit from the ASEAN Statistical Yearbook 2019.

*** Refers to demand deposits.

Source: ADB Asia SME Monitor 2020 database. Data from Annual Economic Report 2010 (data on 2007 and 2008) and Annual Economic Report 2013 (data on 2009-2013); updated by the Bank of the Lao PDR.

Table 6.4: Nonbank Finance

End of period data

Item	2010	2011	2012	2013	2014	2015	2016	2017	2018	2019
NUMBER OF NONBANK FINANCE INSTITUTIONS										
Microfinance institutions	30	42	54	60	67	92	107	123	124	96
Credit unions/cooperatives	--	--	--	--	--	--	--	--	--	26
Finance companies	--	--	--	--	--	--	--	--	--	--
Pawnshops	--	--	25	30	31	29	27	29	27	26
Leasing companies	3	5	6	11	13	21	29	31	29	29
Factoring companies	--	--	--	--	--	--	--	--	--	--
Insurance companies	--	--	--	--	--	--	--	--	--	--
Others: Money transfer shops	--	--	5	5	5	5	5	5	5	5
MICROFINANCE INSTITUTIONS										
Financing outstanding, total (KN million)	49,209	93,042	103,110	173,620	237,477	319,998	517,795	777,559	1,055,912	1,294,060
Financing growth (%)	--	89.1	10.8	68.4	36.8	34.7	61.8	50.2	35.8	22.6
Total financing to GDP (%)	0.1	0.1	0.1	0.2	0.2	0.3	0.4	0.6	0.7	0.8
Annual financing rate (%, on average)	--	--	--	--	--	--	--	--	--	--
Gross nonperforming financing (NPFs) (KN million)	--	--	--	--	--	--	--	--	--	74,235
Gross NPFs to total financing (%)	--	--	--	--	--	--	--	--	--	0.1
Number of customers financed, total	18,958	19,070	21,018	31,251	40,826	46,015	61,587	70,157	87,613	97,573
Financing outstanding by sector (% share)										
Agriculture, forestry, and fisheries	--	--	--	13.9	15.9	--	22.8	18.8	20.1	13.0
Manufacturing	--	--	--	--	--	--	--	1.4	1.2	0.2
Transportation and communication	--	--	--	0.1	0.7	--	--	0.1	--	0.1
Construction	--	--	--	0.3	0.9	--	0.6	1.2	1.9	2.6
Wholesale and retail trade	--	--	--	60.5	52.0	--	38.3	37.5	31.4	25.5
Other services	--	--	--	3.7	1.6	--	1.8	2.0	1.9	4.9
Others*	--	--	--	21.5	29.0	--	36.5	39.0	43.5	53.7
Financing outstanding by region (% share)										
Capital city	--	--	--	--	--	--	--	--	--	--
Others	--	--	--	--	--	--	--	--	--	--
PAWNSHOPS										
Financing outstanding, total (KN million)	--	--	--	--	--	--	1,696	3,884	2,682	6,319
Financing growth (%)	--	--	--	--	--	--	--	129.0	(30.9)	135.6
Total financing to GDP (%)	--	--	--	--	--	--	0.001	0.003	0.002	0.004
Annual financing rate (%, on average)	--	--	--	--	--	--	--	--	--	--
Gross nonperforming financing (NPFs) (KN million)	--	--	--	--	--	--	--	--	--	--
Gross NPFs to total financing (%)	--	--	--	--	--	--	--	--	--	--
Number of customers financed, total	--	--	--	--	--	--	685	1,658	1,539	2,177
Financing outstanding by sector (% share)										
Agriculture, forestry, and fisheries	--	--	--	--	--	--	--	--	--	--
Manufacturing	--	--	--	--	--	--	--	--	--	--
Transportation and communication	--	--	--	--	--	--	--	--	--	--
Construction	--	--	--	--	--	--	--	--	--	--
Wholesale and retail trade	--	--	--	--	--	--	--	--	--	--
Other services	--	--	--	--	--	--	--	--	--	--
Others	--	--	--	--	--	--	--	--	--	--
Financing outstanding by region (% share)										
Capital city	--	--	--	--	--	--	--	--	--	--
Others	--	--	--	--	--	--	--	--	--	--
LEASING COMPANIES										
Financing outstanding, total (KN million)	--	--	--	285,445	193,511	515,490	941,785	1,415,065	3,749,693	4,775,000
Financing growth (%)	--	--	--	--	(32.2)	166.4	82.7	50.3	165.0	27.3
Total financing to GDP (%)	--	--	--	0.3	0.2	0.4	0.7	1.0	2.5	2.9
Annual financing rate (%, on average)	--	--	--	--	--	--	--	--	--	--
Gross nonperforming financing (NPFs) (KN million)	--	--	--	--	--	--	--	--	--	--
Gross NPFs to total financing (%)	--	--	--	--	--	--	--	--	--	--
Number of customers financed, total	--	--	--	--	--	--	--	--	--	110,801
Financing outstanding by sector (% share)										
Agriculture, forestry, and fisheries	--	--	--	--	--	--	--	--	--	--
Manufacturing	--	--	--	--	--	--	--	--	--	--
Transportation and communication	--	--	--	--	--	--	--	--	--	--
Construction	--	--	--	--	--	--	--	--	--	--
Wholesale and retail trade	--	--	--	--	--	--	--	--	--	--
Other services	--	--	--	--	--	--	--	--	--	--
Others	--	--	--	--	--	--	--	--	--	--
Financing outstanding by region (% share)										
Capital city	--	--	--	--	--	--	--	--	--	--
Others	--	--	--	--	--	--	--	--	--	--

GDP = gross domestic product

* Includes households, and materials and technical supplies.

Source: ADB Asia SME Monitor 2020 database. Data from Bank of the Lao PDR.

Table 6.5: Capital Markets

End of period data

Item	2011	2012	2013	2014	2015	2016	2017	2018	2019
EQUITY MARKET									
Main Board									
Index: LSX Composite Index	899	1,215	1,253	1,414	1,174	1,015	998	836	728
Market capitalization (KN million)	4,638,300	8,136,540	8,826,800	10,968,690	12,047,100	10,414,100	11,352,400	9,868,000	9,618,492
Growth (%)	--	75.4	8.5	24.3	9.8	(13.6)	9.0	(13.1)	(2.5)
Trading value (KN million)	301,490	123,790	188,890	156,320	200,000	113,000	343,000	92,000	74,019
Trading volume (million of shares)	40.0	23.0	26.2	26.8	31.3	22.5	51.0	19.8	18.9
Number of listed companies	2	2	3	4	5	5	6	9	11
Number of IPOs	2	0	1	1	1	0	1	3	2
Number of delisted companies	--	0	0	0	0	0	0	0	0

IPO = initial public offering.

Source: ADB Asia SME Monitor 2020 database. Data from Lao Securities Exchange (LSX).

Table 6.6: Policies and Regulations

Regulations		
Name		**Outline**
Nonfinance regulations		
Decree No.42/PM/2004 on the Promotion and Development of Small and Medium-sized Enterprises (SMEs)		SME definition (with numeric criteria), directions on SME promotion with action plans, establishment of the SME Promotion and Development Fund, and organizational arrangements stipulated.
Law No.011/NA/2011 on Small and Medium sized Enterprises Promotion		New SME definition (but no numeric criteria) and SME promotion activities stipulated; establishment of SME Promotion Fund.
Decree No. 25/GOL/2017 on Small and Medium Enterprise Classification		New SME definition with sector classification.
Finance regulations		
Law No.05/NA/1995 on the Bank of the Lao PDR (BOL)		Central bank's responsibility for regulating and supervising both banks and nonbank financial institutions stipulated.
Law No.03/NA/2006 on Commercial Banks		Regulation on commercial banks.
Law No.06/NA/2005 on Secured Transactions		Security over movable and immovable properties, guarantees (personal or by legal entity), and security registration.
Decree No.460/G/2012 on Microfinance Institutions (MFIs)		Government regulation on deposit and non-deposit taking MFIs and microfinance projects.
Regulation No.02/BOL/2008 for Non-Deposit Taking Microfinance Institutions		Central bank regulation on non-deposit taking MFIs.
Regulation No.03/BOL/2008 for Savings and Credit Unions		Central bank regulation on savings and credit unions.
Regulation No.04/BOL/2008 for Deposit Taking Microfinance Institutions		Central bank regulation on deposit taking MFIs.
Law No.21/NA/2012 on Securities		Regulation on securities issuance.
Law No.33/NA on the Approval of the Law on Securities		Law outlining the approval of the Law on Securities.
Regulators and Policymakers		
Name		**Responsibility**
Bank of the Lao PDR (BOL)		Regulate and supervise banks and nonbank financial institutions (including finance companies, leasing companies, and MFIs).
Department of SME Promotion, Ministry of Industry and Commerce (MOIC)		Responsible for SME national development policies, strategies, and promotion.
Department of Industry and Commerce, MOIC [as of July 2018, Office of Industry and Commerce of Province (OICP)]		Responsible for SME local policy implementation.
SME Promotion and Development and National Productivity Committee (SMEPDC)		Serve as direct counselors for the government on the different policies and measures on SME promotion and development, and supervise implementation of the SME Development Plan 2011–2015.
Lao Securities Commission Office (LSCO)		Regulate and supervise the securities market.
Policies		
Name	**Responsible Entity**	**Outline**
SME Development Strategy 2006–2010	MOIC	1) Creating an enabling regulatory and administrative environment. 2) Enhancing competitiveness. 3) Expanding domestic and international markets. 4) Improving access to finance. 5) Encouraging and creating favorable conditions for establishing business member organizations. 6) Enhancing entrepreneurial attitude and characteristics within society.
SME Development Plan 2011–2015	MOIC	1) Improving the regulatory environment and public administration of economic activities. 2) Improving access to finance. 3) Formation of new entrepreneurs. 4) Increasing the provision of supports and business development services (BDS). 5) Enhancing the business linkages between large firms and SMEs. 6) Promoting the increase of productivity for upgrading the quality and standard of products and services of SMEs. 7) Enhancing access to markets and enlarging markets for SMEs.
SME Promotion Activities by Law (2011)	MOIC	1) Creating an enabling environment. 2) Access to finance. 3) Policy on customs and taxation. 4) Creating and developing entrepreneurs. 5) Business development consultation. 6) Cooperation among SMEs, large firms, and foreign investment firms. 7) Increasing productivity. 8) Market access and expansion. 9) Business clustering. 10) Allocating business location. 11) Promoting advanced technology utilization. 12) Using and protecting intellectual property. 13) Providing and accessing information.
SME Development Plan 2016–2020	MOIC	1) Promote productivity, technology, and innovation. 2) Promote the access to sources of funds. 3) Promote the access to business development counseling. 4) Access and expand markets. 5) Entrepreneurial development. 6) Create favorable environment to start and operate a business. 7) Customs, tax, and financing.
Strategic Plan for Capital Market Development 2016–2025	LSCO	Overall Targets: 1) Ensuring the necessary conditions and environment required for enterprises to raise capital through capital markets. 2) Creating capital market instruments and procedures that support enterprise reform, especially to improve, strengthen, and enhance competitiveness of state-owned enterprises. 3) Developing a comprehensive regulatory framework suitable for the domestic capital market conditions in line with international practices. 4) Ensuring that the LSX Securities Depository Center (SDC) and securities intermediaries operate smoothly with limited risk, with the ability to integrate regionally and internationally. 5) Developing modern information and communications technology systems that are well-suited to the desired level of capital market growth. 6) Increasing participation from the public, expanding the investor base, and ensuring a greater balance between institutional and individual investors. 7) Having sufficient quantity and quality of capital market regulators, experts at the LSX, SDC and securities professionals. 8) Being able to integrate the Lao PDR capital market regionally and internationally.
Lao PDR Financial Inclusion Roadmap 2018–2025	BOL	Key Components: 1) Improving the availability and sustainability of credit. 2) Consumer protection and empowerment. 3) Strengthening village funds. 4) Payment ecosystem development. 5) Extending the outreach of banks and other financial service providers (financial outreach).

Source: ADB Asia SME Monitor 2020 database. Data from Bank of the Lao PDR, Ministry of Industry and Commerce (Department of SME Promotion), SME Development Plan 2011-2015, and Lao Securities Commission Office.

Country Review

Malaysia

Overview

Malaysia's economic growth decelerated from 4.8% in 2018 to 4.3% in 2019, in part due to slower exports and investments affected by global trade tensions. Its working age population is 22.9 million (fourth quarter of 2019).[66] Private sector businesses are dominated by micro, small, and medium-sized enterprises (MSMEs), which accounted for 98.5% of total enterprises in 2015. MSMEs employed 66.2% of the workforce and contributed 38.3% of country's gross domestic product (GDP) in 2018. Most MSMEs are in services. The services sector holds great promise in accelerating national economic growth, especially led by internationalized MSMEs, young entrepreneurs, and start-ups. While the growth of bank credit to MSMEs is likely decelerating, alternative funding opportunities for them are expanding through increasing digital financial services and dedicated stock markets for small and medium-sized enterprises (SMEs). MSME policymaking and coordination are centralized within the Ministry of Entrepreneur Development and Cooperatives. Promoting MSMEs exposed to global markets is key to boosting national economic productivity and to bolster inclusive growth in Malaysia.

1. MSME Development

- The services sector, primarily distributive trade, dominates MSME activity, which tends to be concentrated in urban areas such as in the capital, Kuala Lumpur, and Selangor State; there are few women-owned MSMEs.
- Most MSME employees work in services, and are concentrated in urban areas; women constitute one-third of MSME employees.
- GDP of MSMEs is growing faster than the overall economy, but their share of total GDP remains small; MSME labor productivity has improved gradually; more than half of MSME gross value added comes from urban areas. MSME dynamics could be strengthened further to boost national productivity.
- Most MSMEs market domestically with limited global value chain participation; MSME exports remain low but growing, and internationalizing MSMEs could boost inclusive growth.
- E-commerce is rapidly transforming the MSME business landscape but remains small in scale; more innovation is needed for MSME business.
- Business networking communities help MSMEs grow by facilitating business matching and skill training.

Scale of MSMEs

In Malaysia, an MSME is defined as a manufacturing firm with annual sales not exceeding RM50 million or with a maximum 200 full-time employees, or in services and other sectors, a firm with annual sales not exceeding RM20 million or with a maximum 75 full-time employees (Table 7.1).

An economic census conducted every 5 years monitors the number of MSMEs. The latest available data are for 2015 based on the Economic Census 2016. In 2015, there were 907,065 MSMEs, or 98.5% of all enterprises (Figure 7.1A and Table 7.2). The compound annual growth rate (CAGR) from 2011 to 2015 was 7.3%. By sector,

66 Department of Statistics Malaysia, Official Portal (http://www.dom.gov.my/). Working age refers to those aged 16-64 years old.

89.2% of MSMEs were in services, including transport and storage, wholesale and retail trade, telecommunications, and real estate, followed by manufacturing (5.3%); construction (4.3%); primary industries like agriculture, forestry, and fisheries (1.1%); and mining and quarrying (0.1%) (Figure 7.1B). The sector composition hardly changed from 2010 to 2015. By region, 14.7% of MSMEs were in Kuala Lumpur (up from 13.1% in 2010), while the remaining 85.3% were spread across the 13 states and other federal territories, the largest being Selangor (19.8%), the large state surrounding Kuala Lumpur. In short, more than one-third of Malaysia's MSMEs were in the large, mostly urban region of Kuala Lumpur and Selangor. Seventy percent of MSMEs had been operating for 5–24 years, while 22% were operating less than 5 years as of 2015.

There were 186,930 women-owned MSMEs in 2015, a relatively low 20.6% share of total MSMEs, but with an 8.0% CAGR over 2010. 92.7% of women-owned MSMEs were engaged in the services sector.

Figure 7.1: Number of MSMEs

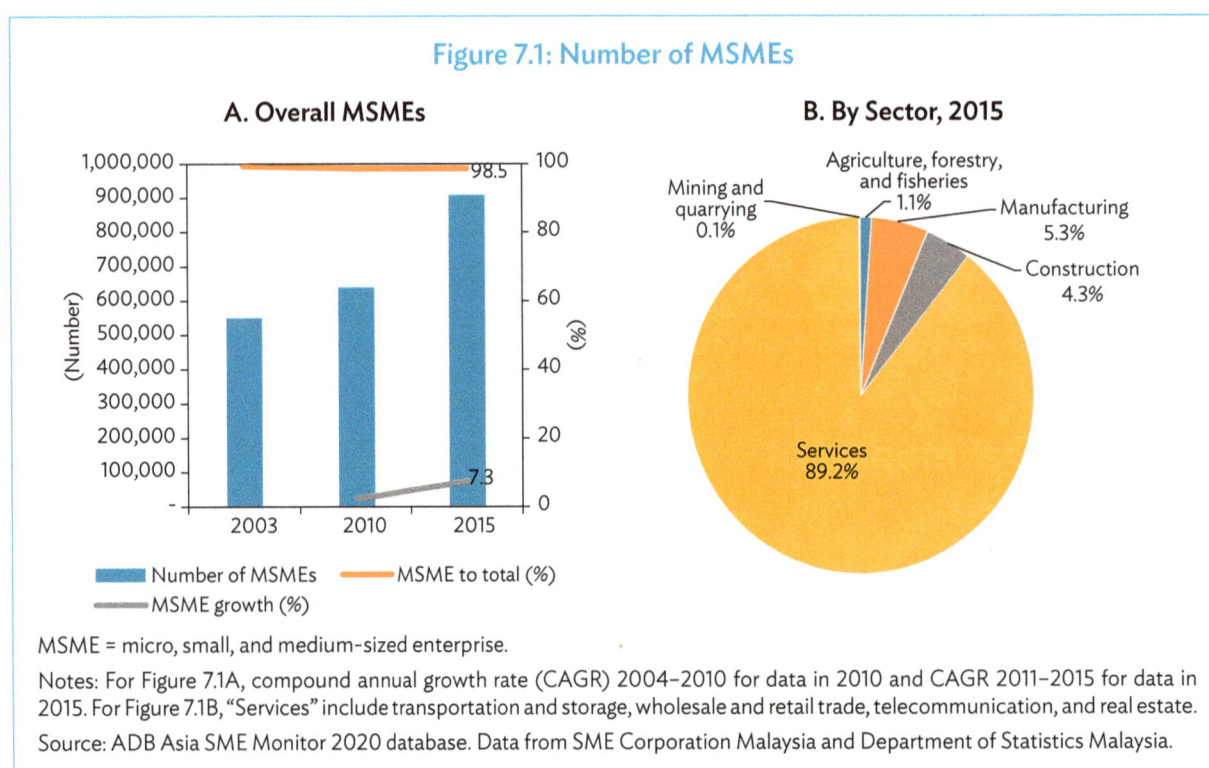

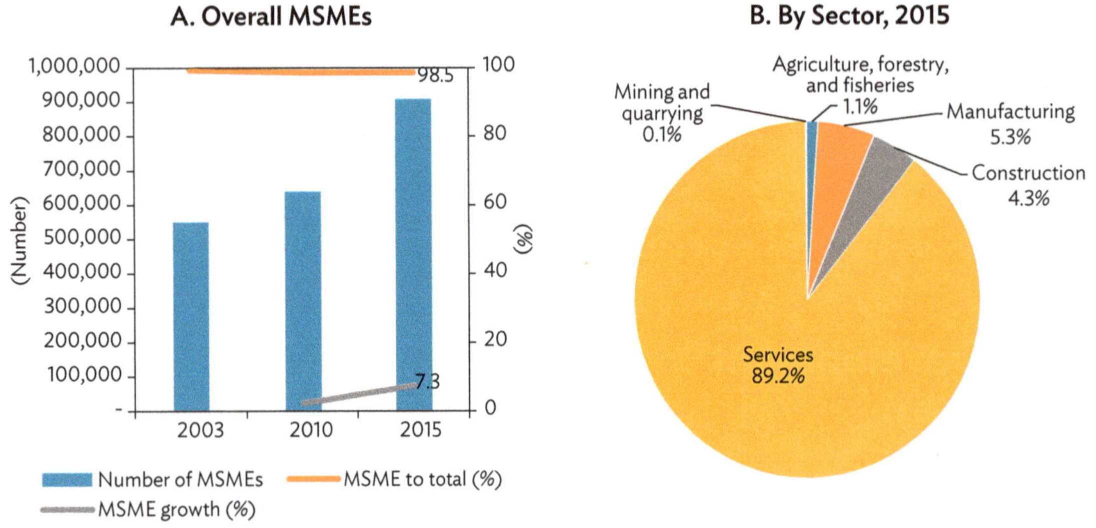

MSME = micro, small, and medium-sized enterprise.

Notes: For Figure 7.1A, compound annual growth rate (CAGR) 2004–2010 for data in 2010 and CAGR 2011–2015 for data in 2015. For Figure 7.1B, "Services" include transportation and storage, wholesale and retail trade, telecommunication, and real estate.

Source: ADB Asia SME Monitor 2020 database. Data from SME Corporation Malaysia and Department of Statistics Malaysia.

Employment

Employment data are updated annually, yet the number of MSME employees is not officially disclosed as the Department of Statistics Malaysia is reviewing and developing a methodology for estimating MSME employment levels, linked to the government's SME Master Plan 2012–2020 (as of March 2020).[67] Using this method, The employed by MSMEs accounted for 66.2% of the total workforce in Malaysia in 2018 (Figure 7.2A). The number of MSME employees increased 3.2%, but growth has been slowing. By sector, 62.3% of MSME employees were in services, followed by manufacturing (16.4%), primary industries (10.7%), construction (10.3%), and mining and quarrying (0.3%) in 2018 (Figure 7.2B). By region, 15.7% of MSME employees worked in Kuala Lumpur with the remaining 84.3% outside of capital in 2015 (Economic Census 2016). More than 38% of MSME employees were concentrated in Selangor and Kuala Lumpur urban areas.

[67] The Department of Statistics Malaysia publishes the total number of employed persons; however, it is not used as the denominator for calculating the number of MSME employees.

In 2015, the share of female employees to total MSME employees remained relatively small in Malaysia (33.6%) (Economic Census 2016). More women could join if there were more flexible working arrangements, a greater digital presence, available childcare services, and by encouraging female entrepreneurs.

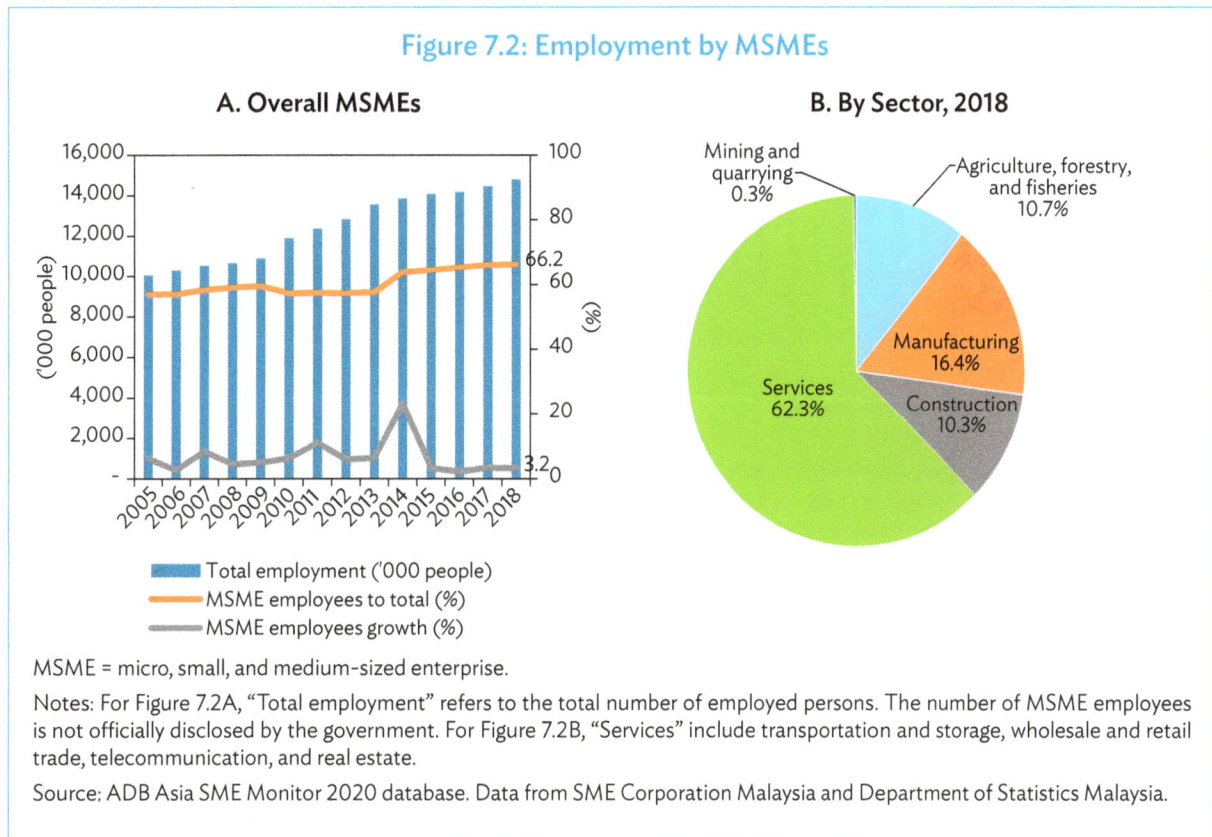

Figure 7.2: Employment by MSMEs

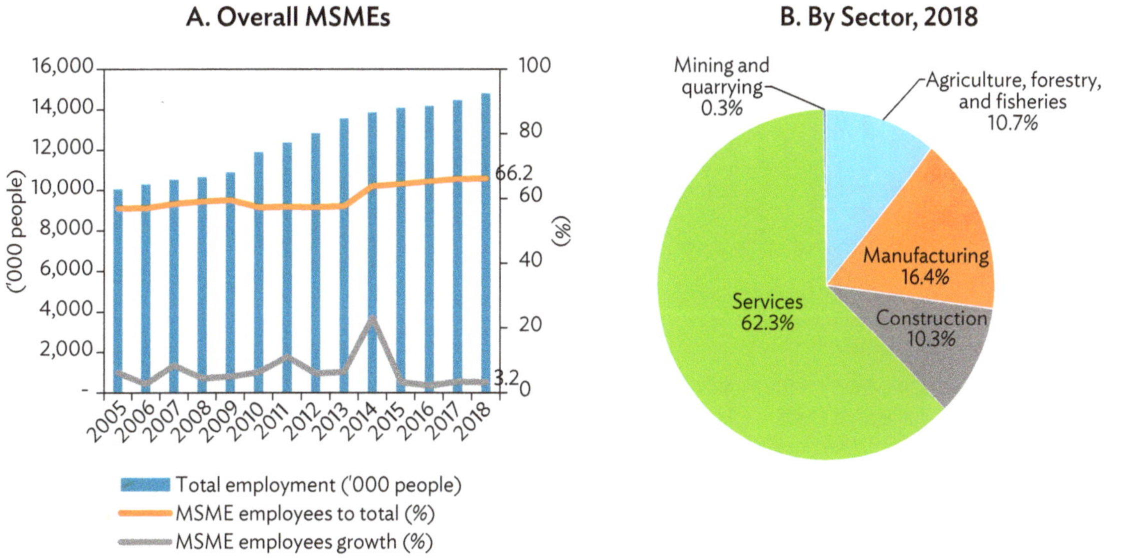

MSME = micro, small, and medium-sized enterprise.

Notes: For Figure 7.2A, "Total employment" refers to the total number of employed persons. The number of MSME employees is not officially disclosed by the government. For Figure 7.2B, "Services" include transportation and storage, wholesale and retail trade, telecommunication, and real estate.

Source: ADB Asia SME Monitor 2020 database. Data from SME Corporation Malaysia and Department of Statistics Malaysia.

Business Productivity

Lower exports and investments due to global trade tensions contributed to a drop in GDP growth from 4.8% in 2018 to 4.3% in 2019 (footnote 66). MSMEs contributed RM521.7 billion or 38.3% of Malaysia's GDP in 2018, a 6.2% increase but down from 7.1% in 2017 (Figure 7.3A). Decreased foreign demand was partly a factor for slowing growth of MSME GDP, but it was not significant as most MSMEs were not exposed to global markets. In Malaysia, MSME GDP is monitored based on real GDP at constant 2015 prices.

By sector, services accounted for 62.4% of MSME GDP in 2018, followed by manufacturing (20.1%), primary industries (10.1%), construction (5.9%), and others (1.6%) including mining and quarrying (0.5%) (Figure 7.3B). By region, 23% of MSME gross value added came from businesses in Kuala Lumpur with the remaining 77% from outside the capital city in 2015 (Economic Census 2016). Combined, Selangor and Kuala Lumpur contributed 48.8% of MSME gross value added.

Labor productivity in MSMEs, calculated as real value added per employee, has gradually increased to RM73,399 in 2018, 2.9% higher than 2017, but lower than the 3.6% rise in 2017. MSME labor productivity growth was led by mining and quarrying (8.3% annual growth), services (3.8%), and manufacturing (3.1%).[68]

[68] SME Corporation Malaysia. SME Annual Report 2018/2019.

Figure 7.3: MSME Contribution to Gross Domestic Product

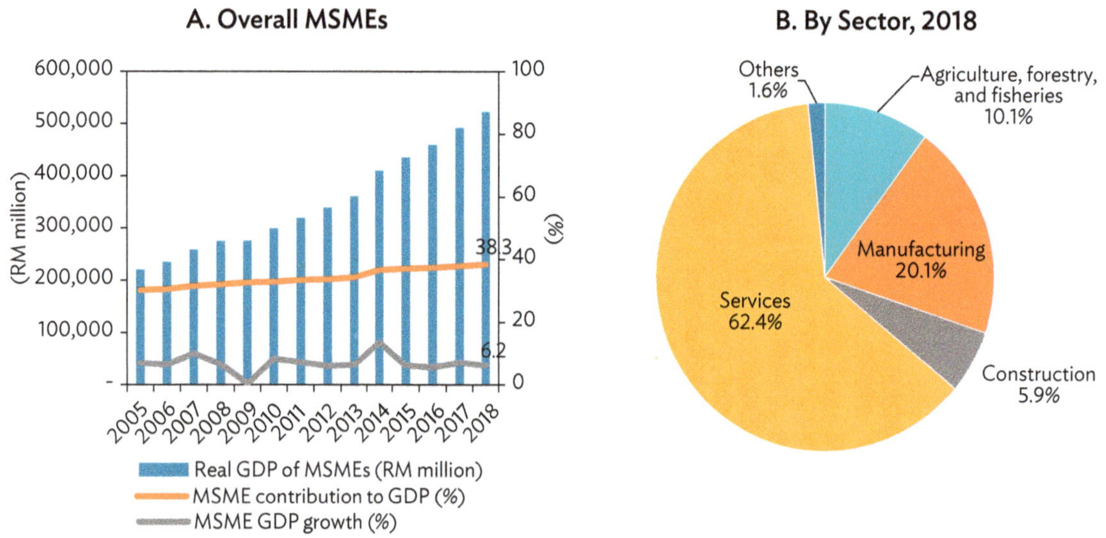

GDP = gross domestic product; MSME = micro, small, and medium-sized enterprise.

Notes: Figure 7.3A is based on real GDP. MSME GDP at constant 2015 prices (figures for 2003-2014 were adjusted based on 2015 constant prices). For Figure 7.3B, "Services" include transportation and storage, wholesale and retail trade, telecommunication, and real estate. "Others" include mining and quarrying, and import duties.

Source: ADB Asia SME Monitor 2020 database. Data from SME Corporation Malaysia and Department of Statistics Malaysia.

MSME GDP growth was higher than non-MSME, but its contribution to GDP remains small, suggesting that strengthened sector dynamics could boost national productivity.

Market Access

Most MSMEs target domestic markets, using self-generated marketing channels with few linkages with other business partners. According to the 2018 SME survey conducted by SME Corporation Malaysia (SME Corp), MSMEs have not yet successfully joined product supply chains. Just 6.7% of MSMEs surveyed (1,721 firms) sell products to large foreign firms in Malaysia. The SME Input-Output Table: Analysis and Impact (2019) also showed that microenterprises sourced 5% of their inputs from large firms, with small firms 10%, and medium-sized firms 21% for their production processes, while large firms did not rely on MSMEs for their production inputs (SME Corp 2019).

Few MSMEs trade overseas, although MSME exports by value have increased gradually. In 2018, the value of MSME exports was RM171.9 billion, a 3.4% increase over 2017 but lower than growth in 2017 (7.2%) (Figure 7.4A). It was also slightly lower than total exports (3.5% in 2018) (Figure 7.4B). The share of MSME exports to total export value remained at 17.3% in 2018. By sector, services accounted for 50.3% of MSME exports in 2018, followed by manufacturing (48.3%) and agriculture (1.5%). Due to weaker foreign demand, the growth of MSME exports has decelerated in services (from 7.1% in 2017 to 2.0% in 2018) and manufacturing (from 7.8% in 2017 to 5.1% in 2018). MSME-manufactured exports headed mainly to Singapore (18.6% of total MSME exports), the People's Republic of China (8.9%), and the United States (7.8%) (SME Corp 2019). Internationalizing MSMEs by developing domestic and global value chains is key to boost national productivity and inclusive growth in Malaysia. The government has launched several programs to support the internationalization of MSMEs, such as the SME Go Global, Market Development Grant, and export training programs (SME Corp 2019).

Figure 7.4: MSME Exports

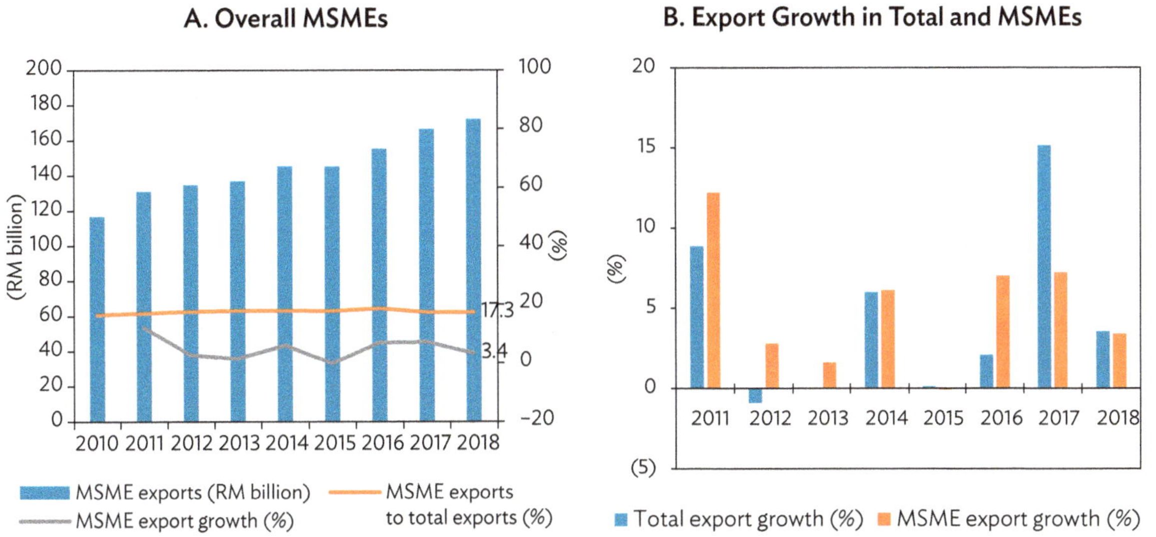

MSME = micro, small, and medium-sized enterprise.

Source: ADB Asia SME Monitor 2020 database. Data from SME Corporation Malaysia.

Technology and Innovation

Information and communications technology (ICT) has become a popular tool for MSMEs. According to the SME Corp's 2018 SME survey, 83.6% of MSMEs surveyed used computers, 82.3% used smartphones or tablets, and 73.3% used the internet for business. The survey also revealed that 37.9% of MSMEs conducted online business and generated an average 30% of sales online. However, their online presence is primarily domestic, and the majority of MSMEs prefer traditional ways of doing business. According to the Economic Census 2016, only 4.8% of MSMEs (or 43,460 out of 907,065) were engaged in e-commerce transactions in 2015, mostly in manufacturing and services.

Business innovation has been slow in most MSMEs. The Economic Census 2016 indicated that only 1.3% of MSMEs surveyed filed business patents, trademarks, or copyrights in 2015, and that only 0.9% of them invested in research and development (R&D) for business innovation during the same period.

The government has implemented several measures to accelerate MSME adoption of technology and innovation. The Malaysia Digital Economy Corporation (MDEC), a government agency established in 1996, helps MSMEs participate in e-commerce business through the Accelerating SME eCommerce Adoption program.

There are around 3,000 technology-based companies and start-ups, including more than 100 fintech companies, operating under the Multimedia Super Corridor, mainly in Kuala Lumpur's Cyberjaya science park, that aims to develop and promote Malaysia's digital economy. E-commerce is rapidly changing the MSME business landscape. According to the MDEC,[69] however, getting new technology out to local economies is a key challenge—it is hard to convince local people to use new technology for business. Enhancing digital literacy for MSMEs is critical to move the government's digital economy agenda forward. MDEC offers incentives for MSMEs to digitize their operations by using new technologies for business.

[69] Interview with the Malaysian Digital Economy Corporation on 24 July 2019.

Box 7.1: Technology Park Malaysia Supports Technology-Based MSMEs

Technology Park Malaysia (TPM), established on 28 November 1996, is a government agency owned by the Ministry of Finance and under the purview of the Ministry of Science, Technology and Innovation. It aims to create a world-class Technopolis that provides an advanced and comprehensive science, technology, and innovation ecosystem in Malaysia.

TPM has two incubation centers and two incubator programs—physical and virtual. The physical incubator program offers fully furnished office space for start-ups in the Technology Park. Around 100 start-ups and micro, small, and medium-sized enterprises (MSMEs) benefit from this program. Monthly rent ranges from $250 to $750. Electricity and internet connection are included. The virtual incubator program offers co-office space in the Technology Park. Again, around 100 start-ups and MSMEs avail of this program. The monthly fee is $70 (around RM300). Internet connection is included. As of July 2019, 25 MSMEs using TPM's incubator programs were listed on Bursa Malaysia, and their businesses are growing. In addition, there is a co-incubator program for Association of Southeast Asian Nations (ASEAN) economies, where incubators and experts are shared among ASEAN members.

TPM supports technology-based start-ups and MSMEs access technology, funds, markets, and infrastructure. As of July 2019, 2,300 MSMEs participated in its 160 programs, amounting to RM10.5 billion. TPM has 35 expert partners comprising more than 150 coaches, trainers, industrial mentors, intellectual property (IP) experts, and subject matter consultants. TPM connects MSMEs to these 35 expert partners as hands-on support. It also provides facilities for engineering and biotechnology manufacturing with fully equipped machinery, laboratories, and tools for accreditation of Hazard Analysis Critical Control Points, Good Manufacturing Practice, HALAL certification, and MS 2717:2019.

Aside from connecting MSMEs with government funding institutions, TPM also actively channels MSMEs to angel investors by working closely with the Malaysian Business Angel Network (MBAN). MBAN was established in 2013 and has 243 accredited business angels. Their average investment size ranges from RM10,000 to RM1 million with an average 3-year exit, with some ranging as long as 5–7 years. Business angels do not provide financial management outsourcing to MSMEs but link them to finance and nonfinancial options. Business angels receive a RM500,000 tax incentive per transaction from the government.

Source: Interview with the general manager of Technology Park Malaysia on 24 July 2019.

Networking and Support

The Malaysian International Chamber of Commerce and Industry has been serving private sector businesses since 1837. With headquarters in Kuala Lumpur and seven branch networks nationwide, it includes around 1,000 member corporations, of which 60% are multinationals and 40% SMEs (400 corporate partners). The chamber is also an advocate for business with government through various national councils covering trade and investment, taxation, logistics and infrastructure, and human capital and education. It facilitates business matching among members through regular and ad hoc business networking events and offers advisory services and capacity-building training programs on legislative issues, corporate governance, and taxation.

Besides the Malaysian International Chamber of Commerce and Industry, there is an active SME Association in Malaysia, established in 1995, that supports SME business development through various skill training programs and business networking events. The SME Association also advocates for SME business with government. It has 3,500 members and 13 branch offices nationwide.

2. Access to Finance

- MSME bank credit growth is likely slowing with fewer borrowers over the past decade, due in part to recent global economic uncertainty.
- However, the government offers a multitude of financial assistance packages to MSMEs through grants, subsidized loans, and credit guarantees, with demand growing among MSMEs.
- Venture capital and private equity play a critical role in filling unmet demand for growth capital financing for high-growth firms; however, investments in start-ups remain small.
- Digital financial services and infrastructure have developed rapidly, with demand for equity crowdfunding (ECF) and peer-to-peer (P2P) financing surging; however, to expand the usage of these new instruments, digital literacy and education should be strengthened further.
- Malaysia has a multitiered equity market, including boards targeting SME issuers such as ACE and LEAP markets; SME demand to use these markets is rising.
- There are several coexisting credit bureaus, raising the argument for a single, centralized entity; a modern secured lending system with a centralized credit registry is being formed.

Bank Credit

As of January 2020, there were 26 licensed commercial banks, 17 Islamic banks, and 11 investment banks operating in Malaysia. There were also six development financial institutions (DFIs),[70] including the Small Medium Enterprise Development Bank Malaysia Berhad (SME Bank). DFIs are specialized financial institutions established by the government with a special mandate to finance strategically important sectors for socioeconomic development.

In 2019, MSME loans outstanding, combining loans from both banking institutions and DFIs, totaled RM278.7 billion, a 12.9% decrease from 2018. They accounted for 14.6% of total bank loans outstanding and 18.5% of GDP (Figure 7.5A and Table 7.3). Banking institutions provided 95% of MSME loans while DFIs served the remaining 5% in 2019.

The sharp decrease in MSME credit in 2019 was caused by a restructuring of MSME loan classifications. Banks have begun reviewing and reclassifying some MSME accounts to non-MSMEs in line with the national MSME definition since January 2018. MSMEs that have grown into large firms through an increase in annual turnover or number of employees (beyond the national definition threshold) are being excluded, along with public listed companies, subsidiaries of public listed companies and large firms, multinational companies, government-linked companies, and state-owned enterprises that were formerly classified as MSMEs.[71] Because of the reclassification, 2019 MSME credit growth is likely underestimated. Bank Negara Malaysia (BNM), the central bank, estimates the adjusted growth for MSME outstanding loans for 2018 in fact up 5.4%, which is consistent with the 2017 growth of 5.3%. Nonetheless, panel data indicates that growth of MSME bank credit has decelerated since 2011, likely affected by increased global economic uncertainty due to trade tensions.

The annual average lending rate on MSME loans was 6.0% in 2019, slightly down from 6.1% in 2018 (Figure 7.5B). The lending rate spread between MSME and non-MSME loans appears to be widening (the annual average lending rate for local currency bank loans in 2019 was 5.0%). There were 115,498 MSME borrowers in 2019, 6.6% less than 2018. But the decrease was also affected by MSME loan reclassification. MSMEs in wholesale and retail trade were the most active borrowers from banks. The average loan size per MSME was RM393,000 as of May

70 There are six development financial institutions: (i) Bank Kerjasama Rakyat Malaysia Berhad (Bank Rakyat); (ii) Bank Pembangunan Malaysia Berhad; (iii) Bank Pertanian Malaysia Berhad (Agrobank); (iv) Small Medium Enterprise Development Bank Malaysia Berhad (SME Bank); (v) Bank Simpanan Nasional; and (vi) Export-Import Bank of Malaysia Berhad (EXIM Bank).

71 The reclassified amount (from MSMEs to non-MSMEs) can be viewed on the BNM website: http://www.bnm.gov.my/index.php?ch=fi&pg=fi_download&ac=445&lang=en.

2019, higher than the RM330,000 average in 2014. While MSME borrowers from banks have moderately dropped in number over the past decade (from 2019), alternative financing options such as ECF, P2P financing platforms, digital financial services, and specialized SME equity markets have begun supplementing MSME bank credit. According to BNM,[72] banks are open to work together with new entrants in the financial sector such as digital finance service providers.

BNM conducted an SME finance survey in 2018, which showed access to finance was not a major constraint for MSME business development. The survey respondents (1,529 formal SMEs and 223 informal businesses) cited increasing competition as the top constraint (69% of respondents), followed by changing consumer demand (51%) and rising input costs (44%). Access to finance ranked eighth (19% of respondents) among various business constraints. More than half of MSMEs surveyed cited public financing schemes—such as grants, soft loans, and credit guarantees—as the most useful tool in easing various business constraints.

Figure 7.5: MSME Loans

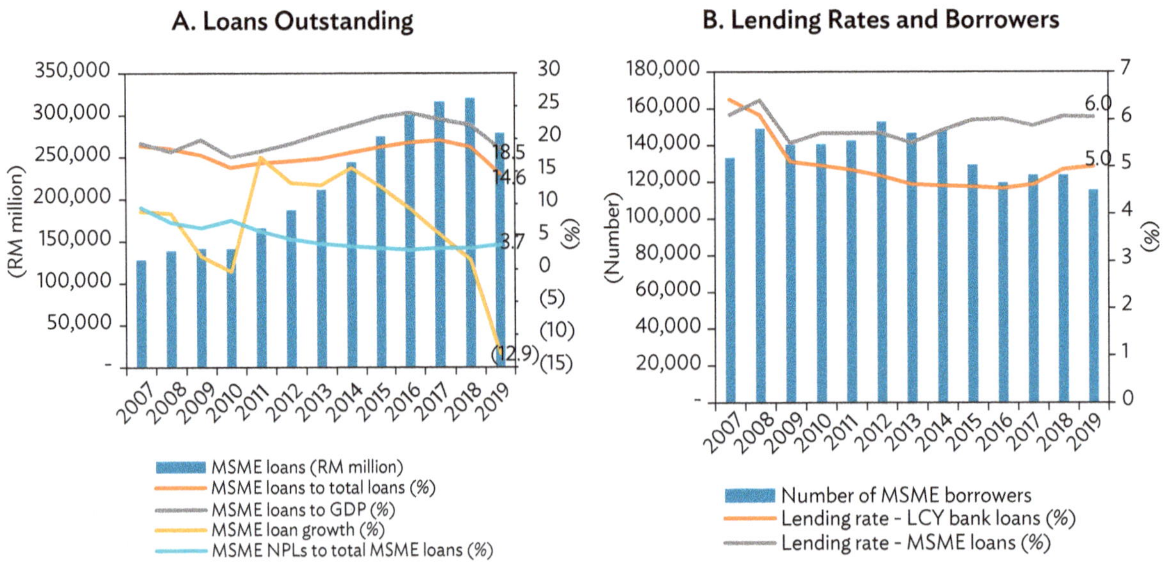

GDP = gross domestic product; LCY = local currency; MSME = micro, small, and medium-sized enterprise.

Source: ADB Asia SME Monitor 2020 database. Data from Bank Negara Malaysia and SME Corporation Malaysia.

Public Financing and Guarantees

The government offers a multitude of financial assistance to MSMEs such as grants, subsidized loans, and credit guarantees. In 2018, the government spent RM13 billion for MSME development through 44 programs related to access to finance. These programs benefited 424,115 MSMEs (SME Corp 2019).

a. Specialized bank for MSMEs

SME Bank, established in 2005, is a government financial institution owned by the Ministry of Finance to provide financial assistance to MSMEs. It offers Islamic financing using partial government subsidies and credit guarantees.

[72] Interview with BNM manager on 23 July 2019.

Major products include (i) working capital financing with a 4%–8% per annum referring to the base financing rate plus 0% up to 2.5% with an average maturity of 3–5 years, (ii) investment capital financing with a loan maturity of 7–10 years, and (iii) hire purchase leasing (a maximum 7-year leasing for buses and tank lorries). SME Bank uses a 70% partial credit guarantee from the Credit Guarantee Corporation Malaysia Berhad (CGC) and Prokhas (a state-owned asset management company) for MSME financing. Remaining financing risks are covered by collateral, including real estate, movable assets, and cash. The bank has developed thematic financing programs focusing on women entrepreneurs, construction and infrastructure projects, tourism, and rural economic development. It also assists MSMEs strengthen their core business, build capacity and capability, and facilitate access to finance through a business accelerator program.

b. Credit guarantees

In Malaysia, credit guarantees for MSMEs are mainly provided by two guarantors: CGC and Prokhas. Prokhas uses government guarantee funds managed by the Syarikat Jaminan Pembiayaan Perniagaan (SJPP).

SJPP, established in 2009, is a state-owned company under the Minister of Finance to manage government guarantee programs addressing MSMEs. As of end-2018, there were seven government guarantee funds that disbursed a total of RM7 billion in 2018 (Table 7.4). SJPP has six product lines covering all MSME sectors: five working capital guarantee schemes for general MSMEs and priority segments (start-ups, *bumiputera* [domestic, Malay-owned MSMEs], exporters, and women) and one digital guarantee scheme. Its credit guarantees range between RM50,000 and RM10 million with guarantee coverage of 70% or 80%, with a guarantee fee of 0.75% or 1.0% per annum, depending on the product. RM2.7 billion was issued through working capital guarantee schemes, benefitting 2,520 MSMEs in 2018 (SME Corp 2019).

CGC is a private credit guarantee corporation, established by BNM and financial institutions in 1972. It actively supports MSME access to finance through various guarantee and direct financing products and services.[73] Since its establishment, CGC has provided more than 460,000 guarantees and financing to MSMEs valued at RM70.8 billion as of end-2018. In 2018, it approved RM3.7 billion in guarantees, benefitting 8,999 MSMEs (Figure 7.6A). Since the third quarter of 2010, CGC has also offered portfolio guarantees. It issued 5,449 letters of guarantees in 2017, a 48% increase from 2016. It also launched an online SME financing and loan referral platform (imSME) in 2018, which refers MSME financing applications to participating financial institutions online. As of January 2020, 25 financial institutions including five DFIs, three agencies, and 12 alternative financiers participated in imSME[74]. The platform financed RM137 million for 1,417 MSMEs as of September 2019 (SME Corp 2019). It also has a financial advisory team to address MSMEs that cannot find suitable financing options.

c. Soft loan programs

As of end-2018, 26 government funds channeled interest rate subsidies to MSME loans, totaling RM3.2 billion disbursed (Figure 7.6B). Subsidized financing programs include the *Syariah*-Compliant SME Financing Scheme (SSFS) implemented by participating Islamic financial institutions. SSFS benefited 476 MSMEs in 2018. The program is supposed to return 2% of its profit to the government (SME Corp 2019). Skim Pembiayaan Mikro, started in 2005, is a non-collateral microcredit program that finances up to RM50,000 for microenterprises, servicing 230,082 firms with approved loans of RM4.1 billion from 2005 to 2018 (SME Corp 2019).

[73] Financing to *bumiputera* MSMEs is done under the Bumiputera Entrepreneur Project Fund-i (TPUB-i) under the Credit Guarantee Corporation Malaysia.

[74] imSME. About imSME. https://imsme.com.my/portal/about-imsme/.

Since 1993, BNM has managed special funds that facilitate concessional loans to MSMEs. In 2018, loans outstanding amounted to RM5.8 billion and served 78,267 MSME accounts. The funds were mainly used for working capital and business expansion of MSMEs.

Figure 7.6: Public Finance and Guarantees

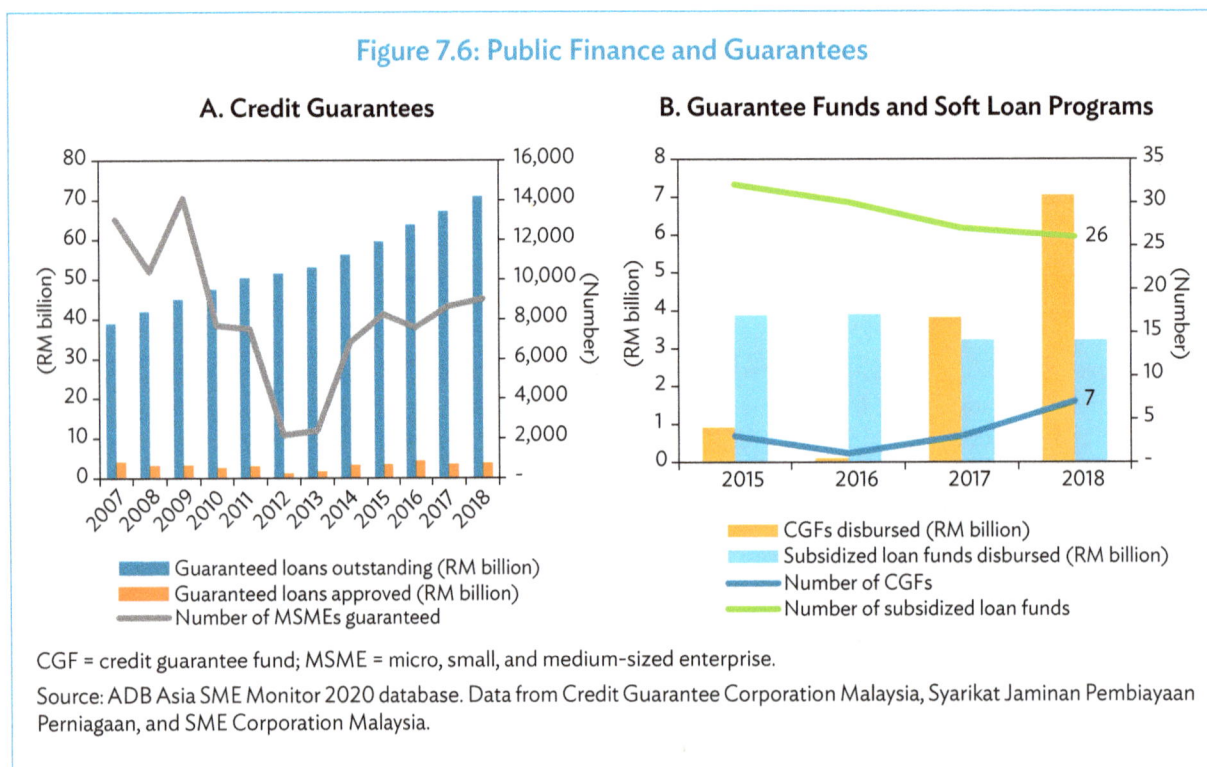

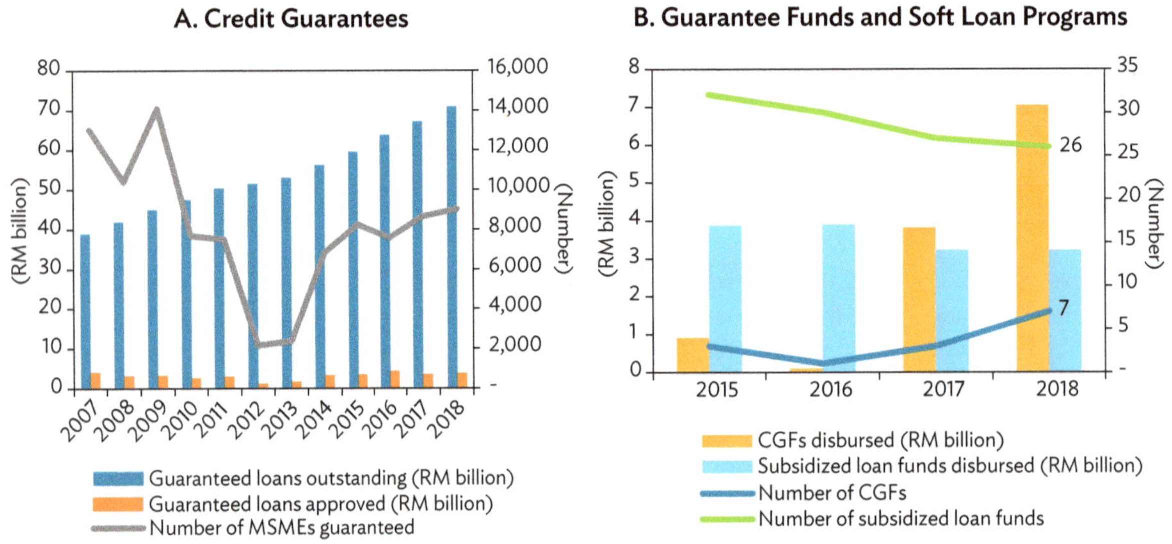

CGF = credit guarantee fund; MSME = micro, small, and medium-sized enterprise.

Source: ADB Asia SME Monitor 2020 database. Data from Credit Guarantee Corporation Malaysia, Syarikat Jaminan Pembiayaan Perniagaan, and SME Corporation Malaysia.

Nonbank Financing

The nonbank finance industry is underdeveloped compared with the banking sector. Financing outstanding of factoring and leasing amounted to RM773 million in 2018, or just 0.05% of total bank credit and a 6.5% decrease from the previous year (Table 7.5). However, demand for alternative or diversified financing has been increasing among high-growth enterprises and start-ups, supported by the advent of advanced technology or the Fourth Industrial Revolution. Venture capital and private equity play a critical role in filling unmet MSME demand for growth capital financing.

There are two types of venture capital and private equity firms registered with the Securities Commission Malaysia (SCM): (i) corporations that directly manage their own funds, and (ii) management corporations that indirectly manage funds from venture capital and private equity firms. As of end-2019, 105 venture capital firms (both corporations and management corporations) and 17 private equity firms were registered with the SCM. The registration of private equity firms started in 2015. Total funds managed by venture capital and private equity firms amounted to RM6,084 million in 2018, a 13.1% decrease from 2017 (Figure 7.7A). However, total investments by venture capital and private equity firms reached RM613 million in 2018, a 47% increase from 2017. Accumulated investments by venture capital and private equity firms was RM3,116 million at end-2018, serving 387 companies.

In 2018, early and expansion stage firms accounted for 87% of the investment by venture capital and private equity firms, with only 0.8% going to seed firms and start-ups (Figure 7.7B). By sector, life sciences accounted for 49.6% of total investments, followed by ICT (22.7%) in 2018. ICT received RM139 million in 2018, a sharp increase from the RM59 million invested in 2017.

Figure 7.7: Nonbank Finance

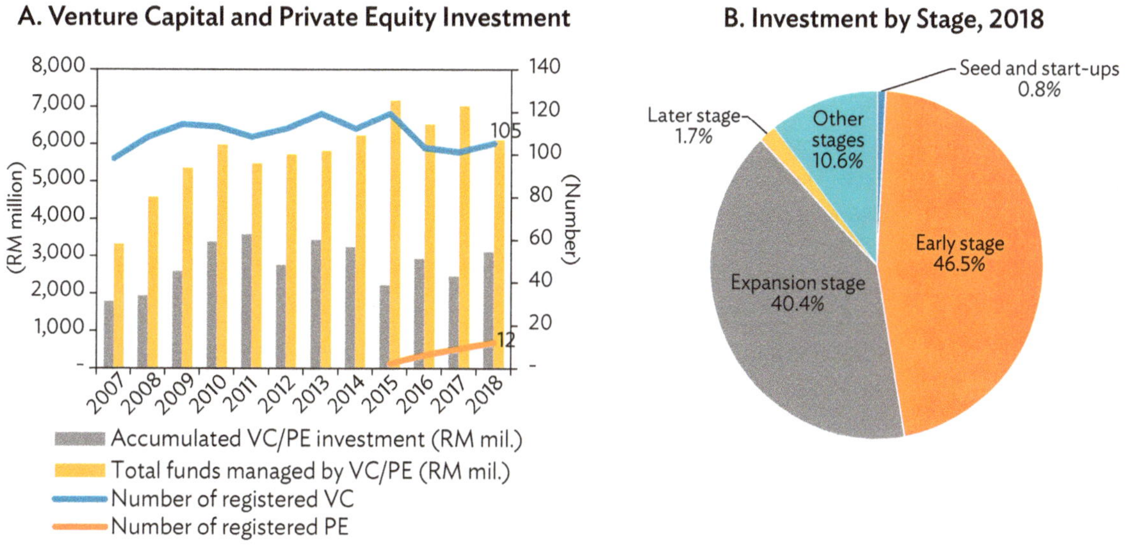

PE=private equity, VC=venture capital.

Source: ADB Asia SME Monitor 2020 database. Data from Securities Commission Malaysia.

Digital Financial Services

In 2011, BNM launched a Financial Inclusion Framework which included strategic targets for developing innovative financial services and channels—including digital financial services (DFS). BNM's Financial Sector Blueprint 2011–2020 accelerated the country's migration to electronic or e-payments. There is an interoperable payment network run by Payments Network Malaysia Sdn Bhd (PayNet). PayNet launched a real-time retail payments platform in 2019 to modernize the country's retail payment system and facilitate other innovative e-payments. PayNet has payment options such as MyDebit (a national debit card), SAN (a shared ATM network), JomPay (a national bill payment platform), among other online networks. As of July 2019, BNM licensed 5 banks and 41 nonbank finance institutions for e-wallet services.

An agent banking system was launched in 2012 to allow customers to access banking services through third-party agents, such as retail outlets and post offices.[75] In 2015, a BNM regulation allowed agents to help open savings accounts through online real-time systems and by using biometric identity verification. As of end-2019, there were 5,532 agent banks that helped open more than 45,000 accounts and process 195 million transactions, amounting to RM16.3 billion.

[75] Bank Negara Malaysia. Financial Stability and Payment Systems Report 2015.

The Interoperable Credit Transfer Framework was launched in July 2018. It allows a payer to instruct an institution to transfer funds to a beneficiary. Under this framework, MSMEs enjoyed fee-free instant transfers up to RM15,000 (SME Corp 2018[76]).

Internet banking and mobile banking have expanded rapidly. Internet banking subscribers rose from 11.9 million in 2011 to 24.5 million in 2019, covering 98.2% of adults aged 15 and above, with mobile banking subscribers expanding from 1.6 million in 2011 to 13.2 million in 2019, 52.9% of the adult population.

The regulatory framework for ECF came out in February 2015, while the framework for P2P financing platforms was launched in April 2016. As of end-2019, 77 ECF issuers successfully raised RM73.7 million. One-half was for RM500,000 and below. Of ECF investors, 53% were retail investors, followed by sophisticated investors (29%), angel investors (16%), and institutional investors (2%). Forty percent were 35 years old or younger. At the same time, 1,866 P2P financing issuers successfully raised RM632.4 million, with 70% for RM50,000 and below. Of P2P financing investors, 95% were retail investors with 62% of them aged 35 years old or below.[77] The demand on ECF and P2P lending has been growing especially in online businesses and digital industries. As of end-2019, 10 ECF platforms and 11 P2P financing platforms were registered with the SCM. Applications for registering ECF and P2P financing is set by SCM in accordance with market demand.

For cyber risk management, SCM organizes and conducts cyber security simulations every year on capital market intermediaries, including SCM-regulated fintech platforms. The SCM does thematic cyber security assessments on fintech platforms to ensure effective cyber measures and controls are in place. A quarterly Cyber Risk Working Group has been held since 2018 to build continuous cyber awareness and educate on emerging cyber threats.

One challenge for the fintech industry is to further strengthen digital literacy and education to potential customers, including MSMEs, so financial institutions and DFS providers can reach out to potential, viable customers, and to establish "trust" among digital finance users—key for developing the fintech industry. There is high demand from MSMEs to use DFS because it requires no collateral and offers fast, low-cost, and easy access to loans. The collaboration between fintech firms and banks would create greater synergy for delivering more demand-driven financial services.

Capital Markets

Malaysia has multitiered equity markets, comprising a main market, the ACE ("Access, Certainty, Efficiency") market, and the LEAP ("Leading Entrepreneur Accelerator Platform") market under Bursa Malaysia. Among them, ACE and LEAP are equity finance platforms that SMEs can tap to fund business growth.

The ACE market is a sponsor-driven market designed for companies with growth prospects. It was launched in August 2009, revamped from the former MESDAQ market. The ACE market requires sponsors to assess the suitability of potential issuers to list. Unlike the main market, ACE does not require a minimum operating track record or profits for listing. It also has eased listing requirements such as a lower minimum number of public shareholders—a minimum of 200 shareholders holding not less than 100 shares each as compared to a minimum 1,000 shareholders holding not less than 100 shares each for the main market.

---

76 SME Corporation Malaysia. SME Annual Report 2017/2018.

77 Securities Commission Malaysia. Crowdfunding Monitor December 2019. https://www.sc.com.my/api/documentms/download.ashx?id=0d6670ca-e336-4405-8236-bb3a1c8d77a2.

A sponsor must remain involved for at least 3 fiscal years after listing or at least 1 fiscal year after the company generates operating revenue, whichever is later. The sponsor who submitted the listing application must act as a sponsor to a company for at least 1 fiscal year after listing. The sponsorship period is liberalized for ACE market companies that have met the quantitative criteria for listing on the main market, from 3 years to just 1 year. As of end-2019, the ACE market had 129 listed companies with a market capitalization of RM18.8 billion, a 55.1% increase over 2018 (Figure 7.8A and Table 7.6). While trading volume fell slightly (by 0.3% in 2019 from the previous year), trading value grew by 8.2% over the same period.

The LEAP market was launched in July 2017 as an advisor-driven market for emerging companies and SMEs. The LEAP market requires advisors to assess the suitability of potential issuers to list. Only sophisticated investors (for example, registered investors with high net worth) specified under the Capital Markets and Services Act 2007 can invest in the LEAP market. The LEAP market offers the eased listing requirements for issuers, which reduces the time and cost of preparing for listing (Table 7.7). Similar to the ACE market, the LEAP market does not require any minimum operating track record or profits for listing. There is no minimum shareholder limit, but at least 10% of the company's shares must be held by the public. Advisors are required to remain involved for at least 3 fiscal years after listing or at least 1 fiscal year after the company has generated operating revenue, whichever is later. The approved advisor who submitted the listing application must continue as advisor for at least 1 fiscal year after listing.

As of end-2019, the LEAP market had 28 listed companies from various sectors including manufacturing and export-oriented electronic services (Figure 7.8B). These listed companies mostly market domestically and include only a few globalized SMEs. The market capitalization of the LEAP market was RM2,435 million in 2019, a sharp 165% increase from RM920 million in 2018. Both trading volume and value have surged since its launch in 2017 (333 million shares traded worth RM33 million in 2019).

While the performance of the main market has been stagnant since 2018 (with flat market capitalization growth in 2019), both ACE and LEAP markets have been growing with increasing number of new listings, especially the LEAP market, suggesting strong demand for equity financing by growing SMEs. However, there are several challenges for these emerging markets: (i) limited number of qualified sponsors and advisors; (ii) cultivating a base of potential SME issuers; and (iii) market liquidity. Principal advisors that can undertake corporate finance and apply to the SCM are limited in number. Bank-backed advisors also show lukewarm interest in the LEAP market. For early-stage financing, high-growth SMEs are likely to reach out to private equity and venture capital financing; thus the challenge to cultivate a base of potential SME issuers. To attract more SMEs to equity markets, Bursa Malaysia has conducted several IPO seminars targeting SMEs since 2018, part of its effort to strengthen capital market literacy among SMEs and enhance awareness of the benefits of listing.

Figure 7.8: Equity Markets

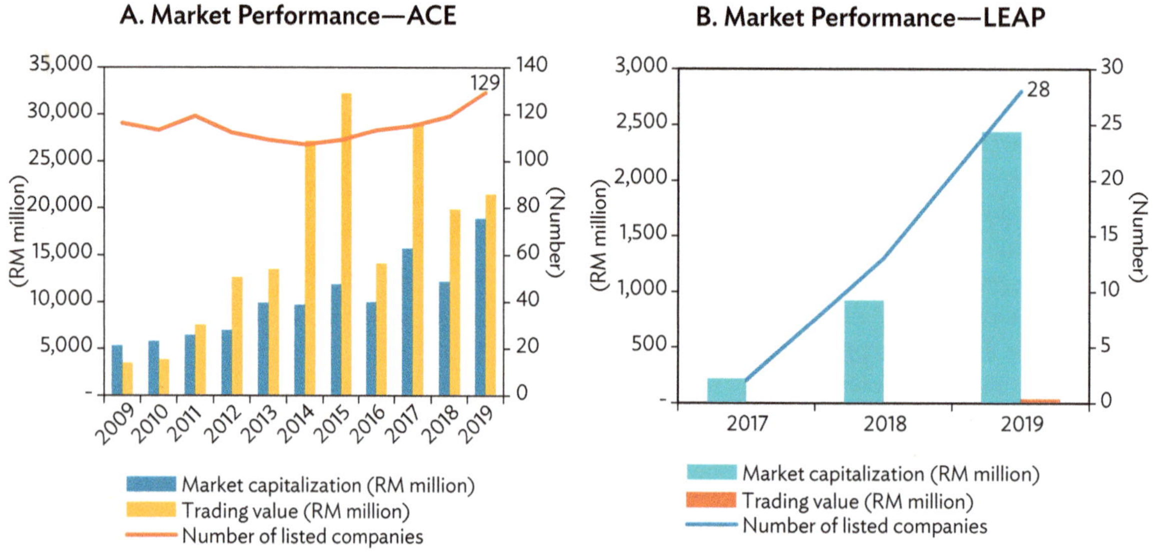

ACE = Access, Certainty, Efficiency; LEAP = Leading Entrepreneur Accelerator Platform.

Source: ADB Asia SME Monitor 2020 database. Data from Bursa Malaysia.

Financial Infrastructure

A secured lending legal system has yet to be fully developed in Malaysia. The government is preparing legislation for a modern, unified movable property security interest legislation and a centralized collateral registry for movable assets, including machinery and equipment, intellectual property, inventories, and agricultural products (as of end-2019).

As early as 1982, BNM operated a public credit registry, aggregating large financing deals from financial institutions to monitor any concentration of credit risks nationally. This evolved into the Central Credit Reference Information System (CCRIS) in 2001. CCRIS aggregates credit data not only from commercial financial institutions, but also from development financial institutions, as well as the national student loan fund.

There are seven private credit bureaus (PCBs) in the country. Their activities are regulated by the Credit Reporting Agencies Act of 2010 which requires PCBs to register with the Registrar of Credit Reporting Agencies under the Ministry of Finance. The BNM-owned public credit registry predominantly serves BNM and banking industry needs and is not governed under the act.

Credit Bureau Malaysia (CBM) is one of the seven PCBs. It was established in 2008 by government initiative to help improve financial inclusion among MSMEs (it was originally named the SME Credit Bureau; following changes in legislation—the Personal Data Protection Act of 2010 and the Credit Reporting Agencies Act of 2010—the SME Credit Bureau expanded coverage to include individuals and was renamed). CBM was a pioneer in introducing credit reports including repayment history and a statistically derived credit score.

CBM, together with two other PCBs have been granted access to credit data from CCRIS and can produce full credit reports for both commercial entities and individuals. Three other PCBs produce credit reports on commercial entities but not individuals. Most PCBs are able to purchase data from the Companies Commission of Malaysia and collect commercial credit repayment data and litigation from public records on their own or in collaboration with other PCBs.

The Financial Information Services Sdn Bhd (FIS), established by the Association of Finance Companies Malaysia and the Association of Hire Purchase Companies of Malaysia in 1986, shares commercial, financial, and other business information with associations' members. Since 2013, FIS Data Reference Sdn Bhd, a subsidiary of FIS, has collected and circulated data to associations' members.

Among the challenges faced by the credit bureau industry is the large number of registered PCBs in relation to population size as well as restrictions on accessing public data.

3. Policies and Regulations

- Malaysia has developed a well-organized centralized policy coordination mechanism for all MSME support measures initiated by line ministries and agencies; the government, under the National Entrepreneur and SME Development Council, has set a long-term strategy for entrepreneurship and SME development.
- Among the multitude of MSME development policies, formalizing informal businesses is critical to accelerate inclusive growth, where business incubation and business development services could be strengthened further.
- The central bank's financial inclusion strategy runs until 2020; another long-term framework for financial inclusion is expected.
- Broadening alternative financing models using digital technology should be promoted along with strengthened financial and digital literacy under a holistic financial inclusion strategy.

MSME Development

MSME development reached another milestone with the establishment of the Ministry of Entrepreneur Development and Cooperatives (MEDAC) in 2018 as a focal ministry for entrepreneurship development policies. MEDAC developed its National Entrepreneurship Policy 2030 (Dasar Keusahawanan Nasional, DKN 2030) as a long-term strategy.

DKN 2030 was launched in July 2019 to build an entrepreneurship culture and create a holistic entrepreneurial ecosystem in the country. It aims to increase qualified, viable, and resilient entrepreneurs, and scale up MSMEs with a global mindset. It consists of six strategic thrusts with 19 strategies (Table 7.8): (i) fostering an entrepreneurship culture across all segments of Malaysian society, (ii) optimizing the regulatory environment and access to finance, (iii) promoting holistic and integrated entrepreneurship development, (iv) accelerating economic growth through innovation-driven enterprises, (v) boosting the entrepreneurial capabilities and performance of MSMEs, and (vi) internationalizing high-growth enterprises.

DKN 2030 has macro targets for MSME development by 2030: (i) raise MSME contributions to GDP to 50% (38.3% in 2018), (ii) increase MSME employment to 80% of the workforce (66.2% in 2018), and (iii) increase MSME contributions to exports by value to 30% (17.3% in 2018).

Following the change in government administration after the 14th general election in 2018, SME Corp, previously under the purview of the Ministry of International Trade and Industry, was placed under MEDAC as an agency to implement national MSME policies, while continuing its strategic role as central coordinating agency and secretariat of the National Entrepreneur and SME Development Council.

MDEC launched the National eCommerce Strategic Roadmap in 2016 to support a national agenda for the digital economy. It targets approximately 50% of MSMEs to enter the international e-commerce arena, ensuring they are able to keep pace with new digital developments.

All MSME policies and strategies initiated by line ministries and agencies are well coordinated. The National SME Development Council, chaired by the Prime Minister, was a top-tier MSME policymaking authority covering all economic sectors. Under the new MEDAC initiatives, the council was reorganized as the National Entrepreneur and SME Development Council in April 2019, with greater emphasis on developing entrepreneurship. A High Level Task Force for Entrepreneur and SME Development acts as a conduit for strengthening cooperation and coordination among line ministries and agencies for effective implementation of entrepreneurship and MSME development policies. The task force established strategic thematic committees covering connectivity, tourism, human capital, and climate change.

Among the multitude of MSME development policies and measures, formalizing informal businesses is critically important to accelerate inclusive growth in Malaysia. There are dedicated agencies that cater to microenterprises by requiring them to formalize their businesses in order to access financing for expansion. In addition to this and conventional measures such as tax incentives, incubator programs and business development services can be further strengthened to create a base of growth-oriented MSMEs.

Financial Inclusion

Financial inclusion offers equal opportunities at all levels of economic society to access formal financial services, generate income, and enjoy enhanced social welfare, with the goal of creating sustainable economic growth. In 2011, BNM developed a long-term Financial Sector Blueprint 2011–2020, with four recommendations for financial inclusion: (i) adopt innovative ways to enhance the outreach of affordable financial services, (ii) expand the range of financial products and services, (iii) strengthen the institutional arrangements to provide financial services to all citizens, and (iv) enhance the knowledge and capacity of those underserved to use financial services.

Based on these recommendations, BNM set out a comprehensive financial inclusion framework through 2020. The framework has four broad strategies and 10 action plans: (i) innovative channels that include the development of agent banking and technology-based channels; (ii) innovative products and services that address flexible microfinancing, micro-savings, and micro-insurance; (iii) effective financial institutions and infrastructure that strengthen DFI capability, organize financial inclusion training, and introduce a Financial Inclusion Index; and (iv) build a well-informed, responsible populace through collaboration with nongovernment organizations (NGOs) and improved financial literacy.

BNM developed the Financial Inclusion Index as a benchmark for measuring how well the financial inclusion strategies stipulated in the framework are implemented. The index has four dimensions: (i) convenient accessibility, (ii) take-up rate for deposit and loan accounts and life insurance, (iii) responsible usage, and (iv) satisfaction level. In 2015, the index showed the positive result. For instance, the dimension of convenient accessibility improved to 99% of the population living in subdistricts with at least one access point in 2015 (82% in 2011), and the dimension of take-up rate increased from 36% of adults with loan accounts in 2011 to 39% in 2015.

In Malaysia, financial institutions are regulated and supervised by three authorities: BNM for the banking sector, SCM for capital markets including emerging digital platforms (ECF and P2P financing platforms), and the Ministry of Housing and Local Government for money lenders. The ministry also offers concessional lending programs to MSMEs. For capital markets, SCM is an approving authority for companies' listing on the main market of Bursa Malaysia, while Bursa Malaysia is a solo approver for listing on the ACE and LEAP markets. For listing on the ACE market, SCM registers the prospectus. The establishment of the LEAP market was in line with the growth strategy of promoting capital formation under the Capital Market Masterplan 2, launched in 2011, with the goal of increasing the number of high-growth firms under the SME Masterplan 2012–2020, and the recommendation of effective intermediation under the Financial Sector Blueprint 2011–2020.

Challenges to promote financial inclusion include strengthening digital finance literacy for the entire population. Mobile phone usage for financial services has generally improved, but not sufficiently in rural areas, where people tend to embrace traditional behavior. How to promote the usage of mobile applications for people to access financial services, or how to reach out to the rural economy is a primary challenge for financial inclusion. Improving people's savings behavior is also a critical challenge. Broadening alternative financing models by using digital technology and innovative instruments should be promoted, together with strengthening financial and digital literacy for all under a holistic financial inclusion strategy.

Data Tables

Table 7.1: MSME Definition

Sector	Item	Micro	Small	Medium
Manufacturing	Annual Sales Turnover	Less than RM300,000 OR	From RM300,000 to less than RM15 million OR	From RM15 million to not exceeding RM50 million OR
	Number of Full-time Employees	Fewer than 5 employees	From 5 to 74 employees	From 75 to not exceeding 200 employees
Services and Other Sectors	Annual Sales Turnover	Less than RM300,000 OR	From RM300,000 to less than RM3 million OR	From RM3 million to not exceeding RM20 million OR
	Number of Full-time Employees	Fewer than 5 employees	From 5 to 29 employees	From 30 to not exceeding 75 employees

MSME = micro, small, and medium-sized enterprise.

Notes: MSME definition has been effective since 1 January 2014.

Source: ADB Asia SME Monitor 2020 database. Data from SME Corporation Malaysia.

Table 7.2: MSME Landscape

End of period data

Item	2003	2004	2005	2006	2007	2008	2009	2010	2011	2012	2013	2014	2015	2016	2017	2018	2019
NUMBER OF ENTERPRISES																	
Number of enterprises, total	552,849	--	--	--	--	--	--	648,260	--	--	--	--	920,624	--	--	--	--
Number of MSMEs	548,267	--	--	--	--	--	--	638,790	--	--	--	--	907,065	--	--	--	--
Number of large enterprises	4,582	--	--	--	--	--	--	9,470	--	--	--	--	13,559	--	--	--	--
MSME to total (%)	99.2	--	--	--	--	--	--	98.5	--	--	--	--	98.5	--	--	--	--
MSME growth (%)[1]	--	--	--	--	--	--	--	2.2	--	--	--	--	7.3	--	--	--	--
MSMEs by sector (% share)																	
Agriculture, forestry, and fisheries	6.2	--	--	--	--	--	--	1.2	--	--	--	--	1.1	--	--	--	--
Manufacturing	7.2	--	--	--	--	--	--	6.0	--	--	--	--	5.3	--	--	--	--
Construction	--	--	--	--	--	--	--	3.3	--	--	--	--	4.3	--	--	--	--
Services[2]	86.6	--	--	--	--	--	--	89.4	--	--	--	--	89.2	--	--	--	--
Mining and quarrying	--	--	--	--	--	--	--	0.1	--	--	--	--	0.1	--	--	--	--
Number of MSMEs by region (% share)																	
Capital city	--	--	--	--	--	--	--	13.1	--	--	--	--	14.7	--	--	--	--
Others	--	--	--	--	--	--	--	86.9	--	--	--	--	85.3	--	--	--	--
EMPLOYMENT																	
Number of employment, total ('000)	--	--	10,045	10,275	10,538	10,660	10,897	11,900	12,352	12,821	13,545	13,853	14,068	14,164	14,450	14,776	--
Number of employment by MSMEs[3]	--	--	--	--	--	--	--	--	--	--	--	--	--	--	--	--	--
Number of employment by large enterprises	--	--	--	--	--	--	--	--	--	--	--	--	--	--	--	--	--
MSME employees to total (%)	56.4	56.6	56.8	56.9	58.2	58.9	59.4	57.1	57.3	57.2	57.5	63.8	64.5	65.3	66.0	66.2	--
MSME employees growth (%)	--	(1.1)	6.1	2.7	8.3	4.4	5.0	6.3	11.0	5.9	6.3	23.1	3.2	2.1	3.4	3.2	--
Employment by MSME by sector (% share)																	
Agriculture, forestry, and fisheries	9.1	8.7	9.2	8.3	8.5	8.0	3.1	3.1	7.7	7.4	7.5	10.2	10.0	9.8	11.0	10.7	--
Manufacturing	22.2	19.6	20.4	19.6	20.4	18.7	21.0	21.2	19.5	19.5	18.9	16.2	16.4	16.5	16.5	16.4	--
Construction	4.4	4.8	5.0	5.3	5.4	5.7	6.4	6.7	6.8	7.1	7.5	10.2	10.6	10.4	10.5	10.3	--
Services[2]	64.2	66.7	65.3	66.8	65.5	67.5	69.5	68.8	66.0	65.9	66.0	63.1	62.7	63.0	61.7	62.3	--
Mining and quarrying	0.2	0.2	0.1	0.1	0.1	0.1	0.1	0.1	0.1	0.1	0.1	0.3	0.3	0.3	0.3	0.3	--
Employment by MSMEs by region (% share)																	
Capital city	--	--	--	--	--	--	--	--	--	--	--	--	15.7	--	--	--	--
Others	--	--	--	--	--	--	--	--	--	--	--	--	84.3	--	--	--	--
CONTRIBUTION TO GDP[4]																	
Real GDP of MSMEs (RM mil.)	190,199	205,999	220,213	234,359	257,883	274,766	275,324	298,180	319,832	339,121	360,916	409,776	435,072	458,686	491,159	521,721	--
MSME contribution to GDP (%)	29.3	29.7	30.2	30.4	31.5	32.0	32.6	32.8	33.4	33.6	34.2	36.6	37.0	37.3	37.8	38.3	--
MSME GDP growth (%)	--	8.3	6.9	6.4	10.0	6.5	0.2	8.3	7.3	6.0	6.4	13.5	6.2	5.4	7.1	6.2	--
MSME Labor productivity growth (%)	--	--	--	--	--	--	--	--	--	0.2	0.1	(7.8)	2.9	3.3	3.6	2.9	--
MSME GDP by sector (% share)																	
Agriculture, forestry, and fisheries	14.3	14.3	13.9	14.1	13.2	12.7	12.8	12.6	12.5	11.9	11.5	11.8	11.4	10.8	10.6	10.1	--
Manufacturing	24.0	24.4	24.1	24.0	23.4	22.1	20.5	21.0	21.2	21.2	20.9	20.4	20.4	20.3	20.2	20.1	--
Construction	3.0	2.8	2.8	2.6	2.7	2.6	2.8	2.9	2.9	3.2	3.4	5.9	6.0	6.0	6.0	5.9	--
Services[2]	58.6	57.8	58.4	58.6	60.0	61.8	63.3	62.5	62.4	62.5	63.0	60.3	60.6	61.2	61.3	62.4	--
Others[5]	0.4	0.5	0.4	0.4	0.4	0.6	0.6	0.8	0.9	1.1	1.2	1.5	1.7	1.7	1.8	1.6	--
MSME GDP by region (% share)																	
Capital city	--	--	--	--	--	--	--	--	--	--	--	--	23.0	--	--	--	--
Others	--	--	--	--	--	--	--	--	--	--	--	--	77.0	--	--	--	--
EXPORTS																	
Total export value (RM million)	--	--	--	--	--	--	--	714,075	777,302	770,202	770,368	816,483	817,370	834,491	960,778	994,860	--
Total export growth (%)	--	--	--	--	--	--	--	--	8.9	(0.9)	0.0	6.0	0.1	2.1	15.1	3.5	--
MSME export value (RM billion)	--	--	--	--	--	--	--	116.8	131.0	134.7	136.9	145.2	145.0	155.1	166.2	171.9	--
MSME export to total export value (%)	--	--	--	--	--	--	--	16.4	16.9	17.5	17.8	17.8	17.7	18.6	17.3	17.3	--
MSME export growth (%)	--	--	--	--	--	--	--	--	12.2	2.8	1.6	6.1	(0.1)	7.0	7.2	3.4	--
IMPORTS																	
Total import value (RM million)	--	--	--	--	--	--	--	583,337	635,316	665,714	683,408	713,863	728,778	751,363	866,524	893,403	--
Total import growth (%)	--	--	--	--	--	--	--	--	8.9	4.8	2.7	4.5	2.1	3.1	15.3	3.1	--
MSME import value (RM million)	--	--	--	--	--	--	--	--	--	--	--	--	--	--	--	--	--
MSME import to total import value (%)	--	--	--	--	--	--	--	--	--	--	--	--	--	--	--	--	--
MSME import growth (%)	--	--	--	--	--	--	--	--	--	--	--	--	--	--	--	--	--

GDP = gross domestic product; MSME = micro, small, and medium-sized enterprise.

1 Compounded annual growth rate (CAGR) 2004–2010 for data in 2010 and CAGR 2011–2015 for data in 2015.

2 Services include transportation and storage, wholesale and retail trade, telecommunication, and real estate.

3 Number of MSME employees is not officially disclosed by the government. The Department of Statistics Malaysia is reviewing and developing a methodology for estimating SME employment and thus can be linked to the SME Master Plan 2012-2020 by the Government of Malaysia.

4 Based on real GDP. SME GDP at constant 2015 prices (figures for 2003-2014 were adjusted based on 2015 constant prices).

5 Others include mining and quarrying, and import duties.

Source: ADB Asia SME Monitor 2020 database. Data from Census of Establishments and Enterprises 2005, Economic Census 2011, Economic Census 2016 by Department of Statistics Malaysia and SME Corporation Malaysia.

Table 7.3: Bank Credit

End of period data

Item	2007	2008	2009	2010	2011	2012	2013	2014	2015	2016	2017	2018	2019
COMMERCIAL BANKS													
Number of commercial banks													
Development financial institutions	6	6	6	6	6	6	6	6	6	6	6	6	6
Banking institutions	47	54	54	55	56	56	55	54	54	54	54	53	53
Credit													
Loans outstanding, total (RM million)	644,237	726,546	783,507	883,285	1,003,504	1,107,999	1,225,656	1,339,718	1,445,105	1,521,428	1,584,340	1,705,749	1,759,124
Loans outstanding in domestic currency (RM million)	--	--	--	--	--	--	--	--	--	--	--	--	--
Loans outstanding in foreign currency (RM million)	--	--	--	--	--	--	--	--	--	--	--	--	--
Loan growth (%)	8.6	12.8	7.8	12.7	13.6	10.4	10.6	9.3	7.9	5.3	4.1	7.7	3.1
Total commercial bank loans to GDP (%)	96.8	94.4	109.9	107.5	110.1	114.1	120.3	121.1	122.8	121.7	115.5	117.9	116.5
Lending rate (%)	6.4	6.1	5.1	5.0	4.9	4.8	4.6	4.6	4.6	4.5	4.6	4.9	5.0
Gross nonperforming loans (NPLs) (RM million)	41,577	34,785	28,669	29,692	26,996	22,538.0	22,790.7	22,179.1	23,180.4	24,515.7	24,499.2	25,245.0	28,071
Gross NPLs to total loans (%)	6.5	4.8	3.7	3.4	2.7	2.0	1.9	1.7	1.6	1.6	1.5	1.5	1.6
Deposits													
Deposits, total (RM million)	864,947	972,092	1,061,863	1,136,212	1,296,545	1,403,568	1,512,712	1,633,779	1,659,149	1,695,467	1,763,423	1,912,171	1,956,371
Deposits in domestic currency (RM million)	--	--	--	--	--	--	--	--	--	--	--	--	--
Deposits in foreign currency (RM million)	22,757	36,302	50,338	53,506	64,612	79,020	75,242	92,815	142,219	138,765	129,460	142,419	152,110
Deposit rate (%)	--	--	--	--	--	--	--	--	--	--	--	--	--
MSME LOANS													
MSME loans outstanding, total (RM million) *	127,984	138,859	141,608	141,159	165,316	187,039	211,038	243,708	274,412	299,733	315,660	320,140	278,701
Development finance institutions	13,847	14,105	16,285	12,805	12,147	12,018	13,303	13,629	14,801	15,448	14,184	15,850	13,281
Banking institutions	114,137	124,753	125,323	128,354	153,168	175,022	197,735	230,079	259,611	284,285	301,476	304,290	265,420
MSME loans to total loans outstanding (%)	18.9	18.4	17.4	15.5	16.2	16.5	16.9	17.9	18.7	19.4	19.8	18.7	14.6
MSME loans to GDP (%)	19.3	18.0	19.9	17.2	18.1	19.3	20.7	22.0	23.3	24.0	23.0	22.1	18.5
MSME loan growth (%) **	8.8	8.5	2.0	(0.3)	17.1	13.1	12.8	15.5	12.6	9.2	5.3	1.4	(12.9)
MSME lending rate (%)	6.1	6.4	5.5	5.7	5.7	5.7	5.5	5.8	6.0	6.0	5.9	6.1	6.0
Nonperforming MSME loans (NPLs) (RM million)	12,083	9,882	8,895	10,590	9,552	8,574	8,216	8,553	8,880	8,874	10,065	10,261	10,399
MSME NPLs to total MSME loans (%)	9.4	7.1	6.3	7.5	5.8	4.6	3.9	3.5	3.2	3.0	3.2	3.2	3.7
Number of MSME loan borrowers ***	132,974	148,803	140,118	140,486	142,378	152,709	146,512	148,005	129,053	119,502	123,784	123,690	115,498
MSME loan borrowers to total bank borrowers (%)	--	--	--	--	--	--	--	--	--	84.9	86.7	86.3	86.9
MSME loan rejection rate (% of total applications)	--	--	--	--	--	--	--	--	--	--	--	--	--
Number of MSME savings account in banks	--	--	--	--	--	--	--	--	--	--	--	--	--
Guaranteed MSME loans (RM million)	--	--	--	--	--	--	--	--	--	--	--	--	--
Non-collateral MSME loans (RM million)	--	--	--	--	--	--	--	--	--	--	--	--	--
MSME loans outstanding by sector (% share)													
Agriculture, forestry, and fisheries	5.1	5.5	6.9	6.8	6.8	7.4	7.3	7.2	6.6	6.0	6.0	5.3	5.1
Manufacturing	23.6	23.0	22.3	22.0	20.8	19.9	18.4	17.2	15.6	14.9	15.1	15.5	15.6
Construction	15.0	14.0	14.2	13.0	11.3	11.6	10.9	11.7	12.8	12.9	12.5	14.1	12.5
Services	47.7	49.7	52.4	55.0	56.9	59.0	59.9	60.7	62.9	64.3	64.7	63.4	65.7
Others	8.7	7.9	4.2	3.2	4.2	2.1	3.5	3.3	2.1	1.9	1.7	1.7	1.1
MSME loans outstanding by region (% share)													
Capital city	--	--	--	--	--	--	--	--	--	--	--	--	--
Others	--	--	--	--	--	--	--	--	--	--	--	--	--
MSME loans outstanding by type of use (% share)													
For working capital	--	--	--	49.4	48.2	46.2	44.6	43.4	43.0	42.5	43.3	43.6	40.1
For capital investment	--	--	--	2.1	2.1	1.7	1.7	1.7	1.5	1.3	1.2	1.2	1.3
Others	--	--	--	48.5	49.7	52.1	53.7	54.9	55.6	56.2	55.5	55.2	58.7
MSME loans outstanding by tenor (% share)													
Less than 1 year	--	--	--	--	--	--	--	--	--	--	--	--	--
1-5 years	--	--	--	--	--	--	--	--	--	--	--	--	--
More than 5 years	--	--	--	--	--	--	--	--	--	--	--	--	--

MSME = micro, small, and medium-sized enterprise.

* Financial institutions conducted a review and reclassification of SME accounts from SMEs to non-SMEs, to follow the national SME definition, starting January 2018. This includes excluding SMEs which have grown into large companies due to increase in annual turnover or number of employees (beyond the national threshold), and exclusion of public listed companies, subsidiaries of public listed companies/large firms, multinational companies, government-linked companies, and state-owned enterprises as SMEs.

** Given the reclassification exercise, the growth numbers is underestimated and may not be truly reflective of actual SME financing growth.

*** Number of new SME loans (development financial institutions plus banking institutions).

Source: ADB Asia SME Monitor 2020 database. Data from Bank Negara Malaysia.

Table 7.4: Public Finance and Guarantees

End of period data

Item	2007	2008	2009	2010	2011	2012	2013	2014	2015	2016	2017	2018	2019
Credit Guarantee Corporation Malaysia													
Outstanding guaranteed loans (RM billion)	38.8	41.8	44.9	47.4	50.3	51.4	52.9	56.1	59.5	63.7	67.1	70.8	--
Growth (%)	--	7.7	7.4	5.6	6.0	2.3	2.9	6.0	6.1	7.1	5.3	5.5	--
Guaranteed loans approved (RM billion)	3.9	3.0	3.1	2.5	2.9	1.1	1.5	3.2	3.4	4.2	3.4	3.7	--
Guaranteed loans disbursed (RM billion)	--	--	--	--	--	--	--	--	--	--	--	--	--
Number of MSMEs guaranteed	13,004	10,368	14,073	7,670	7,504	2,152	2,368	6,839	8,225	7,568	8,637	8,999	--
Accumulated number of MSMEs guaranteed	37,450	388,818	402,891	410,561	418,065	420,190	422,585	429,424	437,649	445,217	453,854	462,853	--
Portfolio guarantees*: number of L/G (new approval)	--	--	--	665	906	351	679	2,689	2,997	3,680	5,449	--	--
MSME access to guarantees (% of total MSMEs)	--	--	--	--	--	--	--	--	--	--	--	--	--
Guaranteed loans to MSME loans (%)	--	--	--	--	--	--	--	--	--	--	--	--	--
Government Credit Guarantee Funds													
Number of funds	--	--	7	7	7	2	2	--	3	1	3	7	--
Number of guarantee schemes (new approval)	--	--	31,890	35,155	35,154	5,842	5,842	--	--	--	--	--	--
Outstanding amount of guarantee schemes (RM billion)	--	--	--	--	--	--	--	--	--	--	--	--	--
Approved amount of guarantee schemes (RM billion)	--	--	2.77	3.52	3.52	0.29	0.30	--	--	--	--	--	--
Disbusred amount of guarantee schemes (RM billion)	--	--	1.38	2.05	2.13	--	--	--	0.91	0.09	3.81	7.03	--
Number of MSMEs benefitted	--	--	--	--	--	--	--	--	--	--	--	--	--
Subsidized Loans													
Number of funds	64	--	47	45	45	35	35	--	32	30	27	26	--
Number of subsidized loans (new approvals)	1,254,317	--	1,815,426	2,138,960	2,176,177	2,333,167	2,382,177	--	--	--	--	--	--
Outstanding loans (RM billion)	--	--	--	--	--	--	--	--	--	--	--	--	--
Approved loans (RM billion)	81.2	--	44.0	48.2	51.9	49.3	52.7	--	--	--	--	--	--
Disbursed loans (RM billion)	77.3	--	67.4	78.5	93.7	42.8	44.6	--	3.9	3.9	3.2	3.2	--
Number of MSMEs benefitted	--	--	--	--	--	--	--	--	--	--	--	--	--
BNM Special Funds for MSMEs													
Number of approved accounts	33,717	37,498	40,331	46,943	50,988	54,379	58,798	62,266	67,063	72,084	75,754	78,267	--
Outstanding financing (RM million)	--	--	--	--	--	--	--	--	--	--	--	--	--

L/G = letter of guarantee; MSME = micro, small, and medium-sized enterprise.

* Credir Guarantee Corporation Malaysia started offering portfolio guarantees from the third quarter of 2010.

Source: ADB Asia SME Monitor 2020 database. Data from Credit Guarantee Corporation Malaysia, Syarikat Jaminan Pembiayaan Perniagaan, Bank Negara Malaysia (BNM), and SME Corporation Malaysia.

Table 7.5: Nonbank Finance

End of period data

Item	2007	2008	2009	2010	2011	2012	2013	2014	2015	2016	2017	2018	2019
Registered Corporations													
Total number of registered corporations	98	108	114	113	108	112	119	112	121	109	110	117	122
Registered VC corporations and management corporations	98	108	114	113	108	112	119	112	119	103	101	105	105
Registered PE corporations and management corporations*	...	...	...	...	...	...	...	...	2	6	9	12	17
Total funds managed by VC/PE firms (RM million)	3,308	4,570	5,347	5,959	5,460	5,698	5,796	6,211	7,154	6,510	7,003	6,084	...
Growth (%)	...	38.1	17.0	11.4	(8.4)	4.4	1.7	7.2	15.2	(9.0)	7.6	(13.1)	...
Investment by VC/PE firms (RM million)	479	477	597	453	253	230	264	318	365	569	418	613	...
Growth (%)	...	(0.5)	25.3	(24.1)	(44.2)	(9.1)	14.7	20.5	14.9	55.9	(26.6)	46.8	...
Accumulated investment by VC/PE firms (RM million)	1,784	1,929	2,586	3,389	3,586	2,757	3,433	3,246	2,221	2,923	2,454	3,116	...
Growth (%)	...	8.1	34.1	31.1	5.8	(23.1)	24.5	(5.4)	(31.6)	31.6	(16.0)	27.0	...
Number of investee companies	121	134	99	84	51	47	56	74	74	87	77	117	...
Accumulated number of investee companies	433	450	445	389	409	466	356	376	...	376	381	387	...
Investment by stage													
Seed firms and start-ups													
Number of investee firms	34	34	17	17	6	5	13	14	17	13	8	5	...
Investment (RM million)	20.6	15.8	54.3	23.4	16.7	13.0	28.7	22.2	37.7	66.0	3.7	4.9	...
Share of total investment (%)	4.3	3.3	9.1	5.2	6.6	5.6	10.9	7.0	10.3	11.6	0.9	0.8	...
Investment growth (%)	...	(23.5)	244.4	(56.9)	(28.6)	(22.3)	121.1	(22.5)	69.7	75.0	(94.4)	32.0	...
Early-stage firms													
Number of investee firms	18	21	16	24	15	13	10	19	34	29	25	35	...
Investment (RM million)	86.2	82.8	88.4	122.1	97.6	38.1	35.2	77.2	234.0	347.2	139.2	285.0	...
Share of total investment (%)	18.0	17.4	14.8	26.9	38.6	16.6	13.3	24.3	64.1	61.0	33.3	46.5	...
Investment growth (%)	...	(4.0)	6.8	38.0	(20.0)	(60.9)	(7.6)	119.4	203.0	48.3	(59.9)	104.8	...
Expansion-stage firms													
Number of investee firms	58	65	49	25	24	19	17	20	22	39	37	61	...
Investment (RM million)	318.5	298.6	317.4	175.6	117.8	104.2	90.8	79.4	85.5	108.6	141.4	248.0	...
Share of total investment (%)	66.5	62.7	53.1	38.8	46.6	45.3	34.4	25.0	23.4	19.1	33.8	40.4	...
Investment growth (%)	...	(6.2)	6.3	(44.7)	(32.9)	(11.6)	(12.9)	(12.6)	7.8	27.0	30.1	75.4	...
Later-stage firms													
Number of investee firms	9	13	12	18	6	10	16	21	1	1	3	9	...
Investment (RM million)	45.7	71.9	104.4	132.1	20.8	74.6	109.0	139.0	8.0	4.0	74.2	10.3	...
Share of total investment (%)	9.5	15.1	17.5	29.2	8.2	32.4	41.3	43.7	2.2	0.7	17.8	1.7	...
Investment growth (%)	...	57.1	45.2	26.6	(84.3)	258.9	46.2	27.4	(94.2)	(50.0)	1,754.4	(86.1)	...
Other stage firms													
Number of investee firms	2	1	5	...	...	...	...	...	...	5	4	7	...
Investment (RM million)	7.9	7.6	32.9	...	...	...	...	...	...	43.7	59.4	65.0	...
Share of total investment (%)	1.7	1.6	5.5	...	...	...	...	...	...	7.7	14.2	10.6	...
Investment growth (%)	...	(4.4)	334.5	...	...	...	...	...	...	...	36.0	9.6	...
Investment by sector													
Information and communications technology (RM million)	88.6	72.4	103.9	137.8	49.3	16.1	58.3	95.9	63.7	32.2	58.6	139.4	...
Share of total investment (%)	18.5	15.2	17.4	30.4	19.5	7.0	22.1	30.2	17.4	5.7	14.0	22.7	...
Manufacturing (RM million)	131.2	58.6	111.7	71.2	29.1	103.4	49.6	96.2	38.8	30.3	102.9	35.9	...
Share of total investment (%)	27.4	12.3	18.7	15.7	11.5	45.0	18.8	30.3	10.6	5.3	24.6	5.9	...
Life sciences (RM million)	86.2	123.4	150.5	112.4	124.7	60.7	59.6	108.8	177.1	414.6	220.2	304.4	...
Share of total investment (%)	18.0	25.9	25.2	24.8	49.3	26.4	22.6	34.2	48.5	72.8	52.7	49.6	...
Others (RM million)	172.9	222.1	231.2	131.9	49.8	49.6	96.3	17.0	85.7	92.4	36.1	133.6	...
Share of total investment (%)	36.1	46.6	38.7	29.1	19.7	21.6	36.5	5.3	23.5	16.2	8.6	21.8	...
Factoring and Leasing													
Financing outstanding (RM million) **	2,000	1,800	1,500	100	700	900	1,100	1,169	1,027	1,072	827	773	...
Growth (%)	...	(10.0)	(16.7)	(93.3)	600.0	28.6	22.2	6.3	(12.1)	4.4	(22.9)	(6.5)	...

PE=private equity, VC=venture capital.

* Registration of PE corporations and management corporations introduced in 2015.

** Data include financing from banks and nonbank finance institutions.

Source: ADB Asia SME Monitor 2020 database. Data from Securities Commission Malaysia; SME Corporation Malaysia, SME Annual Reports (various editions); and Bank Negara Malaysia.

Table 7.6: Capital Markets

End of period data

Item	2009	2010	2011	2012	2013	2014	2015	2016	2017	2018	2019
EQUITY MARKET											
Main Board											
Index	1,273	1,519	1,531	1,689	1,867	1,761	1,693	1,642	1,797	1,691	1,589
Market capitalization (RM million)	984,948	1,260,413	1,270,503	1,450,283	1,683,768	1,633,308	1,673,069	1,649,448	1,881,865	1,680,260	1,682,523
Growth (%)	--	28.0	0.8	14.2	16.1	(3.0)	2.4	(1.4)	14.1	(10.7)	0.1
Trading value (RM million)	292,728	381,050	424,472	390,610	512,382	501,206	464,597	457,859	578,621	579,692	483,252
Trading volume (million shares)	210,404	212,684	249,342	224,218	305,142	397,090	299,068	289,800	430,834	420,154	453,037
Number of listed companies	844	844	822	809	802	799	794	791	788	783	772
Number of IPOs	11	23	17	14	16	12	9	7	6	2	4
Number of delisted companies	25	26	38	30	26	18	14	9	11	11	16
Specialized Board											
ACE											
Index	4,300	4,348	4,069	4,214	5,676	5,653	6,389	4,781	6,604	4,317	5,227
Market capitalization (RM million)	5,293	5,761	6,415	6,935	9,865	9,665	11,853	9,956	15,646	12,141	18,829
Growth (%)	--	8.8	11.4	8.1	42.3	(2.0)	22.6	(16.0)	57.2	(22.4)	55.1
Trading value (RM million)	3,426	3,779	7,520	12,576	13,435	27,120	32,161	14,050	29,040	19,782	21,405
Trading volume (million shares)	16,696	19,248	47,737	76,131	69,781	115,564	139,199	77,808	156,116	104,049	103,750
Number of listed companies	116	113	119	112	109	107	109	113	115	119	129
Number of IPOs	2	6	11	3	1	3	4	5	6	9	11
Number of delisted companies	2	4	5	6	1	1	--	1	2	1	--
Number of companies that moved to the main board	--	--	--	--	--	--	--	--	--	--	--
LEAP											
Market capitalization (RM million)	--	--	--	--	--	--	--	--	213	920	2,435
Growth (%)	--	--	--	--	--	--	--	--	--	332.3	164.7
Trading value (RM million)	--	--	--	--	--	--	--	--	1.4	5.1	33.2
Trading volume (million shares)	--	--	--	--	--	--	--	--	4.8	80.6	332.8
Number of listed companies	--	--	--	--	--	--	--	--	2	13	28
Number of IPOs	--	--	--	--	--	--	--	--	2	11	15
Number of delisted companies	--	--	--	--	--	--	--	--	--	--	--
Number of companies that moved to the main board	--	--	--	--	--	--	--	--	--	--	--

ACE = Access, Certainty, Efficiency; IPO=initial public offering; LEAP = Leading Entrepreneur Accelerator Platform.
Notes: ACE market was introduced in August 2009. Figures in 2009 include data on MESDAQ. LEAP Market was introduced in 2017.
Source: ADB Asia SME Monitor 2020 database. Data from Bursa Malaysia.

Table 7.7: Listing Requirements—Bursa Malaysia

Criteria	Stock: Main Board	Stock: ACE	Stock: LEAP
Quantitative Admission Criteria	a. Profit Test • Uninterrupted profit of 3 to 5 full financial years (FY), with aggregate after-tax profit of at least RM20 million. • After-tax profit of at least RM6 million for the most recent FY. • Have been operating in the same core business over at least the profit track record prior to submission. b. Market Capitalization Test • A total market capitalization of at least RM500 million upon listing. • Incorporated and generated operating revenue for at least one full FY prior to submission. c. Infrastructure Project Corporation Test • Must have the right to build and operate an infrastructure project in or outside Malaysia, with project costs of not less than RM500 million. • The concession or license for the infrastructure project has been awarded by a government or a state agency, in or outside Malaysia, with remaining concession or license period of at least 15 years from the date of submission.	No minimum operating track record or profit requirement.	No minimum operating track record or profit requirement.
Public Spread	• At least 25% of the company's total number of shares. • Minimum of 1,000 public shareholders holding not less than 100 shares each.	• At least 25% of the company's total number of shares. • Minimum of 200 public shareholders holding not less than 100 shares each.	• At least 10% of the company's total number of ordinary shares at admission.
Sponsorship	Not applicable.	• Engage a sponsor to assess the suitability of the company seeking listing. • Secure and maintain the services of a sponsor for at least 3 full FY after listing or at least 1 full FY after the company has generated operating revenue, whichever is later. • Sponsor who submitted the listing application shall act as a sponsor to a company for at least 1 full FY after listing. • ACE Market corporations that have met the main market admission criteria: sponsorship is for one full FY.	• Engage an approved adviser to assess the suitability of the company seeking listing. • Secure and maintain the services of a continuing adviser for at least 3 full FY after listing or at least 1 full FY after the company has generated operating revenue, whichever is later. • Approved adviser who submitted the listing application must act as a continuing adviser to a company for at least 1 full FY after listing.

ACE = Access, Certainty, Efficiency; LEAP = Leading Entrepreneur Accelerator Platform.
Note: Key listing requirements are extracted.
Source: ADB Asia SME Monitor 2020 database. Data from Bursa Malaysia and Securities Commission Malaysia.

Table 7.8: Policies and Regulations

Regulations		
Name		**Outline**
Small and Medium Enterprises Corporation Malaysia Act 1995		Institutional set-up of SME Corporation Malaysia.
Development Financial Institutions Act 2002		Regulation on development financial institutions (DFIs) including the SME Bank.
National SME Development Council Directive 2005		SME definition included. New SME definition was later endorsed in July 2013.
Capital Markets and Services Act 2007		Regulation on capital markets, including equity crowdfunding (ECF) and peer-to-peer (P2P) lending platforms.
Central Bank of Malaysia Act 2009		Roles and functions of central bank, including on Bank Negara Malaysia (BNM)-owned financial institutions.
Credit Reporting Agencies Act 2010		Regulation on credit reporting businesses.
Agent Banking Act 2012		Regulation on agent banking.
Financial Services Act 2013		Regulation on financial institutions.
Regulators and Policymakers		
Name		**Responsibility**
Ministry of Entrepreneur Development and Cooperatives (MEDAC)		Established on 2 July 2018 to support entrepreneurship development as a national economic agenda and to create a conducive and integrated entrepreneurship ecosystem.
National Entrepreneur and SME Development Council (NESDC)		Provide the framework for a cohesive national policy and programs designed to provide necessary support for entrepreneurs and MSMEs to progress up the value chain.
SME Corporation Malaysia (SME Corp.)		Implement MSME development programs.
Bank Negara Malaysia (BNM)		Regulate and supervise banking institutions and development financial institutions.
Securities Commission Malaysia (SCM)		Regulate and supervise nonbank finance institutions and capital markets.
Policies		
Name	**Responsible Entity**	**Outline**
MSME development		
Shared Prosperity Vision 2030 (October 2019)	Economic Planning Unit	Seven strategic thrusts: 1) Key economic growth activities 2) Business and industry ecosystem 3) Human capital 4) Regional inclusion 5) Social well-being 6) Labor market and compensation of employees 7) Social capital
National Entrepreneurship Policy 2030 (Dasar Keusahawanan Nasional, DKN 2030) (11 July 2019)	MEDAC	Six strategic thrusts: 1) Fostering an entrepreneurship culture across all segments of Malaysian society - build a critical mass of entrepreneurs - enhance entrepreneurship education and skills 2) Optimizing the regulatory environment and access to finance - promote good governance - rationalize roles and functions of entrepreneurship development organizations - enhance monitoring and assessment of outcome and impact - enhance and improve regulatory requirement for business - reduce the bankruptcy stigma - improve access to finance and financial inclusion for entrepreneurs and enterprises 3) Promoting holistic and integrated entrepreneurship development - support entrepreneurial endeavor of *bumiputera*, disadvantaged and special focus groups - cooperatives as driver to inclusive socio-economic development - promote social entrepreneurship 4) Accelerating economic growth through innovation-driven enterprises - support the high-growth and innovation-driven enterprise - facilitate technology exchange and innovation 5) Boosting the entrepreneurial capabilities and performance of MSMEs - strengthen the implementation of vendor development program - enhance entrepreneurship skills and capabilities of MSMEs - provision of targeted support for market access especially for *bumiputera* MSMEs - strengthen supply chain management 6) Internationalization of high-growth enterprises - facilitate access for local enterprise especially *bumiputera* to international market - promote networking and business collaboration
Malaysia Productivity Blueprint (2017)	MPC	A holistic measure to target initiatives to raise productivity level at the national, sector, and enterprise levels. Five strategic thrusts: 1) Building workforce of the future 2) Driving digitalization and innovation 3) Making industry accountable for productivity 4) Forging a robust ecosystem 5) Securing a strong implementation mechanism
National eCommerce Strategic Roadmap (2016-2020)	MDEC	The National e-Commerce Strategic Roadmap has been a key guiding document in ensuring the right trajectory for the e-commerce ecosystem, with growth rates expected to be further enhanced to reach more than 20% and GDP contribution reaching as high as RM170 billion by 2020. In order to maximize impact and accelerate the e-commerce GDP growth, the National eCommerce Strategic Roadmap has outlined focused government intervention in six thrust areas, built on good and affordable infrastructure and supportive governance framework. The six thrust areas will enable all key stakeholders in the e-commerce ecosystem to contribute towards the national agenda: 1) Accelerate seller adoption of e-commerce (MSMEs adopting e-commerce, target* of 50% of MSMEs adopting e-commerce by 2020) *target based on total of SMEs in 2015 (650k) 2) Increase adoption of e-procurement by businesses 3) Lift nontariff barriers (e-fulfillment, cross-border, e-payment, consumer protection) 4) Realign existing economic incentives 5) Make strategic investments in select e-commerce player(s) 6) Promote national brand to boost cross-border e-commerce Across these six thrust areas (as above), various programs have been prioritized for the near term to deliver significant impact. These programs are championed by various ministries/agencies and to govern, drive, and foster coordination in the implementation of programs and initiatives, the National eCommerce Council was established. For over 4 years of its implementation, the roadmap has indeed bare fruition particularly in establishing sound e-commerce-supporting infrastructure and policies, as well as making MSMEs in Malaysia to be more e-commerce ready.
SME Masterplan 2012 – 2020 (July 2012)	SME Corp.	Four strategic goals: 1) Increase business formation 2) expand number of high growth firms 3) raise productivity 4) intensify formalization Six high impact programs: 1) Integration of business registration and licensing 2) Technology commercialization platform 3) SME investment partner 4) Going export 5) Catalyst program 6) Inclusive innovation
Access to finance		
Financial Sector Blueprint 2011 – 2020 (2011)	BNM	1) Effectively intermediate for a high value added and high-income economy. 2) Develop deep and dynamic financial markets. 3) Promote financial inclusion for greater shared prosperity. 4) Strengthen regional and international financial integration. 5) Internationalize Islamic finance. 6) Safeguard the stability of the financial system. 7) Promote electronic payments for greater economic efficiency. 8) Empower consumers. 9) Promote talent development to support a more dynamic financial sector.
Financial Inclusion Framework (2011)	BNM	Four broad strategies: 1) Innovative channels. 2) Innovative products and services. 3) Effective financial institutions and infrastructure. 4) Well informed and responsible underserved.
Capital Market Masterplan 2 (2011)	SCM	Growth strategies: 1) Promote capital formation. 2) Expand intermediation efficiency and scope. 3) Deepen liquidity and risk intermediation. 4) Facilitate internationalization. 5) Build capacity and strengthen information infrastructure.

MDEC=Malaysia Digital Economy Corporation, MPC=Malaysia Productivity Corporation.

Source: ADB Asia SME Monitor 2020 database. Data from SME Masterplan 2012-2020, Financial Sector Blueprint 2011 -2020, Capital Market Masterplan 2 (2011), DKN 2030, Malaysia Productivity Blueprint, and National eCommerce Strategic Roadmap.

Country Review

Myanmar

Overview

As of 2018, Myanmar had a labor force population of 22.7 million.[78] Its economy grew by 6.4% in 2018 and 6.8% in 2019.[79] Small and medium-sized enterprises (SMEs) remain a staple of business; they constitute 83.8% of all manufacturing firms. Significant challenges to SME development are similar to those in neighboring countries. Chief among them are access to finance, human capital and skill development, access to markets, and adopting the latest technology. Bank lending to SMEs has been expanding, with major borrowers from conventional trade and manufacturing (although still small in scale). The financial infrastructure that facilitates SME access to finance remains at the infant stage of development. SMEs are a critical component of the overall national blueprint for socioeconomic development. The government is implementing its Financial Inclusion Roadmap 2014–2020.

1. SME Development

- SMEs (in manufacturing) have been gradually growing in number, especially in large cities (although growth is slowing); SMEs must register to enjoy government assistance, especially to access bank credit.
- The majority of employees in small firms are older than those in medium-sized (and large) firms, suggesting more emphasis is needed to attract younger workers to start businesses.
- The Myanma Investment and Commercial Bank is the major source of trade finance; but there are few SME exports.
- The government only recognized the technology sector as distinct from services in 2017; technology policy is new, with the SME Development Agency establishing a technology promotion department.
- There are two incubator programs, one offered by the SME Development Agency and the ASEAN Business Incubator Network, launched in 2018, for start-ups with high levels of management and technical acumen.

Scale of SMEs

The Small and Medium Enterprises Development Law, which went into effect on 9 April 2015, uses industrial sector, number of full-time employees, capital, and turnover/revenue to classify SMEs. In manufacturing, a firm with up to 300 employees (up to 600 employees for labor-intensive manufacturing), and capital not exceeding MK1,000 million is classified as an SME (Table 8.1). In services (except wholesale and retail trade), a firm with up to 100 employees and turnover not exceeding MK200 million is classified as an SME. In wholesale and retail business and other sectors, a firm with up to 60 employees and turnover not exceeding MK100 million (MK300 million for wholesale business) is classified as an SME. There is no separate category for microenterprises. Thus, this country review report uses the term "SME" rather than "micro, small, and medium-sized enterprise (MSME)" used in other country reports.

The SME Development Agency (SMEDA) collects and maintains a national registry of SMEs; there were 70,000 registered SMEs, also known as "members", as of end-2019. Each must apply to become a member, with the

[78] Central Statistical Organization. Labor Market Data. https://www.csostat.gov.mm/Home/NSDP

[79] ADB. 2020. *Asian Development Outlook 2020 Supplement (June 2020)*. Manila.

primary benefit being better access to finance (SMEDA says the only real chance SMEs have of obtaining bank loans is membership in the national registry). Banks use membership as a filter for credit eligibility, and financing benefits such as lower borrowing rates and no collateral.

The SME membership fee (valid for 2 years) is MK5,000 for small enterprises and MK10,000 for medium-sized enterprises. In addition to better access to finance, members get priority for training, services, trade fairs, technology, and market access. While the extent of the informal economy is not quantified, most say it remains significant in Myanmar, both in number of firms and its contribution to gross domestic product (GDP).

The Central Department of Small and Medium Enterprise Development within the Ministry of Planning, Finance, and Industry (MOPFI) has the most complete data and information on SMEs. It classifies SMEs that make industrial products, daily consumer goods, and food products as small and medium industries (SMIs)—essentially in manufacturing, handicrafts, food processing, and related industries.

The number of SMEs remained relatively constant during 2006–2015, from 39,949 firms in 2006 to 39,162 firms in 2015. But since 2016, due to the SME reclassification, it recorded 59,694 firms in 2016 (a 52.4% increase from 2015) and reached 75,116 firms in 2019 (a 5.4% increase from 2018) (Figure 8.1A and Table 8.2).[80] SMEs accounted for 89.9% of total enterprises in 2019.

As of 2019, the food and beverage sector comprised 56.7% of SMIs (manufacturing firms), followed by "other manufacturing" (25.9%), construction materials (9.1%), mineral and petroleum products (6.8%), and garments (1.6%) (Figure 8.1B). As to the growth trend, food and beverages declined by 13.5% from 2011 to 2019, while mineral and petroleum products increased by 66.2% and construction materials increased by 27.0%.

Figure 8.1: Number of SMEs

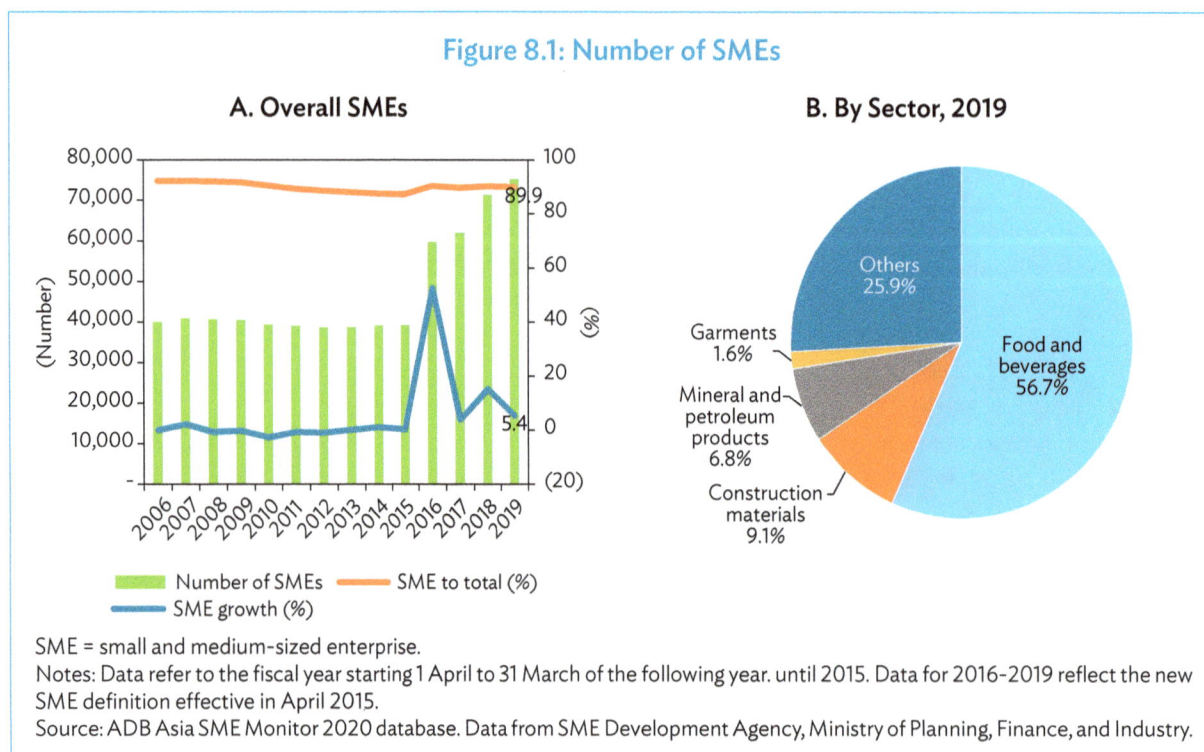

A. Overall SMEs

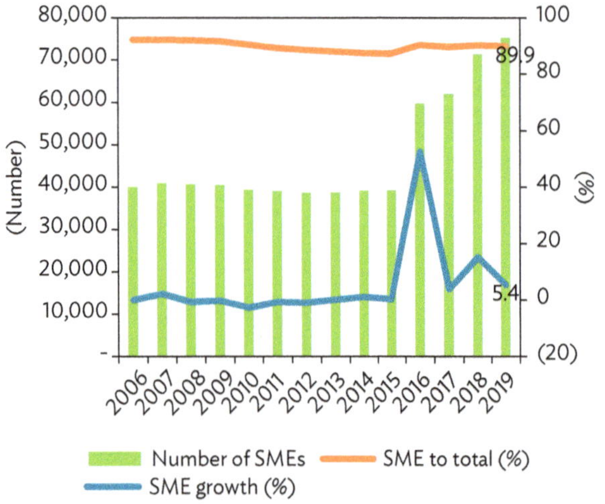

B. By Sector, 2019

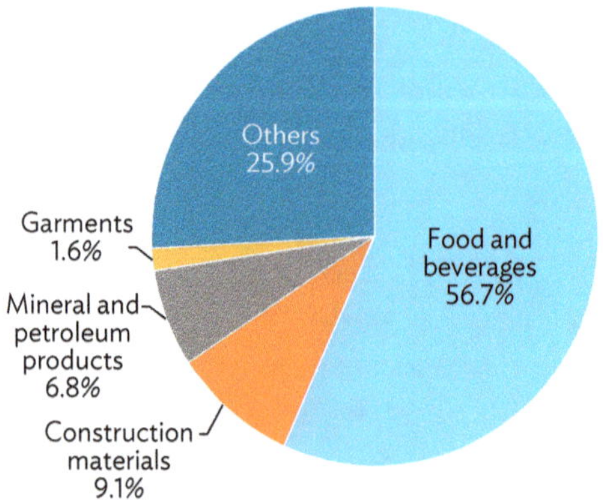

SME = small and medium-sized enterprise.
Notes: Data refer to the fiscal year starting 1 April to 31 March of the following year. until 2015. Data for 2016-2019 reflect the new SME definition effective in April 2015.
Source: ADB Asia SME Monitor 2020 database. Data from SME Development Agency, Ministry of Planning, Finance, and Industry.

[80] Data refer to the fiscal year which starts 1 April and ends 31 March of the following year.

By region, Yangon was home to 15.3% of SMIs in 2019, the capital Naypyitaw 1.7%, and those elsewhere including Mandalay (the second-largest city) 83.0%. During 2012–2019, the share of Yangon-based SMIs to total SMIs grew by 51.4%, followed by Naypyitaw-based SMIs (23.3%), while SMIs share in all other regions declined by 6.2%. SME production appears to be shifting more toward Yangon and the capital than other areas.

Employment

The most recent and complete data available on SME employment is from the Central Statistical Organization under the MOPFI.[81] For the labor force composition by sector showing the percentage of full-time workers,[82] the "repair and installation" and motor vehicle segments employ 100% of their workforce full-time. Rubber and plastics, apparel, and textiles follow with 90% of their workforce full-time. Five industries have 80%–90% full-time (in decreasing order: machinery and equipment, coke and refined petroleum, basic metals, fabricated metal products, and beverages).

The average age of an employee is 32.5 years within a range of 8–90 years (footnote 4). The majority of employees in medium-sized (and large) enterprises are aged 35–44, while the majority of employees in (micro and) small firms are aged 45–54. This suggests that the majority of employees in (micro and) small firms are older than those in medium-sized (and large) firms; there should be more emphasis on incentivizing younger workers to start businesses. By region, the state of Kayin had 99% of its labor force employed full-time, followed by Magway, Chin, and the Mandalay region in central Myanmar.[83]

By trend, total employment decreased from 29.7 million workers in 2010 to 22.5 million workers in 2018, a drop of 24.5% (a compound annual rate of −3.4%) (Figure 8.2A). The largest year-on-year change occurred from 2013 to 2014, when there was a decline of 31.2% from 30.9 million workers to 21.2 million workers. By manufacturing sector, garments accounted for 64.4% of the total, followed by food and beverages (26.4%), construction materials (6.6%), and mineral and petroleum products (2.7%) (Figure 8.2B). By region, two-thirds of total employment was concentrated in Yangon in 2019.

Available data also show that the share of female employees to total employees increased from 37.9% in 2010 to 43.4% in 2018, an increase of 14.5% (a compound annual growth rate of 1.7%).

[81] Central Statistical Organization. 2018. Myanmar Micro, Small and Medium Enterprise Survey 2017. In this report, a microenterprise is defined as a firm with one to nine employees.

[82] Footnote 81. Figure 9.2, p.91.

[83] Footnote 81. Figure 9.1, p.91.

Figure 8.2: Employment by Enterprises

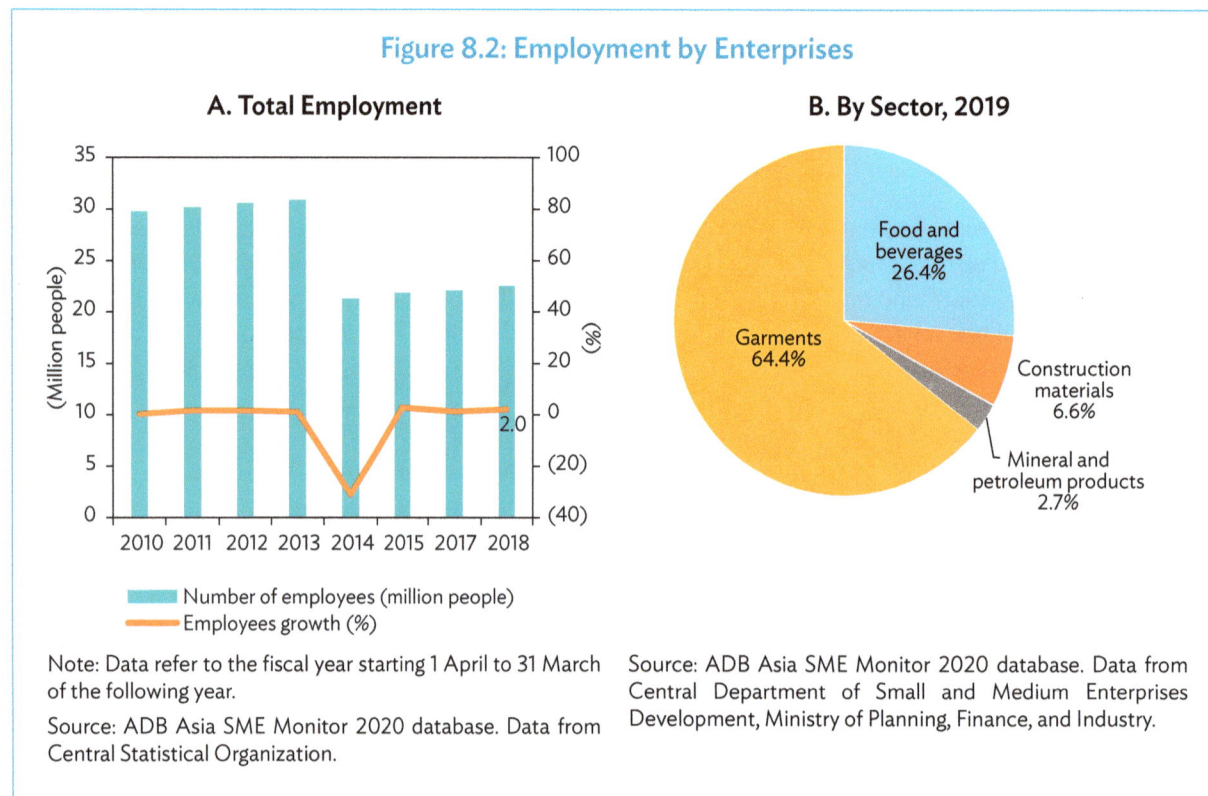

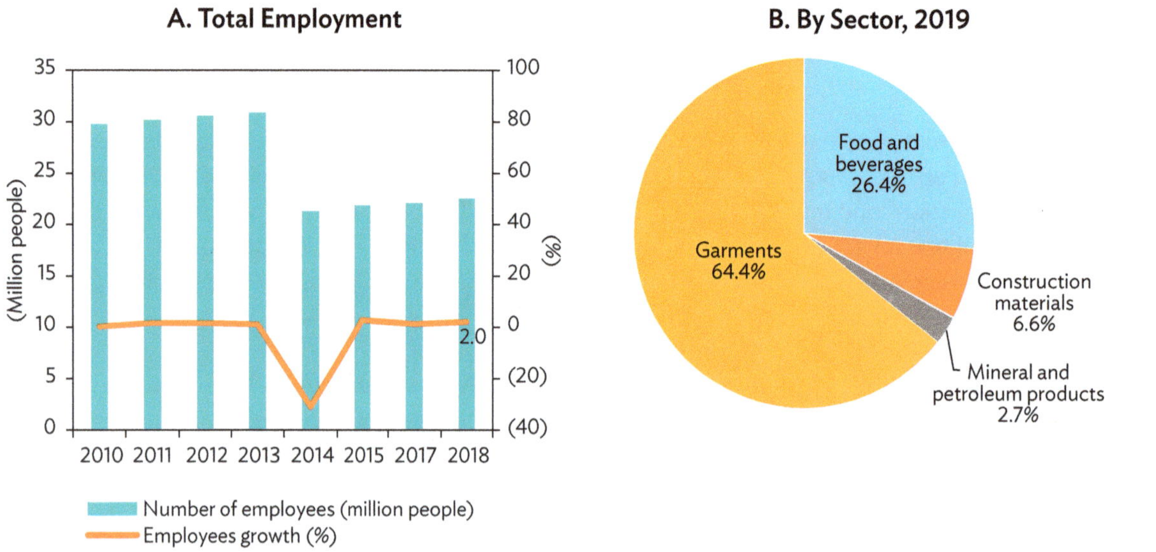

Note: Data refer to the fiscal year starting 1 April to 31 March of the following year.

Source: ADB Asia SME Monitor 2020 database. Data from Central Statistical Organization.

Source: ADB Asia SME Monitor 2020 database. Data from Central Department of Small and Medium Enterprises Development, Ministry of Planning, Finance, and Industry.

Business Productivity

There are no data covering SME contributions to GDP; however, there are data for sector share of GDP from 2004–2017. Manufacturing grew from 11.6% in 2004 to 23.9% in 2017, an increase of 105.9% (a compound annual growth rate of 5.7%). SMEs comprised 87.1%–92.0% of this sector from 2006 to 2019. Agriculture, forestry, and fisheries declined from 48.2% in 2004 to 23.3% in 2017, a decrease of 51.6% (a compound annual rate of –5.4%). Transportation and communication climbed 26.3%, from 10.3% to 13.0% (a compound annual growth rate of 1.8%). Wholesale and retail trade was relatively stable, dropping 6.7% from 22.3% in 2004 to 20.8% in 2017.

Market Access

According to the Myanmar MSME Agency Yangon, which is a branch of SMEDA, market access rivals access to finance as the most important obstacle hindering SME growth. Many SMEs are unable to produce quality products at international standards or delivery their products to relevant markets.

There are no data on SME exports and imports. SMEDA says there is scant overall activity, yet over time it has been growing slowly. Overall trade data for 2004–2018 show exports increased from $2.4 billion to $16.7 billion,[84] an overall gain of 603.2% (a compound annual growth rate of 14.9%). Imports rose from $2.2 billion to $19.3 billion, an increase of 784.1% (a compound annual growth rate of 16.8%).

[84] Exports and imports are calculated using the end-of-period exchange rate. For 2004–2011, the official MK/US$ rate was pegged to special drawing rights. Beginning 1 April 2012, the Central Bank of Myanmar adopted the managed float exchange rate regime.

There are no data on value chain participation, though there are anecdotal examples of individual firms, such as Genius Shan Highlands Coffee. There are very few SMEs from Myanmar participating in value chains.

The Myanma Investment and Commercial Bank (MICB)[85] is the designated (though not only) state bank for trade financing. It says SMEs constitute 60% of their accounts and 40% of loan value (though their definition of an SME differs from the national definition). Almost all of their SME customers are exporters, with products including rubber; beans; other agricultural products; and frozen fish, eel, and shrimp. The average MICB loan ranges from MK300 million to MK500 million, with interest rates from 7% to 10% (as of end-April 2020) and maturities of 1–3 years. MICB says interest rates have been reduced to stimulate the economy in response to the coronavirus disease (COVID-19) pandemic that started mid-March 2020.

Technology and Innovation

According to Seed Myanmar (a private venture capital fund), technology companies were only recognized as a separate sector in 2017, previously being counted among services firms.[86] The use of technology and innovation among SMEs in Myanmar remains low. This is despite the fact that SMEDA has a Technology and Market Promotion Department as one of its three departments. E-commerce is dominated by larger established competitors, making it difficult for SMEs to participate, at least for now (as of end-2019).

Networking and Support

The Union of Myanmar Federation of Chambers of Commerce and Industry is the advocacy group bridging the private sector and government. A key challenge faced by SMEs is the lack of skills and management capacity. There are two separate incubator programs in Myanmar to address these gaps. SMEDA sponsors a program that dispenses technology and offers advisory support (starting with 1 free hour of consultation). SMEDA's incubation program does not offer financial assistance. The second program is the ASEAN Business Incubator Network launched in 2018. This program is for a limited number of SMEs with high levels of business and technology skills. Five Myanmar SMEs qualified in the program's inaugural year.

85 "Myanma" in the company name is Myanmarese language.
86 Interview with Seed Myanmar on 12 August 2019.

2. Access to Finance

- Bank lending to SMEs has been expanding with those in conventional trade and manufacturing major borrowers, although its share of total bank credit remains small.
- The central bank provides assistance to improve SME access to finance; for example, lowering bank collateral requirements.
- The Small and Medium Industrial Development Bank is a major provider of SME bank credit, with loans expanding beyond Yangon.
- The Ministry of Planning, Finance, and Industry and the central bank plan to establish a credit guarantee fund; Myanma Insurance, Myanma Economic Bank, and the Japan International Cooperation Agency (JICA) are important sources of credit guarantees and/or subsidized loans.
- Microfinance institutions (MFIs) are the principal source of nonbank financing, and demand for their credit has grown briskly; conventional trade and agriculture are major consumers of MFI loans.
- The government and central bank are promoting financial inclusion, emphasizing digital financial services; mobile banking is operational, but a national payments system has yet to be developed, while standardized QR code payments infrastructure is being prepared.
- The capital market regulator cites illiquidity as the greatest barrier to market development; SMEs are unlikely to be attractive candidates in capital markets as they lack skills, knowledge, and mindset.
- There are a few private equity and venture capital firms; improving their operating conditions is a future policy area that can boost finance for innovative start-ups.
- A privately-owned credit bureau is scheduled to begin operations in 2020; the MOPFI is drafting a Secured Transactions Law (expected to come into effect in 2020) that will expand the list of allowable collateral and establish a national collateral registry.

Like its neighbors, Myanmar SMEs and associated stakeholders identify access to finance as the paramount challenge to SME development. There are several institutions servicing SME financing, either directly or indirectly: for banking, there are the Central Bank of Myanmar (CBM), the Small and Medium Industrial Development Bank (SMIDB), and MICB; for insurance and guarantees, Myanma Insurance (footnote 85); and for securities, the Securities and Exchange Commission of Myanmar (SECM) and the joint venture Myanmar Securities Exchange Center (MSEC)—both focus on developing national capital markets and SMEs by extension.

Bank Credit

The CBM regulates all bank and nonbank finance institutions (NBFIs). There are nine banks providing loans to SMEs, eight of which are private. Bank credit in 2019 reached MK23.4 trillion ($15.9 billion), up 20.1% from MK19.4 trillion ($12.5 billion) in 2018 (Table 8.3).[87] Fiscal years run from 1 April to 31 March the following year. For 2009–2019, bank loans outstanding climbed from MK657.5 billion to MK23.4 trillion, an overall increase of 3,453% (a compound annual growth rate of 42.9%). By sector, the share of lending for construction grew from 5.7% in 2009 to 18.6% in 2019, other services from 12.5% to 15.6%, and others (sectors not already specified) from 10.2% to 23.7%. Meanwhile, the share of lending for wholesale and trade dropped from 32.3% to 25.7%.

The most recent CBM data on SMEs shows bank credit expanding from MK733.2 billion ($538 million) in 2017 to MK1.1 trillion ($772 million) in 2019, an overall increase of 54.3% (a compound annual growth rate of 24.2%) (Figure 8.3A). Year-on-year growth was 22.3% from 2017 to 2018, and 26.2% from 2018 to 2019. As a percentage of total bank credit, however, SME loans accounted for just 4.5% in 2017, 4.6% in 2018, and 4.8% in 2019. Bank credit to SMEs was equivalent to 1.0% of GDP in 2018. Commercial banks accounted for 94% of SME lending, while other sources (including two-step loans by JICA) comprised the remaining 6%.

[87] Figures converted to US dollars in this report are calculated using International Monetary Fund/International Financial Statistics (IMF/IFS) end-of-period exchange rates in the designated year.

By sector, wholesale and retail trade accounted for 45.6% of SME bank loans in 2019, followed by manufacturing (18.9%) and others (18.3%) (Figure 8.3B). From 2017 to 2019, the share of wholesale and retail trade fell by 12.9%, while "others" increased by 84.3% and other services rose by 40.6%.

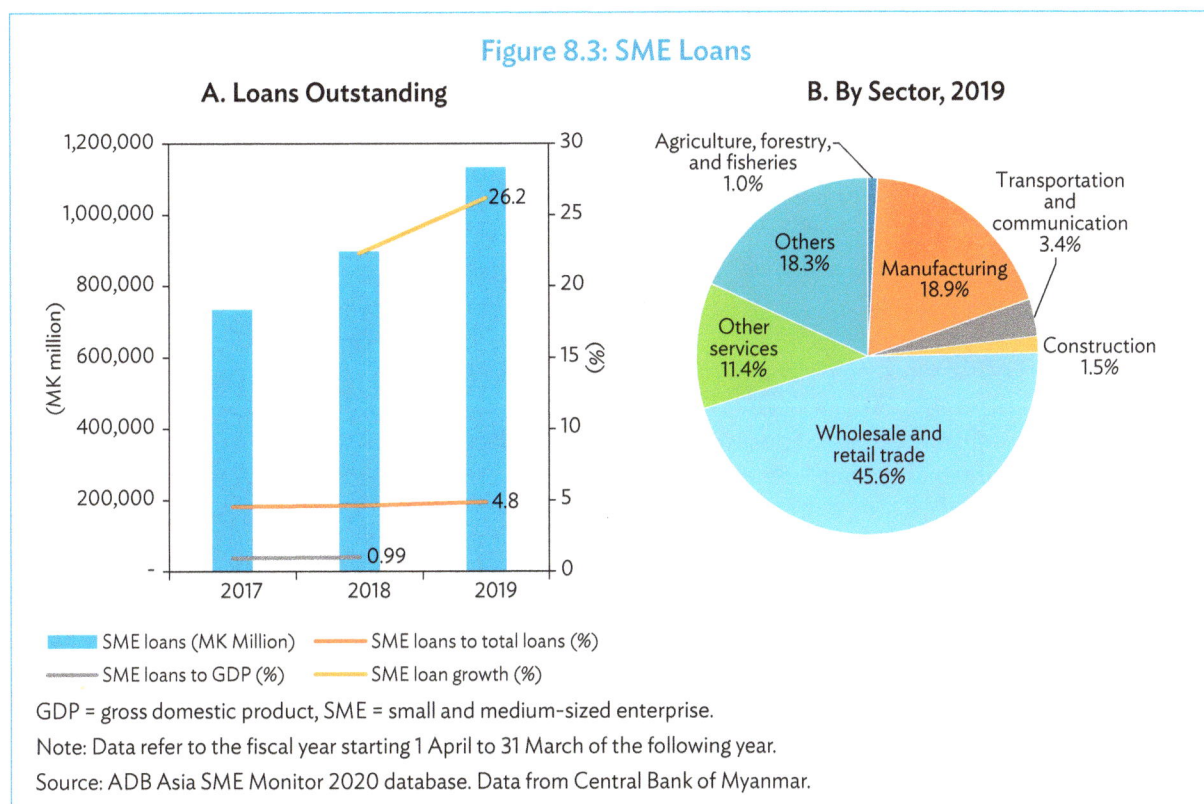

Figure 8.3: SME Loans

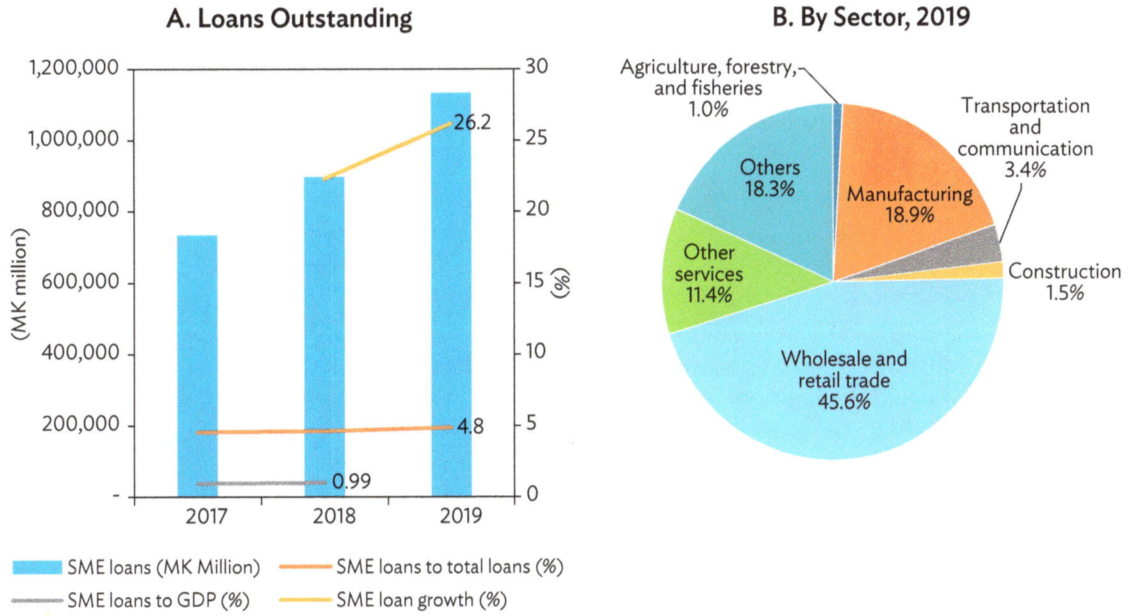

GDP = gross domestic product, SME = small and medium-sized enterprise.

Note: Data refer to the fiscal year starting 1 April to 31 March of the following year.

Source: ADB Asia SME Monitor 2020 database. Data from Central Bank of Myanmar.

Although CBM activities are not directed at SMEs per se, it assists SME development through banking reforms. For example, in January 2019, the CBM issued a circular, Instruction No.1, mandating banks to limit collateral required for loans and to allow non-collateralized loans. Specifically, the circular set a 30% loan/value ratio, an interest rate capped at 13% for collateralized loans, and a ceiling rate of 16% for non-collateralized loans.

The other major provider of bank credit to SMEs is the SMIDB, a private sector bank. SMIDB offers three main loan products for SMEs: corporate loans; JICA's two-step loans (financial intermediation loans as a participating bank); and cash flow base (CFB) loans (which support agriculture, animal husbandry, and light manufacturing).

SMIDB's SME loans outstanding amounted to MK159.8 billion ($109 million) in 2019, a 11.0% increase from the MK143.9 billion ($93 million) in 2018 (Figure 8.4A). It accounted for only 0.7% of total bank credit and just 14.1% of total SME bank loans in 2019. From 2009 to 2019, however, SMIDB outstanding loans increased by 873%, from MK16.4 billion in 2009 to MK159.8 billion in 2019 (a compound annual growth rate of 25.6%).

By sector, wholesale and retail trade received the largest share of SMIDB loans (30.6%) in 2019, followed by manufacturing (21.8%), and others (41.6%) (Figure 8.4B). From 2011 to 2019, wholesale and retail trade increased by 16.2% and "others" rose by a factor of over 13, while manufacturing declined by 60%. Garments and food processing (canning fish) were the major manufacturing subsectors.

By region, SMIDB's loans to SMEs in Yangon were 68.0% of the total in 2011, declining to 59.5% in 2019, a decrease of 12.5%. SME loans in Naypyitaw inched upward from a 2.8% share in 2011 to 3.8% in 2019. SME loans to all other regions grew from 29.3% in 2011 to 36.8% in 2019, an increase of 25.6%.

For CFB loans and corporate lending, the interest rate is 13%—a base rate of 12% plus a 1% service fee. For JICA's two-step loans, the rate is 8.5%. CFB loans are based on borrower cash flows and are non-collateralized. The other two loan products require collateral limited to immoveable property, such as land and buildings. As of 2019, borrowing rates ranged from 8.5% to 16.0%.

For CFB loans, scheduled payments are progressive. For borrowers in light manufacturing, for example, a 3-year CFB loan requires SMIDB to first check the borrower's financial statements and business operations. At the end of the first year, the borrower repays 20%, with the remaining 80% split equally over years 2 and 3. For agriculture borrowers, the loan term is 1 year.

Twelve percent of SMIDB's loan portfolio are JICA's two-step loans, 1% for CFB loans, with the remaining (87%) corporate loans. The average CFB loan size is MK5 million, for corporate loans MK15 million, with a maximum loan size of MK1 billion. Corporate loan size depends on the borrower's collateral. JICA's two-step loans have a maximum size of MK500 million. Manufacturing firms are the main clients for corporate loans. SMIDB's nonperforming loan (NPL) ratio has been stable, if high, 15%-20% over 2014–2019.

Figure 8.4: SME Loans—Small and Medium Industrial Development Bank

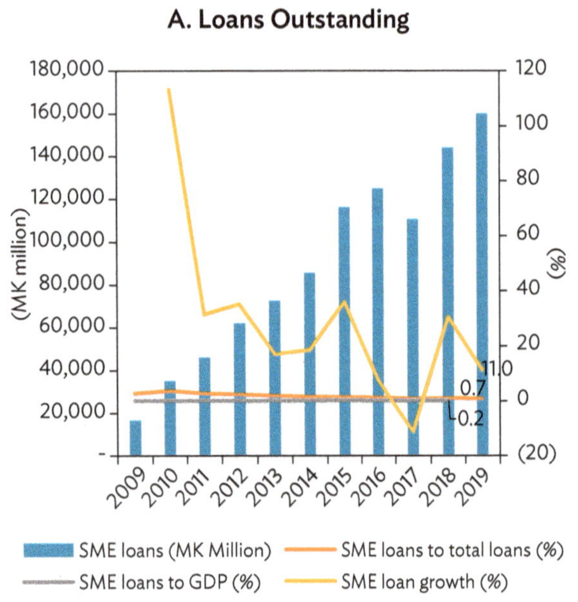

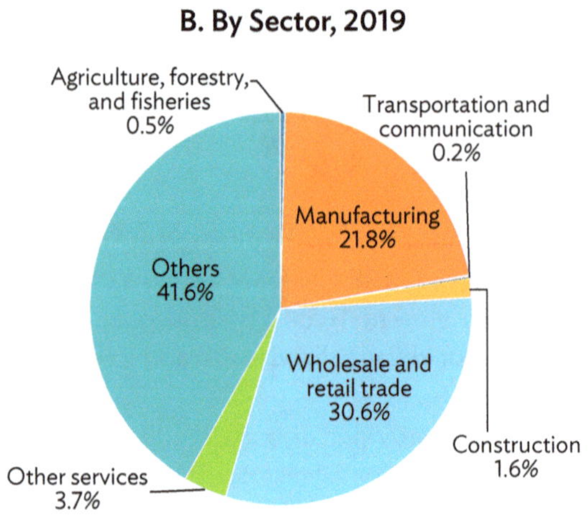

SME = small and medium-sized enterprise, GDP = gross domestic product.

Note: Data refer to the fiscal year starting 1 April to 31 March of the following year.

Source: ADB Asia SME Monitor 2020 database. Data from Small and Medium Industrial Development Bank.

Public Financing and Guarantees

Since 2015, government agency Myanma Insurance has been providing credit insurance and credit guarantee schemes. Credit guarantees are particularly important for SMEs that lack collateral. For a 3-year loan, SMEs with collateral pay a 2% premium for credit insurance/guarantee in the first year, 1.5% in the second, and 1.0% in the third. For SMEs without collateral, the respective premiums are 3.0%, 2.5%, and 2.0%. As mentioned, the average bank lending rate is 13%. MOPFI and central bank, with ADB support, plan to create a credit guarantee fund, after which the credit guarantee function of Myanma Insurance will stop.

According to Myanma Insurance, the average loan size ranges from MK15 million to MK25 million. Myanma Insurance provides credit guarantees for loans up to MK500 million. For 2017–2019, the average credit guarantee insurance premium was MK98.7 million. Only registered SMEs can apply for credit insurance. Commercial trading, such as wholesale and retail trade, is the most common sector covered. There are two types of loans, with and without credit guarantee insurance. There was no lead guarantee scheme as of end-2019.

The Myanma Economic Bank (MEB) (footnote 85) provides subsidized credit to SMEs at 9% per annum, (the deposit rate is 8%). MEB also acts as a conduit for JICA's two-step loans. While both loan types feature below-market interest rates, their terms differ.

JICA is a significant lender in Myanmar and supports SME development through its SME two-step loan scheme, which was in its Phase 2 as of end-2019 (Phase 1 began in 2016). One lending requirement is that at least 80% of loan proceeds must go toward fixed assets/capital. The remainder goes toward working capital needs.

To maximize the accessibility and affordability of its loans, JICA's 8.5% lending rate is just 0.5% higher than the 8.0% minimum deposit rate. SME demand for finance is high, particularly for an affordable product like the JICA two-step loan. However, the number of SMEs that qualify for these loans remains low due to a lack of collateral and a lack of knowledge as to how to apply for a loan and prepare financial statements, among others.

The termination/completion date for a JICA two-step loan project is 8 to 10 years; depending on the disbursement (disbursement under Phase 1 was within 2 years). Outstanding loans can reach a maximum of ¥15 billion, an amount chosen according to JICA policy considering the potential for expansion. JICA is conducting more outreach activities to identify qualified SMEs and entrepreneurs. JICA has a separate two-step loan program for agriculture and agricultural products such as food processing (mill owners), so farmers are ineligible for the SME two-step loan.

Nonbank Financing

Microfinance institutions (MFIs) are the principal conduit for nonbank financing (and are the only source with reliable data). According to the Financial Regulatory Department (FRD) of MOPFI, the number of MFIs increased from 24 in 2012 to 189 in 2019 (Figure 8.5A and Table 8.4),[88] an increase of 688% (a compound annual growth rate of 34.3%).

MFI loans outstanding grew from MK49.2 billion ($58 million) in 2012 to MK1.8 trillion ($1.2 billion) in 2019, an increase of 3,559% (a compound annual growth rate of 67.2%). MFI loans jumped steeply from 2017 to 2018 (up 86.2%) and then again (127.0%) from 2018 to 2019.

[88] The Myanmar fiscal year changed in 2018 from 1 April–31 March to 1 October–30 September. Thus, data for 2012 to 2018 refer to the 1 April–31 March fiscal year, while data for 2019 refer to the revised 1 October–30 September fiscal year.

By sector, the share of MFI loans to wholesale and retail trade was 33.2% in 2019, followed by agriculture, forestry, and fisheries (30.8%) and other services (25.6%) (Figure 8.5B). The share of wholesale and retail trade to total MFI loans grew steadily (55.1% from 2012 to 2019 —a compound annual growth rate of 13.6%). The share of other services grew by 143.5% during the same period (a compound annual growth rate of 6.5%). Agriculture, however, declined by 14.7% (a compound annual decrease of 2.2%).

By region, Yangon accounted for 94.4%–99.3% of MFI lending over the period for any given year. Naypyidaw ranged 0.2%–0.8%, with the remaining regions combined accounting for 0.4%–5.6%. MFI NPLs are negligible, ranging 0.01%–1.1% of the total during 2012–2019.

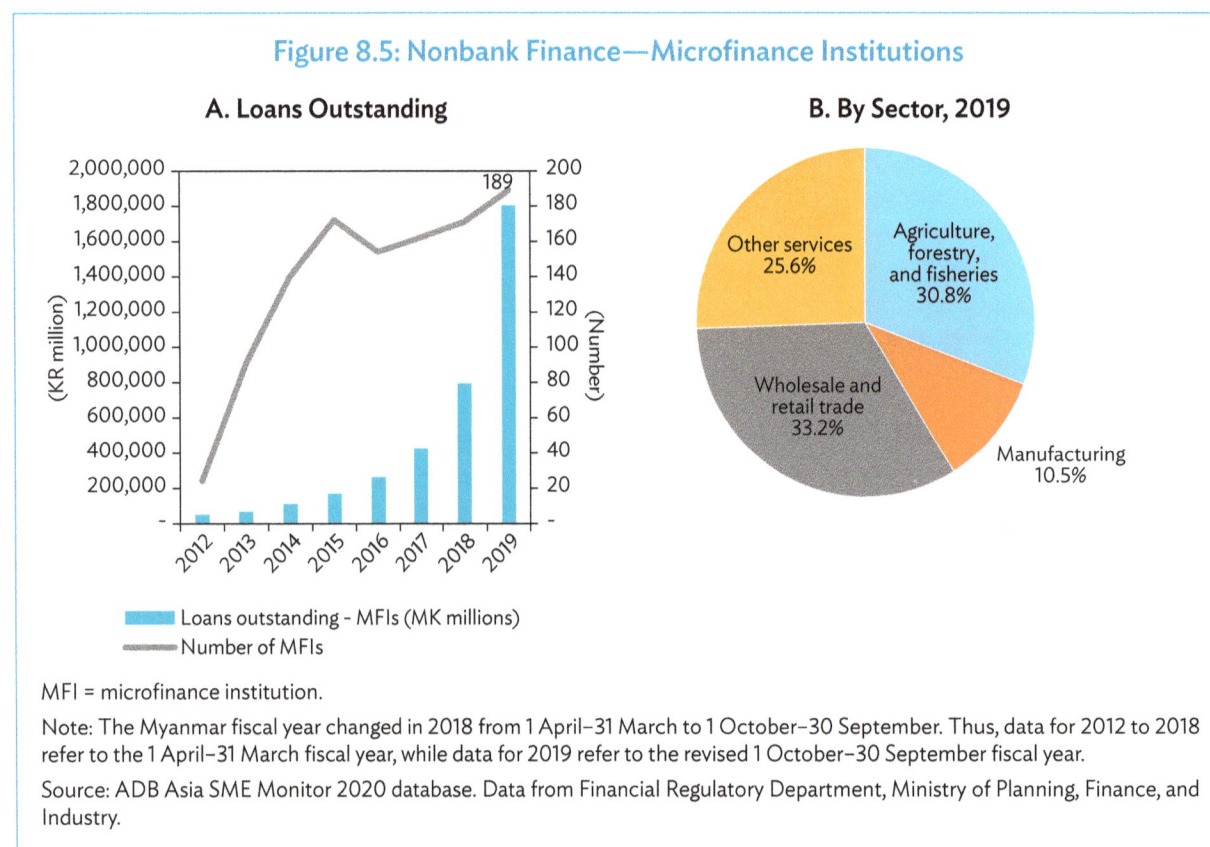

Figure 8.5: Nonbank Finance—Microfinance Institutions

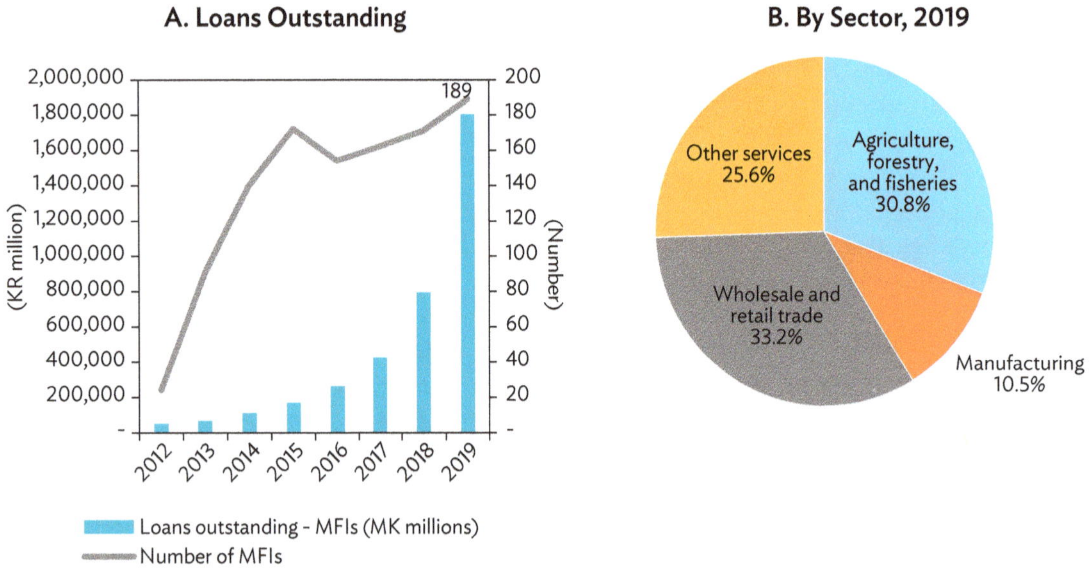

MFI = microfinance institution.

Note: The Myanmar fiscal year changed in 2018 from 1 April–31 March to 1 October–30 September. Thus, data for 2012 to 2018 refer to the 1 April–31 March fiscal year, while data for 2019 refer to the revised 1 October–30 September fiscal year.

Source: ADB Asia SME Monitor 2020 database. Data from Financial Regulatory Department, Ministry of Planning, Finance, and Industry.

Digital Financial Services

MOPFI leads in formulating the national strategy for financial inclusion, which includes digital financial services (DFS). One objective is to upgrade and expand mobile banking payment services. Three telecommunications companies and one NBFI are involved. According to the CBM, the mobile banking system is running, handling 900,000 transactions daily.

According to Seed Myanmar, it is still not possible to digitally transfer money from one bank to another. Less than 5% of the population are banked (have an account). There is no national payments system. The central bank plans to launch the MMQR, a standardized quick response (QR) payment system, possibly in 2020.

In terms of fintech, fully developed crowdfunding is still in the future. There is a peer-to-peer (P2P) lending platform, and a mobile phone application (app) to place buy/sell orders. Digitalization in Myanmar has been discussed at the top level of government ministries (there is a Digital Economy Development Committee), but not specific to SMEs.

While still nascent, there are a few companies ready to engage in DFS (P2P, e-wallet, mobile banking, and equity crowdfunding). Seed Myanmar described the regulatory environment for fintech as "unfriendly," and noted that firms from India and Viet Nam are entering the market.

Capital Markets

To strengthen capital markets, SECM was established in August 2014 under the Securities Exchange Law (20/2013). Prior to SECM, MSEC operated an over-the-counter market until 2015. MSEC is a 50-50 joint venture between MEB and Japan's Daiwa Securities Group. Since becoming regulator, SECM has awarded six securities business licenses and one investment advisory license. MSEC is one of the six securities companies. The Yangon Stock Exchange (YSX) opened 9 December 2015. MSEC supports companies listing on the YSX and accepts buy and sell orders. MSEC has 8,000 accounts, over 95% individual. According to SECM, there are 41,000 accounts total, of which 99% are individuals and 1% institutional investors.

Market performance has been volatile since trading began in March 2016. The YSX Composite Index fell by 27.7% (from 561.5 to 406.2) from 2016 to 2018, then rebounded by 12.8% from 2018 to 458.2 in 2019 (Figure 8.6A). Market capitalization declined 5% from 2016 to 2018, from MK583.9 billion ($430 million) to MK554.6 billion ($358 million), then climbed 13.1% to MK627.4 billion ($428 million) in 2019. Trading value plummeted 82.8% from MK89 million to MK15 million from 2016 to 2017, then skyrocketed 555.1% to MK101 million in 2018 before falling 78.3% to MK22 million in 2019. Trading volume exhibited a pattern similar to trading value. It dropped 77.9% from 12,299 shares in 2016 to 2,715 shares in 2017, then grew 445.2% to 14,802 shares in 2018 before declining 74.0% to 3,845 shares in 2019.[89]

YSX has five listed companies (Figure 8.6B): two in financial services, one special economic zone, First Myanmar Investment, and telecommunication company TMH. There were three listed companies in 2016 with one company listed in both 2017 and 2018. There has been one initial public offering (IPO) in 2018. The three companies in 2016 and one in 2017 were just listing. They did not do any public offering at the time of listing. No companies delisted from 2016 to 2019. The YSX approved a sixth listed company, a firm specializing in logistics, in February 2020. The announcement of trading shares has been postponed because of the COVID-19 pandemic.

There are six brokerage firms/underwriters in Myanmar. Of these, two or three are active (the remainder are dormant). Commissions are a large burden for smaller brokers, even though SECM reduced commission fees twice from 2018 to 2019 to stimulate trading. Foreign countries that have accessed Myanmar capital markets include the Japan, the People's Republic of China, Republic of Korea, and Thailand. Greater foreign activity will improve stock market liquidity.

[89] According to the MSEC, the conglomerate First Myanmar Investment accounted for 50% of total market capitalization in May 2019.

Figure 8.6: Equity Market

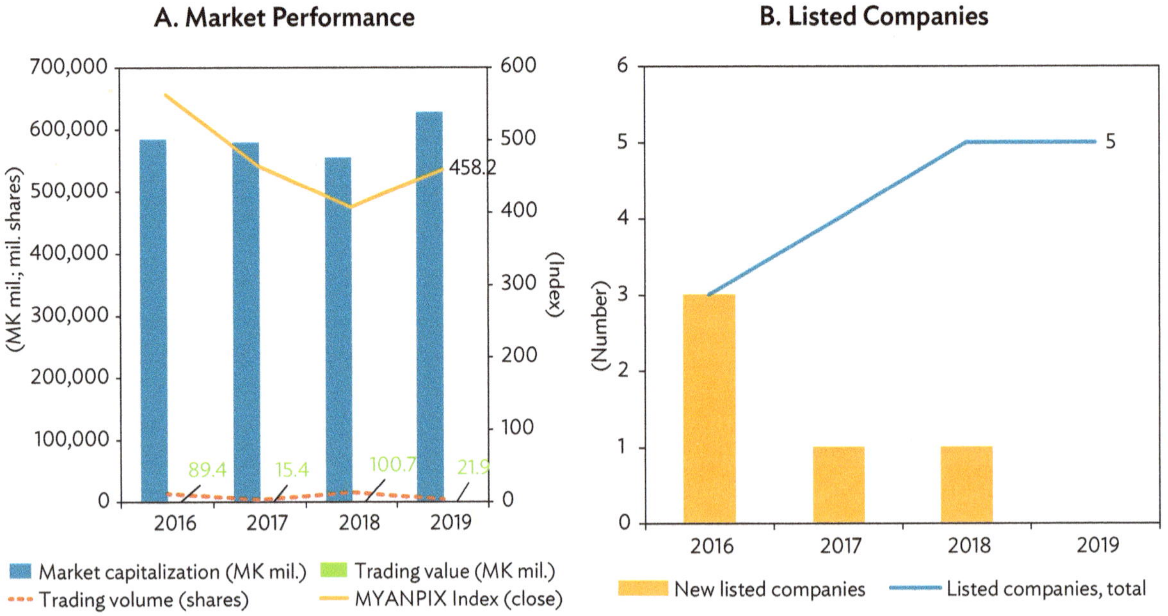

Note: Data are end of year.

Source: ADB Asia SME Monitor 2020 database. Data from Yangon Stock Exchange.

According to SECM and MSEC, illiquidity is the paramount challenge facing capital markets. As of end-2019, there are two to three companies in the pipeline for listing. Liquidity is a problem on both the supply and demand side. To boost liquidity, SECM announced in March 2020 it would allow foreign participation in daily trading of listed companies on the YSX. Of the five listed companies, only three accepted international investors and YSX increased its matching times (the process of matching buy orders to sell orders) from four to seven in March 2020.

There was almost no guidance on corporate governance until 2014. MOPFI formed a team of SECM, the Directorate of Investment and Company Administration (DICA), YSX, and the International Finance Corporation (IFC) to address the corporate governance problem. In April 2019, the team issued the Myanmar Corporate Governance Scorecard 2018: A Report on the Assessment of Myanmar Companies, based on the Asian Corporate Governance Scorecard. SECM, DICA, IFC, and Organisation for Economic Co-operation and Development (OECD) aim to both upgrade corporate governance practices for Myanmar companies and stimulate the interest and trust of potential investors.

According to SECM and MSEC, SMEs are not attractive candidates for capital market participation. Three of the most important reasons are lack of skills, lack of knowledge, and the lack of appropriate mindset. Few SMEs can meet the listing requirements on capital, corporate governance, and financial reporting. And many owners are content with stability and serving very local markets. Despite this, the government is encouraging SMEs to participate in the capital market.

Seed Myanmar and the Myanmar Private Equity and Venture Capital Association have described national private equity overall, and venture capital in particular, as a nascent ecosystem. According to them, there are only a few known venture capital funds for start-ups in Myanmar. There are also emerging markets funds that are broader in scope, supporting both early stage and established businesses.

There are also more than 10 existing private equity companies. One prominent example is Daiwa, which is investing in agriculture and industry. According to Seed Myanmar, there are no more than 50 companies providing private equity, with most investing in asset-heavy, traditional sectors (footnote 86). Less than five companies are investing in technology start-ups. There are about 50 professional business angel investors, both domestic and international. There is no official angel network, with the biggest challenge finding the right pool of available talent.

Financial Infrastructure

As with other nations in the region, Myanmar continues to develop the financial infrastructure necessary to promote SME access to finance. Key institutions such as credit guarantee schemes and credit bureaus are either in the planning stage or nascent. While capital market liquidity has improved, it remains an obstacle. Venture capital and business angel networks are scarcely developed. Use of fintech on any measurable scale is likely several years in the future. The CBM has only partially implemented Basel II capital requirements.

Myanma Insurance notes that an overall lack of information is endemic and hinders the development of credit infrastructure. The regulation establishing a credit bureau was enacted in May 2018. And it is expected to begin operations in 2020. The bureau will be privately owned, with banks holding a 51% share, but a representative from CBM will sit on the Credit Bureau Committee.

There is no collateral registry in Myanmar. Land, buildings, gold, diamonds, savings certificates, credit certificates, savings deposits, and government bonds are all acceptable collateral. MOPFI is in the process of drafting a Secured Transactions Law with the technical assistance of the IFC. The law will serve two main purposes: (i) broadening the range of collateral, especially movable collateral, that will be acceptable to lenders, thereby broadening access to finance, and (ii) establishing a national collateral registry. Multiple stakeholders anticipate that the law will come into effect in 2020.

Several stakeholders note the importance of training to upgrade SME skills for accessing finance and other resources. One key area is in the preparation of financial statements and business plans; the CBM stated that commercial banks cannot rely on SME information because SMEs lack proper accounting and financial reporting methods. Universities have programs specifically for SMEs to address financial statement and business plan preparation.

On market access, MICB sponsors quarterly training seminars for clients covering topics related to exporting, such as changes in regulations and the latest market conditions. The Myanmar MSME Agency Yangon held 72 training sessions during 2016–2019, with 2,133 SME participants and 142 government officials. JICA collaborates with other organizations for training and capacity-building programs for SMEs, with over 1,000 participants in 2019.

On capital markets, MSEC holds monthly seminars with 150–200 participants, and smaller, bi-weekly seminars hosting 30–40 attendees. The number of participants has been growing, indicating that there is strong demand. Also, MSEC has been educating securities companies and providing seminars on a regular basis.

3. Policies and Regulations

- SMEs are a critical component of Myanmar's overall national blueprint for socioeconomic development; the Myanmar Sustainable Development Plan (MSDP) 2018–2030 is the overarching national development strategy, including goals of job creation and private sector-led growth that specifies SME development as the path forward.
- The SME Development Agency (SMEDA) is responsible for translating the broad MSDP vision to the grassroots level of SMEs.
- The Directorate of Investment and Company Administration (DICA) began registering SMEs in 2017, a welcome step toward gathering data and moving more SMEs into the formal economy; a policy focus will be to link this database with others (such as SMEDA's) to give policymakers more information to use and reduce redundancy.
- The Financial Regulatory Department is implementing the Myanmar Financial Inclusion Roadmap 2014–2020; the roadmap sets clear targets and an evaluation framework.

MSME Development

In August 2018, the government released through MOPFI the Myanmar Sustainable Development Plan (MSDP) 2018–2030. The plan consists of three pillars: (i) peace and stability, (ii) prosperity and partnership, and (iii) people and planet. These three pillars contain five goals: (i) peace, national reconciliation, security, and good governance; (ii) economic stability and strengthened macroeconomic management; (iii) job creation and private sector-led growth; (iv) human resources and social development for a 21st century society; and (v) natural resources and the environment for the posterity of the nation. Each goal then specifies up to seven strategies.

The third goal, job creation and private sector-led growth, is particularly germane, as its strategies specify SME development as an engine for job creation. Other strategies address SME concerns over stimulating creativity and innovation, fostering trade, fashioning a business-friendly environment, and widening access to finance. One can infer that SMEs are an important component of the overall national blueprint for socioeconomic development.

The SMEs Development Central Committee's Notification Numbers of January 2018 established the organizational structure governing SMEs. At the apex is a cross-functional, cross-ministerial team known as the SME Central Committee. The committee has no physical office, nor does its Working Committee. Below the Working Committee at the national level is SMEDA, within the Directorate of Industrial Supervision and Inspection under the MOPFI. It is the primary government body for enabling SME development and is responsible for translating the MSDP into action for SMEs. By end-2019, SMEDA had over 300 staff serving each region, state, and union territory, with each regional office focusing on an action plan covering 8–10 items, for example, rice cultivation.

The SME Development Center, forerunner of SMEDA, opened in 2012. The government, recognizing the importance of SMEs to Myanmar's economy, expanded its role nationwide in 2014. From April 2015 to June 2016, the SME Development Law was enacted, and the SME Development Policy and SME Development Rule were both approved. Though these laws and policies precede the MSDP, they are the edifice that supports SMEDA and other government agencies as they act to reform the business environment of Myanmar and promote SME development.

The Myanmar Companies Law No.29/2017 began online SME registration in 2017 under the auspices of DICA. This database, however, is separate from SMEDA's, though there is intent to merge the two databases in the future.

The DICA online registration platform demonstrates progress toward data and statistics gathering on SMEs using modern technology, as well as transitioning more SMEs from the informal to the formal economy.

Financial Inclusion

In addition to overseeing microfinance, the FRD (under MOPFI) is also the focal department for financial inclusion. FRD is implementing the Myanmar Financial Inclusion Roadmap 2014–2020, the first policy aimed at financial inclusion. The stated goals of the program are to increase the financial inclusion rate from 13% to 40%, and the percentage of individuals holding at least one bank account from 6% to 17%. The FRD is introducing a new financial inclusion program (2019–2023), with targets to increase inclusion from 48% to 60% and account holders from 17% to 25%.

According to FRD, there are five pillars for implementing financial inclusion: (i) finance for low-income citizens, (ii) finance for SMEs and emerging farmers, (iii) savings mobilization, (iv) digital financial services, and (v) empowering customers. There is a monitoring and evaluation framework for implementation.

To finance more SMEs and farmers, tactics include encouraging more loans to MFIs, building financial literacy and capacity among SMEs via training, and supporting NBFIs. In addition, both the MEB and the Myanmar Agricultural Development Bank will undergo reforms to focus more on SMEs and farmers. The MEB has three ongoing activities: (i) credit market development, (ii) government pensions, and (iii) government operations. These last two will be reduced so MEB can concentrate more on credit market development.

Because access to finance remains limited, expanding credit is imperative. In agriculture, credit limits are being raised from MK50,000 to MK100,000 per acre, then to MK150,000 per acre. Loans to microenterprises are limited to MK10 million. The FRD says its overarching goal is the development of a credit ecosystem.

There are plans to develop and implement branchless banking and to introduce the standardized MMQR code. The target for mobile banking penetration is to climb from 4% in 2019 to at least 25% by 2023.

Data Tables

Table 8.1: SME Definition

A. Definition until 8 April 2015

Item	Cottage	Small	Medium
Power used (horsepower)	0.25-5 H.P	Over 5 H.P	25-50 H.P
Employees	Not more than 9	Over 10	50-100
Capital investment	...	Up to MK1 million	MK1-5 million
Annual production	...	Up to MK2.5 million	MK2.5-5 million

H.P = horsepower. Note: Small and medium-sized enterprise definition until 8 April 2015. SMEs refer to small and medium industries (manufacturing) under the Private Industrial Enterprise Law No.22/1990 and cottage industries under the Law Amending the Promotion of Cottage Industries Law No.14/2011.

Source: ADB Asia SME Monitor 2020 database. Data from Central Department of Small and Medium Enterprises Development, Ministry of Planning, Finance, and Industry.

B. Definition after 9 April 2015

Sector	Item	Small	Medium
Manufacturing	Capital (C)	Up to MK500 million	MK500 million<C≤MK1,000 million
	Employees	Up to 50	51-300
Labor intensive manufacturing	Capital (C)	Up to MK500 million	MK500 million<C≤MK1,000 million
	Employees	Up to 300	301-600
Wholesale business	Turnover (T)	Up to MK100 million	MK100 million<T≤MK300 million
	Employees	Up to 30	31-60
Retail business	Turnover (T)	Up to MK50 million	MK50 million<T≤MK100 million
	Employees	Up to 30	31-60
Services	Turnover (T)	Up to MK100 million	MK100 million<T≤MK200 million
	Employees	Up to 30	51-100
Other sectors	Turnover (T)	Up to MK50 million	MK50 million<T≤MK100 million
	Employees	Up to 30	31-60

Note: The SME Development Law enacted on 9 April 2015 stipulated the new SME definition.

Source: ADB Asia SME Monitor 2020 database. Data from SME Development Agency, Ministry of Planning, Finance, and Industry.

Table 8.2: SME Landscape

End of period data

Item	2006	2007	2008	2009	2010	2011	2012	2013	2014	2015	2016	2017	2018	2019
NUMBER OF ENTERPRISES														
Number of enterprises, total	43,421	44,381	44,130	44,115	43,478	43,739	43,637	43,976	44,693	44,937	66,191	69,159	79,119	83,591
Number of SMEs*	39,949	40,811	40,529	40,396	39,272	38,978	38,590	38,654	39,062	39,162	59,694	61,949	71,290	75,116
Number of large enterprises	3,472	3,570	3,601	3,719	4,206	4,761	5,047	5,322	5,631	5,775	6,497	7,210	7,829	8,475
SME to total (%)	92.0	92.0	91.8	91.6	90.3	89.1	88.4	87.9	87.4	87.1	90.2	89.6	90.1	89.9
SME growth (%)	--	2.2	(0.7)	(0.3)	(2.8)	(0.7)	(1.0)	0.2	1.1	0.3	52.4	3.8	15.1	5.4
SMEs by sector (% share)														
Food and beverages	--	--	--	--	--	65.5	64.7	63.9	62.7	60.7	59.6	58.4	57.3	56.7
Construction materials	--	--	--	--	--	7.2	7.8	7.8	7.6	8.1	8.4	8.6	8.9	9.1
Mineral and petroleum products	--	--	--	--	--	4.1	4.3	4.7	5.1	5.4	5.8	6.3	6.6	6.8
Garments	--	--	--	--	--	3.6	3.8	4.1	4.5	0.9	1.1	1.2	1.4	1.6
Others	--	--	--	--	--	19.6	19.4	19.6	20.1	24.8	25.0	25.5	25.9	25.9
Number of SMEs by region (% share)**														
Yangon	11.5	11.6	11.4	11.3	11.0	10.5	10.1	9.8	9.7	13.7	13.4	13.2	14.9	15.3
Naypyitaw	--	--	--	--	--	--	1.4	1.3	1.3	1.3	1.5	1.6	1.6	1.7
Others	88.5	88.4	88.6	88.7	89.0	89.5	88.5	88.9	89.0	84.9	85.1	85.2	83.5	83.0
EMPLOYMENT														
Number of employment, total (million)***	--	--	--	--	29.7	30.1	30.5	30.9	21.2	21.8	--	22.0	22.5	--
Number of employment by SMEs	--	--	--	--	--	--	--	--	--	--	--	--	--	--
Number of employment by large enterprises	--	--	--	--	--	--	--	--	--	--	--	--	--	--
SME employees to total (%)	--	--	--	--	--	--	--	--	--	--	--	--	--	--
Employees growth (%)	--	--	--	--	--	1.4	1.4	1.0	(31.2)	2.6	--	--	2.0	--
Share of female employees to total employees (%)	--	--	--	--	37.9	37.9	37.9	37.9	39.3	43.1	--	42.5	43.4	--
Employment by sector (% share)														
Food and beverages	--	--	--	--	--	40.7	34.1	33.4	32.8	31.9	29.9	28.0	27.8	26.4
Construction materials	--	--	--	--	--	4.9	6.2	6.3	6.2	6.5	6.9	7.1	6.7	6.6
Mineral and petroleum products	--	--	--	--	--	2.6	2.8	2.8	2.9	2.9	2.9	2.9	2.7	2.7
Garments	--	--	--	--	--	39.8	44.4	45.4	46.2	58.6	60.4	62.0	62.9	64.4
Others	--	--	--	--	--	11.9	12.5	12.1	11.9	--	--	--	--	--
Employment by region (% share)														
Yangon	--	--	--	--	--	62.5	61.9	62.4	62.7	62.5	63.6	66.4	66.5	66.4
Naypyitaw	--	--	--	--	--	--	0.6	0.6	0.6	0.6	0.6	0.7	0.6	0.6
Others	--	--	--	--	--	--	37.4	36.9	36.7	36.4	35.8	32.9	32.9	33.0
CONTRIBUTION TO GDP														
SME contribution to GDP (MK million)	--	--	--	--	--	--	--	--	--	--	--	--	--	--
SME contribution to GDP (% share)	--	--	--	--	--	--	--	--	--	--	--	--	--	--
SME GDP growth (% share)	--	--	--	--	--	--	--	--	--	--	--	--	--	--
SME GDP by sector (% share)														
Agriculture, forestry, and fisheries	--	--	--	--	--	--	--	--	--	--	--	--	--	--
Manufacturing	--	--	--	--	--	--	--	--	--	--	--	--	--	--
Transportation and communication	--	--	--	--	--	--	--	--	--	--	--	--	--	--
Construction	--	--	--	--	--	--	--	--	--	--	--	--	--	--
Wholesale and retail trade	--	--	--	--	--	--	--	--	--	--	--	--	--	--
Other services	--	--	--	--	--	--	--	--	--	--	--	--	--	--
Others	--	--	--	--	--	--	--	--	--	--	--	--	--	--
SME GDP by region (% share)														
Yangon	--	--	--	--	--	--	--	--	--	--	--	--	--	--
Naypyitaw	--	--	--	--	--	--	--	--	--	--	--	--	--	--
Others	--	--	--	--	--	--	--	--	--	--	--	--	--	--
EXPORTS														
Total export value (MK million)	26,121	34,363	38,681	36,874	49,506	51,916	7,609,500	11,098,204	11,812,738	14,907,328	16,068,728	18,901,836	25,841,600	--
Total export growth (%)	13.7	31.6	12.6	(4.7)	34.3	4.9	14,557.2	45.8	6.4	26.2	7.8	17.6	36.7	--
SME export value (MK million)	--	--	--	--	--	--	--	--	--	--	--	--	--	--
SME export to total export value (%)	--	--	--	--	--	--	--	--	--	--	--	--	--	--
SME export growth (%)	--	--	--	--	--	--	--	--	--	--	--	--	--	--
IMPORTS														
Total import value (MK million)	14,590	17,971	23,901	24,126	27,152	51,085	7,866,855	11,898,484	16,730,930	21,832,872	21,320,895	26,222,586	29,984,750	--
Total import growth (%)	25.9	23.2	33.0	0.9	12.5	88.1	15,299.5	51.2	40.6	30.5	(2.3)	23.0	14.3	--
SME import value (MK million)	--	--	--	--	--	--	--	--	--	--	--	--	--	--
SME import to total import value (%)	--	--	--	--	--	--	--	--	--	--	--	--	--	--
SME import growth (%)	--	--	--	--	--	--	--	--	--	--	--	--	--	--

GDP = gross domestic product, SME = small and medium-sized enterprise. * SMEs refer to small and medium industries (manufacturing) and cottage industries until 2015. Data for 2016-2019 reflect the new SME definition effective in April 2015. ** SMEs refer to small and medium industries (manufacturing) only. *** Data refer to all enterprises (small, medium, and large industries [manufacturing]). Notes: Number of small and medium industries and employees was calculated based on firms located inside of industrial zones. Data refer to fiscal year which starts from 1 April and ends on 31 March of the following year.

Source: ADB Asia SME Monitor 2020 database. Data from SME Development Agency and Central Statistics Office.

Table 8.3: Bank Credit

End of period data

Item	2009	2010	2011	2012	2013	2014	2015	2016	2017	2018	2019
COMMERCIAL BANKS											
Number of commercial banks	18	18	22	22	22	25	25	27	27	27	29
Private sector banks	15	15	19	19	19	22	22	24	24	24	26
State-owned banks	3	3	3	3	3	3	3	3	3	3	3
Credit											
Loans outstanding, total (MK million)	657,465	998,575	1,767,838	2,879,802	4,215,973	6,427,788	9,057,691	12,344,306	16,132,449	19,446,011	23,357,888
Loans outstanding in domestic currency (MK million)	--	--	--	--	--	--	--	--	--	--	--
Loans outstanding in foreign currency (MK million)	--	--	--	--	--	--	--	--	--	--	--
Loan growth (%)	29.1	51.9	77.0	62.9	46.4	52.5	40.9	36.3	30.7	20.5	20.1
Total commercial bank loans to GDP (%)	2.2	2.9	4.4	6.2	8.2	11.1	13.9	17.0	20.2	21.5	--
Lending rate (%)*	17.0	17.0	16.3	13.0	13.0	13.0	13.0	13.0	13.0	13.0	--
Gross nonperforming loans (NPLs) (MK million)	--	--	--	--	--	--	--	--	--	--	--
Gross NPLs to total loans (%)	--	--	--	--	--	--	--	--	--	--	--
Loans outstanding by sector (% share)											
Agriculture, forestry, and fisheries	9.0	7.5	14.6	21.4	16.5	19.8	16.9	12.6	12.2	1.7	2.2
Manufacturing	27.3	27.3	26.5	19.3	16.7	12.6	13.4	11.3	11.3	10.5	12.3
Transportation and communication	3.1	2.3	2.0	1.8	1.6	1.2	1.2	1.1	1.4	2.2	2.0
Construction	5.7	5.0	7.1	8.9	9.9	10.5	12.0	13.6	15.4	18.3	18.6
Wholesale and retail trade	32.3	33.9	31.6	29.9	32.8	27.4	33.3	33.1	33.6	35.5	25.7
Other services	12.5	14.6	11.3	10.2	11.0	9.5	10.7	11.4	12.0	13.0	15.6
Others	10.2	9.4	6.9	8.5	11.4	19.1	12.5	16.8	14.1	18.9	23.7
Deposits											
Deposits, total (MK million)	--	--	7,010,077	11,733,322	16,297,118	19,919,513	25,882,793	32,114,334	--	--	--
Deposits in domestic currency (MK million)	--	--	--	--	--	--	--	--	--	--	--
Deposits in foreign currency (MK million)	--	--	--	--	--	--	--	--	--	--	--
Deposit rate (%)*	12.0	12.0	11.3	8.0	8.0	8.0	8.0	8.0	8.0	8.0	--
SME LOANS**											
SME loans outstanding, total (MK million)	--	--	--	--	--	--	--	--	733,235	896,840	1,131,665
SME loans to total loans outstanding (%)	--	--	--	--	--	--	--	--	4.5	4.6	4.8
SME loans to GDP (%)	--	--	--	--	--	--	--	--	0.9	1.0	--
SME loan growth (%)	--	--	--	--	--	--	--	--	--	22.3	26.2
SME lending rate (%)	--	--	--	--	--	--	--	--	--	--	--
Nonperforming SME loans (NPLs) (MK million)	--	--	--	--	--	--	--	--	--	--	--
SME NPLs to total SME loans (%)	--	--	--	--	--	--	--	--	--	--	--
Number of SME loan borrowers	--	--	--	--	--	--	--	--	7,940	11,042	15,739
SME loan borrowers to total bank borrowers (%)	--	--	--	--	--	--	--	--	--	--	--
SME loan rejection rate (% of total applications)	--	--	--	--	--	--	--	--	--	--	--
Number of SME savings account in banks	--	--	--	--	--	--	--	--	--	--	--
Guaranteed SME loans (MK million)	--	--	--	--	--	--	--	--	--	--	--
Non-collateral SME loans (MK million)	--	--	--	--	--	--	--	--	--	--	--
SME loans outstanding by sector (% share)**											
Agriculture, forestry, and fisheries	--	--	--	--	--	--	--	--	1.3	0.9	1.0
Manufacturing	--	--	--	--	--	--	--	--	22.2	20.8	18.9
Transportation and communication	--	--	--	--	--	--	--	--	3.9	3.8	3.4
Construction	--	--	--	--	--	--	--	--	2.2	2.0	1.5
Wholesale and retail trade	--	--	--	--	--	--	--	--	52.4	50.5	45.6
Other services	--	--	--	--	--	--	--	--	8.1	9.9	11.4
Others	--	--	--	--	--	--	--	--	9.9	12.1	18.3
SMALL AND MEDIUM INDUSTRIAL DEVELOPMENT BANK											
SME loans outstanding, total (MK million)	16,421	34,963	45,846	61,835	72,263	85,512	116,145	124,743	110,498	143,937	159,825
SME loans to total loans outstanding (%)	2.5	3.5	2.6	2.1	1.7	1.3	1.3	1.0	0.7	0.7	0.7
SME loans to GDP (%)	0.06	0.10	0.12	0.13	0.14	0.15	0.18	0.17	0.14	0.16	--
SME loan growth (%)	--	112.9	31.1	34.9	16.9	18.3	35.8	7.4	(11.4)	30.3	11.0
SME NPLs to total SME loans (%)	--	--	--	--	--	--	--	--	--	--	--
SME lending rate (%)	--	--	--	--	--	--	--	--	8.5 ~ 13	--	8.5 ~ 16
SME loans outstanding by sector (% share)											
Agriculture, forestry, and fisheries	--	--	--	5.7	1.4	--	--	--	--	0.3	0.5
Manufacturing	--	--	54.6	40.1	37.3	28.4	26.3	38.1	30.1	19.6	21.8
Transportation and communication	--	--	2.0	1.4	1.8	1.9	0.6	0.4	1.1	0.3	0.2
Construction	--	--	3.5	3.8	6.1	4.2	2.2	2.3	2.1	1.9	1.6
Wholesale and retail trade	--	--	26.3	28.3	30.1	36.7	41.9	37.5	39.1	28.0	30.6
Other services	--	--	10.5	10.0	7.9	10.8	8.2	9.4	7.6	22.9	3.7
Others	--	--	3.1	10.8	15.4	17.9	20.9	12.3	20.0	27.2	41.6
SME loans outstanding by region (% share)											
Yangon	--	--	68.0	69.2	53.3	54.5	59.1	39.6	42.3	57.5	59.5
Naypyitaw	--	--	2.8	9.2	5.3	5.1	3.8	10.0	10.1	2.9	3.8
Others	--	--	29.3	21.6	41.4	40.4	36.9	50.4	47.6	39.6	36.8
SME loans outstanding by type of use (% share)											
For working capital	--	--	--	--	--	--	--	--	--	--	--
For capital investment	--	--	--	--	--	--	--	--	--	--	--
SME loans outstanding by tenor (% share)											
Less than 1 year	--	--	100.0	100.0	100.0	100.0	100.0	100.0	100.0	100.0	100.0
1-5 years	--	--	--	--	--	--	--	--	--	--	--
More than 5 years	--	--	--	--	--	--	--	--	--	--	--

GDP = gross domestic product, SME = small and medium-sized enterprise.

* Based on IMF/IFS data on other depository corporations' rates (percent per annum). ** Based on Central Bank of Myanmar data.

Notes: Data refers to fiscal year which starts from 1 April and ends on 31 March of the following year. Net income represents amounts before tax.

Source: ADB Asia SME Monitor 2020 database. Data from Central Bank of Myanmar and Small and Medium Industrial Development Bank.

Table 8.4: Nonbank Finance

End of period data

Item	2012	2013	2014	2015	2016	2017	2018	2019*
NUMBER OF NONBANK FINANCE INSTITUTIONS								
Microfinance institutions	24	91	140	172	154	162	171	189
Credit unions/cooperatives	--	--	--	--	--	--	--	31,810
Finance companies	--	--	--	--	--	--	--	--
Pawnshops	--	--	--	--	--	--	--	--
Leasing companies	--	--	--	--	--	--	--	--
Factoring companies	--	--	--	--	--	--	--	--
Insurance companies	--	--	--	--	--	--	--	20
Others	--	--	--	--	--	--	--	--
MICROFINANCE INSTITUTIONS								
Financing outstanding, total (MK million)	49,194	67,245	110,069	169,293	260,948	426,016	793,197	1,800,232
Growth (%)	--	36.7	63.7	53.8	54.1	63.3	86.2	127.0
Total financing to GDP (%)	1.68	1.98	2.77	3.66	0.01	0.01	0.01	0.03
Annual financing rate (%, on average)	30.0	30.0	30.0	30.0	30.0	30.0	30.0	30.0
Gross nonperforming financing (NPFs) (MK million)	42.1	40.6	68.0	257.5	1,644.7	2,769.5	9,085.2	14,376.3
Gross NPFs to total financing (%)	0.1	0.1	0.1	0.2	0.6	0.7	1.1	0.01
Number of customers financed, total	426,245	548,881	815,056	1,106,881	1,445,313	2,121,929	3,029,529	5,340,000
Financing outstanding by sector (% share)								
Agriculture, forestry, and fisheries	36.1	38.8	25.4	22.1	23.9	23.5	17.8	30.8
Manufacturing	3.1	2.7	2.7	2.4	2.9	3.3	4.7	10.5
Transportation and communication	--	0.03	0.12	0.24	0.36	0.37	0.30	--
Construction	--	--	0.001	0.120	0.003	0.003	0.003	--
Wholesale and retail trade	21.4	22.7	27.1	27.9	29.4	31.0	35.7	33.2
Other services	10.5	9.6	12.0	14.4	15.4	18.3	19.4	25.6
Others	28.9	26.1	32.6	32.9	28.1	23.5	22.2	--
Financing outstanding by region (% share)								
Yangon	94.4	95.5	96.7	97.5	98.1	98.6	99.3	--
Naypyitaw	--	0.2	0.6	0.7	0.8	0.7	0.4	--
Others	5.6	4.3	2.7	1.8	1.1	0.7	0.4	--

GDP = gross domestic product.

Notes: The Myanmar fiscal year changed in 2018 from 1 April–31 March to 1 October–30 September. Thus, data for 2012 to 2018 refer to the 1 April–31 March fiscal year, while data for 2019 refer to the revised 1 October–30 September fiscal year.

Source: ADB Asia SME Monitor 2020 database. Data from Financial Regulatory Department, Ministry of Planning, Finance, and Industry.

Table 8.5: Capital Markets

End of period data

	2016*	2017	2018	2019
EQUITY MARKET				
Main Board				
MYANPIX (Index)	561.5	463.2	406.2	458.2
Market capitalization (MK million)	583,957	578,721	554,599	627,449
Growth (%)	--	(0.9)	(4.2)	13.1
Trading value (MK million)	89.4	15.4	100.7	21.9
Trading volume (shares)	12,299	2,715	14,802	3,845
Number of listed companies**	3	4	5	5
Number of IPOs	0	0	1	0
Number of delisted companies	0	0	0	0

IPO = initial public offering.

*Yangon Stock Exchange began trading on 25 March 2016.

**The three companies in 2016 and one in 2017 were just listing. They did not do any public offering at the time of listing.

Note: Data are as of the end of the year.

Source: ADB Asia SME Monitor 2020 database. Data from Yangon Stock Exchange.

Table 8.6: Policies and Regulations

Regulations

Name	Outline
Nonfinance regulations	
Private Industrial Enterprise Law No.22/1990	Business registration and regulations. SME definition included.
Law Amending the Promotion of Cottage Industries Law No.14/2011	Cottage industries defined as small-scale industries.
Foreign Investment Law No.21/2012 (amendment)	Regulation and promotion of foreign investment and exports.
SME Development Law No.23/2015	The establishment of the SME Development Agency. The establishment of the SME Development Fund. New SME definition included.
Myanmar Companies Law No. 29/2017	Implementation of an online company registration system under the Directorate of Investment and Company Adminsitration.
SMEs Development Central Committee's Notification Numbers (1/2018),(2/2018),(3/2018), January 2018	Creation of evaluating and reporting body, SME agency, and fund management body.
Finance regulations	
Financial Institutions of Myanmar Law No.16/1990	Regulation on financial institutions (commercial banks, investment/development banks, finance companies, and credit societies).
Myanmar Agricultural and Rural Development Bank Law No.17/1990	Regulation on Agricultural Bank and Rural Development Bank.
Savings Banks Law No. 5/1992	Regulation on savings banks.
Cooperative Society Law No.9/1992	Regulation on credit societies.
Insurance Business Law No. 6/1996	Regulation on insurance companies.
Microfinance Business Law No.13/2011	Regulation on microfinance operations.
Central Bank of Myanmar Law No.16/2013	Stipulate the central bank as a regulator for financial institutions.
Securities Exchange Law No.20/2013	Regulation on securities companies and stock exchange.
Financial Institutions Law No. 20/2016	Regulation on financial institutions (commercial banks, development finance banks, nonbank financial institutions, and scheduled institutions).
Secured Transaction Law (Draft), Forthcoming	Establishment of a modern and formal credit market through which borrowers can take loans using a broad range of moveable assets as collateral and micro, small, and medium-sized enterprises have better access to financing.

Regulators and Policymakers

Name	Responsibility
SMEs Development Central Committee	Formulates policies and guidance to carry out the development of SMEs in accordance with the basic principles contained in the SME Development Law.
SMEs Development Working Committee	Provides information to Central Committee to support the promotion of SMEs.
SME Development Department, Ministry of Planning, Finance, and Industry (MOPFI)	Responsible for SME sector development.
Financial Regulatory Department, MOPFI	Regulate and supervise nonbank financial institutions.
Securities and Exchange Commission, MOPFI	Regulate and supervise securities companies, listed companies and stock exchange.
Central Bank of Myanmar (CBM)	Regulate and supervise financial institutions (banks and nonbank financial institutions).

Policies

Name	Responsible Entity	Outline
Policy of Small and Medium Enterprise Development (2005)	Ministry of Industry (MOPFI, since November 2019)	1) Policy support areas: (i) Human resources (ii) Technology development and innovation (iii) Financial resources (iv) Infrastructure development (v) Market access (vii) Appropriate taxation and procedures (viii) Conducive business environment 2) Role of the SME Development Agency: (i) Registration of SMEs (ii) Financial assistance (iii) Market analysis (iv) Human resource development (v) Monitoring of SME development activities (annual progress report) (vi) SME analysis (to reduce disadvantages of SMEs) (vii) Facilitation of nonfinancial services (business development services) (viii) SME data collection (ix) Connection with international financial institutions and development agencies, business associations, and nongovernment organizations (x) Collaboration with financial institutions 3) Prioritized industries listed in the short-term and long-term perspective
Myanmar Financial Inclusion Roadmap 2014-2020	CBM	1) Strengthened financial sector to better support financial inclusion i) Institutions critical to financial inclusion are created/strengthened ii) Market barriers across product categories are addressed 2) Financial inclusion for three priority segments i) Improved financial access in agriculture ii) Increased financial access for SMEs iii) Financial inclusion and resilience for low-income households

SME = small and medium-sized enterprise.
Source: ADB Asia SME Monitor 2020 database. Data from Ministry of Planning, Finance, and Industry; and Central Bank of Myanmar.

Country Review

Philippines

Overview

The Philippine economy grew by 6.0% in 2019.[90] The country has a working age population of 71.9 million, with a labor force participation rate of 60.3% (43.3 million) and a 5.3% unemployment rate as of January 2019.[91] Micro, small, and medium-sized enterprises (MSMEs) play a critical role in driving the national economy, accounting for 99.5% of total enterprises and 63.2% of the total employed labor force. More than 80% of MSMEs are engaged in services, especially wholesale and retail trade. Access to finance is a chronic problem blocking MSME survival and growth. The share of MSME credit to total bank credit has been falling to a single-digit percentage share since 2013. Meanwhile, microfinance operations by banks have been expanding since 2016, although compliance with mandatory lending to micro and small enterprises has not improved satisfactorily. The nonbank finance industry represented by microfinance institutions and pawnshops is small in scale, but a viable funding source for microenterprises and those self-employed. The capital market has yet to become an alternative funding source for MSMEs to expand. The central bank is promoting digital financial service solutions for MSMEs under its national financial inclusion strategy.

1. MSME Development

- Microenterprises involved in traditional trading activities hold the dominant share of MSMEs in the Philippines; agribusiness and technology-based MSMEs have much growth potential with government support.
- MSMEs account for a moderate share of the country's labor force, especially in services and geographically in Luzon.
- Most MSMEs concentrate on domestic markets and are not well exposed to global markets or value chains; however, a sizable number do operate as sole exporters.
- Technology is spread widely across the Philippines and e-commerce has been growing rapidly; yet there are few domestic e-commerce players, while information technology-business process outsourcing or IT-BPO continues to grow, supported by government programs.
- Philippine Chamber of Commerce and Industry (PCCI), the largest nonprofit business association in the country, plays a critical role in promoting private sector development and advocating policy reforms, including those related to MSMEs.

Scale of MSMEs

The Philippines defines MSMEs by total assets (excluding land) and number of employees (Table 9.1). The asset criterion is a legal definition stipulated in the Small and Medium Enterprise Development Council Resolution No.01 of 2003, where a microenterprise holds assets not more than P3 million, a small enterprise up to P15 million, and a medium-sized enterprise up to P100 million. The employment criterion is used by the Philippine Statistics Authority, where a microenterprise has fewer than 10 employees, a small enterprise less than 100 employees, and a medium-sized enterprise less than 200 employees.

90 ADB. 2020. *Asian Development Outlook 2020 Supplement (June 2020)*. Manila.

91 Working age population is aged 15 years and above. The labor force included 41 million employed and 2.3 million unemployed as of January 2019 (estimates). Philippine Statistics Authority, 4 March 2020.

As of end-2018, there were 998,342 registered MSMEs, an 8.4% increase from 2017. They accounted for 99.5% of all enterprises (Figure 9.1A and Table 9.2). The majority are microenterprises (88.4%), followed by small enterprises (10.6%) and medium-sized enterprises (0.5%).

The main business sector for MSMEs is services, accounting for 86.8% of MSMEs in 2018, with wholesale and retail trade (including the repair of motor vehicles and motorcycles) holding the largest share (46.3% and rising), followed by other services (40.5%)—which includes accommodation and food services (14.5%), other personal services (6.6%), and financial services (4.6%) (Figure 9.1B). Manufacturing's share was 11.7% and is decreasing.

In 2018, by region, 20.4% of MSMEs operate in Metro Manila—the National Capital Region—with the remaining 79.6% spread across the country—Calabarzon (14.8%), Central Luzon (11.6%), Central Visayas (7.1%), Western Visayas (6.2%), and other regions (39.9%).

According to the Bureau of Small and Medium Enterprise Development (BSMED), under the Department of Trade and Industry (DTI), MSME operations in 2019 performed well, with more growing profitable. Agribusiness holds much potential, backed by government support for developing agricultural value chains. Services, including technology-based MSMEs, also have the potential to grow, given the business development support offered by the regional innovation centers established by the Department of Science and Technology (DOST). Construction continues to hire MSME subcontractors, supported by the government's ongoing national infrastructure development projects.[92]

Figure 9.1: Number of MSMEs

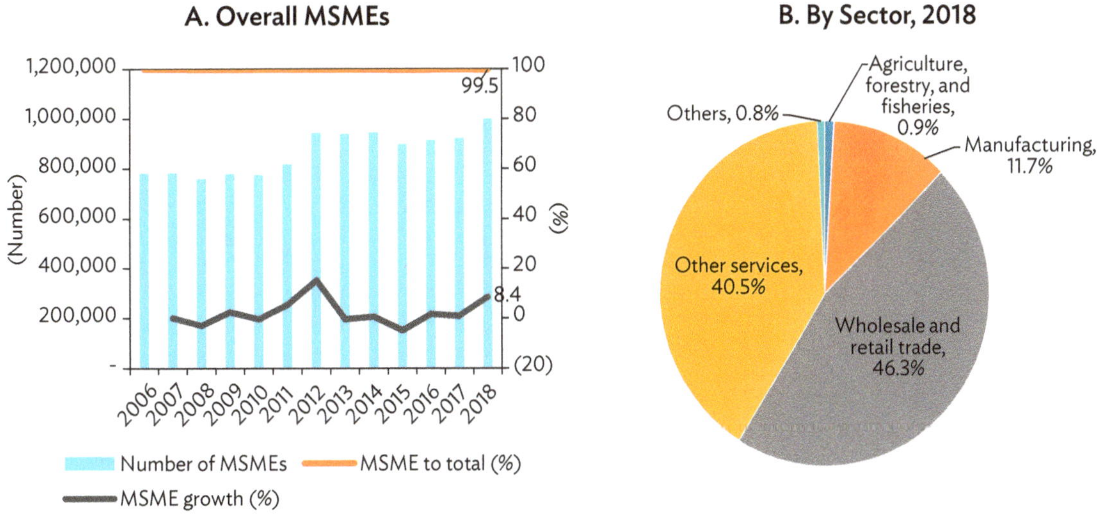

MSME = micro, small, and medium-sized enterprise.

Source: ADB Asia SME Monitor 2020 database. Data from Philippine Statistics Authority, and Bureau of Small and Medium Enterprise Development.

Employment

In 2018, MSMEs had 5,714,262 employees, or 63.2% of total employment, a 16.1% increase from 2017 (Figure 9.2A). Microenterprises held the largest share of total employment (28.9%), followed by small enterprises (27%) and medium-sized enterprises (7.3%). Large firms, which account for just 0.5% of total enterprises, employed 36.8% of the workforce.

92 Interview with the director of the Bureau of Small and Medium Enterprise Development, Department of Trade and Industry, on 25 September 2019.

Of MSME employees, 81.7% worked in services in 2018 with the trend increasing; 35.7% of those were in wholesale and retail trade, followed by other services (46%)—including accommodation and food services (15.4%) (Figure 9.2B). Manufacturing had 13.4% of MSME employees, with its share declining.

By region, 28.4% of MSME employees worked in the National Capital Region, with the remaining 71.6% spread across the country—Calabarzon (14.4%), Central Luzon (10.6%), Central Visayas (7.9%), Western Visayas (5.6%), and other regions (33.1%) in 2018.

Figure 9.2: Employment by MSMEs

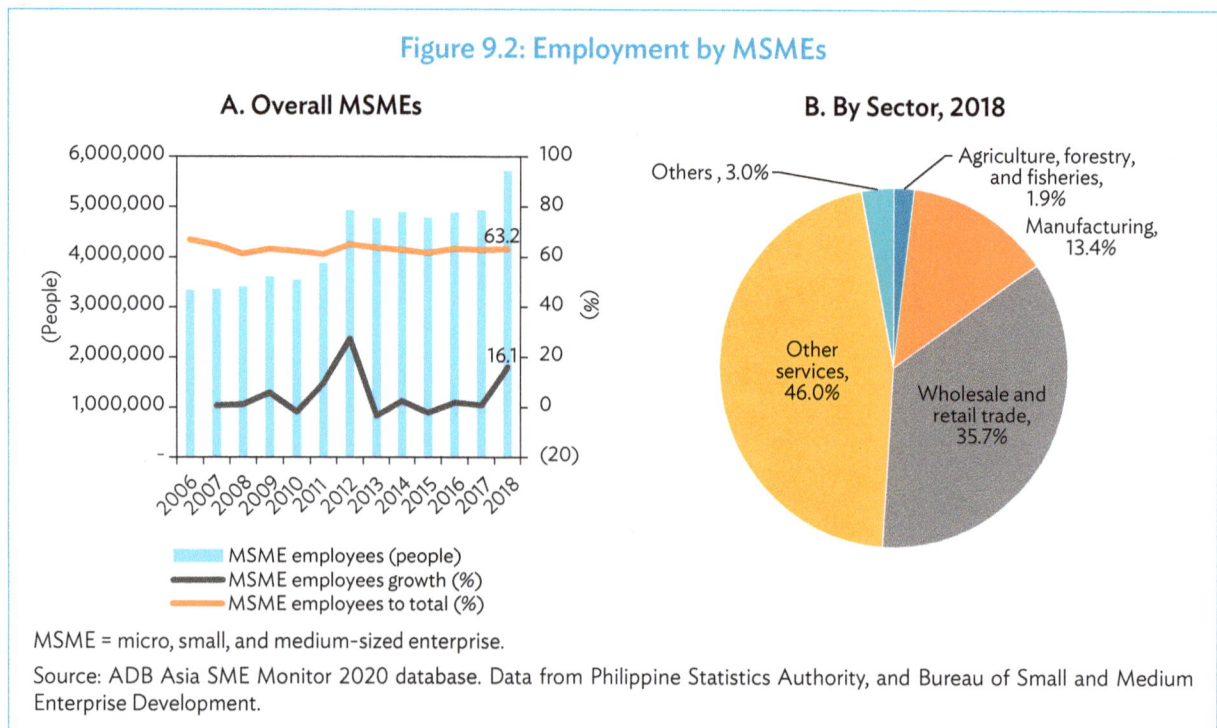

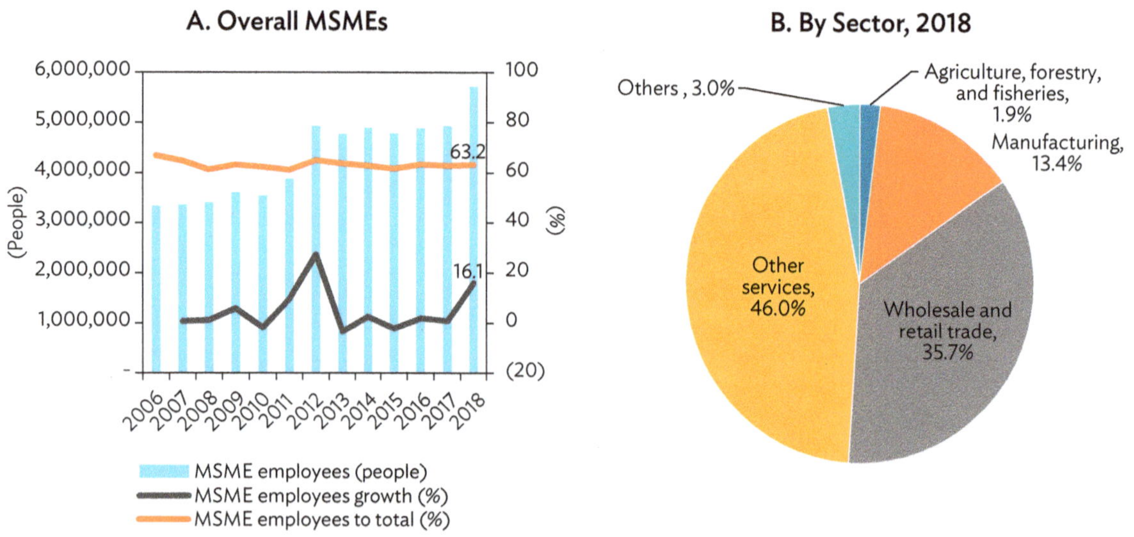

MSME = micro, small, and medium-sized enterprise.

Source: ADB Asia SME Monitor 2020 database. Data from Philippine Statistics Authority, and Bureau of Small and Medium Enterprise Development.

Business Productivity

The latest data on MSME contributions to the Philippines' gross value added (GVA) is from 2006. At that time, MSMEs generated P752 billion, or 35.7% of GVA, with small enterprises accounting for 20.5% of total GVA, followed by medium-sized enterprises (10.3%) and microenterprises (4.9%). MSMEs in manufacturing accounted for 6.9%, wholesale and retail trade 6.6%, and financial services 6% of total GVA in 2006.

Market Access

Philippine MSMEs operate mostly within limited domestic markets using their own marketing channels. Most have yet to join global value chains, and a small number of MSMEs trade internationally. Those that export, however, do have an impact. According to the DTI, MSMEs accounted for 25% of total export value in the Philippines,[93] with 60% of country's exporters categorized into MSMEs. They are normally sole exporters or subcontractors with large multinational firms supplying inputs.

[93] Government of the Philippines, Department of Trade and Industry. 2018 MSME Statistics. https://www.dti.gov.ph/resources/msme-statistics/ (Accessed on 30 March 2020).

Technology and Innovation

Information and communications technology has high penetration in the Philippines, although still in a relatively early stage of development. The number of mobile cellular subscriptions surged from 115.8 million in 2017 to 134.6 million in 2018, or 126 subscriptions per 100 people.[94] Internet penetration also improved from 55.5% of the total population in 2016 to 60.1% in 2017.

E-commerce has been expanding rapidly, with most service providers foreign companies—such as Lazada (Singapore, owned by the Alibaba Group based in the People's Republic of China), Shopee (Singapore), Zalora (Singapore), Carousell (Singapore), and eBay (the United States [US]).[95] Philippine-oriented e-commerce providers have a growing presence, however, such as online shopping by Globe Telecom, one of the major telecommunications companies.

Although domestic MSMEs do not yet have a large share of the e-commerce industry, mobile-based ride-hailing services such as Angkas have become popular. Founded in 2017, Angkas is a Manila-based motorcycle ride-sharing and delivery service company with over 27,000 biker partners covering Metro Manila and Cebu.[96]

IT-BPO continues to grow, represented by call centers and computer-related services such as software/game developers, animation, and IT engineering.[97] As of June 2016, 851 establishments were registered as BPO companies, of which 50.4% were call centers and 46.2% providing computer-related services. The BPO industry had 575,600 employees, 87.6% working at call centers. BPOs hold great potential for developing start-ups and MSMEs, and hence creating new jobs. The Department of Information and Communications Technology is promoting "digitaljobsPH" (formerly Rural Impact Sourcing Program), which offers capacity development training to promote online freelancers or internet-based home businesses, including MSMEs, to encourage e-commerce. During 2018–2019, more than 2,000 people graduated from the program, and 700 MSMEs (online businesses) were created backed by this program.[98]

The Philippine Innovation Act (Republic Act No.11293) was enacted on 17 April 2019 to create and promote an innovation ecosystem driven by MSMEs. It established the National Innovation Council to coordinate all innovation related strategies initiated by government agencies. The council develops innovation strategies to promote MSME internationalization and participation in domestic and global value chains.

Networking and Support

The Philippine Chamber of Commerce and Industry (PCCI) was established in 1978 as a merger of two chambers (the Chamber of Commerce of the Philippines and the Philippine Chamber of Industry). It is the country's largest non-profit business community, with around 35,000 regular members, including MSMEs and a network of 123 local chambers. The PCCI plays a critical role in promoting private sector development including MSMEs and advocates policy reforms promoting MSMEs, among others. Its SME Committee supports MSME development through training programs and seminars that facilitate business networking. It also promotes the ASPIRE (Agribusiness Support for Promotion and Investment in Regional Exposition) program in collaboration with the Department of Agriculture and the DTI. The program promotes agri-product development and improves market access for farmers, fisherfolk, and MSMEs through business matching venues with potential partners, supply chain actors, and customers.

94 World Bank database (https://data.worldbank.org/indicator/). Accessed on 30 March 2020.
95 Referred to ASEAN UP (https://aseanup.com/top-e-commerce-sites-philippines/). Accessed on 30 March 2020.
96 Angkas homepage (https://angkas.com/about/). Accessed on 30 March 2020.
97 Philippine Statistics Authority (http://www.psa.gov.ph/content/20152016-industry-profile-business-process-outsourcing-first-series-0). Accessed on 30 March 2020.
98 digitaljobsPH (https://digitaljobs.ph/about/). Accessed on 30 March 2020.

2. Access to Finance

- Access to finance is a chronic barrier for MSMEs to survive and grow; the share of MSME credit to total bank credit has been falling to less than 10% since 2013.
- Microfinance operations by banks have been expanding since 2016, although compliance with mandatory lending levels to micro and small enterprises has not improved.
- A centralized credit guarantee system started in 2019. Mandatory lending scheme under the Magna Carta has lapsed, while a new scheme targeting innovative activities services start-ups and MSMEs. Soft loan programs continue to serve microenterprises.
- The nonbank finance industry represented by microfinance institutions and pawnshops is small in scale but remains a viable funding source for microenterprises and the self-employed.
- The central bank continues to promote the establishment of a digital financial ecosystem as part of its financial inclusion strategy. Infrastructure such as a national payment switch, digital ID, and standardized QR codes helps boost digital financial service solutions.
- The capital market has yet to be an effective alternative funding venue for growing MSMEs; the QBO Innovation Hub platform is expected to create a potential issuer base for the SME Board by supporting the country's start-up ecosystem.
- The credit bureau and secured lending legal systems have been established as key credit infrastructure supporting MSME access to finance.

Bank Credit

As of end-2019, there were a total of 547 banks—46 universal and commercial banks, 50 thrift banks, and 451 rural and cooperative banks—operating in the Philippines, with 12,870 offices nationwide (both head and branch offices).[99] The bank credit market has been expanding with P18.4 trillion in total assets in 2019, an 8.4% increase from 2018. The loan portfolio was P10.8 trillion, or 58.7% of the bank asset total.

There were P588.8 billion in MSME loans outstanding in 2019, or 6.1% of banks' total loan portfolio (Figure 9.3A and Table 9.3). The share has declined by almost half (from 11.7%) since 2010. The share of MSME nonperforming loans (NPLs) to total MSME loans was 5.8% in 2019, over twice as high as the gross NPL ratio of 2.0%.

Under the 1991 Magna Carta for MSMEs—which provided mandatory credit allocations to MSMEs (Republic Act No.6977 of 1991)—banks are required to allocate 8% of their loan portfolio to micro and small enterprises (MSEs) and 2% to medium-sized enterprises (MEs), for a 10% mandatory MSME allocation. Although the effectivity of mandatory credit lapsed on 16 June 2018, the central bank, Bangko Sentral ng Pilipinas (BSP), continues to monitor banks' quarterly exposures to MSMEs.[100] In 2019, banks set aside P579.1 billion for MSME loans, a slight increase from the P574.8 billion allocated in 2018. MSEs received P228.4 billion (2.8% of total lending) and MEs P350.8 billion (4.3)[101] (Figure 9.3B and Table 9.3a). This was below the 8% mandatory allocation for MSEs, but over the 2% mandatory allocation for MEs.

[99] Bangko Sentral ng Pilipinas. 2020. *Report on the Philippine Financial System - 2nd Semester 2019.*

[100] Following the lapse of the effectivity of the mandatory credit, the BSP issued a memorandum to all banks (Memorandum No. M-2018-022) covering the extension of submission of compliance reports and enjoining banks to continue submitting their quarterly exposures to MSMEs.

[101] The BSP continues to compute the percentage of loans to MSMEs with respect to the total loan portfolio in the banking system. Undercompliance and corresponding penalties, however, no longer apply starting from the third quarter of 2018.

The compliance ratio for MSE loans has been declining over the years, from 10% in 2008 to 2.8% in 2019, falling below 8% since 2011, when the ratio dropped to 7.6%. By type of bank, only rural and cooperative banks met the required 8% allocation target (24.3% in 2019). For MEs, the 2% mandatory allocation was met by all banks. As with MSEs, the share of loans to MEs also continued to decline, however, from 9.0% in 2008 to 4.3% in 2019.

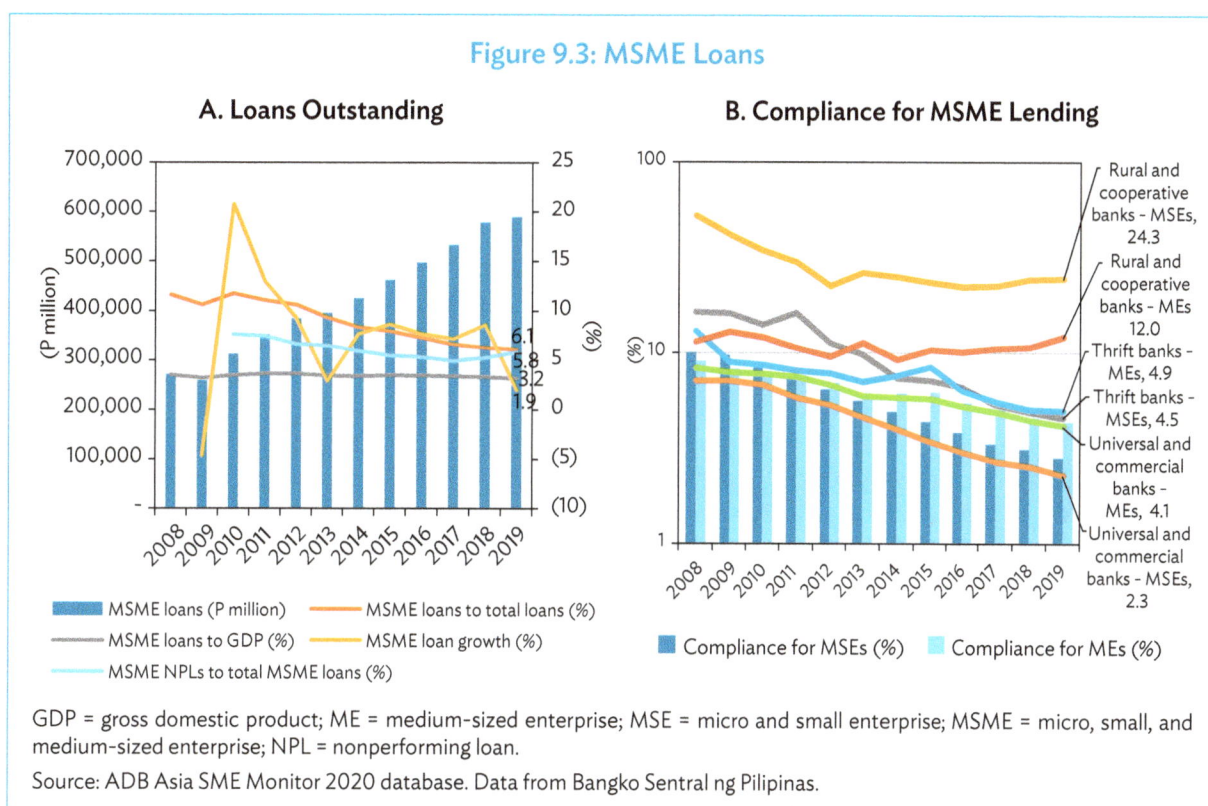

Figure 9.3: MSME Loans

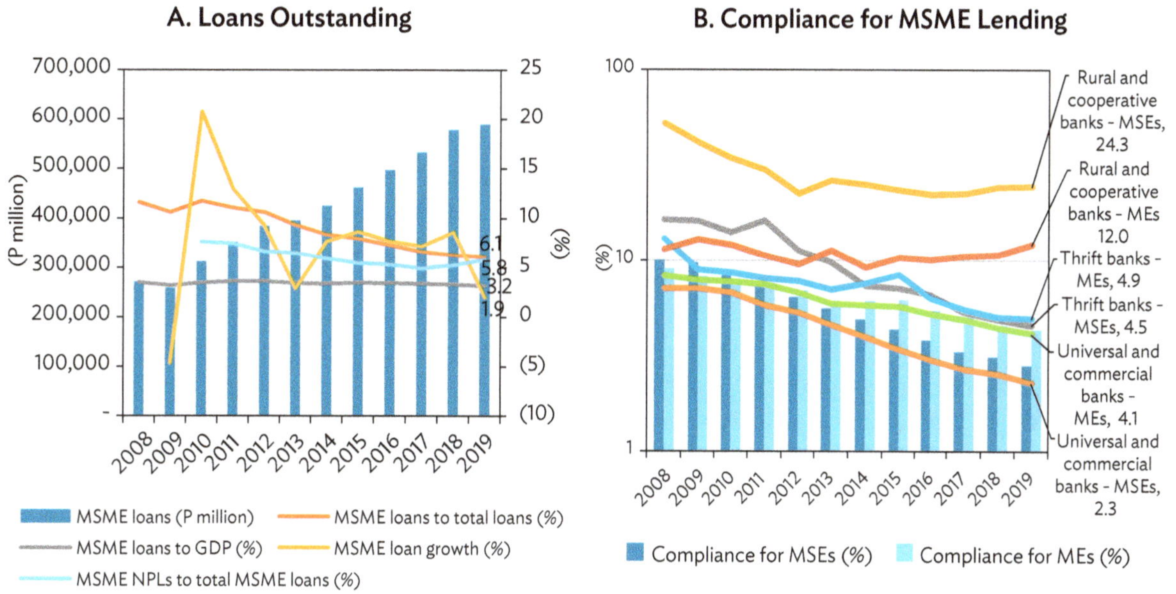

GDP = gross domestic product; ME = medium-sized enterprise; MSE = micro and small enterprise; MSME = micro, small, and medium-sized enterprise; NPL = nonperforming loan.

Source: ADB Asia SME Monitor 2020 database. Data from Bangko Sentral ng Pilipinas.

Microfinance remains critical for enhancing access to finance for the poor, low-income households, and MSMEs. As of end-2019, 154 of the 547 banks had microfinance operations (Table 9.3b). Savings in microfinance-focused banks reached P10.8 billion in 2019, while loans outstanding was P27.3 billion, catering to over 2.4 million borrowers. Retail microfinance loans are classified into four major products: (i) microenterprise loans, (ii) microfinance plus, (iii) micro-agri loans, and (iv) micro-housing loans. Microenterprise loans (P22.9 billion) accounted for 83.8% of the total microfinance loans by banks in 2019.

Following the Barangay Micro Business Enterprises (BMBE) Act of 2002, banks and government financial institutions could also provide loans to village-oriented micro businesses or BMBEs.[102] As of end-2019, there were 20 banks[103] servicing BMBEs with loans outstanding of P74.9 million, directly serving 4,050 borrowers (Table 9.3c). This was a significant drop from 2018 BMBE data, showing a 60.2% decrease in loans outstanding (from P188.3 million), and a 9.3% decline in the number of borrowers (4,467).

102 A barangay micro business enterprise (BMBE) is defined as a business entity engaged in the production, processing, or manufacturing of products or commodities, including agro-processing, trading and services, with total assets (including loans but excluding land), of not more than P3 million, and registered through DTI's Negosyo Centers (one-stop service centers for MSMEs). Republic Act No.9178 of 2002.

103 The 20 banks include one universal and commercial bank, one thrift bank, 16 rural banks, and two cooperative banks.

Public Financing and Guarantees

a. Credit guarantees

The Philippine Guarantee Corporation (PhilGuarantee) was established on 1 September 2019 to create a centralized credit guarantee system in the country. It merged five guarantee corporations: (i) the Philippine Export-Import Credit Agency (PhilEXIM), (ii) the Home Guaranty Corporation, (iii) the Industrial Guarantee and Loan Fund, (iv) the Agricultural Guarantee Fund Pool, and (v) the credit guarantee function of the Small Business Corporation (SBC) (President Executive Order No.58 of 2018). BSP supervises PhilGuarantee, whose base organization is PhilEXIM. It is headquartered in Manila with a branch office in Cebu, with 220 staff members as of September 2019. The PhilGuarantee product line was still being planned in 2019, absorbing existing outstanding guarantees from PhilEXIM, which provided (i) guarantees on short-term loans to SME exporters of up to 90% coverage of the principal of an approved loan (maximum P20 million), and (ii) 1-year portfolio guarantees for SME exporters with the guaranteed amount from P50 million to P300 million (a minimum of five accounts in a portfolio). PhilGuarantee offers credit guarantees to partner banks including universal and commercial banks and cooperative banks. It tentatively targets manufacturing and medium-sized enterprises with assets excluding land from P15 million to P100 million for credit guarantees.[104]

After the launch of the PhilGuarantee, SBC stopped offering new credit guarantees for MSMEs, but still services outstanding guarantees. As of August 2019, SBC had guaranteed P78.4 million in loans servicing 80 MSMEs (Figure 9.4A and Table 9.4). The number of MSMEs guaranteed rose sharply in 2017, due to the credit risk guarantee fund portfolio of P672.4 million with contingent liabilities of P537.9 million covering 14,497 MSMEs.

b. Mandatory lending scheme

The 1991 Magna Carta for MSMEs expired in June 2018. Accordingly, the 10% mandatory lending allocation for MSMEs expired as well. Meanwhile, the Philippine Innovation Act enacted in April 2019 stipulated a new mandatory lending scheme for innovation activities, targeting start-ups and MSMEs. Under the new scheme, banking institutions must set aside at least 4% of their loanable funds for innovation development credit.[105] The innovation development credit and financing program is a special loan program designed to generate and scale up innovation in accordance with the National Innovation Agenda and Strategy Document. The document covers development of new technologies, product innovation, process innovation, organizational innovation, and marketing innovation. In case of a banking institution's noncompliance with the 4% credit allocation, the BSP will impose administrative sanctions and other penalties.

c. Soft loan programs

The Access of Small Enterprises to Sound Lending Opportunity (ASENSO) is a government funding program for MSME loans by government financial institutions. It began as the SME Unified Lending Opportunities for National Growth program in 2003 and was reorganized as ASENSO in 2013. As of end-2016 (latest available data), P37.4 billion was released to government financial institutions, such as the Land Bank of the Philippines, the Development Bank of the Philippines, and the SBC for providing MSME loans (Figure 9.4B and Table 9.4).

104 Interview with the president of the PhilGuarantee on 26 September 2019.

105 While the Magna Carta for MSMEs lapsed, Congress moved to discuss a possible extension. The 4% mandatory credit under the Philippine Innovation Act is a separate issuance and does not intend to replace the mandatory Magna Carta credit allocation for MSMEs.

Under Executive Order No.58 of 2018, SBC transferred its guarantee functions to PhilGuarantee in 2019, shifting its business initiatives to financing microenterprises. DTI launched the P3 Program (Pondo sa Pagbabago at Pag-Asenso) in March 2017 to finance unserved and underserved microenterprises and entrepreneurs in the poorest provinces. The government, through its yearly General Appropriations Act, set P3 Program funding at P1 billion in 2017, P1 billion in 2018, and P1.5 billion in 2019. SBC, the financing arm of DTI, is the implementing agency of P3.

P3 offers two product lines: retail and wholesale loans. SBC's retail loan scheme lends directly to target microenterprises, with loanable amounts from P5,000 to P200,000 per transaction, loan tenors of up to 2 years, with a monthly interest rate of 2.5% (with an add on rate of 18% per annum). The P3 wholesale loan scheme intermediates lending through qualified participating financial institutions, such as cooperatives, rural banks, and microfinance institutions. The maximum loanable amount is P200 million for wholesale loans. The on-lending rate from the P3 fund to participating financial institutions is 2.0% per annum. The relending rate to microenterprise borrowers cannot exceed 30% a year. As of August 2019, the NPL ratio was 5.12% for retail loans and 1.97% for wholesale loans, based on BSP NPL guidelines. As of October 2019, SBC had around 94,000 P3 Program borrowers.

SBC also has regular or corporate-funded wholesale and retail lending programs with the maximum loanable amount of P285 million and P2 million, respectively. According to SBC, demand for MSME credit is growing, but a lack of proper financial records and reports of businesses (such as financial statements and collateral) remain critical barriers for these enterprises to access formal financial services.[106]

Figure 9.4: Public Finance and Guarantees

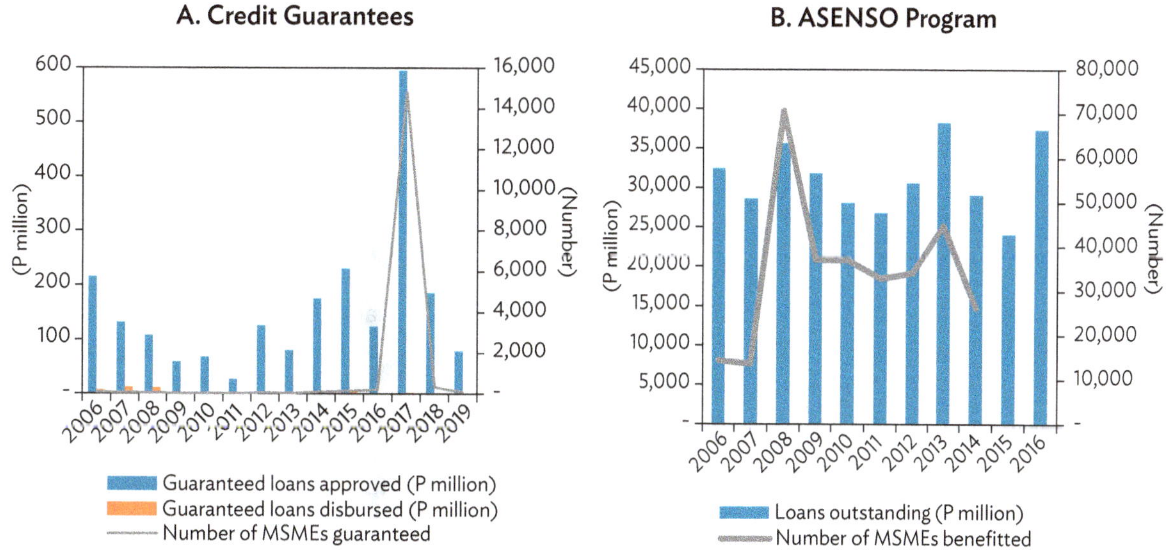

ASENSO = Access of Small Enterprises to Sound Lending Opportunity; MSME = micro, small, and medium-sized enterprise.

In Figure 9.4A, 2019 data are as of August.

Source: ADB Asia SME Monitor 2020 database. Data from Small Business Corporation.

[106] Interview with Small Business Corporation on 10 October 2019.

Nonbank Financing

Nonbank finance institutions (NBFIs) in the Philippines are classified into two types: NBFIs with and without quasi-banking functions. BSP regulates and supervises NBFIs with quasi-banking functions and some NBFIs without quasi-banking functions, such as non-stock savings and loan associations (NSSLAs), pawnshops, and money service businesses (MSBs). The Securities and Exchange Commission (SEC) monitors NBFIs without quasi-banking functions registered with the SEC.

NBFIs with quasi-banking functions are financial institutions that facilitate bank-related financial services, supervised and authorized by BSP (footnote 99). As of end-2019, eight NBFIs with quasi-banking functions (head offices) were operating (two investment houses, five financing companies, and one other NBFI). They posted a modest 1.0% decline in total assets, from P282.2 billion in 2018 to P279.4 billion in 2019, following a decrease in cash and due from banks and investments used to pay off costly borrowings. This partially offset gains from the expansion of the industry's total loan portfolio,[107] which grew 12.8% from P189.9 billion in 2018 to P214.1 billion in 2019. Financing companies with quasi-banking functions accounted for 99.1% (P212.2 billion) of the loan portfolio by NBFIs with quasi-banking functions. The NPL ratio increased to 4.7% in 2019 from 3.9% in 2018.

NBFIs without quasi-banking functions totaled 2,010 firms (head offices) as of end-2019, including 19 financing companies, 18 electronic money issuers, 63 NSSLAs, 1,077 pawnshops, and 785 MSBs.[108] NSSLAs are non-stock and non-profit corporations accumulating members' savings for lending to households by providing long-term financing for home building and/or development, and for personal finance. NSSLAs had combined assets of P205.0 billion in 2019, or 79.1% of total NBFI assets, representing a 15.4% increase over 2018 (P177.1 billion). NSSLA financing outstanding amounted to P213.5 billion as of the second quarter of 2019, an 8.1% increase from end-2018 (Figure 9.5A and Table 9.5).

BSP-registered pawnshops increased by 14.0% in 2019, while MSBs expanded by 24.1%. The emergence of digital platforms creates both new opportunities and risks for pawnshops and MSBs, and is a significant component of their business strategies. They provide access to financial services for the unbanked and underbanked Filipino households and businesses, which make these pawnshops and MSBs vulnerable to credit risk, foreign exchange exposure of foreign exchange departments and money changers, operational risks, and technological risks. Outstanding pawnshop financing amounted to P17.1 billion in 2018, which is small in scale but sharply up (46.6%) from 2017 (Figure 9.5A).

The SEC supervises microfinance nongovernment organizations (microfinance NGOs) as registered nonprofit organizations (besides registered NBFIs without quasi-banking functions). The Microfinance NGOs Act (Republic Act No.10693 of 2015) established the Microfinance NGOs Regulatory Council (MNRC) as an accrediting body for microfinance NGOs. Accreditation started in 2018 but benefits started in 2017. Accredited microfinance NGOs are entitled to a preferred tax rate of 2% on gross receipts from microfinance operations, which was reduced from 5%. The lower tax rate is expected to encourage a shift from informal to formal (SEC-registered) microfinance institutions. As of end-2019, 28 microfinance NGOs were accredited by the MNRC. Accreditation is valid for 3 years. Microfinance NGOs play a critical role in financing MSMEs.

The Cooperative Development Authority (CDA) regulates and supervises cooperatives, including credit unions. As of end-2018, 11,939 credit unions and cooperatives operated in the country. Outstanding financing was P313.3

107 Inclusive of Interbank Loans Receivable.

108 Excludes pawnshops multi-functioning as MSBs.

billion in 2018, a 31.2% increase from 2017 (Figure 9.5B). The ratio of gross NPLs to total loans was 9.4% in 2018, down from 10.4% in 2017.

The nonbank finance industry is small in scale and NBFIs do not specially target MSMEs for financing; however, they are a viable funding source for MSMEs, especially microenterprises and the self-employed.

Figure 9.5: Nonbank Finance

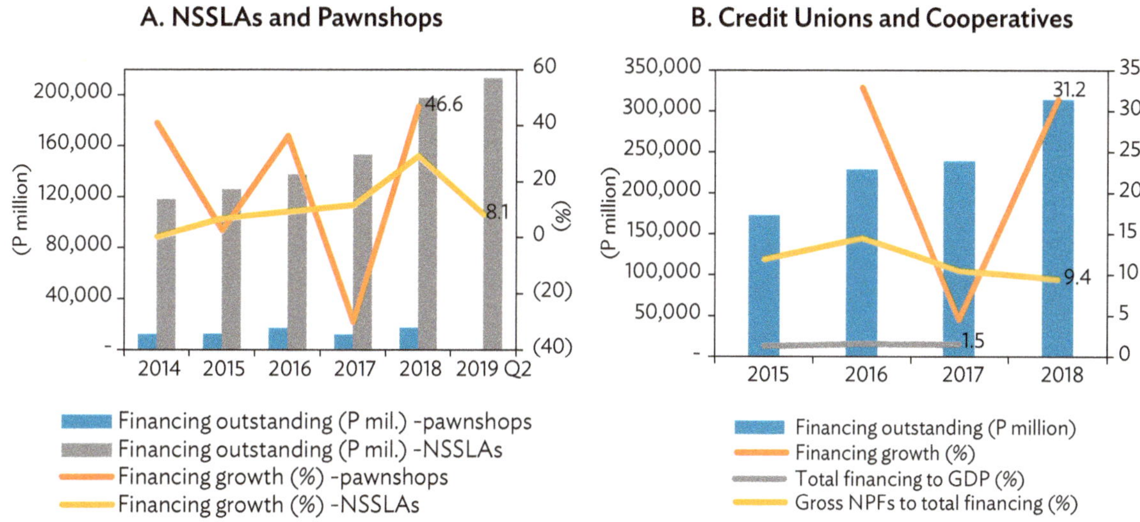

GDP = gross domestic product, NPF = nonperforming finance, NSSLA = non-stock savings and loan association.

Source: ADB Asia SME Monitor 2020 database. Data from Bangko Sentral ng Pilipinas.

Digital Financial Services

Advanced technology plays a critical role in catalyzing the development of financial products and services—to increase access to finance for the traditionally unserved and underserved segments of society and enterprises. BSP is promoting the establishment of a digital financial ecosystem as part of its financial inclusion strategy. It focuses on three strategic pillars: (i) an efficient retail payment system that facilitates delivery of digital financial services; (ii) an expansive network of low-cost nodes, or "touch points," to attract new clients, facilitate digitization, disburse cash, and provide access to other financial transactions; and (iii) a democratized access to a transaction account wherein every person is able to open an account and use digital financial services. BSP has issued regulations and supportive legislation that form the foundation for digital financial inclusion.

a. Efficient retail payment system

The National Payment Systems Act (Republic Act No.11127 Series of 2018) is landmark legislation that provides a comprehensive legal and regulatory framework for payment systems.[109] BSP uses the National Retail Payment System (Circular No.980 Series of 2017) framework to promote interoperability—to allow digital financial

[109] The National Payment Systems Act mandates BSP to oversee payment systems in the Philippines and use its supervisory and regulatory powers to ensure the stability and effectiveness of the monetary and financial system.

transactions to be sent and received from one account to any other account, whether held in a bank or e-money issuer. As of April 2020, there were over 50 PESONet (batch electronic fund transfer) and over 40 InstaPay (real-time, low-value electronic fund transfer) participants.[110]

The BSP also issued policies (Circular No.1055 Series of 2019) on standardizing a national quick response (QR) code to promote interoperable QR payment services. In November 2019, a pilot peer-to-peer payment structure using standardized "QRPh" codes was launched in collaboration with the payments industry.

b. Expansive network of low-cost touch points

Cash agent (Circular No.940 Series of 2017) and branch-lite unit (Circular No.987 Series of 2017) regulations allow banks to overcome hurdles in establishing physical presence in every location of the country. Cash agents allow banks to serve clients by accepting and disbursing cash for, and on behalf of, the bank. Branch-lite units provide a wide range of products and services depending on the market needs of a specific locality. In 2019, there were over 17,000 cash agents operating in the country.[111] And there were over 2,000 branch-lite units in 871 local government units, 195 of which served solely by a branch-lite unit.

c. Democratized access to a transactional account

The Philippine Identification System (PhilSys) is a national identification (ID) system for all citizens and resident foreigners in the country, simplifying public and private transactions. PhilSys is designed to attract the unbanked to join the financial system. This can be an important tool for client onboarding, especially for those currently unable to open a formal account due to lack of an acceptable ID (see financial Infrastructure section).

BSP also issued a framework for basic deposit accounts (Circular No.992 Series of 2018) to simplify ownership of a transaction account, considered the cornerstone of financial inclusion. Basic deposit accounts meet the need of the unbanked for a low-cost, no-frills account.[112] As of the fourth quarter of 2019, there were 119 banks offering basic deposit accounts to four million depositors with total deposits amounting to P3.5 billion. In addition, BSP updated reduced know-your-customer rules for certain low-risk accounts and applies technology for face-to-face contract requirements (Circular No.950 Series of 2017). It also allows the acceptance of national IDs for the client onboarding process.

Capital Markets

The Philippine Stock Exchange (PSE) created the Small and Medium Enterprise Board (SME Board) in July 2001, with one listed company, establishing a three-board system together with the First Board and Second Board. In June 2013, the PSE stock market was reorganized into a two-board system: a Main Board and Small, Medium, and Emerging Board (SME Board, the same name as the previous board). The revamped SME Board strengthened listing rules to remove non-SME listing. The definition of SMEs in the capital market differs from the national definition, and is based on the size of capital and profitability (earnings before interest, taxes, depreciation, and amortization [EBITDA]). There are three underwriters operating in the SME Board.

110 Under PESONet, fund transfers and/or payment instructions are processed in bulk and cleared at batch intervals, enabling each payee to receive the full value in their account within the same banking day (provided the payment instruction was sent prior to the cut-off time). InstaPay is designed to facilitate small value payments particularly useful for purchasing retail goods, paying toll fees and tickets, and for e-commerce, helping MSMEs, among others.

111 Preliminary data for 2019 based on banks implementing/piloting the cash agent model.

112 Features of the basic deposit account include low opening amount capped at P100, no maintaining balance, no dormancy charges, and simplified identification requirements.

The SME equity market is small with low liquidity. As of end-2019, the market capitalization of the SME Board was P11.6 billion with an annual trading value of P8.6 billion (Figure 9.6A and Table 9.6). Five companies were listed on the SME Board at the time, one listed in August 2019 (Figure 9.6B). Three companies successfully migrated from the SME Board to the Main Board (in 2007, 2009, and 2015). The total market capitalization of the SME Board increased sharply from P871 million in 2013 to P34.5 billion in 2014 due to two large-scale initial public offerings (IPOs) in 2014 (Double Dragon Properties and mobile technology firm Xurpas); however, Double Dragon Properties moved to the main board in 2015, contributing to a drop in market capitalization of the SME Board that year. The typical issuing size on the SME Board is P400 million-P500 million, and mainly for land acquisition or technology upgrading.

The listing requirements in the SME Board are concessional as compared to the Main Board (Table 9.7). A company applying for SME Board listing must have a minimum authorized capital stock of P100 million (P500 million on the Main Board), of which at least 25% is subscribed and fully paid. It must have a minimum of 200 stockholders (1,000 for Main Board listing). The applicant should also have a cumulative EBITDA of at least P15 million (P50 million for Main Board listing) for the 3 fiscal years immediately preceding the listing application. Applicants for SME Board are mostly technology-based or food service firms. Due to the small number of listed companies on the SME Board, the PSE is working on easing listing rules to attract more SMEs to the board while addressing investor protection.[113] The PSE offers capital market literacy and training programs to potential SME issuers in partnership with the Development Bank of the Philippines, PCCI, and other private sector organizations.

As a public-private partnership between the DOST, DTI, J.P.Morgan, and Ideaspace Foundation, the QBO Innovation Hub was launched in 2016 to support creating a Philippine start-up ecosystem and offer incubation programs for start-ups. As of September 2019, around 400 start-ups had signed up for QBO, which helps develop the potential base of issuers for the SME Board.

Figure 9.6: Equity Market

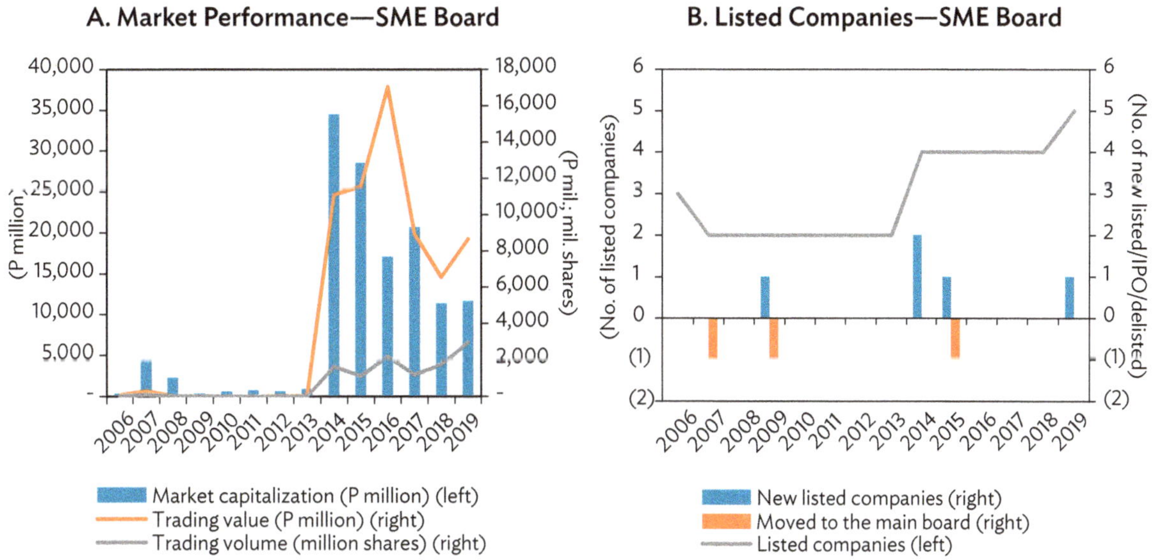

SME =small and medium-sized enterprise.

Source: ADB Asia SME Monitor 2020 database. Data from Philippine Stock Exchange.

[113] Interview with the Philippine Stock Exchange on 24 September 2019.

Financial Infrastructure

The Philippines' credit bureau system and secured lending legal system are key credit infrastructure supporting MSME access to finance.

The Credit Information Corporation was founded in 2008 under the Credit Information Systems Act of 2008 (Republic Act No.9510). It compiles basic credit data as a central repository and offers standardized information on credit history and financial conditions of corporate and personal borrowers for member financial institutions. Its credit data are collected from various sources including banks, insurance firms, credit card firms, credit cooperatives, and utility companies. It operates under the SEC and is supervised by the Governance Commission for Government Owned and Controlled Corporations.

The Personal Property Security Act (Republic Act No.11057) was enacted in August 2018 to allow financial institutions to use movable assets (such as receivables, equipment, inventory, and intellectual property rights) as collateral for MSME loans and to strengthen the country's financial infrastructure with a centralized electronic registry on personal property. The electronic registry was established under the Land Registration Authority.

BSP and the CDA continue to work on promoting strong and effective Credit Surety Fund cooperatives. These funds offer a maximum 80% surety cover for loans granted by banks to borrowers that typically have difficulty in accessing credit. Credit Surety Funds are in the process of registering as fund cooperatives under the Credit Surety Funds Act (R.A. No. 10744 Series of 2015).

The Philippine Identification System Act or the PhilSys Law (Republic Act No.11055 Series of 2017) gives Filipinos and foreign residents a unique, trusted, verifiable biometric-based digital identity. This will be required to participate in and benefit from the digital finance ecosystem being developed. Not only will it address the persistent issue on the lack of acceptable IDs, but it can also boost account ownership by enabling remote and more seamless onboarding. PhilSys will also enable online identity verification that can support the digitalization of financial services.

The Credit Risk Database (CRD) will help generate scoring models predicting the creditworthiness of MSMEs. This will improve their access to finance through risk-based lending and lessen the dependence of banks on collateral. Preparatory activities such as bank interviews and preparatory surveys to understand the volume and nature of data, and organization of a project implementation unit are underway (as of June 2020).

3. Policies and Regulations

- The Micro, Small, and Medium Enterprise Development (MSMED) Council plays a key role in creating a mid-term MSME development strategy; the MSME Development Plan 2017–2022 strategically focuses on improving the business climate, accessing finance, enhancing management and labor capacities, accessing technology and innovation, and accessing markets.
- Ongoing corporate income tax and incentives reform benefits MSMEs, given that a high corporate income tax is a heavy burden on MSME operations.
- DOST offers several programs that help MSMEs upgrade their technology as well as provide soft loans for financing start-ups and innovative MSMEs.
- The National Strategy for Financial Inclusion promotes effective access to diversified financing options across socioeconomic segments, including MSMEs, with a centralized coordination body to implement and monitor strategic actions.

MSME Development

The 1991 Magna Carta for MSMEs (Republic Act No.6977) was the core legal framework to set up a coordination body and agency to support MSME development and entrepreneurship. It was amended three times (Republic Acts No.8289 of 1997, No.9501 of 2008, and No.10644 of 2014), and legally expired on 16 June 2018. However, in practical terms, it remains at least partially valid. The Magna Carta has three main components: (i) creation of the Micro, Small, and Medium Enterprise Development Council (MSMED Council); (ii) creation of the Small Business Corporation (SBC); and (iii) a 10% mandatory lending allocation for MSMEs. While the mandatory lending scheme expired with the Magna Carta, the Philippine Innovation Act of 2019 set a new mandatory scheme for innovative start-ups and MSMEs.

The MSMED Council helps create the mid-term MSME development strategy. The latest is the MSME Development Plan 2017–2022. It was developed in line with the long-term national development vision by 2040 called "AmBisyon Natin 2040" formulated by the National Economic and Development Authority in March 2016. The MSME Development Plan 2017–2022 has three focal areas: (i) business environment, (ii) business capacity, and (iii) business opportunities. These pillars have five thematic strategies.

The business environment focal area addresses two strategies: (i) improve the business climate to better deliver MSME assistance services, streamline business permits and licensing, and reduce the regulatory burden for MSMEs; and (ii) improve access to finance to simplify MSME loan requirements, build capacities of financial institutions, provide financial literacy training for MSMEs, and promote alternative financing models for MSMEs. The business capacity focal area adds two strategies: (iii) enhance management and labor capacities to promote entrepreneurship, equal opportunities for women and youth, human resource development, and advocacy campaigns on MSME-related policies and regulations; and (iv) improve access to technology and innovation to promote internationally harmonized industry performance standards, MSME clustering, and the commercialization of technology. The third focal area on business opportunities adds one more: (v) improve access to markets by establishing mechanisms that facilitate MSME regulatory compliance and promotes their participation in market promotion activities and e-commerce.

The Barangay Micro Business Enterprises (BMBE) Act of 2002 (Republic Act No.9178) offers several preferential treatments and assistance services for BMBEs, including (i) tax exemptions, (ii) exemptions from the coverage of the minimum wage law, (iii) a special credit window for BMBEs, (iv) training on technology transfer and management, and (v) marketing and trade promotion.

The Bureau of Small and Medium Enterprise Development (BSMED) under the DTI is an implementing agency for government programs and policies related to MSME development. BSMED is also the secretariat of the MSMED Council, a coordinating body of national policies and strategies on MSME development. BSMED monitors MSMEs through regional networks of business support centers for MSMEs called "Negosyo Centers" located in all provinces and municipalities. The Negosyo Centers were created under the Go Negosyo Act of 2014 (Republic Act No.10644). As of September 2019, around 1,700 Negosyo Centers operated across the country, offering online registration and assistance services for MSMEs. BSMED uses the client profile monitoring system (CPMS) operated by DTI to collect MSME data.

The Department of Finance does not target MSMEs specifically in its policy support, but ongoing comprehensive tax reform programs include certain benefits for MSMEs. The department is leading the Tax Reform for Acceleration and Inclusion. The regulation on Package 1 of the tax reform program (Republic Act No.10963) was enacted in December 2017 and implemented in January 2018. It lowered personal income taxes and simplified taxes for small and micro self-employed businesses (an 8% flat tax rate on gross sales and reduced payment frequency from 8 to 4 times). A Package 2 dealing with corporate income taxes and incentives reform was being discussed by Congress as of end-2019.[114] It proposes to gradually lower the corporate income tax rate from 30% to 20%—by 1% annually through 2029—as the Philippines has the highest corporate income tax rate among Association of Southeast Asian Nations (ASEAN) economies. Package 2 targets all enterprises and benefits MSMEs as well, given the heavy burden taxes bring to operations.

The DOST offers several programs supporting MSMEs in upgrading technology. The Small Enterprise Technology Upgrading Program (SET-UP), started in 1992, was a DOST initiative helping small enterprise business development. It ended in 2019, with DOST planning to relaunch an improved program (as SET-UP 2.0). The program supported around 45,000 MSMEs from 1992 to 2007 (latest available data), covering food, furniture, gifts, decor, handicrafts, horticulture, aquaculture, health products, and information and communications technology. DOST established innovation centers in every region to support local MSMEs develop innovative products and services. It helps MSMEs connect research and development (R&D) firms through its Collaborative Research and Development to Leverage Philippine Economy (CRADLE) Program.

DOST also has a soft loan program for financing start-ups and innovative MSMEs that develop new technology for business, known as the Venture Financing Program. On average, the financing program supports 5–10 projects a year, with maximum financing per project at P2 million with average financing of P300,000–P1.5 million. It offers zero-interest rate loans payable in 3 years with 6-month grace period. From its start in 1992 to the end of 2019, the financing program assisted more than 100 MSMEs. Funded start-ups and MSMEs must share their licenses of technology developed through the program with DOST. Participating firms are mostly export-oriented food businesses and fabrication companies. Some are also aligned with the wood and decor industries, health-related test kits, and other science and technology-based enterprises.

114 Package 2 is being deliberated in the Senate plenary. The Department of Finance proposed some changes to the proposal including the following that would benefit MSMEs: (i) an accelerated reduction of corporate income tax rate - immediate cut from 30% to 25% and (ii) extended availment of net operating loss carry-over (NOLCO) from 3 years to 5 years for losses incurred in 2020 (as of May 2020).

Financial Inclusion

BSP continues to create an enabling policy environment for financial inclusion, along with organized public and private sector support through its National Strategy for Financial Inclusion (NSFI). The NSFI, launched in July 2015, promotes effective access to diversified financing options across all socioeconomic segments, especially the traditionally unserved and underserved, including low-income households and MSMEs. The NSFI has four strategic pillars: (i) policies and regulations that facilitate access to a wide range of financial products and services for all, (ii) financial education and consumer protection, (iii) advocacy programs, and (iv) data collection and measurement for proper monitoring. It offers a comprehensive framework for financial inclusion through close coordination and cooperation between public and private sectors, addressing access, usage, and the quality of financial products and services, resulting in enhanced welfare across all socioeconomic segments.

As the governing body tasked to drive NSFI implementation, the Financial Inclusion Steering Committee (FISC)[115] adopted two focal areas: (i) digital finance; and (ii) agriculture value chain finance. FISC has harnessed the NSFI as a platform to deepen collaboration for initiatives in financial education, digital IDs, use of transaction accounts, digital payments, agriculture value chains, and MSME financing.

FISC wants to ensure more Filipinos can open and regularly use a digital transaction account, so they can fully participate and benefits from an inclusive digital finance ecosystem. BSP is working with the Department of Labor and Employment to promote transaction accounts for paying worker salaries and for disbursements. Similarly, BSP is actively working with the Department of Social Welfare and Development to facilitate the adoption of transaction accounts for disbursing government cash transfers.

BSP has secured ADB support for a pilot agriculture value chain finance project to increase interest and the capacity of banks to undertake value chain financing. Under this initiative, strong value chains will allow farmers and agribusiness MSMEs to adopt modern technologies and access high-value markets, thereby increasing productivity and income.

The BSP was also able to secure support from the Japan International Cooperation Agency to develop a CRD in the country. By predicting the creditworthiness of MSMEs, the CRD can lessen the dependence of banks on collateral and promote MSME financing.

Other ongoing efforts for MSME development include capacity development among Negosyo Center business counsellors and financial literacy for their MSME clients. The development and design of a dedicated MSME survey is also in the pipeline to generate new and more granular data on MSMEs to support evidence-based policymaking and provide market insight for financial service providers. There are likewise ongoing discussions to implement a digital supply chain finance platform that can help deploy bank funds to smaller firms that banks may be unable or unwilling to serve using a traditional financing approach.

115 The FISC was established in June 2016 under the President Executive Order No.208 of 2016. It includes 19 government agencies as members, with BSP as the chair and secretariat.

Data Tables

Table 9.1: MSME Definition

Item	Micro	Small	Medium
Total assets excluding land*	Up to P3 million	More than P3 million to P15 million	More than P15 million to P100 million
Number of employees**	1–9	10–99	100–199

MSME = micro, small, and medium-sized enterprise.

* Legislated definition of MSMEs as provided by the Small and Medium Enterprise Development Council Resolution No.01 Series of 2003 dated 16 January 2003. ** Definition used by the Philippine Statistics Authority.

Source: ADB Asia SME Monitor 2020 database. Data from Magna Carta for Micro, Small and Medium Enterprises; Bureau of Micro, Small and Medium Enterprise Development; and National Statistics Office.

Table 9.2: MSME Landscape

End of period data

Item	2006	2007	2008	2009	2010	2011	2012	2013	2014	2015	2016	2017	2018	2019
NUMBER OF ENTERPRISES														
Number of enterprises, total	783,065	783,869	761,409	780,437	777,687	820,255	944,897	941,174	946,988	900,914	915,726	924,721	1,003,111	--
Number of MSMEs	780,469	781,201	758,436	777,357	774,664	816,759	940,886	937,327	942,925	896,839	911,768	920,677	998,342	--
Micro	720,191	720,084	697,077	710,822	709,899	743,250	844,764	846,817	851,756	806,609	820,795	828,436	887,272	--
Small	57,439	58,198	58,292	63,529	61,979	70,222	92,027	86,762	87,283	86,367	86,955	88,412	106,175	--
Medium	2,839	2,919	3,067	3,006	2,786	3,287	4,095	3,748	3,886	3,863	4,018	3,829	4,895	--
Number of large enterprises	2,596	2,668	2,973	3,080	3,023	3,496	4,011	3,847	4,063	4,075	3,958	4,044	4,769	--
MSME to total (%)	99.7	99.7	99.6	99.6	99.6	99.6	99.6	99.6	99.6	99.5	99.6	99.6	99.5	--
MSME growth (%)	--	0.1	(2.9)	2.5	(0.3)	5.4	15.2	(0.4)	0.6	(4.9)	1.7	1.0	8.4	--
MSMEs by sector (% share)														
Agriculture, forestry, and fisheries	0.7	0.7	0.7	0.7	0.6	0.6	0.9	0.9	0.9	0.9	1.0	1.0	0.9	--
Manufacturing	14.9	14.9	14.7	14.4	14.4	13.7	12.5	12.5	12.5	12.7	12.7	12.6	11.7	--
Transportation and communication	--	--	--	--	--	--	--	--	--	--	--	--	--	--
Construction	--	--	--	--	--	--	--	--	--	--	--	--	--	--
Wholesale and retail trade	50.1	50.1	49.9	49.6	49.7	47.0	46.4	46.4	46.4	46.2	46.1	46.0	46.3	--
Other services	33.7	33.8	34.2	34.8	34.8	38.1	39.4	39.5	39.6	39.2	39.5	39.6	40.5	--
Others*	0.5	0.5	0.5	0.5	0.5	0.6	0.8	0.7	0.7	0.7	0.7	0.7	0.8	--
Number of MSMEs by region (% share)														
Capital city	25	25	26	27	27	26	22.4	22	22	21	20.4	21	20.4	--
Others	75	75	74	73	73	74	77.6	78	78	79	79.6	79	79.6	--
EMPLOYMENT														
Number of employment, total	4,984,883	5,187,793	5,544,590	5,689,939	5,669,297	6,345,742	7,598,591	7,489,611	7,789,257	7,766,689	7,710,908	7,832,089	9,043,063	--
Number of employment by MSMEs	3,327,855	3,355,742	3,395,505	3,595,641	3,532,935	3,872,406	4,930,851	4,770,445	4,891,836	4,784,870	4,879,179	4,922,251	5,714,262	--
Micro	1,667,824	1,661,884	1,663,382	1,731,082	1,729,100	1,778,353	2,316,664	2,326,509	2,372,678	2,285,634	2,345,992	2,369,748	2,610,221	--
Small	1,279,018	1,297,792	1,314,065	1,449,033	1,417,672	1,642,492	2,061,090	1,932,857	1,986,823	1,968,452	1,981,316	2,024,470	2,445,111	--
Medium	381,013	396,066	418,058	415,526	386,163	451,561	553,097	511,079	532,335	530,784	551,871	528,033	658,930	--
Number of employment by large enterprises	1,657,028	1,832,051	2,149,085	2,094,298	2,136,362	2,473,336	2,667,740	2,719,166	2,897,421	2,981,819	2,831,729	2,909,838	3,328,801	--
MSME employees to total (%)	66.8	64.7	61.2	63.2	62.3	61.0	64.9	63.7	62.8	61.6	63.3	62.8	63.2	--
MSME employees growth (%)	--	0.8	1.2	5.9	(1.7)	9.6	27.3	(3.3)	2.5	(2.2)	2.0	0.9	16.1	--
Share of female employees to total employees (%)	38.7	38.8	38.5	39.0	39.2	39.3	39.2	39.3	39.5	39.6	38.9	37.9	38.2	--
Employment by MSME by sector (% share)														
Agriculture, forestry, and fisheries	2.3	2.3	2.2	2.0	2.0	1.8	2.2	2.2	2.2	2.2	2.1	2.1	1.9	--
Manufacturing	19.4	19.5	18.7	17.7	17.5	16.7	16.6	16.5	16.1	16.0	15.6	15.3	13.4	--
Transportation and communication	--	--	--	--	--	--	--	--	--	--	--	--	--	--
Construction	--	--	--	--	--	--	--	--	--	--	--	--	--	--
Wholesale and retail trade	35.5	35.3	35.1	34.8	35.0	33.9	35.7	35.8	35.5	35.7	35.5	35.4	35.7	--
Other services	40.3	40.3	41.4	42.7	42.7	44.7	42.5	42.5	43.1	43.0	43.6	44.0	46.0	--
Others*	2.5	2.5	2.5	2.8	2.8	2.9	3.0	3.1	3.2	3.2	3.2	3.2	3.0	--
Employment by MSMEs by region (% share)														
Capital city	35.3	35.6	35.8	37.8	37.5	37.2	32.0	31.5	31.8	30.8	29.6	30.1	28.4	--
Others	64.7	64.4	64.2	62.2	62.5	62.8	68.0	68.5	68.2	69.2	70.4	69.9	71.6	--
CONTRIBUTION TO GDP**														
MSME contribution to GDP (P million)	751,943	--	--	--	--	--	--	--	--	--	--	--	--	--
MSME contribution to GDP (% share)	35.7	--	--	--	--	--	--	--	--	--	--	--	--	--
MSME GDP growth (%)	--	--	--	--	--	--	--	--	--	--	--	--	--	--
MSME GDP by sector (% share)***														
Agriculture, forestry, and fisheries	1.0	--	--	--	--	--	--	--	--	--	--	--	--	--
Manufacturing	19.3	--	--	--	--	--	--	--	--	--	--	--	--	--
Transportation and communication	--	--	--	--	--	--	--	--	--	--	--	--	--	--
Construction	--	--	--	--	--	--	--	--	--	--	--	--	--	--
Wholesale and retail trade	18.4	--	--	--	--	--	--	--	--	--	--	--	--	--
Other services	41.9	--	--	--	--	--	--	--	--	--	--	--	--	--
Others	19.3	--	--	--	--	--	--	--	--	--	--	--	--	--
MSME GDP by region (% share)														
Capital city	--	--	--	--	--	--	--	--	--	--	--	--	--	--
Others	--	--	--	--	--	--	--	--	--	--	--	--	--	--
EXPORTS														
Total export value (P million)	2,920,983	2,981,846	2,849,943	2,587,015	3,133,507	3,109,661	3,254,826	3,232,795	3,652,888	3,782,890	4,069,198	4,904,037	5,521,318	5,594,831
Total export growth (%)	--	2.1	(4.4)	(9.2)	21.1	(0.8)	4.7	(0.7)	13.0	3.6	7.6	20.5	12.6	1.3
MSME export value (P million)	--	--	--	--	--	--	--	--	--	--	--	--	--	--
MSME export to total export value (%)	--	--	--	--	--	--	--	--	--	--	--	--	--	--
MSME export growth (%)	--	--	--	--	--	--	--	--	--	--	--	--	--	--
IMPORTS														
Total import value (P million)	3,032,905	2,988,588	3,039,737	2,677,363	3,296,732	3,462,678	3,599,262	3,718,554	4,113,553	4,568,699	5,416,117	6,460,981	7,732,833	7,839,162
Total import growth (%)	--	(1.5)	1.7	(11.9)	23.1	5.0	3.9	3.3	10.6	11.1	18.5	19.3	19.7	1.4
MSME import value (P million)	--	--	--	--	--	--	--	--	--	--	--	--	--	--
MSME import to total import value (%)	--	--	--	--	--	--	--	--	--	--	--	--	--	--
MSME import growth (%)	--	--	--	--	--	--	--	--	--	--	--	--	--	--

GDP = gross domestic product; MSME = micro, small, and medium-sized enterprise.

* Includes construction, electricity, gas and water supply, and mining.

** Based on gross value added (GVA) which refers to the total payment to factors of production, i.e., wages, interest, profits, and rents. It also includes capital consumption allowance and indirect taxes.

*** Based on GVA; computation based on available data in the MSME Development Plan 2011-2016.

Source: ADB Asia SME Monitor 2020 database. Data from Philippine Statistics Authority, Bureau of Small and Medium Enterprise Development, and MSME Development Plan 2011-2016.

Table 9.3: Bank Credit

End of period data

Item	2008	2009	2010	2011	2012	2013	2014	2015	2016	2017	2018	2019
COMMERCIAL BANKS[1]												
Number of operating banks, total	--	785	758	726	696	673	648	632	602	587	571	547
Universal and commercial banks	--	38	38	38	37	36	36	40	42	43	45	46
Thrift banks	--	73	73	71	70	71	69	68	60	55	54	50
Rural and cooperative banks	--	674	647	617	589	566	543	524	500	489	472	451
Credit												
Loans outstanding, total (P million)	--	--	--	--	3,630,906	4,259,771	5,116,991	5,820,814	6,856,476	8,100,477	9,282,980	9,716,174
Loans outstanding in domestic currency (P million)	--	--	--	--	--	--	--	--	--	--	--	--
Loans outstanding in foreign currency (P million)	--	--	--	--	--	--	--	--	--	--	--	--
Loan growth (%)	--	--	--	--	--	17.3	20.1	13.8	17.8	18.1	14.6	4.7
Total bank loans to GDP (%)[2]	--	--	--	--	34.4	36.9	40.5	43.7	47.4	51.2	53.3	52.2
Lending rate (%)[3]	8.8	8.5	7.7	6.6	5.7	5.8	5.5	5.6	5.6	5.6	6.1	7.1
Gross nonperforming loans (NPLs) (P million)	119,259	114,903	116,899	106,095	105,309	135,543	134,831	136,504	144,158	152,985	177,845	224,105
Gross NPLs to total loans (%)[4]	4.1	3.6	3.6	2.8	2.5	2.8	2.3	2.1	1.9	1.7	1.8	2.0
Deposits												
Deposits, total (P million)	--	--	--	--	5,753,629	7,608,868	8,524,553	9,231,344	10,506,562	11,726,967	12,764,135	13,669,469
Deposits in domestic currency (P million)	--	--	--	--	--	--	--	--	--	--	--	--
Deposits in foreign currency (P million)	--	--	--	--	--	--	--	--	--	--	--	--
Deposit rate (%)[5]	2.2	2.1	1.6	1.6	1.3	0.8	0.6	0.7	0.7	0.7	0.9	1.2
MSME LOANS[1]												
MSME loans outstanding, total (P million)	270,526	257,894	311,452	351,693	384,082	395,031	425,155	461,650	496,863	532,198	577,719	588,837
MSME loans to total loans outstanding (%)	11.6	10.6	11.7	11.0	10.6	9.3	8.3	7.9	7.2	6.6	6.2	6.1
MSME loans to GDP (%)[6]	3.5	3.2	3.5	3.6	3.6	3.4	3.4	3.5	3.4	3.4	3.3	3.2
MSME loan growth (%)	--	(4.7)	20.8	12.9	9.2	2.9	7.6	8.6	7.6	7.1	8.6	1.9
MSME lending rate (%)	--	--	--	--	--	--	--	--	--	--	--	--
Nonperforming MSME loans (NPLs) (P million)	--	--	23,656	26,078	25,347	25,512	25,097	25,209	26,217	25,989	30,030	32,020
MSME NPLs to total MSME loans (%)	--	--	7.6	7.4	6.6	6.5	5.9	5.5	5.3	4.9	5.2	5.8
Number of MSME loan borrowers	432,061	749,111	1,140,207	792,965	902,681	836,651	1,466,675	1,589,185	1,642,865	1,603,181	1,712,488	1,651,501
MSME loan borrowers to total bank borrowers (%)	--	--	--	--	--	--	--	--	--	--	--	--
MSME loan rejection rate (% of total applications)	--	--	--	--	--	--	--	--	--	--	--	--
Number of MSME savings account in banks	--	--	--	--	--	--	--	--	--	--	--	--
Guaranteed MSME loans (P million)	--	--	--	--	--	--	--	--	--	--	--	--
Non-collateral MSME loans (P million)	--	--	--	--	--	--	--	--	--	--	--	--
MSME loans outstanding by sector (% share)												
Agriculture, forestry, and fisheries	--	--	--	--	--	--	--	--	--	--	--	--
Manufacturing	--	--	--	--	--	--	--	--	--	--	--	--
Transportation and communication	--	--	--	--	--	--	--	--	--	--	--	--
Construction	--	--	--	--	--	--	--	--	--	--	--	--
Wholesale and retail trade	--	--	--	--	--	--	--	--	--	--	--	--
Other services	--	--	--	--	--	--	--	--	--	--	--	--
Others	--	--	--	--	--	--	--	--	--	--	--	--
MSME loans outstanding by region (% share)												
Capital city	--	--	--	--	--	--	--	--	--	--	--	--
Others	--	--	--	--	--	--	--	--	--	--	--	--
MSME loans outstanding by type of use (% share)												
For working capital	--	--	--	--	--	--	--	--	--	--	--	--
For capital investment	--	--	--	--	--	--	--	--	--	--	--	--
MSME loans outstanding by tenor (% share)												
Less than 1 year	--	--	--	--	--	--	--	--	--	--	--	--
1-5 years	--	--	--	--	--	--	--	--	--	--	--	--
More than 5 years	--	--	--	--	--	--	--	--	--	--	--	--

GDP = gross domestic product; MSME = micro, small, and medium-sized enterprise.
1. Pertains to Philippine Banking System data.
2. Computed as total loan portfolio over GDP (at current prices).
3. Refers to bank average lending rate.
4. Computed as gross NPL over gross total loan portfolio.
5. Refers to savings deposit rate.
6. Percentage of MSME loans to GDP (at current prices).
Source: ADB Asia SME Monitor 2020 database. Data from Bangko Sentral ng Pilipinas.

Table 9.3a: Compliance with MSME Loans Required

End of period data

Item	2008	2009	2010	2011	2012	2013	2014	2015	2016	2017	2018	2019
Net loan portfolio (P million)	1,637,533	1,728,628	1,881,138	2,303,436	2,912,347	3,309,653	4,003,526	4,702,652	5,462,190	6,438,258	7,495,487	8,148,659
Min. amount required to be set aside (P million)*	163,753	172,863	188,114	230,344	291,235	330,965	400,353	470,265	546,219	643,826	749,549	814,866
Total funds set aside for MSMEs (P million)	310,882	309,356	308,554	348,915	387,681	387,031	440,173	495,779	505,082	537,638	574,784	579,130
Compliance Ratio												
Compliance for MSEs (%)	10.0	9.7	8.5	7.6	6.4	5.6	4.9	4.4	3.8	3.3	3.1	2.8
Universal and commercial banks	7.1	7.1	6.8	5.8	5.3	4.6	4.0	3.4	3.0	2.7	2.5	2.3
Thrift banks	16.4	16.1	14.0	16.2	11.3	9.8	7.4	7.1	6.6	5.4	4.9	4.5
Rural and cooperative banks	51.8	41.1	34.1	29.6	22.3	26.0	24.8	23.2	22.0	22.3	24.0	24.3
Compliance for MEs (%)	9.0	8.2	7.9	7.6	6.9	6.1	6.1	6.2	5.4	5.0	4.6	4.3
Universal and commercial banks	8.3	7.9	7.7	7.4	6.7	5.9	5.8	5.7	5.2	4.9	4.4	4.1
Thrift banks	12.9	8.9	8.6	8.0	7.8	7.0	7.6	8.4	6.3	5.5	5.0	4.9
Rural and cooperative banks	11.4	12.8	12.0	10.5	9.5	11.2	9.1	10.3	10.0	10.5	10.6	12.0

ME = medium-sized enterprise; MSE = micro and small enterprise; MSME = micro, small, and medium-sized enterprise.
* 8% of net loan portfolio to MSEs and 2% to MEs. Note: Compliance required under the Republic Act No.6977 (amended by R.A. No.8289 and No.9501).
Source: ADB Asia SME Monitor 2020 database. Data from Bangko Sentral ng Pilipinas.

Table 9.3b: Microfinance Exposures of Microfinance-Oriented and Engaged Banks

End of period data

Item	2012	2013	2014	2015	2016	2017	2018	2019
Number of banks with microfinance operations	187	182	176	170	168	162	159	154
Number of microfinance borrowers	1,137,813	1,049,988	1,229,825	1,471,896	1,686,152	1,956,276	1,986,683	2,410,677
Amount of microfinancing portfolio (P million)	8,414	8,701	11,373	11,256	13,741	17,111	22,615	27,295
Growth (%)	--	3.4	30.7	(1.0)	22.1	24.5	32.2	20.7
Savings component (P million)	6,432	3,065	3,708	4,465	5,660	7,676	9,527	10,755
Growth (%)	--	(52.3)	21.0	20.4	26.8	35.6	24.1	12.9
Loans by Purpose								
Microenterprise loans (P million)	6,926	7,377	9,396	9,763	11,957	14,235	18,641	22,880
Microfinance plus (P million)	83	111	217	356	404	777	969	1,163
Micro-agri loans (P million)	496	295	343	288	303	721	1,092	1,327
Micro-housing loans (P million)	242	263	334	615	876	1,003	1,396	1,535
Others (P million)	667	655	1,083	234	201	376	517	389
Total (P million)	8,414	8,701	11,373	11,256	13,741	17,111	22,615	27,295

Source: ADB Asia SME Monitor 2020 database. Data from Bangko Sentral ng Pilipinas.

Table 9.3c: Retail Loans to Barangay Micro Business Enterprises

End of period data

Item	2013	2014	2015	2016	2017	2018	2019
Number of banks servicing BMBEs, total					8	20	20
Universal and commercial banks	--	--	--	--	1	1	1
Thrift banks*	--	--	--	--	1	1	1
Rural and cooperative banks*	--	--	--	--	6	18	18
BMBE loans outstanding, total (P million)					58.0	188.3	74.9
Universal and commercial banks	--	--	--	--	5.9	5.1	5.3
Thrift banks*	--	--	--	--	0.5	0.6	0.7
Rural and cooperative banks*	--	--	--	--	51.7	182.7	68.9
Number of BMBE borrowers, total	26,195	3,466	3,072	1,787	2,530	4,467	4,050
Universal and commercial banks	--	2	3	4	8	7	7
Thrift banks*	25,364	116	110	112	98	107	113
Rural and cooperative banks*	831	3,348	2,959	1,671	2,424	4,353	3,930
Number of non-BMBE borrowers, total	836,651	1,466,675	1,589,185	1,642,865	1,603,181	1,712,488	1,651,501
Universal and commercial banks	199,072	174,064	182,868	193,256	185,361	217,197	91,156
Thrift banks*	136,777	167,208	307,595	283,795	236,010	237,603	275,458
Rural and cooperative banks*	500,802	1,125,403	1,098,722	1,165,814	1,181,810	1,257,688	1,284,887
Number of borrowers - grand total	862,846	1,470,141	1,592,257	1,644,652	1,605,711	1,716,955	1,655,551

* Reporting banks only.

Source: ADB Asia SME Monitor 2020 database. Data from Bangko Sentral ng Pilipinas.

Table 9.4: Public Finance and Guarantees

End of period data

Item	2006	2007	2008	2009	2010	2011	2012	2013	2014	2015	2016	2017	2018	2019*
SBC's Credit Guarantees														
Outstanding guaranteed loans (P million)	--	--	--	--	--	--	--	--	--	--	--	--	--	--
Loan origination (P million)	316.1	212.6	166.5	82.5	136.6	40.2	182.6	134.0	284.6	332.9	177.6	914.1	318.7	112.0
Guaranteed loans approved (P million)**	215.0	131.3	107.8	58.3	66.9	26.4	125.6	80.3	175.0	229.7	123.3	594.9	185.2	78.4
Guaranteed loans disbursed (P million)	6.22	11.61	10.45	--	1.12	2.11	--	--	0.97	7.56	--	1.43	0.36	0.58
Number of MSMEs guaranteed***	64	43	36	17	10	9	44	22	91	142	181	14,799	327	80
Accumulated number of MSMEs guaranteed	--	--	--	--	--	--	--	--	--	--	--	--	--	--
MSME access to guarantees (% of total MSMEs)	--	--	--	--	--	--	--	--	--	--	--	--	--	--
Guaranteed loans to MSME loans (%)	--	--	--	--	--	--	--	--	--	--	--	--	--	--
ASENSO Program														
Total funds released for MSME loans (P million)	32,406.6	28,576.3	35,595.8	31,809.3	28,080.0	26,795.0	30,583.0	38,220.0	29,093.0	24,040.0	37,351.0	--	--	--
Land Bank of the Philippines	16,214.4	16,352.8	20,001.4	21,883.3	21,937.0	21,126.0	23,263.0	31,640.0	28,202.0	23,537.0	26,632.1	--	--	--
Development Bank of the Philippines	11,051.2	8,514.5	11,630.5	7,592.1	3,282.0	3,434.0	4,192.0	4,484.0	3,651.9	--	9,672.1	--	--	--
Small Business Corporation	3,443.0	2,689.7	3,004.8	1,825.2	2,459.0	1,784.0	2,015.0	1,603.0	490.3	409.7	861.7	--	--	--
Other GFIs****	1,698.2	1,019.3	959.2	508.6	402.0	451.0	1,112.0	493.0	685.7	93.4	185.5	--	--	--
Number of MSMEs benefitted	14,284	13,585	70,666	36,994	36,892	32,808	34,054	44,677	26,149	--	--	--	--	--

ASENSO = Access of Small Enterprises to Sound Lending Opportunity; GFI = government financial institution; MSME = micro, small, and medium-sized enterprise; SBC = Small Business Corporation.

* Data as of August 2019.

** Guaranteed amount is computed as approved credit line or loan amount x guarantee cover (%). Based on historical data, average guarantee cover is 70%, but there were special cases where the guarantee cover is below 70% such as in 2010.

*** The big jump in 2017 was brought by credit risk guarantee fund portfolio amounting to P672.35 million with contingent liability at P537.86 million on 14,497 MSMEs.

**** Other participating GFIs are National Livelihood Development Corporation, Philippine Export-Import Credit Agency, Quedan and Rural Credit Guarantee Corporation, and Social Security System.

Source: ADB Asia SME Monitor 2020 database. Data from Small Business Corporation.

Table 9.5: Nonbank Finance

End of period data

Item	2009	2010	2011	2012	2013	2014	2015	2016	2017	2018	2019
NUMBER OF NONBANK FINANCE INSTITUTIONS											
Microfinance institutions[1]	--	--	--	--	--	--	--	2,603	2,861	2,861	3,887
Credit unions/cooperatives	--	--	--	--	--	--	9,432	12,363	11,138	11,939	--
Finance companies	591	594	589	576	595	613	621	642	673	707	774
Pawnshops	14,800	15,596	16,729	17,335	17,652	17,422	16,128	16,698	16,582	12,107	13,801
Leasing companies	--	--	--	--	--	--	--	--	--	--	--
Factoring companies	--	--	--	--	--	--	--	--	--	--	--
Insurance companies	--	--	--	--	--	--	--	--	--	--	--
Non-stock savings and loans associations (NSSLAs)	--	--	--	--	--	199	200	199	197	196	200
Investment houses	32	31	28	28	27	27	27	28	27	27	26
Mutual fund/Investment companies	46	51	52	52	55	58	59	62	64	70	70
CREDIT UNIONS AND COOPERATIVES											
Financing outstanding, total (P million)	--	--	--	--	--	--	172,192	228,538	238,753	313,339	--
Growth (%)	--	--	--	--	--	--	--	32.7	4.5	31.2	--
Total financing to GDP (%)	--	--	--	--	--	--	1.3	1.6	1.5	--	--
Annual lending rate (%, on average)	--	--	--	--	--	--	--	--	--	--	--
Gross nonperforming loans (NPLs) (P million)	--	--	--	--	--	--	20,356	32,840	24,868	29,302	--
Gross NPLs to total loans (%)	--	--	--	--	--	--	11.8	14.4	10.4	9.4	--
Number of customers financed, total	--	--	--	--	--	--	--	--	--	--	--
Financing outstanding by region (% share)											
Capital city (NCR)	--	--	--	--	--	--	30.0	32.9	32.6	34.5	--
Others	--	--	--	--	--	--	70.0	67.1	67.4	65.5	--
PAWNSHOPS											
Financing outstanding, total (P million)[2,3]	6,544	5,947	7,711	8,876	8,538	12,007	12,299	16,741	11,677	17,116	--
Growth (%)	--	(9.1)	29.7	15.1	(3.8)	40.6	2.4	36.1	(30.3)	46.6	--
Total financing to GDP (%)[2,3]	0.001	0.001	0.001	0.001	0.001	0.001	0.001	0.001	0.001	0.001	--
Annual financing rate (%, on average)	--	--	--	--	--	--	--	--	--	--	--
Gross nonperforming financing (NPFs) (P million)	--	--	--	--	--	--	--	--	--	--	--
Gross NPFs to total financing (%)	--	--	--	--	--	--	--	--	--	--	--
Number of customers financed, total	--	--	--	--	--	--	--	--	--	--	--
Financing outstanding by region (% share)											
Capital city (NCR)	--	28.1	28.7	30.3	30.1	24.6	25.1	22.7	2.8	--	--
Others	--	71.9	71.3	69.7	69.9	75.4	74.9	77.3	97.2	--	--
NON-STOCK SAVINGS AND LOANS ASSOCIATIONS (NSSLAs)											
Financing outstanding, total (P million)[4,5]	--	--	--	--	--	118,194	125,976	137,469	153,169	197,477	213,452
Growth (%)	--	--	--	--	--	--	6.6	9.1	11.4	28.9	8.1
Total financing to GDP (%)	--	--	--	--	--	0.009	0.009	0.009	0.010	0.011	0.011
Annual financing rate (%, on average)	--	--	--	--	--	--	--	--	--	--	--
Gross nonperforming financing (NPFs) (P million)	--	--	--	--	--	--	--	--	--	--	--
Gross NPFs to total financing (%)	--	--	--	--	--	--	--	--	--	--	--
Number of customers financed, total	--	--	--	--	--	--	--	--	--	--	--
Financing outstanding by region (% share)											
Capital city (NCR)	--	--	--	--	--	--	--	--	--	--	--
Others	--	--	--	--	--	--	--	--	--	--	--

GDP = gross domestic product, NCR = National Capital Region.

1. Bangko Sentral ng Pilipinas (BSP) data on microfinance institutions (2016–2018) are based only from a sample of microfinance nongovernment organizations (NGOs) that responded to the BSP data request. 2019 data is based on the 28 microfinance NGOs accredited by the Microfinance NGO Regulatory Council.
2. Financing pertains to borrowings or loans and notes payable.
3. Revised 2013 and 2014 data for pawnshops financing.
4. Financing outstanding for NSSLAs covers loans and discounts - loans, past due loans and discounts, and items in litigation. Data in 2019 as of the second quarter.
5. Increase in financing outstanding in 2017 is due to inclusion of salary-based general purpose consumption loans.

Source: ADB Asia SME Monitor 2020 database. Data from Bangko Sentral ng Pilipinas, Cooperative Development Authority, and Securities and Exchange Commission.

Table 9.6: Capital Markets

End of period data

Item	2004	2005	2006	2007	2008	2009	2010	2011	2012	2013	2014	2015	2016	2017	2018	2019
EQUITY MARKET																
Main Board																
Index	1,823	2,096	2,983	3,622	1,873	3,053	4,201	4,372	5,813	5,890	7,231	6,952	6,841	8,558	7,466	7,815
Market capitalization (P million)	4,766,409	5,948,447	7,172,864	7,972,331	4,069,931	6,031,882	8,865,558	8,696,247	10,929,506	11,930,423	14,217,248	13,437,055	14,421,746	17,562,463	16,135,383	16,693,763
Growth (%)	--	24.8	20.6	11.1	(48.9)	48.2	47.0	(1.9)	25.7	9.2	19.2	(5.5)	7.3	21.8	(8.1)	3.5
Trading value (P million)	206,563	383,412	572,583	1,337,970	763,887	994,130	1,207,383	1,422,586	1,771,699	2,546,172	2,119,049	2,139,852	1,912,466	1,949,411	1,730,263	1,763,938
Trading volume (million of shares)	284,340	317,615	601,165	1,157,753	373,000	540,808	429,566	1,056,593	1,043,117	515,134	813,579	492,164	440,092	439,365	402,114	329,366
Number of listed companies	234	236	239	244	246	248	253	253	254	257	263	265	265	267	267	268
Number of IPOs	2	2	5	11	2	2	5	6	7	10	5	3	4	4	1	3
Number of delisted companies	3	0	2	6	0	1	0	6	6	7	1	2	4	2	1	3
Specialized Board																
SME Board																
Index	--	--	--	--	--	--	--	--	--	--	--	--	--	--	--	--
Market capitalization (P million)	263	290	322	4,509	2,226	335	549	713	586	871	34,470	28,513	17,029	20,657	11,308	11,587
Growth (%)	--	10.2	10.9	1,302.5	(50.6)	(84.9)	63.6	29.9	(17.8)	48.5	3,857.5	(17.3)	(40.3)	21.3	(45.3)	2.5
Trading value (P million)	2	107	51	282	14	20	1	5	12	11	11,072	11,559	17,033	8,953	6,559	8,640
Trading volume (million of shares)	1	26	9	77	7	16	0	2	2	1	1,614	1,098	2,178	1,182	1,733	2,938
Number of listed companies	3	3	3	2	2	2	2	2	2	2	4	4	4	4	4	5
Number of IPOs	--	--	--	--	--	1	--	--	--	--	2	1	--	--	--	1
Number of delisted companies	--	--	--	--	--	--	--	--	--	--	--	--	--	--	--	--
Moved to the main board	--	--	--	1	--	1	--	--	--	--	--	1	--	--	--	--
Moved from the main board	--	--	--	--	--	--	--	--	--	--	--	--	--	--	--	--

IPO = initial public offering, SME = small and medium-sized enterprise.

Source: ADB Asia SME Monitor 2020 database. Data from Philippine Stock Exchange.

Table 9.7: Listing Requirements—Philippine Stock Exchange

Criteria	Stock	
	Main Board	SME Board
Track record	a. Cumulative consolidated earnings before interest, taxes, depreciation and amortization (EBITDA), excluding non-recurring items, of at least P50 million for 3 full fiscal years immediately preceding the application for listing; b. A minimum EBITDA of P10 million for each of the 3 fiscal years; and c. The applicant company must be engaged in materially the same business(es) and must have a proven track record of management throughout the last 3 years prior to the filing of the application. Exceptions to the 3-year track record requirement: i. The applicant company has been operating for at least 10 years prior to the filing of the application and has a cumulative EBITDA of at least P50 million for at least 2 of the 3 fiscal years immediately preceding the filing of the listing application; ii. The applicant company is a newly formed holding company which uses the operational track record of its subsidiary. However, the newly formed holding company is prohibited from divesting its shareholdings in the said subsidiary for a period of 3 years from the listing of its securities. The prohibition shall not apply if a divestment plan is approved by majority of the applicant company's stockholders.	a. Cumulative earnings before interest, taxes, depreciation and amortization (EBITDA), excluding non-recurring items, of at least P15 million for 3 fiscal years immediately preceding the application for listing; b. A positive EBITDA was generated in at least 2 of the last 3 fiscal years, including the fiscal year immediately preceding the filing of the application; and c. The applicant company must be engaged in materially the same business and must have a proven track record of management throughout the last 3 years prior to the filing of the application for listing. The applicant company shall demonstrate its stable financial condition and prospects for continuing growth by providing a business plan indicating the steps that have been taken and to be undertaken in order to advance its business over a period of 5 years. As a general rule, financial projections are not required, but should there be references made in the business plan to future profits or losses, or any other item that would be construed to indicate forecasts, then the applicant company is required to include financial projections in the business plan duly reviewed by an independent accounting firm.
Minimum capital	• Minimum authorized capital stock of P500 million, of which, at least 25% is subscribed and fully paid. At listing, the market capitalization of the applicant company must be at least P500 million.	• Minimum authorized capital stock of P100 million, of which, at least 25% is subscribed and fully paid.
Minimum number of shareholders	• Upon listing, at least 1,000 stockholders each owning stocks equivalent to at least one board lot.	• Upon listing, at least 200 stockholders each owning stocks equivalent to at least one board lot.
Restrictions	a. No divestment of shares in operating subsidiary - A newly formed holding company which invokes the operational track record of its subsidiary to qualify for the track record requirement of profitable operations, is prohibited from divesting its shareholdings in the said subsidiary for a period of 3 years from the listing of its securities. The prohibition shall not apply if a divestment plan is approved by majority of the applicant company's stockholders. b. No secondary offering for companies invoking exemption of track record and operating history requirements, such as mining, petroleum, and renewable energy companies, and newly formed holding companies during the initial public offering.	a. No listing of holding, portfolio and passive income companies; b. No change in primary purpose and/or secondary purpose for a period of 7 years following its listing; and c. No offering of secondary securities for companies exempt from the track record and operating history requirements such as mining, petroleum, and renewable energy companies.

Note: selected criteria only.

Source: ADB Asia SME Monitor 2020 database. Data from Philippine Stock Exchange.

Table 9.8: Policies and Regulations

Regulations	
Name	**Outline**
Nonfinance Regulations	
Magna Carta for Micro, Small and Medium Enterprises (MSMEs) (R.A. No.6977 of 1991, as amended by R.A. No.8289 of 1997, R.A. No.9501 of 2008, and R.A. No.10644 of 2014)	1) Creation of the MSME Development Council. 2) Establishment of the Small Business Guarantee and Finance Corporation (Small Business Corporation [SBC]). 3) Mandatory allocation of credit resources for MSMEs. 4) Preparation of MSME Development Plan.
Barangay Micro Business Enterprises (BMBE) Act of 2002, (R.A. No.9178 as amended by R.A. No.10644 of 2014)	1) Exemption from income tax for income arising from operation of BMBEs. 2) Exemption from the coverage of the Minimum Wage Law. 3) Priority access for financing requirements through a special credit window. 4) Assistance programs for technology transfer, production and management training, and marketing assistance programs.
Small and Medium Enterprise Development Council Resolution No.01 Series of 2003	Legislated definition of MSMEs.
Philippine Cooperative Code of 2008 (R.A. No.9520)	1) Foster the creation and growth of cooperatives as a practical vehicle for promoting self-reliance and harnessing people power toward the attainment of economic development and social justice. 2) Encourage the private sector to undertake the actual formation and organization of cooperatives and shall create an atmosphere that is conducive to the growth and development of these cooperatives.
Go Negosyo Act of 2014 (R.A. No.10644)	1) Establishment of Negosyo Centers in all provinces, cities and municipalities to promote ease of doing business and facilitate access to services for MSMEs within its jurisdiction. 2) Technology transfer, production and management training, and marketing assistance for MSMEs. 3) Establishment of a Philippine Business Registry Databank under the Department of Trade and Industry (DTI) to serve as a database of all business enterprises in the country. 4) Expansion of MSME Development Council and Advisory Unit. 5) Establishment of a start-up fund for MSMEs to provide financing for the development and promotion of MSMEs in priority sectors of the economy to be sourced from the MSME Development Fund and BMBE Fund.
Tax Reform for Acceleration and Inclusion Act of 2017 (TRAIN Law) (R.A. No.10963)	1) Increases the threshold of value-added tax (VAT) registration to P3 million. 2) Lower personal income taxes that cover micro or small self-employed and professionals. 3) Simplified flat tax system for micro or small self-employed and professionals earning below the VAT threshold.
Ease of Doing Buisness and Efficient Government Service Delivery Act of 2018 (R.A. No.11032)	1) Reduced processing time (i.e., 3 working days for simple transactions; 7 working days for complex transactions, and 21 working days for highly technical transactions). 2) Simplified steps for securing documentation requirements (i.e., unified business application form; automation of local government units' system of issuance of business permits and licenses; establishment of a business one-stop shop). 3) Establishment of a Citizen's Charter. 4) Zero contact policy. 5) Setting up of a central business portal and Philippine Business Databank. 6) Interconnectivity infrastructure development. 7) Creation of the Anti-Red Tape Authority. 8) Penalties.
Philippine Identification System Act of 2018 (R.A. No.11055)	Establish a national digital ID system called PhilSys.
Cooperative Development Authority Charter Act of 2019 (R.A. No.11364)	The act mandates the Cooperative Development Authority (CDA) to promote the viability and growth of cooperatives as instruments of equity, social justice and economic development.
Philippine Innovation Act of 2019 (R.A. No.11293)	The act aims to facilitate the development of strategies toward promoting MSMEs' internationalization and participation in domestic and global value chains. A new mandatory lending scheme for innovation activities, targeting start-ups and MSMEs, is stipulated.
Pantawid Pamilyang Pilipino Program (4Ps) Act of 2019 (R.A. No. 11310)	Stipulate the national social protection and human development program.
Innovative Startup Act of 2019 (R.A. No. 11337)	The act aims to create initiatives that provide benefits and incentives to stratups and start-up enablers.
Finance Regulations	
Pawnshop Regulation Act of 1973 (Presidential Decree No.114)	Regulate and supervise pawnshops.
Non-Stock Savings and Loan Association Act of 1997 (R.A. No.8367)	Regurate and supervise non-stock savings and loan associations (NSSLAs).
Credit Information Systems Act of 2008 (R.A. No.9510)	Establish and supervise the Credit Information Corporation.
Microfinance NGOs Act of 2015 (R.A. No.10693)	1) Strengthen nongovernment organizations (NGOs) engaged in microfinance for the poor. 2) Pursue a program of poverty eradication wherein poor Filipino families shall be encouraged to undertake entrepreneurial activities to meet their minimum basic needs. The Microfinance NGOs Regulatory Council was established as an accrediting body for microfinance NGOs.
President Executive Order No.208 of 2016 on the National Financial Inclusion Steering Committee	Institutionalize the Financial Inclusion Steering Committee.
BSP Circular No.940 Series of 2017 on Cash Agents	Regulate and supervise cash agents (branchless banking).
BSP Circular No.944 Series of 2017 on virtual currency exchanges	Regulate and supervise virtual currency exchanges.
BSP Circular No.980 Series of 2017 on The National Retail Payment System	Operationalize the National Retail Payment System.
President Executive Order No.58 of 2018 on the Philippine Guarantee Corporation	Merger of five guarantee corporations namely: the Philippine Export-Import Credit Agency, the Home Guaranty Corporation, the Industrial Guarantee and Loan Fund, the Agricultural Guarantee Fund Pool, and credit guarantee function of the Small Business Corporation to create the Philippine Guarantee Corporation.
Personal Property Security Act of 2018 (R.A. No.11057)	Establish a centralized electronic registry on personal property and supervise movable asstes.
National Payment Systems Act of 2018 (R.A. No.11127)	Provide a comprehensive legal and regulatory framework for the national payment systems, which appointed the BSP as the regulator of the national payment systems.
Philippine Stock Exchange Consolidated Listing and Disclosure Rules (Article III, Part E)	SME board listing rules.
SEC Circular No.1 Series of 2017 on Rules of the Capital Contribution and Corporate and Trade Names of Microfinance NGO	Microfinance NGOs are required to be established as non-stock, non-profit corporations with capital contribution of at least P1 million.
SEC Circular No.2 Series of 2017 on Clarification of the Three-Year Consecutive Microfinance Operations Requirement	Only microfinance NGOs that have been operating for at least three (3) consecutive years may be accredited by the council.
SEC Circular No.1 Series of 2018 on Accreditation of Microfinance NGOs (Circulars No.2-No.4 for related amendments and guidelines)	Set the applicable performance standards, and identify the information in the audited financial statements and operational reports to be used as basis in the computation of ratios and indicators embodied in such standards.
SEC Circular No.5 Series of 2018 on Adoption of Philippine Financial Reporting Standards (PFRS) for Small Entities	The PFRS allows small entities to comply with the financial reporting requirements without undue cost or burden by reducing choices for accounting treatment, eliminating topics that are not generally relevant to small entities, simplifying methods for recognition and measurement, and reducing disclosure requirements.
SEC Circular No.1 Series of 2019 on Compliance of Microfinance NGOs with the Truth in Lending Act (R.A. No.3765)	Microfinance NGOs are required to provide certain minimum information to borrowers, including the computation of interest.
SEC Circular No.2 Series of 2019 on Standard Chart of Accounts for Microfinance NGOs	Adoption of the financial reporting framework, Standard Chart of Accounts for microfinance NGOs which shall be used from 2020, etc.
SEC Circular No.14 Series of 2019 on Rules and Regulations Governing Crowdfunding	Govern the operation and use of equity-based and lending-based crowdfunding.

continued on next page

Table 9.8 continued

Regulators and Policymakers	
Name	**Responsibility**
Department of Trade and Industry (DTI)	Primary government agency responsible for promoting an enabling environment to MSMEs and their development.
Micro, Small and Medium Enterprise Development Council (MSMED Council)	Chaired by the DTI secretary. Formulate MSME promotion policies and provide guidance on implementing MSME programs.
Bureau of Small and Medium Enterprise Development (BSMED), DTI	Act as the secretariat of MSMED Council. Advocate SME policies, programs, and projects.
Financial Inclusion Steering Committee (FISC)	A coordinating body of implementing the National Strategy for Financial Inclusion (NSFI).
Bangko Sentral ng Pilipinas (BSP)	Regulate and supervise banks and NBFIs.
Securities and Exchange Commission (SEC)	Regulate and supervise the capital markets and participants.
Microfinance Non-Government Organization Regulatory Council (MNRC)	Institute and operationalize a system of accreditation for microfinance NGOs and monitor their performance to ensure continuing compliance with the financial standards, social performance standards, governance standards, and other provisions of the Microfinance NGOs Act.
Cooperative Development Authority (CDA)	Promote the growth and viability of cooperatives as instruments of equity, social justice and, economic development. Regulate all cooperatives in the Philippines.

Policies		
Name	**Responsible Entity**	**Outline**
Small and Medium Enteprise Development Plan (2004–2010)	MSMED Council	Increase the contribution of SMEs as an important engine of growth: 1) Increased productivity 2) Increased production output and sales 3) Contirbution to growth of exports 4) New creative enterprises
Micro, Small and Medium Enteprise Development Plan (2011-2016)	MSMED Council	Increase the contribution of SMEs as an important engine of growth through: 1) Enabling business environment 2) Access to finance 3) Access to markets 4) Increasing productivity and efficiency
Micro, Small and Medium Enterprise Development Plan (2017-2022)	MSMED Council	Increase the contribution of MSME as key drivers of inclusive economic growth through: 1) Improved business climate 2) Improved access to finance 3) Enhanced management and labor capacities 4) Improved access to technology and innovation 5) Improved access to market
Philippine Development Plan (2011–2016)	National Economic Development Authority and other government agencies including the DTI	1) Anticorruption/transparency, accountable, and participatory governance 2) Poverty reduction and empowerment of the poor and vulnerable 3) Rapid, inclusive, and sustained economic growth 4) Just and lasting peace and the rule of law 5) Integrity of the environment and climate change mitigation and adaptation
Philippine Development Plan (2017–2022)	National Economic Development Authority and other government agencies including the DTI	1) Malasakit - Enhancing the social fabric 2) Pagbabago - Inequality-reducing transformation 3) Patuloy na Pag-unlad - Increasing growth potential
The National Strategy for Financial Inclusion (NSFI) (2015)	FISC	1) Policy and regulation that facilitate access to a wide range of financial products and services for all 2) Financial education and consumer protection 3) Advocacy programs 4) Data and measurement for proper monitoring
Bangko Sentral ng Pilipinas (BSP) Initiatives on MSMEs	BSP	1) Promoting innovative approaches in MSME financing: - Agriculture value chain finance. - Regulatory incentives to promote MSME lending. 2) Putting in place the needed financial and digital infrastructure: - Development of enabling market infrastructure. 3) Bridging the information gap: - MSME Finance Survey. 4) Facilitating strategic partnerships.

R.A. = Republic Act.

Source: ADB Asia SME Monitor 2020 database. Data from Bangko Sentral ng Pilipinas, Bureau of Small and Medium Enterprise Development, Cooperative Development Authority, Department of Finance, National Economic Development Authority, Securities and Exchange Commission.

Country Review

Singapore

Overview

Singapore remains the most developed economy within the Association of Southeast Asian Nations (ASEAN). Its per capita gross domestic product (GDP) was S$88,991 ($66,056) in 2019.[116] Real GDP growth decelerated from 3.4% in 2018 to 0.7% in 2019. Singapore had a resident working age population (20-64 years) of 2.6 million people in 2019. Its infrastructure, use of technology, access to finance, and capital markets are highly advanced. In 2019, small and medium-sized enterprises (SMEs) accounted for 99.5% of Singaporean firms, employed 71.4% of the workforce and contributed 44.7% of GDP. SMEs are domestically focused with few incentives to develop global exposure, partly due to a lack of financial access. In 2018, SME access to bank credit was just 5.8% of total bank loans and 15.1% of GDP, with growth decelerating. Nonbank and market-based financing as well as digital financial services could be a viable alternative to traditional bank credit for SMEs.

1. SME Development

- The number of SMEs has grown since 2014, with their share of total enterprises remaining high.
- Over time, SMEs have employed a stable, high percentage of the Singaporean workforce.
- SMEs remain an important contributor to the country's productivity; enterprises in manufacturing and services account for the majority of nominal value added, with SMEs contributing nearly half of the total.
- SMEs are domestically focused; they do not generally tap global business opportunities and have little interest in internationalization.
- The government's SME Go Digital program promotes technology and efficiency by applying digital solutions to SME businesses.
- The Singapore Business Federation, the leading business chamber, promotes the growth and vibrancy of the business community; it offers networking opportunities, business development services, and advocacy.

Scale of SMEs

In Singapore, an enterprise is classified as simply an SME or non-SME. There is no microenterprise category.[117] The definition of SMEs is based on annual sales (turnover) and number of workers. SMEs have no more than S$100 million in annual turnover, or no more than 200 workers (Table 10.1). The Standards, Productivity, and Innovation Board of the Ministry of Trade and Industry (MTI) has followed this definition since April 2011. The Singapore Department of Statistics (DOS) uses this definition in collecting data on SMEs.

According to SingStat, the DOS statistical data portal, there were 273,100 SMEs in 2019, 3% more than the 263,800 in 2018 (Figure 10.1 and Table 10.1). The number grew 11.9% from 2014 to 2019, a compound annual growth rate of 2.3%. The SME share of total enterprises has remained a constant 99.5% over the period, suggesting they are a backbone of the economy. Distribution by sector is unavailable, and there are no reliable estimates of the number

116 Department of Statistics Singapore. https://www.singstat.gov.sg/ Accessed 21 May 2020.

117 This country report uses "SME" rather than "micro, small, and medium-sized enterprise (MSME)," the term used in other country reports.

of informal SMEs. The "gig economy" appears to be growing, but it is unknown how many are employed or how many businesses it supports.[118]

Employment

SingStat revealed that SMEs employed 2.5 million workers in 2019, a 1.8% increase over 2018 (Figure 10.2). They accounted for 71.4% of the total workforce. The number of SME employees and their share of the total have been relatively stable from 2014 to 2019. There is no data available covering sector and regional distribution of SME employees.

Business Productivity

SMEs contributed S$207 billion in 2019 in terms of nominal value added, a 1.4% increase from the S$204 billion in 2018 (Figure 10.3). They accounted for 44.7% of total enterprise nominal value added in 2019. SME nominal value added growth from 2014 to 2019 was 15.2%, or a compound annual growth rate of 2.9%. However, their share of total nominal value added of all enterprises declined from 50.1% in 2014 to 44.7% in 2019, a 10.6% decrease at a compound annual rate of –2.2%. SME dynamics could be strengthened further to boost national productivity.

In terms of average overall sector contributions to GDP, manufacturing contributed 19.7% of GDP during 2014–2018, followed by wholesale and retail trade (17.6%) and business services (17.6%). Contributions to GDP remained relatively stable during the period, with manufacturing growing from 19.0% in 2014 to 21.9% in 2018 (up a cumulative 15.0%), while construction declined from 5.1% in 2014 to 3.6% in 2018 (down 29.9%).

Market Access

Singapore is an international trading hub with a competitive economy in Asia. According to SingStat (2019), direct manufactured exports increased 12.5% from S$189.9 billion in 2013 to S$213.7 billion in 2017. Over the same period, direct exports as a percentage of manufacturing output increased 5.1% from 66.5% to 69.9%. Direct exports as a percentage of total sales grew 5.4% from 66.4% to 70.0%.

For the merchandise trade sector, total exports increased 1.3%, from S$526.1 billion in 2014 to S$532.5 billion in 2019. Imports increased 0.9%, from S$485.6 billion in 2013 to S$489.7 billion in 2019 (Enterprise Singapore). In 2019, the three leading export destinations were the People's Republic of China (PRC) (S$70.4 billion); Hong Kong, China (S$60.5 billion); and Malaysia (S$56.1 billion). The top three export commodities were machinery and equipment (S$258.4 billion), mineral fuels and lubricants (S$88.5 billion), and chemicals and chemical products (S$74.8 billion).

There is no data available for SME exports. However, they appear to shy away from global business. According to the 2018 SME survey by QBE Insurance (Singapore),[119] only 14% of local SMEs surveyed were willing to internationalize their business, while half have no interest in participating in global markets, mainly due to a lack of financing and unfamiliarity with foreign markets. Supporting SMEs to join global value chains, changing the mindset of SME owners toward global business, and enhancing access to diversified financing options would be needed to promote SME internationalization.

[118] Government of Singapore, Ministry of Manpower. Labour Force in Singapore 2018. https://stats.mom.gov.sg/Pages/Labour-Force-In-Singapore-2018.aspx.

[119] QBE. QBE Insights. https://www.qbe.com/sg/newsroom/qbe-insights.

Figure 10.1: Number of SMEs

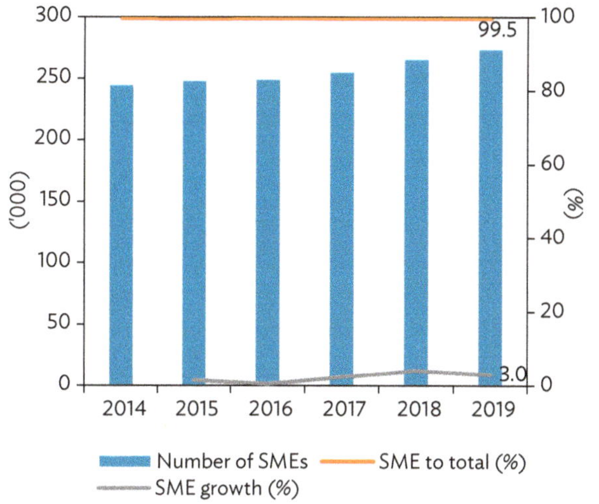

SME = small and medium-sized enterprise.

Source: ADB Asia SME Monitor 2020 database. Data from Singapore Department of Statistics.

Figure 10.2: Employment by SMEs

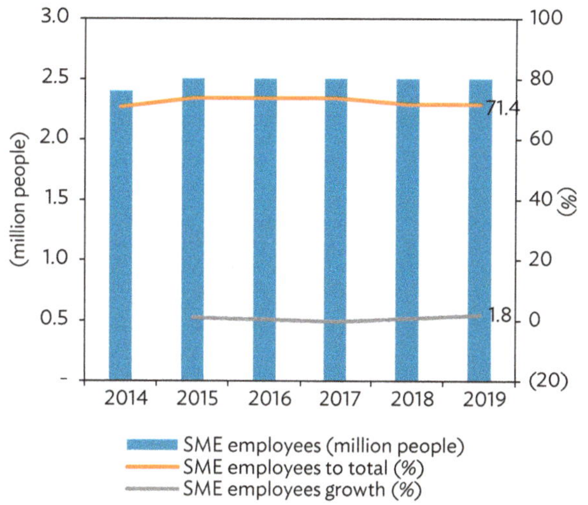

SME = small and medium-sized enterprise.

Source: ADB Asia SME Monitor 2020 database. Data from Singapore Department of Statistics.

Figure 10.3: SME Value Added

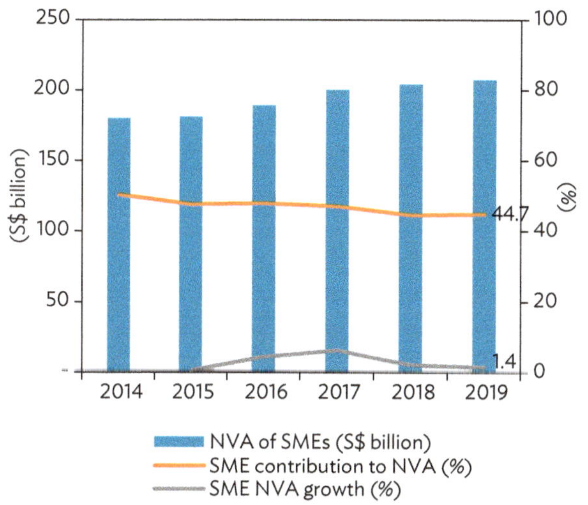

NVA = nominal value added, SME = small and medium-sized enterprise.

Source: ADB Asia SME Monitor 2020 database. Data from Singapore Department of Statistics.

Technology and Innovation

Enterprise Singapore and the Infocomm Media Development Authority (IMDA), launched the SMEs Go Digital program in April 2017 to enable SMEs to find digital solutions for their business. According to SingStat, Go Digital offers several initiatives:

Industry Digital Plans (IDPs). Sector-specific IDPs provide SMEs with a step-by-step guide on available digital solutions they can adopt, and offer relevant training for employees at different stages of business growth. The digital plans are aligned with Industry Transformation Maps for each sector and act as a common reference for relevant SMEs. These plans cover accountancy, construction and facilities management, environmental services, food services, hotels, logistics, media, retail, sea transport, security, and wholesale trade.

Pre-approved solutions with grant support. To make it easy for SMEs to adopt the digital solutions recommended in industry digital plans, IMDA provides a list of pre-approved, market-proven, and cost-effective solutions supported by reliable vendors. These cover, for example, environmental services, food services, retail, security, wholesale trade, and logistics. SMEs can view the solutions online and apply for a Productivity Solutions Grant through the Business Grants Portal.[120] A grant can help offset the costs of adopting these solutions.

[120] Business Grants Portal. www.businessgrants.gov.sg.

Start Digital. This initiative, launched in January 2019, helps newly incorporated SMEs and those yet to go digital and get started with foundational digital solutions. SMEs can select any two solutions from five categories to include in their Start Digital Pack: (i) accounting, (ii) human resource management system and payroll, (iii) digital marketing, (iv) digital transactions, and (v) cybersecurity. The solutions are offered by bank and telecommunication partners at competitive prices. SMEs that sign up for a minimum 18-month contract receive cost waivers for at least 6 months.

Grow Digital. This new initiative supports SMEs willing and ready to seize business opportunities in overseas markets. Through Grow Digital, SMEs can go onto pre-approved IMDA business-to-consumer and business-to-business e-commerce platforms with regional or global reach. These platforms give SMEs a head start in going global without having an overseas physical presence. Grow Digital provides SMEs other benefits: (i) smart matching to connect SME suppliers with potential overseas clients, (ii) optimized listing on international e-markets, (iii) prompt access to financing offers facilitated via these platforms, (iv) cross-border e-payment facilities that alleviate currency risk, and (v) integration with logistics companies to facilitate last-mile delivery.

Pilot projects. In collaboration with industry leaders and information and communication (infocomm) media solution providers, IMDA pilots new digital solutions that both meet the needs of new industry players and hold the potential to scale up and have an impact on the industry. Solutions proven effective and useful to SMEs in that industry can be considered for pre-approval and support under the PSG.

SME Digital Tech Hub. The SME Digital Tech Hub provides digital consultancy to SMEs that need expert advice in specialized areas such as artificial intelligence, cybersecurity, data analytics, and the internet of things. It also provides free advisory clinics for SMEs and recommends suitable infocomm technology vendors and consultants.[121]

Digital Project Management Services. This initiative provides a ready pool of skilled digital project managers that SMEs can engage at subsidized fees to help with implementing their digital solutions. It aims to help SMEs realize the full benefits of going digital, and include services like the review of business processes and job redesign.

Networking and Support

The Singapore Business Federation is the country's leading business chamber. It promotes the growth and vibrancy and champions the interests of Singapore's business community.[122] Under the Singapore Business Federation Act, all Singapore-registered companies with share capital of S$500,000 and above are members of the federation. As of 2020, it represented about 27,200 companies, as well as key local and foreign business chambers located in Singapore.

The Singapore Business Federation functions as a bridge between Singapore's business community and the government. It represents the business community in building bilateral, regional, and multilateral relationships. It offers a comprehensive suite of initiatives and services: (i) advocating for members' interests locally and participating in prominent international business forums; (ii) helping businesses explore opportunities globally through its network of business groups in ASEAN, the PRC and North Asia, Africa, the Middle East, and other frontier and emerging markets; (iii) supporting companies as they go international through market events, overseas business missions, and meetings with visiting business delegations; and (iv) enabling enterprises through capability building focusing on internationalization and digitalization.

121 For more information, please refer to: www.digitaltechhub.sg.

122 Singapore Business Federation. Overview. https://www.sbf.org.sg/about-us/overview-about-us/.

2. Access to Finance

- SME bank loans have grown steadily over the past decade; however, loans have declined slightly as a percentage of total bank credit.
- Enterprise Singapore streamlined its financing programs under an umbrella Enterprise Financing Scheme to support SMEs across each stage of their business cycle.
- Nonbank financing has expanded, with finance companies, the primary providers, offering three main products: housing loans, hire purchase loans, and other loans and advances.
- The Monetary Authority of Singapore is promoting digital finance through a variety of programs using sophisticated technology, such as blockchains and artificial intelligence.
- Singapore has the most highly developed capital markets in the region, with separate stock indices for large companies and SMEs.
- There are several credit bureaus in Singapore, and well-developed laws governing collateral.

Compared with other ASEAN members, Singapore offers relatively affordable access to SME finance. Credit from banks and nonbank financial institutions is readily available. Capital markets are highly developed and digital financial services, including fintech, are the most advanced in the region.

Bank Credit

The number of commercial banks grew 13.9% from 115 in 2004 to 131 in 2019 (Table 10.3). The largest growth was in wholesale banks, which increased from 37 in 2004 to 97 in 2019 (up 162.6%, or a compound annual growth rate of 6.6%). Five new wholesale banks opened in 2019. Offshore banks dwindled from 50 in 2004 to 0 in 2019. In April 2016, the Monetary Authority of Singapore (MAS) stopped issuing offshore bank licenses and began to convert existing offshore banks to wholesale banks over time.[123]

According to MAS, outstanding loans increased from S$641.1 billion in 2010 to S$1.4 trillion as of end-2019 (up 114.5% at a compound annual growth rate of 10.0%). Loans held in domestic currency (domestic banking units) accounted for 50.5%, while those held in foreign currency (Asian currency units) accounted for the rest. Domestic banking unit loans have been over 50% throughout the 2010–2019 period.

Outstanding SME loans grew from S$46.4 billion in 2010 to S$76.6 billion in June 2019 (up 65.0% at a compound annual growth rate of 5.7%) (Figure 10.4A). The percentage of SME loans to total loans declined from 7.2% in 2010 to 5.8% in 2018, a drop of 20.0%. Growth has zigzagged. SME loans accounted for 14.2% of GDP in 2010 and 15.1% in 2018, an increase of 6.6%. The ratio peaked at 17.6% in 2014.

SME nonperforming loans (NPLs) as a percentage of total SME loans grew from 1.5% in 2010 to 4.2% in 2019. While the average lending rate for SMEs is unavailable, the prime lending rate varied from 5.25% in 2014 to 5.35% in September 2019.

As of June 2019, agriculture, forestry, and fisheries accounted for the largest share of SME loans (37%), followed by construction (26%) and other services (17%) (Figure 10.4B). SME loans secured by property rose from 52.3% in 2010 to 63.7% in June 2019, those secured by "others" fell from 24.8% to 17.1%, and those unsecured 22.9% to 19.2%. Over the period, loans secured by property grew by 21.7% overall, while loans secured by others fell 30.8% and unsecured loans declined 16.2%.

[123] Monetary Authority of Singapore. Annual Report 2015/16. https://www.mas.gov.sg/annual_reports/annual20152016/chapter_2/banking.html.

Public Financing and Guarantees

In October 2019, Enterprise Singapore placed its existing financing schemes under an umbrella policy known as the Enterprise Financing Scheme[124]. The objective was to increase access to finance through each stage of an SME's life cycle and share the risk of loan default with participating financial institutions. The financing scheme consists of six areas/products: (i) SME working capital loans to finance daily operations and cash flow; (ii) SME fixed-asset loans to finance domestic and foreign fixed assets; (iii) venture debt loans to finance innovative start-ups using venture debt and warrants; (iv) trade loans to finance imports and exports and to provide guarantees, including (a) inventory/stock financing, (b) structured pre-delivery working capital, (c) factoring/bill of invoice/AR discounting, and (d) overseas working capital loans; (v) project loans to finance secured overseas projects; and (vi) mergers and acquisitions loans for acquiring enterprises, particularly to internationalize operations.

Figure 10.4: SME Loans

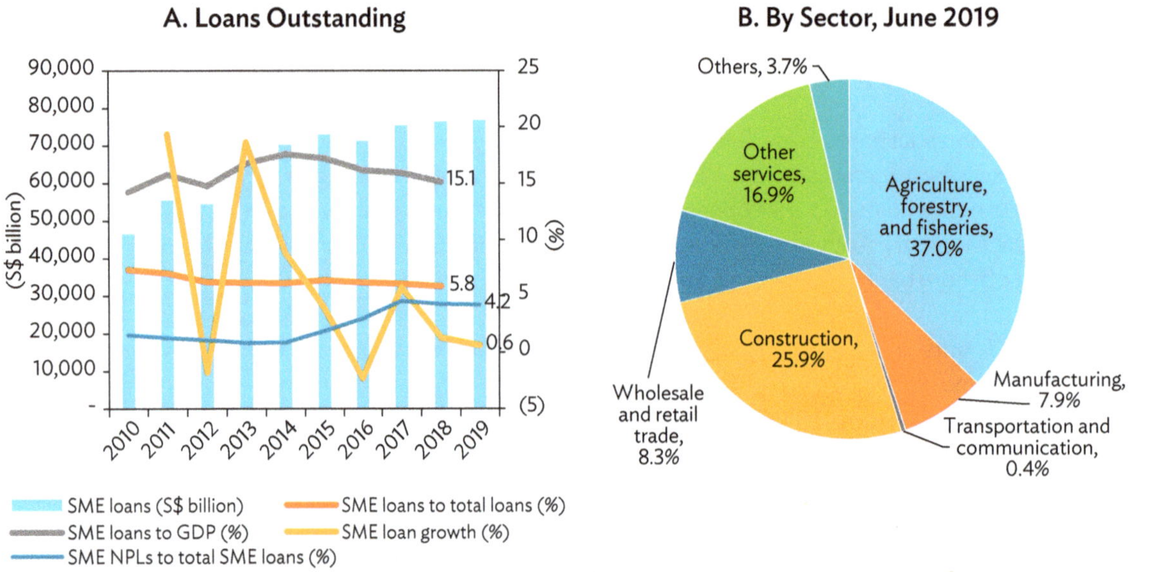

NPL = nonperforming loan, SME = small and medium-sized enterprise.

Source: ADB Asia SME Monitor 2020 database. Data from Monetary Authority of Singapore.

Nonbank Finance

The nonbank finance industry does not normally target SMEs. But the industry plays a critical role supplementing bank credit in financing SMEs and those self-employed. Finance companies are the primary form of nonbank financing in Singapore; there were three firms as of 2019 offering housing, hire-purchase finance, and other types of loans (Figure 10.5 and Table 10.4).

124 Enterprise Singapore. https://www.enterprisesg.gov.sg/financial-assistance/loans-and-insurance/loans-andinsurance/enterprise-financing-scheme/overview.

Nonbank financing grew 113.9% (a compound annual growth rate of 5.3%) from S$6.9 billion in 2004 to S$14.7 billion as of August 2019. As a percentage of GDP, lending from finance companies decreased by 18.1% from 3.5% to 2.9% over the period; however, the trend was stable within a 2.5% to 3.7% range over 15 years.

Housing loans increased from S$952 million in 2004 to S$1.3 billion in 2019, up 41.5% overall (a compound annual growth rate of 2.4%). Hire-purchase lending (for vehicles) declined by 1.6%, from S$2.4 billion to S$2.3 billion. Other loans and advances grew 209.9% (an 8.0% compound annual growth rate) from S$3.6 billion to S$11.0 billion. As of August 2019, housing loans accounted for 9.2% of nonbank financing, hire-purchase loans 15.8%, and other loans and advances the remaining 75.0% (in 2004, the percentages were 13.8%, 34.4%, and 51.8%, respectively). Housing loans fell at a compound annual rate of 2.7%, hire-purchase loans dropped by 5.1%, and other loans and advances grew 7.5%.

For a 3-year hire-purchase loan for new vehicles, interest rates ranged from a high of 5.7% in both 2006 and 2007 to a low of 3.4% in both 2011 and 2012. The range for 15-year housing loans was from a low of 2.9% for the years 2012–2014 to a high of 5.7%, again for both 2006 and 2007—interest rate data for nonbank financing covers 2004 to 2017, when the rate for vehicle loans was 5.1% and 3.2% for housing loans.

Outstanding nonperforming finance amounted S$14.8 million in 2018 (1.0% of nonbank financing) and S$19.7 million as of August 2019 (1.3%). Nonbank finance companies lent the equivalent of 2.2% of bank lending in 2004, declining to 1.1% in August 2019. There is no information available on lending by sector.

Figure 10.5: Nonbank Finance—Finance Companies

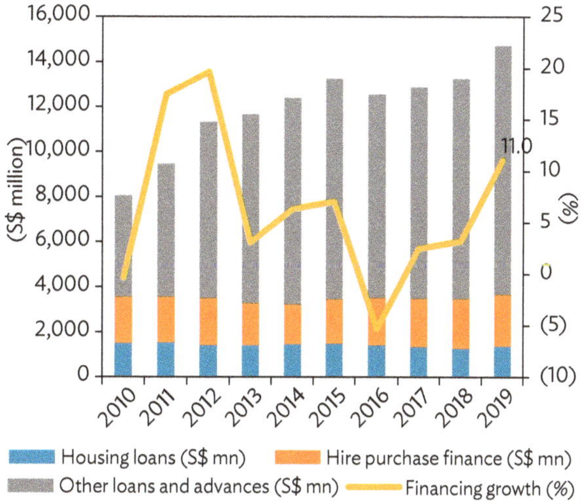

Source: ADB Asia SME Monitor 2020 database. Data from Monetary Authority of Singapore.

Digital Financial Services

According to MAS, fintech and digital financial services figure prominently in both current and future plans for financing SMEs. As of 2019, there were over 1,100 fintech firms in Singapore, and investment in fintech reached a record high of over S$1 billion.[125]

Beyond fintech, MAS is promoting digital financial services in myriad areas. The Global Trade Connectivity Network is a program for digitizing trade finance that uses distributed ledger technology to facilitate payments. Project Ubin is a partnership between MAS and Singaporean industries to use both blockchain and distributed ledger technology for payments and securities settlement. E-payments are already well-developed, with several different national platforms available. MAS also promotes SME digitization with its Business sans Borders, which applies artificial intelligence to locate prices and sales opportunities, access global supply chains, and utilize various digital solutions in business operations.[126]

In 2020, MAS received 21 applications for five available digital banking licenses.[127] Two licenses (from seven bids) allow full service to retail and corporate clients, with the remaining three (of 14 bids) for "wholesale" banking for non-retail customers.

Capital Markets

Singapore has highly developed capital markets, with separate indexes for major companies (Strait Times Index) and for SMEs (Catalist) on the Singapore Exchange. From 2004 to 2019, the Strait Times Index climbed from 2,066 to 3,223, an overall increase of 56.0% (a compound annual growth rate of 3.0%) (Table 10.5). The Catalist Index declined from 797 in 2008 to 272 in 2019 (an overall decrease of 65.8% at a compound annual rate of –9.3%) (Figure 10.6A).

Catalist was launched in November 2007 as a sponsor-supervised listing platform for fast-growing local and international companies, modeled on the London Stock Exchange's Alternative Investment Market. Catalist was created as merger of SESDAQ and a second board of the Singapore Exchange. It allows a sponsor to determine the suitability of a company for listing without Singapore Exchange reviewing the admission of the company.[128] Catalist market capitalization increased by 175.4% from 2008 to 2019 (a compound annual growth rate of 9.6%), from S$3.6 billion to S$9.8 billion. Trading value fell by 68.0% from S$9.4 billion in 2017 to S$3.0 billion in 2019. Trading volume, however, fell from 139.7 million in 2017 to 49.5 million in 2019, a decrease of 64.6% (a compound annual rate of –40.0%).

On the main board (Strait Times), the number of listed companies declined 5.1% from 762 in 2004 to 723 in 2019. The number of IPOs fell from 35 in 2008 to just 13 in 2019, a decrease of 62.9% (a compound annual rate of –8.6%). On Catalist, the number of listed companies increased from 133 in 2008 to 216 in 2019, an increase of 62.4% (a compound annual growth rate of 4.5%) (Figure 10.6B). From 2008 to 2019, 120 companies were newly listed, while 34 companies were delisted, for an average net annual gain of seven new companies over the period.

---

125 Monetary Authority of Singapore. Fintech and Innovation. https://www.mas.gov.sg/development/fintech.

126 https://www.mas.gov.sg/news/media-releases/2019/business-sans-borders-achieves-successful-poc-to-enhance-sme-access-to-trade-opportunities

127 C.Y. Ting. 2020. 21 applications submitted for up to 5 Singapore digital bank licences: MAS. The Straits Times. 7 January. https://www.straitstimes.com/business/banking/21-applications-submitted-for-5-singapore-digital-bank-licences.

128 Singapore Exchange News Release dated 26 November 2007.

Figure 10.6: Equity Market

A. Market Performance—Catalist

B. Listed Companies—Catalist

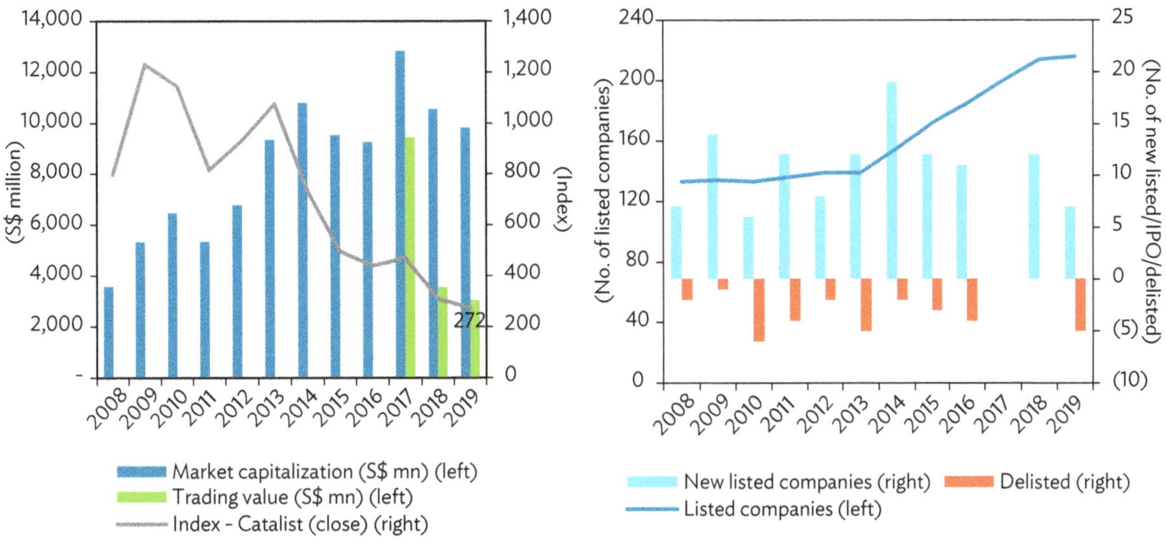

IPO = initial public offering.

Source: ADB Asia SME Monitor 2020 database. Data from Singapore Exchange.

Source: ADB Asia SME Monitor 2020 database. Data from Singapore Exchange and World Federation of Exchanges.

Bond market data for 2014–2018 covers both local currency (in S$) and foreign currency bond issuance ($). Local currency bond issuance grew by 29.0% (a compound annual growth rate of 5.2%) from S$422.3 billion to S$544.7 billion. Foreign currency bond issuance grew 38.5% (a compound annual growth rate of 6.7%) from US$11.7 billion in 2014 to US$16.2 billion in 2018.

Financial Infrastructure

Credit Bureau Singapore is the oldest and largest credit bureau. There is also the Consumer Credit Bureau sponsored by the Post Office Savings Bank, and the Singapore Commercial Credit Bureau supported by Dun & Bradstreet, serving both corporate and individual customers.

Under Singapore law, all kinds of collateral may be used to secure debt, including movable assets. The most common collateral is real estate, but financial assets such as receivables and equity stocks may be used.[129]

In a monograph first issued in 2013 and revised in 2018, MAS specified safety and efficiency as the primary objectives for financial market infrastructure. MAS oversees a variety of financial market infrastructures, categorized as electronic payment systems and capital market infrastructure. There is a regulatory framework and routine inspection of the entire financial market infrastructure network.

129 ICLG.com. Singapore: Lending and Secured Finance Laws and Regulations 2020. https://iclg.com/practice-areas/lending-and-secured-finance-laws-and-regulations/singapore.

3. Policies and Regulations

- The Ministry of Trade and Industry (MTI) has an Economic Strategy to improve productivity, create good jobs, and improve the quality of life for all Singaporeans.
- The Research, Innovation, and Enterprise 2020 Plan builds the innovative capacity of Singaporean enterprises and leverages science and technology for sustainable economic growth.
- Industry Transformation Maps set goals and tactics for each industrial sector to enhance growth and competitiveness.
- Enterprise Singapore is the primary agency responsible for SME development; its Strategic Plan—supporting the MTI Economic Strategy—aims to raise productivity, stimulate innovation, build enterprise capabilities and human capital, and accelerate internationalization.
- The Monetary Authority of Singapore (MAS) uses a Financial Services Transformation Map designed to make Singapore a regional and global hub for a variety of financial products and services; its goals also align with the MTI Economic Strategy.

SME Development

The government is using several major initiatives to bolster SME development. The first is MTI's Economic Strategy, which covers market, industry, enterprise and ecosystem development. These work in tandem to meet the overall MTI vision of promoting economic growth and creating good jobs, to enable Singaporeans to improve their lives.

Supporting the overall vision of the Economic Strategy is the Enterprise Singapore Strategic Plan. As lead agency for developing local enterprises, Enterprise Singapore adopts four strategies: (i) build enterprise capabilities, (ii) develop human capital, (iii) strengthen the enterprise ecosystem, and (iv) establish strong networks and partnerships. These will help SMEs keep pace with the evolving, increasingly complex business landscape locally and abroad. The strategic plan focuses on three key priorities: (i) raising productivity, (ii) strengthening innovation, and (iii) accelerating internationalization. First, Enterprise Singapore helps the large base of micro and small enterprises improve productivity by adopting technology, automation, and digitalization beginning with incorporation. Second, Enterprise Singapore supports companies develop new technologies or adopt technological solutions to create their own intellectual property to distinguish themselves from competitors. And third, Enterprise Singapore helps the broader base of SMEs venture overseas for the first time and supports those with existing market presence to expand their overseas footprint.

A second MTI program is the Research, Innovation, and Enterprise 2020 Plan. As innovation comprises both upstream research and downstream application, the plan also supports SME development. Its broad thrust is to support research, build the innovation capacity of enterprises to drive economic growth, and leverage science and technology for addressing national challenges.

As each industry is different, MTI introduced Industry Transformation Maps in 2016. Each map is tailored to the specific needs of particular industries and brings together relevant stakeholders, coordinated by a lead government agency. While these maps do not focus on SMEs, they benefit them via overall industrial development. Each ITM integrates four pillars of transformation: (i) productivity, (ii) jobs and skills, (iii) innovation, and (iv) trade and internationalization. These are mutually reinforcing to maximize impact.

Enterprise Singapore sponsors a third program directed toward SMEs called "Key Strategies—2019 and Beyond". The philosophy behind the plan is to "take a holistic, enterprise-centric approach to support willing and committed companies through transformation and growth."[130] There are three priorities: (i) raising productivity, (ii) strengthening innovation, and (iii) accelerating internationalization. The program provides Productivity Solutions Grants and acquaints SMEs with the Go Digital program. It connects SMEs with "innovation agents", experts in both management and technology. And it supports a "Plug and Play Network" for SMEs to access foreign markets.

The Key Strategies plan has also set four strategies: (i) build enterprise capabilities, (ii) develop human capital, (iii) strengthen the enterprise ecosystem, and (iv) establish strong networks and partnerships. Enterprise Singapore also runs 13 SME Centers to assist with building skills. It partners with Workforce Singapore and SkillsFuture Singapore to help develop human capital, works within the context of the Industry Transformation Maps, and collaborates with trade associations and chambers.

Financial Inclusion

Singapore is one of the world's international financial hubs. There is no financial inclusion strategy per se given the already high level of development in banking, insurance, and capital markets. Financial sector has its own Industry Transformation Map for future development.

MAS has a vision of Singapore as "a leading global financial center in Asia that connects global markets, supports Asia's development, and serves Singapore's economy."[131] It sets annual targets, including 4.3% value-added growth, 3,000 net jobs, with 1,000 or more in fintech, and productivity growth of 2.4%.

MAS uses three strategies: to become (i) a leading international wealth management hub, (ii) an Asian hub for fund management and domiciliation, and (iii) a global foreign exchange price discovery and liquidity center within Asia. MAS is cooperating with the financial services sector to become a regional leader in enterprise financing, infrastructure financing, fixed-income products, and insurance.

MAS espouses five tactics in building innovation and technology: (i) encourage financial institutions to enhance connectivity and fintech innovation, (ii) collaborate with financial institutions to create common utilities such as electronic payments, (iii) facilitate and invest in research and development, (iv) expand the web of cross-border cooperation agreements with other fintech centers, and (v) use technology to simplify regulatory compliance.

MAS uses three tactics for creating jobs and boosting skills: (i) build a strong local pipeline of specialized talent; (ii) re-skill and re-deploy professionals into job-growth areas; and (iii) facilitate job placement. Thus, the financial inclusion strategies and tactics MAS sets out support the overall MTI economic strategy.

[130] Enterprise Singapore. Key Strategies—2019 and Beyond. https://www.enterprisesg.gov.sg/about-us/strategic-plan.

[131] Monetary Authority of Singapore. Financial Services Industry Transformation Roadmap. https://www.mas.gov.sg/development/financial-services-industry-transformation-roadmap.

Data Tables

Table 10.1: SME Definition

Item	SME	Non-SME
Annual Sales	≤S$100 million	>S$100 million
Employees	≤200 employees	>200 employees

SME = small and medium-sized enterprise.
Source: ADB Asia SME Monitor 2020 database. Data from Singapore Department of Statistics, Ministry of Trade and Industry.

Table 10.2: SME Landscape

End of period data

Item	2014	2015	2016	2017	2018	2019
NUMBER OF ENTERPRISES						
Number of enterprises, total ('000)	244.1	247.6	248.7	254.6	265.1	273.1
Number of SMEs	242.8	246.2	247.4	253.3	263.8	271.8
Number of large enterprises	1.3	1.3	1.3	1.3	1.3	1.3
SME to total (%)	99.5	99.4	99.5	99.5	99.5	99.5
SME growth (%)	--	1.4	0.5	2.4	4.1	3.0
SMEs by sector (% share)						
Agriculture, forestry, and fisheries	--	--	--	--	--	--
Manufacturing	--	--	--	--	--	--
Transportation and communication	--	--	--	--	--	--
Construction	--	--	--	--	--	--
Wholesale and retail trade	--	--	--	--	--	--
Other services	--	--	--	--	--	--
Others	--	--	--	--	--	--
Number of SMEs by region (% share)						
Capital city	--	--	--	--	--	--
Others	--	--	--	--	--	--
EMPLOYMENT						
Number of employment, total (million people)	3.4	3.4	3.4	3.4	3.5	3.5
Number of employment by SMEs	2.4	2.5	2.5	2.5	2.5	2.5
Number of employment by large enterprises	1.0	1.0	1.0	1.0	1.0	1.0
SME employees to total (%)	70.6	73.5	73.5	73.5	71.4	71.4
SME employees growth (%)	--	0.9	0.4	(0.4)	0.7	1.8
Share of female employees to total employees (%)	--	--	--	--	--	--
Employment by SME by sector (% share)						
Agriculture, forestry, and fisheries	--	--	--	--	--	--
Manufacturing	--	--	--	--	--	--
Transportation and communication	--	--	--	--	--	--
Construction	--	--	--	--	--	--
Wholesale and retail trade	--	--	--	--	--	--
Other services	--	--	--	--	--	--
Others	--	--	--	--	--	--
Employment by SMEs by region (% share)						
Capital city	--	--	--	--	--	--
Others	--	--	--	--	--	--
CONTRIBUTION TO GDP						
NVA of enterprises (S$ billion)	359	381	396	426	459	463
NVA of SMEs (S$ billion)	180	181	189	200	204	207
SME contribution to total enterprises NVA (%)	50.1	47.5	47.7	46.9	44.4	44.7
SME NVA growth (%)	--	0.5	4.4	6.2	2.0	1.4
SME GDP by sector (% share)						
Agriculture, forestry, and fisheries	--	--	--	--	--	--
Manufacturing	--	--	--	--	--	--
Transportation and communication	--	--	--	--	--	--
Construction	--	--	--	--	--	--
Wholesale and retail trade	--	--	--	--	--	--
Other services	--	--	--	--	--	--
Others	--	--	--	--	--	--
SME GDP by region (% share)						
Capital city	--	--	--	--	--	--
Others	--	--	--	--	--	--
EXPORTS						
Total export value (S$ billion)	526.1	491.8	466.9	515.0	555.7	532.5
Total export growth (%)	0.1	(6.5)	(5.1)	10.3	7.9	(4.2)
SME export value (S$ billion)	--	--	--	--	--	--
SME export to total export value (%)	--	--	--	--	--	--
SME export growth (%)	--	--	--	--	--	--
IMPORTS						
Total import value (S$ billion)	478.6	423.4	403.3	452.1	500.2	489.7
Total import growth (%)	(1.4)	(11.5)	(4.7)	12.1	10.6	(2.1)
SME import value (S$ billion)	--	--	--	--	--	--
SME import to total import value (%)	--	--	--	--	--	--
SME import growth (%)	--	--	--	--	--	--

GDP = gross domestic product, NVA = nominal value added, SME = small and medium-sized enterprise.
Notes: 1. Enterprises comprise companies, businesses, nonprofit organizations, ministries, statutory boards, and government and/or government-aided schools. 2. SMEs are defined as enterprises with operating receipts not more than $100 million or employment not more than 200 workers; microenterprises are included. 3. Employment of enterprises refers to total employment excluding foreign domestic activities. 4. Value added of enterprises refers to gross value added less ownership of dwellings.
Source: ADB Asia SME Monitor 2020 database. Data from Singapore Department of Statistics.

Table 10.3: Bank Credit

End of period data

Item	2010	2011	2012	2013	2014	2015	2016	2017	2018	2019*
COMMERCIAL BANKS										
Number of commercial banks, total	120	120	123	123	124	126	124	128	127	131
Local banks	7	6	6	6	5	5	5	5	4	4
Full banks	18	18	18	17	18	18	18	19	19	20
Qualifying full banks	7	8	8	10	10	10	10	10	10	10
Wholesale banks	46	50	52	53	55	56	53	57	92	97
Offshore banks	42	38	39	37	36	37	38	37	2	0
Credit										
Loans outstanding, total (S$ million)	641,056	796,447	879,193	1,052,150	1,148,901	1,149,349	1,155,499	1,248,433	1,314,154	1,369,840
Loans outstanding in domestic currency (S$ million)[1]	322,744	420,456	490,707	574,274	607,201	599,756	617,347	651,932	671,735	692,401
Loans outstanding in foreign currency (S$ million)[2]	318,312	375,992	388,487	477,875	541,700	549,593	538,151	596,502	642,419	677,440
Loan growth (%)	13.5	24.2	10.4	19.7	9.2	0.0	0.5	8.0	5.3	4.2
Total commercial bank loans to GDP (%)	--	--	--	--	--	--	--	--	--	--
Loans in domestic currency (%)[1]	98.7	119.7	133.1	149.2	152.2	141.6	140.2	138.1	133.4	136.4
Loans in foreign currency (%)[2]	97.3	107.0	105.3	124.2	135.8	129.8	122.2	126.4	127.6	133.5
Lending rate (%)[3]	5.4	5.4	5.4	5.4	5.4	5.4	5.4	5.3	5.3	5.3
Gross nonperforming loans (NPLs) (S$ million)[2]	--	--	--	--	--	--	--	--	24,443	27,397
Gross NPLs to total loans (%)	--	--	--	--	--	--	--	--	1.9	2.0
Deposits										
Deposits, total (S$ million)	433,758	483,110	518,841	537,583	550,364	560,011	596,612	606,387	627,768	683,521
Deposits in domestic currency (S$ million)	429,824	478,180	513,634	530,815	541,079	549,501	588,229	598,533	619,048	664,802
Deposits in foreign currency (S$ million)	3,934	4,930	5,207	6,767	9,285	10,510	8,383	7,854	8,720	18,719
Deposit rate (%)[3]	0.13	0.11	0.11	0.10	0.11	0.14	0.14	0.16	0.16	0.16
SME LOANS										
SME loans outstanding, total (S$ million)	46,424	55,381	54,371	64,468	70,130	72,835	71,135	75,207	76,159	76,590
SME loans to total loans outstanding (%)	7.2	7.0	6.2	6.1	6.1	6.3	6.2	6.0	5.8	--
SME loans to GDP (%)	14.2	15.8	14.7	16.8	17.6	17.2	16.2	15.9	15.1	--
SME loan growth (%)	--	19.3	(1.8)	18.6	8.8	3.9	(2.3)	5.7	1.3	0.6
SME lending rate (%)	--	--	--	--	--	--	--	--	--	--
Nonperforming SME loans (NPLs) (S$ million)[4]	696	698	574	536	602	1,379	2,115	3,380	3,233	3,211
SME NPLs to total SME loans (%)	1.5	1.3	1.1	0.8	0.9	1.9	3.0	4.5	4.2	4.2
Number of SME loan borrowers	--	--	--	--	--	74,608	77,347	78,854	77,198	77,468
SME loan borrowers to total bank borrowers (%)	--	--	--	--	--	--	--	--	--	--
SME loan rejection rate (% of total applications)	--	--	--	--	--	--	--	--	--	--
Number of SME savings account in banks	--	--	--	--	--	--	--	--	--	--
Guaranteed SME loans (S$ million)	--	--	--	--	--	--	--	--	--	--
Non-collateral SME loans (S$ million)	--	--	--	--	--	--	--	--	--	--
SME loans outstanding by sector (% share)										
Agriculture, forestry, and fisheries	--	--	--	--	--	--	--	--	--	37.0
Manufacturing	--	--	--	--	--	--	--	--	--	7.9
Transportation and communication	--	--	--	--	--	--	--	--	--	0.4
Construction	--	--	--	--	--	--	--	--	--	25.9
Wholesale and retail trade	--	--	--	--	--	--	--	--	--	8.3
Other services	--	--	--	--	--	--	--	--	--	16.9
Others	--	--	--	--	--	--	--	--	--	3.7
SME loans outstanding by region (% share)										
Capital city	--	--	--	--	--	--	--	--	--	--
Others	--	--	--	--	--	--	--	--	--	--
SME loans outstanding by type of use (% share)										
For working capital	--	--	--	--	--	--	--	--	--	--
For capital investment	--	--	--	--	--	--	--	--	--	--
SME loans outstanding by tenor (% share)										
Less than 1 year	--	--	--	--	--	--	--	--	--	--
1-5 years	--	--	--	--	--	--	--	--	--	--
More than 5 years	--	--	--	--	--	--	--	--	--	--
SME loans outstanding by type of collateralisation (% share)										
Secured by property	52.3	45.6	53.9	53.8	59.0	62.8	65.0	62.0	63.3	63.7
Secured by others	24.8	24.7	20.9	25.7	24.1	16.5	15.8	17.1	16.0	17.1
Unsecured	22.9	29.7	25.3	20.5	16.9	20.7	19.2	20.9	20.7	19.2

GDP = gross domestic product, SME = small and medium-sized enterprise.

* Data for commercial banks are as of end-2019 while data for SME loans are as of June 2019.

1 Data refer to domestic banking unit, which holds holds its domestically focused operations denominated in Singapore dollars.

2 Data refer to Asian currency unit, which holds holds its offshore operations entirely denominated in foreign currency.

3 Prime lending rate and bank savings rate, respectively.

4 Calculated using nonperforming loan ratio.

Source: ADB Asia SME Monitor 2020 database. Data from Monetary Authority of Singapore.

Table 10.4: Nonbank Finance

End of period data

Item	2010	2011	2012	2013	2014	2015	2016	2017	2018	2019*
NUMBER OF NONBANK FINANCE INSTITUTIONS										
Microfinance institutions	--	--	--	--	--	--	--	--	--	--
Credit unions/cooperatives	--	--	--	--	--	--	--	--	--	--
Finance companies	3	3	3	3	3	3	3	3	3	3
Pawnshops	--	--	--	--	--	--	--	--	--	--
Leasing companies	--	--	--	--	--	--	--	--	--	--
Factoring companies	--	--	--	--	--	--	--	--	--	--
Insurance companies	158	157	164	168	177	181	185	182	182	184
Others	--	--	--	--	--	--	--	--	--	--
FINANCE COMPANIES										
Financing outstanding, total (S$ million)	8,058	9,460	11,312	11,654	12,385	13,252	12,547	12,849	13,254	14,712
Housing loans	1,486	1,517	1,403	1,394	1,448	1,476	1,397	1,334	1,258	1,347
Hire-purchase finance	2,070	2,038	2,090	1,892	1,779	1,978	2,113	2,151	2,206	2,327
Lease finance	--	--	--	--	--	--	--	--	--	--
Other loans and advances**	4,503	5,905	7,819	8,368	9,158	9,798	9,036	9,365	9,790	11,038
Financing growth (%)	(0.4)	17.4	19.6	3.0	6.3	7.0	(5.3)	2.4	3.2	11.0
Total financing to GDP (%)	2.5	2.7	3.1	3.0	3.1	3.1	2.9	2.7	2.6	2.9
Annual financing rate (%)										
Hire-purchase of new vehicles (3 years)	3.6	3.4	3.4	4.1	4.1	4.9	5.0	5.1	4.9	4.9
Housing loans (15 years)	4.4	4.3	2.9	2.9	2.9	3.2	3.4	3.2	3.2	3.3
Gross nonperforming financing (NPFs) (S$ million)	--	--	--	--	--	--	--	--	14.8	19.7
Gross NPFs to total financing (%)	--	--	--	--	--	--	--	--	1.0	1.3
Number of customers financed, total	--	--	--	--	--	--	--	--	--	--
Financing outstanding by sector (% share)										
Agriculture, forestry, and fisheries	--	--	--	--	--	--	--	--	--	--
Manufacturing	--	--	--	--	--	--	--	--	--	--
Transportation and communication	--	--	--	--	--	--	--	--	--	--
Construction	--	--	--	--	--	--	--	--	--	--
Wholesale and retail trade	--	--	--	--	--	--	--	--	--	--
Other services	--	--	--	--	--	--	--	--	--	--
Others	--	--	--	--	--	--	--	--	--	--
Financing outstanding by region (% share)										
Capital city	--	--	--	--	--	--	--	--	--	--
Others	--	--	--	--	--	--	--	--	--	--

* Data as of August 2019.

** Includes block discounting.

Source: ADB Asia SME Monitor 2020 database. Data from Monetary Authority of Singapore.

Table 10.5: Capital Markets

End of period data

Item	2008	2009	2010	2011	2012	2013	2014	2015	2016	2017	2018	2019
EQUITY MARKET												
Main Board												
Index: Strait Times Index	1,762	2,898	3,190	2,646	3,167	3,167	3,365	2,883	2,881	3,403	3,069	3,223
Market capitalization (S$ million)*	384,663	675,670	829,162	775,780	934,543	939,896	997,576	904,770	925,994	1,052,167	936,869	937,830
Growth (%)	(50.4)	75.7	22.7	(6.4)	20.5	0.6	6.1	(9.3)	2.3	13.6	(11.0)	0.1
Trading value (S$ million)	--	--	--	--	--	--	--	--	--	242,536	254,388	233,174
Trading volume (million of shares)	--	--	--	--	--	--	--	--	--	218,121	170,725	147,600
Number of listed companies*	767	773	778	773	776	776	775	769	757	750	741	723
Number of IPOs	35	22	32	22	22	27	32	15	18	24	17	13
Number of delisted companies	--	--	--	--	--	--	--	--	--	--	--	--
Specialized Board												
Catalist												
Index	797	1,231	1,145	816	930	1,076	736	497	441	470	310	272
Market capitalization (S$ million)	3,562	5,325	6,462	5,347	6,782	9,326	10,791	9,521	9,233	12,819	10,534	9,809
Growth (%)	--	49.5	21.4	(17.3)	26.8	37.5	15.7	(11.8)	(3.0)	38.8	(17.8)	(6.9)
Trading value (S$ million)	--	--	--	--	--	--	--	--	--	9,420	3,522	3,017
Trading volume (million of shares)	--	--	--	--	--	--	--	--	--	139,682	64,512	49,519
Number of listed companies**	133	134	133	136	139	139	155	172	185	200	214	216
Number of IPOs**	7	14	6	12	8	12	19	12	11	--	12	7
Number of delisted companies**	2	1	6	4	2	5	2	3	4	--	--	5
Moved to the main board	--	--	--	--	--	--	--	--	--	--	--	--

IPO = initial public offering.

* Refers to the total equity market.

** For years 2008 to 2016, data refers to Alternative/SME board from the World Federation of Exchanges database, while for years 2017 to 2019, data are from Singapore Exchange Market Report.

Source: ADB Asia SME Monitor 2020 database. Data from Singapore Exchange and World Federation of Exchanges.

Table 10.6: Policies and Regulations

Regulations		
Name		**Outline**
Nonfinance regulations		
Enterprise Singapore Board Act (2018)		Establishes Enterprise Singapore as a statutory board under the Ministry of Trade and Industry.
Finance regulations		
Finance Companies Act 43 of 1967 (Chapter 108) [amended in 1995]		Regulate finance companies.
Hire-Purchase Act 1 of 1969 (Chapter 125) [amended in 2014]		Principally regulates the form and content of hire-purchase agreements, and spells out the rights and duties of parties to such agreements.
Banking Act 41 of 1970 (Chapter 19) [amended in 2008]		Regulate commercial banks.
Electronic Transactions Act 16 of 2010 (Chapter 88) [amended in 2011]		Legal framework for e-commerce and and e-payment issues.
Personal Data Protection Act No.26 of 2012		Consumer protection in digital transactions.
Credit Bureau Act No.27 of 2016		Regulate credit bureaus.
Regulators and Policymakers		
Name		**Responsibility**
Enterprise Singapore (ESG)		Government agency which champions local enterprise development and works with companies to build capabilities, innovate, and internationalize.
Monetary Authority of Singapore (MAS)		Integrated financial regulator that oversees all financial institutions in Singapore which includes banks, insurers, capital market intermediaries, financial advisors, and stock exchanges.
Ministry of Trade and Industry (MTI)		Responsible for the formulation of policies related to trade and industry in Singapore, including strategies to develop small and medium-sized enterprises.
Ministry of Finance (MOF)		MOF aims to advance the well-being and development of Singapore through finance; strives to achieve a balanced budget through prudent and sustainable fiscal policies; fosters a regulatory environment conducive to business and enterprise; ensures prudent investment of the government's reserves and other public funds; and sets policies for government procurement, customs regulation, accounting standards, and business regulation.
Policies		
Name	**Responsible Entity**	**Outline**
MTI's Economic Strategy	MTI	These strategies are intended to promote economic growth and create good jobs for Singaporeans: 1) Market Development 2) Industry Development 3) Enterprise Development 4) Ecosystem Development
Industry Transformation Maps	MTI	Consists of a growth and competitiveness plan for each industry, supported by four pillars: 1) Productivity 2) Jobs and Skills 3) Innovation 4) Trade and Internationalization
Enterprise Singapore's Strategic Plan	ESG	1) Build enterprise capabilities 2) Develop human capital 3) Strengthen enterprise ecosystem 4) Establish strong networks and partnerships
Research, Innovation and Enterprise 2020 Plan	National Research Foundation	Support research, build up innovation capacity of companies to drive economic growth, and leverage on science and technology to address national challenges.

Source: ADB Asia SME Monitor 2020 database. Data from Enterprise Singapore, and Ministry of Trade and Industry.

Country Review

Thailand

Overview

Economic growth slowed to 2.4% in 2019.[132] Escalating trade tensions between the United States (US) and People's Republic of China (PRC) contributed to lower international trade and affected domestic investment. Thailand had a 38.4 million-strong labor force and low 0.9% unemployment rate in 2018.[133] Micro, small, and medium-sized enterprises (MSMEs) play a key role in Thailand's economic growth. In 2018, they accounted for 99.8% of total enterprises, employed 85.5% of the workforce, and contributed 43% of gross domestic product (GDP). The majority of MSMEs are engaged in services. MSMEs generate one-third of exports by value. But recent trade tensions slowed demand. Growth in the traditional MSME credit market has stagnated. Instead, emerging digital finance platforms—such as debt and equity crowdfunding and peer-to-peer (P2P) lending—has begun to serve unmet demand from emerging and high-growth firms and start-ups. Developing innovation-driven MSMEs is a key policy pillar of Thailand's long-term national economic development plan.

1. MSME Development

- The majority of MSMEs are microenterprises or sole proprietorships engaged in wholesale and retail trade; there appears to be high scrap-and-build condition of business.
- The services sector accounts for a large portion of MSME employment; large profitable firms create more jobs than MSMEs.
- MSME contribution to GDP has grown moderately, less affected by declining international trade; it was mainly supported by the services sector.
- MSMEs do not contribute significantly to international trade (by value); those engaged in global business face chronic trade deficits.
- Thailand's e-commerce market has been growing rapidly; domestic e-commerce start-ups are gradually increasing, creating more business opportunities for MSMEs.
- Chambers of commerce play a critical role in supporting MSME business development and innovation by supporting young entrepreneurs, training programs, and one-stop services.

Scale of MSMEs

Thailand modified its definition of enterprises in November 2019, introducing microenterprises as a new segment along with new revenue criterion (Table 11.1). Under the old definition, a small and medium-sized enterprise (SME) is defined as the firm having up to 200 employees or fixed assets (excluding land) of less than B200 million in manufacturing and services (excluding wholesale and retail trading). An SME in the wholesale trade had up to 50 employees or fixed assets less than B100 million, while an SME in retail trade had up to 30 employees or fixed assets less than B60 million. Under the new definition, an MSME in manufacturing is defined as the firm having up to 200 employees or revenue (annual income) of less than B500 million, while an MSME in services and trading has up to 100 employees or annual

[132] ADB. 2020. *Asian Development Outlook 2020 Supplement (June 2020)*. Manila

[133] National Statistical Office. Statistical Yearbook Thailand 2019. Labor force refers to population aged 15 years old and over.

revenue less than B300 million. This section uses the old definition as past data have yet to be updated to reflect the new definition. It does cite the provisional analysis of MSMEs under the new definition made by the Office of Small and Medium Enterprises Promotion (OSMEP).[134] Throughout this country report, the term "MSME" is collectively used.

As of the end of 2018, there were around 3.08 million MSMEs, or 99.8% of total enterprises, a 1.0% growth in number from the previous year (Figure 11.1A and Table 11.2). By type of business, sole proprietorships and others accounted for 74.3% of MSMEs in 2018, followed by juristic entities (23.0%) and community enterprises (2.7%) (OSMEP 2019). By sector, 41.6% of MSMEs were engaged in wholesale and retail trade, followed by other services (39.8%), manufacturing (17.1%), and agribusiness (1.5%) in 2018 (Figure 11.1B). By region, 18.2% of MSMEs were in the capital city Bangkok, while the remaining 81.8% were located in provinces, with the central provinces of Nakhon Pathom, Nonthaburi, Pathum Thani, and Samut Prakan having the second-largest density of MSMEs (8.5% in 2018) (OSMEP 2019).

OSMEP's White Paper on SME 2019 provisionally analyzed the MSME structure under the new definition, with MSMEs accounting for 99.5% of total enterprises in 2018, of which 85.7% were microenterprises, 12.5% small enterprises, and 1.3% medium-sized enterprises. Most of the firms categorized as small enterprises under the old definition moved to the new microenterprise classification. The share of MSMEs to total enterprises decreased by 0.2% in 2018 under the new definition.

There were 71,815 MSMEs newly established in 2018, a 2.7% decrease from the previous year. Meanwhile, 21,676 MSMEs were closed or liquidated in 2018, a drop of 1.8% from 2017 (OSMEP 2019). Wholesale and retail trade (except for motorcycle sales) covered 31.5% of newly established MSMEs, while 33.4% of MSMEs that closed business were in the same sector, suggesting that the scrap and build of businesses is relatively high in the wholesale and retail trade sector.

In Thailand, the Department of Business Development under the Ministry of Commerce has managed business registration since 1923. In April 2017, the department launched an online business registration database, called DBD DataWarehouse+. As of September 2019, 1.5 million enterprises were registered online, of which 700,000 are active while the remaining 800,000 are in liquidation or changed business type.[135]

Figure 11.1: Number of MSMEs

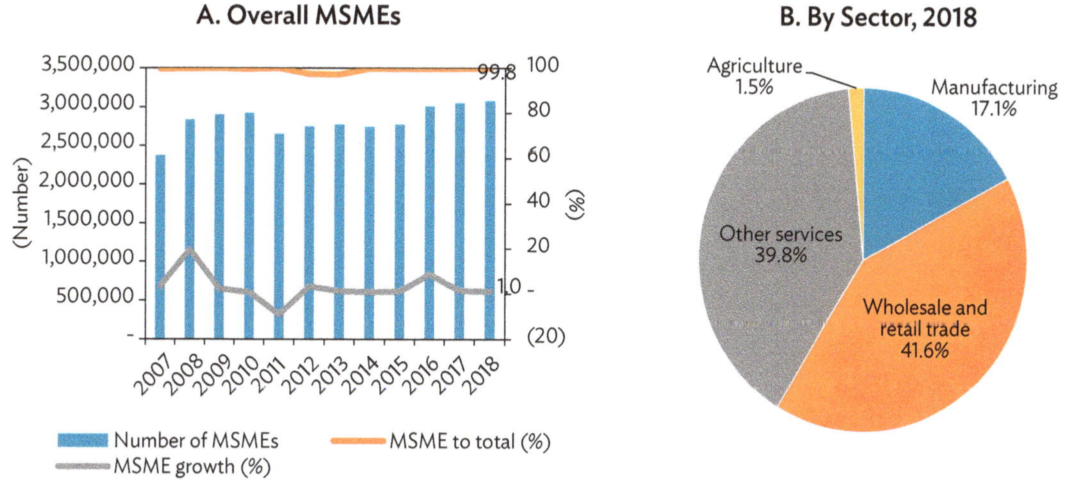

MSME = micro, small, and medium-sized enterprise.

Source: ADB Asia SME Monitor 2020 database. Data from Office of Small and Medium Enterprise Promotion.

[134] Office of Small and Medium Enterprises Promotion (OSMEP). 2019. White Paper on SME 2019.

[135] The critical challenge in creating the MSME database is how to encourage MSMEs to register on the database. There is a huge data gap between active MSMEs and registered MSMEs.

Employment

MSMEs employed 13.9 million workers in 2018, a 4.7% increase from the previous year, and accounted for 85.5% of Thailand's total workforce (Figure 11.2A). By type of business, sole proprietorships and others accounted for 36.0%of total MSME employees, followed by juristic entities (64.0%) in 2018 (OSMEP 2019). By sector, 31.8% of MSME employees were engaged in wholesale and retail trade, followed by other services (43.4%), manufacturing (24.3%), and agribusiness (0.5%) in 2018 (Figure 11.2B). By region, 30.2% of MSME employees worked in the capital city Bangkok with the remaining 69.8% located in provinces in 2018. Central provinces outside Bangkok had the second-largest number of employees by MSMEs (13.6% in 2018) (OSMEP 2019).

Based on the new definition, in 2018, MSME employees accounted for 68.5% of Thailand's workforce, with 30.5% in microenterprises, 25.4% in small enterprises, and 12.7% in medium-sized enterprises. More than half of small enterprises under the old definition shifted to the new classification of microenterprises, medium-sized and large firms. The share of MSME employees to total employees dropped sharply, by 19.8% in 2018, based on revenue. This suggests that firms with high earnings moderately absorbed jobs while MSMEs under the new definition created less jobs.

In 2019, female workers accounted for 45.6% of the total workforce[136]; a relatively high business participation by women. However, there is no breakdown on women working for MSMEs.

Figure 11.2: Employment by MSMEs

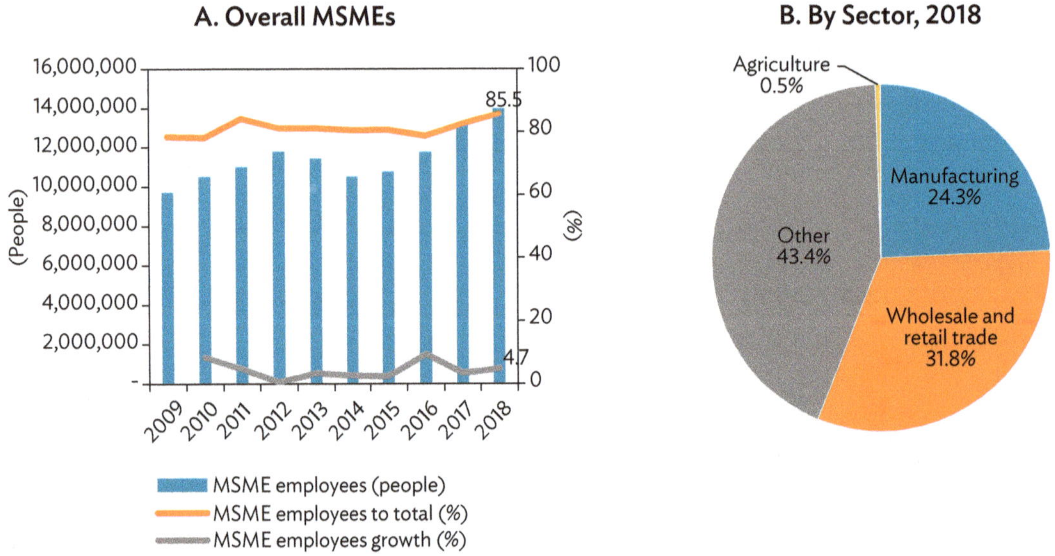

MSME = micro, small, and medium-sized enterprise.

Source: ADB Asia SME Monitor 2020 database. Data from Office of Small and Medium Enterprise Promotion.

Business Productivity

Real GDP in Thailand slowed to 2.4% in 2019 (ADB), affected by global trade tensions. In tandem, MSME exports were negatively affected as well. However, it does not seriously affect overall MSME performance as most MSMEs market domestically. In fact, MSME contributions to GDP have moderately increased. In 2018, MSMEs contributed 43.0% of GDP or B7 trillion, a 7.0% increase over 2017 (Figure 11.3A). By sector, the services sector,

136 National Statistical Office, Labor Force Survey. Data as of the fourth quarter of the year.

combining wholesale and retail trade and other services (including accommodation and catering, fright delivery and storage, and financial services and insurance), accounted for 70.5% of total MSME GDP in 2018, followed by manufacturing, including food and beverages, chemicals, and petroleum-related products (22.6%) (Figure 11.3B). Regional distribution data are unavailable.

Figure 11.3: MSME Contribution to Gross Domestic Product

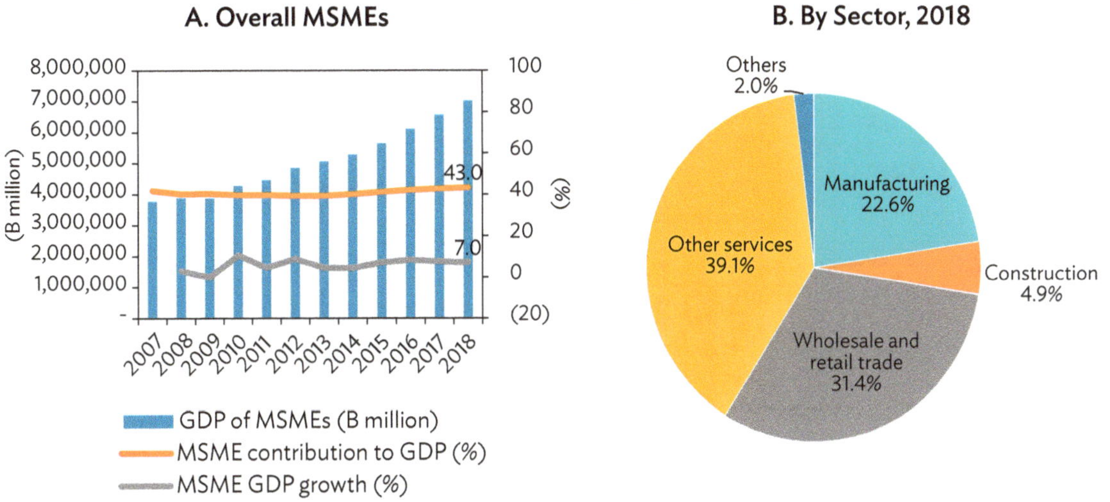

GDP = gross domestic product; MSME = micro, small, and medium-sized enterprise.

Source: ADB Asia SME Monitor 2020 database. Data from Office of Small and Medium Enterprise Promotion.

Market Access

Thailand's exports by value have been declining, affected by the escalated trade tensions between the US and PRC, along with shrinking foreign demand generally. In 2018, MSME exports amounted to B2,325 billion or 28.7% of the total export value, an almost flat growth of 0.5% from the previous year (Figure 11.4A). MSME export growth has been below total export growth since 2017 (Figure 11.4B). MSME imports reached B2,979 billion, or 36.8% of the total import value in 2018, an 8.5% increase from the previous year. MSME import growth has exceeded total import growth since 2015 (Figure 11.4C).

MSMEs mainly imported gems and jewelry; electrical appliances and parts; and machinery, computers, and accessories; to use them as capital goods and raw materials for production and use for domestic consumption (OSMEP 2019). This suggests that MSMEs somewhat rely on imported goods for production. Since 2010, MSME imports have exceeded exports, generating a chronic MSME international trade deficit.

OSMEP also analyzed the impact of new definition on the performance of MSME exports and imports. Under the new definition, MSMEs contributed 12.5% of total export value in 2018, a sharp drop from 28.7% under the old definition. Instead, the share of large firms to total exports increased from 69.7% to 86.0% under the new definition. MSME imports traced the same trend. MSMEs contributed 16.2% of the total import value in 2018, a sharp drop from the 36.8% under the old definition. Instead, the share of large firms to total imports increased from 60.4% to 81.0% under the new definition. This shows a smaller MSME contribution to international trade and the MSME international trade deficit.

MSME participation in domestic and global value chains is limited. Under the national economic development plan (Thailand 4.0), the government promotes the creation of industrial clusters as high-potential production bases, targeting specific clusters such as the automotive and parts industry, electronics, the digital industry, agro-processing, and garments. Developing these clusters offers greater opportunities for MSMEs to participate in domestic and global value chains and improves both market access and production efficiency.

Figure 11.4: MSME Exports and Imports

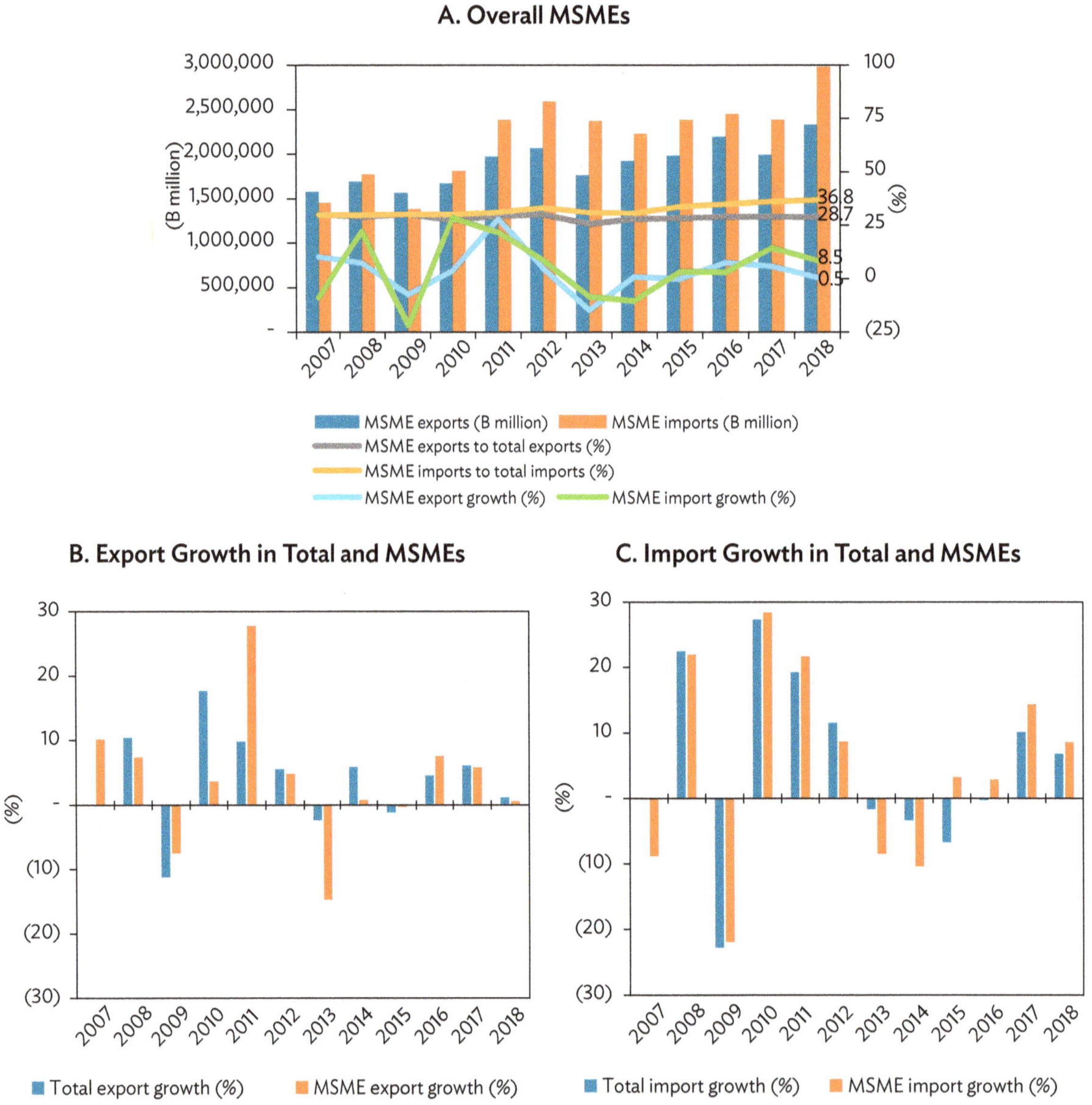

MSME = micro, small, and medium-sized enterprise.

Source: ADB Asia SME Monitor 2020 database. Data from Office of Small and Medium Enterprise Promotion.

Technology and Innovation

The mobile communications market has been growing sharply, reaching B283 billion in 2017, a 17.1% increase from the previous year.[137] Internet users increased to 36 million people in 2018, or more than half of the population, of which 94.7% accessed the internet via smartphones (footnote 133). Those using the internet for work numbered 3 million in 2018, a 35.4% increase from 2017. Internet and mobile phones have become popular tools for people in business and daily life. Accordingly, the e-commerce market has been growing rapidly in Thailand.

According to JP Morgan (2019 Payments Trend), Thailand's e-commerce market was valued at $26.2 billion in 2017, up a sharp 26.8% from 2016. The largest e-commerce category is travel (56.9% of e-commerce merchants), followed by consumer electronics (15.3%). Multinational e-commerce platforms such as Lazada and Shopee have a large presence in Thailand's online shopping industry. Domestic e-commerce players such as JIB (online technology product sales) and online travel start-ups have also gradually grown in number.

Thailand 4.0 addresses the development of technology clusters and future industries, including e-commerce and fintech, to strengthen national competitive advantage. The corresponding SME promotion master plan has encouraged a shift from traditional MSMEs to "smart" MSMEs, promoting e-commerce for marketing, which offers greater business opportunities for Thai MSMEs and start-ups.

Networking and Support

The Thai Chamber of Commerce (TCC) is the largest business network in Thailand with 123,932 members—with 7,181 members in Bangkok (mostly MSMEs), 45,164 from 76 provincial chambers of commerce, 38,475 from 138 trade associations, 7,330 from 35 foreign chambers of commerce, and 18,117 from the University of Thai Chamber of Commerce. TCC has targeted 300,000 MSME members by 2021.

TCC organizes the Young Entrepreneur Chambers of Commerce to support its young entrepreneur members (355 in Bangkok and 4,937 in provincial areas as of September 2019). The number of young entrepreneurs is increasing in Thailand. They are spread widely across the country and increasing in number. The University of TCC conducts research on MSMEs.

TCC works on two main activities: (i) capacity-building programs and (ii) Member Development Centers (formerly SME Smart Centers). Capacity-building programs are organized for members each month. TCC provides at least one training program a month, covering topics such as filing taxes and legal issues. The programs encourage MSMEs to network. TCC promotes financial literacy among members and collaborates with other institutions such as the Stock Exchange of Thailand (SET) for training. SME Smart Centers started in 2015. In April 2019, the name was changed to Member Development Centers, though its functions have not changed. The centers offer one-stop services for MSME members. They provide advisory services (on market access, for example) and help with certifications, such as certificates for agriproducts, and connect them to financial institutions. Only selected MSME members can receive services from the centers. For these MSMEs, TCC assesses their growth potential through interviews. TCC members from large firms support MSME members by offering advice through the centers. On average, 150 MSMEs contact the centers each month (as of September 2019). TCC views services, agriculture, and tourism as the business sectors with the greatest growth potential.

[137] Statistical Yearbook Thailand 2018.

2. Access to Finance

- The credit market in Thailand has been slowing, especially for MSMEs, affected by weakening domestic demand and investment, the result of declining exports.
- A specialized bank offers concessional loans to MSMEs, accepting interest rate subsidies from the government; public credit guarantees are also critical to promote MSME access to bank credit, offering tailor-made products and services.
- The nonbank finance industry is small and plays a limited role in meeting MSME financing demand.
- The electronic payment system has developed along with the pilot national digital identity system; digital finance platforms such as debt and equity crowdfunding and P2P lending have begun serving unmet demand from emerging and high-growth firms and start-ups.
- Although the capital market appears stagnant, the mai, a market for high-growth MSMEs, has seen a steady stream of its listed companies migrate to the main board, an important role in supporting the growth cycle of enterprises.
- One private credit bureau operates in Thailand. A secured lending system with a centralized collateral registry has been operating since 2015.

Bank Credit

The banking sector is the main funding source for enterprises in Thailand, including MSMEs. As of end-2019, 30 registered commercial banks and 8 specialized financial institutions (SFIs)—composed of six deposit-taking and two non-deposit-taking SFIs—operate in the country. SFIs enable specific government policies and programs, which include the Small and Medium Enterprise Development Bank. Total assets, combining commercial banks and SFIs, accounted for 60.4% of total financial institutions' assets[138] as of end-2019.[139]

Outstanding MSME loans from commercial banks and SFIs totaled B6,581 billion in 2019, of which B4,939 billion were from commercial banks with the remaining B1,643 billion from SFIs (Figure 11.5A and Table 11.3). MSME loans by commercial banks accounted for 30.9% of bank loans outstanding—and 30.3% of GDP—in 2019. However, the growth in MSME lending has been decelerating, with flat annual growth in 2019—less than the slow growth in total credit (3.5%). Weakening domestic demand and investment accompanying economic uncertainty and declining exports contributed to the slowdown of the credit market, especially for MSMEs. MSME nonperforming loans (NPLs) by commercial banks totaled B231 billion or 4.7% of the total MSME loans in 2019, which exceeded the total NPLs by commercial banks in the same period (3.0%).[140]

By sector, services (wholesale and retail trade and other services) accounted for 65.1% of the MSME loans by commercial banks in 2019, followed by manufacturing (18.9%) (Figure 11.5B). Bank of Thailand, the central bank, uses the old definition of SMEs for its MSME loan statistics. Commercial banks define MSMEs more practically depending on their individual operations and market segmentation.

The Bank of Thailand promotes MSME access to finance under the Financial Sector Masterplan Phase III for 2016–2020, highlighting the development of the MSME financial database and credit guarantees. The central bank plans to establish a financial data center in 2020. There are several MSME-related databases overseen by different government agencies, such as OSMEP (SME white paper) and the Ministry of Industry (SME Input-

138 Thailand's financial institutions include savings cooperatives and credit unions, mutual funds, insurance firms, leasing firms, credit card and personal loan firms, provident funds, government pension fund, asset management firms, securities firms, agricultural cooperatives, and pawnshops, besides commercial banks and specialized financial institutions.

139 Bank of Thailand. Financial Stability Report 2019.

140 Bank of Thailand criteria categorizes loan assets into five levels: (i) pass, (ii) special mention, (iii) substandard, (iv) doubtful, and (v) doubtful of loss. Nonperforming loans are ranked substandard, doubtful, and doubtful of loss. Please refer to: https://www.bot.or.th/Thai/FIPCS/Documents/FPG/2559/EngPDF/25590128.pdf.

Output Table). The Bank of Thailand is proposing a centralized MSME database that will link all MSME data in the country, including that shared by government agencies, academia, and the MSMEs themselves.

Figure 11.5: MSME Loans

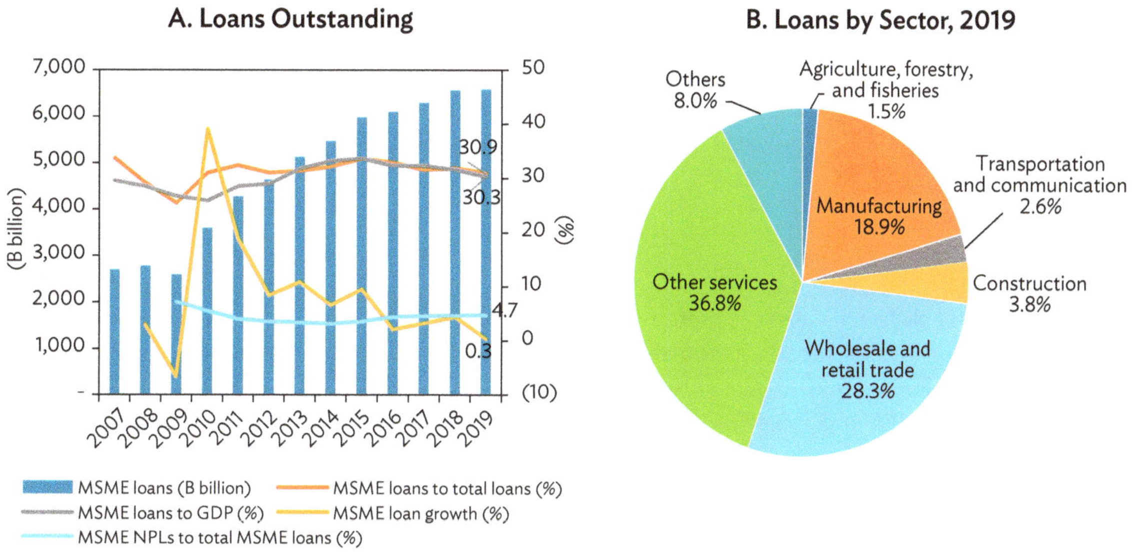

GDP = gross domestic product; MSME = micro, small, and medium-sized enterprise; NPL = nonperforming loan.

Source: ADB Asia SME Monitor 2020 database. Data from Bank of Thailand.

Public Financing and Guarantees

a. Specialized bank for MSMEs

The Small and Medium Enterprise Development Bank (SMEDB) is one of six deposit-taking SFIs in Thailand. SMEDB has 95 branches across the country and 300,000 MSME customers. In 2018, SMEDB developed a mobile application for financial services delivery called the SME D Bank Application, which covers mobile credit and financial services (D-Digital), online finance knowledge sharing (D-Development), and mobility counter services that send bank staff to local areas to serve customers (D-Delivery). The mobility counter service covers all areas of the country, with bank staff visiting customers within 3 days, and with loans approved within 7 days. As of September 2019, there were 1,000 D-Delivery units covering MSMEs in 7,255 villages (districts). About 50,000 MSMEs use SME D Bank Application, increasing online credit.

SMEDB offers several loan products for MSMEs: (i) Strengthen SMEs Loan (interest at 0.65% per month, a B15 million maximum loan amount, with maximum maturity of 7 years); (ii) Local Economy Loan (minimum loan rate of 3.875% per annum, maximum loan amount of B5 million, and maximum maturity of 7 years); (iii) Micro SMEs Loan (1% annual interest rate, B1 million maximum loan, and 7-year maximum maturity); (iv) Transformation Loan for machine improvement (4% annual interest rate, B15 million maximum loan, and 7-year maximum maturity); and (v) SMART SMEs Loan (1% minimum loan rate per annum, B15 million maximum loan, and 10-year maximum maturity). These products accept interest rate subsidies, which enables SMEDB to offer concessional loans to MSMEs as opposed to commercial banks with their annual lending rates of 6%–7%.

Depending on the industry and the loan product, the average loan term of SMEDB credit is 3–4 years for firms in services and 5–7 years for manufacturing firms, with the average loan size around B3 million per customer. The

NPL ratio was high at 30% before 2015, but has decreased to 20% as of September 2019. Nonetheless, it remains very high compared with commercial bank NPL ratios of 3%-5%. Some MSMEs suffer from natural disasters. The services sector (such as retail trade) account for 78% of MSME borrowers, followed by manufacturing (11%). Most borrowers using SMEDB credit are new customers.

Besides SMEDB, the Government Savings Bank (GSB) has a refinancing scheme for MSMEs, which offers concessional financial intermediation lending. It lends to commercial banks at a low 0.1% interest rate, and then commercial banks relend to MSMEs at a 4% per annum rate. The loan tenor is up to 7 years. Banks require collateral for loans, generally real estate but movable assets also qualify. Collateral requirements are at individual bank discretion.

b. Public credit guarantees

Public credit guarantees play a critical role in promoting MSME access to bank credit, especially supporting MSMEs amid economic downturns. Guaranteed loans outstanding have been increasing since a portfolio guarantee scheme (PGS) was launched in 2009. By 2019, guarantees reached B389 billion (11.1% of total MSME loans in 2019, 1% higher than 2018) (Figure 11.6 and Table 11.4). However, growth in guaranteed loans has been decelerating since 2016, corresponding to the slowing growth of the MSME credit market in general.

The Thai Credit Guarantee Corporation (TCG) is a single state-funded guarantee institution in Thailand. TCG provides three main credit guarantee products targeting MSMEs: (i) portfolio guarantees, (ii) guarantees for start-ups and innovative businesses, and (iii) guarantees for micro community businesses (Table 11.5). New regulations on credit guarantees were issued in 2018 to diversify TCG's guarantee services.

TCG launched the PGS in 2009 as part of economic stimulus measures against the 2008–2009 global financial crisis. The PGS phase 8 program covers 2019–2020. Under the PGS, when prosecuted, TCG guarantees 100% of the payment stated in each letter of guarantee issued to participating banks in case that the nonperforming guarantee does not exceed 18.75% of the average guarantee outstanding in each portfolio that pools all guaranteed MSME loans from the participating bank every year. In case that the nonperforming guarantee falls between 18.75% and 34.82%, TCG guarantees 70% of the payment stated in the letter of guarantee. PGS targets Thai SMEs with a guarantee limit of B100 million or less. The maximum coverage per portfolio is not more than 30% of the total portfolio on average.

Startup and Innobiz is a package guarantee scheme for new Thai MSMEs (operating 3 years or less) or innovative businesses. It was launched in 2019 and continues until 2021. The guarantee limit is B40 million or less. Maximum coverage per package is not more than 27%–32% of total packages. TCG guarantees 100% or 50% of the payment depending on the level of the NPLs.

Micro3 is a package guarantee scheme from 2018 through 2020 for micro business owners and peddlers. The guarantee limit is between B10,000–B200,000, with maximum coverage per package not more than 28%–38% of the total package amount, depending on fee rate (the 18% government subsidy plus guarantee fee). TCG guarantees 100% of the payment with the maximum 28%–38% claim on the total package amount.

The Fiscal Policy Office (FPO) under the Ministry of Finance has proposed a new credit guarantee scheme to the TCG, a B150 million program (total outstanding guaranteed loans) for high-potential MSMEs with no collateral. The new scheme would include flexible partial guarantees. In line with this, TCG plans to launch a risk-based credit guarantee product in 2020, which will use a fixed or flexible guarantee ratio. The credit scoring model for MSMEs is also being developed.

Nonbank Financing

The nonbank finance industry is small and plays a limited role in meeting MSMEs financing demand. As of the third quarter of 2019, total assets of savings cooperatives accounted for 6.7% of total financial institutions' assets, followed by leasing firms (2.0%) and pawnshops (0.2%) (footnote 139). According to the Bank of Thailand, there were 1,995 savings cooperatives and credit unions, 771 leasing firms, and 689 pawnshops in 2019 (Figure 11.7 and Table 11.6). The structure of nonbank finance industry has been unchanged since 2015.

Figure 11.6: Credit Guarantees—Thai Credit Guarantee Corporation

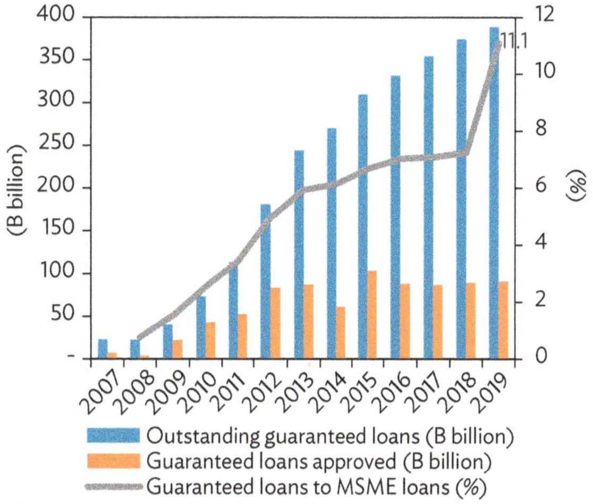

MSME = micro, small, and medium-sized enterprise.

Source: ADB Asia SME Monitor 2020 database. Data from Thai Credit Guarantee Corporation.

Digital Financial Services

In 2019, the Electronic Transactions Development Agency (ETDA) under the Ministry of Digital for Economy and Society developed a national digital identity (NDID) system, with related legislation and pilot testing. The NDID is a project under Bank of Thailand's regulatory sandbox and has been implemented initially in payment, banking, and government (health care) services. It is the core infrastructure for electronic transactions, using e-authentication between service providers and customers through mobile devices. It includes biometrics along with fingerprint and facial recognition, and should help develop digital business and mobile banking, benefitting MSME business and access to finance.

Figure 11.7: Number of Nonbank Finance Institutions

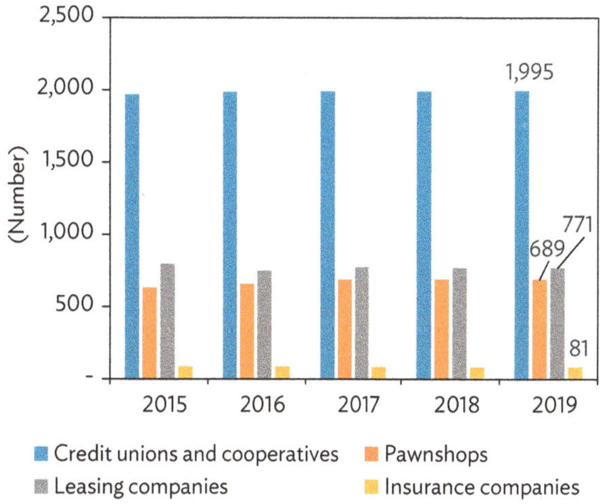

Source: ADB Asia SME Monitor 2020 database. Data from Bank of Thailand.

Thailand's national e-payment system, PromptPay, was launched in 2017. It is a money transfer platform that uses the recipient's national identity number or mobile phone number to access a bank account, instead of using the bank account number. There is no transfer fee. PromptPay enables MSMEs to lower their business costs and the government to efficiently collect MSME taxes. In 2019, the Bank of Thailand issued policy guidelines on a standardized Thai quick response (QR) code for payment transactions.

The Bank of Thailand has also promoted agent banking, allowing customers to access banking services through authorized third-party agents such as retail outlets. The central bank is also developing new digital financial services, such as e-factoring, as alternative MSME financing tool. According to the Thai FinTech Association, there are 70–80 active fintech firms as of October 2019.

While the MSME credit market has had relatively stagnant growth, emerging digital finance platforms—such as debt crowdfunding, equity crowdfunding (ECF), and P2P lending—have started serving unmet demand from emerging and high-growth firms and start-ups. In Thailand, the Securities and Exchange Commission (SEC) supervises crowdfunding platforms while the Bank of Thailand supervises P2P lenders.

The SEC enacted a series of regulations on fintech and digital finance platforms in 2019, including rules and regulations on a digital asset exchange, debt crowdfunding, and ECF. The SEC's crowdfunding notification (No.21/B.E.2562) stipulates that crowdfunding portals should be incorporated in Thailand with a minimum paid-up capital of B5 million. Crowdfunding portals can operate within the scope of SEC-licensed activities. Issuers can offer not more than B100,000 to each retail investor, and the total value of securities offered should not exceed B20 million within the first year of the offering.

As of October 2019, two licensed ECF platforms are operating—*Live* launched by the SET and *Sinwattana* operated by the Phoenixict group—and 10 debt crowdfunding platforms under the SEC approval process. Crowdfunding remains in the infant stage of development. *Live*, launched in May 2018, is operated by the SET subsidiary Live Fincorp. It aims to support start-ups and social enterprises as a new engine of growth, whose objective is different from the SET's mai market that aims to support high potential growth SMEs. *Live* is a sponsor-driven off-exchange market targeting angel investors. *Sinwattana* was launched in 2019 to serve unbanked start-ups. By end-2019, *Sinwattana* had two ECF restaurant projects. According to the SEC, although crowdfunding demand is increasing, more market awareness among potential issuers and investors is needed through outreach campaigns.

In 2019, the Bank of Thailand issued a notification on P2P lending platforms (No.4/B.E.2562). It defines a P2P platform provider as a person who provides an electronic system or network for P2P lending, and a P2P lender as a natural person or juristic person who offers a loan through an electronic system or network, excluding crowdfunding providers. P2P platform providers should be incorporated in Thailand with a minimum paid-up capital of B5 million. The credit limit for P2P lending depends on the size of the lender's average monthly income: up to 1.5 times average monthly income for those with an average monthly income below B30,000 and up to 5 times for lenders with average monthly income of B30,000 or more.

Capital Markets

The Thai capital market has been shrinking since 2017, with low liquidity and a decreasing trend in the number of retail investors. The market for alternative investment (mai), launched in 1998 to support SME financing, has seen lower market capitalization since 2017, and has performed worse than SET's main board. As of end-2019, the mai had 169 listed companies with market capitalization of B215 billion, a 10.7% decrease from end-2018 (Figure 11.8A and Table 11.7). The trading value in 2019 fell to B177 billion from B310 billion in 2018. However, the mai has consistently seen its listed companies move on to the main board, playing the critical role of supporting the growth cycle of enterprises. As of end-2019, a total of 26 companies have shifted from the mai to the SET's main market. In 2019, six companies listed in the mai moved to the main board (Figure 11.8B).

By sector, as of 3 September 2019, 28.2% of issuers on the mai are in services, followed by manufacturing (23.3%) and property and construction (15.3%). Domestic individuals (retail investors) are the main investors in mai stocks, accounting for 94.2% of total trading in 2019 (3 September), while foreign investors rose to 4.7%.

Listing requirements for the mai are eased as compared to for the SET's main board. But they have tightened since January 2017. For instance, required paid-up capital after an initial public offering (IPO) increased from a minimum B20 million to a minimum B50 million. And required net profit increased from zero to a minimum of B10 million in the most recent year (Table 11.8).

There are three critical challenges for SMEs to tap capital markets: (i) a lack of proper business accounting, (ii) a less ambitious growth mindset among SME owners, and (iii) the relatively high cost for listing. Thai capital markets need to attract more investors and issuers, as many remain unconvinced capital markets are good for investment or funding. Instead, crowdfunding is growing as an alternative funding option for SMEs and start-ups.

Given this widely held perception, the SEC started a capital market literacy program in 2017 to inform the public about the mai and crowdfunding. The literacy program is conducted each month, targeting both investors and firms (including SMEs) and covering all regions of Thailand. Given that SME financial management is weak, the SEC is collaborating with both domestic and foreign fintech companies to help SMEs improve their financial management via online platforms. The SEC is also collaborating with certified public accountants (CPAs) and accountant associations to help SMEs improve business accounting. It also facilitates matching investors with SMEs as part of the national SME development policy.

The SET launched the Social Impact Platform in 2016, not as an investment platform, but as a business matching platform between social enterprises and large firms. Through this platform, the SET provides training to social enterprises in areas such as marketing.

During its early years, the mai had tax incentive schemes including a corporate tax deduction for newly listed firms. It boosted the number of mai listed companies in 2004 and 2005, but was removed in 2005 as the government uniformly reduced corporate taxes for all firms. For mai listed companies and investors, however, some tax benefits remain, such as tax exemptions on dividends received from other company shares (for listed companies), and capital gains tax exemptions (for individual investors).

Venture capital and private equity investments are growing but remain small. According to the SET, the size of venture capital fund is around B30 billion. Venture capital firms focus mainly on established firms and do not target SMEs. The Thai Venture Capital Association was established in 1994, to support a venture capital fund targeting SME entrepreneurs. The government offers a tax incentive scheme for venture capital firms and angel investors to invest in high-technology and startup industries, not limited to SMEs.

Figure 11.8: Equity Markets

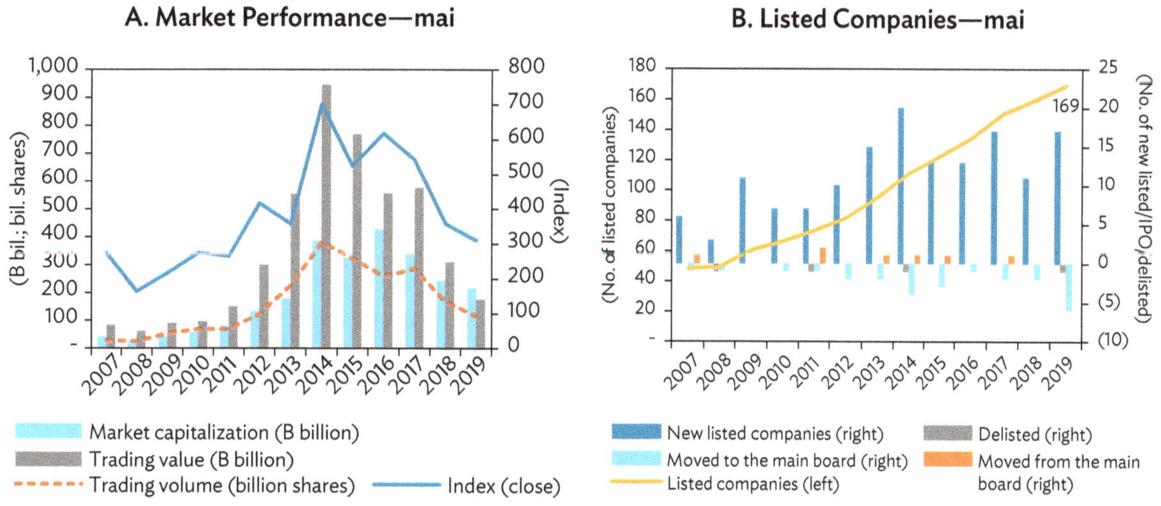

IPO = initial public offering.

Source: ADB Asia SME Monitor 2020 database. Data from Stock Exchange of Thailand.

Financial Infrastructure

A credit bureau system was developed after the 1997–1998 Asian financial crisis. The National Credit Bureau, a single private sector credit bureau, was created as a result of merging the Central Credit Information Services with the Thai Credit Bureau in 2005. The National Credit Bureau collects credit information on consumers and corporates from its 103 members, including commercial banks, specialized financial institutions, and nonbank finance institutions, with 3-year data retention. It offers both positive and negative information on consumers and corporates, exclusively to members. As of February 2020, the bureau held data on 28.5 million people (107.3 million accounts) and 333,000 companies (4.3 million accounts). Its services include consumer and corporate credit reporting, bankruptcy checking for financial institutions, and consumer and SME (corporate) credit scoring.

Thailand uses a collateral-based lending approach. Movable assets such as machinery and equipment are used for collateral to reduce credit risk. In 2015, the Business Collateral Act was introduced, along with a centralized collateral registry. The act aims to strengthen the legal system for lending. Prior to its enactment, borrowers could not retain possession of movable assets pledged as collateral for the duration of the security period. Out-of-court enforcement options were limited as well. The act removes these prohibitions and provides borrowers with greater access to credit.

3. Policies and Regulations

- The 5-year master plan on MSMEs focuses on technology and innovation and value-added MSMEs, promoting a shift from traditional to smart MSMEs.
- National policies on MSME support are well coordinated with a focal agency and cross-agency collaboration, covering both financial and nonfinancial support.
- A comprehensive national strategy for financial inclusion has yet to be developed, while the nationwide SMEs Promotion Plan and the central bank's Financial Sector Master Plan cover key policy actions on financial inclusion.
- Several government agencies have their own financial support measures for target MSMEs, suggesting a need to develop a national financial inclusion strategy with a holistic approach to create greater synergy for inclusive finance.

MSME Development

Thailand 4.0, launched in 2016, is the country's fourth national economic development plan.[141] It covers the development of new growth industries to drive sustainable economic growth, including MSMEs and start-ups. It promotes innovative enterprises that use advanced technology in five clusters—food, health, automation, digital, and creative industries. It aims to facilitate a shift from traditional famers and MSMEs to smart farmers and MSMEs, and to promote start-ups. It targets increasing MSMEs contribution to GDP to 50% by 2021.

OSMEP is a focal government agency under the Office of the Prime Minister in implementing and coordinating MSME development policies with relevant line ministries and the private sector. The National Board of SMEs Promotion, chaired by the Prime Minister, is a centralized body that formulates country's MSME development policies and supervises OSMEP operations.

The centralized budget system for MSME policies, the SME Promotion Integrated Budget, was launched in 2017. Funds are allocated to agencies and line ministries responsible for MSME support so as their functions avoid any

141 The past economic plans focused on agricultural development (Thailand 1.0), light industries (Thailand 2.0), and heavy industries (Thailand 3.0).

budget overlap. This system is linked to OSMEP's 5-year master plan for MSME support. OSMEP acts as the secretariat for all MSME promoting agencies—9 ministries and 30 agencies, including both government and private sector organizations. OSMEP monitors and evaluates activities using the SME Promotion Integrated Budget. TCG receives funding aside from the SME Promotion Integrated Budget for its MSME credit guarantee business.

Under the SME Promotion Integrated Budget, OSMEP allocated B2,000 million to financial support for MSMEs as a rescue fund for those affected by calamity or disaster, and for "turnaround" MSMEs. OSMEP's soft loan program targets these turnaround MSMEs, defined as an MSME whose income declined by 20% over the previous 3 years. The program accepts a 3% interest rate subsidy from the government to provide concessional loans to the target MSMEs. OSMEP has a B10,000 million budget for its soft loan program, separate from the SME Promotion Integrated Budget.

The latest 5-year master plan for MSMEs is the Fourth SMEs Promotion Plan covering 2017–2021. In line with Thailand 4.0, the Fourth Plan focuses on nine policy actions: (i) elevate productivity, technology, and innovation; (ii) promote capital access; (iii) promote market access and internationalization; (iv) develop entrepreneurship; (v) create high value-added start-ups; (vi) promote MSME clusters; (vii) strengthen fundamental enterprises; (viii) develop tools for efficient implementation; and (ix) revise laws, regulations, and privileges that support MSMEs. Policy measures focus on supporting start-up accelerators, incubators, and access to finance (venture capital financing and crowdfunding) to create high value-added start-ups.

To support the shift from traditional to smart MSMEs, policy measures seek more balanced support for access to finance (credit insurance, soft loans, credit scoring, subsidies, and financial literacy); marketing (promoting public procurement and e-commerce); innovation (digitizing MSMEs); infrastructure; and entrepreneurship (one-stop services). Promoting the internationalization of MSMEs is also a policy target, which includes encouraging business matching, linkages between MSMEs and large firms, foreign investment by MSMEs (through the foreign investment information center), and consulting services for product standardization.

The Fifth SMEs Promotion Plan for 2022–2026 is being prepared, placing greater focus on technology and innovation, and value-added MSMEs. The Fifth Plan will address priority sectors such as textiles, electronics, and tourism. Aviation, logistics, health care and wellness, and tourism are new sectors covered in the Fifth Plan. It pays attention to information and technology for upgrading MSME businesses, such as robotics and artificial intelligence in health care and tourism. Foreign direct investment to MSMEs is also addressed. OSMEP will give special privileges to investors for technology-based MSMEs.

OSMEP works with other agencies such as the Ministry of Science and Technology (MOST)[142] which has around 90 incubation centers across the country, including university-collaboration centers. As of September 2019, there are only five active incubators. The MOST provides technology and skill support for technology-based start-ups, while OSMEP supports those incubated at MOST. It offers grant for start-ups to scale up and for marketing, called the Startup Voucher, launched in 2016. The average amount of voucher is around B800,000, but it depends on the startup's proposal. Some technology start-ups can request up to B1 million.

OSMEP operates one-stop service (OSS) windows for MSMEs, covering Bangkok and all provinces. Launched in 2014, OSS was implemented in phases in different areas of the country. To avail of OSS services, MSMEs must become an OSS member by registering with the Ministry of Commerce. OSS gathers information on MSMEs to monitor their business development. There are around 700,000 OSS members, which it helps register at the Ministry of Commerce. OSS acts as a referral center for MSMEs, answering questions and introducing them to appropriate agencies (business matching). Around 180,000 MSMEs use OSS support services yearly.

[142] The MOST was renamed the Ministry of Higher Education, Science, Research and Innovation in May 2019.

FPO offers tax incentives for MSMEs, including corporate income tax exemption for firms with less than B300,000 income and tax reductions for depreciation of machines (programs, hardware, buildings, factories, and machines under certain conditions for the information and technology industry). Start-ups benefit from tax exemptions for the first 5 years, while angel investors receive tax incentives for investing in start-ups (personal income tax exemptions). FPO supervises six deposit-taking specialized financial institutions[143] (state-owned banks) and government financial institutions, which include two major government entities for supporting MSMEs—SMEDB and TCG. FPO has a 5-year strategy for state-owned banks. The latest strategy was for 2014–2019. FPO is preparing a new strategy for 2020–2024. The MSME support component will be incorporated, addressing the use of new technology, new data systems, and access to finance. The finance support will include a new design for information-based lending, the use of artificial intelligence, and advanced technology (the new lending scheme and scope of information are being prepared).

Box 11.1: The National Innovation Agency Supports Technology-Based Innovation by MSMEs

The National Innovation Agency (NIA) was established in 2003 under the Ministry of Science and Technology (MOST)—renamed the Ministry of Higher Education, Science, Research and Innovation (MHESI) in May 2019—to promote private sector-led innovation. NIA provides both financial and nonfinancial support for technology-based innovation through start-ups and micro, small, and medium-sized enterprises (MSMEs). NIA uses the Office of Small and Medium Enterprises Promotion definition for MSMEs in implementing policy. Start-ups and MSMEs can apply directly to the NIA for support; there are committees that assess and decide which projects qualify for support.

NIA's financial support includes the following programs:

- The Seed Funding Program finances technology-based start-ups and MSMEs that conduct prototype testing of innovative products and services. The program targets (i) thematic innovation (such as medical, tourism, food, and aviation/drones) and (ii) open innovation (anyone can apply). The financing cap is $100,000 per project for thematic innovation and $50,000 per project for open innovation. As of September 2019, the program received more than 2,000 applications, of which 200 companies were accepted.
- The zero-interest rate loan program is used to support commercializing new technology. The loan interest rate is covered by the NIA. The financing cap is $100,000 per project (covering interest only). The program approved all applications submitted as of September 2019.

NIA also offers nonfinancial support via advisory services for technology-based enterprises at any stage of research and development (R&D), prototype testing, commercialization, and business expansion. Any enterprise (not only MSMEs but large firms as well) can apply for this support. The nonfinancial support includes the following programs:

- Mind Credit is a financial consulting service. Twenty projects (mostly MSMEs) were approved in 2018.
- A technical and academic training program is provided regularly for start-ups and MSMEs, covering a range of entrepreneurship knowledge.
- The government procurement program supports innovative enterprises that are expanding. The program started in 2018 and aims to improve a company's business concept/model so they can successfully participate in government procurement. Ten projects were approved as of September 2019. For instance, a start-up company Que Que (established in 2016) developed a mobile application for restaurant booking. As the service can expand into patients booking services in public hospitals, the company received a grant of $100,000 to develop this new business model.

NIA's support focuses on innovation and commercialization, rather than R&D. In Thailand, support for R&D is mainly provided by MHESI. In 2019, $300 million was allocated to the Thailand Science Research and Innovation Fund. The fund aims at leveraging R&D capability of the country and promoting industrial R&D.

continued on next page

143 The six specialized financial institutions are (i) Small and Medium Enterprise Development Bank, (ii) Government Savings Bank, (iii) Bank for Agriculture and Agricultural Cooperatives, (iv) Export-Import Bank of Thailand, (v) Islamic Bank of Thailand, and (vi) Government Housing Bank.

Box 11.1 continued

Although MSMEs are not yet involved in infrastructure projects, technology-based start-ups and MSMEs can be involved in public/government projects, but the problem is how they can approach local governments, according to the NIA. Barriers MSMEs must overcome to participate in infrastructure projects are (i) weak MSME budgets with minimal finance, (ii) local government perceptions of MSMEs as high risk, and (iii) worries over MSMEs ability to comply with standard government procurement regulations. Small infrastructure projects not viable for large companies could become easier to bid by technology-based MSMEs.

The potential for innovation in Thailand are in industries such as (i) food processing and agribusiness (domestic and international); (ii) services like tourism and health care; and (iii) renewable energy, for example small solar power systems and wind turbines, and biomass/biogas digester systems, according to the NIA.

NIA also provides training programs for innovation, at least one course each month. These include general and thematic courses on entrepreneurship, branding, and marketing. NIA trains around 30–40 participants per program. The incubation program offers training on how to innovate business for start-ups. The acceleration program offers mentoring and networking for start-ups and MSMEs. Thai Union (the largest canned tuna product exporter) is a partner in one of the acceleration programs. The program is also open to start-ups from other countries.

Source: Interview with NIA managers, 13 September 2019.

Financial Inclusion

A comprehensive national strategy for financial inclusion has yet to be developed in Thailand. But OSMEP's SMEs Promotion Plan and the Bank of Thailand's Financial Sector Master Plan cover key policies for financial inclusion.

The Financial Sector Master Plan Phase III for 2016–2020 has four components: (i) digitization and efficiency (promoting digital banking and electronic payments); (ii) regionalization (promoting Qualified ASEAN Banks and cross-border payments); (iii) access (agent banking for households, availing of financial databases, credit guarantees for MSMEs, and market-based corporate financing); and (iv) enablers (developing financial professionals and promoting financial literacy and consumer protection).

In line with the master plan, the Bank of Thailand focuses on five key policies to support MSMEs: (i) increasing access to MSME funding to promote electronic financial transactions (such as e-factoring) and alternative finance channels (for example, P2P lending); (ii) increasing efficiency and reducing costs to promote electronic payments (PromptPay) with standardized QR codes and developing fintech; (iii) mitigating risks, increasing access to credit guarantees via TCG and secured lending that facilitates the use of movable assets as collateral for loans; (iv) enhancing databases for credit assessment, for developing MSME and credit bureau databases, data exchange protocols, and alternative information for credit assessment (such as payment and transaction data); and (v) empowering, to enhance financial literacy for MSMEs (such as foreign exchange risk management).

FPO has also developed the Act on Community-based Financial Institutions (2019), which reinforces the role of community-based financial institutions in supporting local borrower financing demand. Under this law, a designated community-based financial institution will be granted a legal status to facilitate its operation. It also sets out rules governing operations to ensure risk management standards are met.

The SEC, which regulates capital markets, focuses on three key policies that promote MSME development: (i) to create and amend rules and regulations that facilitate SMEs to issue stocks and convertible bonds via the stock exchange, improving listing criteria to match the capability of potential medium-sized issuers and reducing listing costs; (ii) to reach out to SMEs and people in provinces—the SEC launched a Caravan Project in June 2019 to enhance the capital market literacy of local SMEs and people as potential issuers (covering Khon Kaen, Udon Thani, and Chiang Mai provinces in 2019); and (iii) to launch a new investment channel for SMEs as an alternative for investors undertaking SME risk. These policies are the foundation for SME support under the planned SEC capital market master plan. For financial literacy and capacity-building programs for SMEs, the SEC is cooperating with various agencies on capacity-building programs on capital markets with the Bank for Agriculture and Agricultural Cooperatives and the Department of Industrial Promotion. Aside from the Caravan Project, the SEC has opened a clinic for regulatory advice and consultation on digital asset business licenses and fundraising activities for potential issuers.

Overall, national policies advocating MSMEs are well coordinated with a focal agency and cross-agency collaboration, covering both financial and nonfinancial support. In addition, several line ministries and financial authorities have implemented their own financing support measures targeting MSMEs, suggesting the need for a comprehensive national strategy for financial inclusion to create greater synergy for inclusive finance.

Data Tables

Table 11.1: MSME Definition

A. Definition before November 2019

Sector	Item	Small	Medium
Manufacturing	Employees	Not more than 50	51-200
	Fixed Assets (excluding Land)	Not more than B50 million	More than B50 million and less than B200 million
Service	Employees	Not more than 50	51-200
	Fixed Assets (excluding Land)	Not more than B50 million	More than B50 million and less than B200 million
Trading: Wholesale	Employees	Not more than 25	26-50
	Fixed Assets (excluding Land)	Not more than B50 million	More than B50 million and less than B100 million
Trading: Retail	Employees	Not more than 15	16-30
	Fixed Assets (excluding Land)	Not more than B30 million	More than B30 million and less than B60 million

B. Definition after November 2019

Sector	Item	Micro	Small	Medium
Manufacturing	Employees	1-5	6-50	51-200
	Revenue	B1.8 million and less	More than B1.8 million and less than or equal to B100 million	More than B100 million and less than B500 million
Services and Trading	Employees	1-5	6-30	31-100
	Revenue	B1.8 million and less	More than B1.8 million and less than or equal to B50 million	More than B50 million and less than B300 million

MSME = micro, small, and medium-sized enterprise.
Note: Manufacturing includes the agriculture sector.
Source: ADB Asia SME Monitor 2020 database. Data from Office of Small and Medium Enterprises Promotion.

Table 11.2: MSME Landscape

End of period data

Item	2007	2008	2009	2010	2011	2012	2013	2014	2015	2016	2017	2018	2019
NUMBER OF ENTERPRISES													
Number of enterprises, total	2,375,368	2,836,377	2,900,759	2,924,912	2,652,854	2,781,945	2,844,757	2,744,198	2,773,625	3,013,722	3,053,468	3,084,291	--
Number of MSMEs	2,366,227	2,827,633	2,896,106	2,913,167	2,646,549	2,739,142	2,763,997	2,736,744	2,765,986	3,004,679	3,046,790	3,077,822	--
Number of large enterprises	9,141	4,586	4,653	9,140	6,253	7,591	7,349	7,062	7,156	9,025	6,662	6,455	--
MSME to total (%)	99.6	99.7	99.8	99.6	99.8	97.2	97.2	99.7	99.7	99.7	99.8	99.8	--
MSME growth (%)	3.3	19.5	2.4	0.6	(9.2)	3.2	1.2	0.8	1.1	8.6	1.3	1.0	--
MSMEs by sector (% share)													
Agriculture, forestry, and fisheries	--	0.2	--	--	--	--	--	1.7	1.3	1.4	1.5	1.5	--
Manufacturing	28.2	19.3	18.9	18.7	17.8	18.7	17.4	18.0	18.2	17.3	17.3	17.1	--
Transportation and communication	--	--	--	--	--	--	--	--	--	--	--	--	--
Construction	--	--	--	--	--	--	--	--	--	--	--	--	--
Wholesale and retail trade	41.1	46.7	47.3	47.5	44.5	43.5	43.5	42.4	42.3	41.7	41.6	41.6	--
Other services	30.0	33.8	33.6	33.8	37.7	37.8	39.1	37.9	38.1	39.6	39.6	39.8	--
Others*	0.7	--	--	--	--	--	--	--	--	--	--	--	--
Number of MSMEs by region (% share)													
Capital city	30.7	28.9	20.0	19.7	19.6	19.8	20.1	17.9	17.9	18.1	18.1	18.2	--
Others	69.3	71.1	80.0	80.3	80.4	80.2	80.0	82.1	82.1	81.9	81.9	81.8	--
EMPLOYMENT													
Number of employment, total	11,711,334	--	12,405,597	13,496,173	13,107,263	14,662,812	14,098,563	13,078,147	13,363,054	14,780,001	15,299,865	16,322,746	--
Number of employment by MSMEs	8,900,567	--	9,701,354	10,507,507	10,995,977	11,783,143	11,414,702	10,501,166	10,749,735	11,747,093	13,088,802	13,950,241	--
Number of employment by large enterprises	2,810,767	--	2,704,243	2,988,581	2,111,229	2,251,547	2,682,323	2,575,949	2,612,287	3,032,908	2,211,063	2,372,491	--
MSME employees to total (%)	76.0	--	78.2	77.9	83.9	81.0	81.0	80.3	80.4	78.5	82.2	85.5	--
MSME employees growth (%)	3.1	--	--	8.3	4.6	0.5	3.3	2.6	2.4	9.3	3.3	4.7	--
Share of female employees to total employees (%)	--	--	--	--	--	45.8	46.2	46.0	46.2	45.5	45.3	45.6	45.6
Employment by MSME by sector (% share)													
Agriculture, forestry, and fisheries	--	--	--	--	--	--	--	0.6	0.6	0.6	0.5	0.5	--
Manufacturing	38.9	--	34.2	33.3	29.6	32.7	23.7	23.1	22.8	21.9	23.8	24.3	--
Transportation and communication	--	--	--	--	--	--	--	--	--	--	--	--	--
Construction	--	--	--	--	--	--	--	--	--	--	--	--	--
Wholesale and retail trade	27.3	--	30.0	30.0	34.8	33.2	31.7	31.6	31.4	31.5	32.4	31.8	--
Other services	33.8	--	35.8	35.8	35.6	34.1	44.7	44.8	45.2	46.0	43.3	43.4	--
Others*	--	--	--	--	--	--	--	--	--	--	--	--	--
Employment by MSMEs by region (% share)													
Capital city	51.4	--	34.3	31.6	25.1	24.2	33.5	30.7	30.8	29.6	29.1	30.2	--
Others	48.6	--	65.7	68.4	74.9	75.8	66.5	69.3	69.2	70.4	70.9	69.8	--
CONTRIBUTION TO GDP													
GDP of MSMEs (B million)	3,758,130	3,863,743	3,858,146	4,258,542	4,445,932	4,831,990	5,044,252	5,261,090	5,631,426	6,099,185	6,557,750	7,013,971	--
MSMEs contribution to GDP (% share)	41.4	39.8	39.9	39.4	39.3	39.1	39.1	39.8	41.0	41.9	42.4	43.0	--
MSME GDP growth (%)	--	2.8	(0.1)	10.4	4.4	8.7	4.4	4.3	7.0	8.3	7.5	7.0	--
Labor productivity (B thousand)	422.2	--	397.7	405.3	404.3	410.1	441.9	501.0	523.9	519.2	501.0	502.8	--
MSME GDP by sector (% share)													
Agriculture, forestry, and fisheries	--	--	--	--	--	--	--	--	--	--	--	--	--
Manufacturing	25.9	26.5	25.5	26.9	26.1	24.6	24.4	24.4	23.7	23.3	23.1	22.6	--
Transportation and communication	--	--	--	--	--	--	--	--	--	--	--	--	--
Construction	5.8	5.7	5.8	5.9	5.7	5.9	5.7	5.3	5.6	5.4	5.0	4.9	--
Wholesale and retail trade	28.4	29.1	30.2	30.0	29.8	29.8	28.9	29.1	29.5	30.3	30.9	31.4	--
Other services	36.3	36.9	36.6	35.4	36.5	37.9	39.2	39.3	39.4	39.0	39.2	39.1	--
Others*	3.6	1.7	1.9	1.8	1.9	1.9	1.9	1.8	1.8	1.9	1.8	2.0	--
MSME GDP by region (% share)													
Capital city	--	--	--	--	--	--	--	--	--	--	--	--	--
Others	--	--	--	--	--	--	--	--	--	--	--	--	--
EXPORTS													
Total export value (B million)	5,302,119	5,851,371	5,194,597	6,113,336	6,707,990	7,078,420	6,909,741	7,313,066	7,227,161	7,550,704	8,006,265	8,093,441	--
Total export growth (%)	--	10.4	(11.2)	17.7	9.7	5.5	(2.4)	5.8	(1.2)	4.5	6.0	1.1	--
MSME export value (B million)	1,576,000	1,691,000	1,564,000	1,669,000	1,971,000	2,065,460	1,761,800	1,922,500	1,978,300	2,190,500	1,990,420	2,325,852	--
MSME export to total export value (%)	30.1	28.9	30.1	27.3	29.4	29.9	25.5	27.9	28.2	29.0	28.9	28.7	--
MSME export growth (%)	10.1	7.3	(7.5)	3.6	27.7	4.8	(14.7)	0.7	(0.3)	7.5	5.8	0.5	--
IMPORTS													
Total import value (B million)	4,870,186	5,962,483	4,601,982	5,856,591	6,982,728	7,786,132	7,657,346	7,403,898	6,906,078	6,888,187	7,587,118	8,098,098	--
Total import growth (%)	--	22.4	(22.8)	27.3	19.2	11.5	(1.7)	(3.3)	(6.7)	(0.3)	10.1	6.7	--
MSME import value (B million)	1,453,000	1,772,000	1,384,000	1,810,000	2,383,000	2,588,300	2,369,200	2,226,300	2,382,200	2,445,800	2,382,921	2,979,699	--
MSME import to total import value (%)	29.8	29.8	30.1	30.0	31.0	33.1	30.9	30.6	33.8	34.9	36.2	36.8	--
MSME import growth (%)	(8.8)	21.9	(21.9)	28.3	21.6	8.6	(8.5)	(10.4)	3.2	2.8	14.3	8.5	--

GDP = gross domestic product, MSME = micro, small, and medium-sized enterprise.
Note: Data based on the SME definition effective until November 2019. The new definition was implemented after November 2019, but the past data have yet to reflect the new definition (as of the end of 2019). * Includes mining and electricity, gas and water supply.
Source: ADB Asia SME Monitor 2020 database. Data from Office of Small and Medium Enterprise Promotion, SME White Paper (various editions); National Statistical Office.

Table 11.3: Bank Credit

End of period data

Item	2007	2008	2009	2010	2011	2012	2013	2014	2015	2016	2017	2018	2019
COMMERCIAL BANKS													
Number of banks													
Commercial banks (CBs)	34	34	32	32	31	31	30	30	31	30	30	30	30
Public financial institutions (PFIs)	8	8	8	8	8	8	8	8	8	8	8	8	8
Credit													
Loans outstanding, total (B billion)	7,994	9,527	10,178	11,617	13,224	14,954	16,369	17,030	17,815	18,550	19,970	20,607	21,319
Total loans - PFIs[1] (B bil.)	1,765	1,978	2,370	2,854	3,442	3,677	4,026	4,157	4,597	4,922	5,240	5,492	5,690
Total loans - CBs (B bil.)	6,229	7,549	7,807	8,763	9,782	11,278	12,342	12,873	13,218	13,627	14,730	15,115	15,629
Loans outstanding in domestic currency (B billion)	--	--	--	--	--	--	--	--	--	--	--	--	--
Loans outstanding in foreign currency (B billion)	--	--	--	--	--	--	--	--	--	--	--	--	--
Loan growth (%)	--	19.2	6.8	14.1	13.8	13.1	9.5	4.0	4.6	4.1	7.7	3.2	3.5
Total commercial bank loans to GDP (%)	68.6	77.8	80.8	81.1	86.5	91.3	95.6	97.3	96.2	93.6	95.3	92.6	--
Lending rate (%)[2]	5.7	5.8	4.3	4.4	5.3	5.1	5.0	4.9	4.6	4.3	4.3	4.1	--
Gross nonperforming loans (NPLs) (B billion)[3]	--	--	376	313	266	254	266	277	338	386	429	444	465
Gross NPLs to total loans (%)[3]	--	--	0.3	0.2	0.1	0.1	0.1	0.1	2.6	2.8	2.9	2.9	3.0
Deposits													
Deposits, total (B billion)	6,605	7,156	7,121	7,490	7,991	10,220	11,177	12,010	12,303	12,599	13,238	13,759	14,333
Deposits in domestic currency (B billion)	--	--	--	--	--	--	--	--	--	--	--	--	--
Deposits in foreign currency (B billion)	--	--	--	--	--	--	--	--	--	--	--	--	--
Deposit rate (%)[4]	0.8	0.8	0.5	0.5	0.9	0.7	0.5	0.4	0.3	0.3	0.3	0.3	0.3
MSME LOANS													
MSME loans outstanding, total (B billion)	2,688	2,768	2,585	3,594	4,272	4,627	5,123	5,460	5,974	6,096	6,288	6,560	6,581
MSME loans - PFIs[1] (B bil.)	--	--	--	790	1,038	1,047	1,019	1,066	1,343	1,392	1,457	1,568	1,643
MSME loans - CBs (B bil.)	2,688	2,768	2,585	2,804	3,234	3,579	4,104	4,393	4,631	4,703	4,831	4,992	4,939
MSME loans to total loans outstanding (%)[3]	33.6	29.1	25.4	30.9	32.3	30.9	31.3	32.1	33.5	32.9	31.5	31.8	30.9
MSME loans to GDP (%)[3]	29.6	28.5	26.8	25.9	28.6	29.0	31.8	33.2	33.7	32.3	32.3	31.6	30.3
MSME loan growth (%)	--	3.0	(6.6)	39.0	18.9	8.3	10.7	6.6	9.4	2.0	3.2	4.3	0.3
MSME lending rate (%)	--	--	--	--	--	--	--	--	--	--	--	--	--
Nonperforming MSME loans (NPLs) (B billion)[3]	--	--	184	153	130	125	136	137	164	205	220	230	231
MSME NPLs to total MSME loans (%)[3]	--	--	7.1	5.4	4.0	3.5	3.3	3.1	3.5	4.4	4.5	4.6	4.7
Number of MSME loan borrowers	--	--	--	--	--	--	--	--	--	--	--	--	--
MSME loan borrowers to total bank borrowers (%)	--	--	--	--	--	--	--	--	--	--	--	--	--
MSME loan rejection rate (% of total applications)	--	--	--	--	--	--	--	--	--	--	--	--	--
Number of MSME savings account in banks	--	--	--	--	--	--	--	--	--	--	--	--	--
Guaranteed MSME loans (B billion)	--	--	--	--	--	--	--	--	--	--	--	--	--
Non-collateral MSME loans (B billion)	--	--	--	--	--	--	--	--	--	--	--	--	--
MSME loans outstanding by sector (% share)* **													
Agriculture, forestry, and fisheries	3.1	2.8	2.7	2.5	2.1	2.1	2.0	1.9	1.9	1.8	1.7	1.6	1.5
Manufacturing	27.9	26.7	26.3	25.8	24.8	23.6	23.0	22.6	21.8	20.6	21.0	20.4	18.9
Transportation and communication	2.4	2.7	2.8	2.6	2.7	3.0	3.0	3.0	3.2	2.8	2.4	2.5	2.6
Construction	4.2	4.1	3.9	3.9	3.6	3.5	3.3	3.2	3.2	3.5	3.4	3.7	3.8
Wholesale and retail trade	26.2	25.8	27.0	27.9	28.8	30.5	30.6	30.3	29.3	29.4	28.9	28.5	28.3
Other services	32.7	34.4	33.9	34.2	34.6	33.3	33.5	34.0	34.6	34.9	35.7	35.5	36.8
Others[5]	3.4	3.5	3.4	3.1	3.4	4.0	4.6	5.0	6.0	7.0	7.1	7.8	8.0
MSME loans outstanding by region (% share)													
Capital city	--	--	--	--	--	--	--	--	--	--	--	--	--
Others	--	--	--	--	--	--	--	--	--	--	--	--	--
MSME loans outstanding by type of use (% share)													
For working capital	--	--	--	--	--	--	--	--	--	--	--	--	--
For capital investment	--	--	--	--	--	--	--	--	--	--	--	--	--
MSME loans outstanding by tenor (% share)													
Less than 1 year	--	--	--	--	--	--	--	--	--	--	--	--	--
1-5 years	--	--	--	--	--	--	--	--	--	--	--	--	--
More than 5 years	--	--	--	--	--	--	--	--	--	--	--	--	--

GDP = gross domestic product; MSME = micro, small, and medium-sized enterprise.
Revision to the MSME data from 2007 to 2019 to be in line with MSME definition by the Ministry of Industry.

1 Six PFIs combined: Small and Medium Enterprise Development Bank, Government Savings Bank, Islamic Bank of Thailand, Bank for Agriculture and Agricultural Cooperatives, Export-Import Bank of Thailand, and Government Housing Bank. Total loan excludes personal, financial, and public administration and large debtors who borrow over B100 million.
2 Weighted average of minimum lending rate for commercial banks; interest rates used for retail customers.The figures have been quoted by five commercial banks (Bangkok Bank, KrungThai Bank, The Siam Commercial Bank, Kasikorn Bank, and Bank of Ayudhya).
3 Based on commercial bank loans.
4 Refers to savings deposit rate (minimum).
5 Others include mining, electricity, gas, and water supply.
Source: ADB Asia SME Monitor 2020 database. Data from Bank of Thailand.

Table 11.4: Public Finance and Guarantees

End of period data

Item	2007	2008	2009	2010	2011	2012	2013	2014	2015	2016	2017	2018	2019
Thai Credit Guarantee Corporation*													
Outstanding guaranteed loans (B billion)	22.3	21.9	39.9	72.9	113.0	180.5	243.6	269.5	308.9	331.0	353.9	373.8	388.7
Growth (%)	--	(1.8)	82.5	82.8	55.1	59.6	35.0	10.6	14.6	7.1	6.9	5.6	4.0
Guaranteed loans approved (B billion)	6.4	3.3	21.6	42.6	52.4	82.8	87.1	61.1	102.8	87.5	86.6	88.9	90.6
Guaranteed loans disbursed (B billion)	--	--	--	--	--	--	--	--	--	--	--	--	--
Number of MSMEs guaranteed	--	--	--	--	--	--	--	--	--	--	--	--	--
Accumulated number of MSMEs guaranteed	--	--	--	--	--	--	--	--	--	--	--	--	--
MSME access to guarantees (% of total MSMEs)	--	--	--	--	--	--	--	--	--	--	--	--	--
Guaranteed loans to MSME loans (%)**	--	0.8	1.5	2.6	3.4	5.0	5.9	6.1	6.7	7.0	7.1	7.2	11.1
Portfolio Guarantees													
Number of Letter of Guarantee (accumulated)	8,999	8,631	13,084	24,593	39,045	59,469	81,002	97,421	162,813	200,090	293,316	327,725	350,803
Number of Letter of Guarantee (new approval)	2,298	1,366	5,763	13,346	17,641	24,357	28,029	25,250	79,249	56,507	119,149	80,917	91,489

MSME = micro, small, and medium-sized enterprise.

* Guaranteed loans outstanding are the aggregate amount of the government support program and the Thai Credit Guarantee Corporation's own support program. The government support program accounted for around three-fourths of Thai Credit Guarantee Corporation's total guarantee amounts.
** Based on commercial bank loans.

Source: ADB Asia SME Monitor 2020 database. Data from Thai Credit Guarantee Corporation.

Table 11.5: Credit Guarantee Schemes—Thai Credit Guarantee Corporation

Item	Y2015-2016 PGS5 (Revised)	Y2016-2017 PGS6	Y2017-2018 PGS6 (Revised)	Y2018-2019 PGS7	Y2019-2020 PGS8	Y2016-2019 Startup and Innovation	Y2019-2021 Startup and Innobiz	Y2016-2017 Micro2	Y2018-2020 Micro3
Limit of Scheme	฿100,000 million	฿19,000 million	฿81,000 million	฿64,000 million	฿150,000 million	฿1,994 million	฿8,000 million	฿13,500 million	฿15,000 million
Target Group	General Thai SMEs/Thai SMEs who invest in other countries	General Thai SMEs/Thai SMEs who invest in other countries	General Thai SMEs/Thai SMEs who invest in other countries	General Thai SMEs/Thai SMEs who invest in other countries	General Thai SMEs/Thai SMEs who invest in other countries	New SMEs having year in business not more than 3 years or Innovation business	New SMEs having year in business not more than 3 years or Innovation business	Micro community businesses owners/peddlers/ other professions	Micro community businesses owners/peddlers/ other professions
Guarantee Limit	Not more than ฿40 million	Not more than ฿40 million	Not more than ฿40 million	Not more than ฿40 million	Not more than ฿100 million	Not more than ฿20 million	Not more than ฿40 million	฿10,000–฿200,000	฿10,000–฿200,000
Guarantee Fee/year	1.75% (Total subsidized fee by the government 4%)	1.75%	1.75% (Total subsidized fee by the government 4%)	1.0%, 1.5%, 1.75% (Total subsidized fee by the government 2.25%)	1.0%, 1.5%, 1.75% (Total subsidized fee by the government 3.5%)	1%–2% (1st year fee is subsidized by the government)	1.0%, 1.5% (Total subsidized fee by the government 2%)	1%–3% according to customer risk assessed by the bank (1st year fee is subsidized by the government)	1%–2% according to customer risk assessed by the TCG (1st year fee is subsidized by the government)
Terms and Conditions of SMEs	Fixed assets (excluding land) not more than ฿200 million	Fixed assets (excluding land) not more than ฿200 million	Fixed assets (excluding land) not more than ฿200 million	Fixed assets (excluding land) not more than ฿200 million	Fixed assets (excluding land) not more than ฿200 million	Having experience not more than 3 years and fixed assets not more than ฿200 million or Innovation business	Having experience not more than 3 years and fixed assets not more than ฿200 million or Innovation business	Having explicit business location and fixed assets not more than ฿5 million	Having explicit business location and fixed assets not more than ฿5 million
Tenor	Not more than 7 years	Not more than 10 years	Not more than 10 years	Not more than 10 years	Not more than 10 years	Not more than 10 years	Not more than 10 years	At least 3 years but not more than 10 years	Not more than 10 years
Type of Guarantee	Portfolio Guarantee Scheme	Portfolio Guarantee Scheme	Portfolio Guarantee Scheme	Portfolio Guarantee Scheme	Pool Package Guarantee Scheme	Package Guarantee Scheme	Package Guarantee Scheme	Package Guarantee Scheme	Package Guarantee Scheme
Max Coverage per Portfolio	Not more than 22.5% of total portfolio	Not more than 23.75% of total portfolio	Not more than 30% of total portfolio	average Not more than 24.25% of total portfolio	average Not more than 30% of total portfolio	Not more than 27%–37% of total portfolio depend on fee rate	Not more than 27%–32% of total portfolio depend on fee rate	Not more than 30% and 50% depend on fee rate (subsidy from the government 20% plus guarantee fee)	Not more than 28% and 38% depend on fee rate (subsidy from the government 18% plus guarantee fee)
Obligation per letter of guarantee	• Pay 100% in case of NPG ≤15%	• Pay 100% in case of NPG≤20%	• Pay 100% in case of NPG≤20%	• Pay 100% in case of NPG≤17.5%	• Pay 100% in case of NPG≤18.75%	Pay 100% 80% 50% depend on NPL level (Max claim 27%–37%)	Pay 100% 50% depend on NPL level(Max claim 27%–32%)	Pay 100% Max claim 30%–50%	Pay 100% Max claim 28%–38%
	• Pay 50% in case 15% < NPG ≤30%	• Pay 50% in case 20% < NPG ≤25%	• Pay 50% in case 20% < NPG ≤40%	• Pay 50% in case 17.5% < NPG ≤32.5%	• Pay 70% in case 18.75% < NPG ≤34.82%				
		• Pay 25% in case 25% < NPG ≤30%		depend on each subprogram	depend on each subprogram				

NPG = nonperforming guarantee, PGS = portfolio guarantee scheme, SME = small and medium-sized enterprise, TCG = Thai Credit Guarantee Corporation.
Source: ADB Asia SME Monitor 2020 database. Data from Thai Credit Guarantee Corporation.

Table 11.6: Nonbank Finance

End of period data

Item	2015	2016	2017	2018	2019
NUMBER OF NONBANK FINANCE INSTITUTIONS					
Microfinance institutions	--	--	--	--	--
Credit unions/cooperatives	1,969	1,986	1,990	1,990	1,995
Finance companies	--	--	--	--	--
Pawnshops	628	658	688	689	689
Leasing companies	796	751	775	771	771
Factoring companies	--	--	--	--	--
Insurance companies	86	84	83	82	81
Others	--	--	--	--	--

Source: ADB Asia SME Monitor 2020 database. Data from Bank of Thailand.

Table 11.7: Capital Markets

End of period data

Item	2007	2008	2009	2010	2011	2012	2013	2014	2015	2016	2017	2018	2019
EQUITY MARKET													
Main Board													
Index	858.1	450.0	734.5	1,032.8	1,025.3	1,391.9	1,298.7	1,497.7	1,288.0	1,542.9	1,753.7	1,563.9	1,579.8
Market capitalization (B billion)*	6,636	3,568	5,873	8,335	8,408	11,831	11,497	13,856	12,283	15,079	17,587	15,978	16,747
Growth (%)	--	(46.2)	64.6	41.9	0.9	40.7	(2.8)	20.5	(11.4)	22.8	16.6	(9.1)	4.8
Trading value (B billion)**	4,189	3,920	4,338	6,938	7,040	7,616	11,777	10,193	9,997	12,260	11,652	13,820	12,802
Trading volume (billion of shares)**	605	839	890	1,093	973	1,296	2,768	2,771	2,487	2,670	2,296	3,086	3,953
Number of listed companies	470	472	472	472	470	476	489	502	517	522	538	545	556
Number of IPOs	7	9	7	4	5	8	13	17	23	11	22	8	13
Number of delisted companies	8	8	7	5	6	4	1	7	9	8	7	3	8
Specialized Board													
mai													
Index	272.4	162.9	215.3	272.8	264.2	415.7	356.8	700.1	522.6	616.3	540.4	356.4	309.6
Market capitalization (B billion)*	38	22	39	55	77	133	177	383	323	425	339	241	215
Growth (%)	--	(42.1)	76.6	40.9	40.2	72.1	33.3	116.0	(15.6)	31.5	(20.3)	(28.9)	(10.7)
Trading value (B billion)**	83	61	90	96	151	299	553	946	768	556	575	310	177
Trading volume (billion shares)**	25	23	50	67	66	123	224	380	322	258	284	168	115
Number of listed companies	48	49	60	66	73	81	95	111	122	134	150	159	169
Number of IPOs	6	3	11	7	7	10	15	20	13	13	17	11	17
Number of delisted companies	0	1	0	0	1	0	0	1	0	0	0	0	1
Moved to the main board	1	1	0	1	1	2	2	4	3	1	2	2	6
Moved from the main board	1	0	0	0	2	0	1	1	1	0	1	0	0

IPO = initial public offering.

* Excluding depositary receipts, unit trusts, derivative warrants, debentures and convertible debentures.

** Excluding debentures and convertible debentures.

Source: ADB Asia SME Monitor 2020 database. Data from Stock Exchange of Thailand.

Table 11.8: Listing Requirements—Stock Exchange of Thailand

Criteria	Stock	
	Main Board	mai
Par value	B0.50/share	B0.50/share
Paid-up capital after IPO	≥ B300 million	≥ B50 million
Shareholders' equity	≥ B300 million + equity >0 before IPO	≥ B50 million + equity >0 before IPO
Track record	≥ 3 years	≥ 2 years
Net profit	• Total net profit in the latest 2 or 3 years ≥ B50 million • + most recent year ≥ B30 million • + accumulative in the most recent quarter > 0	• Profit in most recent year ≥ B10 million • + accumulative in the most recent quarter > 0
Market capitalization test	Market capitalization ≥ B7.5 billion and EBIT latest year + profit accumulative in the most recent quarter > 0	Market capitalization ≥ B1 billion and EBIT latest year + profit accumulative in the most recent quarter > 0
Same management	≥ 1 year	≥ 1 year
Free float	• Number of free float requirement: no less than 1,000 shareholders • Percentage of free float requirement: - No less than 25% of paid-up capital (paid-up capital < B3 billion) - No less than 20% of paid-up capital (paid-up capital > B3 billion)	• Number of free float requirement: no less than 300 shareholders • Percentage of free float requirement: - No less than 25% of paid-up capital (paid-up capital < B3 billion) • No less than 20% of paid-up capital (paid-up capital > B3 billion)
Shares offering	• No less than 15% of paid-up capital (paid-up capital < B500 million) • No less than 10% of paid-up capital or no less than B75 million, whichever is higher (paid-up capital ≥ B500 million)	No less than 15% of paid-up capital
Silent period	• Applicable to strategic shareholders • 55% of paid-up capital cannot be traded. • For the period of 1 year, after 6 months may sell 25% of locked up amount.	• Applicable to strategic shareholders • 55% of paid-up capital cannot be traded. For the period of 1 year, after 6 months may sell 25% of locked up amount.
Independent directors	At least one-third of all directors and at least three directors	At least one-third of all directors and at least three directors
Audit committee	At least three directors + one need to be knowledgeable in accounting	At least three directors + one need to be knowledgeable in accounting
Internal audit	Good internal audit	Good internal audit
Company/shareholding structure	• No conflict of interest • Distinct management and authorization system	• No conflict of interest • Distinct management and authorization system
Financial advisor	• Approved by the SEC	Approved by the SEC
Financial statement/ auditor	• Financial statements complied with the SEC standards • Approved by the SEC	• Financial statements complied with the SEC standards • Approved by the SEC
Chief financial officer (CFO) * applicable in 2019	• Bachelor's degree • Have worked with the company at least 1 year prior to the listing date • Have experiences on accounting 3 years out of 5 latest years • Attend the orientation course at least 12 hours and maintain the refreshed course at least 6 hours per annum	• Bachelor's degree • Have worked with the company at least 1 year prior to the listing date • Have experiences on accounting 3 years out of 5 latest years • Attend the orientation course at least 12 hours and maintain the refreshed course at least 6 hours per annum
Financial statement standards * applicable in 2024	• IPO companies must adopt PAEs (publicly accountable entities) accounting standard for 3 years before submitting the filing.	• IPO companies must adopt PAEs (publicly accountable entities) accounting standard for 3 years before submitting the filing.

EBIT = earnings before interest and taxes, IPO = initial public offering, SEC = Securities and Exchange Commission.

Source: ADB Asia SME Monitor 2020 database. Data from Stock Exchange of Thailand.

Table 11.9: Policies and Regulations

Regulations	
Name	**Outline**
Nonfinance Regulations	
SMEs Promotion Act B.E.2543 (2000) [amendments: No.2/B.E.2561 (2018) and Ministerial Regulation on SME Definition/B.E.2562 (2019)]	SME promotion policies. Establishment of the Office of Small and Medium Enterprises Promotion (OSMEP). Amendment of the Act in 2018 and Ministerial Regulation on SME Definition in 2019 includes the new definition of MSMEs.
Electronic Transactions Act, B.E.2544 (2001) and amendments	Regulation on electronic transaction service providers and consumer protection.
Bankruptcy Act B.E.2559 (2016)	Regulation on business rehabilitation.
Finance Regulations	
Small Industry Credit Guarantee Corporation Act B.E.2534 (1991) and No.2/B.E.2560 (2017)	Regulation on credit guarantee operations for banks, addressing SME loans. The 2017 amendment added guarantees for nonbanks and factoring and hire-purchase leasing.
Securities and Exchange Act B.E.2535 (1992) as amended	Regulation on capital markets.
Credit Information Business Act B.E.2545 (2002) [amendments: B.E.2549 (2006) and B.E.2551 (2008)]	Regulation on credit information business.
Small and Medium Enterprise Development Bank of Thailand Act B.E.2545 (2002)	Establishment of the Small and Medium Enterprise Development Bank of Thailand.
Financial Institutions Business Act B.E. 2551 (2008)	Regulation on commercial banking and financing business.
Business Collateral Act B.E. 2558 (2015)	Range of eligible collateral for loans expanded to movable assets.
Royal Decree on Tax Exemption and Support for the Implementation of Taxes under the Revenue Code B.E. 2558 (2015)	Requiring the financial statements submitted to the Revenue Department as an evidence in applying for a loan with a financial institution.
Payment Systems Act B.E.2560 (2017)	Regulations on national payment system.
Bank of Thailand Notification No.4/B.E.2562 on the Determination of Rules, Procedures, and Conditions for Peer-to-Peer Lending Businesses and Platforms (2019)	Regulation on peer-to-peer (P2P) lending platforms. Procedures on regulatory sandbox (BOT).
Securities and Exchange Commission Notification No.21/B.E.2562 on the Offering of Securities for Sale through Crowdfunding Portals (2019)	Regulations and procedures on equity crowdfunding portals and investor protection.
Securities and Exchange Commission Rules on Digital Asset Exchange B.E.2562 (2019)	Regulations and procedures on digital asset companies that trade in an online exchange platform.
Community-based Financial Institutions Act B.E.2562 (2019)	Regulations on the operational structure and rules on community-based finance business.
Bank of Thailand Notification on Rules, Procedures, and Conditions for Undertaking of Personal Loan Business	Regulations and procedures on personal loan business.
Bank of Thailand Notification on Rules, Procedures, and Conditions for Undertaking of Nano Finance Business	Regulations and procedures on nano finance business.
Bank of Thailand Notification on Rules, Procedures, and Conditions for Conducting Credit Card Business	Regulations and procedures on credit card business.

Regulators and Policymakers	
Name	**Responsibility**
Office of National Economic and Social Development Board (NESDB)	Formulate national long-term strategies, including SME policies.
National Board of SMEs Promotion	Stipulate SME promotion policies and plans, and supervise the OSMEP's operations.
Office of Small and Medium Enterprises Promotion (OSMEP)	Plan and coordinate SMEs promotion policies.
Fiscal Policy Office, Ministry of Finance (FPO)	Formulate national fiscal and economic policies, and supervise pico finance lenders.
Bank of Thailand (BOT)	Monetary policy, financial stability, regulate and supervise commercial banks, specialized financial institutions, some nonbank finance institutions, and payment service providers.
Securities and Exchange Commission (SEC)	Regulate and supervise capital markets (inluding mai).

Policies		
Name	**Responsible Entity**	**Outline**
The First SMEs Promotion Plan (2002-2006)	OSMEP	1) Reinvigorate SMEs as key economic and social mechanism. 2) Build and improve infrastructure and reducing obstacles in business operations. 3) Reinforce SMEs to attain sustainable growth. 4) Capacity building for SMEs in the export sector. 5) Create and develop new entrepreneurs. 6) Promote the role of community enterprises.
The Second SMEs Promotion Plan (2007-2011)	OSMEP	1) Create new entrepreneurs and promote capacity building among existing entrepreneurs. 2) Upgrade productivity and innovative capability in manufacturing sector. 3) Enhance efficiency and reduce modern trade effects in trade sector. 4) Promote value creation and value added in service sector. 5) Promote SMEs in regional and local areas. 6) Develop enabling factors favorable to business operation.
The Third SMEs Promotion Plan (2012-2016)	OSMEP	1) Develop enabling factors and a conducive business environment for Thai SMEs. 2) Build and strengthen Thai SMEs competitiveness. 3) Promote balanced growth for regional Thai SMEs. 4) Build and strengthen business capability of Thai SMEs for international economic integration.
The Fourth SMEs Promotion Plan (2017-2021)	OSMEP	1) Elevate productivity, technology, and innovation. 2) Promote capital access. 3) Promote market access and internationalization. 4) Develop and promote entrepreneurship. 5) Develop tools for efficient implementation. 6) Revise regulation, laws, and privileges supportive to SMEs. 7) Create high value-added start-ups. 8) Promote SME clusters. 9) Strengthen fundamental enterprise.

continued on next page

Table 11.9 continued

Policies		
Name	Responsible Entity	Outline
National Strategy 2018-2037 and Master Plan (October 2019)	NESDB	1) Create national security for public contentment. 2) Enhance different capacities to promote constant economic development. 3) Promote multidimensional human capital development for righteous, skillful, and quality citizens. 4) Broaden opportunities and promote equality in society. 5) Improve quality of life based on green growth. 6) Reform government administration with a focus on public interest.
Thailand 4.0 (2016)		1) Prepare Thais for Thailand becoming a First World nation. 2) Develop technology cluster and future industries. 3) Incubate entrepreneurs and develop networks of innovation-driven enterprise. 4) Strengthen the internal economy through the mechanism of 18 provincial clusters and 76 provinces. 5) Integrate with ASEAN and connect Thailand to the global community.
The Twelfth National Economic and Social Development Plan (2017-2021)	NESDB	1) Strengthen and realize the potential of human capital. 2) Create a just society and reduce inequality. 3) Strengthen the economy, and underpin sustainable competitiveness. 4) Environment-friendly growth for sustainable development. 5) Reinforce national security for the country's progress towards prosperity and sustainability. 6) Public administration, corruption prevention, and good governance in Thai society. 7) Advance infrastructure and logistics. 8) Develop science, technology, research, and innovation. 9) Regional, urban, and economic zone development. 10) International cooperation for development.
The Bank of Thailand's 3-Year Strategic Plan (2017-2019)	BOT	1) Monetary stability. 2) Financial stabililty. 3) Financial institutions stability. 4) Payments system stability. 5) Financial system development. 6) Connectivity. 7) Financial inclusion, market conduct, and sustainability. 8) Data systems and analytics. 9) Research excellence. 10) Human resource. 11) Organizational capablity. 12) Stakeholders engagement.
Financial Sector Master Plan Phase III (2016-2020)	BOT	1) Facilitate access to alternative funding channels (e.g., P2P lending, crowdfunding, and venture capital) and promote e-financial transactions (e.g., e-factoring and e-claims) which aim to reduce existing gaps in the credit and financing market for SMEs. 2) Promote development of digital solutions that could address SMEs pain points, increse efficiency, and reduce costs, e.g., standardized QR code and PromptPay (low-cost fund transfer service). 3) Support Thai Credit Guarantee Corporation in the development of effective credit guarantee mechanisms to mitigate risks for SMEs. 4) Encourage the National Credit Bureau to expand its coverage to include more types and a larger number of members, and to offer bureau scoring services both for individuals and juristic persons; promote the usage of alternative information for credit assessment (e.g., payment and transactional data). 5) Support the implementation of government policies on SMEs development such as encouraging the government's SME One-Stop Service Center in its role as an information center and a resource for helping SMEs develop their capabilities.
Payment Systems Roadmap No. 4 (2019-2021)	BOT	1) Develop infrastructure that is interoperable, secure, and in compliance with international standards to support innovations and cross-boarder connectivity. 2) Promote the development of various service innovations that meet users' needs. 3) Integrate payment data for utilization, develop data integration, and analyze by using technologies. 4) Maintain stability, sound risk management, responsive supervision and examination, and customer protection. 5) Improve access, raise awareness and understanding, and promote continuous usage.
The Third Thai Capital Market Development Plan (2016-2021)	FPO	SME related measure: "Promoting Capital Market to be source of finance for SMEs and Innovation."
Policy Guidelines for the Specialized Financial Institutions with regards to SMEs (2016-2020)	FPO	1) Promote financial access for SMEs at appropriate cost. 2) Support SMEs in targeted industries (innovative, green, and agriculture SMEs). 3) Develop financial products suitable for micro SMEs as well as enable capable SMEs to become exporters. 4) Advocate for financial literacy.

SME = small and medium-sized enterprise.
Source: ADB Asia SME Monitor 2020 database. Data from Office of Small and Medium Enterprises Promotion, Bank of Thailand, and Securities and Exchange Commission.

Country Review

Viet Nam

Overview

Viet Nam has a labor force population of 55.4 million (aged 15 years and above). Its economy remains robust, growing by 7.0% in 2019.[144] As of 2018, micro, small, and medium-sized enterprises (MSMEs) represented 97.2% of all firms and employed 38.0% of the labor force. They play a pivotal role as a growth driver of the economy. They are mainly engaged in traditional trade or low-tech industries. Innovation and internationalization is key for strengthening MSME dynamics and boosting national productivity. The bank credit market has expanded at a slower pace since 2018, while bank credit to MSMEs has grown moderately, supported by a multitude of government support measures. Microfinance helps fill unmet financing demand from MSMEs. Digital financial services (DFS) have yet to emerge, but a newly launched financial inclusion strategy supports its development. Access to finance, a dearth of qualified managers, and access to technology and information remain critical hurdles to cross for continued MSME and overall economic development.

1. MSME Development

- An increasing number of MSMEs are engaged in traditional trade and low-tech industries; informal household businesses are deep-rooted in the economy, and one important policy objective is to absorb more into the formal economy.
- MSMEs in manufacturing account for a large number of jobs; as they shrink in number, job absorption by MSMEs weakens accordingly; promoting new and innovative start-ups are expected to create new jobs.
- MSME capital and profitability have expanded; the business community recognizes MSMEs' large contribution to gross domestic product (GDP), underpinned by household businesses.
- There are few globalized MSMEs; internationalization of MSMEs is a policy support priority designed to promote their participation in global value chains.
- E-commerce and other digital industries offer huge opportunities for new and innovative business for domestic MSMEs; developing business clusters and linking MSMEs with government projects will encourage more innovative businesses.
- Business communities play a key role in voicing positions on government policies involving business development and thematic global agendas such as gender mainstreaming.

Scale of MSMEs

On 12 June 2017, the National Assembly passed the Support for Small and Medium Sized Enterprises (SME Support Law)—Law No.04/2017/QH14—which stipulates criteria for defining MSMEs: an annual average number of employees participating in social insurance not greater than 200, and satisfying one of the following criteria; (i) total capital is not greater than D100 billion; or (ii) revenue from the previous year is not greater than D300 billion. The law also states that MSMEs will be identified by industry and that the government will provide detailed guidance. On 11 March 2018, the National Assembly passed the guidelines for the SME Support Law—Decree

[144] General Statistics Office of Viet Nam (https://www.gso.gov.vn/) and; ADB. 2020. *Asian Development Outlook 2020 Supplement (June 2020)*. Manila.

No.39/2018/ND-CP—which sets criteria for MSME classification (Table 12.1). This decree superseded a 2009 decree (Decree No.56/2009/ND-CP), which used the same sectors with different criteria. Microenterprises were identified only by employment: 10 workers or fewer. Small and medium-sized enterprises were defined using thresholds for employment and total capital, but not revenue.

The number of MSMEs (private and domestically owned) has grown exponentially since 2007. There were 143,622 in 2007 and 593,629 as of 2018 (Figure 12.1A and Table 12.2).[145] Overall, the number of MSMEs for 2007–2018 increased by 313.3% (a compound annual growth rate of 13.8%). Year-on-year, the growth rate has been volatile, ranging from a high of 29.8% in 2008 to a low of 6.9% in 2012. The number of MSMEs grew by 9.9% in 2017 and 9.1% in 2018. MSMEs have also grown as a share of total enterprises, increasing from 96.3% in 2007 to 98.0% in 2015 and 2016, before dipping to 97.1% in 2017 and edging up to 97.2% in 2018.

By sector as of 2018, wholesale and retail trade accounted for 39.0% of MSMEs, followed by other services (22.3%), manufacturing (15.1%) and construction (13.3%) (Figure 12.1B). The sector share has remained steady for trade and construction during 2007–2018, but dropped 19.0% for manufacturing, from 18.6% to 15.1%. Other services has grown 38.9%, from 16.1% in 2007 to 22.3% in 2018.

The Agency for Business Registration, under the Ministry of Planning and Investment, had 760,000 enterprises registered as of end-2019, including foreign-owned and state-owned enterprises. Foreign-owned enterprises are categorized as privately held foreign direct investment (FDI) firms that have at least 50% foreign ownership. Although a small portion of MSMEs, there were 2,662 state-owned MSMEs operating as of 2016, of which 111 were microenterprises, 1,039 small enterprises, and 392 medium-sized enterprises.

According to the General Statistics Office, there are 5 million household businesses (sole proprietorships or personal home businesses), mostly engaged in agri-business. Of these household businesses, 1.6 million are registered with the remaining 3.4 million unregistered, i.e., informal businesses. One primary policy goal for MSME development is to register informal businesses and move them out of the shadow economy.

Figure 12.1: Number of MSMEs

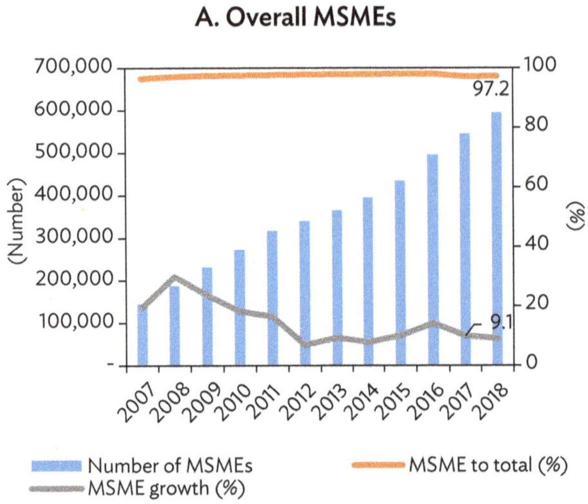

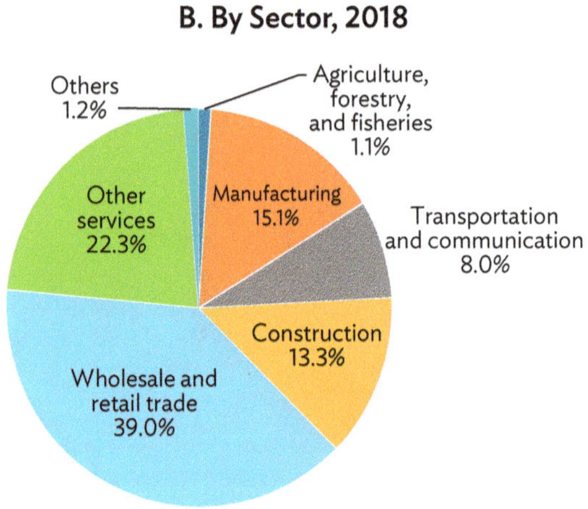

MSME = micro, small, and medium-sized enterprise.

Source: ADB Asia SME Monitor 2020 database. Data from Agency for Enterprise Development, Ministry of Planning and Investment; and General Statistics Office.

[145] The most recent General Statistics Office MSME data is for 31 December 2018. Data for the end of 2019 will not be available until March 2021.

Employment

During 2007–2018, MSMEs employed an average 43.2% of the labor force, ranging from a high of 46.8% in 2011 to a low of 38.0% in 2018, gradually trending downward (Figure 12.2A). By number of people with jobs, MSME employment grew 98.5% (a compound annual growth rate of 6.4%), from 2.8 million in 2007 to 5.6 million in 2018. Year-on-year, growth has varied considerably, ranging from 18.1% in 2008 to –10.8% in 2017. There was double-digit growth from 2007 to 2011, single-digit growth for 2012–2016, a decline in 2017 and a 1.6% rebound in 2018. Although MSME data are unavailable, there are data for female labor participation for 2010–2018; relatively stable, ranging from 46.1% in 2017 to 48.8% in 2014.

By sector, the largest employer is manufacturing (26.4% of the MSME workforce in 2018), followed by wholesale and retail trade (26.1%) and construction (18.6%) (Figure 12.2B). From 2007 to 2018, manufacturing dropped by 32.6% (from 39.2% in 2007 to 26.4% in 2018), while other services grew 89.4% (from 9.5% to 18.0%). Wholesale and retail trade expanded 31.0% (from 19.9% in 2007 to 26.1% in 2018).

Figure 12.2: Employment by MSMEs

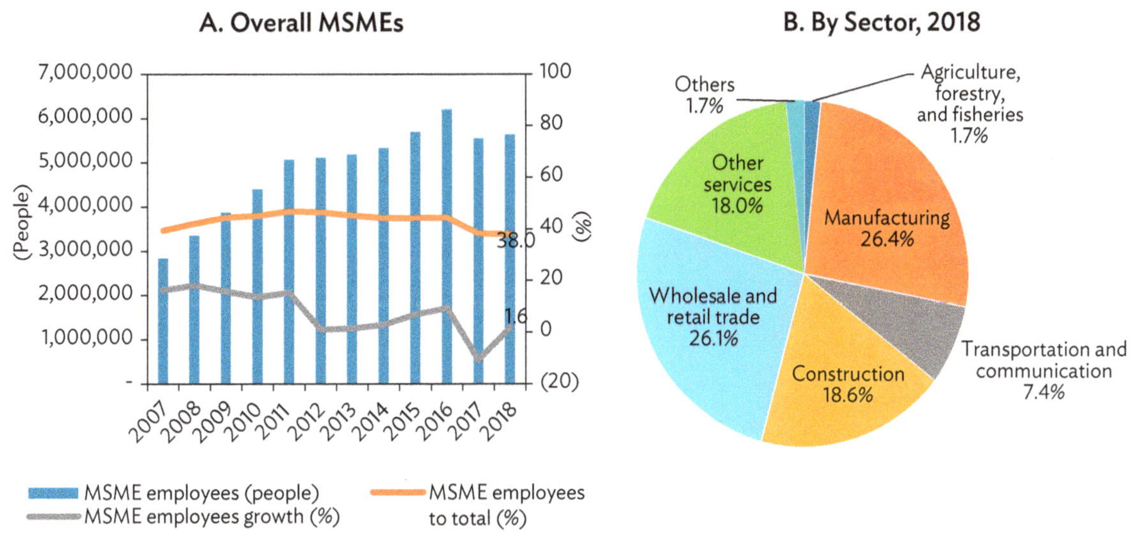

MSME = micro, small, and medium-sized enterprise.

Source: ADB Asia SME Monitor 2020 database. Data from Agency for Enterprise Development, Ministry of Planning and Investment; and General Statistics Office.

Business Productivity

Key financial and productivity metrics for MSMEs during 2007–2018 were total capital, fixed assets and long-term investment, and net income. All three surged during the period. Capital grew from D1.4 quadrillion ($86.9 billion)[146] in 2007 to D11.8 quadrillion ($518.4 billion) by 2018, an overall increase of 744.6% (a compound annual growth rate of 21.4%). Fixed assets and long-term investments rose from just D519.9 trillion ($32.3 billion) in 2007 to D4.2 quadrillion ($182.8 billion) in 2018, an increase of 702.4% (a compound annual growth rate of 20.8%). Net income was D1.7 quadrillion ($104.2 billion) in 2007, expanding to D6.4 quadrillion ($282.2 billion) in 2018, an overall increase of 283.4% (a compound annual growth rate is 13.0%).

[146] Conversion from Vietnamese dong (D) to US dollar in this report is calculated by using International Monetary Fund/International Financial Statistics (IMF/IFS) end-of-year exchange rates.

According to the Vietnam Chamber of Commerce and Industry (VCCI),[147] MSMEs (private and domestically owned firms) contributed approximately 40% of GDP in 2018, higher than the contribution of foreign-owned enterprises (FDI firms). Household businesses accounted for 30% of the MSME contribution and 12% of GDP in 2018.

Market Access

MSME businesses are typically focused on the domestic market. Their exposure to global markets is still limited, and internationalization of MSMEs is one policy target for the government's MSME support. The Vietnam Trade Promotion Agency (VIETRADE), under the Ministry of Industry and Trade, encourages MSMEs to export. There are three support mechanisms: (i) trade promotion activities via policies and exhibitions, (ii) policies and mechanisms to access foreign markets and to join global value chains, and (iii) market information support and training programs.[148]

In the first quarter of 2019, FDI firms were only 2.2% of all firms, but accounted for 70% of exports by value ($55 billion according to VIETRADE). There are no data on the share of FDI firms that are MSMEs. While VIETRADE prioritizes domestic companies, it also helps FDI firms that partner with domestic companies, including MSMEs.

VIETRADE provides technical support for exporting rather than subsidies. From 2015 to 2018, 30,000 enterprises received VIETRADE support, mostly MSMEs. VIETRADE does not collect data on MSMEs that export, but estimates that 20% of MSMEs are involved either in direct or indirect exports. Top destinations include the People's Republic of China, the United States, the European Union, and Japan. Direct exports are mainly in footwear and aquaculture products such as catfish (*basa*) and shrimp.

By sector, the textile, garments, and apparel industry holds the largest share of MSME exports, with FDI firms driving the sector. Year-on-year, mobile phones and components are growing fastest. VIETRADE does not prioritize sectors for exporting, with companies from any sector eligible for support.

VIETRADE is also trying to link Vietnamese MSMEs with global value chains. Most MSMEs are engaged in low value-added activities such as raw material supply or packaging. Less than 1% of MSMEs engage in outward FDI, for example, in logistics services, where Vietnamese MSMEs establish branches in the Lao PDR, Cambodia, and Myanmar.

While there are no data on MSME exports and imports, there are US dollar data for total exports and imports for 2007–2018. Exports climbed from $55.0 billion in 2007 to $258.5 billion in 2018, an increase of 369.8% (a compound annual growth rate of 15.1%). Total imports grew from $69.9 billion in 2007 to $255.8 billion (a compound annual growth rate of 12.5%).

Technology and Innovation

The number of mobile cellular subscriptions has been surging, from 120 million in 2017 to 141 million in 2018.[149] Individuals using the internet also increased sharply, from 58.1% of the population in 2017 to 70.4% in 2018. Accordingly, the e-commerce market has been rapidly expanding. The Vietnam E-Business Index 2019 indicated that e-commerce revenue—from online retailing, travel ticketing, entertainment, and shopping—surged from $4 billion in 2015 to $7.8 billion in 2018 (a compound annual growth of 30%).[150] E-commerce and other digital industries offer

[147] Interview with the director of VCCI on 7 August 2019.
[148] Interview with the director of the Vietnam Trade Promotion Agency on 6 August 2019.
[149] World Bank database (https://data.worldbank.org/indicator/). Accessed on 30 March 2020.
[150] The Vietnam E-Commerce Association. 2019. Vietnam E-Business Index 2019.

huge opportunities for new and innovative businesses for domestic start-ups and MSMEs. Technology and innovation underpin sustainable economic growth, promoted by several government policy measures.

The Ministry of Science and Technology (MOST)—the focal agency for relevant regulations—supports science and innovative start-ups. MSMEs using their own or university-based science and technology for production and services are defined as tech start-ups.

The 2017 SME Support Law elevated the Master Plan 844 of 2016 as a policy enjoying full legal status. The targets of the master plan include innovative start-ups and their supporting network of universities, incubators, and the like. The master plan is designed to develop a national ecosystem for improving innovative capacity, establishing incubators, and incentivizing venture capital for start-ups.

According to MOST, the environment for tech start-ups is getting better.[151] The number of new technology firms and organizations supporting them are increasing, along with the amount of venture capital financing, the number of new deals, and the value of those deals.

MOST cited big data, machine learning through artificial intelligence, and blockchain technology as popular among the younger generation of Vietnamese inventors. These technologies are widely used in health care, logistics, tourism, education, renewable energy, and environmental protection. Both central and provincial governments are encouraging “smart” technology for developing public and business products and services in urban and rural areas.

One trend is clustering technology start-ups. The minimum size of a cluster is three to four firms, with a maximum of over 100 firms. Building clusters is popular in fintech and health care industries. For example, there is a cluster of more than 100 MSMEs that uses big data to analyze phone traffic, determining which products to market to telecommunication companies.

Master Plan 844 directs state-owned enterprises, state-backed business associations, and government agencies to seek out technology-based start-ups to solve procurement problems, among others. Large state-owned enterprises have budgets to hire technology-based start-ups and MSMEs. An example is Vingroup, which uses tech firms to handle its e-commerce. It shows how state-owned enterprises can help technology-based start-ups, and illustrates the benefits of corporate-level support and cooperation between the public and private sectors.

Networking and Support

VCCI offers business development services and networking opportunities. It has 200,000 members: 15,000 are direct members with the remaining 185,000 indirect members. Direct members are business associations and the like. Only 100–200 members are large enterprises; the remainder MSMEs.

VCCI has two broad areas of support. The first is policy development, where it is actively involved in drafting laws, decrees, and circulars pertaining to enterprises. For example, VCCI was part of the drafting team of the 2017 SME Support Law. It is a conduit for obtaining grassroots feedback from businesses on legislation drafts. The second area of support is to service MSMEs. VCCI sponsors promotional activities, exhibitions, and training that benefits MSMEs. For example, it promotes partnerships with foreign firms and connects MSMEs with overseas businesses. Ongoing projects include technical assistance to the agriculture sector and rural areas, helping

[151] Interview with the director general of MOST on 8 August 2019.

MSMEs join global value chains. It is partnering with Microsoft to build MSME capacities and with Facebook to build MSME marketing skills.

Another support organization is the Women's Initiative for Startups and Entrepreneurship (WISE), a non-profit organization to empower women and build the next generation of women entrepreneurs. It inspires, motivates and supports women in starting, innovating and growing their business. WISE enjoys government support. The 2017 SME Support Law formally defines women-owned MSMEs as those with at least 51% female ownership and at least one female executive. It also calls for giving women-owned MSMEs priority for support services. In 2017, 21% of MSMEs were female-owned; the government wants to increase this to 30% by 2025.

WISE has built a community of 12,000 women in startups and businesses, provided training for nearly 4,000 women across the country, motivated women to start business through different start-up competitions, challenges, and incubation programs. Over the last 3 years (2017–2019), WISE has run two cohorts (20 companies) of female founder accelerators which have raised around $2 million. Through its signature acceleration programs, women role models are identified and promoted, developing leadership and entrepreneurship among young women. WISE mentors and coaches, provides business connections and information sharing, along with research and advocacy to nurture women entrepreneurship.

According to WISE, female-owned MSMEs are most prevalent in fashion, beauty products, tourism, food and beverage, health care, education, and agriculture.[152] It wants to encourage more women to consider high-tech sectors. It is working to establish a network of angel investors dedicated to investing in female-owned start-ups. WISE is also working to advertise the accomplishments of female entrepreneurs, for example, ELSA, an English language pronunciation application that a Vietnamese woman developed in Silicon Valley.

2. Access to Finance

- While growth in commercial bank lending slowed, bank credit to MSMEs expanded moderately due to a multitude of government support measures.
- While there is no specialized bank for MSMEs, state policy banks help support their access to finance to adhere to government policies.
- State-owned funds help MSMEs access finance from different thematic angles by supporting tech-based startups, social enterprises, and women entrepreneurs, using credit guarantees and interest subsidies.
- Although the nonbank finance industry is small-scale, licensed microfinance institutions and People's Credit Funds have supplemented unmet financing demand from MSMEs.
- Digital financial services have yet to emerge in Viet Nam, but the newly launched financial inclusion strategy will support its development.
- There is no dedicated SME capital market in Viet Nam, but UPCoM (Unlisted Public CoMpany), a trading venue for unlisted stocks, offers equity financing opportunities for growing and viable SMEs.
- The credit bureau system will need more diverse data sources to develop a sophisticated credit information system, while a collateral registry or secured lending legal system needs to be developed; financial literacy must be more widespread before MSMEs can take advantage of available financial services and infrastructure.

Every stakeholder mentioned access to finance as the main barrier for MSME development. Although access to finance has improved since 2014, there is still room for improvement. The government is addressing this concern with two separate strategies for financial inclusion and capital market reform.

152 Interview with the chief executive of WISE on 9 August 2019.

Bank Credit

As of end-2018, there were 97 commercial banks operating in Viet Nam—7 state-owned banks, 2 policy banks (the Vietnam Bank for Social Policies and Vietnam Development Bank), 28 joint stock banks, 2 joint venture banks, 9 fully foreign-owned banks, and 49 foreign bank branches (Table 12.3).

The bank credit market has been growing steadily. During 2012–2019, bank loans outstanding increased by 165.1%, from D3.1 quadrillion ($148.4 billion) to D8.2 quadrillion ($353.9 billion) (a compound annual growth rate of 14.9%)—year-on-year growth was 13.6% from 2018 to 2019 (Figure 12.3A). Loans as a percentage of GDP increased steadily from 95.2% in 2012 to 130.1% in 2018,[153] an increase of 36.6% (a compound annual growth rate of 5.3%).

As of 2019, sectors categorized as "others," such as education, health care, and services, accounted for the largest share of bank loans (37.2%), followed by wholesale and retail trade (22.5%) and manufacturing (19.0%) (Figure 12.3B). During 2012–2019, the wholesale and retail trade share to total loan portfolio averaged 19.7%, ranging from 17.8% in 2015 to 22.5% in 2019, continuing its upward trend. In manufacturing, however, while its share averaged 23.6%, it ranged from 29.3% in 2012 to 19.0% in 2019, a clear downward trend. Construction and agriculture, forestry, and fisheries have been relatively stable at 9%–10% of the loan portfolio.

The nonperforming loan (NPL) ratio declined over 2012–2019, from 4.1% to 1.6% as of end-2019. The average lending rate is 7.5%–9.0% for short-term borrowing (<12 months), while medium-term (1–7 years) and long-term (7+ years) rates are 11%–14%. MSMEs receive a 2% interest rate subsidy if they borrow from one of the 10 state-run funds that the Ministry of Finance oversees (see Public Financing and Guarantees).

Commercial banks can accept movable assets as collateral. With no movable asset registry, however, commercial banks must review and assess movable asset values internally. Viet Nam does have a Land Registry Office for immovable assets such as land and buildings. Four types of collateral are registered: land (technically, land use rights); assets on land such as homes and buildings; airplanes; and ships. The Ministry of Justice supervises the Land Registry Office.

While growth in commercial bank lending has slowed, bank credit to MSMEs has expanded moderately from a multitude of government support measures. No MSME credit data is publicly available, but according to the State Bank of Vietnam (SBV), the MSME credit market has been growing robustly since 2015. Year-on-year growth was 12.1% from 2014 to 2015, 14.2% in 2016, 14.4% in 2017, and 15.5% in 2018.[154] By sector, services, including wholesale and retail trade, accounted for 55% of MSME loans outstanding in 2018, followed by "industry" (manufacturing) and construction (40%).

Most MSME loans come from banks rather than nonbank financial institutions (NBFIs). Only 2%–3% are from NBFIs, mostly from leasing companies and microfinance institutions (MFIs). The SBV maintains it is difficult for MSMEs to access credit because they have limited financial capacity and are not adept at writing credible business plans. They are also weak in information technology and accounting, and do not have accurate financial data.

153 The most recent year for GDP data is 2018.
154 Interview with the SBV on 6 August 2019.

Figure 12.3: Bank Loans

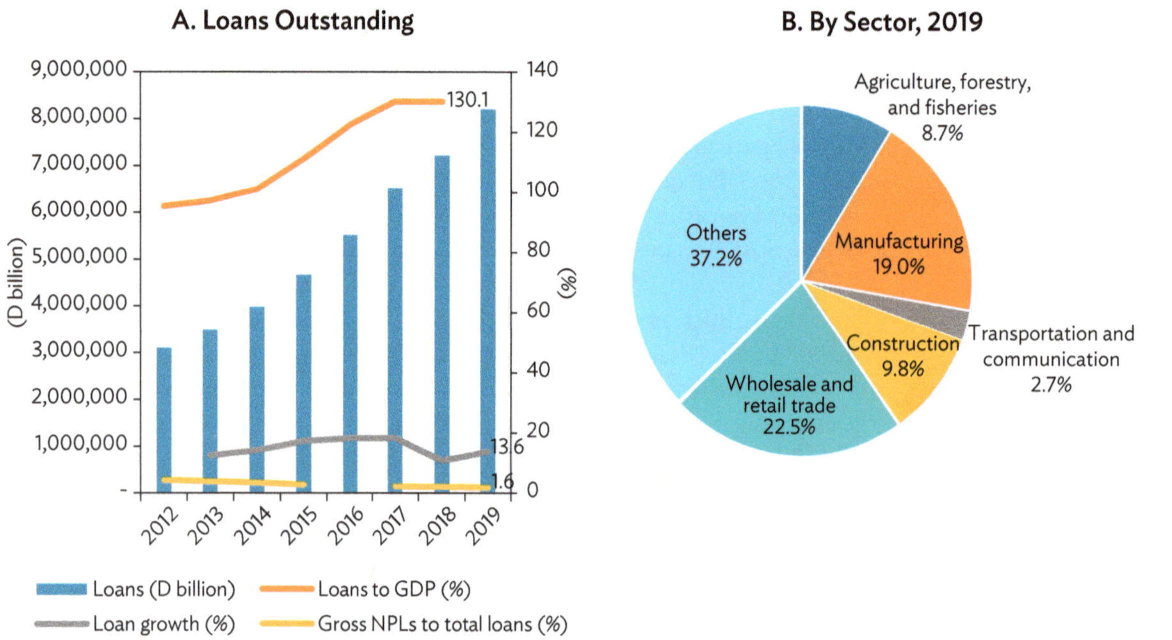

GDP = gross domestic product, NPL = nonperforming loan.

Source: ADB Asia SME Monitor 2020 database. Data from State Bank of Vietnam.

Public Financing and Guarantees

a. Specialized bank for MSMEs

There is no specialized bank for MSMEs in Viet Nam, but two policy banks partly support MSME access to finance in line with government policies. One is the Vietnam Development Bank (VDB).[155]

Over time, VDB has absorbed four functions. The first is to provide investment credit. VDB provides preferential loans to priority government development projects (Decree No.32/2017/ND-CP, issued 31 March 2017 to govern state investment credit). Sectors include energy, infrastructure, agriculture, industry (manufacturing), and health, among others. MSMEs often find it difficult to participate in development projects due to a lack of capital, expertise, and other resources.

Second is to provide export credit, short-term support for eligible export products as defined by the government. These stopped in 2017.

Third is to administer official development assistance guarantees to support projects defined and selected by the government. These are government-to-government transactions; very little goes to MSMEs.

[155] The other is the Vietnam Bank for Social Policies.

The fourth is a credit guarantee program. Credit guarantees are not a regular function of the VDB, but a temporary government measure in response to the economic downturn. Many MSMEs benefited from the program. It was initiated only for 2009–2010; after that, the guarantee program stopped. However, the VDB continues to manage the remaining long-term loans that were guaranteed during the period. There were over D10 trillion in original credit guarantees covering construction and construction materials, transport, manufacturing and processing, education, and aquaculture. As of end-2019, VDB continued to hold credit guarantees for 45 loans worth over D800 billion, in textiles, packaging, processing, plastic production, aquaculture, and transportation.

The VDB is undergoing a restructuring that should be completed by the end of 2020. Due to the risk associated with credit guarantees, the Ministry of Finance has declared a moratorium on the VDB issuing credit guarantees for new loans, and it has no plans to issue credit guarantees.

b. Credit guarantees

Viet Nam first developed a credit guarantee scheme for MSMEs in 2001 (under Decree No.193/2001/QD-TTg), revising it in March 2018 (under Decree No.34/2018/ND-CP).[156] Credit guarantees can operate according to non-profit principles and using the model of a one-member limited company with 100% charter public sector capital. Credit guarantee funds must have a minimum of D100 billion at the time of chartering, and MSMEs must own at least 20% of the capital to be guaranteed. The total credit guarantee leverage cannot exceed 15% of the charter capital of a credit guarantee fund for a single customer and 20% for a customer and related party.

For credit guarantee schemes, the Decree No.34/2018/ND-CP implements the MSME Credit Guarantee Fund, which falls under SVB and Ministry of Finance responsibility. The decree sets five conditions for MSME borrowers: (i) it should be a feasible investment project, (ii) it should have an approved business plan, (iii) it should have equity capital worth at least 20% of the project, (iv) it must not have tax arrears of over 1 year, and (v) it must have collateral.

c. Soft loan programs

A concessional credit program for agricultural and rural development was laid out in 2015 (Decree No.55 of 2015, superseded by the Decree No.116 of 2018), which specifically targets agricultural technology development. Up to 80% of program funds can be allocated as uncollateralized loans, with interest rates 0.5%–1%, lower than the market rate for a comparable loan.

In addition, the Ministry of Finance manages 10 state-owned funds for MSMEs:

(i) SME Development Fund, under the Ministry of Planning and Investment, with D1 trillion in capital funded by the Ministry of Finance;
(ii) National Foundation for Science and Technology Development Fund, with D1 trillion in capital, supporting MSMEs in science and technology;
(iii) Fund for Science and Technology Innovation, a separate fund from National Foundation for Science and Technology Development, with D500 billion in capital funded by the Ministry of Finance, also for high-tech MSMEs;
(iv) Environment Protection Investment Fund, with D600 billion in capital, supporting MSMEs engaged in environment protection, such as waste management;

[156] L. N. Dang and A. T. Chuc. 2019. Challenges in Implementing the Credit Guarantee Scheme for Small and Medium-sized Enterprises: The Case of Viet Nam. *ADBI Working Paper Series*. No.941.

(v) Cooperative Development Support Fund, supporting cooperative-typed MSMEs;
(vi) Farmer Support Fund;
(vii) Women Support Fund, with D100 billion, offering concessional loans for women;
(viii) Credit Guarantee Fund, having 27 locally run credit guarantee funds in the larger provinces (the number is expected to grow further);
(ix) Local Development Investment Fund, having 44 investment funds with D20 trillion in total capital;
(x) Ho Chi Minh Financial Investment Company (formerly a Local Development Investment Fund) Investment Fund, the largest and best-performing fund with D5 trillion in capital.

Both the central and provincial budgets contribute capital to these funds, which are mobilized through credit guarantees and interest subsidies. VDB mobilizes the most, providing D10 trillion via bonds.

MSMEs have priority. They are targeted borrowers with certain funds such as the Farmer Support Fund, Environment Protection Investment Fund, and Cooperative Development Support Fund. The funds are not for profit and thus can provide lower interest rates, generally 2%–3% below market rates for comparable loans. The average short-term borrowing rate (<12 months) is 5.5%–6%, while medium- and long-term rates range 9%–11%. The medium term is 1–7 years and with long-term loans over 7 years.

The interest rate subsidy is 2% on average. However, the subsidy is being phased out due to its cost; it is cheaper to provide loans at lower rates than to subsidize the interest. As of August 2019, most funds had abandoned the subsidy, except the Environment Protection Investment Fund and the Cooperative Development Support Fund.

Nonbank Financing

The nonbank finance industry is small in scale. As of end-June 2019, there were four licensed MFIs, one cooperative bank, 26 finance and leasing companies, and 1,183 People's Credit Funds operating in the country (Table 12.4). People's Credit Funds, introduced in 1993, are credit institutions established on a voluntary basis as cooperatives. There was a Central People's Credit Fund as an apex fund for all People's Credit Funds, but it shifted legal status to a cooperative bank in July 2013. Total financing outstanding for nonbank finance institutions—combined MFIs and People's Credit Funds—amounted to D102 trillion in the second quarter of 2019, or 1.3% of total bank loans outstanding (D7.7 quadrillion).

Although relatively small-scale, microfinance from licensed MFIs and People's Credit Funds has effectively supplemented some of the unmet MSME financing demand. During 2011–2019 (second quarter), MFI loans increased from D419.0 billion ($20.1 million) to D6.0 trillion ($258.7 million) (Figure 12.4A). This 1,329.4% growth represents a compound annual growth rate of 42.6%. Loans by People's Credit Funds increased from D23.7 trillion ($1.3 billion) to D96.1 trillion ($4.2 billion) during 2010–2019 (second quarter) (Figure 12.4B), a 305.3% gain (a compound annual growth rate of 17.9%). Since 2013, however, growth has decelerated (to 6.2% in the second quarter of 2019). As a percentage of GDP, MFI loans accounted for 0.02% in 2011 and 0.10% in 2018. People's Credit Fund loans accounted for 1.1% in 2010 and 1.6% in 2018.

NPLs for MFIs are negligible, less than 0.4% of outstanding loans from 2011 to June 2019. There is no data for NPLs for People's Credit Funds. By sector, SBV reports that manufacturing MSMEs account for 40%–50% of MFI loans.

Figure 12.4: Nonbank Finance

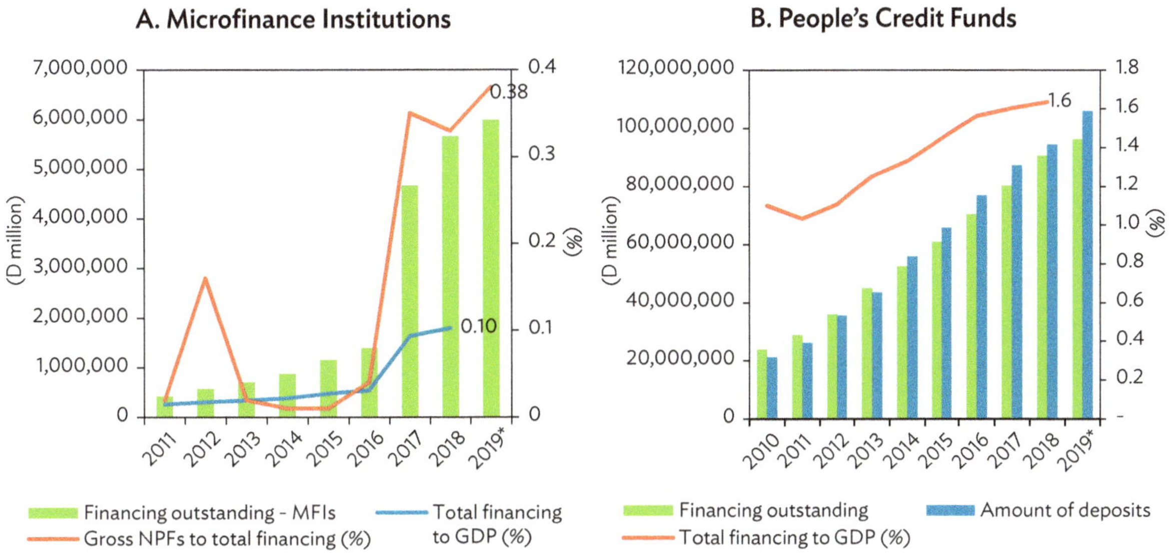

GDP = gross domestic product, MFI = microfinance institution, NPF = nonperforming finance.

* Data for 2019 as of the second quarter.

Source: ADB Asia SME Monitor 2020 database. Data from State Bank of Vietnam.

Digital Financial Services

Digital financial services (DFS) remain nascent in Viet Nam. SBV has a Fintech Working Group that is exploring peer-to-peer lending. The State Securities Commission (SSC) is researching the feasibility of crowdfunding; its usefulness will depend upon the risk appetite and financial sophistication of the investors and offering firms. There is a dearth of MSMEs with the requisite skills and capabilities to employ these kinds of DFS effectively. Additionally, using DFS to reach the unbanked is a key tactic of SBV's financial inclusion strategy and Ministry of Finance.

Capital Markets

Viet Nam's capital market is comprised of two state-owned stock exchanges (the Ho Chi Minh Stock Exchange and the Hanoi Stock Exchange) and a central depository (the Vietnam Securities Depository). The SSC regulates and supervises stock markets under the Securities Law of 2006. The Hanoi Stock Exchange has a market for unlisted public companies and privatized state-owned enterprises, called UPCoM (Unlisted Public CoMpanies). Operating since 2009, UPCoM is not a dedicated MSME market, but an equity financing venue MSMEs can tap.

In the UPCoM, companies are not listed but registered. It targets (i) public companies ineligible for listing; (ii) public companies eligible for listing but unlisted on the stock exchange; (iii) delisted companies that remain public companies (for example, companies delisted due to mergers and acquisitions); and (iv) unlisted privatized state-owned enterprises following regulations on privatization.

UPCoM has three equity boards and one "warning list" since 2017: (i) UPCoM SMALL with shareholder equity values from $450,000 to $14 million; (ii) UPCoM MEDIUM with shareholder equity values from $14 million to $45 million; and (iii) UPCoM LARGE with shareholder equity values more than $45 million. UPCoM SMALL holds 61% of UPCoM registered companies, 14% are UPCoM MEDIUM. Trading settlement is T+2.

UPCoM's market capitalization rose steadily from D16.2 trillion ($857.7 million) in 2010 to D912 trillion ($39.4 billion) as of end-2019, larger than the Hanoi Stock Exchange main board (D192 trillion) (Figure 12.5A and Table 12.5). The 5,516.2% increase during 2010–2019 translates into a compound annual growth rate of 56.5%. Trading value climbed from D2.3 trillion ($119.7 million) in 2010 to D73.5 trillion ($3.2 billion) by end-2019, an increase of 3,141.2% (a compound annual growth rate of 47.2%). Trading volume climbed from 152 million shares in 2010 to 3.7 billion shares in 2019, an increase of 2,307.1% (a compound annual growth rate of 42.4%).

The UPCoM offers eased requirements on registration for issuers. A company seeking UPCoM registration should have D10 billion or more in capital and at least 100 investors, excluding professional securities investors (Table 12.6). In addition, privatized state-owned enterprises conducting initial public offerings (IPOs) must register their shares on the UPCoM market. The company should also register at the Vietnam Securities Depository.

Since 2010, registration in UPCoM has grown from 109 to 872 companies as of end-2019 (Figure 12.5B), or a 700.0% increase (a compound annual growth rate of 26.0%). The number of newly registered companies dropped from 82 in 2010 to 7 in 2012, but increased each year from 2013 to 2017, before dropping back from 285 new firms in 2017 to 137 in 2018, and then 108 in 2019. An average 10.2 firms deregistered each year over 2010–2019; however, 21 delisted in 2018, and 24 in 2019.

The Hanoi Stock Exchange says liquidity is the primary challenge for Viet Nam's capital markets, both for equity and corporate bonds.[157] Only the Masan Group has issued bonds, (two issuances). One measure to expand liquidity is increasing the trading band by 15%. Another is to use "mark-to-market," and to implement margin trading. UPCoM has two major tasks: (i) support registration and (ii) improve transparency and corporate governance. Since 2009, the Hanoi Stock Exchange has the UPCoM Watch, monitoring registered companies since 2009. Companies can earn UPCoM Premium status for good financial reporting and information disclosure. If not, they earn Warning Status or Suspended Status. Since 2018, it has an Information Disclosure, Evaluation and Award for large public companies on UPCoM market to promote good corporate governance.

A new securities law (Securities Law No.54/2019/QH14) may alter UPCoM's role. Passed in November 2019 by the National Assembly, the law will become effective 1 January 2021. According to the SSC, a Vietnam Stock Exchange and Vietnam Securities Clearing and Settlement Corporation will be established and operate no later than 1 January 2023. Article 42 of the law authorizes the Vietnam Stock Exchange and its subsidiaries to organize trading markets for securities. Article 52 states that the government will own more than 50% of the charter capital/total voting shares of the Vietnam Securities Clearing and Settlement Corporation, which will operate in compliance with both the securities law and the 2014 Enterprise Law (No.68/2014/QH13) that became effective 1 July 2015.

Developing a venture capital and business angel industry is essential for expanding the capital market's investor base. According to the SSC, there are 47 venture capital funds in Viet Nam.[158] Business angels include the WISE network investing in women-owned businesses. But there are no data on the number of angel investors or the size of their investments.

157 Interview with the Hanoi Stock Exchange on 6 August 2019.
158 Interview with the director general of the SSC on 7 August 2019.

Figure 12.5: Equity Market

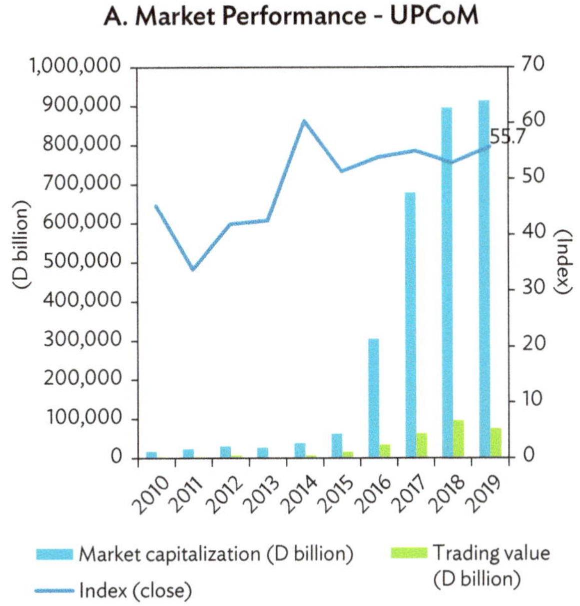

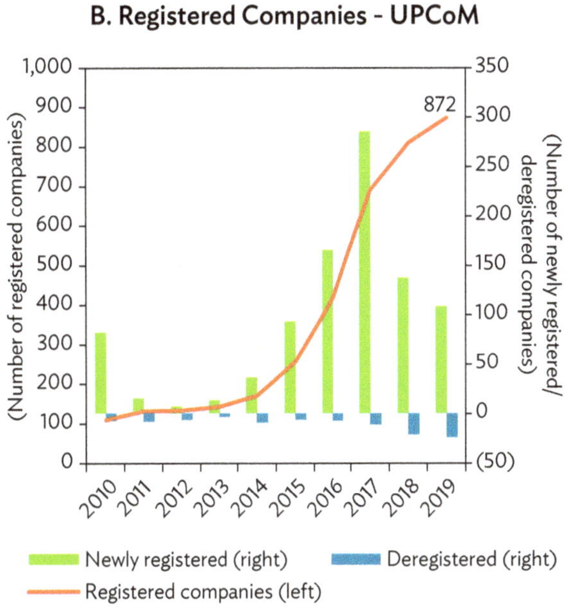

UPCoM = Unlisted Public CoMpanies.

Source: ADB Asia SME Monitor 2020 database. Data from Hanoi Stock Exchange.

Financial Infrastructure

There are two credit bureaus in Viet Nam: (i) the Credit Information Center (CIC) under the SBV and (ii) the Private Credit Bureau (PCB) licensed by SBV. The CIC is a major provider of credit information, holding records for more than 40 million borrowers. PCB was established in 2007 as the only private sector credit bureau, but received a license to operate from the SBV in 2013. Both CIC and PCB maintain their own data.

As of January 2020, PCB had a database of 26 million borrowers, of which 99% are individuals and the remainder MSMEs. For the 200,000 MSMEs, there are between 750,000–800,000 loans on record. The average loan size is for D2.3 billion.

PCB has over 33 members and currently receives data from 24 banks and financial companies. Setting up these data connections with banks and finance companies is the biggest constraint to creating more private credit bureaus. Banks and financial companies must submit their data to CIC, but becoming a member and contributing data to PCB is voluntary and contract-based. Because many organizations continue to upgrade their data collection systems, they lack the resources to connect to PCB and use automated programming interface services, which enables data submission and transmission.

PCB updates contracts with members monthly, and updates borrower data and requests in real time. PCB is a full-fledged credit bureau, gathering a firm's complete credit history covering both positive and negative information. PCB provides both personal historical data and a credit report. It provides value-added services such as credit scores, portfolio management, benchmarking reports, and "skip tracing" (or locating a debtor who has "skipped" or left town) to support organizations manage risk according to a product lifecycle.

PCB utilizes CRIF—a global company specializing in credit bureau and business information—to provide the online platform for its data services. Aside from supporting PCB in providing its platform, CRIF also plays a role as strategic shareholder. It advises on credit solutions and helps PCB in market analysis, sales, and management, among others.

The authorization for data access to broader sources is key for developing the credit information system, which in turn will help narrow the supply-demand gap confronting MSME financing. A comprehensive national data infrastructure that links tax records, social insurance data, business registration and operations information, and telecom data would be ideal, but probably sometime in the future.

There is no collateral registry or secured lending legal system assessing movable assets such as machinery and equipment, inventory, accounts receivable, and intellectual property rights. Accepting movable assets as loan collateral is at the lender's discretion.

Financial literacy and education programs play a critical role to help MSMEs tap available financial services and infrastructure, and to examine appropriate financing opportunities. This is especially important when setting up new and innovative financial services, including DFS solutions or funding opportunities beyond traditional bank credit. The SSC trains MSMEs on how to access capital markets and prepare necessary financial disclosures and reports. Most MSMEs are unaware of the various financial products available. VCCI also provides training to MSMEs on access to finance. For example, it supports Microsoft YouthSpark Career Readiness and Business Insights, among others, which uses financial training programs for MSMEs and start-ups to improve financial management capacity, create business plans, and learn the necessary skills in the fields of finance, taxation, and accounting. VCCI also offers other support, such as business cluster development that helps MSMEs join agricultural value chains, and boost competitiveness through participation in the global value chains.

WISE also provides a curriculum to women entrepreneurs. Topics include business management, accounting and bookkeeping, access to finance and loan applications, and marketing. WISE has trained 3,000 women from the start of 2017 to August 2019. In addition, WISE promotes a mobile platform for self-learning in partnership with the Cherie Blair Foundation for Women in the United Kingdom. The mobile phone application (app) offers modules on the skills cited above.

3. Policies and Regulations

- The 2017 SME Support Law offers the basis for a medium- to long-term policy framework for MSME development; it comprehensively addresses finance and nonfinance measures, including the creation of state funds, tax incentives, and capacity development programs.
- The government's support emphasizes drawing informal MSMEs into the formal economy, promoting innovative and tech-based MSMEs, and increasing MSME participation in global value chains.
- The central bank and the government have formulated a national financial inclusion strategy and roadmap, supporting overall MSME development and sustainable economic growth; digital financial services merits more policy focus given its potential widespread benefits.
- Capital market development will help innovative small businesses tap growth capital and boost productivity, thus contributing to inclusive growth.

MSME Development

In 2016, the National Assembly of Viet Nam passed a 5-year Socio-Economic Development Plan for 2016–2020 (Resolution No.142/2016/QH13). In brief, the plan sets out several primary economic objectives. They include macroeconomic stability, restructuring for greater competitiveness and efficiency, development of human resources and scientific/technical capabilities, and sustainable growth. The plan also includes specific targets for 2020, such as an average annual GDP growth of 6.5%–7.0%, per capita GDP of $3,200–$3,500, industry and services accounting for 85% of GDP, and total factor productivity 30%–35% of growth.

Given that MSMEs are the backbone of the economy, the government established guidelines in 2018 for the 2017 law on MSME support (Decree No.39/2018/ND-CP). The decree had four main MSME components: (i) MSME sector development policy, (ii) MSME definition, (iii) enhancing the functions of the SME Development Promotion Council, and (iv) establishing the SME Development Fund. The rules included support for creative start-ups and MSMEs participating in industrial clusters and value chains, support for information, consultancy, and human resource development, and support for boosting women-owned businesses and female-held jobs. In short, Decree No.39 set out the tactics for fulfilling the long-term national economic development strategy for relevant line ministries to follow. For example, the Ministry of Planning and Investment issued Circular No.06/2019/TT-BKHDT in 2019 to offer guidance on how MSMEs could connect to the consultancy network for business advice, as well as Circular No.05/2019/ TT-BKHDT offering training incentives for women-owned MSMEs.

Master Plan 844 is the governing policy on technology. There are several supporting ancillary decrees:

- Decree No.38/2018/ND-CP, effective March 2018, offers guidance on investing in innovative start-ups and provides venture capital regulations.
- Decree No.76/2018/ND-CP, effective December 2018, outlines policies on the commercialization of research to help implement the Technology Transfer Law of 2017.
- Decree No.13/2019/ND-CP, effective March 2019, offers tax breaks and exemptions/reductions in leasing fees for science and technology firms.

It is clear that Master Plan 844 supports creative start-ups and aims to fulfill several primary long-term objectives of the plan relating to competitiveness, efficiency, and the development of human resources and technical capabilities.

MSMEs are not prioritized for public procurement. However, there are several set-asides for MSMEs, for example, small contracts (D20 billion or less), which simply reflect the economic reality that small projects are not feasible for large companies. In general, MSMEs lack the resources to compete effectively for public procurement. In fact, MSME loans range from D7 billion to D20 billion precisely to enable MSMEs to obtain the contracts large companies do not want, but not to enable them to bid for contracts larger firms might bid for.

One issue plaguing MSMEs is brand management, and by extension, market access. To help address this, VIETRADE manages a National Brand Program, where the best quality companies become role models for the rest. These companies are typically large firms—the banking and consumer product companies with outstanding brand management. VIETRADE uses them to generate interest among MSMEs to build and protect their brands, and then provides support for their brand development and management.

Financial Inclusion

Since June 2016, SBV has issued several circulars to support MSME access to finance. These aim to (i) create policies credit institutions can implement and (ii) provide incentives to credit institutions who lend to MSMEs, by allowing them to have higher credit growth. The rate for MSMEs is 1%–2% lower than the market rate as long as the MSME is in good financial condition.

As part of overall economic restructuring toward greater efficiency and competitiveness, the 5-Year Socio-Economic Development Plan specifies reforms for financial markets—banking, insurance, and capital markets. For banks, it requires bringing standards up to international levels, which in the future should only help MSMEs obtain bank credit.

The government drafted a national financial inclusion strategy (beginning in 2018) which the Prime Minister signed in February 2020.[159] SBV is the lead agency for this strategy, though the Ministry of Finance and various other national and international agencies play various roles. The financial inclusion strategy has three components: (i) situation assessment, (ii) directions and solutions, and (iii) a roadmap. The overall focus is to use fintech for rural MSMEs and households to enhance access to finance. Its implementation remains at a very early stage.

A key player in financial inclusion is the Vietnam Bank for Social Policies, a state-run policy bank that provides support and policies to poor households. The bank accounts for 80% of all microfinancing. It is important for financial inclusion as it reaches out to remote areas and marginalized communities in increasing access to financial services. Under the financial inclusion strategy, the bank will receive increased support to improve operations and expand its outreach.

There are two tax incentives for MSMEs, the primary one a 5% rate reduction on corporate taxes. The second is a tax exemption for state-run funds. This lowers operational costs and enables them to lend to MSMEs at lower interest rates.

Capital market development will help innovative small businesses tap growth capital and boost their productivity; thus contributing to inclusive growth. To improve liquidity and transparency of the capital markets, the government enacted the Viet Nam Capital Market Development Strategy starting in 2015. It is a 5-year plan that includes financial services and insurance sectors. In March 2019, the Prime Minister approved a new plan (Plan No.242/QD-TTg) to continue the process of reforming capital markets and related industries through 2025.[160] Key elements of the new plan include revising current securities laws to restructure and expand capital markets, using the capital markets to restructure and privatize state-owned enterprises, and launching new investment products such as covered warrants and bond futures.

Securities Law No.54, approved in 2019, stipulates (Article 42) that the Vietnam Stock Exchange and its subsidiaries will be able to organize a trading market for the securities of innovative start-up businesses. In this way, access to capital markets can be improved for high-tech MSMEs. As mentioned, the law will become effective on 1 January 2021 with full compliance not until 1 January 2023.

Financial inclusion supports overall MSME development and sustainable economic growth in Viet Nam. Digital financial services merit more policy focus given its widespread potential benefits.

159 *Viet Nam News*. 2020. PM ratifies national financial inclusion strategy until 2025. 2 February. https://vietnamnews.vn/economy/591722/pm-ratifies-national-financial-inclusion-strategy-until-2025.html.

160 *Viet Nam News*. 2019. PM passes securities market plan. 8 March. https://vietnamnews.vn/economy/506634/pm-passes-securities-market-plan.html#sxHdM8tSH6FG7LQo.97.

Data Tables

Table 12.1: MSME Definition

A. Definition until 11 June 2017

Sector	Item	Micro	Small	Medium
Agriculture, forestry, and fisheries	Total capital	--	Less than or equal to D20 million	More than D20 billion but less than or equal to D100 billion
	Number of employees	1-10	11-200	201- 300
Industry and construction	Total capital	--	Less than or equal to D20 million	More than D20 billion but less than or equal to D100 billion
	Number of employees	1-10	11-200	201- 300
Commerce and services	Total capital	--	Less than or equal to D10 million	More than D10 billion but less than or equal to D50 billion
	Number of employees	1-10	11-50	51-100

Source: ADB Asia SME Monitor 2020 database. Data from Decree No. 56/2009/ND-CP.

B. Definition after 12 June 2017

Sector	Item	Micro	Small	Medium
Agriculture, forestry, and fisheries	Number of employees (with insurance)	1-10	11-100	101-200
	Total revenue	Not more than D3 billion	Not more than D50 million	Not more than D200 billion
	Total capital	Not more than D3 billion	Not more than D20 million	Not more than D100 billion
Industry and construction	Number of employees (with insurance)	1-10	11-100	101-200
	Total revenue	Not more than D3 billion	Not more than D50 million	Not more than D200 billion
	Total capital	Not more than D3 billion	Not more than D20 million	Not more than D100 billion
Commerce and services	Number of employees (with insurance)	1-10	11-50	51-100
	Total revenue	Not more than D10 billion	Not more than D100 million	Not more than D300 billion
	Total capital	Not more than D3 billion	Not more than D50 million	Not more than D100 billion

MSME = micro, small, and medium-sized enterprise.
Source: ADB Asia SME Monitor 2020 database. Data from Law No.04/2017/QH14; Decree No.39/2018/ND-CP.

Table 12.2: MSME Landscape

End of period data

Item	2007	2008	2009	2010	2011	2012	2013	2014	2015	2016	2017	2018*	2019
NUMBER OF ENTERPRISES													
Number of enterprises, total	149,069	192,179	236,584	279,360	324,691	346,777	373,213	402,326	442,485	505,059	560,413	610,637	--
Number of MSMEs**	143,622	186,379	230,365	272,283	316,941	338,916	365,181	393,915	433,453	495,010	544,212	593,629	--
Number of large enterprises	5,447	5,800	6,219	7,077	7,750	7,861	8,032	8,411	9,032	10,049	16,201	17,008	--
MSME to total (%)	96.3	97.0	97.4	97.5	97.6	97.7	97.8	97.9	98.0	98.0	97.1	97.2	--
MSME growth (%)	19.6	29.8	23.6	18.2	16.4	6.9	9.4	7.9	10.0	14.2	9.9	9.1	--
MSMEs by sector (% share)													
Agriculture, forestry, and fisheries	1.6	1.1	1.0	0.9	1.0	1.0	1.0	0.9	0.9	0.9	1.0	1.1	--
Manufacturing	18.6	18.2	17.5	15.7	15.7	15.7	15.2	15.2	14.8	14.5	14.2	15.1	--
Transportation and communication	6.5	5.3	5.7	6.7	7.6	7.6	7.5	7.8	8.1	8.3	8.3	8.0	--
Construction	14.0	14.6	15.0	15.5	13.7	14.2	14.1	13.8	14.0	13.0	13.2	13.3	--
Wholesale and retail trade	41.5	42.3	41.4	40.9	40.3	39.5	40.3	40.0	39.7	40.0	39.8	39.0	--
Other services	16.1	16.7	17.8	18.9	20.4	20.7	20.6	21.0	21.4	22.2	22.4	22.3	--
Others	1.7	1.7	1.6	1.4	1.4	1.4	1.3	1.2	1.2	1.1	1.1	1.2	--
Number of MSMEs by region (% share)													
Capital city	--	--	--	--	--	--	--	--	--	--	--	--	--
Others	--	--	--	--	--	--	--	--	--	--	--	--	--
MSMEs by type of ownership (% share)													
State-owned enterprises	1.3	1.0	0.8	0.7	0.6	0.6	0.5	0.5	0.4	0.3	0.2	0.2	--
Non-state-owned enterprises	96.1	96.7	97.0	97.2	97.1	97.3	97.2	97.3	97.4	97.4	97.6	97.8	--
Foreign-invested enterprises	2.6	2.3	2.2	2.1	2.3	2.1	2.2	2.2	2.2	2.3	2.2	2.1	--
EMPLOYMENT													
Number of employment, total	7,225,364	7,948,618	8,718,967	9,741,735	10,815,999	11,005,298	11,464,897	12,048,834	12,856,856	14,012,276	14,518,326	14,817,812	--
Number of employment by MSMEs	2,834,950	3,347,883	3,872,711	4,394,037	5,060,430	5,107,958	5,179,702	5,321,882	5,682,980	6,205,320	5,538,134	5,627,952	--
Number of employment by large enterprises	4,390,414	4,600,735	4,846,256	5,347,698	5,755,569	5,897,340	6,285,195	6,726,952	7,173,876	7,806,956	8,980,192	9,189,860	--
MSME employees to total (%)	39.2	42.1	44.4	45.1	46.8	46.4	45.2	44.2	44.2	44.3	38.1	38.0	--
MSME employees growth (%)	16.2	18.1	15.7	13.5	15.2	0.9	1.4	2.7	6.8	9.2	(10.8)	1.6	--
Share of female employees to total employees (%)	--	--	--	48.4	48.3	48.5	48.6	48.8	48.5	48.5	46.1	46.7	--
Employment by MSME by sector (% share)													
Agriculture, forestry, and fisheries	2.6	2.3	2.0	1.8	1.8	1.7	1.7	1.7	1.6	1.5	1.7	1.7	--
Manufacturing	39.2	37.0	34.7	33.3	31.9	31.6	31.7	31.7	31.5	31.2	26.3	26.4	--
Transportation and communication	4.9	4.8	5.0	5.3	5.6	5.8	5.8	6.0	6.4	6.6	7.5	7.4	--
Construction	21.1	21.2	22.7	23.3	23.7	23.5	22.8	22.2	22.1	21.6	20.3	18.6	--
Wholesale and retail trade	19.9	21.6	21.8	21.8	21.8	22.0	22.3	22.2	22.3	22.5	25.4	26.1	--
Other services	9.5	10.5	11.1	11.9	12.9	13.3	13.5	13.9	14.1	14.6	17.2	18.0	--
Others	2.8	2.7	2.6	2.5	2.3	2.2	2.2	2.2	2.1	2.0	1.7	1.7	--
Employment by MSMEs by region (% share)													
Capital city	--	--	--	--	--	--	--	--	--	--	--	--	--
Others	--	--	--	--	--	--	--	--	--	--	--	--	--
CONTRIBUTION TO GDP													
GDP of MSMEs (D billion)	--	--	--	--	--	--	--	--	--	--	--	--	--
MSME contribution to GDP (%)	--	--	--	--	--	--	--	--	--	--	--	--	--
MSME GDP growth (%)	--	--	--	--	--	--	--	--	--	--	--	--	--
MSME GDP by sector (% share)													
Agriculture, forestry, and fisheries	--	--	--	--	--	--	--	--	--	--	--	--	--
Manufacturing	--	--	--	--	--	--	--	--	--	--	--	--	--
Transportation and communication	--	--	--	--	--	--	--	--	--	--	--	--	--
Construction	--	--	--	--	--	--	--	--	--	--	--	--	--
Wholesale and retail trade	--	--	--	--	--	--	--	--	--	--	--	--	--
Other services	--	--	--	--	--	--	--	--	--	--	--	--	--
Others	--	--	--	--	--	--	--	--	--	--	--	--	--
MSME GDP by region (% share)													
Capital city	--	--	--	--	--	--	--	--	--	--	--	--	--
Others	--	--	--	--	--	--	--	--	--	--	--	--	--
EXPORTS													
Total export value ($ million)	55,021	69,691	62,862	79,697	105,597	124,149	142,743	161,267	173,267	189,081	228,169	258,472	--
Total export growth (%)	22.5	26.7	(9.8)	26.8	32.5	17.6	15.0	13.0	7.4	9.1	20.7	13.3	--
MSME export value ($ million)	--	--	--	--	--	--	--	--	--	--	--	--	--
MSME export to total export value (%)	--	--	--	--	--	--	--	--	--	--	--	--	--
MSME export growth (%)	--	--	--	--	--	--	--	--	--	--	--	--	--
IMPORTS													
Total import value ($ million)	69,942	88,670	78,136	94,760	118,609	124,830	145,853	162,849	181,791	191,736	230,215	255,767	--
Total import growth (%)	39.8	26.8	(11.9)	21.3	25.2	5.2	16.8	11.7	11.6	5.5	20.1	11.1	--
MSME import value ($ million)	--	--	--	--	--	--	--	--	--	--	--	--	--
MSME import to total import value (%)	--	--	--	--	--	--	--	--	--	--	--	--	--
MSME import growth (%)	--	--	--	--	--	--	--	--	--	--	--	--	--
Financial indicators of MSMEs (D billion)													
Total capital	1,401,076	2,108,421	3,191,115	4,681,677	5,369,536	5,930,800	6,904,707	7,427,608	9,629,698	10,808,009	9,012,689	11,833,344	--
Fixed assets and long-term investment	519,916	849,831	1,128,917	1,877,337	1,839,961	2,107,379	2,623,265	2,573,198	3,378,248	4,056,818	3,067,317	4,171,933	--
Growth (%)	--	63.5	32.8	66.3	(2.0)	14.5	24.5	(1.9)	31.3	20.1	(24.4)	36.0	--
Net income	1,679,861	2,973,456	3,351,404	3,641,191	4,673,543	5,032,576	5,307,303	5,929,294	6,699,548	7,889,252	5,800,528	6,440,126	--
Growth (%)	47.0	77.0	12.7	8.6	28.4	7.7	5.5	11.7	13.0	17.8	(26.5)	11.0	--

GDP = gross domestic product; MSME = micro, small, and medium-sized enterprise. * Preliminary data. ** Active enterprises based on labor scale.
Note: MSME classification prior to 2017 is based on Decree No: 56/2009/ND-CP, while for 2017 onward follows Decree No.39/2018/ND-CP.
Source: ADB Asia SME Monitor 2020 database. Data from Agency for Enterprise Development, Ministry of Planning and Investment; and General Statistics Office.

Table 12.3: Bank Credit

End of period data

Item	2012	2013	2014	2015	2016	2017	2018	2019*
COMMERCIAL BANKS								
Number of commercial banks, total	99	102	96	95	96	97	97	--
State-owned banks	5	5	5	7	7	7	7	--
Policy banks	2	2	2	2	2	2	2	--
Joint stock banks	34	33	33	28	28	28	28	--
Joint venture banks	4	4	4	3	2	2	2	--
Fully foreign-owned banks	5	5	5	5	6	9	9	--
Foreign bank branches	49	53	47	50	51	49	49	--
Credit								
Loans outstanding, total (D billion)	3,090,904	3,477,985	3,970,548	4,655,890	5,505,406	6,512,018	7,211,175	8,195,428
Loans outstanding in domestic currency (D billion)	--	--	--	--	--	--	--	--
Loans outstanding in foreign currency (D billion)	--	--	--	--	--	--	--	--
Loan growth (%)	--	12.5	14.2	17.3	18.2	18.3	10.7	13.6
Total commercial bank loans to GDP (%)	95.2	97.0	100.8	111.0	122.3	130.1	130.1	--
Lending rate (%)**	13.5	10.4	8.7	7.1	7.0	7.1	7.4	7.7
Gross nonperforming loans (NPLs) (D billion)	126,727	125,555	129,043	118,725	--	129,589	137,733	131,127
Gross NPLs to total loans (%)	4.1	3.6	3.3	2.6	--	2.0	1.9	1.6
Loans outstanding by sector (% share)								
Agriculture, forestry, and fisheries	9.6	10.6	10.5	10.0	10.2	9.8	9.2	8.7
Manufacturing	29.3	27.8	25.6	23.3	21.8	21.7	19.9	19.0
Transportation and communication	4.3	3.6	3.3	3.3	3.5	3.7	3.0	2.7
Construction	9.3	10.0	9.5	9.7	9.2	9.9	9.7	9.8
Wholesale and retail trade	19.5	19.3	18.6	17.8	18.2	20.1	21.8	22.5
Other services	--	--	--	--	--	--	--	--
Others	28.0	28.7	32.5	35.9	37.1	34.8	36.4	37.2
Deposits								
Deposits, total (D billion)***	405,455	510,539	615,364	729,555	862,391	1,004,102	1,089,015	--
Deposits in domestic currency (D billion)	--	--	--	--	--	--	--	--
Deposits in foreign currency (D billion)	--	--	--	--	--	--	--	--
Deposit rate (%)**	10.5	7.1	5.8	4.7	5.0	4.8	4.7	4.8

GDP = gross domestic product, SME = small and medium-sized enterprise.

* Data at the end of 2019, calculated from the State Bank of Vietnam data (https://www.sbv.gov.vn/webcenter/portal/en/home/sbv/statistic/).

** Based on International Monetary Fund/International Finance Statistics (IMF/IFS) data on other depository corporations' rates (percent per annum).

*** Refers to demand deposits.

Source: ADB Asia SME Monitor 2020 database. Data from State Bank of Vietnam and IMF/IFS.

Table 12.4: Nonbank Finance

End of period data

Item	2010	2011	2012	2013	2014	2015	2016	2017	2018	2019*
NUMBER OF NONBANK FINANCE INSTITUTIONS										
Microfinance institutions	--	1	2	2	2	3	3	4	4	4
Credit unions/cooperatives**	--	--	--	1	1	1	1	1	1	--
Finance companies***	17	18	18	17	17	16	15	16	26	--
Pawnshops	--	--	--	--	--	--	--	--	--	--
Leasing companies	13	12	12	12	11	11	11	11	--	--
Factoring companies	--	--	--	--	--	--	--	--	--	--
Insurance companies	--	--	--	--	--	--	--	--	--	--
Others: People's Credit Funds	1,057	1,095	1,132	1,144	1,145	1,147	1,166	1,178	1,183	--
MICROFINANCE INSTITUTIONS										
Financing outstanding, total (D million)	--	419,034	570,035	700,936	865,576	1,145,916	1,385,887	4,662,572	5,657,270	5,989,843
Growth (%)	--	--	36.0	23.0	23.5	32.4	20.9	236.4	21.3	5.9
Total financing to GDP (%)	--	0.02	0.02	0.02	0.02	0.03	0.03	0.09	0.10	--
Annual financing rate (%, on average)	--	--	--	--	--	--	--	--	--	--
Gross nonperforming financing (NPFs) (D million)****	--	84	912	140	87	115	554	16,319	18,669	22,761
Gross NPFs to total financing (%)	--	0.02	0.16	0.02	0.01	0.01	0.04	0.35	0.33	0.38
Number of customers financed, total	--	--	730,000	770,000	--	--	--	--	--	--
Financing outstanding by sector (% share)										
Agriculture, forestry, and fisheries	--	--	--	--	--	--	--	--	--	--
Manufacturing	--	--	--	--	--	--	--	--	--	--
Transportation and communication	--	--	--	--	--	--	--	--	--	--
Construction	--	--	--	--	--	--	--	--	--	--
Wholesale and retail trade	--	--	--	--	--	--	--	--	--	--
Other services	--	--	--	--	--	--	--	--	--	--
Others	--	--	--	--	--	--	--	--	--	--
Financing outstanding by region (% share)										
Capital city	--	--	--	--	--	--	--	--	--	--
Others	--	--	--	--	--	--	--	--	--	--
PEOPLE'S CREDIT FUNDS										
Financing outstanding, total (D million)	23,708,082	28,657,846	35,879,999	44,856,836	52,355,614	60,735,042	70,315,079	80,233,476	90,483,103	96,096,713
Growth (%)		20.9	25.2	25.0	16.7	16.0	15.8	14.1	12.8	6.2
Total financing to GDP (%)	1.1	1.0	1.1	1.3	1.3	1.4	1.6	1.6	1.6	--
Annual financing rate (%, on average)	--	--	--	--	--	--	--	--	--	--
Gross nonperforming financing (NPFs) (D million)	--	--	--	--	--	--	--	--	--	--
Gross NPFs to total financing (%)	--	--	--	--	--	--	--	--	--	--
Number of customers financed, total	950,000	--	1,070,000	1,120,000	--	--	--	--	--	--
Amount of deposits (D million)	21,026,791	25,960,294	35,461,422	43,464,491	55,797,836	65,709,710	76,818,112	87,131,348	94,329,445	105,865,312
Number of depositors	--	--	1,260,000	1,310,000						
Financing outstanding by sector (% share)										
Agriculture, forestry, and fisheries	--	--	--	--	--	--	--	--	--	--
Manufacturing	--	--	--	--	--	--	--	--	--	--
Transportation and communication	--	--	--	--	--	--	--	--	--	--
Construction	--	--	--	--	--	--	--	--	--	--
Wholesale and retail trade	--	--	--	--	--	--	--	--	--	--
Other services	--	--	--	--	--	--	--	--	--	--
Others	--	--	--	--	--	--	--	--	--	--
Financing outstanding by region (% share)										
Capital city	--	--	--	--	--	--	--	--	--	--
Others	--	--	--	--	--	--	--	--	--	--

GDP = gross domestic product, SME = small and medium-sized enterprise.

* Data as of Q2 2019.

** Refers to cooperative bank.

*** Since 2018, data includes both finance companies and leasing companies.

**** Calculated using gross NPFs to total financing (%).

Source: ADB Asia SME Monitor 2020 database. Data from State Bank of Vietnam.

Table 12.5: Capital Markets

End of period data

Item	2009	2010	2011	2012	2013	2014	2015	2016	2017	2018	2019
EQUITY MARKET											
Main Board - HOSE											
Index	495	484.7	351.6	413.7	504.6	545.6	579.0	664.9	984.2	892.5	961.0
Market capitalization (D billion)	495,094	591,345	453,784	678,403	842,105	985,258	1,146,925	1,491,778	2,614,150	2,875,544	3,279,616
Growth (%)	--	19.7	(23.3)	49.5	24.1	17.0	16.4	30.1	75.2	10.0	14.1
Trading value (D billion)	422,460	376,512	159,154	216,881	260,985	533,053	482,047	602,026	1,041,234	1,337,557	988,147
Trading volume (billion of shares)	10	12	8	14	16	30	28	32	48	49	44
Number of listed companies	196	275	301	308	301	305	307	320	344	373	378
Number of IPOs	--	--	--	15	4	--	19	19	31	35	6
Number of delisted companies	--	--	--	9	11	--	17	6	7	6	--
Main Board - HNX											
Index	168.17	114.24	58.74	57.09	67.84	82.98	79.96	80.12	116.86	104.23	102.51
Market capitalization (D million)	123,574,000	131,817,647	83,721,034	86,543,004	106,870,618	136,017,407	151,607,768	151,812,749	222,894,000	192,136,000	192,029,579
Growth (%)	--	6.7	(36.5)	3.4	23.5	27.3	11.5	0.1	46.8	(13.8)	(0.1)
Trading value (D million)	197,358,000	241,695,822	95,847,067	109,679,474	82,081,933	199,527,092	135,035,878	129,651,787	161,054,000	196,859,000	102,362,000
Trading volume (million of shares)	5,760	8,755	7,944	12,138	10,575	16,982	11,554	11,615	13,911	13,043	7,907
Number of listed companies	257	367	393	396	377	365	377	376	384	376	367
Number of IPOs	--	15	7	5	14	37	64	30	10	10	4
Number of delisted companies	6	3	3	11	30	25	18	16	13	18	20
UpCoM - HNX											
Index	53.8	45.2	33.8	41.8	42.5	60.3	51.3	53.8	54.9	52.8	55.7
Market capitalization (D million)	4,259,814	16,237,680	22,663,598	28,868,424	25,745,000	37,169,559	61,033,252	303,359,258	677,705,000	893,777,000	911,940,645
Growth (%)	--	281.2	39.6	27.4	(10.8)	44.4	64.2	397.0	123.4	31.9	2.0
Trading value (D million)	545,479	2,266,651	2,280,259	5,065,137	510,679	5,410,073	14,288,085	31,946,171	60,457,000	93,764,000	73,466,370
Trading volume (million of shares)	40	152	120	185	80	547	934	2,083	3,130	4,736	3,665
Number of registered companies	34	109	131	132	142	169	256	417	690	810	872
Number of newly registered companies	--	82	15	7	13	36	93	165	285	137	108
Number of deregistered companies	--	7	8	6	3	9	6	7	11	21	24
Number of securities firms (UPCoM members)	--	91	92	88	84	84	75	73	74	74	74

HNX = Hanoi Stock Exchange, HOSE = Ho Chi Minh Stock Exchange, IPO = initial public offering, UPCoM = Unlisted Public CoMpanies.
Source: ADB Asia SME Monitor 2020 database. Data from Hanoi Stock Exchange (for HNX main board and UpCoM data), State Securities Commission of Vietnam, and Ho Chi Minh Stock Exchange (for HOSE main board data).

Table 12.6: Listing Requirements—Hanoi Stock Exchange

Criteria	HNX - Main Board	HNX - UPCoM
Capital size	• D30 billion or more.	• D10 billion or more.
Years in operation	• At least 1 year as a joint stock company (except for state-owned enterprises equitization coupled with listing).	• n/a,
Profitability	• Minimum 5% of return on equity (ROE) in the previous year • Profitable in the previous year • No overdue debt for more than 1 year • No accumulated loss as of the year of listing registration • Compiles with the provisions of law on accounting and financial statements	• n/a, • n/a, • n/a, • n/a, • n/a,
Public exposure	• At least 15% of the voting shares should be held by at least 100 shareholders who are not major shareholders (except for state-owned enterprises equitize following to regulations of Prime Minister). • Shareholders being members of the BOD, Board of Supervisory, BOM, chief accountant; major shareholders affiliated to BOD, BOM, Board of Supervisory, chief accountant must commit to hold 100% of their shares for 6 months since listing time and 50% of their shares in the next 6 months excluding any shares held by any of the abovementioned individuals as representative of the state owner. • Valid listing dossiers according to the regulation.	• Owned by at least 100 investors, excluding professional securities investors. • n/a, • n/a,
Others	• Registered for depository at the Vietnam Securities Depository.	• Registered for depository at the Vietnam Securities Depository.

BOD = Board of Directors, BOM = Board of Management, HNX = Hanoi Stock Exchange, UPCoM = Unlisted Public CoMpanies.
Source: ADB Asia SME Monitor 2020 database. Data from Hanoi Stock Exchange.

Table 12.7: Policies and Regulations

Name	Outline
Regulations	
Nonfinance regulations	
Law No.21/2008 on High Technology	Including the national policy to promote technology and innovation targeting small and medium-sized enterprises (SMEs).
Prime Minister Decision No.844/2016/QD-TTg on Supporting the National Innovative Startup Ecosystem to 2025 (Master Plan 844)	Supporting the development of the national innovative startup ecosystem by 2025, including funding support.
Decree No.78/2015/ND-CP and Decree No.108/2018/ND-CP on Business Registration	Regulation on business registration procedures.
Law No.07/2017/QH14 on Technology Transfer	Regulation on technology transfer.
Decree No.76/2018/ND-CP on Guidelines for the Technology Transfer Law	Formulating policies on commercialization of research products to guide in the implementation of the Technology Transfer Law (2017).
Law No.04/2017/QH14 on Support for Small and Medium-sized Enterprises (SME Support Law)	1) Micro, small, amd medium-sized enterprise (MSME) sector development policy. 2) MSME definition. 3) Enhance the functions of SME Development Promotion Council. 4) Establishment of SME Development Fund.
Decree No.39/2018/ND-CP on Guidelines for the SME Support Law	Guidelines for the SME Support Law (2017).
Decree No.13/2019/ND-CP on Science and Technology Enterprises	Offers tax breaks and exemptions/reductions in leasing fees for science and technology firms.
Decree No.55/2019/ND-CP providing legal assistance for SME	Providing legal support for SMEs.
Circular No.05/2019/TT-BKHĐT support for human resource development	Support to enhance capacity for SMEs on human resource development.
Circular No.06/2019/TT-BKHDT guidelines for organization and operation of consultant network, consultancy support for SME	Support SMEs in consultancy through the consultant network.
Circular No.32/2018/TT-BKDTBXH guidelines for vocational training for labor of SME	Support for vocational training for workers working in SMEs.
Prime Minister Decision No.939/2017/QĐ-TTg on approving the project supporting women in starting their businesses in the period of 2017-2025	Supporting women in starting their businesses in the period of 2017–2025.
Decision No.1665 / QD-TTg dated October 30, 2017 of the Prime Minister on the approval of the Scheme on Supporting Start-Up Students by 2025	Supporting start-up students by 2025.
Directive No.09/CT-TTg dated February 18, 2020, on creating conditions for Supporting Startup Enterprises	Interdisciplinary directive on promoting the development of innovative start-ups.
Finance regulations	
Decree No.48/2001/ND-CP on People's Credit Fund	Establishment and operations of the People's Credit Fund.
Law No.18/2003/QD on Cooperatives	Regulation on cooperatives.
Decree No.165/2007/ND-CP on Microfinance Institutions (amendment of Decree No.28/2005/ND-CP)	Regulation on microfinance institutions (MFIs).
Law No.47/2010/QH12 on Credit Institutions	Regulation on banks and nonbank finance institutions.
Law No.62/2010/QH12 on Securities	Regulation on capital markets.
Decree No.03/2011/ND-CP on Promulgating the Regulation on Guaranteeing Commercial Bank Loans to SMEs	Special treatments to promote SME access to finance through guarantee by the Vietnam Development Bank.
Prime Minister Decision No.2195/2011/QD-TTg on Approving the Proposal for Building and Developing the Microfinance System in Vietnam up to 2020	1) Creating a comprehensive legal framework for microfinance operations. 2) Enhancing policymaking and regulatory capacity of government agencies. 3) Strengthening capacity of MFIs. 4) Conducting advocacy activities to raise awareness of microfinance. 5) Other supporting solutions (funding facilitation for microfinance operations, establishment of training institutes, microfinance database, and establishment of a microfinance association).
Prime Minister Decision No.254/2012/QD-TTg on Approving the Project on Restructuring the System on Credit Institutions During 2011-2015	Focus on achieving healthy financial conditions and increasing capability of credit institutions; improve the safety and efficiency of credit institutions; enhance the discipline and market principle in banking activities.
State Bank of Vietnam (SBV) Circular No.16/2013/TT-NHNN on the maximum interest rate of dong short-term loans imposing on credit institutions and foreign bank branches	Concessional lending rate for SMEs (9%).
SBV Document No.884/2013/NHNN-TTGSNH on Transforming the Central People's Credit Fund into the Cooperative Bank of Vietnam	Converting the legal status of the Central People's Credit Fund into the cooperative bank.
SBV Circular No.04/2015/TT-NHNN on People's Credit Funds	Revised regulation on People's Credit Funds.
Decree No.102/2017/ND-CP on Registration of Security Interests	Providing procedures and requirements for registration of security measures and improved information for secured assets.
Decree No.34/2018/ND-CP on Establishment and Operation of Credit Guarantee Funds and relevant documents (Circular No.45/2018/TT-NHNN, Circular No.15/2019/TT-BTC, Circular No.57/2019/TT-BTC)	Establishment and operations of credit guarantee funds for MSMEs.
Decree No.38/2018/ND-CP on Investment for Small and Medium Startups and Innovative Firms	Guidance on investment in innovative start-ups. Start-ups receive support from the state budget with no more than 30% of total investment mobilized from investment funds.
Decree No.57/2018/ND-CP on Incentive Policies for Enterprises Investing in Agriculture and Rural Areas	Policies on supporting enterprises investing in agriculture and rural areas.
Decree No.116/2018/ND-CP on Credit Policy for Agricultural and Rural Development (amendment of Decree No.55/2015/ND-CP)	A special credit program for agricultural and rural development. Decree No.116 specially targets technological development in agriculture.

continued on next page

Figure 12.7 continued

Prime Minister Decision No.242/2019/QD-TTg on Approving the Restructuring Securities and Insurance Markets		Outlines the plan to restructure the securities and insurance markets by 2020 and vision to 2025.
Decree No.39/2019/ND-CP on organization and operation of Small and Medium Enterprise Development Fund and relevant documents		Organization and operation of Small and Medium Enterprise Development Fund.
Circular No.132/2018/TT-BTC providing guidance on accounting regimes for micro enterprise		Create easier procedures on accounting system for microenterprises.
Law No.54/2019/QH14 on Securities		New regulation on capital markets.
Regulators and Policymakers		
Name		**Responsibility**
State Bank of Vietnam (SBV)		Regulate and supervise banks and nonbank financial institutions.
Ministry of Planning and Investment (MPI)		Formulate MSME development policies.
Agency for Enterprise Development, MPI		Executing agency of the MSME development policies.
Ministry of Finance (MOF)		Supervise state-owned financial institutions and regulate state-run funds supporting MSMEs.
Ministry of Science and Technology (MOST)		Support innovative and technology-based start-ups and MSMEs.
Ministry of Industry and Trade (MOIT)		Formulate industry development policies.
State Securities Commission on Vietnam (SSC)		Regulate and supervise capital markets.
SME Development Promotion Council		Advisory body to Prime Minister related to MSME development policies.
Policies		
Name	**Responsible Entity**	**Outline**
5 Year SME Development Plan 2006–2010 (2005)	MPI	A comprehensive MSME development policy package prepared by all economic ministries/agencies. Specific targets: 1) Newly established MSMEs of 320,000 (22% annual growth). 2) Newly established MSMEs in disadvantaged provinces with annual increase of 15% by 2010. 3) MSMEs having direct exports: 3%–6%. 4) 2.7 million new jobs created by MSMEs in 2006–2010. 5) Additional 165,000 technical workers in MSMEs.
5 Year SME Development Plan 2011–2015 (2012)	MPI	A comprehensive MSME development policy package prepared by all economic ministries/agencies. Specific targets: 1) Newly established MSMEs of 350,000 during 2011–2015. 2) MSMEs having direct exports: 25% of total export nationwide. 3) Investment from MSMEs: 35% of total investment. 4) MSME contribution to GDP: 30%; MSME contribution to total revenue of state budget: 30%. 5) 2.5 million to 4.0 million new jobs created by MSMEs in 2011–2015.
Restructuring securities and insurance markets by 2020 and vision to 2025 (2019)	SSC	Restructuring the securities market until 2025 with aim to be an instrument for medium- and long-term capital raising for the Vietnamese economy and businesses. Key components: 1) Revise current securities law to restructure and expand the capital markets. 2) Use the capital markets to restructure and privatize state-owned enterprises. 3) Launch new investment products such as covered warrants and bond futures.
National Financial Inclusion Strategy (2020)	SBV	1) Situation assessment. 2) Directions and solutions. 3) Roadmap.

Source: ADB Asia SME Monitor 2020 database. Data from State Bank of Vietnam, Ministry of Planning and Investment, Ministry of Finance, State Securities Commission of Vietnam, Agency for Business Registration, Hanoi Stock Exchange.

www.ingramcontent.com/pod-product-compliance
Lightning Source LLC
Chambersburg PA
CBHW050041220326
41599CB00045B/7244
* 9 7 8 9 2 9 2 6 2 4 2 1 7 *